A PRACTICAL GRAMMAR OF THE SANSKRIT LANGUAGE

A PRACTICAL GRAMMAR OF THE SANSKRIT LANGUAGE

Arranged with Reference to

The Classical Languages of Europe,

For the use of

English Students

by

MONIER WILLIAMS, M.A.

SECOND EDITION

GYAN

Published by

GYAN

Gyan Publishing House
5, Ansari Road
Daryaganj, New Delhi-110002
Phone: 011-47034999, 9811692060
E-mail: books@gyanbooks.com

Distribution Network
gyanbooks.com
India, USA, Canada, UK, Australia, France

ISBN : 978-81-212-2983-8 (PB)
sFirst Published, 1857

2nd Impression 2021

Printed at: Gyan Press, Delhi.

A
Practical Grammar of the Sanskrit Language
Author: Monier Williams

A PRACTICAL GRAMMAR OF THE SANSKRIT LANGUAGE,

ARRANGED WITH REFERENCE TO

THE CLASSICAL LANGUAGES OF EUROPE,

FOR THE USE OF

ENGLISH STUDENTS.

BY

MONIER WILLIAMS, M.A.

PROFESSOR OF SANSKRIT AT THE EAST-INDIA COLLEGE, HAILEYBURY;
MEMBER OF THE ROYAL ASIATIC SOCIETY, AND OF THE ORIENTAL SOCIETY OF GERMANY;
FORMERLY BODEN SCHOLAR IN THE UNIVERSITY OF OXFORD.

SECOND EDITION.

OXFORD:
AT THE UNIVERSITY PRESS.
M.DCCC.LVII.

PREFACE.

IN 1846 I published a Grammar of the Sanskṛit language, which I entitled 'An elementary Grammar, arranged according to a new Theory.' This work is now out of print, and a new edition is required. The increasing experience which, during the subsequent ten years, I have derived from my duties as Sanskṛit Professor at the East-India College, where every student without exception is compelled by statute to acquire this language, has led me to modify some of the views I expressed in my first Grammar respecting the Indian grammatical system. I have consequently felt myself called upon to re-write the book; and although I have seen no reason to depart materially from the arrangement originally adopted, yet I am confident that the present enlarged and more complete work will be found even better adapted than its predecessor to the practical wants of the European student.

At the best, a grammar is regarded by an European as a necessary evil, only to be tolerated because unavoidable. Especially must it be so in the case of a language confessedly more copious, more elaborate and artificial, than any other language of the world, living or dead. The structure of such a language must of necessity be highly complex. To the native of Hindústán this complexity is a positive recommendation. He views in it an evidence and a pledge of the sacred and unapproachable character of the tongue which he venerates as divine. To him the study of its intricate grammar is an end, complete and satisfying in itself. He wanders with delight in its perplexing mazes; and values that grammar most which enters most minutely into an abstract analysis of the construction of the language, apart from its practical bearing on the literature or even on the formation of his own vernacular dialect. But the matter-of-fact temperament of an European, or at least of an Englishman, his peculiar mental organization, his hereditary and educational bias, are opposed to all such purely philosophical ideas of grammatical investigation. A Sanskṛit grammar intended for his use must be plain, straightforward, practical: not founded on the mere abstract theory of native grammarians, not moulded in servile conformity to Indian authority, but constructed independently from an examination of the literature, and with direct reference to the influence exercised by Sanskṛit on the spoken dialects of India and the cognate languages of Europe. To the English student, as a general rule, all grammatical study is a disagreeable necessity—a mere means to an end—a troublesome road that must be passed in order that the goal of a sound knowledge of a language may be attained. To meet his requirements the ground must be cleared of needless obstacles, its rough places made smooth, its crooked places straight, and the passage over it facilitated by simplicity and perspicuity of arrangement, by consistency and unity of design, by abundance of example and illustration, by synoptical tables, by copious indices, by the various artifices of typography.

Before directing attention to the main features of the plan adopted in the present volume, and indicating the principal points in which it either differs from or conforms to the Indian system of grammatical tuition, I will endeavour to explain briefly what that system is; on what principles it is based; and in what relation it stands to the literature.

It might have been expected that in Sanskṛit, as in

other languages, grammatical works should have been composed in direct subservience to the literature. But without going the length of affirming that the rules were anterior to the practice, or that grammarians in their elaborate precepts aimed at inventing forms of speech which were not established by approved usage, certain it is that in India we have presented to us the curious phenomenon of a vast assemblage of purely grammatical treatises, the professed object of which is not so much to elucidate the existing literature, as to be studied for their own sake, or as ancillary to the study of the more abstruse work of the first great grammarian, Páṇini. We have, moreover, two distinct phases of literature; the one, simple and natural—that is to say, composed independently of grammatical rules, though of course amenable to them; the other, elaborate, artificial, and professedly written to exemplify the theory of grammar. The literary compositions which preceded the appearance of Páṇini's aphorisms, probably about the 2d century B. C., belong of course to the first of these phases. Such are the Vedas, the code of Manu, and the two epic poems of the Rámáyaṇa and Mahá-bhárata*. The Vedas, indeed, which are referred back to a period as early as the 12th or 13th century B. C., abound in obsolete and peculiar formations, mixed up with the more recent forms of grammar with so much irregularity as to lead to the inference, that the language at that time was too unsettled and variable to be brought under subjection to a system of strict grammatical rules; while the simplicity of the style in the code of Manu and the two epic poems is a plain indication that a grammar founded on and intended to be a guide to the literature as it then existed, would have

* That Páṇini was subsequent to the Mahá-bhárata may be conjectured from the circumstance that in the chapter on patronymics the examples given in the Vártikas or supplementary rules (probably nearly as ancient as the Sútras) seem to be taken from the names of the chiefs and warriors of that poem.

differed from the Páṇiníya Sútras as a straight road from a labyrinth.

What then was the nature of Páṇini's extraordinary work, which caused so complete a revolution in the character of Sanskṛit literary composition? It consisted of about four thousand Sútras or aphorisms, composed with the symbolic brevity of the most concise *memoria technica.* These were to the science of Sanskṛit grammar what the seed is to the tree, the bud to the full-blown flower. They were the germ of that series of grammatical treatises which, taking root in them, speedily germinated and ramified in all directions. Each aphorism, in itself more dark and mystic than the darkest and most mystical of oracles, was pregnant with an endless progeny of interpretations and commentaries, sometimes as obscure as the original. About one hundred and fifty grammarians and annotators followed in the footsteps of the great Father of Sanskṛit grammar, and, professing to explain and illustrate his dicta, made the display of their own philological learning the paramount aim and purpose of their disquisitions.

It cannot be wondered, when all the subtlety of the Indian intellect expended itself in this direction, that the science of Sanskṛit grammar should have been refined and elaborated by the Hindús to a degree wholly unknown in the other languages of the world. The highly artificial writings of later times resulted from such an elaboration, and were closely interwoven with it; and although much of the literature was still simple and natural, the greater part was affected by that passion for the display of philological erudition which was derived from the works of Páṇini and his disciples. Poetry itself became partially inoculated with the mania. Great poets, like Kálidása, who in the generality of their writings were remarkable for majestic simplicity and vigour, condescended in some of their works to humour the taste of the day by adopting a pedantic and obscure style; while others, like Bhaṭṭi, wrote long poems, either with the avowed object of exemplifying grammar, or with the ill-concealed motive of exhibiting their own familiarity with the niceties and subtleties of speech.

Indeed it is to be regretted that the Paṇḍits of India should have overlaid their system, possessing as it does undeniable excellencies, with a network of mysticism. Had they designed to keep the key of the knowledge of their language, and to shut the door against the vulgar, they could hardly have invented a method more perplexing and discouraging to beginners. Having required, as a preliminary step, that the student shall pass a noviciate of ten years in the grammar alone, they have constructed a complicated machinery of signs, symbols, and indicatory letters, which may be well calculated to aid the memory of the initiated natives, but only serves to bewilder the English tyro. He has enough to do, in conquering the difficulties of a strange character, without puzzling himself at the very threshold in a labyrinth of symbols and abbreviations, and perplexing himself in his endeavour to understand a complicated cipher, with an equally complicated key to its interpretation. Even Colebrooke, the profoundest Sanskṛit scholar of his day, imbued as he was with a predilection for every thing Indian, remarks on the eight lectures or chapters, which, with four sections under each, comprise all the celebrated Páṇiníya Sútras, and constitute the basis of the Hindú grammatical system;—'The outline of Páṇini's arrangement is simple, but numerous exceptions and frequent digressions have involved it in much seeming confusion. The first two lectures (the first section especially, which is in a manner the key of the whole grammar) contain definitions; in the three next are collected the affixes by which verbs and nouns are inflected. Those which appertain to verbs occupy the third lecture; the fourth and fifth contain such as are affixed to nouns. The remaining three lectures treat of the changes which roots and affixes undergo in special cases, or by general rules of orthography, and which are all effected by the addition or by the substitution of one or more elements. The apparent simplicity of the design vanishes in the perplexity of the structure. The endless pursuit of exceptions and limitations so disjoins the general precepts, that the reader cannot keep in view their intended connexion and mutual relation. He wanders in an intricate maze, and the clue of the labyrinth is continually slipping from his hand.' Again; 'The studied brevity of the Páṇiníya Sútras renders them in the highest degree obscure; even with the knowledge of the key to their interpretation, the student finds them ambiguous. In the application of them, when understood, he discovers many seeming contradictions; and, with every exertion of practised memory, he must experience the utmost difficulty in combining rules dispersed in apparent confusion through different portions of Páṇini's eight lectures.'

That the reader may judge for himself of the almost incredible brevity and hopeless obscurity of these grammatical aphorisms, it may be worth while here to furnish him with one or two examples. The closing Sútra at the end of the eighth lecture is as follows: 'अ अ *a a*.' Will it be believed that this is interpreted to mean, 'Let short *a* be held to have its organ of utterance contracted, now that we have reached the end of the work, in which it was necessary to regard it as being otherwise?'

Another example, taken from the third section of the eighth lecture, may be useful as showing that grammatical theory is sometimes not strictly carried out in practice. The Sútra (VIII. 3. 31) is as follows: 'शि तुक् *śi tuk*.' This is interpreted to signify, that 'when न् *n* comes at the end of a word, and श *ś* follows, the augment त् *t* may be inserted, and न् श may then be written in three ways, thus; ञ्छ, ञ्श, ञ् श.' But if we examine the best MSS. and printed works throughout the whole compass of the literature, we shall find that in practice न् श are constantly left unchanged. The same may be said of न् ज, which by another Sútra ought to pass into ज्ञ. See rr. 55, 56. *a.* pp. 30, 31, of this book.

My aim has been, in the present work, to avoid the mysticism of Indian grammarians, without ignoring the best parts of their system, and without rejecting such of their technical symbols as I have found by experience to be really useful in assisting the memory.

With reference to my first chapter, the student will doubtless be impatient of the space devoted to the explanation of the alphabet. Let him understand at the outset, that a minute and accurate adjustment of the mutual relationship of letters is the very hinge of the whole subject of Sanskṛit grammar. It is the point which distinguishes the grammar of this language from that of every other. In fact, Sanskṛit, in its whole structure, is an elaborate process of combining letters according to prescribed rules. Its entire grammatical system, the regular formation of its nouns and verbs from crude roots, its theory of declension and conjugation, and the arrangement of its sentences, all turn on the reciprocal relationship and interchangeableness of letters, and the laws which regulate their euphonic combination. These laws, moreover, are the key to the influence which this language has exercised on the study of comparative philology. Such being the case, it is scarcely possible for a Sanskṛit grammar to be too full, luminous, and explicit in treating of the letters, their pronunciation, classification, and mutual affinities.

With regard to the second chapter, which contains the rules of Sandhi or euphonic combination, I have endeavoured as far as possible to simplify a part of the grammar which is the great impediment to the progress of beginners. There can be little doubt that the necessity imposed on early students of conquering these rules at the commencement of the grammar, is the cause why so many who address themselves energetically to the study of the language are compelled after the first onset to retire from the field dispirited, if not totally discomfited. The rules for the combination and permutation of letters form, as it were, a mountain of difficulty to be passed at the very beginning of the journey; and the learner cannot be convinced that, when once surmounted, the ground beyond may be more smooth than in other languages, the ingress to which is comparatively easy. My aim has been to facilitate the comprehension of these rules, not by omission or abbreviation, but by a perspicuous method of arrangement, and by the exhibition of every Sanskṛit word with its equivalent English letters. The student must understand that there are two distinct classes of rules of Sandhi, viz. those which affect the final or initial letters of complete words in a sentence, and those which relate to the euphonic junction of roots or crude bases with affixes and terminations. Many of the latter class come first into operation in the conjugation of the more difficult verbs. In order, therefore, that the student may not be embarrassed with these rules, until they are required, the consideration of them is reserved to the middle of the volume. (See p. 124.)

As to the chapter on Sanskṛit roots and the formation of nominal bases, the place which it occupies before the chapter on declension, although unusual, scarcely calls for explanation; depending as it does on the theory that nouns as well as verbs are derived from roots, and that the formation of a nominal base must precede the declension of a noun, just as the formation of a verbal base must be anterior to the conjugation of a verb. Consistency and clearness of arrangement certainly require that an enumeration of the affixes by which the bases of nouns are formed should precede their inflection. The early student, however, may satisfy himself by a cursory observation of the eight classes under which these affixes are distributed. Some of the most uncommon, which are only applicable to single words, have been omitted. Moreover, in accordance with the practical character of the present Grammar, the servile and indicatory letters of Indian grammarians, under which the true affix is often concealed, if not altogether lost, have been discarded. For example, the adjective *dhana-vat*, 'rich,' is considered in the following pages to be formed by the affix *vat*, and not, as in native Grammars, by *matup;* and the substantive *bhoj-ana*, 'food,' is considered to be formed with the affix *ana*, and not, as in native Grammars, by *lyuṭ*.

In my explanation of the inflection of the base of both nouns and verbs, I have, as before, treated both declension and conjugation as a process of *Sandhi;* that is to say, *junction* of the crude base, as previously formed from the root, with the terminations. But in the present Grammar I have thought it expedient to lay more stress on the general scheme of terminations propounded by native grammarians; and in the application of this scheme to the base, I have referred more systematically to the rules of euphonic combination, as essential to a sound acquaintance with the principles of nominal and verbal inflection. On the other hand, I have in the present work deviated from the Indian system by retaining स् *s* as a final in the declension of nouns and conjugation of verbs, for the practical reason of its being more tangible and easy to apprehend than the symbol *Visarga* or *ḥ*, which is imperceptible in pronunciation. (See the observations under changes of final *s*, pp. 32, 33.) Even in native Grammars those terminations, the finals of which are afterwards changed to Visarga, are always regarded as originally ending in स् *s;*

and the subsequent resolution of *s* into *h*, when the termination is connected with the base, is a source of confusion and uncertainty. Thus *s* is said to be the termination of the nominative case; but the nominative of अग्नि *agni*, 'fire,' would according to the Indian system be written अग्निः *agnih*, which is scarcely distinguishable in pronunciation from the base *agni*. In the following pages, therefore, the nominative is given *agnis;* and the liability of *agnis* to become *agnih* and *agnir* is explained under the head of changes of final *s* (at p. 33). This plan (which is that of Professor Bopp) has also the advantage of exhibiting the resemblance between the system of inflection in Sanskṛit and Latin and Greek.

The difficulty experienced in comprehending the subject of Sanskṛit conjugation has led me to give abundant examples of verbs conjugated at full. I have of course deviated from the Indian plan of placing the third person first. I have, moreover, deemed it advisable to exhibit the English equivalents of Sanskṛit words in the principal examples under each declension and conjugation, knowing by experience the thankfulness with which this aid is received by early students, not thoroughly familiar with the Devanágarí character. The numerous examples of verbs, primitive and derivative, will be found to include all the most useful in the language. In previous Grammars it has been usual to follow the native method of giving only the 3d pers. sing. of each tense, with an occasional indication of any peculiarities in the other persons. The present Grammar, on the other hand, exhibits the more difficult tenses of *every verb in full*, referring at the same time for the explanation of every peculiar formation to the rule, in the preceding pages, on which it depends. This is especially true of the 2d and 3d preterites, as these constitute the chief difficulty of the Sanskṛit verb; and I have constantly found that even advanced students, if required to write out these tenses, will be guilty of inaccuracies, notwithstanding one or two of the persons may have been given for their guidance.

In the chapter on compound words I have again endeavoured, without ignoring the Indian arrangement, to disembarrass it of many elements of perplexity, and to treat the whole subject in a manner more in unison with European ideas. The explanations I have given rest on actual examples selected by myself from the Hitopadeśa and other standard works in ordinary use. Indeed this chapter and that on syntax constitute perhaps the most original part of the present volume. In composing the syntax, the literature as it exists has been my only guide. All the examples are taken from classical authors, so as to serve the purpose of an easy delectus, in which the learner may exercise himself before passing to continuous translation. The deficiency of native Grammars on this important subject is only to be accounted for on the supposition that their aim was to furnish an elaborate analysis of the philosophical structure of the language, rather than a practical guide to the study of the literature.

The exercises in translation and parsing, in the last chapter of this volume, will, it is hoped, facilitate the early student's first effort at translation. Two fables from the Hitopadeśa are given, as before, with a translation and grammatical analysis; but I have thought fit to omit the story of Vedagarbha and the selections from Manu, which I appended to my first Grammar. The Sanskṛit of the former is too modern and interspersed with Bengálí idioms, while that of the latter is too advanced. I have therefore substituted for the one some easy sentences selected from classical sources; and for the other, a few simple fables from the Pańcha-tantra, the book from which a great part of the Hitopadeśa itself is drawn. Every word in these selections is explained either by notes at the foot of the page or by references to the preceding pages of the Grammar.

The separation of words by the free use of the Virâma, and the employment of a dot underneath to mark the division, whenever the blending of vowels or the association of crude bases in a compound make junction unavoidable, may offend the eye of the Oriental scholar, if habituated to the Indian system of writing; but the beginner can scarcely be expected to know which is the final and which the initial letter of words thus joined together. Why, therefore, refuse him a clue to guide him in his search for the word in the dictionary? and why, by uniting those parts of a sentence which admit of separation, superadd an unnecessary source of perplexity to the necessary difficulty, unknown in other languages, resulting from the blending of vowels and the composition of words? It may be quite true that, according to native authorities, the Virâma ought only to be employed when no *Sandhi* takes place; and that, according to the strict interpretation of the word *Sandhi*, actual contact ought to ensue whenever a law of euphony comes into operation. But does euphonic connexion necessarily imply contact? and may not words be mutually affected by euphonic laws, without being actually joined together?

The system of uniting words which are really distinct may commend itself to the natives of Hindústán, as tending to reduce the labour of writing; but in Europe, where abundant punctuation is deemed essential to facilitate reading, the absence of spaces must always be regarded as productive of unnecessary hindrance. The student has already sufficient obstacles to surmount in the Deva-nágarí character and the rules for the permutation of letters. The changes required by these rules will cause no embarrassment, provided separation be permitted, in accordance with the European method. Thus the Latin scholar, if acquainted with the laws of permutation, would not be embarrassed by the sentence *Uby ad Dianæ venerir itav at sinistram* (euphonically changed from *ubi ad Dianæ veneris ito ad sinistram*); but he would, to say the least, be unnecessarily hindered if this permuted sentence were linked together into two words, thus — *Ubyaddianæ veneriritavatsinistram.* Nor is it easy to understand why the slight spaces between the words in the first case should be deemed incompatible with the operation of euphonic laws. If such separation, therefore, is only to be effected in Sanskṛit by extending the legitimate functions of the Viráma, the facilities afforded by modern typography ought to leave us free to do so. The only cases in which it is undesirable to separate distinct words, acted on by *Sandhi*, are when two vowels blend into one, and when final *u* and *i* are changed into their corresponding semivowels *v* and *y*.

In regard to the general scope of the book, it remains to state that my aim has been to minister to the wants of the earliest as well as the more advanced student. I have therefore employed types of two different sizes. The larger attracts the eye to those parts of the subject to which the attention of the beginner may advantageously be confined. The smaller generally contains such matter as offers no claim to immediate consideration.

Under the conviction that the study of Sanskṛit ought to possess charms for the classical scholar, independently of its wonderful literature, I have taken pains to introduce in small type the most striking comparisons between this language and Latin and Greek. I am bound to acknowledge that I have drawn nearly all the materials for this important addition to the book from the English translation of Bopp's Comparative Grammar, by my friend and colleague Professor Eastwick.

One point more remains to be noticed. The want of an Index was felt to be a serious defect in my first Grammar. This omission is now supplied. Two full Indices have been appended to the present work, the one English, and the other Sanskrit. The latter will enable the student to turn at once to any noun, verb, affix, idiom or peculiar formation explained in the foregoing pages.

In conclusion, I desire to take this opportunity of expressing to the Delegates of the Oxford University Press my grateful and respectful sense of the advantages the volume derives from their favour and patronage *.

M. W.

EAST-INDIA COLLEGE, HAILEYBURY,
January 1857.

* Not the least of these advantages has been the use of a press which, in its appointments and general efficiency, stands unrivalled. The judgment and accuracy with which the most intricate parts of my MS. have been printed, have excited a thankfulness in my mind, which those only can understand who know the toil of correcting the press, when much Oriental type is interspersed with the Roman, and when a multitude of minute diacritical points, dots, and accents have to be employed to represent the Deva-nágarí letters. If many errors are discovered in the following pages, they must be laid at my own door ; and I have nothing to urge in palliation, excepting that I have spared no pains to avoid inaccuracies, and that the work of one man, however careful and laborious, cannot be expected to be free from the imperfection incidental to all human performances.

CONTENTS.

PAGE.

INTRODUCTORY REMARKS xix

MODIFICATIONS OF THE SANSKRIT ALPHABET xxv

CHAP. I.—LETTERS 1

Pronunciation 7

Classification 11

Accentuation 14

Method of writing 16

CHAP. II.—SANDHI OR EUPHONIC PERMUTATION OF LETTERS 19

Sect. I. Changes of vowels 19

Sect. II. Changes of consonants 26

CHAP. III.—SANSKRIT ROOTS, AND THE FORMATION OF NOMINAL BASES 39

Formation of the base of nouns by affixes 44

CHAP. IV.—DECLENSION OF NOUNS. GENERAL OBSERVATIONS 53

Sect. I. Declension of nouns, whose bases end in vowels 60

Sect. II. Declension of nouns, whose bases end in consonants 71

Sect. III. Adjectives 86

Sect. IV. Numerals 90

CHAP. V.—PRONOUNS 94

CHAP. VI.—VERBS. GENERAL OBSERVATIONS 101

Terminations 104

Summary of the ten conjugations 110

Formation of the base in the four conjugational tenses :

Of verbs of the first, fourth, sixth, and tenth classes 117

Of verbs of the second, third, and seventh classes 126

Of verbs of the fifth, eighth, and ninth classes 132

Formation of the base in the six non-conjugational tenses :

Second preterite; formation of the base 134

First and second future; formation of the base 140

Third preterite; formation of the base 146

Benedictive; formation of the base 152

Conditional; formation of the base 153

Infinitive; formation of the base 154

Passive verbs; formation of the base 154

Causal verbs; formation of the base 158

Desiderative verbs; formation of the base 163

Frequentative or intensive verbs; formation of the base 165

Nominal verbs 168

Participles 170

Participial nouns of agency 182

PAGE.

Examples of verbs conjugated at full :
Table of verbs of the ten conjugations conjugated at full 184
Table of passive verbs conjugated at full 192
Auxiliary verbs conjugated 197
Verbs of the first class conjugated 198
Verbs of the fourth class conjugated 212
Verbs of the sixth class conjugated 217
Verbs of the tenth class conjugated 223
Verbs of the second class conjugated 227
Verbs of the third class conjugated 235
Verbs of the seventh class conjugated 239
Verbs of the fifth class conjugated 244
Verbs of the eighth class conjugated 249
Verbs of the ninth class conjugated 252
Passive verbs conjugated 258
Causal verbs conjugated 260
Desiderative verbs conjugated 262
Frequentative or intensive verbs conjugated 264

CHAP. VII.—INDECLINABLE WORDS.
Adverbs 267
Conjunctions 270
Prepositions 271
Interjections 273

CHAP. VIII.—COMPOUND WORDS.
Sect. I. Compound nouns 273
Tat-purusha or dependent compounds 276
Dwandwa or aggregative compounds 278
Karma-dháraya or descriptive compounds 281
Dwigu or collective compounds 282
Avyayí-bháva or indeclinable compounds 283
Bahu-vríhi or relative compounds 283
Complex compounds 288
Sect. II. Compound verbs 292
Sect. III. Compound adverbs 297

CHAP. IX.—SYNTAX 298

CHAP. X.—EXERCISES IN TRANSLATION AND PARSING 328

SCHEME OF THE MORE COMMON SANSKṚIT METRES 350

ENGLISH INDEX 355

SANSKṚIT INDEX 358

LIST OF COMPOUND OR CONJUNCT CONSONANTS 367

INTRODUCTORY REMARKS.

SANSKRIT is the classical and learned language of the Hindús, in which all their literature is written, and which bears the same relation to their vernacular dialects that Greek and Latin bear to the spoken dialects of Europe. It is one of the family called by modern philologists Arian* or Indo-European; that is to say, it is derived, in common with the languages of Europe, from that primeval but extinct type, once spoken by a tribe in Central Asia, partly pastoral, partly agricultural, who afterwards separated into distinct nationalities, migrating first southwards into Áryávarta or Upper India—the vast territory between the Himálaya and Vindhya mountains—and then northwards and westwards into Europe.

In all probability Sanskṛit approaches more nearly to this primitive type than any of its sister-tongues; but, however this may be, comparative philology has proved beyond a doubt its community with Greek, Latin, Gothic, Lithuanian, Slavonic, Keltic †, and through some of these with Italian, French, Spanish, Portuguese, German, and our own mother-tongue.

The word Sanskṛit (संस्कृत *sanskṛita*) is made up of the preposition *sam* (सं = συν, *con*), 'together,' and the passive participle *kṛita* (कृत = *factus*), 'made,' an euphonic *s* being inserted (see 53. *a.* and 6. *b.* of the following Grammar). The compound means 'carefully constructed,' 'symmetrically formed' (*confectus, constructus*). In this

---

* More properly written Áryan, from the Sanskṛit आर्य *árya*, 'noble,' 'venerable,' 'respectable,' the name assumed by the race who immigrated into Northern India, thence called *Áryávarta*, 'the abode of the Áryans.'

† Zand and old Persian might be added to the list, although the reality of Zand as any thing more than the vehicle of the sacred writings called *Zand-Avastá* (affirmed by the Parsí priests of Persia and India to be the composition of their prophet Zoroaster) has been disputed. Comparative philologists also add Armenian.

sense it is opposed to Prákṛit (प्राकृत *prákṛita*), 'common,' 'natural,' the name given to the vulgar dialects which gradually arose out of it, and from which most of the languages now spoken in Upper India are more or less directly derived. It is probable that Sanskṛit, although a real language—once the living tongue of the Áryan or dominant races, and still the learned language of India, preserved in all its purity through the medium of an immense literature—was never spoken in its most perfect and systematized form by the mass of the people. For we may reasonably conjecture, that if the language of Addison differed from the vulgar and provincial English of his own day, and if the Latin of Cicero differed from the spoken dialect of the Roman plebeian, much more must the most polished and artificial of all languages have suffered corruption when it became the common speech of a vast community, whose separation from the educated classes was far more marked. To make this hypothesis clearer, it may be well to remind the reader, that, before the arrival of the Sanskṛit-speaking immigrants, India was inhabited by a rude people, called 'barbarians' or 'outcastes' (*Mlechchhas, Nisháḍas, Dasyus*, &c.) by Sanskṛit writers, but probably the descendants of various Scythian hordes who, at a remote period, entered India by way of Bilúchistán* and the Indus. The more powerful and civilised of these aboriginal tribes appear to have retired before the Áryans into Southern India, and there to have retained their independence, and with their independence the individuality and essential structure of their vernacular dialects. But in Upper India the case was different. There, as the Áryan race increased in numbers and importance, their full and powerful language forced itself on the aborigines. The weak and scanty dialect of the latter could no more withstand a conflict with the vigorous Sanskṛit, than a puny dwarf the aggression of a giant. Hence the aboriginal tongue gradually wasted away, until its identity became merged in the language of the Áryans; leaving, however, a faint and skeleton-like impress of itself on the purer Sanskṛit of the educated classes, and disintegrating it into Prákṛit, to serve the purposes of ordinary speech †.

* The Brahuí, a dialect of Bilúchistán, still preserves its Scythian character.

† The cerebral letters in Sanskṛit, and words containing cerebral letters, are probably the result of the contact of Sanskṛit with the language of the Scythian

Prákṛit, then, was merely the natural process of change and corruption which the refined Sanskṛit underwent in adapting itself to the exigencies of a spoken dialect *. It was, in fact, the provincial Sanskṛit of the mass of the community; whilst Sanskṛit, properly so called, became, as it is to this day, the language of the Bráhmaṇs and the accomplishment of the learned †.

This provincial Sanskṛit assumed of course different modifications, according to the circumstances of the district in which the corruption took place; and the various modifications of Prákṛit are the intermediate links which connect Sanskṛit with the dialects at present spoken by the natives of Hindústán.

They have been analyzed and assorted by Vararuchi, the ancient grammarian, who was to Prákṛit what Páṇini was to Sanskṛit grammar. The most noticeable varieties were the *Mágadhí*, spoken in Magadha or Bihár; the *Maháráshṭrí*, spoken in a district stretching from Central to Western India; and the *Śaurasení*, spoken on the banks of the Jamná, in the neighbourhood of the ancient Mathurá ‡. These patois modifications of Sanskṛit are employed as the language of the inferior characters in all the Hindú dramas which have come

tribes: and a non-Sanskṛit, or, as it may be called, a Scythian element, may be traced with the greatest clearness in the modern dialects of Hindústán. In all of these dialects there is a substratum of words, foreign to Sanskṛit, which can only be referred to the aboriginal stock. See the last note at the bottom of p. xxii.

* It would be interesting to trace the gradual transition of Sanskṛit into Prákṛit. In a book called the *Lalita-vistara*, the life and adventures of Buddha are narrated in pure Sanskṛit. It is probably of no great antiquity, as the Buddhists themselves deny the existence of written authorities for 400 years after Buddha's death (about B. C. 543). But subjoined to the Sanskṛit version are *gáthás* or songs, which repeat the story in a kind of mixed dialect, half Sanskṛit, half Prákṛit. They were probably rude ballads, which, though not written, were current among the people soon after Buddha's death. They contain Vaidik as well as more modern formations, interspersed with Prákṛit corruptions (ex. gr. शृणुहि for शृणु, which is Vaidik; and धरेन्ति for धारयन्ति, which is Prákṛit), proving that the language was then in a transition state.

† The best proof of this is, that in the Hindú dramas all the higher characters speak Sanskṛit, whilst the inferior speak various forms of Prákṛit. It is idle to suppose that Sanskṛit would have been employed at all in dramatic composition, had it not been the spoken language of a section of the community.

‡ Arrian (ch. VIII) describes the *Suraseni* as inhabiting the city of Methoras.

down to us, some of which date as far back as the 2d century B. C., and the first of them is identical with *Páli*, the sacred language of the Ceylon Buddhists *. Out of them arose *Hindí* (termed *Hindústání* or *Urdú*, when mixed with Persian and Arabic words), *Maráthí*, and *Gujaráthí*, the modern dialects spread widely over the country. To these may be added, *Bengálí*, the language of Bengal, which bears a closer resemblance to its parent, Sanskṛit, than either of the three enumerated above; *Uriya*, the dialect of Orissa, in the province of Cuttack; *Sindhí*, that of Sindh; *Pañjábí*, of the Pañjáb; *Káśmírian*, of Káśmír; and *Nipálese*, of Nipál †.

The four languages of Southern India, viz. 1. Tamiḷ ‡, 2. Telugu (the Ándhra of Sanskṛit writers) §, 3. Kanarese (also called Kannaḍi or Karṇáṭaka), and 4. Malayálam (Malabar) ||, although drawing largely from Sanskṛit for their literature, their scientific terms, their religion, their laws, and their social institutions, are proved to be distinct in their structure, and are referred, as might have been expected from the previous account of the aborigines, to the Scythian, or, as it is sometimes termed, the Tatar or Turanian type ¶.

* Páli, which is identical with the Mágadhí Prákṛit, is the language in which the sacred books of the Buddhists of Ceylon are written. Buddhist missionaries from Magadha carried their religion, and ultimately (after the decay of Buddhism in India) their language, into that island. Páli (meaning in Singhalese 'ancient') is the name which the priests of Ceylon gave to the language of the *old* country, whence they received their religion.

† For an account of some of these dialects, see Prof. H. H. Wilson's very instructive Preface to his 'Glossary of Indian Terms.'

‡ Often incorrectly written Tamul, and by earlier Europeans erroneously termed Malabar. The cerebral *l* at the end has rather the sound of *rl*.

§ Sometimes called Gentoo by the Europeans of the last generation.

|| A fifth language is enumerated, viz. Tuḷu or Tuḷuva, which holds a middle position between Kanarese and Malayálam, but more nearly resembles the former. It is spoken by only 150,000 people. Added to this, there are four rude and uncultivated dialects spoken in various parts of Southern India, viz. the Tuda, Kôta, Gônd, and Ku or Khond; all of which are affiliated with the Southern group.

¶ This is nevertheless consistent with the theory of a remote original affinity between these languages and Sanskṛit and the other members of the Indo-European family. The various branches of the Scythian stock, which spread themselves in all directions westward, northward, and southward, must have radiated from a common centre with the Áryans, although the divergence of the latter took place at a much

Sanskṛit is written in various Indian characters, but the character which is peculiarly its own is the Nágarí or Deva-nágarí, i. e. that of 'the divine, royal, or capital city.' The earliest form of this character cannot be traced back to a period anterior to the 3d century B. C.*; and the more modern, which is the most perfect, comprehensive, and philosophical of all known alphabets, is not traceable for several centuries *after* Christ. The first is the corrupt character of the various inscriptions which have been discovered on pillars and rocks throughout India, written in Mágadhí Prákṛit, spoken at the time of Alexander's invasion over a great part of Hindústán. These inscriptions are ascertained to be addresses from the Buddhist sovereigns of Magadha to the people, enjoining the practice of social virtues and reverence for the priests. They are mostly in the name of Piya-dasi † (for Sanskṛit Priya-darśí), supposed to be an epithet of Aśoka, who is known to have reigned at some period between the 2d and the 3d century B.C. by his being the grandson of Chandra-gupta, probably identical with Sandrakottus, described by Strabo as the most powerful Rájá, immediately succeeding Alexander's death. He was one of the kings of Magadha (Bihár), whose court was at Pálibothra or Páṭali-putra (Patna), and who claimed the title of Samráṭs or universal monarchs; not without reason, as their addresses are found in these inscriptions at Delhi, and at Kuttack in the south, and again as far west as Gujarát, and again as far north as the Pañjáb. The imperfect form of Nágarí which the corrupt character exhibits is incompatible with Sanskṛit orthography. It may therefore be conjectured that a more perfect alphabet existed, which bore

later period. It is to be observed, that in the South-Indian dialects the Scythian element constitutes the bulk of the language. It may be compared to the warp, and the Sanskṛit admixture to the woof. In the Northern dialects the grammatical structure and many of the idioms and expressions are still Scythian, but the whole material and substance of the language is Sanskṛit. See, on this subject, the able Introduction of the Rev. R. Caldwell to his 'Comparative Grammar of the Drávidian or South-Indian Languages,' lately published.

* Mr. James Prinsep, whose table of modifications of the Sanskṛit alphabet follows these Remarks, placed the earliest form, apparently on insufficient grounds, as far back as the 5th century B. C.

† The regular Prákṛit form would be Pia-dassi. Probably the spoken Prákṛit of that period approached nearer to Sanskṛit than the Prákṛit of the plays.

the same relation to the corrupt form that Sanskṛit bore to Prákṛit. Nor does it militate against this theory that the perfect character is not found in any ancient inscription, as it is well known that the Bráhmaṇs, who alone spoke and understood the pure Sanskṛit, and who alone would therefore need that character, never addressed the people, never proselytized, never sought political power, and never cared to emerge from the indolent apathy of a dignified retirement.

A table of the various modifications of the Deva-nágarí alphabet, both ancient and modern, from the date of the earliest inscriptions to the present time, follows this page. The perfection of the modern character, and the admirable manner in which it adapts itself to the elaborate and symmetrical structure of the Sanskṛit language, will be apparent from the first chapter.

MODIFICATIONS

OF THE

SANSKṚIT ALPHABET.

MODIFICATIONS OF THE SANSKṚIT ALPHABET.

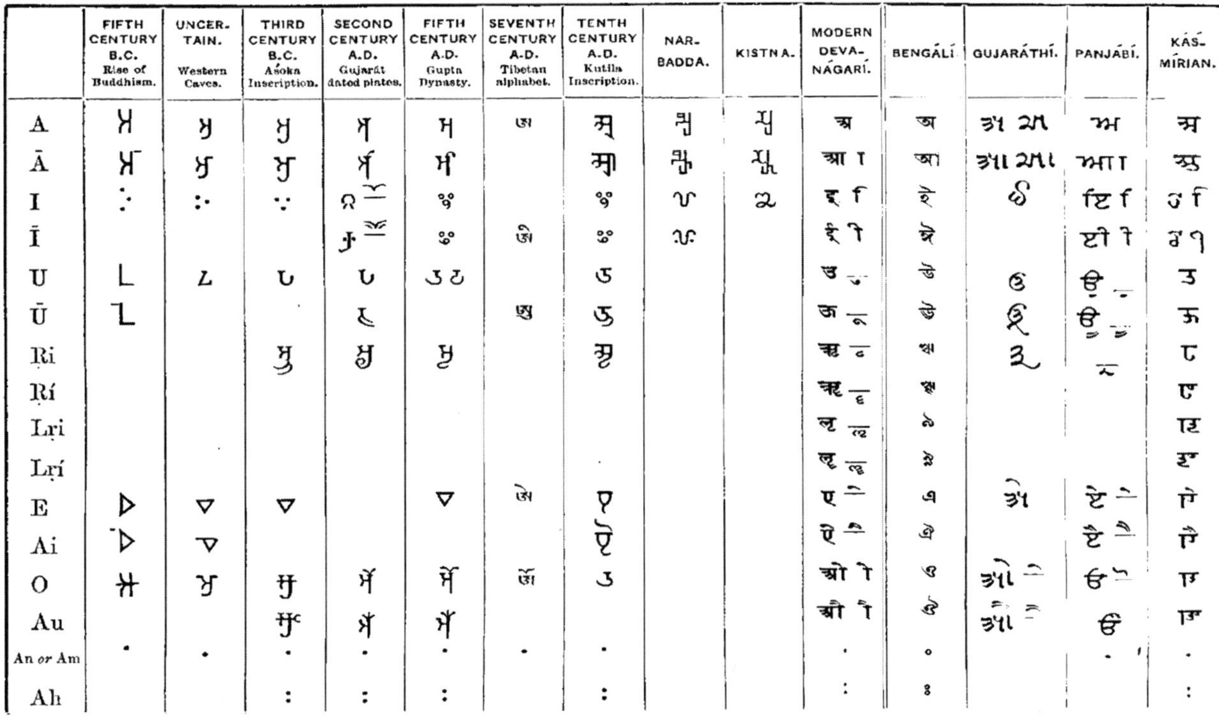

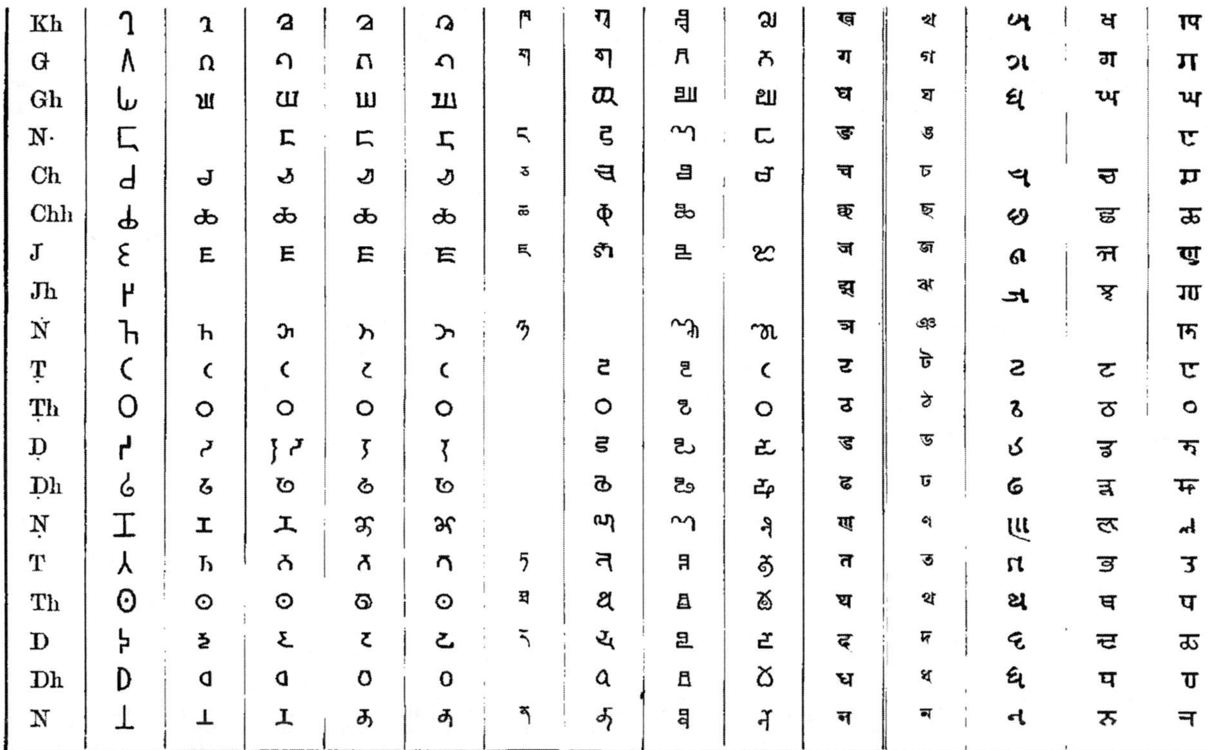
Kh
G
Gh
N·
Ch
Chh
J
Jh
Ṅ
Ṭ
Ṭh
Ḍ
Ḍh
Ṇ
T
Th
D
Dh
N

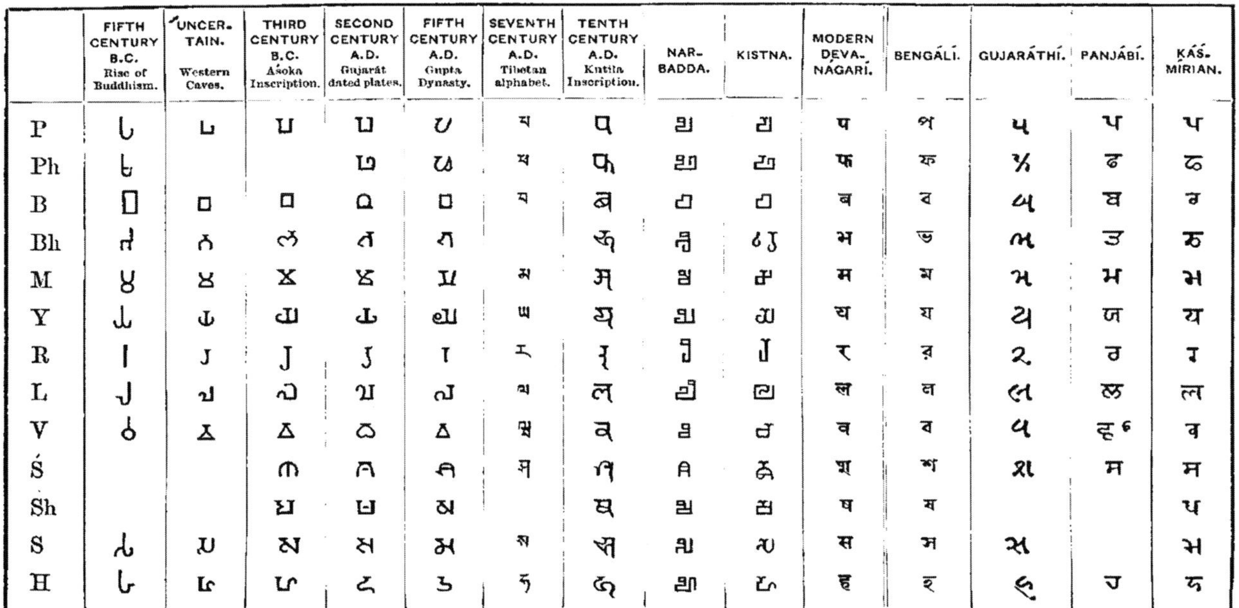

MODERN CONJUNCTION OF CONSONANTS.

क्त kt, क्र kr, क्ल kl, क्व kw, क्ष ksh, ख्य khy, ग्न gn, ग्र gr, ग्ल gl, घ्र ghr, ङ्क n·k, ङ्ग n·g, च्च chch, च्छ chchh, च्य chy, ज्ज jj, ज्व jw, ज्ञ jñ, ञ्च ñch, ञ्छ ñchh, ञ्ज ñj, ट्ट ṭṭ, ण्ट ṇṭ, ण्ठ ṇṭh, ण्ड ṇḍ, त्त tt, त्न tn, त्म tm, त्य ty, त्र tr, त्स ts, द्ध ddh, द्भ dbh, द्य dy, द्र dr, द्व dw, न्त nt, न्द nd, न्न nn, प्त pt, प्य py, प्र pr, प्ल pl, ब्द bd, ब्र br, भ्य bhy, भ्र bhr, म्भ mbh, म्य my, म्ल ml, ल्प lp, व्य vy, व्व vv, श्च śch, श्य śy, श्र śr, ष्ट shṭ, ष्ठ shṭh, ष्य shy, स्त st, स्य sy, स्र sr, स्स ss, ह्ण hṇ, ह्म hm, ह्ल hl, क्त्य kty, क्त्व ktw, क्ष्म kshm, क्ष्य kshy, क्ष्व kshw, ङ्क्य n·ky, ङ्क्ष n·ksh, ङ्ग्य n·gy, ङ्घ्य n·ghy, च्छ्व chchhw, त्त्व ttw, त्स्न tsn, द्ग्र dgr, द्द्य ddy, द्द्व ddw, द्ध्य ddhy, द्ध्व ddhw, द्भ्य dbhy, द्र्य dry, द्व्य dwy, न्त्य nty, प्त्य pty, ष्ट्र shṭr, ङ्क्त्य n·kty, ङ्क्त्व n·ktw.

SANSKRIT GRAMMAR.

CHAPTER I.

LETTERS.

1. THE Deva-nágarí character, in which the Sanskṛit language is written, is adapted to the expression of almost every known gradation of sound; and every letter has a fixed and invariable pronunciation.

There are fourteen vowels and thirty-three simple consonants. To these may be added the nasal symbol, called *Anuswára*, and the symbol for a final aspirate, called *Visarga* (see No. 6). They are here exhibited in the dictionary order *. All the vowels, excepting *a*, have two forms; the first is the initial, the second the medial or non-initial.

VOWELS.

अ *a*, आ ा *á*, इ ि *i*, ई ी *í*, उ ु *u*, ऊ ू *ú*, ऋ ृ *ri*, ॠ ॄ *rí*. ऌ ॢ *lri*, ॡ ॣ *lrí*, ए े *e*, ऐ ै *ai*, ओ ो *o*, औ ौ *au*.

Nasal symbol, ं *n* or *m*. Symbol for the final aspirate, ः *h*.

CONSONANTS.

Gutturals,	क *k*	ख *kh*	ग *g*	घ *gh*	ङ *n·*
Palatals,	च *ch*	छ *chh*	ज *j*	झ *jh*	ञ *ṅ*
Cerebrals,	ट *ṭ*	ठ *ṭh*	ड *ḍ*	ढ *ḍh*	ण *ṇ*
Dentals,	त *t*	थ *th*	द *d*	ध *dh*	न *n*
Labials,	प *p*	फ *ph*	ब *b*	भ *bh*	म *m*
Semivowels,	य *y*	र *r*	ल *l*	व *v*	
Sibilants,	श *ś*	ष *sh*	स *s*		
Aspirate,	ह *h*				

The compound or conjunct consonants (see No. 5) may be multiplied to the extent of four or five hundred. The most common

* The character ळ *lr* is not given, as being peculiar to the Vedas. See 16. *a*.

are given here; a fuller list will be found at the end of the volume; and some varieties in a different type are exhibited at the end of the Table of Modifications, opposite to page 1.

THE MORE COMMON OF THE COMPOUND OR CONJUNCT CONSONANTS.

क्क *kk*, क्त *kt*, क्र or क्र *kr*, क्ल *kl*, क्व *kw*, क्ष *ksh*, ख्य *khy*, ग्न *gn*, ग्र *gr*, ग्ल *gl*, घ्र *ghr*, ङ्क *n·k*, ङ्ग *n·g*, च्च *chch*, च्छ *chchh*, च्य *chy*, ज्ज *jj*, ज्ञ *jñ*, ज्व *jw*, ञ्च *ñch*, ञ्छ *ñchh*, ञ्ज *ñj*, ट्ट *ṭṭ*, ट्य *ṭy*, ड्ग *ḍg*, ड्य *ḍy*, ण्ट *ṇṭ*, ण्ठ *ṇṭh*, ण्ड *ṇḍ*, ण्ण *ṇṇ*, ण्य *ṇy*, त्त *tt*, त्थ *tth*, त्न *tn*, त्म *tm*, त्य *ty*, त्र or त्र *tr*, त्व *tw*, त्स *ts*, थ्य *thy*, द्ग *dg*, द्ध *ddh*, द्भ *dbh*, द्म *dm*, द्य *dy*, द्र *dr*, द्व *dw*, ध्य *dhy*, ध्व *dhw*, न्त *nt*, न्द *nd*, न्न *nn*, न्य *ny*, प्त *pt*, प्य *py*, प्र *pr*, प्ल *pl*, ब्ज *bj*, ब्द *bd*, ब्य *by*, ब्र *br*, भ्य *bhy*, भ्र *bhr*, म्भ *mbh*, म्म *mm*, म्य *my*, म्ल *ml*, य्य *yy*, र्क *rk*, र्म *rm*, ल्प *lp*, ल्ल *ll*, व्य *vy*, व्र *vr*, श्च *śch*, श्य *śy*, श्र *śr*, श्ल *śl*, श्व *św*, ष्ट *shṭ*, ष्ठ *shṭh*, ष्ण *shṇ*, ष्य *shy*, स्क *sk*, स्ख *skh*, स्त *st*, स्थ *sth*, स्न *sn*, स्म *sm*, स्य *sy*, स्र *sr*, स्व *sw*, स्स *ss*, ह्म *hm*, ह्य *hy*, ह्ल *hl*, क्त्य *kty*, क्त्र *ktr*, क्त्व *ktw*, क्ष्ण *kshṇ*, क्ष्म *kshm*, क्ष्य *kshy*, ग्न्य *gny*, ग्भ्य *gbhy*, ग्र्य *gry*, ङ्क्त *n·kt*, ङ्क्य *n·ky*, च्छ्य *chchhy*, च्छ्र *chchhr*, ण्ड्य *ṇḍy*, त्स्न *tsn*, त्म्य *tmy*, त्र्य *try*, त्स्य *tsy*, त्त्र *ttr*, त्त्व *ttw*, द्द्य *ddy*, द्ध्य *ddhy*, द्भ्य *dbhy*, द्र्य *dry*, न्त्य *nty*, म्ब्य *mby*, र्द्र *rdr*, र्य्य *ryy*, र्व्व *rvv*, ष्ट्र *shṭr*, स्थ्न *sthn*, स्त्य *sty*, स्त्र *str*, त्स्न्य *tsny*, न्त्र्य *ntry*, र्त्स्य *rtsy*, र्त्स्न्य *rtsny*.

OF THE METHOD OF WRITING THE VOWELS.

Observe—In reading the following pages for the first time, it is recommended that the attention be confined to the large type.

2. The short vowel अ *a* is never written unless it begin a word, because it is supposed to be inherent in every consonant. Thus. *ak* is written अक्, but *ka* is written क; so that in such words as कनक *kanaka*, नगर *nagara*, &c., no vowel has to be written. The mark ् under the *k* of अक्, called Viráma (see No. 9), indicates a consonantal stop, that is, the absence of any vowel, inherent or otherwise, after the consonant.

a. The other vowels, if written after a consonant, take the place of the inherent *a*. They assume two forms, according as they are initial or not initial. Thus, *ik* is written इक्, but *ki* is written कि.

b. Observe here, that the short vowel *i*, when *not initial*, is always written *before* the letter *after* which it is pronounced. Hence. in writing the English word *sir*, the letters in Sanskṛit would be arranged thus, *isr* सिर्.

c. The only assignable reason for this peculiarity is, that the top of the non-initial ि *i*, if written in its right place, might occasionally interfere with a subsequent letter, especially with the letter *r*, as the first member of a conjunct consonant. This will be evident to any one who tries in writing the word *kirk* in Sanskṛit to retain the *i* in its proper place.

3. The long vowels ा *á* and ी *í*, not initial, take their proper place after a consonant. The vowels *u*, *ú*, *ṛi*, *ṛí*, *lṛi*, not initial, are written *under* the consonants after which they are pronounced; as, कु *ku*, कू *kú*, कृ *kṛi*, कॄ *kṛí*, कॢ *klṛi*; excepting when *u* or *ú* follows र *r*, in which case the method of writing is peculiar; thus, रु *ru*, रू *rú*.

a. The vowels *ṛi*, *ṛí*, *lṛi* and *lṛí* are peculiar to Sanskṛit. See No. 11. *c*. ऌ *lṛi* occurs in only one word, viz. कॢप् 'to make.' The long ॡ *lṛí* is not found in any word in the language, and is useless excepting as contributing to the completeness of the alphabet.

b. The vowels *e* and *ai*, not initial, are written above the consonants after which they are pronounced; thus, के *ke*, कै *kai*. The vowels *o* and *au* (which are formed by placing े and ै over ा *á*), like ा *á*, take their proper place after their consonants; thus, को *ko*, कौ *kau*.

OF THE METHOD OF WRITING THE CONSONANTS.

4. The consonants have only one form, whether initial or not initial. And here note this peculiarity in the form of the Devanágarí letters. In every consonant, excepting those of the cerebral class, and in some of the initial vowels, there is a perpendicular stroke; and in all the consonants without exception, as well as in all the initial vowels, there is a horizontal line at the top of the letter. In two of the letters, ध *dh* and भ *bh*, this horizontal line is broken; and in writing rapidly, the student should form the perpendicular line first, then the other parts of the letter, and lastly the horizontal line. The natives, however, sometimes form the horizontal line first.

OF THE COMPOUND CONSONANTS.

5. Every consonant is supposed to have the vowel अ *a* inherent in it, so that it is never necessary to write this vowel, excepting at the beginning of a word. Hence when any simple consonants stand alone in any word, the short vowel अ *a* must always be pronounced after them; but when they appear in conjunction with any other vowel, this other vowel of course takes the place of short अ *a*. Thus such a word as कलानतया would be pronounced *kalánatayá*, where long आ *á* being written after *l* and *y* takes the place of the inherent vowel. But supposing that instead of *kalánatayá* the word had to

be pronounced *klántyá*, how are we to know that *kl* and *nty* have to be uttered without the intervention of any vowel? This occasions the necessity for compound consonants. *Kl* and *nty* must then be combined together; thus, क्ल, न्त्य, and the word is written क्लान्त्या. And here we have illustrated the two methods of compounding consonants; viz. 1st, by writing them one above the other; 2dly, by placing them side by side, omitting in all, except the last, the perpendicular line which lies to the right. Observe, however, that some letters change their form entirely when combined with other consonants. Thus र, when it is the *first* letter of a compound consonant, is written above the compound in the form of a semicircle, as in the word कूर्म *kúrma;* and when the *last*, is written below in the form of a small stroke, as in the word क्रमेण *krameṇa.* So again in क्ष* *ksha* and ज्ञ† *jña* the simple elements क ष and ज ञ are hardly traceable. In some compounds the simple letters slightly change their form; as, श *śa* becomes श्‍ in श्च *ścha;* द् *d* with य *y* becomes द्य *dya;* द् *d* with ध *dh* becomes द्ध *ddha;* द् *d* with भ *bh* becomes द्भ *dbha;* त *t* with र *r* becomes त्र *tra* or त्र *tra;* क *k* with त *t* becomes क्त *kta.* Most of the other compound consonants are readily resolvable into their component parts. The student should direct his first attention to the compound consonants given in the list opposite to page 1. He should afterwards study the list at the end of the book.

Observe—Two aspirated letters never occur in the same compound. When an aspirated letter has to be doubled, the first is expressed by the unaspirated letter of the same species.

OF THE SYMBOLS AND MARKS.

6. The Sanskṛit alphabet possesses certain symbols and indicatory marks. Of these the most useful are the nasal symbol *Anuswára* and the symbol for a final aspirate called *Visarga.*

Anuswára, 'after-sound,' (called so because it is always the final or closing nasal sound of a syllable, and can never be used like a consonant or any nasal letter to begin a syllable,) is denoted by a dot placed over the horizontal line of a letter. It is a weaker and

* Sometimes formed thus क्ष, and pronounced *ky* in Bengálí. In Greek and Latin it always passes into ξ and *x*. Compare दक्षिण, dexter, δεξιός.

† This compound is sometimes pronounced *gya* or *nya*, though it will be more convenient to represent it by its proper equivalent *jña*.

thicker nasal than the five consonantal nasals. Although it is properly the nasal of the semivowels, sibilants, and *h*, and is then expressible by the English *n*, yet it is ordinarily used as a short substitute for any of the five nasals, ङ *ṅ*, ञ *ñ*, ण *ṇ*, न *n*, and म *m*, when no vowel intervenes between these letters and a following consonant. Thus the five English words *ink*, *inch*, *intrust*, *ant*, *imp*, which illustrate the five nasal sounds, might either be written इङ्क्, इञ्च्, इण्ट्रस्त्, आन्त्, इम्प्, or with Anuswára इंक्, इंच्, इंट्रस्त्, आंत्, इंप्. It is most conveniently used as a substitute for the म् *m* which is the original final of accusative cases singular, nominative cases neuter, and some indeclinable words *; (thus एनं *enam*, 'him,' for एनम्; दानं *dánam*, 'a gift,' for दानम्; सं *sam*, 'with,' for सम्; इदानीं *idáním*, 'now;') passing, however, again into म् *m* when followed by a vowel; (as, दानम् आप्नोति *dánam ápnoti*, 'he receives a gift;') and passing optionally into ङ्, ञ्, ण्, न् or म् when followed by consonants of the guttural, palatal, cerebral, dental, and labial classes respectively; (as, दानं ददाति or दानन् ददाति 'he gives a gift,' संडीन or सण्डीन 'flight.') Hence it appears, that as the final of a complete word it may generally be represented by the English *m*.

a. It is never admitted as a substitute for a final न् *n* when originally the *final* of a word, (as in accusative cases plural, in the locative cases of pronominals, in the 3d pers. plur. and present participles of verbs,) unless the next word begin with *t* or *ch*, when by the laws of euphony a sibilant is interposed before the initial *t* or *ch*. See 53 and 54.

b. It must never be forgotten that it is peculiarly the nasal of the aspirate ह *h*, the semivowels य *y*, र *r*, ल *l*, व *v*, and the three sibilants श *ś*, ष *sh*, स *s*; and it must always take the place of any other nasal that has to precede these letters *in the same word* †. Thus the preposition सम् *sam* and the participle स्मृत *smṛita*, when united in one word, are written संस्मृत; सम् *sam* and हार *hára*, संहार; सम् *sam* and राग *rága*, संराग; but in each of these cases the Anuswára takes the sound of the nasal of the class to which the following letter belongs. Thus संस्मृत is sounded as if written सन् स्मृत; संहार as if written सङ् हार; संलाप as if written सन् लाप. In these cases Anuswára not being the final of a complete word will be most conveniently transliterated by the English *n*.

7. Another nasal symbol called *Chandra-vindu* (lunar mark) or *Anunásika*, written

---

* Prof. Bopp objects to this practice; but by Paṇini (VIII. 3, 23) a final म् *m* is convertible to Anuswára before *any* consonant. See Bopp's Comparative Grammar, Eastwick's translation, p. 7, note.

† सम्राज्, 'an universal monarch,' is the only word that violates this rule. The word सम्यच्, 'just,' is compounded of समि and अच्.

over a letter thus ँ, is sometimes employed. It is rather the sign of the nasality of the letter over which it is written, than the representative of any actual nasal sound. Thus in the rules of combination, when final न *n* assimilates with ल *l*, the mark ँ placed over *l*, though not pronounced, indicates the nasal origin of the लँ. It is a kind of silent Anuswára.

8. The symbol *Visarga*, 'rejection,' (called so because often rejected,) usually written thus :, but more properly in the form of two small circles ः, is used to represent a weaker aspiration than the letter ह *h*, and that at the end of a word. It expresses an euphonic transition of final स् *s* and र् *r* into a kind of imperceptible breathing. But this symbol, although never the representative of ह *h*, but rather of a weak and almost imperceptible final aspirate, which, under certain circumstances, takes the place of final *s* and *r*, may nevertheless be conveniently transliterated by the English *h* at the end of a word, and that without danger of being confounded with ह, which can never occur as a final letter. At the same time it should be borne in mind that Visarga is less than *h*, and is in fact no consonant, but only a symbol for *s* and *r* whenever the usual consonantal sound of these letters is deadened at the end of a sentence or through the influence of a *k*, *p* or *s* commencing the next word. Observe, however, that all those inflections of nouns and persons of verbs, which as standing separate from other words are by some made to end in Visarga, may most conveniently be allowed to retain their final स् *s*; only bearing in mind that this *s* is liable at the end of a sentence, or when followed by certain consonants, to pass into an imperceptible breathing, as in the French *les* or the English *isle, viscount;* in all which cases it might be expressed by Visarga, thus ले: &c. So again, in French infinitives, such as *aller*, the final *r* is silent; and in many English words, such as *bar*, *tar*, the sound of *r* is very indistinct; and these also might be written in Sanskṛit with Visarga, अल्ले:, बा: &c.

a. An *Ardha-visarga*, 'half-visarga,' or modification of the symbol Visarga, in the form of two semicircles ᳵ, is sometimes employed before *k*, *kh* and *p*, *ph*. Before the two former letters this symbol is properly called *Jihvá-múlíya*, and the organ of its enunciation said to be the root of the tongue. Before *p* and *ph* its proper name is *Upadhmáníya*, and its organ of utterance is then the lips.

The following are other marks:

9. The *Virámo* or 'stop,' placed under a consonant (thus क् *k*),

indicates the absence of the inherent अ *a*, by help of which the consonant is pronounced.

10. The mark ऽ, sometimes called *Ardhákára*, 'half the letter *a*,' placed between two words, denotes the elision of an initial अ *a* after ए *e* or ओ *o* final preceding. It corresponds to our apostrophe. Thus, तेऽपि *te 'pi* for ते अपि *te api*.

a. The half pause । is a stop or mark of punctuation, usually placed at the end of the first line of a couplet or stanza.

b. The whole pause ॥ is placed at the end of a couplet, and corresponds to a full stop.

c. The mark of repetition ० indicates that a word or sentence has to be repeated.

PRONUNCIATION OF SANSKRIT VOWELS AS COMPARED WITH THOSE OF OTHER LANGUAGES.

11. The vowels in Sanskṛit are pronounced for the most part as in Italian or French, though occasional words in English may exemplify their sound.

a. Since अ *a* is inherent in every consonant, the student should be careful to acquire the correct pronunciation of this letter. There are many words in English which afford examples of its sound, such as *vocal, cedar, zebra, organ*. But in English the vowel *u* in such words as *fun, bun, sun*, frequently represents this obscure sound of *a*; and even the other vowels may occasionally be pronounced with this sound, as in *her, sir, son*.

b. The long vowel आ *á* is pronounced as *a* in the English *last, bard, cart*; इ *i* as the *i* in *pin, sin*; ई *í* as the *í* in *marine*; उ *u* as the *u* in *push*; ऊ *ú* as the *u* in *rude*.

c. The vowel ऋ *ṛi*, peculiar to Sanskṛit, is pronounced as the *ri* in *merrily*, where the *i* of *ṛi* is less perceptible than in the syllable *ri*, composed of the consonant *r* and the vowel *i* *. ॠ *ṛí* is pronounced as the *ri* in *chagrin*, being hardly distinguishable from the syllable री; ए *e* as the *e* in *prey*; ओ *o* as in *so*; ऐ *ai* as *ai* in *aisle*; औ *au* as *au* in the German *baum* or as *ou* in the English *our*. ऌ *lṛi* and ॡ *lṛí* do not differ in sound from the letter ल *l* with the vowels *ṛi* and *ṛí* annexed, but the vowel ऌ *lṛi* only occurs in one word, viz.

* There does not, however, seem to be much difference practically between the pronunciation of the vowel *ṛi* and the syllable रि *ri*, though grammarians assert that the *i* of the vowel is less distinctly enunciated.

क्लृप् *kḷrip*, 'to make;' and its long form is not found in any word in the language. As to the Vaidik ळ *ḷra*, see 16. *a*.

d. Hence it appears that every simple vowel in Sanskṛit has a short and a long form, and that each vowel has one invariable sound; so that the beginner can never be in doubt what pronunciation to give it, as in English, or whether to pronounce it long or short, as in Latin.

e. Note, however, that Sanskṛit possesses no short *ĕ* and *ŏ* in opposition to the long diphthongal sounds of *e* and *o*.

f. In comparing Sanskṛit words with Greek and Latin, it will be found that the Sanskṛit अ *a* usually answers to the Greek ο; sometimes to ε (especially in vocative cases); and rarely to α. In Latin, the Sanskṛit अ *a* is represented by *u* as well as by *a*, *e*, and *o*. Again, the Sanskṛit आ *á* is generally replaced by the Greek η or ω, rarely by a long alpha. In Latin it is represented by long *a* or even by long *e*. See Bopp's Comparative Grammar, Eastwick's translation, p. 4 &c.

g. Although for all practical purposes it is sufficient to regard vowels as either short or long, it should be borne in mind that native grammarians give eighteen different modifications of each of the vowels *a*, *i*, *u*, *ṛi*, and twelve of *ḷri*, which are thus explained:—Each of the first four vowels is supposed to have three prosodial lengths, a short (*hraswa*), a long (*dírgha*), and a prolated (*pluta*); the long being equal to two, and the prolated to three short vowels. Each of these three modifications may be uttered with a high tone, or a low tone, or a tone between high and low; or in other words, may have the acute, or the grave, or the circumflex accent. This gives nine modifications to *a*, *i*, *u*, *ṛi*; and each of these again may be regarded either as nasal or non-nasal, according as it is pronounced with the nose and mouth, or with the mouth alone. Hence result eighteen varieties of every vowel, excepting *ḷri*, *e*, *ai*, *o*, *au*, which have only twelve, because the first does not possess the long and the last four have not the short prosodial time.

PRONUNCIATION OF SANSKṚIT CONSONANTS AS COMPARED WITH THOSE OF OTHER LANGUAGES.

In the first arrangement of the alphabet most of the consonants are distributed under the five heads of gutturals, palatals, cerebrals, dentals, and labials, according to the organ principally employed in pronouncing them, whether the throat, the palate, the top of the palate, the teeth, or the lips. This classification of letters is more fully explained at No. 18.

12. क *ka*, ग *ga*, च *cha*, ज *ja*, त *ta*, द *da*, प *pa*, ब *ba*. These consonants are pronounced as in English, but ग has always the sound of *g* in *gun*, *give*, never of *g* in *gin*. Observe; च *cha* is a simple consonantal sound, and not an aspirate: it is pronounced as *ch* in

church, and is a modification or softening of *ka*, just as *ja* is of *ga*, the organ of utterance being in the palate, a little in advance of the throat. Hence, in Sanskṛit and its cognate languages, the palatals *ch* and *j* are often exchanged with the gutturals *k* and *g*. See note, p. 13.

Observe, that द् *d* often passes into θ in Greek.

13. ख *kha*, घ *gha*, छ *chha*, झ *jha*, थ *tha*, ध *dha*, फ *pha*, भ *bha*. These are the aspirated forms of the preceding consonants. In pronouncing them the sound of *h* must be distinctly added to the unaspirated consonantal sound. Thus ख is pronounced like *kh* in *ink-horn*, not like the Greek χ; थ as *th* in *ant-hill*, not as in *think;* फ as *ph* in *uphill*, not as in *physic*. When, however, they are rapidly enunciated they are hardly distinguishable from their respective unaspirated equivalents.

a. The Sanskṛit थ *th* generally becomes τ in Greek, and ध *dh* becomes θ, while छ *chh* generally passes into $\sigma\kappa$. Again, Sanskṛit भ *bh* generally passes into ϕ and *f*, or sometimes in Latin into *b*.

b. With a view to the comparison of Sanskṛit words with Greek and Latin, it is important to remember that the aspirates of the different classes are easily interchangeable in different languages; thus *dh* and *bh* in Sanskṛit may become *f* (or *ph*) in Latin; *gh* in Sanskṛit may become θ in Greek &c.

14. ट *ṭa*, ठ *ṭha*, ड *ḍa*, ढ *ḍha*. The sound of these cerebral letters is in practice hardly to be distinguished from the sound of the corresponding dental consonants. Properly, however, the cerebrals should be uttered with a duller and deeper intonation, produced by turning back the tip of the tongue towards the palate, or top of the head (*cerebrum*). Thus a Hindú would distinguish the pronunciation of the *t* and *d* in the English words *trust* and *drip* from that of the same letters in the words *tun* and *din*. He would write the former with the cerebral *ṭ* and *ḍ*, ट्रस्ट्, ड्रिप्; and the latter with the dental, तुन्, दिन्.

a. In Bengal the cerebral ड *ḍa* and ढ *ḍha* have nearly the sound of a dull *r*. Thus विडालः *viḍálah*, 'a cat,' is pronounced *virálah*. In all corruptions of Sanskṛit (especially in Prákṛit) the cerebral letters often take the place of dentals. In Sanskṛit the cerebrals are rarely found at the beginning of words.

15. ङ *ṅa*, ञ *ña*, ण *ṇa*, न *na*, म *ma*. Each of the five classes of consonants in Sanskṛit has its own nasal sound, represented by a separate nasal letter. In English and most other languages the same fivefold division of nasal sounds might be made, though we have only one nasal letter to express the guttural, palatal, cerebral,

and dental nasal sounds. The truth is, that in all languages the nasal letters take their sound from the organ employed in uttering the consonant that follows them. Thus in English it will be found that guttural, palatal, cerebral, dental, and labial nasals are followed by consonants of the same classes, as in *ink, sing, inch, intrust, ant, imp.* If such words existed in Sanskṛit, the distinction of nasal sounds would be represented by distinct letters; thus, इङ्क्, सिङ्ग्, इञ्च्, इण्ट्रस्ट्, आन्त्, इम्प्. Compare 6.

a. The guttural nasal ङ is rarely found by itself at the end of a word in Sanskṛit, never at the beginning. In the nominative cases प्राङ्, प्रत्यङ् &c. it probably has the sound of *ng* in *sing*, where the sound of *g* is almost imperceptible. The palatal ञ is only found in conjunction with palatal consonants, as in ञ्च *ñch*, ञ्ज *ñj*, ञ्छ *chñ*, and ज्ञ *jñ*. This last may be pronounced like *ny*, or like *gn* in the French *campagne*. In Bengal, however, it always has the sound of *gy*: thus राज्ञा is pronounced *rágyá*. The cerebral nasal ण *ṇ* is found at the beginning of words and before vowels, as well as in conjunction with cerebral consonants. It is then pronounced, as the other cerebrals, by turning the tip of the tongue towards the palate. The dental and labial nasals न *na* and म *ma* are pronounced with the same organs as the class of letters to which they belong. [See 21.]

16. य *ya*, र *ra*, ल *la*, व *va*, are pronounced as in English. Their relationship to the vowels *i, ṛi, lṛi, u*, respectively, should never be forgotten. See No. 22. *a.* When व *v* is the last member of a conjunct consonant it is pronounced like *w*, as द्वार *dwára;* but not after *r*, as सर्व *sarva.*

a. The character ळ *ḷra* is peculiar to the Vedas. It is a form of the semivowel ल *l*, and represents a liquid sound formed by curving back the tongue against the roof of the mouth.

b. The semivowels are so soft and vowel-like in their nature that they readily flow into each other. Hence *l* and *r* are sometimes exchangeable.

17. श *śa*, ष *sha*, स *sa*, ह *ha*. Of these, श *śa* is a palatal sibilant, and is pronounced as an aspirated *s*. ष *sha* is a cerebral, and is a more strongly aspirated sibilant, but its pronunciation is hardly to be distinguished from that of the palatal. The dental स *sa* is pronounced as the common English *s*. The same three sibilants exist in English, though represented by one character, as in the words *sure, session, sun.* ह *ha* is pronounced as in English, and is guttural.

a. The guttural origin of ह *ha* is proved by its passing into *k* at the end of Sanskṛit words, and into χ, κ, and *c*, in Greek and Latin; as, हृदय, καρδία, *cor.*

b. Note that श *śa*, although a palatal, might be called half a guttural. It is certainly guttural in its origin, as all the palatals are. This is well illustrated by its constant transition into κ and c in Greek and Latin words. Compare अश्रु δάκρυ, अश्व equus, श्वन् κύων. It is moreover interchanged with क *k* in Sanskṛit words.

OF THE CLASSIFICATION OF LETTERS.

18. In the first arrangement of the alphabet all the consonants, excepting the semivowels, sibilants, and *h*, were distributed under the five heads of gutturals, palatals, cerebrals, dentals, and labials. We are now to show that *all the forty-seven* letters, vowels, semivowels, and consonants, may be referred to one or other of these five grand classes, according to the organ principally concerned in their pronunciation, whether the throat, the palate, the top of the palate, the teeth, or the lips.

a. We are, moreover, to point out that all the letters may be regarded according to another principle of division, and may be all arranged under the head of either HARD or SOFT, according as the effort of utterance is attended with expansion (*vivára*), or contraction (*samvára*), of the throat.

b. The following tables exhibit this twofold classification, the comprehension of which is of the utmost importance to the study of Sanskṛit grammar.

	VOWELS AND DIPHTHONGS.	HARD CONSONANTS.	CORRESPONDING SOFT CONSONANTS.	NASALS.	ASPIRATE AND SEMI-VOWELS.	SIBI-LANTS.
Gutturals	अ *a* आ *á*	क *ka* ख *kha*	ग *ga* घ *gha*	ङ *n·a*	ह *ha*	
Palatals	इ *i* ई *í* ए *e* ऐ *ai*	च *cha* छ *chha*	ज *ja* झ *jha*	ञ *ña*	य *ya*	श *śa*
Cerebrals	ऋ *ṛi* ॠ *ṛí*	ट *ṭa* ठ *ṭha*	ड *ḍa* ढ *ḍha*	ण *ṇa*	र *ra*	ष *sha*
Dentals	ऌ *ḷri* ॡ *ḷrí*	त *ta* थ *tha*	द *da* ध *dha*	न *na*	ल *la*	स *sa*
Labials	उ *u* ऊ *ú* ओ *o* औ *au*	प *pa* फ *pha*	ब *ba* भ *bha*	म *ma*	व *va*	

The first two consonants in each of the above five classes and the sibilants are hard; all the other letters are soft, as in the following table:

HARD OR SURD LETTERS.			SOFT OR SONANT LETTERS.	
Gutturals,	क *ka** ख *kha**		अ *a* आ *á*	ग *ga** घ *gha** ङ *n·a* ह *ha*
Palatals,	च *cha** छ *chha**	श *śa*	इ *i* ई *í* ए *e* ऐ *ai*	ज *ja** झ *jha** ञ *ña* य *ya*
Cerebrals,	ट *ṭa** ठ *ṭha**	ष *sha*	ऋ *ṛi* ॠ *ṛí*	ड *ḍa** ढ *ḍha** ण *ṇa* र *ra*
Dentals,	त *ta** थ *tha**	स *sa*	ऌ *ḷri* ॡ *ḷrí*	द *da** ध *dha** न *na* ल *la*
Labials,	प *pa** फ *pha**		उ *u* ऊ *ú* ओ *o* औ *au*	ब *ba** भ *bha** म *ma* व *va*

c. Observe, that although ए *e*, ऐ *ai*, are more conveniently connected with the palatal class, and ओ *o*, औ *au*, with the labial, these letters are really diphthongal, being made up of *a* + *i*, *á* + *i*, *a* + *u*, *á* + *u*, respectively. Their first element is therefore guttural.

d. Note also, that it is most important to observe which hard letters have kindred soft letters, and *vice versa*. The kindred hard and soft are those in the same line marked with a star in the above table; thus *g*, *gh*, are the corresponding soft letters to *k*, *kh*; *j*, *jh*, to *ch*, *chh*, and so with the others.

In order that the foregoing classification may be clearly understood, it is necessary to remind the student of the proper meaning of the term vowel and consonant, and of the relationship which the nasals, semivowels, and sibilants, bear to the other letters.

19. A vowel is defined to be a vocal emission of breath from the lungs, modified and modulated, but not interrupted by the play of one or other of five organs, viz. the throat, the palate, the tongue, the teeth, or the lips*.

a. Hence अ *a*, इ *i*, उ *u*, ऋ *ṛi*, ऌ *lṛi*, with their respective long forms, are simple vowels, belonging to the guttural, palatal, labial, cerebral, and dental classes respectively, according to the organ principally concerned in their modulation. But ए *e*, ऐ *ai*, ओ *o*, औ *au*, are diphthongal or compound vowels, as explained above at 18. *c.*† So that *e* and *ai* are half guttural, half palatal; *o* and *au* half guttural, half labial.

b. The vowels are of course considered to be soft letters.

20. A consonant is not the modulation, but the actual stoppage, of the vocal stream of breath by one or other of the five organs, and cannot be enunciated excepting in conjunction with a vowel.

a. All the consonants, therefore, are arranged under the five heads of gutturals, palatals, cerebrals, dentals, and labials, according to the organ concerned in *stopping* the vocal sound.

b. Again, the first two consonants in each of the five classes, and the sibilants, are called *hard* or *surd*, because the vocal stream is

---

* See Proposals for a Missionary Alphabet, by Prof. Max Müller.

† If the two vowels *a* and *i* are pronounced rapidly they naturally form the sound *e* pronounced as in *prey*, or as *a* and *i* in *sail*; and so with the other diphthongs. The sound of *ai* in *aisle* may readily be resolved into *á* and *i*, and the sound of *ou* in *out* into *á* and *u*.

abruptly and completely interrupted, and no murmuring sound (*aghosha*) allowed to escape: while all the other letters are called *soft* or *sonant*, because the vocal sound is less suddenly and completely arrested, the effect of stopping it being attended with a low murmur (*ghosha*).

c. Observe, that the palatal stop is only a modification of the guttural, the point of contact being moved a little more forward from the throat towards the palate *. The cerebral (*múrdhanya*) stop is a modification of the dental, the difference being, that whereas in the dental consonantal sound the tip of the tongue is brought into direct contact with the teeth; in the cerebral it is first curled back, so as to strike the dome of the palate, thus producing a more obtuse sound.

d. The name *cerebral* is retained in deference to established usage. Perhaps a more significant translation of *múrdhanya* would be *supernal*. The head or brain is certainly not the organ of enunciation of any letter. *Múrdhan* here denotes the *upper part* of the palate. But the inaccuracy involved in the word *cerebral* hardly justifies the substitution of *supernal*.

21. A nasal or narisonant letter is a soft letter, in the utterance of which the vocal stream of breath incompletely arrested, as in all soft letters, is forced through the nose instead of the lips. As the soft letters are of five kinds, according to the organ which interrupts the vocal breathing, so the nasal letters are five, guttural, palatal, cerebral, dental, and labial. See 15.

22. The semivowels *y*, *r*, *l*, *v* (called *antahstha* because in the first arrangement of the alphabet they *stand between* the other consonants and the sibilants) are formed by a vocal breathing, which is only half interrupted, the several organs being only slightly touched by the tongue. They are, therefore, soft or sonant consonants, approaching nearly to the character of vowels; in fact, half vowels, half consonants.

a. Each class of soft letters (excepting the guttural) has its own corresponding semivowel to which it is related. Thus the palatal soft letters इ *i*, ई *í*, ए *e*, ऐ *ai*, ज *j*, have य *y* for their kindred semivowel. (Compare Sanskṛit *yuvan* with Latin *juvenis* &c.) Similarly

---

* The relationship of the palatal to the guttural letters is proved by their frequent interchangeableness in Sanskṛit and in other languages. See 176, and compare *church* with *kirk*, Sanskṛit *chatwár* with Latin *quatuor*, Sanskṛit *cha* with Latin *que* and Greek *καί*, Sanskṛit *jánu* with English *knee*, Greek *γόνυ*, Latin *genu*. Prof. Müller proposes to represent the palatals च and ज by *k* and *g* in Italics.

र *r* is the kindred semivowel of the cerebral soft letters ऋ *ṛi*, ॠ *ṛí*, and ड *ḍ*; ल *l* of the dentals ऌ *lṛi*, ॡ *lṛí*, and द *d**; and व *v* of उ *u*, ऊ *ú*, ओ *o*, औ *au*, and ब *b*. The guttural soft letters have no semivowel in Sanskṛit, unless the aspirate ह *h* be so regarded.

23. The sibilants or hissing sounds (called *winds* by the native grammarians) are hard letters, which, nevertheless, strictly speaking, have something the character of vowels. The organs of speech in uttering them, although not closed, are more contracted than in vowels, and the vocal stream of breath in passing through the teeth experiences a friction which causes sibilation.

a. Sanskṛit does not recognise any guttural sibilation, though the palatal sibilant is really half a guttural. See 17. *a.* The aspirate ह *h* might perhaps be regarded as a guttural *flatus* or wind without sibilating sound. The labial sibilation denoted by the letter *f*, and the soft sibilation denoted by *z*, are unknown in Sanskṛit.

ACCENTUATION.

24. Accentuation in Sanskṛit is confined to the Vedas. In common pronunciation the tone or intonation of vowels in all Sanskṛit words is equal. This general monotonous intonation is called by Páṇini *eka-śruti*, the one level, as it were, of pronunciation. But in the Vaidik hymns a rise and fall of the voice seems to have been recognised †. Hence arose the three tones or accents. First, the low tone, common to all vowels in ordinary speech. This tone is marked by the grave accent, and a syllable thus uttered is said to be *anudátta* (unacute, grave). Next, the high tone, produced by the sudden raising of the voice. This tone is marked by the acute accent, and is described by grammarians as the result of employing in the enunciation of the vowel what they call the upper half of the organ of utterance, whether the throat, palate, teeth, or lips. A syllable thus uttered is said to be *udátta* (acutely accented). Lastly, the mixed tone, a tone half high, half low, which is thus produced. In pronouncing the syllable immediately following the high-toned syllable, the voice, unable to lower itself abruptly to the level of the low intonation, passes into a tone partly high, partly low. A syllable uttered with this mixed intonation is said to be *swarita*, or marked with a combination of the acute and grave accent, commonly called the circumflex accent.

Practically, therefore, there are only three tones or accents recognised in Sanskṛit, the *anudátta*, the *udátta*, and the *swarita*.

---

* That ल *l* is a dental, and kindred to द *d*, is proved by its interchangeableness with *d* in cognate languages. Thus *lacryma*, δάκρυμα. Compare also दीप् with λαμπ.

† According to Professor Bopp, accentuation in the Vedas has nothing to do with chanting, but is etymological, like the Greek accent.

25. Nevertheless, there is yet another tone noticed by Páṇini, and called by him *sannatara* or *anudáttatara*, i. e. more grave than the common grave intonation. It is thus explained: the exertion of the voice required to produce the acute or high tone (*udátta*) is so great that in order to attain the proper pitch the voice is obliged to lower the tone of the preceding syllable as much below the ordinary low intonation as the syllable that bears the *udátta* is raised above it. Consequently the syllable preceding another that bears the acute accent, and which is originally pronounced with the grave tone (*anudátta*), becomes more than grave (*anudáttatara*) *.

---

* The three accents are thus marked in the Ṛig-veda.

A small horizontal stroke under a syllable marks the *anudátta* or low tone; and in the Pada, if it extend under all the syllables of the same word, it indicates that the whole word is *anudátta* unaccented or pronounced in the low tone (thus समः). But in the Sanhitá, where the distinction of *anudáttatara* is admitted, the stroke under a syllable is always the mark of the *anudáttatara*, never of the *anudátta*, the mere absence of accent not being marked at all.

When a syllable having the horizontal mark underneath is followed by one bearing no mark, the latter is considered to be *udátta*, acutely accented; and when followed by two syllables, bearing no mark, both are considered to be *udátta*.

The *swarita* or circumflex accent is denoted by a small perpendicular stroke above the syllable. Thus in the word चकार the syllable च is *anudáttatara*, का is *udátta*, and र is *swarita*.

All the syllables (in a single word or sentence) which follow a syllable bearing the *swarita* are supposed to be *anudátta* unaccented or pronounced in the same tone, until the horizontal stroke, or *anudáttatara* mark under a syllable, appears again. In fact, the *anudáttatara* mark is the beginning of a series of three accents, of which the *swarita* is the end; and the appearance of this mark prepares the reader for the occurrence of an *udátta* immediately following, and of a *swarita*. The latter, however, may sometimes be retarded by a new *udátta* syllable, which shows that the accents have nothing to do with chanting. Nevertheless a *swarita* mark does not necessarily imply an *anudáttatara* mark preceding, as in the word अक्रन्दः at the beginning of a line, where the *swarita* merely shows that the first syllable is *udátta*. Again, in the Pada, where each word stands separately, there may be no *swarita* following an *udátta*, as पश्चा । जातं. It must also be borne in mind that frequently where a *swarita* is immediately followed by an *udátta* syllable, the *swarita* becomes changed to *anudáttatara*: thus in दिवा पतयंतं the *swarita* of प becomes so changed, because of the *udátta* following.

With regard to the *swarita* mark, it may either indicate a dependent *swarita*, produced by an *udátta* immediately preceding, or an independent, i. e. either a *swarita* as such, or a *swarita* produced by the suppression of a syllable bearing the *udátta*, as in तन्वा contracted from तनुवा, where the middle syllable is properly *udátta*. In the latter case, if the syllable bearing the *swarita* is long, and another

OF THE INDIAN METHOD OF WRITING.

26. According to Hindú grammarians every syllable ought to end in a vowel *, and every final consonant ought to be attracted to the beginning of the next syllable; so that where a word ends in a consonant, that consonant ought to be pronounced with the initial letter of the next word. Hence in some Sanskṛit MSS. all the syllables are separated by slight spaces, and in others all the words are joined together without any separation. Thus the two words आसीद् राजा *ásíd rájá* would in some books be written आ सी द्रा जा and in others आसीद्राजा. In Sanskṛit works printed in Europe, the common practice is to separate only those words the final or initial letter of which are not acted on by the rules of combination. In such books *ásíd rájá* would be written together, आसीद्राजा, because the final द् is the result of an euphonic change from त्, caused by the following र *r*. There seems, however, but little reason for considering the mere spaces left between the words of a sentence to be incompatible with the operation of euphonic laws; especially as the absence of such spaces must always cause more or less impediment even to the fluent reader. Therefore in many books recently printed in Europe, every uncompounded word capable of separation by the use of the Viráma is separated. Thus *pitur dhanam ádadáti* is written पितुर् धनम् आददाति, and not पितुर्धनमाददाति. The only cases in which separation is undesirable, are where the final vowel of one word blends with the initial vowel of the next into one long similar or dissimilar vowel, and where final *u* and *i* are changed into their corresponding semivowels *v* and *y*.

The following words and passages in the Sanskṛit and English character, are given that the Student, before proceeding further in the Grammar, may exercise himself in reading the letters and in

---

word follows beginning with an *udátta*, then that syllable and all preceding syllables in the same word receive the *anudáttatara* mark, and the figure ३ is inserted to carry the *swarita*, having also the *anudáttatara* mark beneath; thus तन्वा३ममं.
If the syllable bearing the independent *swarita* be short, then the figure १ carries the *swarita*, with an *anudáttatara* under it; thus क्ष१तत्.

* Unless it end in Anuswára or Visarga *ḥ*, which in theory are the only consonantal sounds allowed to close a syllable. That Anuswára is not a full consonant is proved by the fact that it does not impede the operation of rule 70.

transliteration; that is to say, in turning Sanskṛit letters into the English equivalents, and *vice versa*.

To be turned into English letters.

अक, अज, अश, आस, आप, इल, इष, ईड, ईर, उख, उच, ऊह, ऋण, ऋज, एध, ओख, कण, कित, कुमार, क्षम, क्षिप, क्षुध, क्षै, क्लृप, खन, खिद, गाह, गुज, गृध, गॄ, घृण, घुष, चकास, चक्ष, चित, छिद, छो, जीवा, झष, टीका, ठः, डीनं, ढौक, णिद, तापः, तडागः, दया, दम्भकः, दशरथः, दुरालापः, देव, धूपिका, धृतः, नटः, नील, नेम, परिदानं, पुरुषस्, पौरः, पौरुषेयी, पुरोडाशः, बहुः, बालकस्, भोगः, भोजनं, मुखं, मृगः, मेदस्, मेदिनी, यकृत्, योगः, रेणु, रेचक, रै, रैवत, रुजा, रूपं, रुरुदिषु, लोह, वामः, वैरं, शक्, शौरः, षट्, साधुः, हेमकूटः, हेमन्.

To be turned into Sanskṛit letters.

Ada, asa, ali, ádi, ákhu, ágas, iti, íśah, íhá, udára, upanishad, uparodha, úru, úsha, ṛishi, eka, kakud, kaṭu, koshah, gaura, ghaṭa, chaitya, chet, chhalam, jetṛi, jhirí, ṭagara, ḍamara, ḍhála, ṇama, tatas, tathá, tṛiṇa, tushára, deha, daitya, dhavala, nanu, nayanam, nidánam, pitṛi, bhauma, bheshajam, marus, mahat, yuga, rush, rúḍhis, lauha, vivekas, śatam, shodaśan, sukhin, hṛidaya, tatra, adya, buddhi, arka, kratu, ansa, an·ka, an·ga, añchala, añjana, kaṇṭha, aṇḍa, anta, manda, sampúrṇa.

The following story has the Sanskṛit and English letters interlineated.

अस्ति हस्तिनापुरे विलासो नाम रजकः। तस्य गर्द-
asti hastinápure viláso náma rajakah tasya garda-

भोऽतिभारवाहनाद् दुर्बलो मुमूर्षुर् अभवत्। ततस् तेन
bho 'tibháraváhanád durbalo mumúrshur abhavat tatas tena

रजकेनासौ व्याघ्रचर्मणा प्रछाद्यारण्यसमीपे शस्यक्षेत्रे
rajakenásau vyághracharmaṇá prachhádyáraṇyasamípe śasyakshetre

मोचितः । ततो दूराद् अवलोक्य व्याघ्रबुद्ध्या क्षेत्रप-
mochitah tato dúrád avalokya vyághrabuddhyá kshetrapa-

तयः सत्वरं पलायन्ते । अथ केनापि शस्यरक्षकेण धूसर-
tayah satwaram paláyante atha kenápi śasyarakshakeṇa dhúsara-

कम्बलकृततनुत्राणेन धनुःकाण्डं सज्जीकृत्यावनतकायेन
kambalakṛitatanutráṇena dhanuhkáṇḍam sajjíkṛityávanatakáyena

एकान्ते स्थितं । ततस् तं च दूरे दृष्ट्वा गर्दभः पुष्टाङ्गो
ekánte sthitam tatas tam cha dúre dṛishṭwá gardabhah pushṭán-go

गर्दभीयमिति मत्वा शब्दं कुर्वाणस् तदभिमुखं धावितः ।
gardabhíyamiti matwá śabdam kurváṇas tadabhimukham dhávitah

ततस् तेन शस्यरक्षकेण गर्दभोऽयमिति ज्ञात्वा लीलयैव
tatas tena śasyarakshakeṇa gardabho 'yamiti jñátwá lílayaiva

व्यापादितः ॥
vyápáditah.

The following story is to be turned into Sanskrit letters.

Asti śríparvatamadhye brahmapurákhyam nagaram. Tatra śaila-śikhare ghaṇṭákarṇo náma rákshasah prativasatíti janapravádah śrúyate. Ekadá ghaṇṭám ádáya paláyamánah kaśchich chauro vyághreṇa vyápáditah. Tatpáṇipatitá ghaṇṭá vánaraih práptá. | Te vánarás tám ghaṇṭám anukshaṇam vádayanti. Tato nagarajanair manushyah khádito dṛishṭah pratikshaṇam ghaṇṭáráváścha śrúyate. Anantaram ghaṇṭákarṇah kupito manushyán khádati ghaṇṭám cha vádayati ityuktwá janáh sarve nagarát paláyitáh. Tatah karálayá náma kuṭṭinyá vimṛiśya markaṭá ghaṇṭám vádayanti swayam vijñáya rájá vijñápitah. Deva yadi kiyaddhanopakshayah kṛiyate tadáham enam ghaṇṭákarṇam sádhayámi. Tato rájñá tushṭena tasyai dhanam dattam. Kuṭṭinyá cha maṇḍalam kṛitwá tatra gaṇeśádigauravam darśayitwá swayam vánarapriyaphalányádáya vanam praviśya phalányákírṇáni. Tato ghaṇṭám parityajya vánaráh phalásaktá babhúvuh. Kuṭṭiní cha ghaṇṭám gṛihítwá nagaram ágatá sakalalokapújyá 'bhavat.

Observe, that *m* at the end of a word may most conveniently be transliterated by the symbol Anuswára, and *vice versa;* thus, *brahmapurákhyam nagaram* ब्रह्मपुराख्यं नगरं. Strictly, however, the first of these Anuswáras, being influenced by the following *n*, is equivalent in sound to *n*, and the two words might have been written *brahmapurákhyan nagaram* ब्रह्मपुराख्यन् नगरं. Similarly, *pratikshaṇam* before *ghaṇṭárávas* is written प्रतिक्षणं, though equivalent in sound to प्रतिक्षणङ्, in consequence of the following घ.

CHAPTER II.

SANDHI OR EUPHONIC COMBINATION OF LETTERS.

We are accustomed in Greek and Latin to certain euphonic changes of letters. Thus *rego* makes, in the perfect, not *regsi*, but *reksi* (*rexi*), the soft *g* being changed to the hard *k* before the hard *s*. Similarly, *veho* becomes *veksi* (*vexi*). In many words a final consonant assimilates with an initial; thus *συν* with *γνώμη* becomes *συγγνώμη*; *ἐν* with *λάμπω*, *ἐλλάμπω*. *Suppressus* is written for *subpressus*; *appellatus* for *adpellatus*; *immensus* for *inmensus*; *affinitas* for *adfinitas*; *colloquium* for *conloquium*; *irrogo* for *inrogo*. These laws for the euphonic junction of letters are applied throughout the whole range of Sanskṛit grammar; and that, too, not only in uniting different parts of one word, but in combining words in the same sentence. Thus, if the sentence "*Rara avis in terris*" were Sanskṛit, it would require, by the laws of Sandhi or combination, to be written *Rarávir ins terriḥ;* and might even be joined together thus, *Raráviriinsterriḥ*. The learner must not be discouraged if he is unable to understand *all* the laws of combination at first. He is recommended, after reading those that are printed in large type, to pass at once to the declension of nouns and conjugation of verbs. To attempt to commit to memory a number of rules, the use of which is not fully seen till he comes to read and construct *sentences*, must only lead to a loss of time and patience.

Sect. I.—CHANGES OF VOWELS.

27. Nevertheless, there are some changes of letters which come into immediate application in the formation and declension of nouns, and the conjugation of verbs; and amongst these, the changes of vowels called Guṇa and Vṛiddhi should be impressed on the memory,

before another step is taken in the study of the Grammar. When the vowels इ *i* and ई *í* are changed to ए *e*, this is called the Guṇa change, or *qualification*; when *i* and *í* are changed to ऐ *ai*, this is called the Vṛiddhi change, or *increase**. Similarly, उ *u* and ऊ *ú* are often changed to their Guṇa ओ *o*, and Vṛiddhi औ *au*; ऋ *ṛi* and ॠ *ṛí* to their Guṇa अर् *ar*, and Vṛiddhi आर् *ár*; and अ *a*, though it have no corresponding Guṇa change, has a Vṛiddhi substitute in आ *á*.

28. Let the student, therefore, never forget the following rules. There is no Guṇa substitute for अ *a*, but आ *á* is the Vṛiddhi substitute for अ *a*; ए *e* is the Guṇa, and ऐ *ai* the Vṛiddhi, for इ *i* and ई *í*; ओ *o* is the Guṇa, and औ *au* the Vṛiddhi, for उ *u* and ऊ *ú*; अर् *ar* is the Guṇa, and आर् *ár* the Vṛiddhi, for ऋ *ṛi* and ॠ *ṛí*; अल् *al* is the Guṇa, and आल् *ál* the Vṛiddhi, for ऌ *lṛi* and ॡ *lṛí*. Moreover, ऐ *ai* is the Vṛiddhi of the Guṇa ए *e*, and औ *au* the Vṛiddhi of the Guṇa ओ *o*.

a. Observe—It will be convenient in describing the change of a vowel to its Guṇa substitute, to speak of that vowel as *gunated*; and in the case of the Vṛiddhi change, to speak of it as *vriddhied*.

b. In the conjugation of verbs the vowels of roots cannot be gunated or vriddhied, if they are followed by double consonants, i. e. if they are long by position; nor can a vowel long by nature be so changed, unless it be final. The vowel अ *a* is of course incapable of Guṇa.

29. Again, let him bear in mind that the Guṇa sounds ए *e*, ओ *o*, and अर् *ar*, are diphthongal, that is, composed of two simple vowel sounds. Thus, ए *e* is made up of अ *a* and इ *i*; ओ *o* of अ *a* and उ *u*; अर् *ar* of अ *a* and ऋ *ṛi*; so that a final अ *a* will naturally coalesce with an initial इ *i* into ए *e*; with an initial उ *u* into ओ *o*; with an initial ऋ *ṛi* into अर् *ar*. Compare 18. *c*.

a. Similarly, the Vṛiddhi diphthong ऐ *ai* is made up of *á* and *i*; and औ *au* of *á* and *u*. Hence, *a* with *e* will blend into *ai* (for $e = a + i$ and $a + a + i$ will equal $á + i$ or *ai*). Similarly, *a* will blend with ओ *o* into औ *au*. Compare 18. *c*.

b. Since the sound *ai* is composed of *á* and *i*, it may be asked, How is it that long *á* as well as short *a* blends with *i* into *e* (see 32), and not into *ai*? In answer to this, Professor Bopp (Comparative Grammar, p. 2) maintains that a long vowel

* गुण *guṇa* in Sanskṛit means 'quality,' and वृद्धि *vṛiddhi*, 'increase.' It will be convenient to Anglicise these words, and write Guṇa, Vṛiddhi.

at the end of a word naturally shortens itself before an initial vowel. His opinion is, that the very meaning of Guṇa is the prefixing of short *a*, and the very meaning of Vṛiddhi, the prefixing of long *á*, to a simple vowel. He therefore holds that the Guṇa of *i* is originally *a i*, though the two simple vowels blend afterwards into *e*. Similarly, the original Guṇa of *u* is *a u*, blending afterwards into *o*; the original Guṇa of *ṛi* is *a ṛi*, blending into *ar*.

c. Hence it appears, that, since the Sanskṛit *a* answers to the Greek ε or ο (see 11. *f*.), the practice of gunating vowels is not peculiar to Sanskṛit alone. The Sanskṛit एमि *emi*, 'I go,' which in the plural becomes इमस् *imas*, is originally *a i mi*, corresponding to the Greek εἶμι and ἴμεν. Similarly in Greek, the root φυγ (ἔφυγον) is in the present φευγω. Compare also the Sanskṛit *veda* (*vaida*), 'he knows,' with Greek οἶδα; and compare λέλοιπα, perfect of λιπ, with the Sanskṛit 2d preterite.

30. Again, let him never forget that य *y* is the kindred semivowel of इ *i*, ई *í*, ए *e*, and ऐ *ai*; व *v* of उ *u*, ऊ *ú*, ओ *o*, and औ *au*; र *r* of ऋ *ṛi* and ॠ *ṛí*; and ल *l* of ऌ *lṛi* and ॡ *lṛí*. So that *i*, *í*, *e*, *ai*, at the end of words, when the next begins with a vowel, may often pass into *y*, *y*, *ay*, *áy*, respectively; *u*, *ú*, *o*, *au*, into *v*, *v*, *av*, *áv*; and *ṛi*, *ṛí*, into *r*. [NB. *lṛi* is not found as a final.]

In order to impress the above rules on the mind, the substance of them is embodied in the following table:

Simple vowels,	*a* or *á*	*i* or *í*	*u* or *ú*	*ṛi* or *ṛí*	*lṛi* or *lṛí*
Guṇa substitute,		*e*	*o*	*ar*	*al*
Vṛiddhi substitute,	*á*	*ai*	*au*	*ár*	*ál*
Simple vowels,		*i* or *í*	*u* or *ú*	*ṛi* or *ṛí*	*lṛi* or *lṛí*
Semivowel substitute,		*y*	*v*	*r*	*l*
Guṇa,		*e*	*o*		
Guṇa resolved,		*a* + *i*	*a* + *u*		
With semivowel substitute,		*ay*	*av*		
Vṛiddhi,		*ai*	*au*		
Vṛiddhi resolved,		*á* + *i*	*á* + *u*		
With semivowel substitute,		*áy*	*áv*		

The succeeding rules will now explain themselves.

31. If a word ends in अ *a* or आ *á*, when the similar vowels अ *a* or आ *á* follow, then the final and initial vowel blend into one long similar vowel: thus

न + अस्ति *na + asti* becomes नास्ति *násti*, 'there is not.'

जीवा + अन्त *jívá + anta* = जीवान्त *jívánta*, 'the end of life.'

a. The same rule applies to the other vowels, इ *i*, उ *u*, ऋ *ṛi*, short or long: thus

अधि + ईश्वर *adhi + íśwara* becomes अधीश्वर *adhíśwara*, 'the supreme lord.'

ऋतु + उत्सव *ṛitu + utsava* = ऋतूत्सव *ṛitútsava*, 'the festival of the season.'

पितृ + ऋद्धि *pitṛi + ṛiddhih* = पितॄद्धि *pitṛíddhi*, 'the father's prosperity.'

32. If a word ends in अ *a* or आ *á*, when the dissimilar vowels इ *i*, उ *u*, ऋ *ṛi*, short or long, follow, then *a* or *á* blends with *i* or *í* into ए *e*; with *u* or *ú* into ओ *o**; with *ṛi* or *ṛí* into अर् *ar*: thus

परम + ईश्वर *parama + íśwara* becomes परमेश्वर *parameśwara*, 'the mighty lord.'

हित + उपदेश *hita + upadeśa* = हितोपदेश *hitopadeśa*, 'friendly instruction.'

गङ्गा + उदक *gan·gá + udaka* = गङ्गोदक *gan·godaka*, 'Ganges water.'

तव + ऋद्धि *tava + ṛiddhi* = तवर्द्धि *tavarddhi*, 'thy growth.'

Similarly, तव + ऌकार *tava + ḷrikára* becomes तवल्कार *tavalkára*, 'thy letter ḷṛi.'

33. If a word ends in अ *a* or आ *á*, when the dissimilar vowels ए *e*, ओ *o*, ऐ *ai*, or औ *au*, follow, then *a* or *á* blends with *e* into *ai*; with *ai* also into *ai*; with *o* into *au*; with *au* also into *au*: thus

पर + एधित *para + edhita* becomes परैधित *paraidhita*, 'nourished by another.'

विद्या + एव *vidyá + eva* = विद्यैव *vidyaiva*, 'knowledge indeed.'

देव + ऐश्वर्य्य *deva + aiśwarya* = देवैश्वर्य्य *devaiśwarya*, 'divine majesty.'

अल्प + ओजस् *alpa + ojas* = अल्पौजस् *alpaujas*, 'little energy.'

गङ्गा + ओघ *gan·gá + ogha* = गङ्गौघ *gan·gaugha*, 'the torrent of the Ganges.'

---

* The blending of *a* and *i* into the sound *e* is recognised in English in such words as *sail*, *nail*, &c.; and the blending of *a* and *u* into the sound *o* is exemplified by the French *faute*, *baume*, &c.

ज्वर + औषध *jwara + aushadha* = ज्वरौषध *jwaraushadha*, 'fever-medicine.'

34. If a word ends in इ *i*, उ *u*, ऋ *ṛi*, short or long, when any dissimilar vowel follows, the former letters pass into their kindred semivowels; viz. *i* or *í* into *y**; *u* or *ú* into *v**; *ṛi* or *ṛí* into *r*: thus

अग्नि + अस्त्र *agni + astra* becomes अग्न्यस्त्र *agnyastra**, 'firearms.'

प्रति + उवाच *prati + uvácha* = प्रत्युवाच *pratyuvácha*, 'he spoke in reply.'

तु + इदानीं *tu + idáním* = त्विदानीं *twidáním**, 'but now.'

मातृ + आनन्द *mátṛi + ánanda* = मात्रानन्द *mátránanda*, 'the mother's joy.'

35. If a word ends in ए *e* or ओ *o*, when the next begins with अ *a*, then *e* and *o* remain unchanged, and the initial अ *a* is cut off: thus

ते + अपि *te + api* becomes तेऽपि *te 'pi*, 'they indeed!' [See 10.]

गृहे + अस्ति *gṛihe + asti* = गृहेऽस्ति *gṛihe 'sti*, 'he is in the house.'

सो + अपि *so + api* = सोऽपि *so 'pi*, 'he indeed!'

हतो + अस्मि *hato + asmi* = हतोऽस्मि *hato 'smi*, 'I am undone!'

36. If a word ends in ए *e* or ओ *o*, when the next begins with any other vowel except अ *a*, then *e* is changed to *ay*, and *o* to *av*; and if both the words are complete words, the *y* of *ay*, and more rarely the *v* of *av*, may be dropped, leaving the *a* uninfluenced by the following vowel: thus

ते + आगताः *te + ágatáh* becomes तयागताः *tayágatáh*, and then त आगताः *ta ágatáh*, 'they have come.'

Similarly, विष्णो + इह *vishṇo + iha* becomes विष्णविह *vishṇaviha*, and then विष्ण इह *vishṇa iha*, 'O Vishṇu, here!'

a. But if ए *e* and ओ *o* be the finals of roots or nominal bases, and these have to be joined with the initial vowels of terminations, affixes, &c., even though the initial vowel be अ *a* or ए *e* or ओ *o*, then final *e* must still be changed to *ay*, and final *o* to *av*, and both *y* and *v* must be retained: thus

जे + अति *je + ati* becomes जयति *jayati*, 'he conquers†.'

---

* So in English we pronounce a word like *million* as if written *millyon*; and we write *evangelist* for *euangelist*.

† In English we respect this law in writing, though not in pronouncing such words as *saying*, *playing*, &c.

अग्ने + ए *agne* + *e* = अग्नये *agnaye*, 'to fire.'

भो + अति *bho* + *ati* = भवति *bhavati* 'he is.'

गो + ईश्वर *go* + *íśwara* = गवीश्वर *gavíśwara*, 'owner of kine.'

गो + ओकस् *go* + *okas* = गवोकस् *gavokas*, 'the abode of cattle.'

37. If a word ends in ऐ *ai* or औ *au*, when any vowel, similar or dissimilar, follows, *ai* is changed to *áy*, and *au* to *áv*: thus

कस्मै + अपि *kasmai* + *api* becomes कस्मायपि *kasmáyapi*, 'to any one whatever.'

रै + अः *rai* + *ah* = रायः *ráyah*, 'riches.'

ददौ + अन्नं *dadau* + *annam* = ददावन्नं *dadávannam*, 'he gave food.'

नौ + औ *nau* + *au* = नावौ *návau*, 'two ships.'

a. If both the words be complete words, the *y* and *v* are occasionally dropped, but not so usually as in the case of *e* at 36: thus कस्मा अपि *kasmá api* for कस्मायपि *kasmáyapi*, and ददा अन्नं *dadá annam* for ददावन्नं *dadávannam*.

38. There are some exceptions (*pragrihya*) to the above rules. The most noticeable is that of nominative and accusative cases dual, ending in *í*, *ú*, or *e*. These are never acted on by following vowels: thus,

हरी एतौ *harí etau*, 'these two Haris.'

विष्णू इमौ *vishnú imau*, 'these two Vishnus.'

सुते एते *sute ete*, 'these two daughters.'

The same applies to अमी *amí*, nom. pl. m. of the pronoun अदस्.

a. A vocative case in *o*, when followed by the particle *iti*, may remain unchanged, as विष्णो इति *vishno iti*, or may follow 36.

b. Particles, when simple vowels, and आ *á* and ओ *o*, as the finals of interjections, remain unchanged, as आ एवं *á evam*, 'Ah, indeed!' अहो इन्द्र *aho indra*, 'Ho, Indra.'

c. The ओ *o* of गो *go*, 'a cow,' may become अव *ava* in certain cases, as गो + इन्द्र *go*+*indra* becomes गवेन्द्र *gavendra*, 'lord of kine.'

The following table exhibits all the combinations of vowels at one view. Supposing a word to end in *ú*, and the next word to begin with *au*, the student must carry his eye down the first column (headed "final vowels") till he comes to *ú*, and then along the top horizontal line of "initial vowels," till he comes to *au*. At the junction of the perpendicular column under *au* and the horizontal line beginning *ú*, will be the required combination, viz. *v au*.

INITIAL VOWELS.	*a*	*á*	*i*	*í*	*u*	*ú*	*ṛi*	*ṛí*	*e*	*ai*	*o*	*au*
FINAL VOWELS.												
a	*á*	*á*	*e*	*e*	*o*	*o*	*ar*	*ar*	*ai*	*ai*	*au*	*au*
á	*á*	*á*	*e*	*e*	*o*	*o*	*ar*	*ar*	*ai*	*ai*	*au*	*au*
i	*y a*	*y á*	*í*	*í*	*y u*	*y ú*	*y ṛi*	*y ṛí*	*y e*	*y ai*	*y o*	*y au*
í	*y a*	*y á*	*í*	*í*	*y u*	*y ú*	*y ṛi*	*y ṛí*	*y e*	*y ai*	*y o*	*y au*
u	*v a*	*v á*	*v i*	*v í*	*ú*	*ú*	*v ṛi*	*v ṛí*	*v e*	*v ai*	*v o*	*v au*
ú	*v a*	*v á*	*v i*	*v í*	*ú*	*ú*	*v ṛi*	*v ṛí*	*v e*	*v ai*	*v o*	*v au*
ṛi	*r a*	*r á*	*r i*	*r í*	*r u*	*r ú*	*ṛí*	*ṛí*	*r e*	*r ai*	*r o*	*r au*
ṛí	*r a*	*r á*	*r i*	*r í*	*r u*	*r ú*	*ṛí*	*ṛí*	*r e*	*r ai*	*r o*	*r au*
e	*e* ’ *ay a*	*a á* *ay á*	*a i* *ay i*	*a í* *ay í*	*a u* *ay u*	*a ú* *ay ú*	*a ṛi* *ay ṛi*	*a ṛí* *ay ṛí*	*a e* *ay e*	*a ai* *ay ai*	*a o* *ay o*	*a au* *ay au*
ai	*áy a*	*áy á*	*áy i*	*áy í*	*áy u*	*áy ú*	*áy ṛi*	*áy ṛí*	*áy e*	*áy ai*	*áy o*	*áy au*
o	*o** ’	*av á*	*av i*	*av í*	*av u*	*av ú*	*av ṛi*	*av ṛí*	*av e*	*av ai*	*av o*	*av au*
au	*áv a*	*áv á*	*áv i*	*áv í*	*áv u*	*áv ú*	*áv ṛi*	*áv ṛí*	*áv e*	*áv ai*	*áv o*	*áv au*

Observe, that in the above table the final letter, in its changed state, has been printed, for greater clearness, separate from the initial; except in those cases where the blending of the two vowels made this impossible.

* If the initial *a* belong to a termination, affix, &c., and not to a complete word, then *a* is not cut off, and *o* becomes *av* before it. See 36. *a*.

SECT. II.—CHANGES OF CONSONANTS.

39. Before proceeding to the combination of consonants, let the letters be again regarded as divided into two grand classes of Hard and Soft, as explained at 20. *b*.

HARD OR SURD.			SOFT OR SONANT.							
k	*kh*		*g*	*gh*	*ṅ*	*h*	*a*	*á*		
ch	*chh*	*ś*	*j*	*jh*	*ñ*	*y*	*i*	*í*	*e*	*ai*
ṭ	*ṭh*	*sh*	*ḍ*	*ḍh*	*ṇ*	*r*	*ṛi*	*ṛí*		
t	*th*	*s*	*d*	*dh*	*n*	*l*	*ḷṛi*	*ḷṛí*		
p	*ph*		*b*	*bh*	*m*	*v*	*u*	*ú*	*o*	*au*

Note—In the following rules it may generally be observed, that final consonants have a tendency to adapt themselves to initial, rather than initial to final.

GENERAL RULES.

40. If two hard or two soft consonants come together, one at the end and the other at the beginning of a word or affix, there is generally no change; and similarly, if a soft consonant ends a word, when a vowel follows: thus,

विद्युत् प्रकाशते *vidyut prakáśate*, 'the lightning shines.'

कुमुद् विकसति *kumud vikasati*, 'the lotus blossoms.'

दृशद् अधोगच्छति *dṛiśad adhogachchhati*, 'the rock descends.'

विद्युत् + सु *vidyut* + *su* = विद्युत्सु *vidyutsu*, 'in lightnings.'

a. Observe, however, that the unaspirated form of a final letter is substituted for the aspirated, as चित्रलिख् + करोति *chitralikh* + *karoti* becomes चित्रलिक् करोति *chitralik karoti*.

41. If any hard letter ends a word, root, or crude base, when any soft initial letter follows, the hard (unless affected by some special rule) is changed to its own unaspirated soft: thus

वाक् + देवी *vák* + *deví* becomes वाग्देवी *vágdeví*, 'the goddess of eloquence.'

वाक् + ईश *vák* + *íśa* = वागीश *vágíśa*, 'the lord of speech.'

चित्रलिख् + लिखति *chitralikh* + *likhati* = चित्रलिग् लिखति *chitralig likhati*, 'the painter paints.'

विट् + भव *viṭ* + *bhava* = विड्भव *viḍbhava*, 'generated by filth.'

a. There is an option allowed before nasals; that is, when any nasal begins the next word, the final of the last word is usually (though not necessarily) changed to the nasal of its own class: thus

वाक् + मय *vák + maya* becomes वाङ्मय *váṅ-maya*, 'full of words.'
विट् + मय *viṭ + maya* = विण्मय *viṇmaya*, 'full of filth.'
तत् + मात्र *tat + mátra* = तन्मात्र *tanmátra*, 'that element.'
तत् + नेत्रं *tat + netram* = तन् नेत्रं *tan netram*, 'that eye.'
अप् + मूलं *ap + múlam* = अम्मूलं *ammúlam*, 'water and roots.'

b. Rule 41 applies to terminations of nouns or verbs beginning with consonants, but not to terminations beginning with vowels. In the latter case, the final hard consonant is supposed to attract the initial vowel, and thus, losing its character of a final letter, is not made soft: thus वाक् + भिस् *vák+bhis* becomes वाग्भिस् *vágbhis*, 'by words;' but वाच् + आ *vách+á* becomes वाचा *váchá*, 'by a speech;' not वाजा *vájá*. चित्रलिख् + सु *chitralikh+su* is चित्रलिक्षु *chitraliksu*, 'in painters;' but चित्रलिख् + आ *chitralikh+á* remains चित्रलिखा *chitralikhá*, 'by a painter.'

c. Of course, rule 41 does not apply to final sibilants, as they have no corresponding soft letters. The rules for sibilants are given at 61.

42. If a soft letter ends a word, root, or crude base, when any hard initial letter follows, the soft is changed to its own unaspirated hard: thus

कुमुद् + फुल्लति *kumud + phullati* becomes कुमुत् फुल्लति *kumut phullati*, 'the lotus blossoms.'
समिध् + प्रदीप्यते *samidh + pradípyate* = समित् प्रदीप्यते *samit pradípyate*, 'the fuel is ignited.'

Note—Similarly in Latin, a soft guttural or labial often passes into a hard before *s* and *t*; thus *reg+si* becomes *recsi* (*rexi*), *scrib+si* becomes *scripsi*.

a. The same may take place at the end of a sentence or before a pause, as फुल्लति कुमुत् *phullati kumut*.

b. Soft letters, which have no corresponding hard, such as the nasals, semivowels, and ह *h*, are changed by special rules.

c. If the final be an aspirated soft letter, and belongs to a root whose initial is ग *g*, द *d*, or ब *b*, then the aspirate, which is suppressed in the final, is transferred back to the initial letter of the root; as बुध् + करोति *budh+karoti* becomes भुत् करोति *bhut karoti*, 'he who knows acts;' दध् + तस् *dadh + tas* becomes धत्तस् *dhattas*, 'they two place;' and see 306. *a*, 299. *a*.

Note—Greek recognises a similar principle in θρὶξ, τριχὸς, τρέχω, θρέξω, &c.

43. The following consonants are not allowed to remain unchanged at the end

of words *, under any circumstances: that is to say, they undergo modifications, even at the end of a sentence; and when they are combined with the initial letters of succeeding words, or with the initial *consonants* of affixes, these modifications must take place before rules 41 and 42 are applied. 1st, A conjunct consonant of any kind; 2d, an aspirated consonant; 3d, the aspirate ह *h*; 4th, the palatal letters च् *ch*, छ् *chh*, ज् *j*, झ् *jh* (when originally palatal, and not the result of the euphonic changes of final त् *t* and द् *d* at 47); 5th, the sibilants श् *ś* and ष् *sh*.

a. With regard to 1, when a word ends in a single or conjunct consonant, and a termination to be affixed consists of a single consonant, then, to avoid the concurrence of silent consonants at the end of a word, the first only of the conjunct consonants is allowed to remain, and the termination is dropped: thus चरन्त् + स् *charant+s* leaves चरन् *charan*, 'going;' अवेद् + स् *aved+s* leaves अवेत् *avet* or अवेद् *aved*. So in Latin, *mulsi* is written for *mulg-si*; *sparsi* for *sparg-si*, &c.

b. With regard to 2, the unaspirated form is substituted for the aspirated.

c. With regard to 3, a final ह *h* (which is of very rare occurrence) is usually changed either to क् *k* or ट् *ṭ*. See 17. *a.*

d. With regard to 4, palatals, as being derived from gutturals (see 20. *c.*), generally revert to their originals; i. e. final च *ch* and झ् *jh* are usually changed to क् (see 12), but छ *chh* may become ट् *ṭ*; ज *j* becomes ग *g*, but sometimes ट् *ṭ* or ड् *ḍ*.

e. With regard to 5, final श् *ś* and ष् *sh* usually pass into either क् *k* or ट् *ṭ*. (See 17. *b.*)

The above changes must hold good, whatever may be the initial letter of a following word; but rules 41 and 42 must be afterwards applied. They also hold good before all terminations or affixes beginning with strong consonants; but before vowels (except the affix *a* at 80. I.) and weak consonants (i. e. nasals and semivowels) the finals remain unchanged. See 41. *b*, and *vách* at 176.

44. The special rules for the changes of consonants are very numerous. but since few words in Sanskṛit end in any other consonants than त् *t* and द् *d*, the nasals न् *n* and म् *m*, the dental sibilant स् *s*, and the semivowel र् *r*, it will be sufficient for all practical purposes to notice these special rules under four heads; 1st, the changes of final त् and द्; 2dly, the changes of the nasals; 3dly, the changes of final स्; 4thly, the changes of final र्.

CHANGES OF FINAL त् *t* AND द् *d*.

45. By the general rule (41), final त् *t* becomes द् *d* before soft consonants, and before all vowels (as मरुत् + वाति *marut + váti* becomes मरुद् वाति *marud váti*, 'the wind blows').

* Excepting in roots, standing by themselves, or, if used as nouns, before terminations beginning with vowels.

a. There is an exception in the case of *vidyut* + *vat*, making *vidyutwat*, 'possessed of lightning.'

46. And final द् *d* becomes त् *t* before hard consonants (as दृशद् + पतति *dṛiśad* + *patati* becomes दृशत् पतति *dṛiśat patati*, 'the stone falls'). See 42.

47. And final त् *t* or द् *d* becomes न् *n* before all nasals, See 41. *a.* But final त् *t* or द् *d* before initial च *ch*, ज *j*, ल *l*, श *ś*, and ह *h*, undergoes special changes: thus—

Final त् t *or* द् d *before* च ch, ज j, ल l.

48. If त् *t* or द् *d* ends a word, when an initial च *ch*, ज *j*, or ल *l*, follows, then त् *t* or द् *d* assimilates with these letters: thus

भयात् + लोभात् + च *bhayát* + *lobhát* + *cha* becomes भयाल् लोभाच् च *bhayál lobhách cha*, 'from fear and avarice.'

तद् + जीवनं *tad* + *jívanam* = तज् जीवनं *taj jívanam*, 'that life.'

a. A final त् *t* or द् *d* also assimilates with a following छ *chh*, झ *jh*, but as, by 43. *b*, an aspirate is not allowed at the end of a word, the combination will be *ch chh*, *j jh*. They also assimilate with the cerebral letters ट *ṭ*, ड *ḍ*: thus तत् + डीनं *tat* + *ḍínam* becomes तड् डीनं *taḍ ḍínam*.

b. Observe—When छ *chh* is the *original* initial letter of a word, and a previous word ends in a short vowel (or even a long vowel), then त् *t*, changeable to च् *ch* by 48. *a*, may be inserted: thus वि + छेद *vi* + *chheda* may be written विच्छेद *vichchheda*.

Final त् t *or* द् d *before* श ś.

49. If त् *t* or द् *d* ends a word, when an initial श *ś* follows, then त् *t* or द् *d* is changed to च् *ch*, and the initial श *ś* is usually changed to छ *chh*: thus तत् + श्रुत्वा *tat* + *śrutwá* becomes तच् छ्रुत्वा *tach chhrutwá*, 'having heard that.'

Final त् t *or* द् d *before* ह h.

50. If त् *t* ends a word, when initial ह *h* follows, the final त् *t* is changed to द् *d* (by 41), and the initial ह *h* to ध *dh*: thus तत् + हरति *tat* + *harati* becomes तद् धरति (or तद्धरति) *tad dharati*, 'he seizes that.'

51. By a similar rule, and on the same principle, are written words ending in क् *k*, followed by initial ह *h*; thus वाक् + हरति *vák* + *harati* becomes वाग् घरति *vág gharati*, 'speech captivates.' Similarly, roots ending in ट *ṭ*, followed by a termination beginning with ह *h*; thus द्विट् + हि *dwiṭ* + *hi* becomes द्विड्ढि *dwiḍḍhi*.

CHANGES OF THE NASALS.

Changes of final न् n.

52. If the letter न् *n*, preceded by a *short* vowel, ends a word, when the next begins with any vowel, the *n* is doubled: thus

आसन् + अत्र *ásan + atra* becomes आसन्न् अत्र *ásann atra*, 'they were there.'

तस्मिन् + उद्याने *tasmin + udyáne* = तस्मिन्न् उद्याने *tasminn udyáne*, 'in that garden.'

53. If न् *n* ends a word, when an initial त *t*, च *ch*, or ट *ṭ*, follows, a sibilant is inserted between the final and initial letter, according to the class of the initial letter; and the न् *n* then passes into Anuswára by 6. *b*: thus

अस्मिन् + तडागे *asmin + taḍáge* becomes अस्मिंस्तडागे or अस्मिंस् तडागे *asmins taḍáge*, 'in this pool.'

कस्मिन् + चित् *kasmin + chit* = कस्मिंश्चित् *kasminśchit* *, 'in a certain person.'

महान् + टङ्कः *mahán + ṭan·kah* = महांष्टङ्कः *mahánshṭan·kah*, 'a large axe.'

a. A similar euphonic *s* is inserted between the prepositions *sam, ava, pari, prati*, and certain words which begin with *k*, as संस्कार *sanskára*, परिष्कार *parishkára*, प्रतिष्कार *pratishkára*, &c. (see 70); just as in Latin, between the prepositions *ab* and *ob*, and *c*, *q*, and *p*.

b. न् *n* at the end of a root, or incomplete word, is not amenable to this rule: thus हन् + ति *han+ti* is हन्ति *hanti*, 'he kills.' The word प्रशान् *praśán* (nom. of *praśám*) is also an exception; as, प्रशान् तनोति 'the peaceful man spreads.'

54. Rule 53 describes the only cases in which न् *n*, when originally the final of a word, can pass into Anuswára: thus, combinations like तान् जानाति or तान् ददाति can never be written तां जानाति, तां ददाति.

55. If न् *n* ends a word, when the next begins with श *ś*, then both न् *n* and श *ś* may remain unchanged or be combined in either of the two following ways: 1st, the final न् *n* may be changed to ञ *ñ*; thus महान् + शूरः *mahán+śúrah* may be written महाञ् शूरः 'a great hero:' 2dly, the श *ś* may be changed to छ *chh*; thus महाञ् छूरः.

56. If न् *n* ends a word, when the next begins with ल *l*, the *n* assimilates with the *l*, and the mark ँ is placed over the preceding vowel: thus पक्षान् + लुनाति *pakshán+lunáti* becomes पक्षाँल्लुनाति or पक्षाँल् लुनाति 'he clips the wings.' See 7. Similarly, ἐν with λάμπω becomes ἐλλάμπω; and *con* with *ligo*, *colligo*.

---

* The same holds good before छ *chh*, and before थ *th*, ठ *ṭh*; but the two latter are never likely to occur.

a. Final न् *n*, before ज *j* or झ *jh*, is sometimes (but very rarely) written in the palatal form ञ्; and before ड *ḍ*, ढ *ḍh*, in the cerebral form ण.

57. न *n* as the final of crude bases is rejected before terminations and affixes beginning with consonants: thus

धनिन् + भिस् *dhanin + bhis* becomes धनिभिस् *dhanibhis*, 'by rich people.'

धनिन् + त्व *dhanin + twa* = धनित्व *dhanitwa*, 'the state of being rich.'

a. As the final of a root it is rejected before those terminations beginning with consonants (excepting nasals and semivowels), which have no symbol indicative of Guṇa. (See 307 and 318.)

b. Also, when the word ending in न् *n* is the first (or any but the last) member of a compound word, even though the next member of the compound begins with a vowel: thus

राजन् + पुरुष *rájan + purusha* becomes राजपुरुष *rája-purusha*, 'the king's servant.'

राजन् + इन्द्र *rájan + indra* = राजेन्द्र *rájendra*, 'the chief of kings.'

स्वामिन् + अर्थं *swámin + artham* = स्वाम्यर्थं *swámyartham*, 'on account of the master.'

Change of न n, *not final, to* ण ṇ.

58. If न *n* (*not final*) follows any one of the three cerebral letters, ऋ *ṛi*, र *r*, ष *sh*, in *the same word*, then न *n* must be changed to the cerebral ण *ṇ*, even though क *k*, ग *g*, प *p*, ब *b*, (or their aspirates,) ह *h*, य *y*, व *v*, or म *m*, intervene. Thus the nom. plur. of शुष्कं पुष्पं 'a withered flower,' is शुष्काणि पुष्पाणि *śushkáṇi pushpáṇi* (not शुष्कानि पुष्पानि). Similarly, the accus. case of ब्रह्महन् *brahmahan*, 'a bráhman slayer,' is ब्रह्महणं; the imperative of क्षिप् *kship*, 'to throw,' is क्षिपाणि; the nom. plur. of वर्मन् *varman*, 'armour,' is वर्माणि; the instrum. sing. of मृग *mṛiga*, 'a deer,' is मृगेण. But the intervention of a dental, or cerebral consonant, or of any palatal except *y*, or of any letter whatever (excepting a nasal, a semivowel, or ह *h*) if conjunct with the nasal, prevents the operation of this rule. Thus the instrum. case of शृगाल *śṛigála*, 'a jackal,' is शृगालेन; the nom. plur. of वर्त्मन् *vartman*, 'a word,' is वर्त्मानि; and in further illustration of the same law, may be taken सर्जन *sarjana*, 'abandoning;' क्रीडन *kríḍana*, 'playing;' प्राप्नोति *prápnoti*, 'he obtains;' राज्ञा *rájñá*, 'by a king.' But वृक्ण is sometimes written वृक्ण.

Changes of final म् m.

59. If म् *m* ends a word or root, when any consonant follows, then म् *m* may pass into Anuswára, or may optionally, before those consonants which have a corresponding nasal, be changed to this nasal:

thus गृहम् + जगाम *griham + jagáma* is written either गृहं जगाम or गृहञ् जगाम 'he went home:' so also *sam + ḍína* becomes either संडीन or सण्डीन 'flight;' *sam + chaya*, either संचय or सञ्चय 'collection;' *sam + nyása*, either संन्यास or सन्न्यास 'abandonment;' *gam + tá*, either गंता or गन्ता. But although म् *m* may in these cases pass into Anuswára, the latter must always take the sound of the nasal to which it may optionally be changed.

60. When the next word begins with a vowel, then म् *m* must always be written: thus गृहमायाति or गृहम् आयाति *griham áyáti*, 'he comes home.'

CHANGES OF FINAL स् *s*.

61. Nearly every nominative case, and many other cases of nouns, in Sanskrit, besides many inflections of verbs, end in स् *s*, which is changeable to श् *ś*, and is liable to be represented by : Visarga (i. e. the symbol for a final aspirate), or to pass into र् *r*, or to be liquefied into उ *u*, or to be dropped altogether, according to the nature of the initial letter following*. *At every step these changes will meet the eye*: therefore let the student master the following five rules, before he attempts to read a single sentence of the most elementary Sanskrit work.

Observe—The following rules are designated by Indian grammarians, "rules for the changes of Visarga." This exaltation of a mere symbol to the place of the letter which it represents, tends, however, to embarrass the subject unnecessarily, and imparts to Visarga itself a nature so Protean, that the student is continually foiled in his effort to apprehend a character which is liable to become now *s*, now *r*, now *u*, now *y*, now to be dropped, and now to return to its original form. It seems a simpler and preferable course (the result being in the end equivalent) to start from the tangible character स् *s*, which Visarga, under certain circumstances, represents; or, in other words, to regard Visarga as no letter at all, but a mere symbol for final स् *s*, and, as we shall afterwards see at 71, for final र् *r*, when these letters are pronounced with an imperceptible aspiration (compare rule 8), as they are always pronounced before क *k*, प *p*, स *s*, श *ś*, and at the end of a sentence.

---

* The interchangeableness of *s* with *r* and *h* is not unknown in other languages. Thus the Latin *flos* becomes in the genitive *floris*; *genus* becomes *generis*: and many other Latin words, such as *labor*, *robur*, were originally written either *labor* or *labos*, *robur* or *robus*. Again, the initial aspirate in many Greek words passes in Latin into *s*; as, ἕξ, *sex*, &c.

First Rule.—*When does final* स् s *remain unchanged, or become* श् ś, ष sh?

62. Before त *t*, च *ch*, and ट *ṭ*, respectively. Before त *t*, and its aspirate, it remains unchanged. Before च *ch*, and its aspirate, it passes into the palatal sibilant श् *ś*. Similarly, before ट *ṭ*, and its aspirate, it passes into the cerebral sibilant ष *sh*. But this latter change can rarely occur, as very few words in Sanskṛit begin with ट *ṭ* or ठ *ṭh*.

a. In some books final स् *s* is allowed to remain unchanged before स *s*, and to assimilate with initial श *ś*.

Second Rule.—*When does final* स् s *pass into Visarya* (:)?

63. Before क *k*, प *p*, and their aspirates, and before the sibilants स *s*, श *ś*.

a. Before a pause, i. e. at the end of a sentence.

b. Observe—When a word stands by itself, final *s* properly passes into Visarga; and this is why, in native grammars, the terminations of nouns and verbs, which appear first in the tabular scheme, as ending in *s*, are made to end in Visarga, when they appear again in declension and conjugation. In the following pages, however, *s* will be preserved as a final, in declension and conjugation, for two reasons: 1st, because it is more tangible, and easy to apprehend, than a symbol which is imperceptible in pronunciation: 2dly, because it enables the classical student to keep in view the resemblance between Sanskṛit and Greek and Latin terminations.

Third Rule.—*When does final* स् s *blend with a preceding* अ a *into the vowel* ओ o?

64. When preceded by short अ *a*, before all *soft* consonants, it is treated as if liquefied into उ *u**, and blends with the *a* into ओ *o*.

a. Similarly, before short अ *a*, which *a* is then cut off.

Fourth Rule.—*When does final* स् s *become* र् r?

65. When preceded by any other vowel but अ *a* or आ *á*, and before all *soft* letters, consonants or vowels.

---

* That is, it is first changed to *r*, as at 65, and *r* is then liquefied into a vowel; just as *l* is often changed to *u* in French. The plural of *animal* is *animaux*, not *animals*.

a. Unless र् *r* itself be the soft letter following, in which case, to avoid the conjunction of two *r*'s, final स् *s* is dropped, and the vowel preceding it (if short) is lengthened.

FIFTH RULE.—*When is final* स् s *dropped?*

66. When preceded by short अ *a*, before any other vowel except short अ *a* *. NB. The अ *a*, which then becomes final, opens on the initial vowel without coalition †.

a. When preceded by long आ *á*, before any soft letter, consonant or vowel. NB. If the initial letter be a vowel, the आ *á*, which then becomes final, opens on it without coalition.

b. When preceded by any other vowel but अ *a* or आ *á*, before the letter *r*, as noticed at 65. *a.*

c. Observe—Although it simplifies the subject to speak of final *s* as dropped in these cases, yet, according to native grammarians, it would be more correct to say that final *s* first passes into Visarga, which is then dropped: otherwise the term Visarga is without meaning. Indian grammarians, however, hold that Visarga undergoes another change before it is dropped, viz. to *y;* and that this *y* is rejected in accordance with 36, 37.

The above five rules are illustrated in the following table, in which the nominative cases नरस् *naras*, 'a man;' नरास् *narás*, 'men;' हरिस् *haris*, 'the god Vishṇu;' रिपुस् *ripus*, 'an enemy;' and नौस् *naus*, 'a ship'—are joined with the verbs *karoti*, 'he does;' *kurvanti*, 'they do;' *khanati*, 'he digs;' *khananti*, 'they dig;' *pachati*, 'he cooks;' *pachanti*, 'they cook;' *sarati*, 'he goes;' *śochati*, 'he grieves;' *tarati*, 'he crosses;' *charati*, 'he moves;' *gachchhati*, 'he goes;' *jayati*, 'he conquers;' *rakshati*, 'he preserves;' *atti*, 'he eats;' *adanti*, 'they eat;' *eti*, 'he goes;' *áyáti*, 'he comes;' *edhate*, 'he prospers.'

---

* That is, it blends with *a* into *o*, as in 64; and *o* becoming *av* before any vowel but *a*, the *v* is rejected by 36. Indian grammarians hold that final *s* or Visarga here becomes *y*, which would also be rejected by 36. This, however, seems rather to apply to 66. *a*.

† This is one of the three cases in which a hiatus of two vowels is admissible in Sanskṛit. The three cases are, 1. when final *s* is rejected from *as* or *ás* (66); 2. when a complete word, ending in *e*, is followed by any other vowel but *a* (see 36); 3. when the dual terminations ई *í*, ऊ *ú*, ए *e*, are followed by vowels (see 38).

First Rule. Final स् *s* remains unchanged, or passes into श् *ś*.	Second Rule. Final स् *s* passes into Visarga.	Third Rule. Final स् *s* blends with *a* into ओ *o*.	Fourth Rule. Final स् *s* becomes र् *r*.	Fifth Rule. Final स् *s* is dropped.
नरस् तरति *naras tarati* नरास् तरन्ति *narás taranti* हरिस् तरति *haris tarati* नौस् तरति *naus tarati* नराश् चरति *naráś charati* नराश् चरन्ति *naráś charanti* हरिश् चरति *hariś charati* नौश् चरति *nauś charati* Final *s* rarely remains unchanged before स *s*, and assimilates with श *ś*: thus, नरस् सरति *naras sarati* नरास् सरन्ति *narás saranti* हरिस् सरति *haris sarati* नरश् शोचति *naraś śochati* नराश् शोचन्ति *naráś śochanti* हरिश् शोचति *hariś śochati*	नरः करोति *narah karoti* नराः कुर्वन्ति *naráh kurvanti* हरिः करोति *harih karoti* नरः खनति *narah khanati* नराः खनन्ति *naráh khananti* हरिः खनति *harih khanati* नरः पचति *narah pachati* नराः पचन्ति *naráh pachanti* हरिः पचति *harih pachati* नरः सरति *narah sarati* नराः सरन्ति *naráh saranti* हरिः सरति *harih sarati* नरः शोचति *narah śochati* नराः शोचन्ति *naráh śochanti* हरिः शोचति *harih śochati* Before a pause, करोति नरः *karoti narah*	नरो गच्छति *naro gachchhati* नरो जयति *naro jayati* नरो याति *naro yáti* नरो रक्षति *naro rakshati* Similarly, final *s* preceded by *a*, before all soft consonants; and also before अ *a*, which अ *a* is then cut off: thus, नरोऽत्ति *naro 'tti* for *naro atti*	हरिर् अत्ति *harir atti* रिपुर् अत्ति *ripur atti* नौर् आयाति *naur áyáti* हरिर् एति *harir eti* रिपुर् एति *ripur eti* नौर् एति *naur eti* हरिर् गच्छति *harir gachchhati* रिपुर् गच्छति *ripur gachchhati* नौर् गच्छति *naur gachchhati* हरिर् याति *harir yáti* रिपुर् याति *ripur yáti* नौर् याति *naur yáti* Similarly, final *s* preceded by any vowel but *a* or *á*, before all soft letters excepting *r*, when final *s* also becoming *r* is rejected, and the preceding vowel lengthened: thus, हरी रक्षति *harí rakshati* रिपू रक्षति *ripú rakshati*	नर आयाति *nara áyáti* नरा अदन्ति *nará adanti* नर ईक्षते *nara íkshate* नरा ईक्षन्ते *nará íkshante* नर एधते *nara edhate* नरा एधन्ते *nará edhante* नरा गच्छन्ति *nará gachchhanti* नरा यान्ति *nará yánti* नरा रक्षन्ति *nará rakshanti* Similarly, final *s* preceded by अ *a*, before all vowels excepting अ *a*; and, final *s* preceded by *á*, before all soft letters, consonants or vowels.

67. There is one common exception to 62, 63, 64: सस् *sas*, 'he,' and एषस् *eshas*, 'this,' the nominative cases of the pronouns तद् *tad* and एतद् *etad* (220, 223), drop the final *s* before any *consonant*, hard or soft; as, स करोति *sa karoti*, 'he does;' स गच्छति *sa gachchhati*, 'he goes;' एष पचति *esha pachati*, 'this man cooks.' But rules 64. *a*, 66 and 63. *a*, are observed: thus, सोऽपि *so 'pi*, 'he also;' स एषः *sa eshah*, 'he himself.' Sometimes *sa* may blend with a following vowel, as सैषः for स एषः.

A remarkable agreement is observable here in the Greek ὁ for ὅς. Compare also the Latin *qui* for *quis*, and *ille, iste, ipse*, for *illus, istus, ipsus*. Bopp considers that the reason why *sa* dispenses with the termination *s* is, that this termination is itself derived from the pronoun *sa*.

a. There is an option allowed when an initial sibilant is compounded with another hard consonant. In that case, the preceding final *s* may be dropped; as, हरि स्कन्दति *hari skandati*, 'Hari goes.'

b. A rare exception to the first rule occurs, when an initial त *t* is compounded with a sibilant. In that case, the preceding final *s* becomes Visarga; as, हरिः त्सरुं गृह्णाति *harih tsarum grihṇáti*, 'Hari grasps the hilt of his sword.'

68. The preceding rules are most frequently applicable to स् *s*, as the final of the cases of nouns and inflections of verbs; but they come equally into operation in substantives or adjectives, whose *base* or *crude form* ends in अस् *as*, इस् *is*, and उस् *us*: thus, by 64, चक्षुस् + ईक्षते *chakshus*+*íkshate* becomes चक्षुर् ईक्षते *chakshur íkshate*, 'the eye sees;' and चक्षुस् + भिस् *chakshus* + *bhis* = चक्षुर्भिस् *chakshurbhis*, 'by eyes.' Similarly, by 65, मनस् + जानाति *manas* + *jánáti* = मनो जानाति *mano jánáti*, 'the mind knows;' and मनस् + भिस् *manas* + *bhis* = मनोभिस् *manobhis*, 'by minds.'

a. Observe—All nouns ending in इस् *is* and उस् *us* may be regarded as ending in इष् *ish* and उष् *ush*, which is the form they necessarily assume in declension before the terminations beginning with vowels (see 70, and compare 41. *b*): thus चक्षुस् + आ *chakshus* + *á* becomes चक्षुषा *chakshushá*, 'by the eye;' but before consonants they must be treated as ending in the dental sibilant. See 165.

69. स् *s* at the end of the first member of a compound word, before hard letters of the guttural or labial classes (क *k*, प *p*, or their aspirates), may follow 63, or is more usually retained, passing sometimes into ष *sh*, according to 70: thus तेजस् + कर *tejas* + *kara* becomes either तेजस्कर or तेजःकर 'causing light;' प्रादुस् + कृत *prádus* + *krita* becomes प्रादुष्कृत *prádushkrita*, 'made manifest;' दिवस् + पति *divas* + *pati* = दिवस्पति 'the lord of day.'

a. Again, in opposition to 64 and 65, a final स् *s* is usually retained before affixes beginning with व *v* and म *m*, passing sometimes into ष *sh*, according to 70: thus तेजस् + विन् *tejas*+*vin* becomes तेजस्विन् *tejaswin*, 'full of light;' भास् + वर *bhás*+*vara* = भास्वर *bháswara*, 'radiant;' and अर्चिस् + मत् *archis* + *mat* = अर्चिष्मत् *archishmat*, 'possessing flame.'

70. स *s*, *not final*, passes into ष *sh* when preceded by any other vowel but अ *a* or आ *á*; also when preceded by the semivowel र् *r*, or by क् *k*:

thus अग्नि + सु *agni + su* becomes अग्निषु *agnishu*, 'in fires;' करो + सि *karo + si* = करोषि *karoshi*, 'thou doest;' बिभर् + सि *bibhar + si* = बिभर्षि *bibharshi*, 'thou bearest;' वाक् + सु *vák + su* = वाक्षु *vákshu*, 'in words.' See 69. and 69. *a*.

a. An intervening Anuswára or Visarga does not prevent the operation of this rule: thus, हवींषि, चक्षूंषि, हविःषु, चक्षुःषु.

CHANGES OF FINAL र् *r*.

71. Most of the changes of final र् *r* are the same as those of final स् *s*.

a. Thus, by 63, प्रातर् + काल *prátar + kála* becomes प्रातःकाल *prátahkála*, 'the time of morning;' and प्रातर् + स्नान *prátar + snána* = प्रातःस्नान *prátahsnána*, 'morning ablution.' But *r* as the final of a root, or as a radical letter, remains unchanged before a sibilant: thus, चर् + सु = चर्षु (No. 70); बिभर् + सि = बिभर्षि.

b. By 62, प्रातर् + तु *prátar + tu* becomes प्रातस्तु *prátastu*; and प्रातर् + च *prátar + cha* = प्रातश्च *prátaścha*.

Note, that the transition of *r* into *s* before *t* is exemplified in Latin by *gestum* from *gero*, *ustum* from *uro*, &c. On the other hand, *r* in the middle of words is preserved before *t* in Sanskṛit, as in *kartum*, &c.

c. By 65, निर् + उक्त *nir + ukta* remains निरुक्त *nirukta*, 'described;' निर् + दय *nir + daya* remains निर्दय *nirdaya*, 'without pity;' and निर् + रस *nir + rasa* is नीरस *nírasa*, 'without flavour.'

d. After the analogy of 65. *a*, final *ar* before initial *r* drops its own *r*, and lengthens the preceding *a*; as पुनर् + रक्षति *punar + rakshati* becomes पुना रक्षति *puná rakshati*, 'again he preserves.'

e. But in opposition to 64 and 66, final अर् *ar*, unlike अस् *as*, remains unchanged before any soft letter (consonant or vowel): thus प्रातर् + आश *prátar + áśa* remains प्रातराश *prátaráśa*, 'morning meal;' पुनर् + याति *punar + yáti* remains पुनर् याति *punar yáti*, 'again he goes.'

72. र् *r* at the end of the first member of a compound, before क *k*, प *p*, and their aspirates, may either become Visarga, by 63, or more usually follows 69, and passes into स् *s*, which is liable to become ष *sh* by 70: thus निर् + फल *nir + phala* becomes निष्फल *nishphala*, 'without fruit.' In the case of दुर् + ख *dur + kha*, दुःख is more common than दुष्ख.

73. र् *r* may optionally double any consonant, except ह *h*, that immediately follows it: thus निर् + दय *nir + daya* may be written निर्द्दय *nirddaya*.

The following table exhibits the more common combinations of consonants at one view. Observe, that in the top line of initial letters the aspirated consonants have been omitted, because it is an universal rule, that whatever change takes place before any consonant, the same holds good before its aspirate.

INITIAL VOWELS AND CONSONANTS.	अ *a*	आ, इ, *á, i,* &c.	क *k*	ग *g*	च *ch*	ज *j*	त *t*	द *d*	न *n*	प *p*	ब *b*	म *m*	य *y*	र *r*	ल *l*	व *v*	श *ś*	स *s*	ह *h*
FINAL CONSONANTS.																			
क् *k* or ग् *g*	*g a*	*g á* &c.	*k k*	*g g*	*k ch*	*g j*	*k t*	*g d*	*n· n*	*k p*	*g b*	*n· m*	*g y*	*g r*	*g l*	*g v*	*k ś*	*k s*	*g gh*
त् *t* or द् *d*	*d a*	*d á* &c.	*t k*	*d g*	*ch ch*	*j j*	*t t*	*d d*	*n n*	*t p*	*d b*	*n m*	*d y*	*d r*	*l l*	*d v*	*ch chh*	*t s*	*d dh*
न् *n*	*nn* a*	*nn* á* &c.	*n k*	*n g*	*nś ch*	*n† j*	*ns t*	*n d*	*n n*	*n p*	*n b*	*n m*	*n y*	*n r*	*l l*	*n v*	*n ś* or *ṅ ś* or *ṅ chh*	*n s*	*n h*
अस् *as*	*o '*	*a á* &c.	*ah k*	*o g*	*aś ch*	*o j*	*as t*	*o d*	*o n*	*ah p*	*o b*	*o m*	*o y*	*o r*	*o l*	*o v*	*ah ś*	*ah s*	*o h*
आस् *ás*	*á a*	*á á* &c.	*áh k*	*á g*	*áś ch*	*á j*	*ás t*	*á d*	*á n*	*áh p*	*á b*	*á m*	*á y*	*á r*	*á l*	*á v*	*áh ś*	*áh s*	*á h*
इस् *is*, ईस् *ís*, उस् *us*, ऊस् *ús*	*ir a*	*ir á*	*ih k*	*ir g*	*iś ch*	*ir j*	*is t*	*ir d*	*ir n*	*ih p*	*ir b*	*ir m*	*ir y*	*í r*	*ir l*	*ir v*	*ih ś*	*ih s*	*ir h*
एस् *es*, ऐस् *ais*	*ur a*	*ur á*	*uh k*	*ur g*	*uś ch*	*ur j*	*us t*	*ur d*	*ur n*	*uh p*	*ur b*	*ur m*	*ur y*	*ú r*	*ur l*	*ur v*	*uh ś*	*uh s*	*ur h*
ओस् *os*, औस् *aus*	&c.	&c.	&c.	&c.	&c.	&c.	&c.	&c.	&c.	&c.	&c.	&c.	&c.	&c.	&c.	&c.	&c.	&c.	&c.
र् *r*, preceded by *any* vowel.	*r a*	*r á* &c.	*h k*	*r g*	*ś ch*	*r j*	*s t*	*r d*	*r n*	*h p*	*r b*	*r m*	*r y*	*r*	*r l*	*r v*	*h ś*	*h s*	*r h*

* *n* is only doubled if preceded by a short vowel.

† A final *n* before *j* is very rarely written in the palatal form ञ *ñ*.

CHAPTER III.

ON SANSKṚIT ROOTS, AND THE FORMATION OF NOMINAL BASES.

Before treating of Sanskṛit nouns, it will be advisable to point out in what respect the peculiar system adopted in their formation requires an arrangement of the subject different from that to which we are accustomed in other languages.

74. In Sanskṛit nouns (including substantives, adjectives, pronouns, and numerals) there is this great peculiarity, that every one of them has two distinct states prior to the formation of the nominative case; viz. 1st, a root; 2dly, coming directly from the root, a state which is sometimes called *the crude form;* that is to say, a state antecedent to inflection, and anterior to any of the cases, even the nominative. This form of the noun is more properly termed *the nominal base,* or *the inflective base* of the noun; that is, the changed form of the root, which serves as the basis on which the system of cases is constructed. In the first place, then, let us inquire what is the root?

There are in Sanskṛit about two thousand elementary sounds, out of which, as out of so many blocks, are carved and fashioned, not only all the nouns, but all the verbs which exist in the language.

a. Though the root may be compared to a rough block, or to the raw material, out of which nouns and verbs are constructed, yet the student must understand that in the dialect of the Vedas, and even in modern classical Sanskṛit, roots are not unfrequently used by themselves as substantives and adjectives, and are very commonly so used at the end of compounds. See 84, 87, and 172.

b. Every one of these roots or primary sounds conveys some simple idea, which appears under different modifications in the derivatives from it. Thus—to mention a few of the most common—the root क्षिप् *kship* conveys the idea of 'throwing;' कृ *kṛi*, of 'doing,' 'making;' क्री *krí*, of 'buying;' हृ *hṛi*, of 'seizing,' 'taking;' युज् *yuj*, 'joining;' अस् *as*, वृत् *vṛit*, 'being;' भू *bhú*, 'becoming;' जीव् *jív*, 'living;' नी *ní*, 'leading;' जि *ji*, 'conquering;' गम् *gam*, या *yá*, चर् *char*, क्रम् *kram*, इ *i*, सृ *sṛi*, स्कन्द् *skand*, 'going;' वद् *vad*, वच् *vach*,

ब्रू *brú*, 'speaking;' बुध् *budh*, ज्ञा *jñá*, 'knowing;' दृश् *driś*, 'seeing;' इष् *ish*, कम् *kam*, 'wishing;' मृ *mri*, 'dying;' दा *dá*, 'giving;' जन् *jan*, 'producing;' धा *dhá*, 'placing;' अद् *ad*, भुज् *bhuj*, भक्ष् *bhaksh*, 'eating;' पा *pá*, 'drinking;' पच् *pach*, 'cooking;' हन् *han*, 'killing;' पत् *pat*, 'falling;' वस् *vas*, 'dwelling;' विश् *viś*, 'entering;' स्था *sthá*, 'standing;' श्रु *śru*, 'hearing;' स्पृश् *spriś*, 'touching;' सिध् *sidh*, साध् *sádh*, 'accomplishing;' कुप् *kup*, क्रुध् *krudh*, 'being angry;' चि *chi*, 'collecting;' घ्रा *ghrá*, 'smelling;' ख्या *khyá*, 'relating;' नश् *naś*, 'perishing;' त्यज् *tyaj*, रह् *rah*, 'quitting;' द्विष् *dwish*, 'hating;' निन्द् *nind*, 'blaming;' द्रु *dru*, 'running;' द्युत् *dyut*, दीप् *díp*, भा *bhá*, शुभ् *śubh*, 'shining;' पू *pú*, 'purifying;' प्रच्छ् *prachchh*, 'asking;' आप् *áp*, लभ् *labh*, 'obtaining;' स्तु *stu*, शंस् *śans*, 'praising;' यत् *yat*, 'striving;' यम् *yam*, 'restraining;' शक् *śak*, 'being able;' तप् *tap*, 'heating;' दह् *dah*, 'burning;' मुच् *much*, 'liberating;' मुह् *muh*, 'being foolish;' युध् *yudh*, 'fighting;' रुह् *ruh*, 'growing;' हस् *has*, 'laughing;' स्वप् *swap*, 'sleeping;' हृष् *hrish*, नन्द् *nand*, ह्लाद् *hlád*, 'being glad;' स्ना *sná*, 'bathing;' रभ् *rabh*, 'beginning;' स्वर् *swar*, 'sounding;' सह् *sah*, वह् *vah*, 'bearing;' स्मृ *smri*, 'remembering;' अर्च् *arch*, 'honouring.'

c. Observe, that it will be convenient, in the following pages, to express the idea contained in the root by prefixing to it the infinitive sign *to*. But the student must not suppose that the sound *kship* denotes any thing more than the mere *idea* of 'throwing;' nor must he imagine that in deriving nouns from it, we are deriving them from the infinitive, or from any part of the verb, but rather from a simple original sound, which is the common source of both nouns and verbs.

75. A cursory glance at the above list of common roots will serve to shew that there are two particulars in which they all agree. Every one of them is monosyllabic, and every one of them contains a single vowel, and no more. In other respects they offer considerable diversity. Some consist of a single vowel only; some begin with one or two consonants, and end in a vowel, but none end in either अ *a* or औ *au*; some begin with a vowel, and end in one or two consonants*; and some begin and end with one or two

* Rule 43, which requires that if a word ends in a conjunct consonant, the last member shall be rejected, is not applicable to roots, unless they are used as complete words in a sentence. Nevertheless, in the case of roots ending in a consonant, preceded by a nasal, the latter is often euphonically dropped, as बन्ध् becomes बध्.

consonants*, inclosing a medial vowel; so that a root may sometimes consist of only one letter, as इ् *i*, 'to go;' and sometimes of five, as स्कन्द् *skand*, 'to move;' प्रच्छ् *prachchh*, 'to ask.'

a. There are a few polysyllabic words recognised as roots, but they are generally the result of the accidental conjunction of a preposition with a monosyllabic root; that is to say, the preposition has been so constantly used in conjunction with the root, that it has at length come to be regarded as part of the root: thus in the roots सङ्ग्राम् *san-grám*, 'to fight,' and अवधीर् *avadhír*, 'to despise,' the prepositions सं *sam* and अव *ava* have combined with the root in this manner. A few other polysyllabic roots are the result of a reduplication of the radical syllable; (as, दरिद्रा *daridrá*, 'to be poor;' जागृ *jágri*, 'to be awake;' चकास् *chakás*, 'to shine;' वेवी *veví*, 'to go,' 'pervade;') and a few are derived from nouns; as, कुमार् 'to play,' from कुमार *kumára*, 'a boy.'

b. Roots beginning with न *n* and स *s* are liable, according to 58 and 70, to be changed to ण *ṇ* and ष *sh*. Hence these roots are invariably exhibited in Native Grammars as beginning with ण and ष, because the Indian system requires that in exhibiting any general type of a class of words, that form should be taken which may occur even under the rarest circumstances. But in this Grammar, roots of which the initials are न *n* and स *s* will be exhibited as beginning with these letters, by reason of their more frequent occurrence.

c. Indian grammarians attach certain symbolical letters and syllables (called *anubandhas* or 'appendages') to particular roots to indicate peculiarities in their conjugation. Thus the letter इ् *i*, placed after a root, marks the insertion of a nasal; as in the root *nid*, which could be written निदि *nidi*, to shew that in conjugation न् *n* is inserted (pres. *nindámi*, &c.). Similarly, इर् *ir* marks two forms of the 3d preterite; thus *śuchir* shews that *śuch* may make either *aśochisham* or *aśucham* in that tense. So also, औ *au* indicates a root which rejects the inserted *i* (see 391); ओ *o* marks the substitution of *na* for *ta* in the pass. participle; उ *u*, the optional insertion of *i* in the indeclinable participle; ऊ *ú*, the optional insertion of *i* in the two futures, &c.

76. The learner is recommended to study attentively the commonest of these roots, or elementary sounds, as given at 74. *b.* He may rest assured, that by pausing for a time at the root, his progress afterwards will be more rapid, when he ascends to the branches which spring from it. For it must never be forgotten, that every word in Sanskrit, whether substantive, adjective, verb, or adverb, stands in close filial relationship to some radical sound. In fact, every root is a common bond of union for a large family of words, which might otherwise appear unconnected; and words

* One root, श्च्युत् *śchyut*, 'to drop,' begins with three consonants.

which, when viewed apart from the root, are isolated symbols, demanding a separate effort of memory for each separate idea which they express, fasten themselves readily on the mind when regarded as so many parts of one original idea, so many branches of a common stock.

Thus, to take any one of the foregoing roots—as, for example, *budh*, 'to know'—we shall find that from it may be drawn out with great regularity, 1st, a set of simple substantives; 2dly, of simple adjectives; 3dly, of simple verbs: thus, *bodha* or *bodhana*, 'knowledge;' *buddhi*, 'intellect;' *bodhaka*, 'an informer;' *bauddha*, 'a Buddhist;' *budha*, 'wise;' *buddhimat*, 'intellectual;' and the following verbs, *bodhati*, 'he knows;' *budhyate*, 'it is known;' *bodhayati*, 'he informs;' *bubhutsate* or *bubodhishati*, 'he wishes to know;' *bobudhyate*, 'he knows well.' And the simple idea contained in the root may be endlessly extended by the prefixing of prepositions; as, *prabodha*, 'vigilance;' *prabudhyate*, 'he awakes.'

77. In the next place we are to inquire what is the base or crude form of the noun. The student should understand, at the outset, the meaning and use of this form. It is an intermediate state between the root and nominative case, the naked form of the noun, which serves as the basis on which to construct its eight cases, beginning with the nominative. In a Greek or Latin dictionary we look for the noun under the nominative case, but in Sanskṛit we look for it under its crude state. Thus, *bodha, bodhana, tat, pañchan, bhavat*, are the crude bases under which the nominative cases *bodhas, bodhanam, sas, pañcha, bhaván*, are to be sought. And here it may be observed, that the base of a noun is no mere grammatical invention. It is, perhaps, more practically useful than the cases derived from it. It is that form of the noun which is always used in the formation of compound words, and in this respect may be regarded as the most general of cases. And since every Sanskṛit sentence contains more compound words than simple, it may with truth be said, that the crude base is the form under which the noun most usually appears.

We may conceive it quite possible that Greek and Latin grammarians might have proceeded on a similar plan, and that they might have supposed a root λεγ, from which was drawn out the nouns λέξις, λεξικὸς, λεκτὸς, καταλογὴ, ἔλλογος, and the verbs λέγω, καταλέγω, ἐλλογέω: so also, a root *scrib*, from which was derived the nouns *scriptio, scriptum, scriptor, scriptura*; and the verbs *scribo, perscribo, ascribo*: or a root *nau*, from which would come *nauta, navis, nauticus, navalis, navigo*, &c. Again, they might have supposed a crude base to each of these nouns, as well as a root; as, for instance, λεξι and λεξικο of λέξις and λεξικὸς, and *navi* of *navis;* and they might have required the student to look for λέξις under λεξι, λέγω under λεγ, *navis* under *navi*, and *navigo* under *nau*. Further than this, they might have shewn that the base was the form used in the formation of compound words, as in λεξικογράφος, *naviger*. But Greek and Latin are too uncertain in their construction to admit of such an analysis being completely carried out.

78. It will be perceived from the foregoing remarks that the consideration of Sanskṛit nouns must divide itself into two heads: 1st, the formation of the base; 2dly, the inflection or declension of the base; that is, the adaptation of the base or modified root to a common scheme of case-terminations.

a. In fact, it will appear in the sequel, that the same system applies both to nouns and verbs. As in verbs (see 248) the formation of a verbal base from a root precedes the subject of verbal inflection or conjugation, so in nouns it is necessary to the clear elucidation of the subject that the method of forming the nominal base from the root should be explained antecedently to declension.

b. Indeed, it must be remembered that nouns, substantive and adjective, in Sanskṛit are classified into separate declensions, according to the finals of their bases, not according to the finals of their cases; and it becomes essential to determine the form of the final syllable of the nominal base before the various declensions can be arranged.

79. The bases of nouns, substantive and adjective, are formed either by adding certain affixes to the root, the vowel of which is liable, at the same time, to be gunated or vriddhied (see 28. *a*); or by adding certain affixes to the bases of nouns already formed. When, however, the root itself is used as a noun, no affix is required, but the root is then also the base. Hence it follows that the final syllable of nominal bases will end in almost any letter of the alphabet. Those bases, however, that end in vowels may be conveniently separated under four classes, each class containing masc., fem., and neuter nouns; the 1st ending in अ *a*, आ *á*, and ई *í*; the 2d in इ *i*; the 3d in उ *u*; and the 4th in ऋ *ṛi*. Those that end in consonants may also be arranged under four classes; the 1st, 2d, and 3d, ending in त् *t* or द् *d*, न् *n*, स् *s*, respectively (compare 44); and the 4th comprising all other final consonants.

a. It will be afterwards shewn, that the first class of nouns, comprising bases in *a*, *á*, and *í*, is by far the most numerous and important. See 109.

Bearing in mind, therefore, that Sanskṛit declension consists in building up a system of cases on a base, by attaching the case-terminations to that base—bearing in mind, moreover, that the whole distinction of declensions depends on the distribution of the bases of nouns under eight classes, according to their final syllables—we are now to explain more precisely, under each of these classes, the method of forming the nominal inflective base by regular derivation from the root.

Observe—It is not intended that the student should dwell long on the following pages printed in small type. He is recommended to read them over rapidly, and to note carefully the final letters of the base under each of the eight classes.

Observe, moreover, that although all the bases of Sanskṛit nouns, without exception, are derived from roots, there are many in which the connection between the noun and its source, either in sense or form, is not very obvious *. The following rules have reference only to those bases whose formation proceeds on clear and intelligible principles.

FORMATION OF THE BASE OR CRUDE FORM OF NOUNS.

80. First Class.—*Comprising Masculine and Neuter bases in* अ a; *Feminine in* आ á *and* ई í.

Formed by adding to roots—

I. अ *a*, forming, 1st (nom. *-as*), after Vṛiddhi of medial *a* of a root, and Guṇa of any other vowel, a large class of masculine substantives; as, from the root *div*, 'to sport,' *deva*, 'a deity.' If a root ends in *ch* or *j*, these letters are changed to *k* and *g* respectively; as, from *pach*, 'to cook,' *páka*, 'cooking;' from *yuj*, 'to join,' *yoga*, 'joining.' See 43. *d*.

II. अ *a*, forming, 2dly (nom. masc. *-as*, fem. *-á*, neut. *-am*), after Guṇa of a final, and sometimes Guṇa of a medial vowel, nouns of agency and adjectives; as, from *plu*, 'to swim,' *plava*, 'what swims;' from *sṛip*, 'to creep,' *sarpa*, 'what creeps.' See 580. Adjectives of this form generally occur at the end of compounds; as, *arin-dama*, 'foe-taming;' *bhayan-kara*, 'fear-causing.' Compare corresponding formations in Greek and Latin; as, ἱππό-δαμος, *veri-dicus*, *grandi-loquus*, *omni-vorus*, &c. When सु εὐ and दुस् δυς are prefixed to these adjectives,

* Thus *purusha*, 'a man,' is said to come from *pur*, 'to precede;' *śṛigála*, 'a jackal,' from *sṛij*, 'to create.'

they are susceptible of a passive sense, both in Sanskrit and Greek; as, सुकर 'easy to be done;' दुष्कर 'hard to be done,' &c. Similarly, εὔφορος, δύςφορος, δύςτομος, &c.

III. अ *a*, forming, 3dly (nom. *-as, -á, -am*), adjectives; as, from *śubh*, 'to shine,' *śubha*, 'beautiful.' Sometimes there is great change of the root; as in *śiva*, 'propitious,' from शी *śí*, 'to sleep;' *sundara*, 'beautiful,' from दृ *dṛi*, 'to respect:' and sometimes the feminine may be formed in *í;* as, *sundarí*. There are very few adjectives formed with this affix.

IV. अक *aka* (nom. *-akas, -aká* or *-iká, -akam*), after Vṛiddhi of a final vowel or medial *a*, and Guṇa of any other vowel. Still more common than *a* to form adjectives and nouns of agency (see 582. *b*); as, from *tap*, 'to burn,' *tápaka*, 'inflammatory;' from *kṛi*, 'to do,' *káraka*, 'a doer.' Observe, *-aká* is generally taken for the feminine of the adjectives, and *-iká* for the feminine of the agents; as, *tápaká, káriká*. Compare Greek forms like φύλακος.

V. अन *ana* (nom. *-anam*), after Guṇa of the root, forming, 1st, a large class of neuter substantives; as, from *ní*, 'to guide,' *nayana*, 'the eye,' 'guidance;' from *dá*, 'to give,' *dána*, 'a gift;' from *dṛip*, 'to make proud,' *darpaṇa*, 'a mirror.' Compare analogous Greek formations in ανο; as, ὄργανον, δρέπανον, &c.

अन *ana*, forming, 2dly (nom. *-anas, -aná, -anam*), nouns of agency (see 582. *c*) and adjectives; as, from *nṛit*, 'to dance,' *nartana*, 'a dancer;' from *śubh*, 'to shine,' *śobhana*, 'bright.' Compare Greek forms like ἱκανός, &c. The feminine of the agents is sometimes in *-aní*.

VI. न *na*. A few abstract nouns are formed with *na;* as, *yajna*, 'sacrifice,' from *yaj; yatna*, 'effort,' from *yat; swapna*, 'sleep,' from *swap*. Compare ὕπνος, *somnus*.

VII. त्र *tra* (nom. *-tram*), after Guṇa of the root; as, from *pá*, 'to drink,' *pátra*, 'a vessel;' from श्रु *śru*, 'to hear,' *śrotra*, 'the organ of hearing.' This affix is used to form neuter nouns denoting some instrument or organ, and corresponds to the Latin *trum* in *aratrum, plectrum*, &c.; and the Greek τρον, θρον in νίπτρον, βάκτρον, βάθρον, &c.

VIII. There are other uncommon affixes to roots to form adjectives and a few substantives in अ *a* (nom. *-as, -á, -am*); as, र *ra*, ल *la*, अल *ala*, अर *ara*, वर *vara*, मर *mara*, इल *ila*, इर *ira*, उर *ura*, उल *ula*, म *ma*, व *va*, त्र *tra*, आक *áka*, एर *era*, उक *uka*, ऊक *úka*, क *ka*. The following are examples of nouns formed with these affixes: *dípra*, 'shining' (compare Greek formations like λάμπ-ρος, &c.; and Latin *pu-rus*, &c.); *chandra*, 'the moon;' *śukla*, 'white;' *chapala*, 'fickle;' *tarala*, 'trembling' (compare Greek forms like τρόχ-αλος, τράπ-ελος; and Latin *tremulus*, &c.); *vaṭara*, 'unsteady' (compare Greek forms like φάνερος, &c.); *jitwara*, 'victorious;' *ghasmara*, 'voracious;' *anila*, 'wind;' *pathila*, 'a traveller' (compare Latin forms like *agilis*, &c.); *chhidira*, 'an axe;' *bhidura*, 'brittle;' *harshula*, 'a lover;' *bhíma*, 'terrible;' *gharma*, m., 'heat;' *yugma*, n., 'a pair;' *dhúma*, m., 'smoke' (compare forms like θύ-μος, ἄνεμ-ος, *fumus, animus*, &c.); *aśwa*, m., 'a horse' (*equus*); *chitra*, 'variegated;' *jalpáka*, 'talkative' (compare forms like *loquacs, loquac*, and φένακς for φένακος); *patera*, 'moving;' *varshuka*, 'rainy;'

jágarúka, 'watchful' (added especially to frequentative or reduplicate forms; as, from *vávad*, 'to speak often;' *vávadúka*, 'loquacious'); *śushka*, 'dry' (from *śush*, 'to dry.' Compare Latin *siccus*).

Formed by adding to the bases of NOUNS—

IX. त्व *twa* (nom. *-twam*), forming neuter abstract substantives from any noun in the language; as, from *purusha*, 'a man,' *purushatwa*, 'manliness.' In adding this affix to bases ending in nasals, the nasal is rejected; as, from *dhanin*, 'rich,' *dhanitwa*, 'the state of being rich.' (See 57.)

X. य *ya*, forming, 1st (nom. *-yam*), neuter abstract substantives aud a few collectives, the first syllable of the noun taking Vṛiddhi; as, from सुहृद् *suhṛid*, 'a friend,' सौहृद्य *sauhṛidya*, 'friendship.' When the base ends in a vowel, this vowel is rejected before *ya* is affixed; as, from *vichitra*, 'various,' *vaichitrya*, 'variety.'

XI. य *ya*, forming, 2dly (nom. *-yas*, *-yá*, *-yam*), adjectives expressing some relationship to the noun; as, from *dhana*, 'wealth,' *dhanya*, 'wealthy.' Sometimes Vṛiddhi takes place; as, from *soma*, 'the moon,' *saumya*, 'lunar.' In this case the fem. is *-yí*. Compare Greek adjectives in *ιος*, and Latin in *ius*.

XII. अ *a* (nom. *-as*, *-í*, *-am*), after Vṛiddhi of the first syllable of the noun, forming innumerable adjectives expressing some relationship to the noun. When the base ends in *a*, no further affix is required, and the only change is the Vṛiddhi of the first syllable; as, from *purusha*, 'a man,' पौरुष *paurusha*, 'manly;' from *Vasishṭha*, *Vásishṭha*, 'a descendant of Vasishṭha.' When in *á* or *í*, this *á* or *í* must be rejected; as, from *sikatá*, 'sand,' *saikata*, 'sandy.' When in *u*, this *u* is gunated, and becomes *av* before this and the three following affixes; as, from *Vishṇu*, 'the god Vishṇu,' *Vaishṇava*, 'a worshipper of Vishṇu;' from *dáru*, 'wood,' *dárava*, 'wooden;' from *manu*, *mánava*, 'a descendant of Manu.' When the initial letter of a word is compounded with *v* or *y*, these latter are resolved into *uv* and *iy*, which are vriddhied; as, सौवर *sauvara*, 'relating to sound,' from *swara*, 'a note;' वैयाघ्र *vaiyághra*, 'relating to a tiger,' from *vyághra*, 'a tiger.' Observe—This applies to the two next affixes also.

Sometimes the neuter form of these adjectives is taken as an abstract substantive; thus, nominative case, *paurusham*, 'manliness;' *śaiśavam*, 'childhood,' from *śiśu*, 'a child;' or, as a collective; thus, *kshaitram*, 'fields,' collectively, from *kshetra*. Observe—This applies to the two next affixes also.

XIII. इक *ika* (nom. *-ikas*, *-ikí*, *-ikam*), after Vṛiddhi of the first syllable of the noun, forming numerous adjectives. Before this affix is added, the final vowel of the base must be rejected; as, from *dharma*, 'religion,' *dhármika*, 'religious;' from *venu*, 'a flute,' *vainavika*, 'a flute-player;' from श्वस् *śwas*, 'to-morrow,' शौवस्तिक *śauvastika*, 'relating to to-morrow.' Compare Latin forms like *bellicus*, *nauticus*, &c.; and Greek πολεμικός, &c.

XIV. एय *eya* (nom. *-eyas*, *-eyí*, *-eyam*), after Vṛiddhi of the first syllable of the noun, forming many adjectives. The final vowel of the base must be rejected; as, from *purusha*, 'a man,' *paurusheya*, 'manly;' from *agni*, 'fire,' *ágneya*, 'fiery.' Compare forms like λεόντειος, λεόντεος; and Latin *igneus*, &c.

XV. ईय *íya* (nom. *-íyas, -íyá, -íyam*), without any change of the noun, except the rejection of final *a;* as, from *parvata,* 'a mountain,' *parvatíya,* 'mountainous.' Sometimes there is Vṛiddhi; as, from *sukha,* 'pleasure,' *saukhíya,* 'pleasurable.' When the final of the base remains, *k* is prefixed to this and the last affix; as, from *para,* 'another,' *parakíya,* 'belonging to another.'

XVI. There are other uncommon affixes to nouns forming adjectives in अ *a* (nom. *-as, -á, -am*); such as *ína, ina, vala, tana;* forming, from *gráma,* 'a village,' *grámíṇa,* 'rustic;' from *ratha,* 'a chariot' (Lat. *rota*), *rathina,* 'having a chariot;' from *śikhá,* 'a crest,' *śikhávala,* 'crested;' from *śwas,* 'to-morrow,' *śwastana,* 'future.' This last answers to the Latin *tinus,* and has reference to *time.* Compare *crastinus,* &c.

XVII. क *ka* (nom. *-kas, -ká, -kam*), added to words to form adjectives and collective nouns, or to express depreciation: thus, *madhuka,* 'sweet,' from *madhu,* 'honey;' *aśwaka,* 'a hack,' from *aśwa,* 'a horse.' It is often redundant.

XVIII. मय *maya* (nom. *-mayas, -mayí, -mayam*), added to words to denote 'made of,' 'full of;' as, from *loha,* 'iron,' *lohamaya,* 'made of iron;' from *tejas,* 'light,' *tejomaya,* 'full of light.'

XIX. तर *tara* (nom. *-taras, -tará, -taram*), तम *tama* (nom. *-tamas, -tamá, -tamam*), इष्ट *ishṭa* (nom. *-ishṭas, -ishṭá, -ishṭam*), added to adjectives to express the degrees of comparison. See 191, 192.

XX. दघ्न *daghna* (nom. *-daghnas, -daghní, -daghnam*), द्वयस *dwayasa* (*-dwayasas, -dwayasí, -dwayasam*), and मात्र *mátra* (*-mátras, -matrí, -mátram*), added to words to denote 'measure' or 'height;' as, *jánu-daghnam jalam,* 'water up to the knees.'

XXI. देशीय *deśíya* (nom. *-deśíyas, -deśíyá, -deśíyam*) and कल्प *kalpa* (nom. *-kalpas, -kalpá, -kalpam*), added to words to denote 'similitude,' but with some inferiority; as, *kavi-kalpa* or *kavi-deśíya,* 'a sort of poet:' or denoting 'nearly,' about;' as, *mṛita-kalpa,* 'nearly dead;' *vinśati-varsha-deśíya,* 'about twenty years of age.'

a. Observe—The affixes त *ta* and इत *ita* (nom. *-tas, -tá, -tam*), forming innumerable passive participles—as, *jita,* 'conquered,' from *ji,* 'to conquer,' &c.—fall under the first class of bases. See 530.

b. So also many other participles formed with *mána, ána, tavya, aníya, ya,* &c. See 526, 527, 568.

c. इत *ita* is said to be added to nouns to form adjectives; as, *phalita,* 'fruitful,' from *phala,* 'fruit;' but these may be regarded as passive participles from nominal verbs. See 551.

By adding to ROOTS—

XXII. आ *á* (nom. *-á*), with no change of the root, forming feminine substantives; as, from *jív,* 'to live,' *jíva,* 'life;' from स्पृह् *spṛih,* 'to desire,' स्पृहा *spṛihá,* 'desire.' Compare Greek formations like φόρα, φύγη; and Latin *fuga,* &c. Occasionally there is Guṇa; as in *lekhá,* 'a line,' from *likh,* 'to write;' *jará,* 'old age,' from *jṛi,* 'to grow old.' This affix is frequently added to the desiderative form of a root; as, from *pipás,* 'to desire to drink,' *pipásá,* 'thirst;' and rarely to the frequentative or intensive; as, from *lolúy*, 'to cut much,' *lolúyá*, 'cutting much.'

A few abstract nouns are formed with ना *ná*: as, *tṛishná*, 'thirst,' from *tṛish*: compare Greek nouns in νη.

By adding to the bases of NOUNS—

XXIII. ता *tá* (nom. *-tá*), forming feminine abstract substantives; as, from *purusha*, 'a man,' *purushatá*, 'manliness.' This affix may be added to any noun in the language, and corresponds to the Latin *tas* in *celeritas*, &c.; and the Greek της in κακότης, πλατύτης (पृथुता).

Also forming collectives; as, बन्धुता 'a number of relations,' from बन्धु 'a relation.'

XXIV. त्रा *trá* (nom. *-trá*), forming a few substantives, derived from neuters in *tra* (see VII), and like them denoting 'the instrument' or 'means;' as, दंष्ट्रा 'a tooth,' 'the instrument of biting,' from *danś*, 'to bite;' यात्रा 'provisions,' 'the means of going,' from *yá*, 'to go.'

XXV. ई *í* (nom. *-í*), forming a large class of feminine substantives, usually derived from masculines in *a*, by changing *a* to *í*; as, from *nada*, 'a river,' fem. *nadí*; from *putra*, 'a son,' fem. *putrí*; from *nartaka*, 'a dancer,' fem. *nartakí*. An affix *ání* is used to denote 'the wife of;' as, from *Indra*, इन्द्राणी (58) 'the wife of Indra.' Compare the Greek αινα in θέαινα, &c.

XXVI. ई *í* (nom. *-í*), forming, 2dly, the feminine of nouns of agency, like दातृ *dátṛi*, 'a giver' (129. *b*), and *kárin*, 'a doer' (160).

XXVII. ई *í* (nom. *-í*), forming, 3dly, the feminine of many adjectives; as of *tanu*, 'thin' (118. *a*), of *dhanavat*, 'rich,' and *dhímat*, 'wise' (140. *b*); of *dhanin*, 'rich' (160), and of comparative degrees like *balíyas* (167). Observe—The feminine of some adjectives formed with the affixes *a*, *ya*, *ika*, and *eya* (XI. XII. XIII. XIV), and of some adjectives like *sundara*, 'beautiful,' is also formed with *í*.

XXVIII. A few roots standing by themselves as substantives, or with prepositions prefixed, or at the end of compounds, may come under this class; as, *bhí*, 'fear,' *ájñá*, 'an order,' from ज्ञा 'to know;' *senání*, 'a general,' from *sená*, 'an army,' and *ní*, 'to lead,' &c. It will be more convenient, however, to consider the declension of monosyllabic nouns in *í* under the 2d class. See 123.

81. SECOND CLASS.—*Masculine, Feminine, and Neuter bases in* इ i.

Formed by adding to ROOTS—

I. इ *i*, forming, 1st (nom. *-is*), a few masculine substantives; as, *agni*, 'fire,' from *an·k*, 'to mark;' *kavi*, 'a poet,' from *ku*, 'to sound;' *ahi*, 'a snake' (ἔχις, *anguis*), from *anh*, 'to move;' *dhwani*, 'sound,' from *dhwan*; *peshi*, 'a thunderbolt,' from *pesh*, 'to crush,' &c. When this affix is added to the root *dhá*, 'to place,' 'to hold,' *á* is dropped, and various prepositions are prefixed; as in *sandhi*, *vidhi*, *nidhi*, &c.

Also a few feminine nouns; as, *kṛishi*, 'ploughing,' from *kṛish*: *lipi*, 'writing,' from *lip*, &c. Compare Greek forms like χάρις, ἐλπίς, μῆνις (मन्युस्).

II. इ *i*, forming, 2dly (nom. *-i*), one or two neuter substantives; as, from *vṛi*, 'to surround,' *vári*, 'water;' from *aksh*, 'to pervade,' *akshi*, 'an eye' (*oculus*, ὄκος).

III. इ *i*, forming, 3dly (nom. *-is*, *-is*, *-i*), a few adjectives; as, from *śuch*, 'to be pure,' *śuchi*, 'pure;' from *budh*, 'to know,' *bodhi*, 'wise.'

IV. मि *mi* (nom. *-mis*), forming a few nouns; as, *bhúmi*, f., 'the earth,' from *bhú*, 'to be' (*humus*); *raśmi*, m., 'a ray,' &c.

V. ति *ti* (nom. *-tis*), forming abstract substantives feminine. This affix bears a great analogy to the passive participle at 531. The same changes of the root are required before it as before this participle; and, in fact, provided the passive participle does not insert *i*, this substantive may always be formed from it, by changing *ta* into *ti*. But if *i* is inserted before *ta*, no such substantive can be formed*: thus, from *vach*, 'to speak,' *ukta*, 'spoken,' *ukti*, 'speech;' from *man*, 'to imagine,' *mata*, 'imagined,' *mati*, 'the mind;' from *dá*, 'to give,' *datta*, 'given,' *datti*, 'a gift.' And when *na* is substituted for *ta* of the passive participle, *ni* is substituted for *ti*; as, from *glai*, 'to be weary,' *glána*, 'wearied,' *gláni*, 'weariness;' from *lú*, 'to cut,' *lúna*, 'cut,' *lúni*, 'cutting:' but not always; as, from पॄ 'to fill,' *púrṇa*, 'full,' *púrtti*, 'fulness.' This affix corresponds to the *tio* of the Latin, added in the same way to passive participles; as, *actus*, *actio*; *junctus*, *junctio* (*yuktis*). Greek exhibits analogous forms in ζεῦξις, πίστις, δόσις.

A few masculine nouns are formed with *ti*; as, *yati*, 'a sage,' from *yam*, 'to restrain;' *jñáti*, 'a relation,' from *jñá*; *pati*, 'a husband' (for *páti*), from *pá*.

Formed by adding to the bases of a few NOUNS ending in *a*—

VI. इ *i* (nom. *-is*), after Vṛiddhi of the first syllable, and after rejection of the final vowel. This affix forms a few patronymics; as, दौष्यन्ति *daushyanti*, 'the son of Dushyanta,' from दुष्यन्त *dushyanta*.

82. THIRD CLASS.—*Masculine, Feminine, and Neuter bases in* उ u.

Formed by adding to ROOTS—

I. उ *u*, forming, 1st (nom. *-us*), substantives of the masculine, and one or two of the feminine gender; as, from *bandh*, 'to bind,' *bandhu*, m., 'a kinsman;' from *kṛi*, 'to do,' *káru*, m., 'an artificer;' from *bhid*, 'to cleave,' *bhidu*, m., 'a thunderbolt;' from *tan*, 'to stretch,' *tanu*, f., 'the body.'

II. उ *u*, forming, 2dly (nom. *-u*), one or two neuter substantives; as, *dáru*, 'wood,' from *dṛí*, 'to cleave' (δόρυ); *madhu*, 'honey' (μέθυ), &c.

III. उ *u*, forming, 3dly (nom. *-us*, *-us* or *ví*, *-u*), sometimes with change of the root, a few adjectives; as, from *swad*, 'to taste,' *swádu*, 'sweet' (ἡδύ); from *tan*, 'to stretch,' *tanu*, 'thin' (compare ταvv); from *langh*, 'to spring,' *laghu*, 'light' (ἐλαχύ); from *prath*, 'to extend,' *pṛithu*, 'broad' (πλατύ). This affix is often added to desiderative roots to form adjectives; as, from *pipás*, 'to desire to drink,' *pipásu*, 'thirsty;' from जिजीविष 'to desire to live,' जिजीविषु 'desirous of living.'

* Nevertheless, गृहीति from गृहीत occurs, though not given in the Dictionary.

Latin has added an *i* to all adjectives formed with *u* in the cognate languages; as, *tenuis* from *tanus; gravis* (for *garuis*) from *gurus*. It has, however, substantives in *u;* as, *currus*, *acus*, &c.

IV. नु *nu* (nom. *-nus*, *-nus*, *-nu*), forming adjectives and substantives; as, from *tras*, 'to fear,' *trasnu*, 'timid;' from *bhá*, 'to shine,' *bhánu*, m., 'the sun;' from *dhe*, 'to drink,' *dhenu*, f., 'a cow;' from *sú*, 'to bear,' *súnu*, m., 'a son.' (Compare Greek forms like λιγνύς.)

V. इष्णु *ishṇu* (nom. *-ishṇus*, *-ishṇus*, *-ishṇu*), with Guṇa of the root, forming adjectives; as, from *kshi*, 'to perish,' *kshayishṇu*, 'perishing.'

VI. There are many other affixes to roots, forming nouns in *u* (nom. *-us*, *-us*, *-u*); as, रु *ru*, नु *nu*, आलु *álu*, स्नु *snu*, आरु *áru*, इत्नु *itnu*, तु *tu*, अथु *athu*, यु *yu*. The following nouns afford examples of these affixes: *bhíru*, 'timid;' *aśru*, n., 'a tear' (for *daśru*, from *danś*, 'to bite,' compare δάκρυ, *lacryma*); *śayálu*, 'sleepy;' *sthásnu*, 'firm;' *śaráru*, 'noxious;' *gadayitnu*, 'loquacious;' *jantu*, m., 'an animal;' *gantu*, m., 'a traveller;' *vepathu*, m., 'trembling;' *manyu*, m., 'wrath' (μένος); and *mṛityu*, m. f., 'death.'

There are a few nouns in long *ú*, which may conveniently be placed under this class. They consist chiefly of roots standing by themselves as substantives, or at the end of compounds: thus, भू f. 'the earth,' स्वयम्भू m. 'the self-existent,' &c. See 125. *a*, 126. *b*.

83. Fourth Class.—*Masculine, Feminine, and Neuter bases in* ऋ ṛi.

Formed by adding to roots—

I. तृ *tṛi*, forming, 1st (nom. *-tá*, *-trí*, *-tṛi*), nouns of agency of three genders, the same change of the root being required which takes place in the first future, and the same euphonic changes of *t* (see 386 and 581): thus, from *kship*, 'to throw,' *ksheptṛi*, 'a thrower;' from *dá*, 'to give,' *dátṛi*, 'a giver;' from बुध् 'to know,' बोद्धृ *boddhṛi*, 'a knower;' from सह् 'to bear,' सोढृ 'patient.' This corresponds to the Latin affix *tor*, and the Greek τηρ: compare *dator*, δοτήρ.

II. तृ *tṛi*, forming, 2dly (nom. *-tá*), nouns of relationship, masculine and feminine; as, *pitṛi*, 'a father,' *mátṛi*, 'a mother.'

84. Fifth Class.—*Masculine, Feminine, and Neuter bases in* त् t *and* द् d.

Formed by adding to roots—

I. त् *t* (nom. *-t*, in all genders), if the root ends in a *short vowel:* forming nouns of agency, substantives and adjectives, of three genders; as, from *kṛi*, 'to do,' *kṛit*, 'a doer;' from *ji*, 'to conquer,' *jit*, 'a conqueror.' This class of nouns are never used, except as the last member of a compound: thus, *karmakṛit*, 'a doer of work.'

Roots already ending in *t* or *d*, taken to form adjectives or nouns of agency, fall under this class; as, from *vid*, 'to know,' *dharmavid*, 'one who knows his duty;'

from अद् 'to eat,' क्रव्याद् 'an eater of flesh.' There are also a few nouns falling under this class, formed by prefixing prepositions to roots ending in *t* or *d* or a short vowel; as, from *vid*, 'to know,' संविद् f. 'an agreement;' from द्युत् *dyut*, 'to shine,' *vidyut*, 'lightning;' from *pad*, 'to go,' *sampad*, 'success.' So also, समित् 'battle,' from इ 'to go;' उपनिषद् 'a theological work,' from सद् *sad*.

One or two roots ending in त् or द् may stand by themselves as substantives: thus, मुद् *mud*, f., 'joy;' चित् *chit*, f., 'the mind.'

The practice of using roots at the end of compounds prevails also in Greek and Latin; as in χέρ-νιψ (-νιβ), βου-πλήξ (-πληγ), &c., *arti-fex* (*-fic*), *carni-fex* (*-fic*), *præ-ses* (*-sid*), &c. And there is a very remarkable agreement between Sanskṛit and Latin in the practice of adding *t* to roots ending in short vowels: thus, *com-it* (*comes*), 'a goer with;' *equ-it* (*eques*), 'a goer on horseback;' *al-it* (*ales*), 'a goer with wings;' *super-stit* (*superstes*), 'a stander by,' &c. Greek adds a similar *t* to roots with a long final vowel; as, ἀ-γνώτ, ἀ-πτώτ, &c. (See Bopp's Comparative Grammar, Eastwick, 1293.)

II. इत् *it* (nom. *-it*, in all genders), after Guṇa of the root, forming a few substantives and adjectives; as, from सृ *sṛi*, 'to flow,' सरित् *sarit*, f., 'a stream;' from हृ 'to seize,' हरित् 'green,' 'Vishṇu.'

III. There are a few other nouns in त् *t* and द् *d*, of uncertain derivation; as, मरुत् m. 'the wind,' शरद् f. 'autumn,' दृशद् f. 'a stone,' कुमुद् n. 'a lotus.'

By adding to the base of NOUNS—

I. वत् *vat* (nom. *-ván*, *-vatí*, *-vat*), if the base ends in *a* or *á**, forming innumerable adjectives; as, from *dhana*, 'wealth,' *dhanavat*, 'possessed of wealth.' This and the next affix are universally applicable, and are of the utmost utility to form adjectives of possession. Sometimes *vat* is added to bases in *s* and *t*; as in तेजस्वत् *tejaswat* (compare 69. *a*) and *vidyutwat* (see 45). Compare Greek forms in εις, εντ; as, χαρίεις, χαρίεντ, δακρυόεις, δακρυόεντ, &c.

II. मत् *mat* (nom. *-mán*, *-matí*, *-mat*), if the base ends in *i*, *í*, or *u*, to form adjectives like the preceding; as, from *dhí*, 'wisdom,' *dhímat*, 'wise;' from *anśu*, 'a ray,' *anśumat*, 'radiant.'

85. SIXTH CLASS.—*Masculine, Feminine, and Neuter bases in* अन् an *and* इन् in.

Formed by adding to ROOTS—

I. अन् *an* (nom. *-á*), forming a few masculine nouns; as, *rájan*, 'a king,' from *ráj*, 'to be glorious;' *takshan*, 'a carpenter,' from *taksh*, 'to cleave;' *ukshan*, 'a bull' (compare English *oxen*), from *uksh*, 'to impregnate;' *snehan*, 'a friend,' from *snih*, 'to love,' &c. Greek and Latin have similar formations in ων, ον, ην, αν, *on* and *in*; as, τέκτον = तक्षन् (τέκτων), εἰκόν (-κων), *homin* (*homo*), &c.

---

* *Vat* is not often found added to feminine bases. It occurs, however, occasionally; as, कान्तावत् 'having a wife,' शिखावत् 'crested.'

II. मन् *man* (nom. *-ma*), after Guṇa of the root, forming neuter substantives; as, from *kṛi*, 'to do,' *karman*, 'a deed.' This affix corresponds to the Latin *men*, in *regimen*, *agmen*, *stamen*, &c.; and to the Greek *μων*, in *μνήμων*, *τλήμων*, &c.: but adjectives in *man*, like शर्मन् 'prosperous,' are very rare in Sanskṛit. A few nouns in *man* are masculine; as, *átman*, 'soul' (nom. *-má*); उष्मन् 'the hot season;' शुष्मन् 'fire;' पाप्मन् 'sin;' सीमन् 'a border;' वेमन् 'a loom.'

III. वन् *van* (nom. *-vá*, *-vá*, *-va*), forming a few substantives and adjectives; as, दृश्वन् 'seeing,' 'a looker,' from *dṛiś*, 'to see.'

By adding to roots or to the base of NOUNS—

IV. इमन् *iman* (nom. *-imá*), forming masculine abstract substantives. If the noun ends in *a* or *u*, these vowels are rejected; as, from *kála*, 'black,' *káliman*, 'blackness;' from *laghu*, 'light,' *laghiman*, 'lightness;' from *mṛidu*, 'soft,' *mradiman*, &c. If it ends in a consonant, this consonant, with its preceding vowel, is rejected; as, from *mahat*, 'great,' *mahiman*, 'greatness.' A medial *ṛi* before a simple consonant is changed to *ra*, but not before a double consonant; as, from कृष्ण 'black,' कृष्णिमन् 'blackness.' A final *ṛi* is gunated; as, *sariman* from *sṛi*; *stariman* from *stṛi* (compare *stramen*); *hariman*, 'time,' from *hṛi*, &c. *Iman* is generally added to *adjectives*, and the same changes take place before it, that take place before the affixes *íyas* and *ishṭha* (see 192): thus, *gariman*, *preman*, *drághiman*, *bhúman*, *prathiman*, &c.

By adding to ROOTS—

V. इन् *in* (nom. *-í*, *-iní*, *-i*), after Vṛiddhi of a final vowel and medial *a*, and Guṇa of any other medial vowel, forming nouns of agency of three genders (see 582. *b*); as, from *kṛi*, 'to do,' *kárin*, 'a doer.' Compare Greek and Latin formations in *ον* and *on*; as, *τέκτον* (*-κτων*), *edon* (*edo*), &c.

By adding to the base of NOUNS—

VI. इन् *in* (nom. *-í*, *-iní*, *-i*), forming innumerable adjectives of possession. The final of a base is rejected before this affix; as, from *dhana*, 'wealth,' *dhanin*, 'wealthy;' from *málá*, 'a garland,' *málin*, 'garlanded;' from *vríhi*, 'rice,' *vríhin*, 'having rice.' Compare Greek and Latin formations in *ων* and *on*; as, *γνάθ-ων*, 'having cheeks;' *nason* (*naso*), 'having a nose.'

VII. विन् *vin* (nom. *-ví*, *-viní*, *-vi*), if the base ends in *á* or *as*, forming a few adjectives; as, from *medhá*, 'intellect,' *medhávin*, 'intellectual;' from *tejas*, 'splendour,' *tejaswin*, 'splendid.' Compare 69. *a*.

86. SEVENTH CLASS.—*Masculine, Feminine, and Neuter bases in* अस् as, इस् is, *and* उस् us.

Formed by adding to ROOTS—

I. अस् *as* (nom. *-as*), after Guṇa, forming a great many neuter substantives; as, from *man*, 'to think,' *manas*, 'the mind;' from *sṛi*, 'to go,' *saras*, 'water.' It also forms one or two masculine and feminine nouns; as, *vedhas*, m., 'Brahmá;'

chandramas, m., 'the moon;' *apsaras*, f., 'a nymph;' *ushas*, f., 'the dawn,' from *ush*, 'to glow:' but in these the nominative is long (*-ás*).

II. इस् *is* or उस् *us* (nom. *-is*, *-us*). In place of *as*, the neuter affixes *is* or *us* are occasionally added; as, from *hu*, 'to offer,' *havis*, 'ghee;' from *chaksh*, 'to speak,' *chakshus*, 'the eye.' See 68. *a*. With *as* compare the Latin *es* in *nubes* (नभस् *nabhas*), *sedes* (सदस् *sadas*), &c.; but especially the *us* and *ur* of words like *genus*, *scelus*, *robur*. Compare also the Greek formations πάθ-ος, ἕδ-ος, μέν-ος, ψεῦδ-ος, &c.

87. Eighth Class.—*Masculine, Feminine, and Neuter bases in* any Consonant, except त् t *and* द् d, न् n, स् s.

Formed by using roots as adjectives, substantives, or nouns of agency—

Any root may be used to form an adjective or a noun of agency, provided it be the last member of a compound word: thus, from शक् 'to be able,' *sarvaśak*, 'omnipotent.' Those roots which end in *t* or *d*, or in a short vowel, having *t* affixed, have been already noticed as falling under the fifth class. This eighth class is intended to comprise all other roots, ending in *any consonant;* as, भुज् *bhuj* (nom. *bhuk*); राज् *ráj* (nom. राट्); प्राच्छ् (nom. प्राट्); बुध् (nom. भुत्); पुर् (nom. पूस्); गिर् (nom. *gís*); दिव् (nom. *dyaus*); स्पृश् (nom. *spṛik*); विश् (nom. विट्); लिह् (nom. लिट्); दुह् (nom. धुक्); पिपक्ष् (nom. *pipak*). There are also one or two other nouns derived from roots falling under this class; as, तृष्णज् 'thirsty' (nom. तृष्णक्); ऋत्विज् 'a priest' (nom. ऋत्विक्); असृज् n. 'blood' (nom. असृक्); and a few substantives formed by prefixing prepositions to roots; as, समिध् f. 'fuel' (nom. समित्), from the root इन्ध् 'to kindle' (see 43 and 75, with note).

A few roots standing by themselves as substantives may fall under this class: thus, युध् f. 'battle' (nom. युत्); क्षुध् f. 'hunger' (nom. क्षुत्); वाच् f. 'speech' (nom. वाक्), from *vach*, 'to speak,' the medial *a* being lengthened. Greek and Latin use a few monosyllabic roots in the same manner; as, ὄψ (ὀπ), φλόξ (φλογ), &c.; and Latin *vox* (*voc*), *lex* (*leg*), *dux* (*duc*).

CHAPTER IV.

DECLENSION; OR INFLECTION OF THE BASE OF NOUNS, SUBSTANTIVE AND ADJECTIVE.

GENERAL OBSERVATIONS.

88. Having explained how the base of nouns is generally formed, we have now to shew how it is inflected.

As, in the last chapter, nouns, substantive and adjective, were arranged under eight classes, according to the final of their bases (the first four classes comprising those ending in vowels, the last four those ending in consonants), so it will be the object of the present chapter to exhibit their declension or inflection under the same eight classes. Moreover, as every class comprised adjectives as well as substantives, so it is intended that the declension of a masculine, feminine, and neuter substantive, exhibited under each, shall serve as the model for the declension of masculine, feminine, and neuter adjectives coming under the same class.

89. The learner will have already gathered that the noun has three genders, and that the gender is, in many cases, determinable from the termination of the base. Thus, all bases in *á*, *í*, and those formed with the affix *ti* (No. 81. V), are feminine: nearly all nouns whose crudes end in *ana*, *twa*, *ya*, *tra* (see under 80), *as*, *is*, *us* (86), and *man* (85. II), are neuter; all in *iman* (85. IV) are masculine; but those in *a*, *i*, *u*, and *ṛi*, are not reducible to rule. The nominative case is, however, in the first of these instances a guide to the gender; as, *devas*, 'a deity,' is masculine; but *dánam*, 'a gift,' neuter. And in other cases the meaning of the word; as, *pitṛi*, 'a father,' is masculine; and *mátṛi*, 'a mother,' feminine.

90. In Sanskṛit, all the relations between the words in a sentence are expressed by inflections. A great many prepositions exist in the language, but they are rarely used alone in government with any case, their chief use being as prefixes to verbs and nouns. The dearth of such useful syntactical auxiliaries leads to the necessity for eight cases, which are regularly built upon the base. These are called, 1. nominative; 2. accusative; 3. instrumental; 4. dative; 5. ablative; 6. genitive; 7. locative; 8. vocative *. Of these, the third and seventh are new to the classical student. The *instrumental* denotes generally the instrument by which a thing is done; as, *tena kṛitam*, 'done by him.' The *locative* generally refers to the place or time in which any thing is done; as, *Ayodhyáyám*, 'in *Ayodhyá*;' *púrvakále*, 'in former time;' *bhúmau*, 'on the ground †.' Hence it follows that the *ablative* is restricted to the sense *from*,

* These cases will sometimes be denoted by their initial letters. Thus N. will denote nominative; I., instrumental.

† Both these cases are used to denote various other relations. See the Chapter on Syntax.

and cannot be used, as in Latin and Greek, to express *by*, *with*, *in*, *at*, *on*, &c.

91. According to the Indian system of teaching, each of these eight cases has three numbers, singular, dual, and plural; and to each belongs a termination which is considered to be peculiarly its own, serving alike for masculine, feminine, and neuter nouns. Again, according to the native system, some of the terminations may be combined with memorial letters to aid pronunciation or assist the memory. Thus the proper termination of the nominative singular is स् *s* (expressible by Visarga before *k*, *p*, and the sibilants, or at the end of a sentence, see 63); but the memorial termination is सु *su*, the letter *u* being only memorial. Similarly, the termination of the nominative plural is *jas*, the *j* being memorial. The two schemes of termination, with and without the memorial letters, are here exhibited. The first is given in small type, as being of no importance excepting as subservient to the second.

Terminations with memorial letters.

	SING.	DUAL.	PLURAL.
Nom.	सु *su*	औ *au*	जस् *jas*
Acc.	अं *am*	औट् *auṭ*	शस् *śas*
Inst.	टा *ṭá*	भ्यां *bhyám*	भिस् *bhis*
Dat.	ङे *n.e*	भ्यां *bhyám*	भ्यस् *bhyas*
Abl.	ङसि *n.asi*	भ्यां *bhyám*	भ्यस् *bhyas*
Gen.	ङस् *n.as*	ओस् *os*	आं *ám*
Loc.	ङि *n.i*	ओस् *os*	सुप् *sup*

Terminations without memorial letters.

	SING.	DUAL.	PLURAL.
Nom.	स् *s*	औ *au*	अस् *as*
Acc.	अं *am*	— *au*	— *as*
Inst.	आ *á*	भ्यां *bhyám*	भिस् *bhis*
Dat.	ए *e*	— *bhyám*	भ्यस् *bhyas*
Abl.	अस् *as*	— *bhyám*	— *bhyas*
Gen.	— *as*	ओस् *os*	आं *ám*
Loc.	इ *i*	— *os*	सु *su*

92. Observe—The vocative is not given in the above general scheme, as it is held to be only another aspect of the nominative, and always coincides with the nom. in the dual and plural. In the singular it is often identical with the base, and has no termination.

a. Observe also—The terminations beginning with vowels will often be called *vowel-terminations;* those beginning with consonants, including the nom. sing., will be called *consonantal-terminations.*

Similarly, those cases which take the vowel-terminations will sometimes be called *vowel-cases;* and those which take the consonantal, *consonantal-cases.*

93. Having propounded the above scheme, which for convenience will be called *the memorial scheme of terminations,* as the general type of the several case-affixes in the three numbers, Indian grammarians proceed to adapt them to every noun, substantive and adjective, in the language, as well as to pronouns, numerals, and participles, whether masculine, feminine, or neuter. In fact, their theory is, that there is but one declension in Sanskṛit, and that the base of a noun being given, and the regular case-terminations being given, the base is to be joined to those terminations according to the usual rules for the combination of final and initial letters, as in the following examples of the two bases, नौ *nau,* f., 'a ship' (*navi, vav*), and हरित् *harit,* m. f., 'green.'

94.

	SINGULAR.	DUAL.	PLURAL.
Nom. voc.	नौस् *naus* *nau + s*	नावौ *návau* *nau + au.* See 37.	नावस् *návas* *nau + as.* 37.
Acc.	नावं *návam* *nau + am.* 37.	— *návau*	— *návas*
Inst.	नावा *nává* *nau + á.* 37.	नौभ्यां *naubhyám* *nau + bhyám*	नौभिस् *naubhis* *nau + bhis*
Dat.	नावे *náve* *nau + e.* 37.	— *naubhyám*	नौभ्यस् *naubhyas* *nau + bhyas*
Abl.	नावस् *návas* *nau + as.* 37.	— *naubhyám*	— *naubhyas*
Gen.	नावस् *návas* *nau + as.* 37.	नावोस् *návos* *nau + os.* 37.	नावां *návám* *nau + am.* 37.
Loc.	नावि *návi* *nau + i.* 37.	— *návos*	नौषु *naushu* *nau + su.* 70.

95.

	SINGULAR.	DUAL.	PLURAL.
Nom. voc.	हरित् *harit* *harit* + *s*. See 43.*a*.	हरितौ *haritau* *harit* + *au*. 41. *b*.	हरितस् *haritas* *harit* + *as*. 41. *b*.
Acc.	हरितं *haritam* *harit* + *am*. 41.*b*.	— *haritau*	— *haritas*
Inst.	हरिता *haritá* *harit* + *á*. 41. *b*.	हरिद्भ्यां *haridbhyám* *harit* + *bhyám*. 41.	हरिद्भिस् *haridbhis* *harit* + *bhis*. 41.
Dat.	हरिते *harite* *harit* + *e*. 41. *b*.	— *haridbhyám*	हरिद्भ्यस् *haridbhyas* *harit* + *bhyas*. 41.
Abl.	हरितस् *haritas* *harit* + *as*. 41.*b*.	— *haridbhyám*	— *haridbhyas*
Gen.	— *haritas*	हरितोस् *haritos* *harit* + *os*. 41. *b*.	हरितां *haritám* *harit* + *ám*. 41. *b*.
Loc.	हरिति *hariti* *harit* + *i*. 41. *b*.	— *haritos*	हरित्सु *haritsu* *harit* + *su*. 40.

96. Unfortunately, however, it happens, that of nouns whose bases end in vowels, नौ *nau*, 'a ship,' is nearly the only one that admits of this regular junction of the base with the case-endings; and, although nouns whose bases end in consonants are numerous, and are generally declined as regularly as *harit*, yet they are numerically insignificant, compared with nouns in *a*, *á*, *i*, *í*, *u*, and *ṛi*, whose declension requires frequent changes in the final of the base, and various modifications, or even substitutions, in the terminations.

97. Thus in the first class of nouns ending in *a* (which will be found to comprise more nouns than all the other seven classes together; compare 80 with 81—87), not only is the final *a* of the base liable to be lengthened and changed to *e*, but also the termination *ina* is substituted for *á*, the proper termination of the instrumental sing. masc.; *ya* for *e* of the dative; *t* for *as* of the ablative; *sya* for *as* of the genitive; *n* for *as* of the accus. plural; *ais* for *bhis* of the instrum. plural. And in many other nouns particular changes and substitutions are required, some of which are determined by the gender.

The annexed table exhibits synoptically the terminations, with the most usual substitutions, throughout all the classes of nouns. Those substitutions marked * are mostly restricted to nouns ending in *a*, and are therefore especially noticeable.

	SINGULAR.	DUAL.	PLURAL.
N.	स् (m. f.), म्* (n.)	औ (m.f.), ई (n.)	अस् (m. f.), इ (n.)
Ac.	अं (m. f.), म्* (m. f. n.)	औ (m.f.), ई (n.)	अस्, म्(m.f.), न्*(m.), इ(n.)
I.	आ (m. f. n.), इन* (m. n.)	भ्यां (m. f. n.)	भिस् (m. f. n.), ऐस्* (m. n.)
D.	ए (m. f. n.), य* (m. n.)	भ्यां (m. f. n.)	भ्यस् (m. f. n.)
Ab.	अस् (m.f.n.), स् (m.f.), त्* (m.n.)	भ्यां (m. f. n.)	भ्यस् (m. f. n.)
G.	अस्(m.f.n.), स्(m.f.), स्य*(m.n.)	ओस् (m. f. n.)	आं (m. f. n.)
L.	इ (m. f. n.), आं* (f.)	ओस् (m. f. n.)	सु (m. f. n.)

a. Comparing the above terminations with those of Latin and Greek, we may remark that *s* enters into the nom. sing. masc., and *m* or *n* into the neuter, in all three languages. In regard to the Sanskṛit dual *au*, the original termination was *á*, as found in the Vedas; and *á* equals the Greek α, ω, and ε. In nom. pl. masc. the *s* appears in many Latin and Greek words. In acc. sing., Sanskṛit agrees with Latin, and frequently with Greek, as the Sanskṛit *m* may be euphonically changed to *n* (ν), if influenced by a dental following (see note to page 18). In the acc. pl. *s* appears in all three languages; and when the Sanskṛit ends in *n*, as in the first class of nouns, this *n* is probably for *ns*, since a preceding *a* is lengthened to compensate for the rejection of *s*. In inst. pl. *bhis* is preserved in the Latin *nobis*, *vobis*, and the Greek φι(ν) for φις (ναῦ-φιν = *naubhis*). The *ais* which belongs to Sanskṛit nouns in *a* is probably a contraction of *ábhis*, since in the Vedas *aśwebhis* for *aśwábhis* is found for *aśwais*, and *vṛikebhis* for *vṛíkais*. The dat. pl. *bhyas* answers to the Latin *bus*. In the gen. sing. all three languages have preserved the *s* (*návas*, *navis*, ναϝος for νηός); and in the gen. pl. *ám* is equivalent to the Greek ων, and the Latin *um* (पदां = ποδῶν, *pedum*). In loc. sing. the Sanskṛit *i* is preserved in the dative of Greek and Latin words (निशि = νυκτί — Compare the expression τῇ αὐτῇ νυκτί — नावि = *navi*). In loc. pl. *su* answers to the Greek σι (नौषु = ναυσί). Sanskṛit bases in *a* prefix *i* to *su*; so that *vṛikaishu* (29. *b*) = λυκοῖσι. The voc. sing. in Greek is generally identical with the base, and the voc. dual and pl. with the nom., as in Sanskṛit: thus λόγε is the voc. sing. of λόγος, τριῆρες of τριήρης, χαρίεν of χαρίεις, βασιλεῦ of βασιλεύς, &c. See Bopp's Comparative Grammar, Eastwick, *passim*.

98. In the following pages no attempt will be made to bring back all nouns to the general scheme of terminations by a detailed explanation of changes and substitutions in every case. But under every one of the eight classes a model noun for the masculine, feminine, and neuter, serving for adjectives as well as substantives,

will be declined at full; and under every case of every noun the method of joining the final letter of the base with the proper terminations will be indicated in English letters.

99. The student must, however, understand, that the division into eight classes, which here follows, is not meant to imply the existence of eight separate declensions in the sense understood by the classical scholar, but is rather intended to shew, that the final letters of the inflective bases of nouns may be arranged under four general heads for vowels, and four for consonants; and that all Sanskṛit nouns, whatever may be the final of their bases, are capable of adaptation to one common scheme of nearly similar case-terminations.

a. In the same manner it will appear in the sequel, that the ten classes into which verbs are divided do not imply ten different conjugations, but rather ten different ways of adapting the bases of verbs to one common scheme of tense-terminations. There is no reason why the same system of generalisation should not have been carried out in Latin and Greek, had the inflection of nouns and verbs in these languages been built upon roots and crude bases.

100. The classical scholar may, if he please, satisfy his own ideas of declension, by regarding masculine and neuter nouns in *a*, like *śiva* of the first class, as his 1st declension; feminine nouns in *á* and *í*, like *śivá* and *nadí* of the first class, as his 2d declension; masculine and feminine nouns in *i* and *u*, like *kavi*, *mati*, *bhánu*, and *dhenu*, of the second and third classes, as his 3d declension; and all the remaining nouns, including the neuters of those in *i* and *u*, and all those contained in the last five classes, as his 4th declension. These four declensions may be traced in regular order in the following pages, and will be denoted by the capital letters A at 103; B at 105; C at 110; D at 114.

101. Observe, that in declining the model nouns, under every inflection, the crude base with the sign +, and after it the termination, will be exhibited in English letters. Moreover, the number of the rule of Sandhi which must come into operation in joining the final of the base with the initial of the termination will generally be indicated. For it is most important to remember, that the formation of every case in a Sanskṛit noun supposes the application of a rule of Sandhi or 'junction;' and that the very meaning of *declension* is the junction of the final syllable of the crude base with the terminations.

102. Not unfrequently, however, in some of the cases, the original final of the base is changed to its Guṇa or Vṛiddhi equivalent (see 27), or to some other

letter (see 43. *b. c. d. e*), before the termination is affixed; and not unfrequently the original termination of the scheme is changed for some other termination, as indicated at 97.

In order, therefore, that the student, without forgetting the original final of the crude base, or the original termination of the memorial scheme, may at the same time observe, 1st, whether in any particular instances the final of the base undergoes any or what modification—2dly, whether the original termination suffers any change—it will be desirable that, whenever in exceptional cases the final vowel of the base is to be gunated or vriddhied, or otherwise changed, this changed form of the base be exhibited in place of the original form: thus, at 103, under the genitive dual *śivayos*, *śive + os* denotes, that before the base *śiva* is joined to the termination *os*, the final letter *a* is to be changed to *e*; and the number indicates the rule of Sandhi which must come into operation in joining *śive* and *os* together. Similarly, whenever the original termination has to be modified, it will be desirable that the termination be exhibited in its altered form: thus, at 103, under the accus. sing., *śiva + m* denotes, that the base is to be joined with *m*, substituted for the original termination *am*. See the table, page 58.

SECTION I.

DECLENSION OF NOUNS, SUBSTANTIVE AND ADJECTIVE, WHOSE BASES END IN VOWELS, OR OF THE FIRST FOUR CLASSES OF NOUNS.

FIRST CLASS OF NOUNS DECLINED.

Masculine and neuter bases in अ a; *feminine bases in* आ á *and* ई í.

Note, that this class comprises by far the greater number of nouns, substantive and adjective, in the language. It answers to a common class of Latin and Greek words in *us* and *ος*, *um* and *ον*, *a* and *α*; such as *lupus*, λύκος (= Sans. *vṛikas*, nom. of *vṛika*); *donum*, δῶρον; *terra*, χώρα (= धरा); and to adjectives like *bonus*, ἀγαθός, &c.

103. (A) Masculine bases in *a*, declined like शिव *śiva*, m., 'the god Śiva,' or as an adjective, 'prosperous.'

The final of the base is lengthened in D. Ab. sing., I. D. Ab. du., G. pl.; and changed to *e* in G. L. du., D. Ab. L. pl.: *n* is euphonically affixed to the final in G. pl.

N.	शिवस् *śivas* *śiva + s*	शिवौ *śivau* *śiva + au*. See 33.	शिवास् *śivás* *śiva + as*. See 31.
Ac.	शिवं *śivam* *śiva + m*	— *śivau*	शिवान् *śiván* *śivá + n*. 31.
I.	शिवेन *śivena* *śiva + ina*. 32.	शिवाभ्यां *śivábhyám* *śivá + bhyám*	शिवैस् *śivais* *śiva + ais*. 33.

D.	शिवाय *śiváya* *śivá+ya*	शिवाभ्यां *śivábhyám* *śivá+bhyám*	शिवेभ्यस् *śivebhyas* *śive+bhyas*
Ab.	शिवात् *śivát* *śivá+t.* 31.	— *śivábhyám*	— *śivebhyas*
G.	शिवस्य *śivasya* *śiva+sya*	शिवयोस् *śivayos* *śive+os.* 36.	शिवानां *śivánám* *śiván+ám*
L.	शिवे *śive* *śiva+i.* 32.	— *śivayos*	शिवेषु *śiveshu* *śive+su.* 70.
V.	शिव *śiva* *śiva* (*s* dropped). 92.	शिवौ *śivau* *śiva+au.* 33.	शिवास् *śivás* *śiva+as.* 31.

104. Neuter bases in *a*, declined like शिव *śiva*, n., 'prosperous.'

The final of the base is lengthened and assumes *n* in N. Ac. V. pl.

N. Ac.	शिवं *śivam* *śiva+m.* 97.	शिवे *śive* *śiva+í.* 32.	शिवानि *śiváni* *śiván+i*

The vocative is शिव *śiva*, शिवे *śive*, शिवानि *śiváni;* all the other cases are like the masculine.

105. (B) Feminine bases in *á*, declined like शिवा *śivá*, f., 'the wife of S'iva,' or as an adjective, 'prosperous.'

The final of the base is changed to *e* before I. sing., N. G. L. V. du.; and to *áyá* before D. Ab. G. L. sing.; and assumes *n* in G. pl.

N.	शिवा *śivá* *śivá* (*s* rejected)	शिवे *śive* *śive* (*au* rejected)	शिवास् *śivás* *śivá+as.* 31.
Ac.	शिवां *śivám* *śivá+am.* 31.	— *śive*	— *śivás*
I.	शिवया *śivayá* *śive+á.* 36.	शिवाभ्यां *śivábhyám* *śivá+bhyám*	शिवाभिस् *śivábhis* *śivá+bhis*
D.	शिवायै *śiváyai* *śiváyá+e.* 33.	— *śivábhyám*	शिवाभ्यस् *śivábhyas* *śivá+bhyas*
Ab.	शिवायास् *śiváyás* *śiváyá+s.* 31.	— *śivábhyám*	— *śivábhyas*
G.	— *śiváyás*	शिवयोस् *śivayos* *śive+os.* 36.	शिवानां *śivánám* *śiván+ám*
L.	शिवायां *śiváyám* *śiváyá+ám.* 31.	— *śivayos*	शिवासु *śivásu* *śivá+su*
V.	शिवे *śive* *śivá+i.* 32.	शिवे *śive* *śive* (*au* rejected)	शिवास् *śivás* *śivá+as.* 31.

106. Feminine bases in *í*, declined like नदी *nadí*, f., 'a river.'

The final of the base becomes *y* before the vowel-terminations, by 34; is changed to *yá* in D. Ab. G. sing.; is shortened in V. sing.; and assumes *n* in G. pl.

N.	नदी *nadí* *nadí* (*s* rejected)	नद्यौ *nadyau* *nadí+au*. 34.	नद्यस् *nadyas* *nadí+as*. 34.
Ac.	नदीं *nadím* *nadí+m*	— *nadyau*	नदीस् *nadís* *nadí+s*
I.	नद्या *nadyá* *nadí+á*. 34.	नदीभ्यां *nadíbhyám* *nadí+bhyám*	नदीभिस् *nadíbhis* *nadí+bhis*
D.	नद्यै *nadyai* *nadyá+e*. 33.	— *nadíbhyám*	नदीभ्यस् *nadíbhyas* *nadí+bhyas*
Ab.	नद्यास् *nadyás* *nadyá+as*. 31.	— *nadíbhyám*	— *nadíbhyas*
G.	— *nadyás*	नद्योस् *nadyos* *nadí+os*. 34.	नदीनां *nadínám* *nadín+ám*
L.	नद्यां *nadyám* *nadí+ám*. 34.	— *nadyos*	नदीषु *nadíshu* *nadí+su*. 70.
V.	नदि *nadi* *nadi* (final shortened)	नद्यौ *nadyau* *nadí+au*. 34.	नद्यस् *nadyas* *nadí+as*. 34.

The classical student will recognise in the terminations of *śiva* and *nadí* many resemblances to the terminations of nouns in Latin and Greek, remembering that the Sanskṛit *a* corresponds to the Latin *u* and the Greek *ο*; the Sanskṛit *m* to the Latin *m* and the Greek *ν*; the Sanskṛit *á* or *í* to the Latin *a* and the Greek *η* or *α*, or in the gen. plur. *ω*; the Sanskṛit *bh* or *bhy* to the Latin *b*. See 11. *f*. and 97. *a*.

107. In accordance with 58, such words as मृग *mṛiga*, m., 'a deer;' पुरुष *purusha*, m., 'a man;' भार्या *bháryá*, f., 'a wife;' कुमारी *kumárí*, f., 'a girl'—must be written, in the inst. sing. m. and the gen. pl. m. f., with the cerebral ण *ṇ*: thus, मृगेण *mṛigeṇa*, पुरुषेण, मृगाणां, पुरुषाणां, भार्याणां, कुमारीणां. When *n* is final, as in the acc. pl. m., it remains unchanged.

a. Observe, monosyllabic nouns in ई *í*, like श्री 'fortune,' भी 'fear,' &c., vary from *nadí* in the manner explained at 123.

b. Observe also, that feminine nouns in ऊ *ú* are declined analogously to *nadí*, excepting in the nom. sing., where *s* is not rejected. See 125.

108. When a feminine noun ending in *á* is taken to form the last member of a compound adjective, it is declined like *śiva* for the masculine and neuter. Thus, taking the feminine noun *vidyá*, 'learning;' whence may be formed the compound *alpavidyá*, 'little learning.' When this is used as a compound adjective, it becomes, in the nom. masc. fem. and neut., *alpavidyas*, *alpavidyá*, *alpavidyam*, 'possessed of little learning.' On the same principle, a masculine noun takes the feminine and

neuter terminations, when forming the last member of a compound adjective; and a neuter noun, the masculine and feminine.

a. When roots ending in *á*, such as *pá*, 'to drink' or 'to preserve,' are taken for the last member of compound words, they form their neuter like the neuter of *śiva;* and for their masculine and feminine assume the memorial terminations regularly, rejecting, however, the final of the base in the Ac. pl. and remaining vowel-cases: thus, सोमपा *soma-pá*, 'a drinker of Soma juice;' N. -पास्, -पौ, -पास्; Ac. -पां, -पौ, -पस्; I. -पा, -पाभ्यां, &c.; D. -पे, &c.

b. हाहा *háhá*, 'a Gandharba,' assumes the terminations regularly throughout: thus, D. sing. हाहै. See 33.

c. The voc. c. of अम्बा *ambá*, 'a mother,' is अम्ब *amba.*

d. जरा *jará*, 'decay,' forms some of its cases from *jaras*, at 171.

109. To convince the student of the absolute necessity of studying the declension of this first class of nouns, he is recommended to turn back to rule 80. He will there find given, under twenty-eight heads, the most usual forms of nouns, substantive and adjective, which follow this declension. All the masculine and neuter substantives in this list are declined like *śiva*, and all the feminine either like *śivá* or *nadí*. Again, all the adjectives in this list follow the same three examples for their three genders. Again, according to *śiva* masc. and neut., and *śivá* fem., are declined all present participles (see 526, 527, 528); all passive past participles, which are the most common and useful of verbal derivatives (see 530); all future passive participles (see 568); all participles of the second future (see 578); many ordinals, like *prathama* (208). Lastly, according to *nadí* feminine, are also declined the *feminines* of innumerable adjectives, see 80. XIII. XIV; the feminines of active participles, like *kṛitavat* (553, and 140. *a*); the feminines of participles of the 2d preterite, like *vividwas* (see 554 and 168); the feminines of many ordinals, like *chaturtha* (209).

SECOND AND THIRD CLASSES OF NOUNS DECLINED.

Observe, that the declension of the 2d and 3d classes of nouns (see 81 and 82) is exhibited together, that their analogy may be more readily perceived.

2d class—Masculine, feminine, and neuter bases in इ *i*.

3d class—Masculine, feminine, and neuter bases in उ *u*.

Note, that the 2d class answers to Latin and Greek words like *ignis*, *turris*, πόλις, πίστις, *mare*, μέλι; and the 3d, to words like *gradus*, βότρυς, ἡδὺς, μέθυ.

110. (C) Masculine bases in इ *i* and उ *u*, declined like अग्नि *agni*, m. (*ignis*), 'fire,' and भानु *bhánu*, m., 'the sun.'

The final of the base is gunated in D. Ab. G. V. sing., N. pl.; lengthened in N. Ac. du., Ac. G. pl.; dropped in L. sing.; and assumes *n* in I. sing., G. pl.

N.	अग्निस् *agnis* *agni+s*	अग्नी *agní* *agní* (*au* rejected)	अग्नयस् *agnayas* *agne+as.* 36.
Ac.	अग्निं *agnim* *agni+m*	— *agní*	अग्नीन् *agnín* *agní+n*
I.	अग्निना *agniná* *agnin+á*	अग्निभ्यां *agnibhyám* *agni+bhyám*	अग्निभिस् *agnibhis* *agni+bhis*
D.	अग्नये *agnaye* *agne+e.* 36.	— *agnibhyám*	अग्निभ्यस् *agnibhyas* *agni+bhyas*
Ab.	अग्नेस् *agnes* *agne+s*	— *agnibhyám*	— *agnibhyas*
G.	— *agnes*	अग्न्योस् *agnyos* *agni+os.* 34.	अग्नीनां *agnínám* *agnín+ám*
L.	अग्नौ *agnau* *agn* (*i* dropped) + *au*	— *agnyos*	अग्निषु *agnishu* *agni+su.* 70.
V.	अग्ने *agne* *agne* (*s* rejected)	अग्नी *agní* *agní* (*au* rejected)	अग्नयस् *agnayas* *agne+as.* 36.

111.	N.	भानुस् *bhánus* *bhánu+s*	भानू *bhánú* *bhánú* (*au* rejected)	भानवस् *bhánavas* *bháno+as.* 36.
	Ac.	भानुं *bhánum* *bhánu+m*	— *bhánú*	भानून् *bhánún* *bhánú+n*
	I.	भानुना *bhánuná* *bhánun+á*	भानुभ्यां *bhánubhyám* *bhánu+bhyám*	भानुभिस् *bhánubhis* *bhánu+bhis*
	D.	भानवे *bhánave* *bháno+e.* 36.	— *bhánubhyám*	भानुभ्यस् *bhánubhyas* *bhánu+bhyas*
	Ab.	भानोस् *bhános* *bháno+s*	— *bhánubhyám*	— *bhánubhyas*
	G.	— *bhános*	भान्वोस् *bhánwos* *bhánu+os.* 34.	भानूनां *bhánúnám* *bhánún+ám*
	L.	भानौ *bhánau* *bhán* (*u* dropped) + *au*	— *bhánwos*	भानुषु *bhánushu* *bhánu+su.* 70.
	V.	भानो *bháno* *bháno* (*s* rejected)	भानू *bhánú* *bhánú* (*au* rejected)	भानवस् *bhánavas* *bháno+as.* 36.

112. Feminine bases in इ *i* and उ *u*, declined like मति *mati*, f., 'the mind,' and धेनु *dhenu*, f., 'a milch cow.'

The final of the base is gunated in D. Ab. G. V. sing., N. pl.; lengthened in N. Ac. du., Ac. G. pl.; dropped in L. sing. (unless the termination be आं); and assumes *n* in the G. pl.

N.	मतिस् *matis* *mati+s*	मती *matí* *matí* (*au* rejected)	मतयस् *matayas* *mate+as.* 36.
Ac.	मतिं *matim* *mati+m*	— *matí*	मतीस् *matís* *matí+s*
I.	मत्या *matyá* *mati+á.* 34.	मतिभ्यां *matibhyám* *mati+bhyám*	मतिभिस् *matibhis* *mati+bhis*
D.	मतये *mataye* * *mate+e.* 36.	— *matibhyám*	मतिभ्यस् *matibhyas* *mati+bhyas*
Ab.	मतेस् *mates* * *mate+s*	— *matibhyám*	— *matibhyas*
G.	— *mates* *	मत्योस् *matyos* *mati+os.* 34.	मतीनां *matínám* *matín+ám*
L.	मतौ *matau* * *mat* (*i* dropped) + *au*	— *matyos*	मतिषु *matishu* *mati+su.* 70.
V.	मते *mate* *mate* (*s* dropped)	मती *matí* *matí* (*au* rejected)	मतयस् *matayas* *mate+as.* 36.

113.

N.	धेनुस् *dhenus* *dhenu+s*	धेनू *dhenú* *dhenú* (*au* rejected)	धेनवस् *dhenavas* *dheno+as.* 36.
Ac.	धेनुं *dhenum* *dhenu+m*	— *dhenú*	धेनूस् *dhenús* *dhenú+s*
I.	धेन्वा *dhenwá* *dhenu+á.* 34.	धेनुभ्यां *dhenubhyám* *dhenu+bhyám*	धेनुभिस् *dhenubhis* *dhenu+bhis*
D.	धेनवे *dhenave* † *dheno+e.* 36.	— *dhenubhyám*	धेनुभ्यस् *dhenubhyas* *dhenu+bhyas*
Ab.	धेनोस् *dhenos* † *dheno+s.*	— *dhenubhyám*	— *dhenubhyas*
G.	— *dhenos* †	धेन्वोस् *dhenwos* *u+os.* 34.	धेनूनां *dhenúnám* *dhenún+ám*
L.	धेनौ *dhenau* † *dhen* (*u* dropped) + *au*	— *dhenwos*	धेनुषु *dhenushu* *dhenu+su.* 70.
V.	धेनो *dheno* *dheno* (*s* dropped)	धेनू *dhenú* *dhenú* (*au* rejected)	धेनवस् *dhenavas* *dheno+as.* 36.

* The D. may also be मत्यै *matyai;* the Ab. and G. मत्यास् *matyás;* the L. मत्यां *matyám.*

† The D. may also be धेन्वै *dhenwai;* the Ab. and G. धेन्वास् *dhenwás;* and the L. धेन्वां *dhenwám.*

114. (D) Neuter bases in इ *i* and उ *u*, declined like वारि *vári*, n., 'water' (Lat. *mare*, Greek ἱδρώς for ἴδρι); and मधु *madhu*, n., 'honey' (μέθυ).

The final of the base assumes *n* before the vowel-terminations, and is lengthened in N. Ac. pl.

N.	वारि *vári* *vári* (*s* rejected)	वारिणी *váriṇí* *várin*+*í*. See 58.	वारीणि *váríṇi* *várín*+*i*. See 58.
Ac.	— *vári*	— *váriṇí*	— *váríṇi*
I.	वारिणा *váriṇá* *várin*+*á*	वारिभ्यां *váribhyám* *vári*+*bhyám*	वारिभिस् *váribhis* *vári*+*bhis*
D.	वारिणे *váriṇe* *várin*+*e*	— *váribhyám*	वारिभ्यस् *váribhyas* *vári*+*bhyas*
Ab.	वारिणस् *váriṇas* *várin*+*as*	— *váribhyám*	— *váribhyas*
G.	— *váriṇas*	वारिणोस् *váriṇos* *várin*+*os*	वारीणां *váríṇám* *várín*+*ám*
L.	वारिणि *váriṇi* *várin*+*i*	— *váriṇos*	वारिषु *várishu* *vári*+*su*. 70.
V.	वारि *vári* or वारे *váre* *vári* or *váre*. 92.	वारिणी *váriṇí* *várin*+*í*	वारीणि *váríṇi* *várín*+*i*

115.

N.	मधु *madhu* *madhu* (*s* rejected)	मधुनी *madhuní* *madhun*+*í*	मधूनि *madhúni* *madhún*+*i*
Ac.	— *madhu*	— *madhuní*	— *madhúni*
I.	मधुना *madhuná* *madhun*+*á*	मधुभ्यां *madhubhyám* *madhu*+*bhyám*	मधुभिस् *madhubhis* *madhu*+*bhis*
D.	मधुने *madhune* *madhun*+*e*	— *madhubhyám*	मधुभ्यस् *madhubhyas* *madhu*+*bhyas*
Ab.	मधुनस् *madhunas* *madhun*+*as*	— *madhubhyám*	— *madhubhyas*
G.	— *madhunas*	मधुनोस् *madhunos* *madhun*+*os*	मधूनां *madhúnám* *madhún*+*ám*
L.	मधुनि *madhuni* *madhun*+*i*	— *madhunos*	मधुषु *madhushu* *madhu*+*su*. 70.
V.	मधु *madhu* or मधो *madho* *madhu* or *madho*. 92.	मधुनी *madhuní* *madhun*+*í*	मधूनि *madhúni* *madhún*+*i*

116. The declension of neuter nouns in *i* and *u* follows the analogy of nouns in *in*. Hence, *vári* serves also as the model for the neuters of adjectives and nouns of agency in *in*, like *dhanin* and *kárin* (159); and the neuters of nouns of agency in *ṛi*, like *dátṛi*, and nouns of relationship like *mátṛi* (130).

117. Although there are not many substantives declined like *agni* and *vári* (81), yet nouns like *mati* are numerous (81. V). Moreover, adjectives like *śuchi*, and compound adjectives ending in *i*, are declined like *agni* in the masc.; like *mati* in the fem.; and like *vári* in the neuter.

118. Again, although there are but few substantives declined like *dhenu* and *madhu*, yet it is important to study their declension, as well as that of the masc. noun *bhánu*; for all simple adjectives like *tanu*, and all like *pipásu* (82), and all other simple adjectives in *u*, and all compound adjectives ending in *u*, are declined like *bhánu* in the masc.; *dhenu* in the fem.; and *madhu* in the neut.

a. Many adjectives in *u*, however, either optionally or necessarily follow the declension of *nadí* in the fem.; as, *tanu*, 'thin,' makes its nom. fem. either *tanus* or *tanwí*; मृदु, 'tender,' makes nom. f. *mṛidwí*: and some optionally lengthen the *u* in the feminine; as, *bhíru*, 'timid,' makes fem. भीरु or भीरू, declinable like nouns in *ú*, 125.

119. When feminine nouns ending in *i* and *u* are taken to form the last member of a compound adjective, they must be declined like *agni* in the masc., and *vári* in the neut. Thus the compound adjective *alpamati*, 'narrow-minded,' in the acc. plur. masc. would be *alpamatín*; fem. *alpamatís*; neut. *alpamatíni*. The same holds good if a masc. or neut. noun be taken to form the last member of a compound.

a. Although adjectives in *i* and *u* are declined like *vári* and *madhu* for the neuter, yet in the D. Ab. G. L. sing., and in the G. L. du., they may optionally follow the masculine form: thus the adjectives *śuchi* and *tanu* will be, in the D. sing. neut., शुचिने or शुचये, तनुने or तनवे; and so with the other cases.

120. There are some useful irregular nouns in इ *i*, declined as follows: सखि m. 'a friend:' N. सखा, सखायौ, सखायस्; Ac. सखायं, सखायौ, सखीन्; I. सख्या, सखिभ्यां, &c.; D. सख्ये, &c.; Ab. सख्युस्, &c.; G. सख्युस्, सख्योस्, &c.; L. सख्यौ, &c.; V. सखे, &c. In some cases it assumes the memorial terminations at 91 more regularly than *agni*.

121. पति m. 'a master,' 'lord' (πόσις), when not used in a compound word, follows *sakhi* in I. D. Ab. G. L. sing. (thus, I. पत्या, D. पत्ये, Ab. G. पत्युस्); in the other cases, *agni*. But this word is generally found at the end of a compound, and then follows *agni* throughout (thus, भूपतिना 'by the lord of the earth').

122. A few neuter nouns, अस्थि n. 'a bone' (ὀστέον), अक्षि n. 'an eye' (*oculus*, ὄκος), सक्थि n. 'a thigh,' दधि n. 'ghee,' drop their final *i* in some of their cases, and are declined in those cases as if they were derived from obsolete forms in *an*; such as अस्थन्, &c. (compare 148): thus, N. Ac. अस्थि, अस्थिनी, अस्थीनि; I. अस्थ्ना, अस्थिभ्यां, &c.; D. अस्थ्ने, &c.; Ab. अस्थ्नस्, &c.; G. अस्थ्नस्, अस्थ्नोस्, अस्थ्नां; L. अस्थ्नि or अस्थनि, अस्थ्नोस्, अस्थिषु.

Hence, according to 58, अक्षि *akshi* will make in I. sing. अक्ष्णा; in D. अक्ष्णे, &c.

123. There are a few useful monosyllabic words in long ई *í primitively* feminine, (i. e. not derived from masculine substantives, see *nadí* and *putrí* at 80. XXV, and not the feminine forms of adjectives or participles, 80. XII. &c.,) whose declension may conveniently be noticed here. Those in long ई *í* vary from the declension of नदी (106) by retaining स् in the nom., and changing the final to *iy* before the vowel-terminations: thus, श्री f. 'prosperity:' N.V. श्रीस्, श्रियौ, श्रियस्; Ac. श्रियं, श्रियौ, श्रियस्; I. श्रिया, श्रीभ्यां, श्रीभिस्; D. श्रिये or श्रियै, श्रीभ्यां, श्रीभ्यस्; Ab. श्रियस् or श्रियास्, श्रीभ्यां, श्रीभ्यस्; G. श्रियस् or श्रियास्, श्रियोस्, श्रियां or श्रीणां; L. श्रियि or श्रियां, श्रियोस्, श्रीषु.

a. Similarly are declined भी f. 'fear,' ह्री f. 'shame,' and धी f. 'understanding.'

b. When these words occur at the end of compound adjectives, the first inflection only of the two exhibited above, in the D. Ab. G. and L. cases sing., and G. plur., is admissible both for m. and f.: thus, N. गतभीस् m. f., 'fearless,' is गतभिये only in D. sing. The compounds shorten the final *í* for the neut. gender, and follow the declension of *vári* (114), but only optionally in the I. D. Ab. G. and L. cases: thus, N. Ac. गतभि; I. गतभिया or गतभिना; D. गतभिये or गतभिने.

c. स्त्री f., 'a woman,' is like श्री, but follows नदी in the nom.; and makes स्त्रीं as well as स्त्रियं in the Ac. sing.; स्त्रीस् as well as स्त्रियस् in the Ac. plur. V. स्त्रि.

124. There are a few primitively feminine words not monosyllabic, such as लक्ष्मी, तन्त्री, तरी, which, like श्री, take *s* in the nom. sing., but in other respects follow नदी: thus, nom. लक्ष्मीस्, लक्ष्म्यौ, लक्ष्म्यस्. When, however, they occur at the end of compounds (as, अत्तलक्ष्मी m. f. 'deprived of fortune'), they may optionally be declined as masculines in the D. Ab. G. and L. cases: thus, D. -लक्ष्म्ये; Ab. G. -लक्ष्म्यस्; L. -लक्ष्मि, &c. The neuter of such compounds follows the rule for गतभी, 123. *b*.

125. Feminine nouns ending in long ऊ *ú* are declined analogously to feminine nouns ending in ई *í*, i. e. like नदी, excepting in the N. sing., where *s* is retained. ऊ *ú* is changed to *v*, wherever ई *í* is changed to *y* (see 34): thus, वधू 'a wife:' N. वधूस्, वध्वौ, वध्वस्; Ac. वधूं, वध्वौ, वधूस्; I. वध्वा, वधूभ्यां, वधूभिस्; D. वध्वै; Ab. G. वध्वास्; L. वध्वां; V. वधु. Similarly, चमू f. 'a host;' श्वश्रू f. 'a mother-in-law.'

a. Again, monosyllabic words in *ú* primitively feminine are declined analogously to श्री f. (110); *ú* being changed to *uv*, wherever *í* is changed to *iy*: thus, भू f. 'the earth:' N.V. भूस्, भुवौ, भुवस्; Ac. भुवं, भुवौ, भुवस्; I. भुवा, &c. Similarly, भ्रू *bhrú*, f., 'the eyebrow' (ὀφρύς); N.V. भ्रूस्, भ्रुवौ, भ्रुवस्, &c.

b. And the same rule holds good with regard to such words at the end of compounds; see 123. *b*: thus, सुभ्रू m. f. 'having beautiful eyebrows:' N.V. sing. सुभ्रूस्; Ac. सुभ्रुवं; I. सुभ्रुवा; D. सुभ्रुवे. &c. Similarly, the neuter will be N. Ac. सुभ्रु; I. सुभ्रुवा or सुभ्रुणा, &c.

126. When a root like नी, 'to lead,' comes at the end of a compound, it assumes the memorial terminations at 91 more regularly than नदी, though like नदी it takes आं for the termination of loc. sing.: thus, सेनानी m. 'one who leads an army,' 'a general:' N. सेनानीस्, सेनान्यौ, सेनान्यस्; Ac. सेनान्यं, &c.; I. सेनान्या.

सेनानीभ्यां, &c.; D. सेनान्ये, &c.; Ab. सेनान्यस्, &c.; G. सेनान्यस्, -न्योस्, -न्यां; L. सेनान्यां, &c.; V. सेनानीस्, &c.

a. In the same way are declined ग्रामणी 'the chief of a village,' जलपी 'a water-drinker,' &c., for both m. and f. The neuter shortens the vowel for the N. Ac. sing., and follows *vári* (114); but in the I. D. Ab. G. L. sing., G. L. du., G. pl., it may optionally agree with the m. and f.

b. Similarly, roots like पू 'to purify,' in a compound like N.V. खलपूस् 'a sweeper;' Ac. खलप्वं, &c. The L. case, however, is खलप्वि. In the same manner, पुनर्भू 'twice-born:' N. पुनर्भूस्; Ac. पुनर्भ्वं, &c.

c. स्वयम्भू, m. f. 'self-existent,' follows the declension of भू 'the earth,' 125. *a.*

FOURTH CLASS OF NOUNS DECLINED.

Masculine, feminine, and neuter bases in ऋ ṛi.

Note, that this class answers to Latin and Greek words like *pater*, πατήρ, δοτήρ, &c.; the vowel *ṛi* being equivalent to *ar*.

127. Masculine bases in *ṛi*, declined like दातृ *dátṛi*, m., 'a giver,' and पितृ *pitṛi*, m., 'a father.' The former is the model of nouns of agency (83); the latter, of nouns of relationship.

In nouns of agency like *dátṛi* the final *ṛi* is vriddhied (28), and in nouns of relationship like *pitṛi* (excepting *naptṛi*, 'a grandson') gunated, in N. sing. du. pl., Ac. sing. du.; but the *r* of *ár* and *ar* is dropped in N. sing., and to compensate in the last case *a* is lengthened. In both nouns of agency and relationship the final *ṛi* is gunated in L.V. sing., and very anomalously changed to *u* in Ab. G. sing. In Ac. G. pl. it is lengthened, and assumes *n* in G. pl.

It is remarkable, that *dátáram*, *dátáras*, &c., bear the same relation to *pitaram*, *pitaras*, &c., that δοτῆρα, δοτῆρες, δοτῆρι, &c., bear to πατέρα, πατέρες, πατέρι, &c. Compare also the Latin *datoris* from *dator* with *patris* from *pater*.

N.	दाता *dátá* *dátá* (*s* rejected)	दातारौ *dátárau* *dátár+au*	दातारस् *dátáras* (δοτῆρες) *dátár+as*
Ac.	दातारं *dátáram* *dátár+am*	— *dátárau*	दातॄन् *dátṛín* *dátṛí+n*
I.	दात्रा *dátrá* *dátṛi+á.* 34.	दातृभ्यां *dátṛibhyám* *dátṛi+bhyám*	दातृभिस् *dátṛibhis* *dátṛi+bhis*
D.	दात्रे *dátre* *dátṛi+e.* 34.	— *dátṛibhyám*	दातृभ्यस् *dátṛibhyas* *dátṛi+bhyas*
Ab.	दातुस् *dátus* *dátu+s*	— *dátṛibhyám*	— *dátṛibhyas*
G.	— *dátus*	दात्रोस् *dátros* *dátṛi+os.* 34.	दातॄणां *dátṛíṇám* *dátṛín+ám*

L.	दातरि *dátari* *dátar + i*	दात्रोस् *dátros* *dátṛi + os.* 34.	दातृषु *dátṛishu* *dátṛi + su.* 70.
V.	दातर् *dátar* *dátar*	दातारौ *dátárau* *dátár + au*	दातारस् *dátáras* *dátár + as*

128.

N.	पिता *pitá* *pitá* (*s* rejected)	पितरौ *pitarau* *pitar + au*	पितरस् *pitaras* (πατέρες) *pitar + as*
Ac.	पितरं *pitaram* *pitar + am*	— *pitarau*	पितॄन् *pitṛín* *pitṛi + n*
I.	पित्रा *pitrá* *pitṛi + á.* 34.	पितृभ्यां *pitṛibhyám* *pitṛi + bhyám*	पितृभिस् *pitṛibhis* *pitṛi + bhis*
D.	पित्रे *pitre* *pitṛi + e.* 34.	— *pitṛibhyám*	पितृभ्यस् *pitṛibhyas* *pitṛi + bhyas*
Ab.	पितुस् *pitus* *pitu + s*	— *pitṛibhyám*	— *pitṛibhyas*
G.	— *pitus*	पित्रोस् *pitros* *pitṛi + os.* 34.	पितॄणां *pitṛíṇám* *pitṛín + ám*
L.	पितरि *pitari* *pitar + i*	— *pitros*	पितृषु *pitṛishu* *pitṛi + su.* 70.
V.	पितर् *pitar* *pitar*	पितरौ *pitarau* *pitar + au*	पितरस् *pitaras* *pitar + as*

Observe—*Pitṛi* seems to be corrupted from *pátri*, 'a protector' (*pá*, 'to protect'). The cognate languages have preserved the root in πατήρ, *pater*, 'father,' &c. The Latin *Jupiter*, however, is literally *Dyu-pitar* (द्यु-पितर्), 'father of heaven.' Prof. Bopp considers that nouns like *pitṛi* &c. are really from a base *pitar*.

a. Observe—नप्तृ *naptṛi*, 'a grandson *,' although a noun of relationship, is declined like दातृ *dátṛi*, requiring the final to be vriddhied in the same cases.

b. There are a few nouns, which neither express relationship nor agency, falling under this class. नृ *nṛi*, m., 'a man,' is declined like *pitṛi* (N. ना *ná*, Ac. नरं, I. न्रा, D. न्रे, Ab. G. नुस्, &c.), but usually makes नृणां *nṛiṇám* in the gen. plur.

c. क्रोष्टृ, 'a jackal,' takes some of its inflections from a form क्रोष्टु: thus, N. क्रोष्टा, -ष्टारौ, -ष्टारस्; Ac. -ष्टारं, -ष्टारौ, -ष्टून् or -ष्टॄन्; I. -ष्ट्रा or -ष्टुना, -ष्टुभ्यां, &c.; D. -ष्ट्रे or -ष्टवे, &c.; Ab. -ष्टुस् or -ष्टोस्, &c.; G. -ष्टुस् or -ष्टोस्, -ष्ट्रोस् or -ष्ट्वोस्, -ष्टूनां; L. -ष्टरि or -ष्टौ, &c.; V. -ष्टर् or -ष्टो.

129. Feminine bases in ऋ *ṛi* belong only to nouns of relationship, like *mátṛi*, 'a mother' (from *má*, 'to create,' 'the producer'); and their declension only differs from *pitṛi*, 'a father,' in the acc. plur.,

* Derived from *na* and *pitṛi*, i. e. 'not the father;' as if any member of the family but the father.

which takes the termination *s* instead of *n*: thus, मातृस्. Compare the Greek μήτηρ, μητέρα, voc. μῆτερ.

a. स्वसृ *swasṛi*, 'a sister,' however, follows दातृ *dátṛi*; but the Ac. pl. is still स्वसॄस्. The lengthening of the penultimate is probably caused by the loss of the *t* from *tṛi*, preserved in the English *sister*. So *soror* for *sostor*.

b. The feminine base of nouns of agency is formed by adding ई *í* to the final ऋ *ṛi*: thus, दातृ + ई, दात्री *dátrí*, f., 'a giver;' and कर्तृ + ई, कर्त्री f. 'a doer.' See 80. XIX. Their declension follows *nadí* at 106.

130. Neuter bases in ऋ *ṛi* belong only to nouns of relationship or of agency, when used at the end of compound adjectives, such as दिव्यमातृ *divya-mátṛi*, agreeing with कुलं, i. e. 'a family having a divine mother,' or द्विमातृ 'having two mothers' (compare διμήτωρ). They follow the declension of *vári* at 114: thus, N. Ac. मातृ, मातृणी, मातॄणि; दातृ, दातृणी, दातॄणि.

131. Before passing to the declension of nouns ending in consonants, it will be necessary to notice a few monosyllabic nouns, whose bases end in ऐ, ओ, and औ, not sufficiently numerous to form a separate class. They are thus declined:

132. रै *rai*, m. f., 'substance,' 'wealth' (Lat. *res*): N. voc. रास्, रायौ, रायस्; Ac. रायं, &c.; I. राया, राभ्यां, राभिस् (*rebus*); D. राये, &c.; Ab. रायस्, &c.; G. रायस्, रायोस्, रायां; L. रायि, &c.

133. गो *go*, m. f., 'a cow' or 'ox' (*bos*, βοῦς): N. voc. गौस्, गावौ, गावस्; Ac. गां, गावौ, गास्; I. गवा, गोभ्यां, गोभिस्; D. गवे, &c.; Ab. गोस्, &c.; G. गोस्, गवोस्, गवां; L. गवि (*bovi*), गवोस्, गोषु. Compare गां with γῆν; *go* meaning also 'the earth.'

134. नौ *nau*, f., 'a ship' (cf. *navis*, ναῦς), is declined at 94, being the most regular of all nouns. With the N. pl. *návas*, compare *naves*, νᾶες (νῆες). The gen. νηός for νᾶος or ναϝος = *návas*.

a. These nouns may occur at the end of compounds; as, बहुरै 'rich,' उपगो 'near a cow,' बहुनौ 'having many ships.' In that case the neuter is बहुरि, उपगु, and बहुनु; of which the inst. cases will be बहुरिणा or बहुराया, उपगुना or उपगवा, बहुनुना or बहुनावा; and so with the other vowel-cases: but बहुरि becomes बहुरा before all consonantal-cases, except the nom. sing.

SECTION II.

DECLENSION OF NOUNS, SUBSTANTIVE AND ADJECTIVE, WHOSE BASES END IN CONSONANTS, OR OF THE LAST FOUR CLASSES OF NOUNS.

135. Observe—The first four classes of nouns, whose declension has just been considered, comprise many more substantives than adjectives. On the other hand, the last four classes, though com-

prehending a few substantives, consist chiefly of adjectives, participles, or roots used as adjectives at the end of compound words. All the nouns under these remaining classes take the memorial terminations at 91 with perfect regularity.

a. In the anomalies the acc. pl., and in neuter anomalies the inst. sing., is generally the guide to the form assumed before the remaining vowel-terminations.

FIFTH CLASS OF NOUNS DECLINED.

Masculine, feminine, and neuter bases in त् t *and* द् d.

This class answers to Latin words like *comes* (from a base *comit*), *eques* (from a base *equit*), *ferens* (from *ferent*); and to Greek words like χάρις (from a base χαριτ), κέρας (from κερατ), χαρίεις (from χαριεντ).

136. Masculine and feminine bases in त् *t*, declined like हरित् *harit*, m. f., 'green' (declined at p. 57); and सरित् f. 'a river.'

Observe—The nom. case sing. is properly *harits*, but *s* is rejected by 43. *a*. The same applies to all nouns ending in consonants. It is remarkable, that Latin and Greek, when the final consonant of the base refuses to combine with the *s* of the nom., prefer rejecting the base-final: thus, χάρις for χαριτς, *comes* (*comis*) for *comits*. But in these languages the final of the base often combines with the *s* of the nominative; as in *lex* (for *leks*), φλόξ (for φλοκς).

N.V.	सरित् *sarit* *sarit+s* (*s* rejected. 43.*a.*)	सरितौ *saritau* *sarit+au*. 41. *b.*	सरितस् *saritas* *sarit+as*. 41. *b.*
Ac.	सरितं *saritam* *sarit+am*. 41. *b.*	— *saritau*	— *saritas*
I.	सरिता *saritá* *sarit+á*	सरिद्भ्यां *saridbhyám* *sarit+bhyám*. 41.	सरिद्भिस् *saridbhis* *sarit+bhis*. 41.
D.	सरिते *sarite* *sarit+e*	— *saridbhyám*	सरिद्भ्यस् *saridbhyas* *sarit+bhyas*
Ab.	सरितस् *saritas* *sarit+as*	— *saridbhyám*	— *saridbhyas*
G.	— *saritas*	सरितोस् *saritos* *sarit+os*	सरितां *saritám* *sarit+ám*
L.	सरिति *sariti* *sarit+i*	— *saritos*	सरित्सु *saritsu* *sarit+su*. 40.

137. Neuter bases in त् *t*, declined like हरित् *harit*, n., 'green.'

These only differ from the masculine and feminine in the N. du. pl., Ac. sing. du. and pl., the usual neuter terminations ई *í*, इ *i* (see 97), being required.

and an euphonic *n* being inserted before the final of the base in N. Ac. pl.: thus,

N. Ac. हरित् *harit*, हरिती *harití*, हरिन्ति *harinti*; I. हरिता *haritá*, हरिद्भ्यां *haridbhyám*, &c.

138. Masculine and feminine bases in द् *d*, like धर्मविद् *dharma-vid*, m. f., 'knowing one's duty'—a compound composed of the substantive *dharma*, 'duty,' and the root *vid*, 'knowing.' See 84. 1.

N.V.	-वित् *-vit* *-vid* + *s*. 42, 43. *a*.	-विदौ *-vidau* *-vid* + *au*	-विदस् *-vidas* *-vid* + *as*
Ac.	-विदं *-vidam* *-vid* + *am*	— *-vidau*	— *-vidas*
I.	-विदा *-vidá* *-vid* + *á*	-विद्भ्यां *-vidbhyám* *-vid* + *bhyám*	-विद्भिस् *-vidbhis* *-vid* + *bhis*
D.	-विदे *-vide* *-vid* + *e*	— *-vidbhyám*	-विद्भ्यस् *-vidbhyas* *-vid* + *bhyas*
Ab.	-विदस् *-vidas* *-vid* + *as*	— *-vidbhyám*	— *-vidbhyas*
G.	— *-vidas*	-विदोस् *-vidos* *-vid* + *os*	-विदां *-vidám* *-vid* + *ám*
L.	-विदि *-vidi* *-vid* + *i*	— *-vidos*	-वित्सु *-vitsu* *-vid* + *su*. 42.

139. Neuter bases in द् *d*, declined like धर्मविद् *dharma-vid*, n., 'knowing one's duty.'

These differ from the masculine and feminine forms in the same cases, and in the same manner, as neuter bases in त् *t*; see 137: thus,

N. Ac. धर्मवित्, धर्मविदी, धर्मविन्दी.

a. So also, कुमुद् n. 'a lotus:' N. Ac. कुमुत्, कुमुदी, कुमुन्दि; I. कुमुदा, &c.

Observe—All the nouns whose formation is explained at 84. I. II. III. follow the declension of हरित् and धर्मविद्.

140. Possessive adjectives formed with the affixes वत् *vat* and मत् *mat*, like धनवत् *dhanavat*, 'rich,' and धीमत् *dhímat*, 'wise,' are declined like *harit* for the masculine; but in the Nom. Voc. sing. du. pl., Ac. sing. du., *n* is inserted before the final of the base, and the preceding *a* is lengthened in N. sing.

N.	धनवान् *dhanaván* *dhanavánt* + *s*. 43. *a*.	धनवन्तौ *dhanavantau* *dhanavant* + *au*	धनवन्तस् *dhanavantas* *dhanavant* + *as*
Ac.	धनवन्तं *dhanavantam* *dhanavant* + *am*	— *dhanavantau*	धनवतस् *dhanavatas* *dhanavat* + *as*

The remaining cases follow हरित्; thus, I. धनवता, &c.; but the vocative singular is धनवन् *dhanavan.*

a. In the same manner are declined active past participles of the form कृतवत्; thus, N. कृतवान्, कृतवन्तौ, कृतवन्तस्, &c. Similarly, धीमत् 'wise:' N. धीमान्, धीमन्तौ, धीमन्तस्; Ac. धीमन्तं, धीमन्तौ, धीमतस्, &c.

b. The feminine bases of adjectives like धनवत् and धीमत्, and participles like कृतवत्, are formed by adding ई *í* to the masculine base; thus, धनवती, धीमती, कृतवती: declined after नदी at 106; thus, Nom. धनवती, धनवत्यौ, धनवत्यस्, &c.

c. The neuter is declined like the neuter of *harit:* thus, N. Ac. धनवत्, धनवती, धनवन्ति.

141. Present participles like पचत् *pachat,* 'cooking' (524), are declined after *dhanavat* (140), excepting in the N. sing., where *a* is not lengthened before *n:* thus, N. sing. पचन् *pachan* (for *pachants* or *pachans*), and not पचान् *pachán:* N. du. pl. पचन्तौ, पचन्तस्; Ac. पचन्तं, पचन्तौ, पचतस्; I. पचता, &c. Compare the declension of Latin participles like *ferens, ferentis, ferentem,* &c.

a. Observe, however, that all reduplicated verbs, such as verbs of the 3d conjugation—all verbs from polysyllabic roots (75. *a*)—and some few other verbs, such as जक्ष् 'to eat,' शास् 'to rule'—which reject the nasal in the 3d pl. of the Parasmai-pada, reject it also in the declension of the pres. participle. Hence the pres. participle of such verbs is declined like *harit,* the N. case being identical with the base: thus, from *dá,* 'to give,' 3d conj., N. sing. du. pl. *dadat, dadatau, dadatas;* Ac. *dadatam,* &c.: from *bhṛi,* 'to bear,' 3d conj., N. sing. du. pl. *bibhrat, bibhratau, bibhratas.* So also, *jágrat* (from *jágṛi*), *śásat* (from *śás*). The rejection of the nasal is doubtless owing to the encumbrance of the syllable of reduplication.

b. In present participles derived from verbs of the 1st, 4th, and 10th conjugations, a nasal is inserted for the feminine base: thus, पचन्ती from पच्, 1st conj. (declined like *nadí* at 106); and this nasal is carried through all the inflections, not merely, as in the masculine, through the first five. So दीव्यन्ती from *div,* 4th conj.; and चोरयन्ती from *chur,* 10th conj. In the 6th conj., and some few verbs of the 8th and 9th, the insertion of the nasal is optional. The same conjugations also insert a nasal in the dual neuter: thus, पचत्, पचन्ती, पचन्ति.

c. The other conjugations, viz. the 2d, 3d, 5th, 7th, 8th, and most verbs of the 9th, follow 140. *b. c,* and insert no nasal for the feminine and neuter; although all but the 3d assume a nasal in the first five inflections of the masculine: thus, *adat* (from *ad,* 2d conj.); N. masc. *adan, adantau, adantas;* fem. *adatí: juhwat* (from *hu,* 3d conj.); N. masc. *juhwat, juhwatau, juhwatas;* fem. *juhwatí: rundhat* (from *rudh,* 7th conj.); N. masc. *rundhan, rundhantau, rundhantas;* fem. *rundhatí.* But *kurvat* (from *kri,* 8th conj.) makes either *kurvatí* or *kurvantí.*

142. The adjective महत्, 'great,' is properly a pres. part. from the root *mah,* 'to increase;' but, unlike present participles, it lengthens the *a* of *at* before *n* in the N. sing. du. pl., Ac. sing. du.: thus, N. महान्, महान्तौ, महान्तस्; Ac. महान्तं, महान्तौ, महतस्; I. महता, &c.; V. महन्, &c.: N. fem. महती, &c., see 140. *a. b:* N. neut. महत्, महती, महान्ति.

a. बृहत् m. f. n. 'great,' जगत् m. f. n. 'moving,' and पृषत् m. f. 'a deer,' follow the declension of pres. part.: thus, N. बृहन्, बृहन्तौ, बृहन्तस्, &c. The feminine is बृहती, &c.

143. When the present participle of भू, 'to be,' is used as an honorific pronoun, it follows धनवत् (at 140), making the *a* of *at* long in the N. sing.: thus, भवान् 'your honour,' and not भवन्. The vocative is भवन्. As a present participle it follows the declension of पचत्, at 141. The feminine of the pronoun is भवती.

144. यकृत् 'the liver' (ἧπαρ, *jecur*), and शकृत् 'ordure,' both neuter nouns, are declined in some of their cases as if their bases were यकन् and शकन्: thus, N. V. यकृत्, यकृती, यकृन्ति; Ac. यकृत्, यकृती, यकृन्ति or यकानि; I. यकृता or यक्ना, यकृद्भ्यां or यकभ्यां, यकृद्भिस् or यकभिस्; D. यकृते or यक्ने, &c.

145. पाद्, 'a foot,' at the end of compounds is contracted into पद् before the Ac. pl. and remaining vowel-terminations: thus, Ac. pl. सुपदस्, from सुपाद्, 'having beautiful feet.'

SIXTH CLASS OF NOUNS DECLINED.

Masculine, feminine, and neuter bases in अन् an *and* इन् in.

Note, that this class answers to Latin and Greek words like *sermo* (for *sermon*), *homo* (for *homin*), δαίμων (for δαιμον).

146. Masculine and feminine bases in अन् *an*, declined like आत्मन् *átman*, m. f., 'soul,' 'self;' यज्वन् *yajwan*, m., 'a sacrificer;' राजन् *rájan*, m., 'a king;' and पीवन् *pívan*, m. f., 'fat.'

If *an* be preceded by *m* or *v* (*w*), at the end of a conjunct consonant, as in *átman*, *yajwan*, the *a* of *an* is retained before all the terminations: but if *an* be preceded by any other consonant, whether conjunct or not, than *m* or *v*, or even by *m* or *v* if not conjunct, as in *rájan* and *pívan*, the *a* of *an* is dropped in the Ac. plur. and before all the other *vowel*-terminations, and the remaining *n* is compounded with the preceding consonant. All masc. and fem. nouns, without exception, ending in *an*, lengthen the *a* in the N. sing. du. pl., Ac. sing. du.; and drop the *n* before all the consonantal-terminations (see 57).

Observe—Latin follows Sanskṛit in suppressing the *n* in the N. masc. and fem., but not in neut.: thus *homo* is the N. of the base *homin*, the stronger vowel *o* being substituted for *i*, just as *í* is substituted for *i* in Sanskṛit; but *nomen* is the N. of the neuter base *nomin*.

147.

N.	आत्मा *átmá* *átmá* (*n* and *s* rejected. 43.*a*, 57.)	आत्मानौ *átmánau* *átmán* + *au*	आत्मानस् *átmánas* *átmán* + *as*
Ac.	आत्मानं *átmánam* *átmán* + *am*	— *átmánau*	आत्मनस् *átmanas* *átman* + *as*
I.	आत्मना *átmaná* *átman* + *á*	आत्मभ्यां *átmabhyám* *átma* (*n* dropped. 57) + *bhyám*	आत्मभिस् *átmabhis* *átma* (*n* dropped. 57) + *bhis*
D.	आत्मने *átmane* *átman* + *e*	— *átmabhyám*	आत्मभ्यस् *átmabhyas* *átma* (*n* dropped. 57) + *bhyas*

Ab.	आत्मनस् *átmanas* *átman + as*	आत्मभ्यां *átmabhyám* *átma* (*n* dropped. 57) + *bhyám*	आत्मभ्यस् *átmabhyas* *átma* (*n* dropped. 57) + *bhyas*
G.	— *átmanas*	आत्मनोस् *átmanos* *átman + os*	आत्मनां *átmanám* *átman + ám*
L.	आत्मनि *átmani* *átman + i*	— *átmanos*	आत्मसु *átmasu* *átma* (*n* dropped. 57) + *su*
V.	आत्मन् *átman* *átman* (*s* rejected)	आत्मानौ *átmánau* *átmán + au*	आत्मानस् *átmánas* *átmán + as*

148. Similarly may be declined पाप्मन् *pápman*, m., 'sin;' उष्मन् *ushman*, m., 'the hot season;' शुष्मन् *śushman*, m., 'fire;' यज्वन् *yajwan*, m., 'a sacrificer:' N. यज्वा, यज्वानौ, यज्वानस्; Ac. यज्वानं, यज्वानौ, यज्वनस्; I. यज्वना, &c.

So also, अध्वन् *adhwan*, 'a road;' दृश्वन् *dṛiśwan*, 'a looker' (85. IV).

149.

N.	राजा *rájá* *rájá* (*n* and *s* rejected. 43.*a*, 57.)	राजानौ *rájánau* *ráján + au*	राजानस् *rájánas* (*reges*) *ráján + as*
Ac.	राजानं *rájánam* *ráján + am*	— *rájánau*	राज्ञस् *rájñas* *rájñ + as*
I.	राज्ञा *rájñá* *rájñ + á*	राजभ्यां *rájabhyám* *rája* (*n* dropped. 57) + *bhyám*	राजभिस् *rájabhis* *rája* (*n* dropped. 57) + *bhis*
D.	राज्ञे *rájñe* *rájñ + e*	— *rájabhyám*	राजभ्यस् *rájabhyas* *rája* (*n* dropped. 57) + *bhyas*
Ab.	राज्ञस् *rájñas* *rájñ + as*	— *rájabhyám*	— *rájabhyas*
G.	— *rájñas*	राज्ञोस् *rájños* *rájñ + os*	राज्ञां *rájñám* *rájñ + ám*
L.	राज्ञि *rájñi* * *rájñ + i*	— *rájños*	राजसु *rájasu* *rája* (*n* dropped. 57) + *su*
V.	राजन् *rájan* *rájan*. 92.	राजानौ *rájánau* *ráján + au*	राजानस् *rájánas* *ráján + as*

Compare the Latin *rex, regem, reges*, &c.

150. According to *rájan* may be declined पीवन् *pívan*, m. f., 'fat:' N. पीवा, पीवानौ, पीवानस्; Ac. पीवानं, पीवानौ, पीव्नस्; I. पीव्ना, &c. सीमन् m. 'a border;' वेमन् m. 'a loom' (85. I).

So also, मूर्द्धन् *múrddhan*, m., 'the head,' makes in the inst. c. मूर्द्ध्ना; and तक्षन् m. 'a carpenter,' तक्ष्णा (58); and लघिमन् *laghiman*, m., 'lightness,' लघिम्ना.

---

* Or राजनि *rájani*.

a. When a feminine base in ई *í* is formed from words like राजन्, it follows the same rule for the rejection of the *a* of *an:* thus, राज्ञी *rájñí*, 'a queen.'

151. There are no simple feminine nouns in *an;* but when masculine nouns are taken to form the last member of a compound adjective, they take a feminine and neuter form; as in *mahátman*, m. f. n., 'magnanimous.' The feminine form is declined precisely like the masculine, and the neuter follows the declension of neuter nouns, 152.

a. But when *rájan* is taken to form a compound of this kind, it is declined like *śiva* (103); as, N. sing. m. *mahárájas;* Ac. *mahárájam*, &c.

152. Neuter bases in अन् *an*, declined like कर्मन् 'an action,' and नामन् 'a name' (*nomen*, ὄνομα*). The retention or rejection of *a* in *an* before the inst. c. sing. and remaining vowel-terminations, as well as optionally before the nom. acc. du., is determined by the same rule as in masculines (146); and the only difference between masculine and neuter nouns is in the nom. and acc. cases, sing., du., and pl.: thus,

N. Ac. कर्म्न्, कर्मणी, कर्माणि; I. कर्मणा, &c.; D. कर्मणे, &c., like आत्मन्.

N. Ac. नामन्, नाम्नी or नामनी, नामानि; I. नाम्ना, &c.; D. नाम्ने, &c., like राजन्. With *námnám* compare Latin *nominum*.

153. So also the neuter nouns जन्मन्, वेश्मन्, अश्मन्, वर्मन्, वर्त्मन्, चर्मन्, छद्मन्, follow the declension of *karman;* but दामन्, सामन्, धामन्, व्योमन्, रोमन् (for रोह्मन् *rohman*, from *ruh*), प्रेमन्, that of *náman*.

154. When neuters in *an* compose the last member of compound adjectives, they may take the masc. or fem. form: thus, विष्णुशर्मनामा पण्डितः 'a Paṇḍit named Vishṇuśarma.'

155. There are a few anomalous nouns in *an:* श्वन् m. 'a dog' (*canis*, κύων); युवन् m. 'a youth;' मघवन् m. 'a name of Indra:' thus declined:

N. श्वा, श्वानौ, श्वानस्; Ac. श्वानं, श्वानौ, शुनस्; I. शुना, श्वभ्यां, श्वभिस्; D. शुने, &c.; Ab. शुनस्, &c.; G. शुनस् (κυνός), शुनोस्, शुनां; L. शुनि, शुनोस्, श्वसु. See 135. *a.* Fem. शुनी, &c. (like *nadí*).

N. युवा, -वानौ, -वानस्; Ac. -वानं, -वानौ, यूनस्; I. यूना, युवभ्यां, युवभिस्; D. यूने, &c.; Ab. यूनस्, &c.; G. यूनस्, यूनोस्, यूनां; L. यूनि, यूनोस्, युवसु. See 135. *a.* Fem. यूनी or युवती (like *nadí*). Neut. युव, यूनी, युवानि, &c.

N. मघवा, -वानौ, -वानस्; Ac. -वानं, -वानौ, मघोनस्; I. मघोना, मघवभ्यां, -वभिस्; D. मघोने, मघवभ्यां, &c.; Ab. मघोनस्, &c.; G. मघोनस्, मघोनोस्, मघोनां; L. मघोनि, मघोनोस्, मघवसु. Fem. मघोनी.

The last may also be declined like a noun in *vat*. See 140.

---

* Greek has a tendency to prefix vowels to words beginning with consonants in the cognate languages. Compare also *nakha*, 'nail,' ὄνυξ; *laghu*, 'light,' ἐλαχυ; भ्रू 'brow,' ὀφρυ.

156. अहन् n., 'a day,' takes its form, before the consonantal-terminations, from an obsolete base, अहस् *ahas:* thus, N. Ac. अहस् (43. *a*), अह्नी or अहनी, अहानि; I. अह्ना, अहोभ्यां, अहोभिस्; D. अह्ने, अहोभ्यां, अहोभ्यस्; Ab. अह्नस्, &c.; G. अह्नस्, अह्नोस्, अह्नां; L. अह्नि or अहनि, अह्नोस्, अहःसु.

a. दिवन् m., 'a day,' in those cases where the *a* of *an* is rejected, lengthens the *i*: thus, Ac. pl. दीव्नस्; I. दीव्ना, &c.

157. अर्य्यमन् m. 'the sun,' पूषन् m. 'the sun,' and ब्रह्महन् m. 'the murderer of a Brahman,' are analogous in not lengthening the *a* of *an* before the N. du. pl., Ac. sing. du.: thus, N. अर्य्यमा, अर्य्यमणौ, अर्य्यमणस्; Ac. अर्य्यमणं, अर्य्यमणौ, अर्य्यम्णस्; I. अर्य्यम्णा, &c. Similarly, N. पूषा, &c.; but the acc. pl., and remaining vowel-terminations, may be optionally formed from a base पूष्: thus, Ac. pl. पूष्णस् or पूषस्. Similarly, N. ब्रह्महा, ब्रह्महणौ, &c.; but in Ac. pl. ब्रह्मघ्नस्; I. ब्रह्मघ्ना, ब्रह्महभ्यां, &c.

158. अर्वन् m. 'a horse,' or m. f. n. 'low,' 'vile,' is declined like nouns in *vat* at 140, excepting in N. sing.: thus, N. अर्वा, अर्वन्तौ, अर्वन्तस्; Ac. अर्वन्तं, &c.

159. Masculine bases in इन् *in*, declined like धनिन् *dhanin*, m., 'rich.'

The *i* of *in* is lengthened in N. sing., and the *n* rejected before all the consonantal-terminations.

N.	धनी *dhaní* *dhaní* (*n* and *s* rejected. 43. *a*, 57.)	धनिनौ *dhaninau* *dhanin + au*	धनिनस् *dhaninas* *dhanin + as*
Ac.	धनिनं *dhaninam* *dhanin + am*	— *dhaninau*	— *dhaninas*
I.	धनिना *dhaniná* *dhanin + á*	धनिभ्यां *dhanibhyám* *dhani* (*n* dropped. 57) + *bhyám*	धनिभिस् *dhanibhis* *dhani* (*n* dropped. 57) + *bhis*
D.	धनिने *dhanine* *dhanin + e*	— *dhanibhyám*	धनिभ्यस् *dhanibhyas* *dhani* (*n* dropped. 57) + *bhyas*
Ab.	धनिनस् *dhaninas* *dhanin + as*	— *dhanibhyám*	— *dhanibhyas*
G.	— *dhaninas*	धनिनोस् *dhaninos* *dhanin + os*	धनिनां *dhaninám* *dhanin + ám*
L.	धनिनि *dhanini* *dhanin + i*	— *dhaninos*	धनिषु *dhanishu* *dhani* (*n* dropped. 57) + *su*. 70.
V.	धनिन् *dhanin* *dhanin*. 92.	धनिनौ *dhaninau* *dhanin + au*	धनिनस् *dhaninas* *dhanin + as*

Observe—A great many adjectives of the forms explained at 85. VI. VII. are declined like धनिन् for the masculine: thus, मेधाविन् *medhávin*, 'intellectual;' N. मेधावी, -विनौ, -विनस्, &c. Also a vast number of nouns of agency, like कारिन् 'a doer,' at 85. V: thus, N. कारी, कारिणौ (58), कारिणस्, &c.

160. The feminine base of such adjectives and nouns of agency is formed by adding ई *í* to the masc. base; as, from धनिन्, धनिनी f.; from कारिन्, कारिणी f.; declined like *nadí* at 106: thus, N. धनिनी, -न्यौ, -न्यस्, &c.

161. The neuter conforms in every respect to the declension of *vári* at 114: thus, N. Ac. धनि, धनिनी, धनीनि.

162. पथिन् m. 'a road,' मथिन् m. 'a churning-stick,' and ऋभुक्षिन् m. 'a name of Indra,' are remarkable as exhibiting both affixes, *an* and *in*, in the same word. They form their N. sing. from the bases पन्थस्, मन्थस्, ऋभुक्षस्; their N. du. pl., Ac. sing. du., from the bases पन्थन्, मन्थन्, ऋभुक्षन्; their Ac. pl., and remaining vowel-terminations, from the bases पथ्, मथ्, ऋभुक्ष्: thus, N. पन्थास् (163), पन्थानौ, पन्थानस्; Ac. पन्थानं, पन्थानौ, पथस्; I. पथा, पथिभ्यां, पथिभिस्; D. पथे, &c.

The compound सुपथिन्, 'having a good road,' is similarly declined for the masc.; the nom. fem. is सुपथी, -थ्यौ, -थ्यस्, like *nadí* at 106; the nom. neut. सुपथि, -पथी, -पन्थानि, &c.

SEVENTH CLASS OF NOUNS DECLINED.

Masculine, feminine, and neuter bases in अस् as, इस् is, *and* उस् us.

Note, that this class answers to Greek and Latin words like *πάθος*, *μένος*, *genus*, *scelus*, &c.

163. Masculine and feminine bases in अस् *as*, declined like चन्द्रमस् *chandramas*, m., 'the moon.'

The *a* of *as* is lengthened in N. sing.

N.	चन्द्रमास् *chandramás* *chandramás* (*s* rejected. 43.*a*.)	चन्द्रमसौ *chandramasau* *chandramas + au*	चन्द्रमसस् *chandramasas* *chandramas + as*
Ac.	चन्द्रमसं *chandramasam* *chandramas + am*	— *chandramasau*	— *chandramasas*
I.	चन्द्रमसा *chandramasá* *chandramas + á*	चन्द्रमोभ्यां *chandramobhyám* *chandramas + bhyám.* 65.	चन्द्रमोभिस् *chandramobhis* *chandramas + bhis.* 65.
D.	चन्द्रमसे *chandramase* *chandramas + e*	— *chandramobhyám*	चन्द्रमोभ्यस् *chandramobhyas* *chandramas + bhyas.* 65.
Ab.	चन्द्रमसस् *chandramasas* *chandramas + as*	— *chandramobhyám*	— *chandramobhyas*
G.	— *chandramasas*	चन्द्रमसोस् *chandramasos* *chandramas + os*	चन्द्रमसां *chandramasám* *chandramas + ám*
L.	चन्द्रमसि *chandramasi* *chandramas + i*	— *chandramasos*	चन्द्रमःसु *chandramahsu* or -स्सु *chandramas + su.* 62. *a*, 63.
V.	चन्द्रमस् *chandramas* *chandramas.* 92.	चन्द्रमसौ *chandramasau* *chandramas + au*	चन्द्रमसस् *chandramasas* *chandramas + as*

a. After the same manner is declined अप्सरस् *apsaras*, f., 'a nymph.'

164. Neuter bases in अस् *as*, declined like मनस् *manas*, n., 'the mind' (*μένος*, *mens*).

These only differ from the masc. and fem. in the N. and Ac. The *a* of *as* is lengthened in the N. plur. instead of the N. sing. न् *n* is inserted before *s* in the N. plur.

N. Ac.V.	मनस् *manas*	मनसी *manasí*	मनांसि *manánsi*
	manas (*s* rejected. 43. *a.*)	*manas* + *í*	*manáns* + *i*

I. मनसा *manasá*, &c., like the masc. and fem.

a. Observe—Nearly all simple substantives in *as* are neuter like *manas;* but when these neuters are taken to form a compound adjective, they are declinable also in the masculine and feminine like *chandramas*. Thus, when *manas* is taken to form the compound adjective *mahámanas*, 'magnanimous,' it makes in the nom. (masc. and fem.) *mahámanás, mahámanasau, mahámanasas*. In the same way are formed *sumanas*, 'well-intentioned,' *durmanas*, 'evil-minded' (nom. *sumanás, durmanás*, &c.); to which a remarkable analogy is presented by the Greek *εὐμενής* and *δυσμενής*, m. f., making in neut. *εὐμενές*, *δυσμενές*, derived from *μένος* *.

165. Neuter bases in इस् *is* and उस् *us* (see 68. *a*) are declined analogously to मनस् *manas* at 164, *i* and *u* being substituted for *a* throughout; and therefore ष *sh* for स *s* (70), and र *r* for ओ *o* (64): thus, हविस् *havis*, n., 'ghee:' N. Ac.V. हविस्, हविषी, हवींषि; I. हविषा, हविर्भ्यां, हविर्भिस्; D. हविषे, हविर्भ्यां, हविर्भ्यस्; Ab. हविषस्, हविर्भ्यां, हविर्भ्यस्; G. हविषस्, हविषोस्, हविषां; L. हविषि, हविषोस्, हविःषु or -ष्षु.

a. Similarly, चक्षुस् *chakshus*, n., 'the eye:' N. Ac. V. चक्षुस्, चक्षुषी, चक्षूंषि; I. चक्षुषा, चक्षुर्भ्यां, चक्षुर्भिस्; D. चक्षुषे, चक्षुर्भ्यां, चक्षुर्भ्यस्; Ab. चक्षुषस्, चक्षुर्भ्यां, चक्षुर्भ्यस्; G. चक्षुषस्, चक्षुषोस्, चक्षुषां; L. चक्षुषि, चक्षुषोस्, चक्षुःषु or -ष्षु.

166. All nouns formed with the affixes *is* and *us* are neuter. There are two, however, in which the final sibilant is part of the root itself, and not of an affix; viz. आशिस् *ásís*, f., 'a blessing' (from the root शास्), and सजुस् m. f. 'an associate' (from जुष्). These follow the analogy of masc. and fem. nouns in *as* (163) in the N. Ac. cases; and, moreover, before the consonantal-terminations, where the final sibilant is changed to *r*, unlike nouns formed with *is* and *us*, they lengthen the *i* and *u* (compare nouns ending in *r* at 180): thus, N. आशीस्, -शिषौ, -शिषस्; Ac. -शिषं, -शिषौ, -शिषस्; I. -शिषा, -शीर्भ्यां, -शीर्भिस्, &c. Again, N. सजूस्, -जुषौ, -जुषस्; Ac. -जुषं, &c.; I. -जुषा, -जूर्भ्यां, &c. Nouns formed from desiderative bases (497), such as जिगदिस् 'desirous of speaking,' are similarly declined. But desiderative nouns of the form पिपक्ष्, विविक्ष्, reject the sibilant in the consonantal-cases, and are declined in those cases as if ending in च् and श्, the finals of their roots. Compare 43. *a.*

* Bopp's Comparative Grammar, § 146.

a. Observe—When neuter nouns in *is* or *us* are taken for the last member of compound adjectives, they are declinable in the masc. and fem. according to the analogy of *chandramas* at 163: thus, उत्पलचक्षुस् m. f. n., 'having lotus eyes,' makes N. masc. and fem. उत्पलचक्षूस्, उत्पलचक्षुषौ, उत्पलचक्षुषस्; and शुचिरोचिस् m. f. n., 'having brilliant rays,' N. masc. and fem. शुचिरोचीस्, शुचिरोचिषौ, शुचिरोचिषस्, &c.

b. दोस् *dos*, m., 'an arm,' follows the declension of nouns in *is* and *us;* but in Ac. pl., and remaining vowel-cases, optionally substitutes *doshan* for its base: thus, N. दोस्, -षौ, -षस्; Ac. -षं, -षौ, -षस् or -ष्णस्; I. दोषा or दोष्णा, दोर्भ्यां, &c.

167. Adjectives in the comparative degree formed with the affix ईयस् *íyas*, m. f. n. (192), follow *chandramas* at 163, but the *a* of *as* is lengthened, and *n* inserted in N. sing. du. pl., Ac. sing. du.: thus, *balíyas*, 'more powerful,' makes N. बलीयान् (for *balíyáns*, *s* rejected by 43. *a*), -यांसौ, -यांसस्; Ac. -यांसं, -यांसौ, -यसस्; I. -यसा, -योभ्यां, &c.; V. -यन्. The fem. बलीयसी follows *mati* at 106. The neut. बलीयस् is like *manas* throughout.

168. Participles of the 2d preterite, formed with *vas*, are similarly declined in N. sing. du. pl., Ac. sing. du. But in Ac. pl., and remaining vowel-cases, *vas* becomes *ush*, and in the consonantal-cases *vat;* so that there are three forms of the base, viz. in *váns*, *ush*, and *vat* *: thus, विविद्वस् (part. of 2d pret., from विद् 'to know'): N. विविद्वान्, विविद्वांसौ, विविद्वांसस्; Ac. विविद्वांसं, विविद्वांसौ, विविदुषस्; I. विविदुषा, विविद्वद्भ्यां, विविद्वद्भिस्; D. विविदुषे, &c. When this participle is formed with *ivas* instead of *vas*, the vowel *i* is usually rejected in the cases where *vas* becomes *ush:* thus, जग्मिवस् (from *gam*, 'to go'): N. जग्मिवान्, &c.; Ac. जग्मिवांसं, जग्मिवांसौ, जग्मुषस्, &c.; I. जग्मुषा, &c. Similarly, *tenivas* (from *tan*, 'to stretch'): N. *teniván*, *tenivánsau*, &c.; Ac. *tenivánsam*, *tenivánsau*, *tenushas*, &c. But not when the *i* is part of the root: thus, चिचिवस् (from चि), निनीवस् (from नी), चकृवस् (from कृ), make in the Ac. pl. चिच्युषस्, निन्युषस्, चक्रुषस्. The N. feminine of these participles is formed from *ush;* and the N. Ac. neuter, sing., du., and plur., from *vat*, *ush*, and *vas*, respectively: thus, N. fem. विविदुषी, &c., declined like *nadí* at 106. Similarly, from the root तुप् comes तुतुपुषी (compare τετυφυῖα). The neuter is N. विविद्वत्, -दुषी, -द्वांसि. Those formed with *ivas* do not retain *i* in the feminine: thus, *tenivas;* N. masc. fem. neut. *teniván*, *tenushí* †, *tenivas*.

a. The root विद्, 'to know,' has an irregular pres. part. विद्वस् *vidwas*, used commonly as an adjective ('learned'), and declined exactly like विविद्वस् above, leaving out the reduplicated *vi*. With reference to 308. *a*, it may be observed, that as a contracted 2d pret. of *vid* is used as a present tense, so a contracted participle of the 2d pret. is used as a present participle.

---

* *Vat* is evidently connected with the Greek οτ. Compare *tutupvat* (from *tup*) with τετυφ-(F)οτ, and *tutupvatsu* with τετυφ-ο(τ)σι.

† There seems, however, much difference of opinion as to the rejection of *i;* and some grammarians make the feminine *tenyushí*, and the I. masc. *tenyushá*.

169. पुंस् m., 'a male,' forms N. sing. du. plur., Ac. sing. du., from पुमस्; but Ac. pl., and remaining vowel-cases, from पुंस्; and I. du., and remaining consonantal-cases, from पुम्: thus, N. पुमान्, पुमांसौ, पुमांसस्; Ac. पुमांसं, पुमांसौ, पुंसस्; I. पुंसा, पुम्भ्यां, पुम्भिस्; D. पुंसे, &c.; Ab. पुंसस्, &c.; G. पुंसस्, पुंसोस्, पुंसां; L. पुंसि, पुंसोस्, पुंसु; V. पुमन्, &c.

170. उशनस् m., 'a name of the planet Venus,' forms N. sing. उशना from a base उशनन् (147). Similarly, पुरुदंशस् m. 'a name of Indra,' and अनेहस् m. 'time.' The other cases are regular. उशनस्, however, may be optionally उशनन् in the vocative.

171. जरस्, f. 'decay' (γῆρας), forms its consonantal-cases from a base जरा; thus, N. sing. जरा (105); I. sing. du. जरसा, जराभ्यां, &c.

EIGHTH CLASS OF NOUNS DECLINED.

Masculine, feminine, and neuter bases in any consonant, except त् t *and* द् d, न् n, स् s.

Note, that examples of Latin and Greek nouns answering to this class are common. See 87.

172. Observe—This class consists principally of roots used as nouns, either alone or at the end of compounds, or preceded by prepositions and adverbial prefixes. Roots ending in त् *t* and द् *d*, employed in this manner, are of common occurrence; but their declension falls under the fifth class at 136. Roots ending in other consonants are not very frequently found, and the only difficulty in their declension arises from their combination with the consonantal-terminations. See 92. *a*.

173. Whatever change, however, takes place in the nom. sing. is preserved before all the consonantal-terminations; remembering only, that before such terminations the rules of Sandhi come into operation.

174. Before the vowel-terminations the final consonant of the root, whatever it may be, is always preserved (41. *b*). If in one or two nouns there may be any peculiarity in the formation of the acc. pl., the same peculiarity runs through the remaining vowel-cases. The terminations themselves undergo no change, but the *s* of the nom. sing. is of course rejected by 43. *a*. There is but one form of declension for both masc. and fem.; the neuter follows the analogy of other nouns ending in consonants at 137.

175. Masculine and feminine bases in क् *k*, ख् *kh*, ग् *g*, घ् *gh*, declined like सर्वशक् *sarva-śak*, m. f., 'omnipotent' (from *sarva*, 'all,' and शक् 'to be able'),

and चित्रलिख् m. 'a painter' (from चित्र 'a painting,' and लिख् 'to write'). N.V. -शक् (43. *a*), -शकौ (41. *b*), -शकस्; Ac. -शकं, -शकौ, -शकस्; I. -शका, -शग्भ्यां (41), -शग्भिस्, &c.; L. pl. -शक्सु (40) or -शक्षु (70). N.V. -लिक् (43. *b*, 43. *a*), -लिखौ (174), -लिखस्; Ac. -लिखं, &c.; I. -लिखा, -लिग्भ्यां (41), -लिग्भिस्, &c.; L. pl. -लिक्षु (40).

a. The neuter is N. Ac.V. -शक्, -शकी, -शङ्कि, &c.; -लिक्, -लिखी, -लिङ्खि, &c.: the rest like the masc. and fem.

176. Masculine and feminine bases in च् *ch*, छ् *chh*, ज् *j*, झ् *jh*, declined like वाच् *vách*, f., 'speech' (from वच् 'to speak'); मांसभुज् *mánsa-bhuj*, m.f., 'flesh-eater' (from मांस *mánsa*, 'flesh,' and भुज् 'to eat'); प्राछ् *práchh*, m. f., 'an asker' (from प्रछ् 'to ask'). A final च् *ch* is changed to क् *k*, a final ज् *j* to ग् *g*, a final छ् *chh* to ट् *ṭ*, before the consonantal-terminations (43. *d*, 92. *a*). Compare the declension of *vách* with that of the Latin *vox*, and the Greek ὄψ or ὀπ for Ϝοπ.

N. V. वाक् (for *váks*, 43. *a*; *vox*, ὄψ), वाचौ (ὄπε), वाचस् (*voces*, ὄπες); Ac. वाचं (*vocem*), वाचौ, वाचस् (ὄπας); I. वाचा, वाग्भ्यां, वाग्भिस्; D. वाचे, वाग्भ्यां, वाग्भ्यस्; Ab. वाचस्, वाग्भ्यां, वाग्भ्यस्; G. वाचस्, वाचोस्, वाचां; L. वाचि (ὀπί), वाचोस्, वाक्सु or वाक्षु.

N. V. -भुक्, -भुजौ, -भुजस्; Ac. -भुजं, &c.; I. -भुजा, -भुग्भ्यां, -भुग्भिस्, &c.

N. V. प्राट्, प्राछौ, प्राछस्; Ac. प्राछं, &c.; I. प्राछा, प्राड्भ्यां, &c.; L. pl. प्राट्सु.

The last optionally substitutes श् *ś* for its final छ् *chh* before the vowel-terminations: thus, N. du. प्राछौ or प्राशौ, &c. पयोमुच्, 'a cloud,' is declined like वाच्.

a. The neuter is N. Ac. वाक्, वाची, वाञ्चि, &c.; भुक्, भुजी, भुञ्जि, &c.; प्राट्, प्राछी, प्राञ्छि, &c.

b. The root अञ्च् *añch*, 'to go,' preceded by certain prepositions and adverbial prefixes, forms a few irregular nouns; such as, प्राञ्च् 'eastern;' अवाञ्च् 'southern;' प्रत्यञ्च् 'western;' उदञ्च् 'northern;' सम्यञ्च् 'going with,' 'fit,' 'proper;' तिर्यञ्च् 'going crookedly, as an animal;' and a few others less common. These reject the nasal in the acc. pl. and remaining cases masculine. In nom. sing. the final च् *ch* being changed to क् *k*, causes the preceding nasal to take the guttural form, and the क् is rejected by 43. *a*. In the acc. plur., and remaining vowel-cases, there is a further modification of the base in all, excepting प्राञ्च् and अवाञ्च्.

N. V. masc. प्राङ्, प्राञ्चौ, प्राञ्चस्; Ac. प्राञ्चं, प्राञ्चौ, प्राचस्; I. प्राचा, प्राग्भ्यां, प्राग्भिस्; D. प्राचे, &c.; L. pl. प्राक्षु. Similarly, अवाञ्च्.

N.V. प्रत्यङ्, प्रत्यञ्चौ, प्रत्यञ्चस्; Ac. प्रत्यञ्चं, प्रत्यञ्चौ, प्रतीचस्; I. प्रतीचा, प्रत्यग्भ्यां, प्रत्यग्भिस्; D. प्रतीचे, &c. Similarly, उदञ्च् and सम्यञ्च्, which make in acc. pl., and remaining vowel-cases, उदीचस्, समीचस्. But तिर्यञ्च् makes in acc. pl., &c., तिरश्चस्.

The feminine, and the neut. dual of these nouns follow the analogy of the acc. pl.: thus, N. fem. प्राची &c., अवाची &c., प्रतीची &c., उदीची &c., समीची &c., तिरश्ची &c., declined like नदी. The neuter is N. Ac.V. प्राक्, प्राची, प्राञ्चि, &c.; प्रत्यक्, प्रतीची, प्रत्यञ्चि, &c.

c. प्राञ्च्, when it signifies 'worshipping,' retains the nasal throughout; but *ch* is rejected before the consonantal-terminations, and the nasal then becomes guttural: thus, N. प्राङ्, प्राञ्चौ, &c.; Ac. प्राञ्चं, &c.; I. प्राञ्चा, प्राङ्भ्यां, &c.

d. असृज् n., 'blood,' is regular: thus, N. Ac. असृक्, असृजी, असृञ्जि, &c.; but it may optionally take the acc. plur., inst. and dat. sing.; and, according to some authorities, all its other inflexions from an obsolete base, असन् *asan*: thus, Ac. pl. असृञ्जि or असानि; I. sing. असृजा or अस्ना, &c.

e. Nouns formed with the roots यज् 'to worship,' राज् 'to shine,' मृज् 'to rub,' भ्राज् 'to shine,' व्रज् 'to wander,' सृज् 'to create,' change the final ज् to ट् or ड् before the consonantal-terminations (43. *d*). In some, however, the final optionally becomes क् *k* or ग् *g*: thus, देवेज् m. 'a worshipper of the gods' (यज् becoming इज्); N. sing. देवेट् or देवेड्: राज् m. 'a ruler;' N. sing. राट्, I. dual राड्भ्यां: परिमृज् 'a cleanser;' N. sing. परिमृट्: विभ्राज् m. f. 'splendid;' N. sing. विभ्राट्: परिव्राज् m. 'a religious mendicant;' N. sing. परिव्राट्: विश्वसृज् 'the creator of the world;' N. sing. विश्वसृट् or विश्वसृक्. ऋत्विज् m., 'a priest,' is regularly ऋत्विक्.

f. अवयज् m., 'an inferior sacrificer,' lengthens the *a* of *yaj* in the N. sing. and in the vowel-cases, and forms the consonantal-cases from an obsolete base, अवयस्; N. sing. du. pl. अवयास्, -याजौ, -याजस्; Ac. -याजं, &c.; I. -याजा, -योभ्यां, &c.

g. भ्रस्ज् or भ्रज्ज्, 'one who fries,' makes N.V. भृट्, भृज्जौ, भृज्जस्; Ac. भृज्जं, &c. Similarly, व्रश्च् 'one who cuts.'

h. ऊर्ज् m. f., 'strong,' makes N.V. ऊर्क्, &c.; Ac. ऊर्जं, &c.; I. ऊर्जा, ऊर्ग्भ्यां, &c. The neuter is N. Ac. V. ऊर्क्, ऊर्जी, ऊंर्जि *unrji*.

177. Masculine and feminine bases in थ् *th*, ध् *dh*, declined like कथ् m. f. 'one who tells,' युध् f. 'battle.' The final aspirate is changed to its unaspirated form before the consonantal-terminations (43. *b*, 41), but not before the vowel (41. *b*). N.V. कत्, कथौ, कथस्; Ac. कथं, &c.; I. कथा, कद्भ्यां, &c. N.V. युत्, युधौ, युधस्; Ac. युधं, &c.; I. युधा, युद्भ्यां, &c. In the case of a root like बुध् m. f., 'one who knows,' the initial ब *b* becomes भ *bh* wherever the final ध् *dh* becomes *t* or *d*, by 42. *c*: thus, N.V. भुत्, बुधौ, बुधस्; Ac. बुधं, &c.; I. बुधा, भुद्भ्यां, &c.

a. The neuter is N. Ac.V. कत्, कथी, कन्थि, &c.; युत्, युधी, युन्धि, &c.

178. Masculine and feminine bases in प् *p*, फ् *ph*, ब् *b*, भ् *bh*, declined like गुप् m. f. 'one who defends,' लभ् m. f. 'one who obtains.' N.V. गुप्, गुपौ, गुपस्; Ac. गुपं, &c.; I. गुपा, गुब्भ्यां, गुब्भिस्, &c. N.V. लप्, लभौ, लभस्; Ac. लभं, &c.; I. लभा, लब्भ्यां, लब्भिस्, &c.

a. The neuter is N. Ac.V. गुप्, गुपी, गुम्पि, &c.; लप्, लभी, लम्भि, &c.

b. अप् f. 'water,' declined only in the plural, is irregular: thus, N.V. आपस्; Ac. अपस्; I. अद्भिस्; D. Ab. अद्भ्यस्; G. अपां; L. अप्सु.

179. Masculine and feminine bases in म् *m*, declined like शम् m. f. 'one who pacifies.' The final *m* becomes *n* before the consonantal-terminations: thus, N.V. शन्, शमौ, शमस्; Ac. शमं, &c.; I. शमा, शन्भ्यां, शन्भिस्, &c.; L. pl. शन्सु.

a. Similarly, प्रशाम् m. f., 'quiet,' makes N. प्रशान्, -शामौ, -शामस्; Ac. प्रशामं, &c.; I. प्रशामा, प्रशान्भ्यां, &c. Compare 53. *b*.

b. The neuter is N. Ac. V. शन्, शमी, शमि, &c.; प्रशान्, -शामी, -शामि, &c.

180. Masculine and feminine bases in र् *r*, declined like चर् m. f. 'one who goes,' गिर् f. 'speech.' If the vowel that precedes final *r* be *i* or *u*, it is lengthened before the consonantal-terminations (compare 166); and final *r*, being a radical letter, does not become Visarga before the *s* of the loc. pl. (71. *a*). N.V. चर्, चरौ, चरस्; Ac. चरं, &c.; I. चरा, चर्भ्यां, चर्भिस्, &c.; L. pl. चर्षु. N.V. गीर्, गिरौ, गिरस्; Ac. गिरं, &c.; I. गिरा, गीर्भ्यां, गीर्भिस्, &c.; L. pl. गीर्षु.

a. The neuter is N. Ac. V. चर्, चरी, चरि, &c.; गीर्, गिरी, गिरि, &c.

b. There is one irregular noun ending in the semivowel व् *v*, viz. दिव् f. 'the sky,' which makes its base द्यौ in N. sing., and द्यु in the other consonantal-cases: thus, N.V. द्यौस्, दिवौ, दिवस्; Ac. दिवं or द्यां, दिवौ, दिवस्; I. दिवा, द्युभ्यां, द्युभिस्, &c.

181. Masculine and feminine bases in श् *ś* and ष् *sh*, declined like विश् m. f. 'one who enters,' दिश् f. 'a quarter of the sky,' द्विष् m. f. 'one who hates,' मृष् m. f. 'one who endures.' N.V. विट् (43. *e*), विशौ, विशस्; Ac. विशं, &c.; I. विशा, विड्भ्यां, &c. N.V. दिक् (43. *e*, 17. *b*), दिशौ, दिशस्; Ac. दिशं, &c.; I. दिशा, दिग्भ्यां, &c. N.V. द्विट् (43. *e*), द्विषौ, द्विषस्; Ac. द्विषं, &c.; I. द्विषा, द्विड्भ्यां, &c. N.V. मृक् (43. *e*), मृषौ, मृषस्; Ac. मृषं, &c.; I. मृषा, मृग्भ्यां, &c.

a. The neuter is N. Ac.V. विट्, विशी, विंशि, &c.; दिक्, दिशी, दिंशि, &c.; द्विट्, द्विषी, द्विंषि, &c.; मृक्, मृषी, मृंषि, &c.

182. Masculine and feminine bases in ह् *h*, declined like लिह् m. f. 'one who licks;' दुह् m. f. 'one who milks.' In roots beginning with द् *d*, the final aspirate becomes क् *k* or ग् *g* (see 17. *a*), in other roots ट् *ṭ* or ड् *ḍ*, before the consonantal-terminations; but in roots whose initial is *d*, the *h*, which disappears as a final, is transferred to the initial *d*, which becomes *dh* wherever final *h* becomes *k* or *g* (compare 42. *c*). N.V. लिट् (43. *c*), लिहौ, लिहस्; Ac. लिहं, &c.; I. लिहा, लिड्भ्यां, &c. N.V. धुक्, दुहौ, दुहस्; Ac. दुहं, &c.; I. दुहा, धुग्भ्यां, धुग्भिस्, &c. But द्रुह् m. f., 'one who injures,' makes N. ध्रुक् or ध्रुट्; and मुह् m. f., 'foolish,' N. मुक् or मुट्.

a. The neuter is N. Ac.V. लिट्, लिही, लिंहि, &c.; धुक्, दुही, दुंहि, &c.

b. उष्णिह् f., 'a particular kind of metre,' changes its final to *k* or *g* before the consonantal-terminations, like roots beginning with *d*. N. उष्णिक्, उष्णिहौ, &c.

c. वाह्, 'bearing' (from the root वह् 'to bear'), changes वा to ऊ *ú* in the acc. plur. and remaining vowel-cases, and before the ई *í* of the fem.; and if the word that precedes it in the compound ends in *a* or *á*, then *a* or *á* combines with *ú* into औ *au* (instead of ओ *o*, by 32): thus, भारवाह् m. f. 'one who bears a burden:' N.V. masc. भारवाट्, भारवाहौ, भारवाहस्; Ac. भारवाहं, भारवाहौ, भारौहस्; I. भारौहा, भारवाड्भ्यां, &c. N. fem. भारौही, &c. But शालिवाह्, 'bearing rice,' makes in Ac. pl. &c. शाल्यूहस्.

श्वेतवाह् m., 'Indra' (who is borne by white horses), may optionally retain वा in Ac. plur. &c.; and in consonantal-cases is declined as if the base were श्वेतवस्: thus, N.V. श्वेतवास्, श्वेतवाहौ, श्वेतवाहस्; Ac. श्वेतवाहं, श्वेतवाहौ, श्वेतौहस् or श्वेतवाहस्; I. श्वेतौहा or श्वेतवाहा, श्वेतवोभ्यां, श्वेतवोभिस्, &c.

d. अनडुह् m., 'an ox' (for अनोवाह्, from अनस् 'a cart,' and वाह् 'bearing'), forms the N.V. sing. from अनडुत्; and N. du. plur., Ac. sing. du., from अनड्वाह्: thus, N. अनड्वान्, अनड्वाहौ, अनड्वाहस्; Ac. अनड्वाहं, अनड्वाहौ, अनडुहस्; I. अनडुहा, अनडुद्भ्यां, अनडुद्भिस्, &c.; L. pl. अनडुत्सु; V. अनड्वन्. At the end of compounds this word makes fem. N. sing. अनडुही; neut. N.V. अनडुत्, अनडुही, अनड्वांहि.

e. नह्, 'binding,' 'tying,' at the end of compounds, changes the final to त् or द्, instead of ट् or ड्: thus, उपानह् f., 'a shoe,' makes N. उपानत्, उपानहौ, उपानहस्; Ac. उपानहं, &c.; I. उपानहा, उपानद्भ्यां, &c. Compare 306. *b.*

183. Masculine and feminine bases in more than one final consonant, declined like वल्ग् m. f. 'one who leaps:' N.V. वल् क् (43. *a*), वल्गौ, वल्गस्; Ac. वल्गं, &c.; I. वल्गा, वल्भ्यां, &c.

a. The neuter is N. Ac.V. वल्क्, वल्गी, वल्गि, &c.

b. गोरक्ष्, 'a cow-keeper,' makes N.V. गोरक् or गोरट्, &c.

SECTION III.

ADJECTIVES.

184. The declension of substantives includes that of adjectives; and, as already seen, the three examples of substantives, given under each class, serve as the model for the three genders of adjectives falling under the same class. Simple adjectives, coming immediately from roots, and not derived from substantives, are not common. Such as do occur belong chiefly to the first, second, and third classes of nouns; 80, 81, 82.

185. Adjectives *formed from substantives* are very numerous, as may be seen by a reference to 80, 84, 85. They belong chiefly to the first, fifth, and sixth classes of nouns.

186. Compound adjectives, whether formed by using roots or substantives at the end of compounds, are most abundant under every one of the eight classes.

The following table exhibits examples of the most common kind of adjectives in the nom. case masc., fem., and neut., and indicates the class to which their declension is to be referred.

187. *Examples of simple adjectives.*

	BASE.	NOM. MASC.	NOM. FEM.	NOM. NEUT.
1ST CLASS.	प्रिय 'dear'	प्रियस्*	प्रिया	प्रियं
	शुभ 'fortunate'	शुभस्	शुभा	शुभं
	सुन्दर 'beautiful'	सुन्दरस्	सुन्दरा or सुन्दरी	सुन्दरं
2D CLASS.	शुचि 'pure'	शुचिस्	शुचिस्	शुचि
3D CLASS.	पाण्डु 'pale'	पाण्डुस्	पाण्डुस्	पाण्डु
	साधु 'good'	साधुस्	साधुस् or साध्वी 106.	साधु
	मृदु 'tender'	मृदुस्	मृद्वी	मृदु
	भीरु 'timid'	भीरुस्	भीरुस् or भीरूस् 125.	भीरु

188. *Examples of adjectives formed from substantives.*

	BASE.	NOM. MASC.	NOM. FEM.	NOM. NEUT.
1ST CLASS.	मानुष 'human'	मानुषस्	मानुषी	मानुषं
	धार्मिक 'religious'	धार्मिकस्	धार्मिकी	धार्मिकं
5TH CLASS.	बलवत् 'strong'	बलवान्	बलवती 106.	बलवत्
	श्रीमत् 'prosperous'	श्रीमान्	श्रीमती 106.	श्रीमत्
6TH CLASS.	सुखिन् 'happy'	सुखी	सुखिनी 106.	सुखि

189. *Examples of compound adjectives.*

	BASE.	NOM. MASC.	NOM. FEM.	NOM. NEUT.
1ST CLASS.	बहुविद्य 'very learned'	बहुविद्यस्	बहुविद्या	बहुविद्यं
2D CLASS.	दुर्बुद्धि 'foolish'	दुर्बुद्धिस्	दुर्बुद्धिस्	दुर्बुद्धि
3D CLASS.	अल्पतनु 'small bodied'	अल्पतनुस्	अल्पतनुस्	अल्पतनु
4TH CLASS.	बहुदातृ 'very liberal'	बहुदाता	बहुदात्री 106.	बहुदातृ
5TH CLASS.	सर्वजित् 'all-conquering'	सर्वजित्	सर्वजित्	सर्वजित्

---

* When it is remembered that *a* is equivalent in pronunciation to *u*, the three genders of this adjective might be written *priyus, priyá, priyum;* thus offering a perfect similarity to Latin adjectives in *us*.

6TH CLASS. { सुजन्मन् 'well-born'	सुजन्मा	सुजन्मा	सुजन्म
7TH CLASS. { गतचेतस् 'deprived of sense'	गतचेतास्	गतचेतास्	गतचेतस्
8TH CLASS. { मर्म्मस्पृश् 'piercing the vitals'	मर्म्मस्पृक्	मर्म्मस्पृक्	मर्म्मस्पृक्

190. *Examples of some other compound adjectives.*

शङ्खध्मा 'a shell-blower' (108. *a.*)	शङ्खध्मास्	शङ्खध्मास्	शङ्खध्मं
नष्टश्री 'ruined' (123. *b.*)	नष्टश्रीस्	नष्टश्रीस्	नष्टश्रि
खलपू 'a sweeper' (126. *b.*)	खलपूस्	खलपूस्	खलपु
दिव्यमातृ 'having a divine mother' (130.)	दिव्यमाता	दिव्यमाता	दिव्यमातृ
बहुरै 'rich' (134. *a.*)	बहुरास्	बहुरास्	बहुरि
बहुगो 'having many cattle' (134. *a.*)	बहुगौस्	बहुगौस्	बहुगु
बहुनौ 'having many ships' (134. *a.*)	बहुनौस्	बहुनौस्	बहुनु

191. The degrees of comparison are formed in two ways; 1st, by adding to the base तर *tara* (nom. *-taras*, *-tará*, *-taram*, cf. Greek *τερος*) for the comparative; and तम *tama* (nom. *-tamas*, *-tamá*, *-tamam*, cf. Latin *timus*, Greek *τατος*) for the superlative: thus, पुण्य *puṇya*, 'holy,' पुण्यतर *puṇyatara*, 'more holy,' पुण्यतम *puṇyatama*, 'most holy,' declined like nouns of the first class at 103. So also, *dhanavat*, 'wealthy,' *dhanavattara*, 'more wealthy,' *dhanavattama*, 'most wealthy.' A final न् is rejected; as, *dhanin*, 'rich,' *dhanitara*, 'more rich,' *dhanitama*, 'most rich' (57). विद्वस्, 'wise,' makes विद्वत्तर, विद्वत्तम. Compare 168. *a.*

192. 2dly, by adding ईयस् *íyas* (nom. *-íyán*, *-íyasí*, *-íyas*, Greek *ιων*, see declension at 167) for the comparative; and इष्ठ *ishṭha* (nom. *-ishṭhas*, *-ishṭhá*, *-ishṭham*, declined at 103, cf. Greek *ιστος*) for the superlative.

a. Note, that while the base of the Sanskṛit comparative affix strictly appears to end in *n* and *s* (*iyans*), the Greek has adhered to the *n* throughout (N. *íyán* = *ιων*, voc. *íyan* = *ιον*); and the Latin has taken the *s* for its neuter (*íyas* = *ius*, neuter of *ior*; *r* being changed to *s*, which so frequently happens). Compare Sanskṛit *garíyas* with *gravius*.

193. In general, before *íyas* and *ishṭha*, the base disburdens itself of a final vowel, or of the more weighty affixes *in*, *vin*, *vat*, *mat*: thus, बलिन् 'strong,' बलीयस् 'more strong' (declined at 167), बलिष्ठ 'strongest' (declined at 103); लघु 'light,' लघीयस् 'lighter,' लघिष्ठ 'lightest;' मेधाविन् 'intelligent,' मेधीयस् 'more intelligent,' मेधिष्ठ 'most intelligent.'

Compare स्वादीयान् (N. of *swádíyas*) from *swádu* with ἡδίων from ἡδύ; and स्वादिष्ठस् with ἥδιστος.

194. But besides the rejection of the final, the base often undergoes considerable change, as in Greek (compare ἐχθίων, ἔχθιστος, from ἐχθρός); and its place is sometimes supplied by a substitute (compare βελτίων, βέλτιστος, from ἀγαθός). The following is a list of the substitutes:

POSITIVE.	SUBSTITUTE.	COMPARATIVE.	SUPERLATIVE.
अन्तिक *antika*, 'near'	नेद *neda*	नेदीयस्	नेदिष्ठ
अल्प *alpa*, 'little'	कण *kaṇa*	कणीयस्	कणिष्ठ
उरु *uru*, 'large'	वर *vara*	वरीयस्	वरिष्ठ (ἄριστο)
कृश *kriśa*, 'thin'	क्रश *kraśa*	क्रशीयस्	क्रशिष्ठ
क्षिप्र *kshipra*, 'quick'	क्षेप *kshepa*	क्षेपीयस्	क्षेपिष्ठ
क्षुद्र *kshudra*, 'small,' 'mean'	क्षोद *kshoda*	क्षोदीयस्	क्षोदिष्ठ
गुरु *guru*, 'heavy'	गर *gara*	गरीयस् (*gravius*)	गरिष्ठ
तृप्र *tripra*, 'satisfied'	त्रप *trapa*	त्रपीयस्	त्रपिष्ठ
दीर्घ *dírgha*, 'long'	द्राघ *drágha*	द्राघीयस्	द्राघिष्ठ
दूर *dúra*, 'distant'	दव *dava*	दवीयस्	दविष्ठ
दृढ *driḍha*, 'firm'	द्रढ *draḍha*	द्रढीयस्	द्रढिष्ठ
परिवृढ *parivriḍha*, 'excellent'	परिव्रढ *parivraḍha*	परिव्रढीयस्	परिव्रढिष्ठ
पृथु *prithu*, 'broad'	प्रथ *pratha*	प्रथीयस्	प्रथिष्ठ
प्रशस्य *praśasya*, 'good'	श्र * *śra*	श्रेयस्	श्रेष्ठ
	ज्या * *jyá*	ज्यायस्	ज्येष्ठ
प्रिय *priya*, 'dear'	प्र * *pra*	प्रेयस्	प्रेष्ठ
बहु *bahu*, 'much'	भू * *bhú*	भूयस्	भूयिष्ठ
बहुल *bahula*, 'much'	बंह *banha*	बंहीयस्	बंहिष्ठ
भृश *bhriśa*, 'excessive'	भ्रश *bhraśa*	भ्रशीयस्	भ्रशिष्ठ
मृदु *mridu*, 'soft'	म्रद *mrada*	म्रदीयस्	म्रदिष्ठ
युवन् *yuvan*, 'young'	यव *yava*	यवीयस्	यविष्ठ
वाढ *váḍha*, 'firm,' 'thick'	साध *sádha*	साधीयस्	साधिष्ठ
वृद्ध *vriddha*, 'old'	वर्ष *varsha*	वर्षीयस्	वर्षिष्ठ
	ज्या * *jyá*	ज्यायस्	ज्येष्ठ
वृन्दारक *vrindáraka*, 'excellent'	वृन्द *vrinda*	वृन्दीयस्	वृन्दिष्ठ
स्थिर *sthira*, 'firm,' 'stable'	स्थ *stha*	स्थेयस्	स्थेष्ठ
स्थूल *sthúla*, 'gross, 'bulky'	स्थव *sthava*	स्थवीयस्	स्थविष्ठ
स्फिर *sphira*, 'turgid'	स्फ *spha*	स्फेयस्	स्फेष्ठ
ह्रस्व *hraswa*, 'short'	ह्रस *hrasa*	ह्रसीयस्	ह्रसिष्ठ

* In the case of श्र and प्र the final vowel is not rejected, but combines with *íyas* and *ishṭha* agreeably to Sandhi. In ज्या and भू, *yas* is affixed in place of *íyas*.

N

195. Sometimes, but very rarely, degrees of comparison may be formed from feminine bases ending in the vowels ई *í* and ऊ *ú*, which may either be retained before *tara* and *tama*, or be shortened: thus, from सती, 'a faithful wife,' सतीतर, सतीतम or सतितर, सतितम.

196. *Tara* and *tama* may sometimes be added to inseparable prepositions; as, उत् 'up,' उत्तर 'higher,' उत्तम 'highest.' Compare in Latin *extimus*, *intimus*, &c.

a. They are sometimes added to pronominal bases (236), and to numerals (209, 211).

197. They may even be added, in conjunction with the syllable आं *ám*, to the inflexions of verbs; as, जल्पतितरां 'he talks more than he ought.'

SECTION IV.

NUMERAL ADJECTIVES.

CARDINALS.

198. The cardinals are, एक 1; द्वि 2; त्रि 3; चतुर् 4; पञ्चन् 5; षष् 6; सप्तन् 7; अष्टन् 8; नवन् 9; दशन् 10; एकादशन् 11; द्वादशन् 12; त्रयोदशन् 13; चतुर्दशन् 14; पञ्चदशन् 15; षोडशन् 16; सप्तदशन् 17; अष्टादशन् 18; नवदशन् or ऊनविंशति 19; विंशति 20; एकविंशति 21; द्वाविंशति 22; त्रयोविंशति 23; चतुर्विंशति 24; पञ्चविंशति 25; षड्विंशति 26; सप्तविंशति 27; अष्टाविंशति 28; नवविंशति or ऊनत्रिंशत् 29; त्रिंशत् 30; एकत्रिंशत् 31; द्वात्रिंशत् 32; त्रयस्त्रिंशत् 33; चतुस्त्रिंशत् 34; पञ्चत्रिंशत् 35; षट्त्रिंशत् 36; सप्तत्रिंशत् 37; अष्टात्रिंशत् 38; नवत्रिंशत् or ऊनचत्वारिंशत् 39; चत्वारिंशत् 40; एकचत्वारिंशत् 41; द्विचत्वारिंशत् or द्वाचत्वारिंशत् 42; त्रिचत्वारिंशत् or त्रयश्चत्वारिंशत् 43; चतुश्चत्वारिंशत् 44; पञ्चचत्वारिंशत् 45; षट्चत्वारिंशत् 46; सप्तचत्वारिंशत् 47; अष्टाचत्वारिंशत् or अष्टचत्वारिंशत् 48; नवचत्वारिंशत् or ऊनपञ्चाशत् 49; पञ्चाशत् 50; एकपञ्चाशत् 51; द्विपञ्चाशत् or द्वापञ्चाशत् 52; त्रिपञ्चाशत् or त्रयःपञ्चाशत् 53; चतुःपञ्चाशत् 54; पञ्चपञ्चाशत् 55; षट्पञ्चाशत् 56; सप्तपञ्चाशत् 57; अष्टपञ्चाशत् or अष्टापञ्चाशत् 58; नवपञ्चाशत् or ऊनषष्टि 59; षष्टि 60; एकषष्टि 61; द्विषष्टि or द्वाषष्टि 62; त्रिषष्टि or त्रयःषष्टि* 63; चतुःषष्टि* 64; पञ्चषष्टि 65; षट्षष्टि 66; सप्तषष्टि 67; अष्टषष्टि or अष्टाषष्टि 68; नवषष्टि or ऊनसप्तति 69; सप्तति 70; एकसप्तति 71; द्विसप्तति or द्वासप्तति 72; त्रिसप्तति or त्रयःसप्तति 73; चतुःसप्तति 74; पञ्चसप्तति 75; षट्सप्तति 76; सप्तसप्तति 77; अष्टसप्तति or अष्टासप्तति 78; नवसप्तति or ऊनाशीति 79; अशीति 80; एकाशीति 81; द्व्यशीति 82; त्र्यशीति 83; चतुरशीति 84; पञ्चाशीति 85; षडशीति 86; सप्ताशीति 87; अष्टाशीति 88; नवाशीति or ऊननवति 89; नवति 90; एकनवति 91; द्विनवति or द्वानवति 92;

* These may also be written त्रयष्षष्टि, चतुष्षष्टि. In fact, rules 62. *a.* and 63. apply equally to initial ष; but षष् and षष्टि, and their derivatives, are the only words beginning with ष ever likely to occur.

त्रिनवति or त्रयोनवति 93; चतुर्नवति 94; पञ्चनवति 95; षण्णवति 96; सप्तनवति 97; अष्टनवति or अष्टानवति 98; नवनवति or ऊनशत 99; शत n. or एकशत n. 100; सहस्र n. or एकसहस्र n. 1000.

199. The numbers between 100 and 1000, and those above 1000, are usually expressed by compounding the adjective अधिक *adhika*, 'more,' 'plus,' with the cardinal numbers: thus, 101 may be expressed by एकाधिकं शतं, i. e. 'a hundred plus one,' or more concisely एकाधिकशत, or even शताधिकैक. Similarly, द्व्यधिकं शतं or द्व्यधिकशत 102; त्र्यधिकं शतं or त्र्यधिकशत 103; त्रिंशदधिकशत 130; पञ्चाशदधिकशत or सार्द्धशत 150; द्विशत or द्वे शते N. du. neut. 200; षड्विंशत्यधिकद्विशत 226; त्रिशत or त्रीणि शतानि N. pl. neut. 300; त्र्यशीत्यधिकत्रिशत 383; चतुःशत or चत्वारि शतानि N. pl. 400; पञ्चाशीत्यधिकचतुःशत 485; पञ्चशत 500; षण्णवत्यधिकपञ्चशत 596; षट्शत 600; षट्षष्ट्यधिकषट्शत 666; सप्तशत 700; अष्टशत 800; नवशत 900; सहस्र or दशशत n. or दशशती 1000; षोडशशत or षट्शताधिकसहस्र 1600; षट्षष्ट्यधिकषोडशशत 1666.

a. The ordinals are sometimes joined to the cardinals to express 111 and upwards: thus, एकादशं शतं 111; विंशं सहस्रं 1020; त्रिंशं शतं 130, &c.

b. Single words are used for the highest numbers: thus, अयुत n. 'ten thousand;' लक्ष n. or लक्षा f. 'a lac,' 'one hundred thousand;' नियुत or प्रयुत m. n. 'one million;' कोटि f. 'a krore,' 'ten millions;' अर्बुद m. n. 'one hundred millions;' महार्बुद m. n. 'one thousand millions;' पद्म m. n. or अब्ज n. 'ten thousand millions;' महापद्म m. n. 'one hundred thousand millions;' खर्व m. n. 'a billion;' महाखर्व m. n. or शङ्कु m. 'ten billions;' शङ्ख m. n. or समुद्र m. 'a hundred billions;' महाशङ्ख 'a thousand billions;' हाहा m. or अन्त m. 'ten thousand billions;' महाहाहा m. or परार्द्ध m. 'one hundred thousand million;' धुन n. 'one million billion;' महाधुन n. 'ten million billion;' अक्षौहिणी f. 'one hundred million billion;' महाक्षौहिणी 'one thousand million billion.'

DECLENSION OF CARDINALS.

200. एक 1, द्वि 2 (*duo*, δύο), त्रि 3 (*tres*, τρεῖς, τρια), चतुर् 4 (*quatuor*), are declined in three genders.

एक *eka*, 'one' (singular only), follows the declension of pronominals (see 237): nom. m. *ekas;* dat. m. *ekasmai;* nom. f. *eká;* dat. f. *ekasyai;* nom. n. *ekam.* It may take the affixes *tara* and *tama:* thus, *ekatara*, 'one of two;' *ekatama*, 'one of many;' which also follow the declension of pronominals.

201. द्वि *dwi*, 'two' (dual only), is declined as if the base were द्व *dwa:* thus, N. Ac. V. m. द्वौ *dwau*, f. n. द्वे *dwe;* I. D. Ab. m. f. n. द्वाभ्यां; G. L. द्वयोस्.

202. त्रि *tri*, 'three' (plural only), is declined in the masculine like the plural of nouns whose bases end in इ *i* at 110, excepting in the gen.: thus, N.V. masc. त्रयस्; Ac. त्रीन्; I. त्रिभिस्; D. Ab. त्रिभ्यस्; G. त्रयाणां; L. त्रिषु. The feminine forms its cases from a base तिसृ: thus, N. Ac. V. fem. तिस्रस्; I. तिसृभिस्; D. Ab. तिसृभ्यस्; G. तिसृणां; L. तिसृषु. The N. Ac. neut. is त्रीणि; the rest as the masculine.

203. चतुर् *chatur*, 'four' (plural only), is thus declined: N.V. masc. चत्वारस् (τέτταρες, τέσσαρες); Ac. चतुरस्; I. चतुर्भिस्; D. Ab. चतुर्भ्यस्; G. चतुर्णां; L. चतुर्षु. N. Ac. V. fem. चतस्रस्; I. चतसृभिस्; D. Ab. चतसृभ्यस्; G. चतसृणां; L. चतसृषु. N. Ac. V. neut. चत्वारि; the rest as the masculine.

204. पञ्चन् *pañchan*, 'five' (plural only), is the same for masc., fem., and neut. It is declined after the analogy of nouns in *an* (147), excepting in N. Ac. The gen. lengthens the penultimate: thus, N. Ac. V. पञ्च (πέντε); I. पञ्चभिस्; D. Ab. पञ्चभ्यस्; G. पञ्चानां; L. पञ्चसु. Similarly are declined, सप्तन् 'seven' (*septem*, ἑπτά), नवन् 'nine' (*novem*), दशन् 'ten' (*decem*, δέκα), एकादशन् 'eleven' (*undecim*), द्वादशन् 'twelve' (*duodecim*), and all other numerals ending in *an*, excepting अष्टन् 'eight.'

205. षष् *shash*, 'six,' and अष्टन् *ashṭan*, 'eight,' are the same for masc., fem., and neut., and are thus declined: N. Ac.V. षट्; I. षड्भिस्; D. Ab. षड्भ्यस्; G. षण्णां *shaṇṇám*; L. षट्सु. N. Ac.V. अष्ट or अष्टौ (*octo*, ὀκτώ); I. अष्टभिस् or अष्टाभिस्; D. Ab. अष्टभ्यस् or अष्टाभ्यस्; G. अष्टानां; L. अष्टसु or अष्टासु.

206. All the remaining cardinal numbers, from ऊनविंशति 'nineteen' to शत 'a hundred,' and सहस्र 'a thousand,' are declined in the singular only, and are the same whether joined with masculine, feminine, or neuter nouns*. Those ending in ति *ti* are declined like the singular of the feminine noun मति *mati* at 112; and those in त् *t* are declined like the singular of सरित् *sarit* at 136: thus, विंशत्या पुरुषैः 'with twenty men;' त्रिंशता पुरुषैः 'with thirty men.' शत 'a hundred' and सहस्र 'a thousand' are neuter, and are declined like the neut. singular of शिव *śiva* at 103: thus, शतं पितरस् 'a hundred ancestors;' एकाधिकशतं

* Although these numerals, when joined with nouns, are declined in the singular, yet when used alone as substantives, to express more than one hundred, or more than one thousand, they may take a dual or plural; as, विंशती 'two twenties;' त्रिंशतौ 'two thirties;' त्रिंशतस् 'many thirties;' शते 'two hundred;' शतानि 'hundreds;' सहस्राणि 'many thousands.'

पितरस् 'a hundred and one ancestors;' सहस्रेण पितृभिस् 'with a thousand ancestors.'

207. The adjective ऊन 'less,' 'minus,' may be placed before a cardinal number, to denote one less than that number, एक 'one' being either expressed or understood: thus, ऊनविंशति or एकोनविंशति 'twenty minus one' or 'nineteen' (compare the Latin *undeviginti*, i. e. *unus de viginti*). And other cardinals, besides एक 'one,' are sometimes prefixed to ऊन, to denote that they are to be deducted from a following number; as, पञ्चोनं शतं or पञ्चोनशतं 'a hundred less five' or 'ninety-five.'

ORDINALS.

208. The ordinals are, प्रथम 'first'* (compare πρῶτος, *primus*); द्वितीय 'second' (δεύτερα); तृतीय 'third' (*tertia*); declined like pronominals at 237, or like *śiva* at 103.

209. चतुर्थ 'fourth'† (τέταρτος); पञ्चम 'fifth;' षष्ठ 'sixth;' सप्तम 'seventh' (*septimus*); अष्टम 'eighth;' नवम 'ninth' (*nonus*); दशम 'tenth' (*decimus*); declined like *śiva* at 103, 104, for the masc. and neut.; and like *nadí* at 106. for the feminine. In *saptama* and *ashṭama* the superlative affix (196. *a*) may be recognised.

210. The ordinals from 'eleventh' to 'twentieth' are formed from the cardinals by rejecting the final *n*: thus, from एकादशन् 'eleven,' एकादश 'eleventh' (Nom. m. f. n. एकादशस्, -शी, -शं, 103, 106, 104).

211. 'Twentieth,' 'thirtieth,' 'fortieth,' and 'fiftieth,' are formed either by adding the superlative affix *tama* (196. *a*) to the cardinal, or by rejecting the final of the cardinal; as, from विंशति 'twenty,' विंशतितम or विंश 'twentieth' (Nom. m. f. n. -मस्, -मी, -मं; -शस्, -शी, -शं, 103, 106, 104). Similarly, त्रिंशत्तम or त्रिंश 'thirtieth,' &c. The intermediate ordinals are formed by prefixing the numeral, as in the cardinals: thus, एकविंशतितम or एकविंश 'twenty-first,' &c.

a. Some grammarians admit a third form of ordinal, ending in *in*: thus, दशिन् 'tenth,' एकादशिन् 'eleventh,' विंशिन् 'twentieth,' त्रिंशिन् 'thirtieth,' चत्वारिंशिन् 'fortieth,' पञ्चाशिन् 'fiftieth.'

212. The other ordinals, from 'sixtieth' to 'ninetieth,' are formed by adding *tama*, or by changing *ti* to *ta*: thus, from षष्टि 'sixty,' षष्टितम or षष्ट 'sixtieth;' from नवति 'ninety,' नवतितम or नवत 'ninetieth.'

---

* Other adjectives may be used to express 'first;' as, आद्यः, -द्या, -द्यं; आदिमः, -मा, -मं; अग्रः, -ग्रा, -ग्रं; अग्रिमः, -मा, मं.

† तुरीयः, -या, -यं; तुर्यः, -र्या, -र्यं — are also used for 'fourth.'

213. 'Hundredth' and 'thousandth' are formed either by adding *tama* to शत and सहस्र, or simply by converting these ordinals into adjectives, declinable in three genders: thus, शततम or शत 'hundredth' (Nom. m. f. n. शततमस्, -मी, -मं; शतस्, -ती, -तं). Similarly, सहस्रतमस्, -मी, -मं, or सहस्रः, -स्री, -स्रं, 'thousandth.'

214. The aggregation of two or more numbers is expressed by modifications of the ordinal numbers: thus, द्वयं 'a duad,' त्रयं 'a triad,' चतुष्टयं 'the aggregate of four.'

215. There are a few adverbial numerals; as, सकृत् 'once,' द्विस् 'twice,' त्रिस् 'thrice,' चतुस् 'four times.' कृत्वस् may be added to cardinal numbers, with a similar signification; as, पञ्चकृत्वस् 'five times.' The neuter of the ordinals may be used adverbially; as, प्रथमं 'in the first place.'

216. *Numerical symbols.*

१	२	३	४	५	६	७	८	९	१०
1	2	3	4	5	6	7	8	9	10

CHAPTER V.

PRONOUNS.

FORMATION OF THE BASE.

217. PRONOUNS have no crude base analogous to that of nouns; that is, no state distinct from all inflexion, serving as the basis on which all the cases are constructed. The reason of this may be, that the pronouns in Sanskṛit, as in all languages, are so irregular and capricious in their formation, that no one base would be equally applicable to all the cases. Thus in the 1st personal pronoun, the base of the nom. sing. would be *ah*, while that of the oblique cases sing. would be *ma*. In the 2d, the base of the sing. is practically *twa*, while that of the dual and plural is *yu*. The 3d would have *sa* for the base of the nom. sing., and *ta* for the other cases.

The question then arises, What form of the pronoun is to be used in the formation of compound words? In the pronouns of the first and second persons, the ablative cases, singular and plural, and in the other pronouns, the nominative and accusative cases singular neuter, are considered as expressive of the most general and comprehensive state of the pronoun. These cases, therefore, discharge the office of a crude base in respect of compound words.

DECLENSION OF THE PERSONAL PRONOUNS.

Observe—In Sanskrit, as in other languages, to denote the general and indefinite character of the first two personal pronouns, no distinction of gender is admitted. For the same reason, the formation of the nom. case of pronouns is made to resemble the neuter, as the most general state. This may also be the reason why the 3d pronoun *sa* drops the *s* of the nom. case before all consonants.

218. मत् *mat* or अस्मत् *asmat*, 'I.'

N. अहं *aham*, 'I'	आवां *ávám*, 'we two'	वयं *vayam*, 'we'
Ac. मां *mám* or मा *má*, 'me'	— *ávám* or नौ *nau*, 'us two'	अस्मान् *asmán* or नस् *nas*, 'us'
I. मया *mayá*	आवाभ्यां *ávábhyám*	अस्माभिस् *asmábhis*
D. मह्यं *mahyam* or मे *me*	— *ávábhyám* or नौ *nau*	अस्मभ्यं *asmabhyam* or नस् *nas*
Ab. मत् *mat*	— *ávábhyám*	अस्मत् *asmat*
G. मम *mama* or मे *me*	आवयोस् *ávayos* or नौ *nau*	अस्माकं *asmákam* or नस् *nas*
L. मयि *mayi*	— *ávayos*	अस्मासु *asmásu*

219. त्वत् *twat* or युष्मत् *yushmat*, 'thou.'

N. त्वं *twam*, 'thou'	युवां *yuvám*, 'you two'	यूयं *yúyam*, 'you' or 'ye'
Ac. त्वां *twám* or त्वा *twá*	— *yuvám* or वां *vám*	युष्मान् *yushmán* or वस् *vas*
I. त्वया *twayá*	युवाभ्यां *yuvábhyám*	युष्माभिस् *yushmábhis*
D. तुभ्यं *tubhyam* or ते *te*	— *yuvábhyám* or वां *vám*	युष्मभ्यं *yushmabhyam* or वस् *vas*
Ab. त्वत् *twat*	— *yuvábhyám*	युष्मत् *yushmat*
G. तव *tava* or ते *te*	युवयोस् *yuvayos* or वां *vám*	युष्माकं *yushmákam* or वस् *vas*
L. त्वयि *twayi*	— *yuvayos*	युष्मासु *yushmásu*

220. तत् *tat* or तद् *tad*, 'he,' 'that.'

MASCULINE.

N. सस् *sas*, 'he'	तौ *tau*, 'they two'	ते *te*, 'they'
Ac. तं *tam*	— *tau*	तान् *tán*
I. तेन *tena*	ताभ्यां *tábhyám*	तैस् *tais* (τοῖς, ταῖς)
D. तस्मै *tasmai*	— *tábhyám*	तेभ्यस् *tebhyas*
Ab. तस्मात् *tasmát*	— *tábhyám*	— *tebhyas*
G. तस्य *tasya*	तयोस् *tayos*	तेषां *teshám*
L. तस्मिन् *tasmin*	— *tayos*	तेषु *teshu*

FEMININE.

N. सा *sá*, 'she'	ते *te*	तास् *tás*
Ac. तां *tám*	— *te*	— *tás*
I. तया *tayá*	ताभ्यां *tábhyám*	ताभिस् *tábhis*
D. तस्यै *tasyai*	— *tábhyám*	ताभ्यस् *tábhyas*

Ab. तस्यास् *tasyás*	ताभ्यां *tábhyám*	ताभ्यस् *tábhyas*
G. — *tasyás*	तयोस् *tayos*	तासां *tásám*
L. तस्यां *tasyám*	— *tayos*	तासु *tásu*

NEUTER.

N. Ac. तत् *tat*, ते *te*, तानि *táni*; the rest like the masculine. Compare the Greek article with the above pronoun.

a. The above pronoun *tat* is sometimes used *emphatically* with the other pronouns, like *ille* and *ipse*: thus, सोऽहं '*ille ego*;' ते वयं '*illi nos*;' स त्वं '*ille tu*;' ते यूयं '*illi vos*;' स एषः '*ille ipse*;' तद् एतत् '*id ipsum*.'

221. There is a modification of the pronoun *tat* (rarely used), formed by inserting *y*: thus, N. स्यस्, त्यौ, त्ये.

a. Observe the resemblance of the Sanskrit personal pronouns to those of the dead and living cognate languages. *Aham* or *ah* is the Greek ἐγώ (Æolic ἐγών), Latin *ego*, German *ich*, English 'I:' *mám* or *má* (the latter being the original form found in the Vedas) equals ἐμέ, *me*; *mahyam* = *mihi*; *mayi* = *mei*: the *mat* of the abl. sing. and of *asmat*, *yushmat*, corresponds to the Latin *met* in *memet*, *nosmet*, &c.: *vayam* or *va* is the English 'we;' *asmán* = *us*; *nas* = *nos*; *twam* = *tu*, 'thou;' *twám* or *twá* = *te*, 'thee;' *tubhyam* = *tibi*; *twayi* = *tui*; *yúyam* = ὑμεῖς, English 'you;' *vas* = *vos*. The 3d personal pronoun corresponds to the Greek article: thus, *tau* = τώ, *tam* = τόν; *tábhyám* = τοῖν, ταῖν; *tais* = τοῖς, ταῖς, &c.

REFLEXIVE PERSONAL PRONOUNS.

222. The oblique cases of आत्मन् *átman*, 'soul,' 'self' (declined at 147) are used reflexively, in place of the three personal pronouns, like the Latin *ipse*.

Thus, *átmánam* (*me ipsum*) *anáhárena hanishyámi*, 'I will kill myself by fasting;' *átmánam* (*te ipsum*) *mritavad darśaya*, 'show thyself as if dead;' *átmánam* (*se ipsum*) *nindati*, 'he blames himself.'

DEMONSTRATIVE PERSONAL PRONOUNS.

223. The third personal pronoun तत् *tat*, 'he,' declined above at 220, is constantly used in a demonstrative sense, to signify 'that' or 'this;' and by prefixing ए *e* to it, another common pronoun is formed, more proximately demonstrative: thus, एतत् *etat* or एतद् *etad*, 'this.' Observe—The first *t* of *etat* may optionally be changed to *n* in the Ac. sing. du. pl., I. sing., G. du., in all three genders: thus,

एतत् *etat* or एतद् *etad*, 'this.'

MASCULINE.

N. एषस् *eshas*. 70.	एतौ *etau*	एते *ete*
Ac. एतं *etam* or एनं *enam*	— *etau* or एनौ *enau*	एतान् *etán* or एनान् *enán*

I.	एतेन *etena* or एनेन *enena*	एताभ्यां *etábhyám*	एतैस् *etais*
D.	एतस्मै *etasmai*	— *etábhyám*	एतेभ्यस् *etebhyas*
Ab.	एतस्मात् *etasmát*	— *etábhyám*	— *etebhyas*
G.	एतस्य *etasya*	एतयोस् *etayos* or एनयोस् *enayos*	एतेषां *eteshám*
L.	एतस्मिन् *etasmin*	— *etayos* or — *enayos*	एतेषु *eteshu*

The feminine is N. एषा *eshá*, एते *ete*, एतास् *etás*; Ac. एतां or एनां, एते or एने, एतास् or एनास्; I. एतया or एनया, एताभ्यां, एताभिस्; D. एतस्यै, &c.

The neuter is N. एतत्, एते, एतानि; Ac. एतत् or एनत्, एते or एने, एतानि or एनानि, &c.

With the above pronoun compare the Latin *iste, ista, istud*: *etam* = *istum*, *etasya* = *istius*, *etat* = *istud*.

224. There is another common demonstrative pronoun, of which इदं *idam*, 'this,' the N. neuter, is considered to be the base (compare the Latin *is, ea, id*). The true base, however, might rather be said to be the vowel इ *i*, which serves also as the source of certain pronominals, such as इतर, ईदृश, इयत्. See 234, 236, and 234. *b*.

MASCULINE.

N.	अयं *ayam*, 'this'	इमौ *imau*, 'these two'	इमे *ime*, 'these'
Ac.	इमं *imam*	— *imau*	इमान् *imán*
I.	अनेन *anena*	आभ्यां *ábhyám*	एभिस् *ebhis**
D.	अस्मै *asmai*	— *ábhyám*	एभ्यस् *ebhyas*
Ab.	अस्मात् *asmát*	— *ábhyám*	— *ebhyas*
G.	अस्य *asya*	अनयोस् *anayos*	एषां *eshám*
L.	अस्मिन् *asmin*	— *anayos*	एषु *eshu*

FEMININE.

N.	इयं *iyam*	इमे *ime*	इमास् *imás*
Ac.	इमां *imám*	— *ime*	— *imás*
I.	अनया *anayá*	आभ्यां *ábhyám*	आभिस् *ábhis*
D.	अस्यै *asyai*	— *ábhyám*	आभ्यस् *ábhyas*
Ab.	अस्यास् *asyás*	— *ábhyám*	— *ábhyas*
G.	— *asyás*	अनयोस् *anayos*	आसां *ásám*
L.	अस्यां *asyám*	— *anayos*	आसु *ásu*

NEUTER.

N. Ac.	इदं *idam*	इमे *ime*	इमानि *imáni*

* This is an example of the old form for the instr. pl. of masculine nouns of the first class, preserved in the Vedas.

225. There is another demonstrative pronoun (rarely used, excepting in nom. sing.), of which अदस्, 'this' or 'that,' is taken as the base, though the true base is अमु *amu*, and in N. sing. असु *asu*. It is thus declined: Masc. N. असौ, अमू, अमी; Ac. अमुं, अमू, अमून्; I. अमुना, अमूभ्यां, अमीभिस्; D. अमुष्मै, अमूभ्यां, अमीभ्यस्; Ab. अमुष्मात्, अमूभ्यां, अमीभ्यस्; G. अमुष्य, अमुयोस्, अमीषां; L. अमुष्मिन्, अमुयोस्, अमीषु. Fem. N. असौ, अमू, अमूस्; Ac. अमूं, अमू, अमूस्; I. अमुया, अमूभ्यां, अमूभिस्; D. अमुष्यै, अमूभ्यां, अमूभ्यस्; Ab. अमुष्यास्, &c.; G. अमुष्यास्, अमुयोस्, अमूषां; L. अमुष्यां, अमुयोस्, अमूषु. Neut. N. Ac. अदस्, अमू, अमूनि.

RELATIVE PRONOUN.

226. The relative is formed by substituting य *y* for the initial letter of the pronoun *tat*, at 220: thus,

यत् *yat* or यद् *yad*, 'who,' 'which.'

MASCULINE.

N.	यस् *yas*	यौ *yau*	ये *ye*, 'who' or 'which'
Ac.	यं *yam*	— *yau*	यान् *yán*
I.	येन *yena*	याभ्यां *yábhyám*	यैस् *yais*
D.	यस्मै *yasmai*	— *yábhyám*	येभ्यस् *yebhyas*
Ab.	यस्मात् *yasmát*	— *yábhyám*	— *yebhyas*
G.	यस्य *yasya*	ययोस् *yayos*	येषां *yeshám*
L.	यस्मिन् *yasmin*	— *yayos*	येषु *yeshu*

The feminine and neuter follow the fem. and neut. of *tat*, at 220. Fem. N. या *yá*, ये *ye*, यास् *yás*; Ac. यां *yám*, &c. &c. Neut. N. Ac. यत् *yat*, ये *ye*, यानि *yáni*; the rest like the masculine.

With the above pronoun compare the Greek relative ὅς, ἥ, ὅ; the Sanskṛit *y* being often represented in Greek words by the *spiritus asper*.

INTERROGATIVE PRONOUNS.

227. The interrogative differs from the relative by substituting *k* instead of *y* for the initial letter of the pronoun *tat*, at 220: thus, Masc. N. कस् *kas*, कौ *kau*, के *ke*, 'who?' 'which?' 'what?' Ac. कं *kam*, 'whom?' &c. Fem. N. का *ká*, के *ke*, कास् *kás*, &c. The N. Ac. Neut. are किं *kim*, के *ke*, कानि *káni*, not *kat* *, *ke*, *káni*. *Kim* is also taken for the base, and occurs in a few compounds; such as किमर्थं 'on what account?' 'why?'

---

* *Kat*, however (= Latin *quod*), was the old form, and is retained in a few words; such as *kachchit*, 'perhaps;' *kadartha*, 'useless' ('of what use?'); *kadadhwan*, 'a bad road' ('what sort of a road?').

a. The true base, however, is *ka*; and to this may be affixed *ti*, to form कति *kati*, 'how many?' (*quot*). The same affix is added to *ta*, the proper base of the third personal pronoun, to form *tati*, 'so many' (*tot*). The Latin *quot* and *tot*, which drop the final *i*, take it again in composition; as, *quotidie*, *totidem*, &c.

INDEFINITE PRONOUNS.

228. The indeclinable affixes *chit*, *api*, and *chana*, affixed (in accordance with the rules of Sandhi) to the several cases of the interrogative pronouns, give them an indefinite signification; as, कश्चित् *kaśchit*, 'somebody,' 'some one,' 'any one,' 'a certain one:' thus declined:

MASCULINE.

N.	कश्चित् *kaśchit*. 62.	कौचित् *kauchit*	केचित् *kechit*, 'some persons'
Ac.	कञ्चित् *kañchit*. 59.	— *kauchit*	कांश्चित् *kánśchit*. 53.
I.	केनचित् *kenachit*	काभ्याञ्चित् *kábhyáñchit*	कैश्चित् *kaiśchit*. 62.
D.	कस्मैचित् *kasmaichit*	— *kábhyáñchit*	केभ्यश्चित् *kebhyaśchit*
Ab.	कस्माच्चित् *kasmáchchit*	— *kábhyáñchit*	— *kebhyaśchit*
G.	कस्यचित् *kasyachit*	कयोश्चित् *kayośchit*	केषाञ्चित् *kesháñchit*
L.	कस्मिंश्चित् *kasminśchit*	— *kayośchit*	केषुचित् *keshuchit*

Similarly, Fem. Nom. काचित्, केचित्, काश्चित्; Ac. काञ्चित्, &c.: and Neut. Nom. Ac. किञ्चित् 'something,' 'any thing,' केचित्, कानिचित्, &c.

229. So also by affixing अपि; as, Masc. Nom. कोऽपि (64. *a*) 'some one,' 'a certain one,' कावपि, केऽपि (37, 35); Ac. कमपि, &c.; I. केनापि, &c. (31); D. कस्मायपि, &c. (37); Ab. कस्मादपि, &c.; G. कस्यापि, &c.; L. कस्मिन्नपि, &c. (52). Fem. Nom. कापि, &c.; Ac. कामपि, &c.; I. कयापि, &c. &c. Neut. Nom. किमपि 'something,' 'any thing,' &c. The affix *chana* is rarely found, excepting in the Masc. Nom. कश्चन 'some one,' 'any one;' and in the Neut. Nom. किञ्चन 'something.'

230. In the same way interrogative adverbs are made indefinite: thus, from *kati*, 'how many?' *katichit*, 'a few;' from *kadá*, 'when?' *kadáchit*, 'at some time;' from *katham*, 'how?' *kathañchana*, 'some how.'

POSSESSIVE PRONOUNS.

231. These are formed by affixing *íya* (80. XV) to those cases of the personal pronouns, ending in *t*, which are used for crude bases: thus, from मत् and अस्मत् 'I,' मदीय *madíya* (45), 'mine,' and अस्मदीय *asmadíya*, 'our;' from त्वत् 'thou,' त्वदीय *twadíya*, 'thine;' from तद् 'he,' तदीय *tadíya*, 'his.' They are declined like nouns of the first class at 103.

Observe, however, that the genitive case of the personal pronouns is more usually used for the possessive: thus, तस्य पुत्रः 'his son;' मम पुत्री 'my daughter.'

REFLEXIVE OR POSSESSIVE PRONOUNS.

232. स्व *swa* (*suus*) is used reflexively, in reference to all three persons, and may stand for 'my own' (*meus*), 'thy own' (*tuus*), 'his own,' 'our own,' &c. (compare σφός, σφή, σφόν). It often occupies the first place in a compound: thus, स्वगृहं गच्छति 'he goes to his own house.' The gen. case of आत्मन् *átman* at 147, or often the crude base, is used with the same signification; as, आत्मनो गृहं or आत्मगृहं गच्छति *. In modern Sanskrit, निज *nija* is often used in place of स्व and आत्म. स्व is declined like *tat* at 220; but the Ab. L. sing. masc. neut. and N. pl. masc. may follow *śiva* at 103.

HONORIFIC OR RESPECTFUL PRONOUN.

233. भवत् *bhavat*, 'your honour,' requiring the 3d person of the verb, is declined like *dhanavat* at 140: thus, N. masc. भवान् *bhaván*, भवन्तौ *bhavantau*, भवन्तस् *bhavantas;* N. fem. भवती *bhavatí*, भवत्यौ *bhavatyau*, भवत्यस् *bhavatyas*, &c.; Voc. भवति (140. *b*). It is constantly used in place of the 2d personal pronoun: thus, भवान् गृहं गच्छतु 'Let your honour go home' for 'Go thou home.'

DERIVATIVE PRONOUNS OF QUANTITY AND SIMILITUDE.

234. Modifications of the demonstrative, relative, and interrogative pronouns may take the affix वत् *vat* to express 'quantity,' and the affix दृश *dṛiśa* or दृश् *dṛiś*† to express 'similitude:' thus, तावत् *távat*, एतावत् *etávat*, 'so many,' 'so much' (*tantus*); यावत् (*quantus*) 'as many,' 'as much' (declined like *dhanavat* at 140); तादृश *tádṛiśa* or तादृश् *tádṛiś*, 'such like' (*talis*, τηλίκος); एतादृश *etádṛiśa* or एतादृश् *etádṛiś*, 'like this or that' (following *śiva*, at 103, for the masc. and neut.; *nadí*, at 106, for the fem. of those ending in श *śa;* and *diś*, at 181, for the masc. fem. neut. of those in श् *ś*). Similarly, यादृश or यादृश् 'as like,' 'how like?' (*qualis*, ἡλίκος); ईदृश or ईदृश् 'so like;' कीदृश or कीदृश् 'how like?' (*qualis?*).

a. Note, that the affix दृश is derived from the root *dṛiś*, 'to see,' 'appear,' and is in fact our English 'like,' *d* being interchangeable with *l*, and *ś* with *k*.

b. कियत् 'how much,' 'how many,' and इयत् 'so much,' are declined like भवत् at 233.

'WHOSOEVER,' 'WHATSOEVER.'

235. Expressed by prefixing the relative to the interrogative: thus, यः कश्चित् 'whosoever,' यत् किञ्चित् 'whatsoever:' or by repeating the relative; as, यो यः, यद् यद्.

---

* Prof. Lassen cites an example from the Rámáyana, in which *átman* refers to the dual: *Putram átmanah sprishṭwá nipetatuh*, 'They two fell down after touching their son.' Anthol. p. 171.

† दृक्ष *dṛiksha*, declined like *śiva* (103), is also used.

PRONOMINALS.

236. There are certain common adjectives which partake of the nature of pronouns, and follow the declension of *tat* at 220.

These are, अन्य 'other,' 'another;' इतर 'other' (cf. Latin *iterum*); अन्यतर 'one of two;' एकतर 'one of two' (ἑκάτερος); एकतम 'one of many;' कतर 'which of the two?' (πότερος for κότερος); कतम 'which of many?' ततर 'that one of two;' ततम 'that one of many;' यतर 'who or which of two;' यतम 'who or which of many.' The above are mostly formed by adding the comparative and superlative affixes to pronominal bases (196. *a*). They are declined like तत् throughout, and make the N. Ac. neut. sing. in *at*.

237. There are others, however, which make *am* instead of *at* in the N. Ac. neuter. The model of these is सर्व *sarva*, 'all:' thus, Masc. N. सर्वस् *sarvas*, सर्वौ *sarvau*, सर्वे *sarve;* Ac. सर्वं *sarvam*, सर्वौ *sarvau*, सर्वान् *sarván;* I. सर्वेण, &c.; D. सर्वस्मै, &c.; Ab. सर्वस्मात्, &c.; G. सर्वस्य *sarvasya*, सर्वयोस् *sarvayos*, सर्वेषां *sarveshám;* L. सर्वस्मिन्, &c. Fem. N. सर्वा *sarvá*, सर्वे *sarve*, सर्वास् *sarvás*, &c. (220). Neut. N. Ac. सर्वं *sarvam*, सर्वे *sarve*, सर्वाणि *sarváṇi*.

238. Like *sarva* are declined उभय 'both' (no sing.); विश्व 'all;' नेम 'half;' अधर 'inferior;' पर 'other;' अपर 'other;' अवर 'posterior;' उत्तर 'superior,' 'north;' दक्षिण 'south,' 'right;' पूर्व 'east,' 'prior;' एक 'one;' अन्तर 'other:' but (with the exception of the first three) these may optionally follow *śiva*, at 103, in the abl. loc. sing. masc. and neut., and the nom. pl. masc.; as, अधरस्मात् or अधरात्, &c.

239. द्वितीय 'second,' तृतीय 'third,' may either follow *sarva* at 237, or *śiva* at 103, and make their feminine in *á*.

240. अल्प 'a few,' अर्द्ध 'half,' कतिपय 'how few?' 'few,' प्रथम 'first,' generally follow *śiva* at 103; but may make their nom. plur. in *e;* as, अल्पे 'few.' उभ, 'both' (*ambo*, ἄμφω), is declined only in the dual; उभौ, उभाभ्यां, उभयोस्.

CHAPTER VI.

VERBS.

GENERAL OBSERVATIONS.

241. ALTHOUGH the Sanskṛit verb offers the most striking and interesting analogies to the Greek, nevertheless so peculiar and artificial is the process by which it is formed, that it would be impossible, in treating of it, to adopt an arrangement which would be likely to fall in with the preconceived notions of the classical student.

There are ten tenses. Seven of them are of common occurrence; viz. 1. the present, 2. the potential, 3. the imperative, 4. the first preterite, 5. the second preterite, 6. the first future, 7. the second future. Three are of rare occurrence; viz. 8. the third preterite, 9. the benedictive, 10. the conditional. There is also an infinitive mood, and several participles. Of these tenses, the present, the three preterites, and the two futures, belong properly to the indicative mood; and the imperative, potential, benedictive, and conditional, are more properly moods than tenses. Since, however, these latter moods do not comprehend other tenses under them, but are susceptible of all times, present, past, and future, it can lead to no embarrassment to consider them as tenses, and to arrange them indiscriminately with the tenses of the indicative. Four of the tenses, viz. the present, potential, imperative, and first preterite, are called *conjugational tenses*, and are placed first in order, because to them alone (as will be hereafter explained at 248) the rules of conjugation have reference.

242. Although the three preterites are used without much distinction, yet it should be observed, that they properly express different degrees of past time. The first preterite corresponds in form to the imperfect of Greek and Latin verbs, and properly has reference to an event doing at some time past, and not ended: it is often, however, used like the Greek aorist. The second preterite is said to have reference to an event done and past at some definite period: it answers in form to the Greek perfect, but may also be used like the aorist. The third preterite refers to an event done and past at some indefinite period: it corresponds in form and sense to the Greek 1st and 2d aorist *. So also, the two futures properly express, the first definite, the second indefinite futurity: the second, however, is the most used, and answers to the Greek future. The potential may generally be rendered in English by some one of the auxiliaries, 'may,' 'can,' 'would,' 'should,' 'ought.' The conditional is used after the conjunction *yadi*, 'if:' it occurs, however, but very rarely, and the potential usually supplies its place in conditional sentences. The benedictive or precative is a tense sometimes used in praying and blessing. There is no pluperfect in Sanskṛit: the sense of this tense is expressed by the indeclinable participle or by the locative absolute; as, *tasminn apakránte*, 'after he had departed.' See Syntax.

* The fact is, that neither one of the three perfects is very commonly used to represent the completeness of an action. This is generally done by employing the passive participle with an instr. case; or by adding *vat* to the pass. part., and combining it with the present tense of *as*, 'to be;' as, *uktaván asmi*, 'I have said.' See Syntax.

The infinitive mood generally has an active, but is capable of a passive signification.

243. Every tense has three numbers, singular, dual, and plural.

To each tense belong two sets of terminations; one for the active or transitive voice, the other for the reflexive voice. The former of these voices is called by Indian grammarians *Parasmai-pada* ('words for another'), because the action is supposed to pass *parasmai*, 'to another;' the latter is called *A'tmane-pada* ('words for oneself'), because the action is supposed to revert *átmane*, 'to oneself.' This distinction, however, is rarely observed, and we find verbs, transitive or intransitive, conjugated indifferently in the Parasmai-pada or A'tmane-pada or both. Some verbs, however, are conjugated only in the A'tmane, and are restricted to either a neuter or reflexive signification; or sometimes, when a verb takes both voices, the A'tmane may yield its appropriate meaning, and give a sense directing the action in some way towards the agent*. Thus, *dá*, 'to give,' with the preposition *á*, 'to,' prefixed, when conjugated in the A'tmane-pada, means 'to give to oneself,' 'to take;' the causal verb *darśayati*, 'he shows,' becomes in the A'tmane *darśayate*, 'he shows himself,' 'appears;' the roots *mud* and *ruch*, meaning 'to be pleased,' 'please oneself,' are confined to the A'tmane; and *yách*, 'to ask,' although possessing both voices, is more commonly used in the reflexive, the act of asking generally tending to the advantage of the asker.

a. Passive verbs are invariably conjugated in the A'tmane-pada. Indeed, in all the tenses, excepting the first four, the passive is generally undistinguishable from the A'tmane-pada of the primitive verb. But in the present, potential, imperative, and first preterite (unlike the Greek, which exhibits a perfect identity between the middle and passive voices in those tenses), the Sanskṛit passive, although still employing the A'tmane-pada terminations, has a special

---

* In Sanskṛit grammar, the term *voice* has reference to the scheme of terminations; so that there are only two voices in Sanskṛit, and they are used indiscriminately. Although the A'tmane-pada, in a few instances, has a middle sense, yet it cannot be said to correspond entirely with the Greek middle voice, the characteristic of which is that it takes a middle inflection, partly active, partly passive. The passive is a distinct derivative from the root, using the A'tmane terminations.

structure of its own, common to all verbs, and distinct from the conjugational form of the A'tmane-pada. Thus the Greek *ἀκούω* makes for both the middle and passive of those four tenses, 1st sing. *ἀκούομαι, ἀκουοίμην, ἀκούου, ἠκουόμην*. But the Sanskrit *śru*, 'to hear,' makes for the conjugational form of the A'tmane, शृण्वे, शृण्वीय, शृणवै, अशृण्वि; while for the passive it is श्रूये, श्रूयेय, श्रूयै, अश्रूये. Compare 253, and see Bopp's Comparative Grammar, Eastwick, 426, 733.

244. As in nouns the formation of an inflective base out of a root precedes the subject of declension, the root requiring some change or addition before the case-terminations can be affixed; so in verbs the formation of a verbal base out of a root must be antecedent to conjugation. Again, as in nouns every case has its own termination, so in verbs each of the three persons, in the three numbers of every tense, has a termination (one for the Parasmai-pada, and one for the A'tmane-pada) which is peculiarly its own. Moreover, as in nouns, so in verbs, some of the terminations may be combined with memorial letters, which serve to aid the memory, by indicating that where they occur peculiar changes are required in the root. Thus the three terminations which belong to the 1st, 2d, and 3d persons of the present tense, Parasmai-pada, respectively, are *mi, si, ti*; and these are combined with the letter P (thus, *mi* P, *si* P, *ti* P), to indicate that the roots of certain verbs must be modified in a particular way, before these terminations are affixed.

245. The annexed tables exhibit, 1st, the memorial scheme of terminations for Parasmai and A'tmane-pada, in all the tenses (the four conjugational being placed first); and 2dly, the same scheme without the memorial letters. Since, however, a very large number of roots require changes in the terminations of some of the tenses, it will be convenient, in the second table, to indicate the conjugations in which these changes occur.

246. *Terminations with memorial letters.*

PARASMAI-PADA. A'TMANE-PADA.

Present tense.

PERS.	SING.	DUAL.	PLURAL.	SING.	DUAL.	PLURAL.
1.	मिप् *mi* P	वस् *vas*	मस् *mas*	ए *e*	वहे *vahe*	महे *mahe*
2.	सिप् *si* P	थस् *thas*	थ *tha*	से *se*	आथे *áthe*	ध्वे *dhwe*
3.	तिप् *ti* P	तस् *tas*	अन्ति *anti*	ते *te*	आते *áte*	अन्ते *ante*

Potential.

1. याम् *yám*	याव *yáva*	याम *yáma*	ईय *íya*	ईवहि *ívahi*	ईमहि *ímahi*
2. यास् *yás*	यातम् *yátam*	यात *yáta*	ईथास् *íthás*	ईयाथाम् *íyáthám*	ईध्वम् *ídhwam*
3. यात् *yát*	याताम् *yátám*	युस् *yus*	ईत *íta*	ईयाताम् *íyátám*	ईरन् *íran*

Imperative.

1. आनिप् *ániP*	आवप् *ávaP*	आमप् *ámaP*	ऐप् *aiP*	आवहैप् *ávahaiP*	आमहैप् *ámahaiP*
2. हि *hi*	तम् *tam*	त *ta*	स्व *swa*	आथाम् *áthám*	ध्वम् *dhwam*
3. तुप् *tuP*	ताम् *tám*	अन्तु *antu*	तां *tám*	आताम् *átám*	अन्ताम् *antám*

First preterite or *imperfect* (requiring the augment *a*).

1. अमिप् *amiP*	व *va*	म *ma*	इ *i*	वहि *vahi*	महि *mahi*
2. सिप् *siP*	तम् *tam*	त *ta*	थास् *thás*	आथाम् *áthám*	ध्वम् *dhwam*
3. दिप् *diP*	ताम् *tám*	अन् *an*	तन् *tan*	आताम् *átám*	अन्त *anta*

Second preterite or *perfect.*

1. णप् *ṇaP*	व *va*	म *ma*	ए *e*	वहे *vahe*	महे *mahe*
2. थप् *thaP*	अथुस् *athus*	अ *a*	से *se*	आथे *áthe*	ध्वे *dhwe*
3. णप् *ṇaP*	अतुस् *atus*	उस् *us*	ए *e*	आते *áte*	इरे *ire*

First future.

1. तास्मि *tásmi*	तास्वस् *táswas*	तास्मस् *tásmas*	ताहे *táhe*	तास्वहे *táswahe*	तास्महे *tásmahe*
2. तासि *tási*	तास्थस् *tásthas*	तास्थ *tástha*	तासे *táse*	तासाथे *tásáthe*	ताध्वे *tádhwe*
3. ता *tá*	तारौ *tárau*	तारस् *táras*	ता *tá*	तारौ *tárau*	तारस् *táras*

Second future.

1. स्यामिप् *syámip*	स्यावस् *syávas*	स्यामस् *syámas*	स्ये *sye*	स्यावहे *syávahe*	स्यामहे *syámahe*
2. स्यसिप् *syasip*	स्यथस् *syathas*	स्यथ *syatha*	स्यसे *syase*	स्येथे *syethe*	स्यध्वे *syadhwe*
3. स्यतिप् *syatip*	स्यतस् *syatas*	स्यन्ति *syanti*	स्यते *syate*	स्येते *syete*	स्यन्ते *syante*

Third preterite or *aorist* (requiring the augment *a*).

1. सम् *sam*	स्व *swa*	स्म *sma*	सि *si*	स्वहि *swahi*	स्महि *smahi*
2. सीस् *sís*	स्तम् *stam*	स्त *sta*	स्थास् *sthás*	साथाम् *sáthám*	ध्वम् *dhwam*
3. सीत् *sít*	स्ताम् *stám*	सुस् *sus*	स्त *sta*	साताम् *sátám*	सत *sata*

Benedictive.

1. यासम् *yásam*	यास्व *yáswa*	यास्म *yásma*	सीय *síya*	सीवहि *sívahi*	सीमहि *símahi*
2. यास् *yás*	यास्तम् *yástam*	यास्त *yásta*	सीष्ठास् *síshṭhás*	सीयास्थाम् *síyásthám*	सीध्वम् *sídhwam*
3. यात् *yát*	यास्ताम् *yástám*	यासुस् *yásus*	सीष्ट *síshṭa*	सीयास्ताम् *síyástám*	सीरन् *síran*

Conditional (requiring the augment *a*).

1. स्यम् *syam*	स्याव *syáva*	स्याम *syáma*	स्ये *sye*	स्यावहि *syávahi*	स्यामहि *syámahi*
2. स्यस् *syas*	स्यतम् *syatam*	स्यत *syata*	स्यथास् *syathás*	स्येथाम् *syethám*	स्यध्वम् *syadhwam*
3. स्यत् *syat*	स्यताम् *syatám*	स्यन् *syan*	स्यत *syata*	स्येताम् *syetám*	स्यन्त *syanta*

247. *The same terminations without memorial letters.*

PARASMAI-PADA. ÁTMANE-PADA.

Present tense.

PERS.	SING.	DUAL.	PLURAL.	SING.	DUAL.	PLURAL.
1.	मि	वस्	मस्	इ 1,4,6,10. ए 2, 3, &c.	वहे	महे
2.	सि or षि	थस्	थ	से or षे	इथे 1,4,6,10. आथे 2,3,7,5,8,9.	ध्वे
3.	ति	तस्	न्ति 1, 4, 6, 10. अन्ति 2,7,5,8,9. अति 3.	ते	इते 1, 4, 6, 10. आते	न्ते 1, 4, 6, 10. अते 2,3,7,5,8,9.

Potential.

In 1, 4, 6, 10.

PERS.	SING.	DUAL.	PLURAL.
1.	इयं	इव	इम
2.	इस्	इतं	इत
3.	इत्	इतां	इयुस्

In 2, 3, 7, 5, 8, 9.

PERS.	SING.	DUAL.	PLURAL.
1.	यां	याव	याम
2.	यास्	यातं	यात
3.	यात्	यातां	युस्

In all the conjugations.

PERS.	SING.	DUAL.	PLURAL.
1.	ईय	ईवहि	ईमहि
2.	ईथास्	ईयाथां	ईध्वं
3.	ईत	ईयातां	ईरन्

Imperative.

PERS.	SING.	DUAL.	PLURAL.	SING.	DUAL.	PLURAL.
1.	आनि	आव	आम	ऐ	आवहै	आमहै
2.	—1,4,6,10,5. हि 2,3,7,5,8,9. धि 2, 3, 7.	तं	त	स्व or ष्व	इथां 1, 4, 6, 10. आथां 2,3,7,5,8,9.	ध्वं
3.	तु	तां	न्तु 1,4,6,10. अन्तु 2,7,5,8,9. अतु 3.	तां	इतां 1, 4, 6, 10. आतां 2,3,7,5,8,9.	न्तां 1, 4, 6, 10. अतां 2,3,7,5,8,9.

In 9, *ána* is substituted for the *hi* of the 2d sing. after roots ending in consonants. A form तात् *tát* (cf. Latin *to*, Greek τω) may be substituted for *hi* and *tu*, and even for *ta*, to imply benediction, chiefly used in the Vedas.

First preterite (requiring the augment *a*).

PERS.	SING.	DUAL.	PLURAL.	SING.	DUAL.	PLURAL.
1.	म् 1,4,6,10. अं 2,3,7,5,8,9.	व	म	इ	वहि	महि
2.	स्	तं	त	थास्	इथां 1, 4, 6, 10. आथां 2,3,7,5,8,9.	ध्वं
3.	त्	तां	न् 1, 4, 6, 10. अन् 2,7,5,8,9. उस् 3.	त	इतां 1, 4, 6, 10. आतां 2,3,7,5,8,9.	न्त 1, 4, 6, 10. अत 2,3,7,5,8,9.

Second preterite.

1.	अ	*इव	*इम	ए	*इवहे	*इमहे
2.	इथ or थ	अथुस्	अ	*इषे	आथे	*इध्वे or *इढ्वे
3.	अ	अतुस्	उस्	ए	आते	इरे

* Only eight roots, viz. श्रु, स्तु, द्रु, स्रु, कृ, भृ, सृ, वृ, reject the initial *i* from the terminations marked with *; and of these eight all but स्तु and वृ reject it also in the 2d sing. The termination इढ्वे in the 2d plural, Átmane-pada, is especially applicable to roots ending in vowels, but is admissible for all others.

First future.

1.	तास्मि	तास्वस्	तास्मस्	ताहे	तास्वहे	तास्महे
2.	तासि	तास्थस्	तास्थ	तासे	तासाथे	ताध्वे
3.	ता	तारौ	तारस्	ता	तारौ	तारस्

Many roots prefix *i* to the terminations of the above tense throughout: thus. 1. इतास्मि *itásmi*, 2. इतासि *itási*, &c.

Second future.

1.	स्यामि	स्यावस्	स्यामस्	स्ये	स्यावहे	स्यामहे
2.	स्यसि	स्यथस्	स्यथ	स्यसे	स्येथे	स्यध्वे
3.	स्यति	स्यतस्	स्यन्ति	स्यते	स्येते	स्यन्ते

Many roots prefix *i* to the terminations of the above tense throughout: thus, 1. इष्यामि *ishyámi*, 2. इष्यसि *ishyasi*, &c.

Third preterite (requiring the augment *a*).

FORM I.—Terminations of the memorial scheme.

1.	सं	स्व	स्म	सि	स्वहि	स्महि
2.	सीस्	स्तं or तं	स्त or त	स्थास् or थास्	साथां	ध्वं or ढ्वं
3.	सीत्	स्तां or तां	सुस्	स्त or त	सातां	सत

The same terminations with *i* prefixed, excepting in 2d and 3d sing., where initial *s* is rejected.

1.	इषं	इष्व	इष्म	इषि	इष्वहि	इष्महि
2.	ईस्	इष्टं	इष्ट	इष्ठास्	इषाथां	इध्वं or इढ्वं
3.	ईत्	इष्टां	इषुस्	इष्ट	इषातां	इषत

FORM II.—Terminations resembling those of 1st preterite.

1.	अम्	आव or व	आम or म	ए or इ	आवहि	आमहि
2.	अस् or स्	अतं or तं	अत or त	अथास्	एथां or आथां	अध्वं
3.	अत् or त्	अतां or तां	अन् or उस्	अत	एतां or आतां	अन्त or अत

Benedictive.

1.	यासं	यास्व	यास्म	सीय	सीवहि	सीमहि
2.	यास्	यास्तं	यास्त	सीष्ठास्	सीयास्थां	सीध्वं (-ढ्वं)
3.	यात्	यास्तां	यासुस्	सीष्ट	सीयास्तां	सीरन्

Many roots prefix *i* to the Átmane, but not to the Parasmai, of the above tense: thus, 1. इषीय *ishíya*, 2. इषीष्ठास् *ishíshṭhás*, &c.

Conditional (requiring the augment *a*).

1.	स्यं	स्याव	स्याम	स्ये	स्यावहि	स्यामहि
2.	स्यस्	स्यतं	स्यत	स्यथास्	स्येथां	स्यध्वं
3.	स्यत्	स्यतां	स्यन्	स्यत	स्येतां	स्यन्त

Many roots prefix *i* to the terminations of the above tense throughout: thus, 1. इष्यं *ishyam*, 2. इष्यस् *ishyas*, &c.

a. As an aid in committing the above terminations to memory, observe that the letter *m* generally enters into the 1st sing. Parasmai; *s* into the 2d sing. Parasmai and Átmane; and *t* into the 3d sing. du. and pl. Parasmai and Átmane of all the tenses. Moreover, that the letter *v* occurs in the 1st dual, *m* in the 1st plural of all the tenses, and *dhw* in every 2d plural Átmane-pada. In the potential and 1st preterite Átmane, and in the 2d preterite Parasmai, *th* is admitted, instead of *s*, into the 2d sing.; and in the 2d pl. of the last tense, *th* has been dropped, owing to the influence of the heavy reduplication. For the same reason the *t* is dropped in the 3d sing. of the 2d pret. Observe also—When the 1st dual Parasmai is *vas*, the 2d and 3d end in *as*, and the 1st plural is *mas*. When the 1st dual Parasmai is *va*, the 2d and 3d end in *tam*, *tám*, and the 1st plural in *ma*. When the 1st dual Átmane is *vahe*, the 1st plural is *mahe*, and the last letter of the remaining terminations is generally *e*. When the 1st dual Átmane is *vahi*, the 2d and 3d end in *ám*; the 1st plural is *mahi*, and the 2d plural is *dhwam*. Note also—The terminations of the 2d future resemble those of the present, with *sya* prefixed. Those of the 1st future also resemble the present, with *tá* or *tás* prefixed. Those of the conditional resemble the 1st preterite, with *sya* prefixed. Those of the 3d preterite also resemble the 1st preterite, with *s* prefixed. Those of the benedictive resemble the potential, with *s* inserted in most of the Parasmai; and with *s* both inserted and prefixed in some of the Átmane.

b. The frequent occurrence of *m* in the 1st sing., of *s* in the 2d, of *t* in the 3d, of *mas* and *ma* in the 1st pl., of *ta* in the 2d pl., and of *ant* in the 3d pl., suggests a comparison with the Greek and Latin verb. We may remark, that *m*, the characteristic of the 1st person sing., is suppressed in the present tense active of all Greek verbs excepting those in *μι* (*asmi* = ἐμμί, *dadámi* = δίδωμι), and also in Latin verbs (except *sum* and *inquam*); but ω and *o* answer to the Sanskṛit *á* of *bharámi* = φέρω, *fero*. In the Greek middle and passive, the *μι*, which originally belonged to all active verbs, appears in *μαι*; while the Sanskṛit, on the other hand, here suppresses the *m*, and contracts *a i* into *e* (see 32); *bhare* (for *bhara-me* for *bhara-mai*) = φέρομαι. Greek has μι in the 1st sing. optative or potential; and in verbs in μι, ν takes the place of the mute *m* of Sanskṛit and Latin: thus, *bhareyam* = φέροιμι, *feram*; *dadyám* = διδοίην, *dem*; *tishṭheyam* = ἱσταίην, *stem*. In the 1st preterite or imperfect, Greek has ν for the Sanskṛit and Latin mute *m*; *atarpam* = ἔτερπον, *adadám* = ἐδίδων, *astṛinavam* = ἐστόρνυν, *avaham* = *vehebam*. In the first Greek aorist, *m* is suppressed, so that Sanskṛit *adiksham* (3d pret.) = ἔδειξα; but not in the 2d aorist, so that *adám* = ἔδων. In the 2d preterite the Sanskṛit *a* = Greek α, *tutopa* = τέτυφα. In the Greek middle and passive futures, *m* is retained, but not in the active; *dásyámi* = δώσω, *dekshyámi* = δείκσω, *dásye* = δώσομαι. As to the 1st person plural, the Sanskṛit *mas* of the pres. is μεν (for μες) in Greek, and *mus* in Latin; *tarpá-mas* = τέρπο-μεν; *sarpá-mas* = ἕρπο-μεν, *serpi-mus*; *dad-mas* = δίδο-μεν, *da-mus*; *tishṭhá-mas* = ἵστα-μεν, *sta-mus*. The Átmane-pada *mahe* answers to the Greek μεθα; *dad-mahe* = διδό-μεθα. As to the other tenses, in the potential 1st pl. *bhare-ma* = φέροι-μες (-μεν), *fera-mus*; *dadyáma* = διδοίημες (-μεν), *demus*; *dadí-mahi* = διδοί-μεθα. In the 1st preterite 1st pl. *abhará-ma* = ἐφέρο-μεν, *fereba-mus*; *avahá-ma* = *veheba-mus*; *adad-ma* = ἐδίδο-μεν; *abhará-mahi* = ἐφερόμεθα. In the 2d future, *dásyá-mas* = δώσο-μεν, *dekshyá-mas* = δείκσο-μεν. In the 2d pers. sing. active, the characteristic *s* has been preserved in all three languages: thus, in the present, the Sanskṛit *asi* = ἐσσί, *es*; *dadá-si* = δίδως, *das*; *bhara-si* = φέρεις, *fers*; *vahasi* = *vehis*. In the Átmane, the Sanskṛit *se* (for *sai*, by 32) answers exactly to the Greek σαι of verbs in μι (*tishṭha-se* = ἵστα-σαι). In other Greek verbs, *s* has been rejected, and εαι contracted into ῃ, something in the way of Sanskṛit (τύπτῃ for τύπτε-σαι). In the 2d dual, *thas* = Greek τον, and in the 2d plur. *tha* = τε and *tis*; *bhara-thas* = φέρε-τον; *tishṭha-tha* = ἵστα-τε, *statis*; *bhara-tha* = φέρε-τε, *fer-tis*. In the 2d pl. Átmane, *bhara-dhwe* = φέρεσθε. As to the other tenses, in the 2d sing. potential, *tishṭhes* = ἱσταίης, *stes*; *dadyás* = διδοίης, *des*; *vahes* = *vehas*; *bhares* = φέροις, *feras*: in 2d du. *bhare-tam* = φέροι-τον: in 2d pl. *tishṭheta* = ἱσταίητε, *stetis*; *dadyáta* = διδοίητε, *detis*; *bhareta* = φέροιτε, *feratis*. In the 2d sing. imperative, *hi* and *dhi* answer to Greek θι. *Dhi* was originally universal in Sanskṛit (see 291), as in Greek verbs in μι; *e-dhi* = ἴσ-θι, *vid-dhi* = ἴσ-θι, *de-hi* = δίδο-θι. Many verbs drop the termination *hi* both in Greek and Sanskṛit; as, भर = φέρε, and compare δείκνυ with *chinu*, &c. In the 2d du. imp. *tam* = τον, and *ta* = τε. In the imperative Átmane, *swa* = the old form σο; *bhara-swa* = φέρε-σο (old form of φέρου); *dat-swa* = δίδο-σο; *áthám* = εσθον, &c. In the 2d sing. 1st pret. *atarpas* = ἔτερπες, *avahas* = *vehebas*, &c. So also, *tam* = τον, *adat-tam* = ἐδίδο-τον, *ta* = τε, *adat-ta* = ἐδίδο-τε. In the Átmane, *thás* is found for *sás* in the 2d sing. of the 1st pret., as well as of the potential; hence *abhara-thás* = ἐφέρε-σο, *adat-thás* = ἐδίδο-σο, *dadí-thás* = διδοι(σ)ο. In the 2d pret. the *tha* of the 2d sing. = Latin *sti*; *dad-itha* = *dedi-sti*, *tasthi-tha* = *steti-sti*, *tutodi-tha* = *tutudi-sti*. In the 3d pret. *adás* = ἔδως, *avákshís* = *vexisti*. In the 3d pers. sing. active, Greek has dropped the characteristic *t* (except in ἐστί = Sansk. *asti*, Lat. *est*); *bharati*

= φέρε(τ)ι, *fert; vahati* = *vehit*. Verbs in μι have changed *t* to *s; dadáti* = δίδωσι (for δίδωτι). In the Átmane, *bharate* = φέρεται. In the potential, *bharet* = φέροι, *dadyát* = διδοίη. In the imperative, *bhara-tu* or *bhara-tát* = φερέ-τω, *fer-to*. In the 1st pret. *avahat* = *vehebat*, *abharata* = ἐφέρετο. In the 2d pret. *tutopa* = τέτυφε. In the 3d pret. *avákshít* = *vexit*, *adikshata* = ἐδείκσατο. As to the 3d pl., in the above tenses, *bharanti* = φέρουσι, *ferunt; vahanti* = *vehunt; bharante* = φέρονται; *dadati* = διδοῦσι; *tishṭanti* = *stant; bhareyus* = φέροιεν; *bharantu* = *ferunto; abharan* = ἔφερον; *abharanta* = ἐφέροντο; *ásan* = ἦσαν; *atarpishus* = ἔτερψαν; *dásyante* = δώσονται. See Bopp's Comparative Grammar, *passim*.

248. The above terminations are supposed to be applicable to all verbs, whether primitive or derivative: and as in nouns, so in verbs, the theory of Indian grammarians is, that before these terminations can be affixed to roots, an inflective base must be formed out of the root. Ten different rules, therefore, are propounded for forming verbal bases out of roots in the first four tenses; while all verbs are arranged under ten classes, according as they follow one or other of these rules. In the other tenses there is only one general rule for forming the base.

These ten classes of verbs are called *the ten conjugations;* and the four tenses, which alone are affected by the conjugational rules (viz. the present, potential, imperative, and first preterite), are called *the conjugational tenses*. It is evident, however, that the ten conjugations are hardly conjugations in the classical sense of the term. They are rather ten rules for moulding and fashioning ten classes of roots into the proper form for receiving a common scheme of terminations in four of the tenses only.

249. The following is a brief summary of the ten rules for forming the base of the four conjugational tenses in the ten classes of verbs, according to the Indian arrangement of the conjugations.

1st class (1st conjugation). Guṇate the vowel of the root (unless it be अ *a* or precede a double consonant, 28. *b*) before *every termination of the four tenses*, and affix the vowel अ *a*—lengthened to आ *á* before initial *m* or *v*—to the root thus guṇated.

2d class (2d conjugation). Guṇate the radical vowel (unless it be अ *a* or precede a double consonant) before those terminations only which are marked with P in the scheme at 246. Before all the other terminations the original vowel of the root must be retained.

3d class (3d conjugation). Reduplicate the initial consonant and vowel of the root, and guṇate the radical but not the reduplicated vowel before the P terminations only, as in the 2d conjugation.

4th class (4th conjugation). Affix य *ya*—lengthened to या *yá* before initial *m* or *v*—to the root, the vowel of which is generally left unchanged.

5th class (5th conjugation). Affix नु *nu* to the root, and guṇate this *nu* into *no* before the P terminations only.

6th class (6th conjugation). Affix अ *a*—lengthened to आ *á* before initial *m* or *v*—to the root, which in other respects generally remains unchanged.

7th class (7th conjugation). Insert न *na* between the vowel and final consonant of the root before the P terminations, and न् *n* before the other terminations. Observe the peculiarity of this conjugation—that the conjugational *na* or *n* is inserted into the *middle* of the root, and not affixed.

8th class (8th conjugation). Affix उ *u* to the root, and guṇate this *u* into *o* before the P terminations only. Observe—As all the roots, except one, in this class, end in *n*, the 8th conjugation will appear to be exactly similar to the 5th.

9th class (9th conjugation). Affix ना *ná* to the root before the P terminations; नी *ní* before all the others, excepting those beginning with vowels, where only न् *n* is affixed.

10th class (10th conjugation). Guṇate the radical vowel throughout all the persons of all the tenses, and affix अय *aya*—lengthened to अया *ayá* before initial *m* or *v*—to the root thus guṇated.

250. It will appear, from a cursory examination of the above rules, that the object of all of them, excepting the 2d, 3d, and 7th, is to insert a vowel, either alone or preceded by *y* or *n*, between the modified root and the terminations; and that the 1st, 4th, 6th, and 10th, agree in requiring that the vowel, which is immediately to precede the terminations, shall be *a*. It will appear, moreover, that the 2d, 3d, and 7th, alone agree in not interposing a vowel between the final of the root and the terminations; and that the 5th, 8th, and 9th, agree in interposing either *u*, *á*, or *í*, after the letter *n*.

a. It must never, however, be forgotten, that the conjugational characteristic, whatever it may be, has reference only to the four conjugational tenses (excepting only in the 10th conjugation), and that in the other tenses the base is formed according to one general rule for all verbs of whatever conjugation; or, in other words, that in these tenses all verbs, of whatever class, are as if they belonged to one common conjugation.

b. It is evident, that a comparison between the difficulty of the Sanskṛit and Greek verb would be greatly to the advantage of the former. The Greek verb has three voices, and about ninety tenses and moods: the Sanskṛit has only two voices, and not more than twenty tenses and moods. Besides which, a far greater number of verbs are susceptible of the three voices in Greek, than of the two in Sanskṛit. Moreover, in Sanskṛit there are no contracted verbs, and no difficulties resulting from difference of dialect; and although there are ten conjugations, yet these have reference to four tenses only; and, under some of these conjugations, only two or three common verbs are contained.

251. Hence it appears, that the very meaning of Sanskṛit conjugation is the *Sandhi* or junction of a verbal base (formed out of a root according to ten rules for four of the tenses, and one general rule for the other tenses) with a common scheme of terminations, and that in conjugating a verb, two things have to be done; 1st, to form the base from the root, in the manner described above; 2dly, to join the base with the terminations, according to the rules of Sandhi.

252. Before proceeding to a detailed explanation of the formation of the verbal base of the simple or primitive verb, under the several classes, it will be worth while to specify the four other verbs deducible from roots, and to explain how they are derived.

a. It has been already shown, at 74, that there are a large number of monosyllabic sounds in Sanskṛit, called *roots*, which are the source of verbs as well as nouns. These roots are in number about two thousand; and the theory of grammarians is, that each of them may serve as the rough block out of which the inflective bases of five kinds of verbs may be fashioned: 1. of a primitive, transitive or intransitive; 2. of a passive; 3. of a causal, having often a causal and often merely a transitive signification; 4. of a desiderative, giving a sense of wishing to the root; and 5. of a frequentative (or intensive), implying repetition, or heightening the idea contained in the root.

b. It will be found, however, in practice, that the greater number of these two thousand roots never occur at all in the form of verbs, nor, indeed, in any other form but that of the nouns to which they give origin; and that the roots in real use, as the source of verbs, are comparatively few. Of these few, moreover, certain particular roots (such, for example, as कृ *kṛi*, 'to do'), as if to compensate for the inactivity of the others, are kept in constant employment; and, by compounding them with prepositions and other prefixes, applied to the expression of the most various and opposite ideas. Nevertheless, theoretically, from every root in the language may be elicited five kinds of verbal bases.

The first, or primitive verb, is formed from the root, according to the ten different rules (or conjugations) applicable to the formation of the base in the first four tenses. The second, or passive, is formed according to the rule for the change of the root, required by the 4th conjugation; viz. the addition of *ya* in the first four tenses. The third, or causal, is formed according to the rule for the change of the root, required by the 10th conjugation; viz. the addition of *aya* to the root in all the tenses excepting the 3d preterite. The fourth, or desiderative, is formed by the addition of *sa* or *isha*, the root also undergoing reduplication. The fifth, or frequentative, is formed like the passive, according to the rule required by the 4th conjugation, and is, in fact, a reduplicated passive verb. It may also be formed analogously to the rule for the 3d conjugation. Thus, take the root शुभ् *śubh*, conveying the idea of 'shining'—from this are elicited, 1st, the primitive verbal base, *śobha*, 'to shine;' 2dly, the passive, *śubhya*, 'to be bright;' 3dly, the causal, *śobhaya*, 'to cause to shine' or 'illuminate;' 4thly, the desiderative, *śuśobhisha*, 'to desire to shine;' 5thly, the frequentative or intensive, *śośubhya* or *śośobh*, 'to shine very brightly.'

a. Note, that as every root may be the source of five different kinds of verbs, so every noun may be the source of a class of verbs (not much used) called *nominal verbs*. A brief explanation of these will be found after frequentatives at 518.

253. It has already been remarked, that the passive can hardly be considered a *voice*, according to the classical acceptation of the term. In Greek and Latin, a verb in the passive voice corresponds in form with the same verb in the active: thus *audior* corresponds with *audio*, ἀκούομαι with ἀκούω, the terminations or system of inflection only being changed. And in Greek, a verb in the passive corresponds with the same verb in the middle voice, both in the form and in the terminations of most of its tenses. But, in Sanskṛit, the form of the passive varies entirely in the conjugational tenses from that of the active verb (unless that verb belong to the 4th conjugation), whilst the terminations may sometimes be the same, viz. those of the Átmane-pada. It is rather a distinct derivative from the root, formed on one invariable principle, without any necessary community with the conjugational structure of the active verb. Thus the root *bhid*, 'to divide,' is of the 7th conjugation, and makes *bhinatti* or *bhinte*, 'he divides;' *dwish*, 'to hate,' is of the 2d conjugation, and makes *dweshṭi* or *dwishṭe*, 'he hates;'

but the passive of both is formed according to one invariable rule, by the simple insertion of *ya*, without reference to the conjugational form of the active: thus, *bhidyate*, 'he is divided;' *dwishyate*, 'he is hated.' See 243. *a*.

a. In fact, though it be a distinct derivative from the root, a passive verb is nothing but a verb of the 4th conjugation restricted to the Átmane-pada: and to say that every root may take a passive form, is to say that roots of the 1st, 2d, 3d, 5th, 6th, 7th, 8th, 9th, and 10th conjugations may all be conjugated in the 4th conjugation, with a passive sense: so that if a root be already of the 4th conjugation, its passive form is generally, though not always, identical with its own Átmane-pada.

b. It might even with reason be suspected, that the occasional assumption of a neuter signification and a Parasmai-pada inflection by a passive verb, was the cause which gave rise to the 4th conjugation. Instances are certainly found of passive verbs taking Parasmai-pada terminations, and many passive verbs (for example, *jáyate*, 'he is born,' from the root *jan*; *púryate*, 'he is filled,' from the root *prí*; and *tapyate*, 'he is heated,' from the root *tap*) are confounded with verbs of this conjugation *. So that it seems not unlikely, that, by making the 4th conjugation, grammarians only meant to say that the passive form of verbs, or the addition of *ya* to the root, is also the form that may be used to express a neuter or intransitive signification; the only difference requisite to be made between the two forms being exactly that which might be expected to exist between them; viz. that the one should take the Átmane-pada; the other, the Parasmai-pada inflection. This fact, at least, is clear that the Parasmai-pada of the 4th conjugation is the form used in numerous roots to yield a neuter signification; and that the Átmane-pada is identical with the form used to yield a passive sense; so that the 4th conjugation can hardly be said to possess an Átmane-pada †. Hence it arises, that many roots appear in the 4th conjugation as neuter verbs, which also appear in some one of the other nine as transitive. For example, *yuj*, 'to join,' when used in an active sense, is conjugated either in the 7th conjugation, or in the causal; when in a neuter, in the 4th. So also, *push*, 'to nourish;' *kshubh*, 'to agitate;' *kliś*, 'to vex;' *sidh*, 'to accomplish.'

254. Similarly, although causal verbs are said to be distinct derivatives from the root, they are in point of fact verbs of the 10th conjugation, inflected either in Parasmai or Átmane. To say, therefore, that every root may take a causal form, is to say that roots of the first nine conjugations may all be conjugated in the

* That the passive does occasionally take the terminations of the Parasmai-pada is shown by Professor Bopp, who gives several instances; as, *chhidyet* for *chhidyeta*, 'it may be cut.' Nal. xiv. 6; *mokshyasi* for *mokshyase*, 'thou shalt be liberated.' Other instances may be found in Westergaard; as, *vidyati* for *vidyate*.

† At any rate, the forms given for the 3d preterites of such verbs as *pad*, 'to go,' *budh*, 'to know' (which are said to be Átmane verbs of the 4th conjugation), could only belong to passive verbs. The forms given by Westergaard are, *apádi*, *abodhi*. See 475.

10th conjugation, with a causal sense; and that if a root be already of the 10th conjugation, it can then have no distinct form for its causal, the primitive verb and the causal being in that case identical (see 289). Indeed, it might reasonably be conjectured, that the occasional employment of a causal verb in a transitive, rather than a causal sense, was the only reason for creating a 10th conjugation. It would certainly simplify the subject, if this conjugation were not separated from the causal; or, in other words, if the addition of *aya* to the root were considered in all cases as the mark of a causal verb. One thing, at least, is plain, that this affix is not the sign of a separate conjugation, in the way that *nu* is the sign of the 5th conjugation, or in the way of any other conjugational syllable; for it is retained in most of the other tenses of the verb, not only in the first four, just as the desiderative *ish* is retained.

255. The subject of verbs, therefore, will divide itself into two heads. In the first place, the formation of the base; 1st of primitive, 2dly of passive, 3dly of causal, 4thly of desiderative, 5thly of frequentative verbs; with their respective participles. In the second place, the exhibition, at full, of the base, united to its terminations, under each of the five forms of verbs consecutively.

Under the first head will be shown, how the root has to be changed before the terminations can be affixed; while the mode of affixing the terminations to the root, thus changed, will at the same time be indicated. Under the second head, the five forms of verbs beginning with primitives will appear conjugated in detail; the base, or changed root, being combined with its terminations in regular sequence.

PRIMITIVE VERBS.

FORMATION OF THE BASE OF THE FIRST FOUR TENSES, IN THE TEN CONJUGATIONS.

256. A brief summary of the formation of the base, in the ten classes of verbs, has already been given at 249; and a great peculiarity has been noted—that the rules of conjugation have reference only to the first four tenses, called *conjugational*, viz. the present, potential, imperative, and first preterite.

Remember, that after passing these four tenses the conjugational structure of the base is forgotten; and in the formation of the bases of the six remaining tenses all roots conform to one general rule, and are as if they belonged to one general conjugation. Hence the six last tenses are called *non-conjugational*. The tenth class alone retains the conjugational structure of the base throughout *most of the non-conjugational tenses*; but as this class consists chiefly of causal verbs, no confusion can arise from this apparent inconsistency. Of the 2000 roots, more than half follow the 1st conjugation, about 130 follow the 4th, about 140 the 6th, and all may follow the 10th (see 289). Of the remaining roots, about 70 follow the 2d, but not more than 20 are *in common use;* about 20 follow the 3d, of which not half are in common use; about 24, of which hardly 6 are common, follow the 7th; about 30, of which 10 are common, the 5th; about 10, of which only 2 are common, the 8th; about 52, of which 15 are common, the 9th.

257. Primitive verbs, therefore, will separate themselves into ten classes, according as they fall under one or other of the ten conjugations; and these ten conjugations may be segregated into three groups.

a. The 1st group is the most important and comprehensive, as comprising verbs of the 1st, 4th, 6th, and 10th classes, which agree in making their inflective bases end in *a*, and in taking substitutions for some of the terminations, as indicated at 247.

b. The 2d group comprises verbs of the 2d, 3d, and 7th classes, which agree in affixing the regular terminations (at 246) to the final letter of the root, without the intervention of a vowel.

c. The 3d group, comprising verbs of the 5th, 8th, and 9th classes, also affixes the regular terminations to the root; but after the intervention of either *u*, *á*, or *í*, preceded by the consonant *n*.

It will be convenient, in giving a detailed explanation of the formation of the base under each conjugation, to adhere to the grouping of the above divisions.

258. Although, to prevent confusion, it is advisable to preserve the Indian classification of verbs into ten classes, and therefore into ten conjugations; yet it would be more in unison with the classical idea of a conjugation, to arrange all verbs under three classes and three conjugations, according to the above grouping. The classical student may, if he please, consider that verbs of the 1st, 4th, 6th, and 10th classes constitute his first conjugation; verbs of the 2d, 3d, and 7th classes, his second conjugation; and verbs of the 5th, 8th, and 9th, his third conjugation.

a. In comparing Sanskṛit verbs with Greek and Latin, observe that the first group of conjugations in Sanskṛit, viz. the 1st, 4th, 6th, and 10th, answers to the Greek first conjugation in ω, the conjugational अ *a* becoming ο or ε in Greek (*tarpámas* = τέρπομεν, *tarpatha* = τέρπετε); and although the Greek first conjugation contains more subdivisions than the first group in Sanskṛit, yet the inflection of these subdivisions is similar. As to the Sanskṛit 10th conjugation, however, it appears to correspond to Greek verbs in αζω and ιζω, which, like the 10th, are generally found in company with other verbs from the same root: thus, καθαρίζω, 'I make pure' (καθαίρω), στενάζω, 'to groan' (στένω), where ζ is substituted for य *y*, as in ζεά for यव 'barley.' To this class also may be referred verbs in *αω* and *εω*: thus *páraydmi* = *περάω*, where the *y* has been dropped, and the two *a*'s combined. Latin verbs in *io*, like *audio* &c., seem to be related to the Sanskṛit 4th class, as well as to the 10th: thus *cupio* answers to *kupyámi;* and the *e* of *audiebam* answers to the *aya* of the 10th, just as in Prákṛit *aya* is contracted into ए *e*. The second and third groups of conjugations in Sanskṛit (viz. the 2d, 3d, 7th, 5th, 8th, and 9th) answer to Greek verbs in *μι*: thus *emi* 2d conj. = *εἶμι*, *dadámi* 3d conj. = *δίδωμι*. The 7th conjugation, however, has no exact parallel in Greek, but many Greek and Latin verbs resemble it in inserting a nasal into the middle of the root; see 342. *a*. The 5th and 8th conjugations answer to Greek verbs in *νυ* and *υ*; and *νυ* and *υ* are lengthened before certain terminations, just as *nu* is guṇated in Sanskṛit: thus *striṇomi* = *στόρνῡμι*, *striṇoshi* = *στόρνῡς*, *striṇoti* = *στόρνῡτι*, *striṇumas* = *στόρνυμες*, &c. The 9th conjugation answers to Greek verbs in *νᾱ* (*νη*): thus *kríṇámi* = *πέρνᾱμι* (*πέρνημι*), *kríṇímas* = *πέρναμες*. Compare also Latin forms in *ni*: thus *sternimus* = Sans. *striṇímas*, from *stṛi*, 9th conj. See Bopp's Comparative Grammar.

FORMATION OF THE BASE IN THE 1ST, 4TH, 6TH, AND 10TH CLASSES OF VERBS.

259. Before entering upon the formation of the base, observe particularly that the 1st, 4th, 6th, and 10th classes take substitutions for some of the terminations, especially in the potential Parasmai, and in the 2d and 3d dual of the present, imperative, and 1st preterite, Átmane-pada. In the 2d sing. imperative they reject the termination *. See the scheme at 247.

260. Observe also, that it is an universal rule in all ten conjugations that the augment अ *a* be prefixed to the base of the 1st preterite; and when the base begins with अ *a* or आ *á*, the augment blends with these vowels into *á*, by 31 (just as in Greek *ε* and *ε* become *ἤ* in *ἤγειρον*, &c.).

a. But when the augment *a* is prefixed to bases beginning with the vowels इ *i*, उ *u*, and ऋ *ṛi*, short or long, it blends with them into ऐ *ai*, औ *au*, आर् *ár* (instead of *e*, *o*, *ar*, by 32). Thus the base इच्छ *ichchha* becomes in the 3d sing. 1st preterite ऐच्छत् *aichchhat*, the base ऊह *úha* becomes औहत *auhata*, and the base ऋध्नो *ṛidhno* becomes आर्ध्नोत् *árdhnot*.

b. This rule applies to two of the non-conjugational tenses also, viz. the 3d preterite and the conditional. Note, that the 1st and 3d preterites and the conditional are the only three tenses that take the augment *a*.

---

* Probably in consequence of the haste with which 'command' is generally expressed.

First class (1*st conjugation*), *containing about* 1000 *primitive verbs.*

261. Rule for the formation of the base in the four conjugational tenses. Guṇate the vowel (except when debarred by 28. *b*) before *every termination of all the four tenses*, and affix the vowel अ *a* to the root so guṇated. Note, that this vowel अ *a* is lengthened into आ *á* before the initial *m* or *v* of a termination, but not when *m* is final, as in the 1st sing. 1st preterite.

262. Thus, from the root बुध् *budh*, 'to know,' is formed the base बोध *bodha*, lengthened into बोधा *bodhá* before *m* and *v* (Pres. 1.* *bodhá* + *mi* = बोधामि *bodhámi*, *bodha* + *si* = बोधसि *bodhasi*, *bodha* + *ti* = बोधति *bodhati*; Du. 1. *bodhá* + *vas* = बोधावस् *bodhávas*, &c.; Átm. Pres. *bodha* + *i* = बोधे *bodhe* by 32, *bodha* + *se* = बोधसे *bodhase*, &c.). See table at 583.

263. Similarly, from जि *ji*, 'to conquer' (see 590), comes the base जय *jaya*, liable to be lengthened into जया *jayá*, as before (36. *a*); from नी *ní*, 'to lead,' the base *naya* or *nayá*; from भू *bhú*, 'to be' (φύω, Lat. *fu*), the bases *bhava* and *bhavá* (Pres. 1. भवामि *bhavámi*, 36. *a*; 2. भवसि *bhavasi*, φύεις, &c., see 584); from सृप् *sṛip*, 'to creep,' the base सर्प *sarpa* or *sarpá* (see 28); from क्लृप् *kḷrip*, 'to make,' the base कल्प *kalpa* or *kalpá*.

a. Note, that *bhú*, 'to be' or 'to become,' is one of the commonest verbs in the language, and like *as*, 'to be,' at 584, 321, is sometimes used as an auxiliary. It is conjugated at full at 585.

264. In the potential the final *a* of the base blends with the initial *i* of the termination by 32 (Pot. 1. *bodha* + *iyam* = बोधेयं *bodheyam*). So also in the Pres. Átm. (बोधे &c.). See table at 583.

265. In the imperative the termination is rejected in the 2d sing. (Imp. 1. *bodha* + *áni* = बोधानि *bodháni*, 2. बोध *bodha*, 3. *bodha* + *tu* = बोधतु *bodhatu*).

266. The base of the 1st preterite has the augment अ *a* prefixed by 260 (1st Pret. 1. *abodha* + *m* = अबोधं *abodham*, 2. *abodha* + *s* = अबोधस् *abodhas*, &c.).

267. Roots like पच् 'to cook,' भिक्ष् 'to beg,' जीव् 'to live' (603), take the inserted अ *a*, liable to be lengthened to आ *á*, but forbid the Guṇa change by 28. *b* (Pres. 1. पचामि &c.; Átm. 1. भिक्षे &c.; Pres. 1. जीवामि &c.).

* 1. stands for 1st singular; Du. 1. for 1st dual; Pl. 1. for 1st plural, &c.

268. There are some roots ending in the Vṛiddhi ऐ *ai* which cannot be guṇated, but suffer the usual change of Sandhi before अ *a* and आ *á* by 37; as, from गै 'to sing,' ग्लै 'to be weary,' त्रै 'to preserve,' ध्यै 'to meditate,' म्लै 'to fade,' are formed the bases *gáya, gláya, tráya, dhyáya, mláya*. See 595. *a*.

269. Some roots of the 1st conj. form their bases in the first four tenses by a change peculiar to themselves, which change is of course discarded in the other tenses: thus, from स्था 'to stand' (see 587), घ्रा *ghrá*, 'to smell' (588), पा 'to drink' (589), ध्मा 'to blow,' म्ना 'to repeat over,' come the bases तिष्ठ *tishṭha*, जिघ्र *jighra*, पिव *piva*, धम *dhama*, मन *mana*, the final *a* being, as before, liable to be lengthened.

a. Note, that the roots स्था *sthá* and घ्रा *ghrá* are properly reduplicated verbs of the 3d class at 330. The reduplicated base, by 331, would be *tasthá, jaghrá*: but as the reduplication is irregular, and the radical *á* is shortened, grammarians place these roots under the 1st class. The Greek ἵστημι, on the other hand, has not shortened its radical vowel in the singular.

270. Again, from दृश् 'to see,' गम् 'to go,' यम् 'to restrain,' सद् 'to sink,' are formed the bases पश्य *paśya*, गच्छ *gachchha*, यच्छ *yachchha*, सीद *sída* (Pres. 1. पश्यामि *paśyámi*, &c.).

271. गुह् 'to conceal' forms गूह *gúha*; गुप् 'to protect,' गोपाय *gopáya*; and दंश् 'to bite,' दश *daśa* (Pres. 1. गूहामि *gúhámi*, &c.).

Fourth class (4th conjugation), containing about 130 primitive verbs.

272. Rule for the formation of the base in the four conjugational tenses. Affix य *ya* to the root. The vowel of the root is not guṇated, and generally remains unchanged. Note, that the inserted य *ya* is liable to become या *yá* before an initial *m* or *v* of the terminations of the four tenses (but not before the *m* of the 1st sing. 1st preterite), as in the 1st class at 261.

273. Thus, from सिध् *sidh*, 'to succeed,' is formed the base सिध्य *sidhya* (Pres. 1. *sidhyá + mi* = सिध्यामि *sidhyámi*, 2. सिध्यसि *sidhyasi*, &c.; Pot. 1. *sidhya + iyam* = सिध्येयं *sidhyeyam*, 2. सिध्येस् *sidhyes*, &c.; Imp. 1. *sidhya + áni* = सिध्यानि *sidhyáni*, &c.; 1st Pret. *asidhya + m* = असिध्यं *asidhyam*, &c.; Átm. Pres. 1. *sidhya + i* = सिध्ये *sidhye*, *sidhya + se* = सिध्यसे *sidhyase*, &c.). See 616.

274. Similarly, from मा *má*, 'to measure,' the base माय *máya* (Pres. 1. Átm. *máya + i* = माये *máye*, &c.); from क्षिप् *kship*, 'to throw,' क्षिप्य *kshipya*; from नृत् *nṛit*, 'to dance,' नृत्य *nṛitya*; from डी 'to fly,' डीय (Pres. Átm. 1. डीये).

275. Roots ending in *am* and *iv*, and one in *ad*, lengthen the vowel; as, from दिव *div*, 'to play,' दीव्य *dívya*; from भ्रम् *bhram*, 'to wander,' भ्राम्य *bhrámya*; from मद् *mad*, 'to be mad,' माद्य *mádya*.

276. If a root contain a nasal it is generally rejected; as, from भ्रंश् 'to fall,' भ्रश्य *bhraśya;* जन् 'to be born' makes जाय *jáya* (Pres. 1. Átm. जाये), lengthening the vowel, to compensate for the loss of *n*.

a. Roots ending in ओ *o* drop this *o* before the conjugational *ya:* thus सो *so*, 'to destroy,' makes its base *sya*.

277. The following are anomalous. From जॄ 'to grow old,' जीर्य *jírya:* from व्यध 'to pierce,' विध्य *vidhya:* from मिद् 'to be viscid,' मेद्य *medya*.

Observe—Although this class includes only 130 primitive verbs (generally neuter in signification), yet every one of the 2000 roots in the language may have a passive form which follows the Átmane-pada of this class.

Sixth class (6th conjugation), containing about 140 *primitive verbs.*

278. Rule for the formation of the base in the four conjugational tenses. Affix the vowel अ *a* to the root, which is not guṇated, and in other respects generally remains unchanged*. Note, that the inserted अ *a* becomes आ *á* before an initial *m* and *v* of the terminations of the four tenses (but not before the *m* of the 1st sing. 1st preterite), as in the 1st and 4th conjugations at 261 and 272.

279. Thus, from क्षिप् *kship*, 'to throw,' comes the base क्षिप *kshipa* (Pres. 1. *kshipá + mi* = क्षिपामि *kshipámi*, 2. *kshipa + si* = क्षिपसि *kshipasi;* Pot. 1. *kshipa + iyam* = क्षिपेयं *kshipeyam*, &c.; Átm. Pres. 1. *kshipa + i* = क्षिपे *kshipe;* see 635); from तुद् *tud*, 'to strike,' तुद *tuda;* from दिश् *diś*, 'to point out,' दिश *diśa*.

280. Roots in इ *i*, उ *u* or ऊ *ú*, ऋ *ṛi* and ॠ *ṛí*, generally change those vowels into इय् *iy*, उव् *uv*, रि *ri*, and इर् *ir* respectively; as, from रि, 'to go,' comes the base रिय *riya:* from नु 'to praise,' नुव *nuva:* from धू 'to agitate,' धुव *dhuva;* from मृ 'to die,' म्रिय *mriya* (626); from कॄ *kṛí*, 'to scatter,' किर *kira* (627).

281. A considerable class of roots, ending in consonants, in this conjugation, insert a nasal before the final consonant in the four tenses; as, from मुच्, 'to let go,' comes the base मुञ्च *muñcha:* from लिप 'to anoint,' लिम्प *limpa:* from कृत् 'to cut,' कृन्त *kṛinta:* from सिच् 'to sprinkle,' सिञ्च *siñcha:* from लुप् 'to break,' लुम्प *lumpa*. Similarly, the roots पिश्, विद्, खिद्.

282. The following are anomalous. From इष्, 'to wish,' comes the base इच्छ *ichchha;* from प्रच्छ 'to ask,' पृच्छ *pṛichchha;* from भ्रज्ज 'to roast,' भृज्ज *bhṛijja;* from व्यच् 'to deceive,' विच *vicha:* from व्रश्च् 'to cut,' वृश्च *vṛiścha*.

---

* Prof. Bopp observes, that the sixth class is only an offshoot of the first, containing the diseased members of that class. Comp. Gram. 1055.

Tenth class of verbs (10*th conjugation*), *containing a few primitive verbs and all causals.*

283. Rule for the formation of the base in the four conjugational tenses. Guṇate the vowel of the root throughout every person of all the four tenses (except when debarred by 28. *b*), and affix अय *aya* to the root so guṇated. Note, that अय *aya* becomes अया *ayá* before an initial *m* or *v* of the terminations of the four tenses, but not before the *m* of the 1st sing. 1st preterite.

284. Thus, from चुर् *chur*, 'to steal,' is formed the base चोरय *choraya* (Pres. 1. *chorayá* + *mi* = चोरयामि *chorayámi*, 2. *choraya* + *si* = चोरयसि *chorayasi*, &c.; Pot. 1. *choraya* + *iyam* = चोरयेयं *chorayeyam*; Imp. 1. *choraya* + *áṇi* = चोरयाणि *chorayáṇi*, &c., see 58; 1st Pret. 1. *achoraya* + *m* = अचोरयं *achorayam*, &c., see 638).

285. Roots ending in vowels take Vṛiddhi instead of Guṇa; as, from प्री 'to please,' प्रायय *práyaya*; from धृ 'to hold,' धारय *dháraya*. But पॄ, 'to fill,' makes पूरय *púraya*.

286. Roots which enclose the vowel अ *a* between two single consonants generally lengthen this vowel; as, from ग्रस् 'to swallow,' ग्रासय *grásaya*: but not always; as, from कथ 'to say,' कथय *kathaya*.

287. कॄत्, 'to celebrate,' 'to praise,' makes कीर्तय *kírtaya* (Pres. कीर्तयामि).

288. A few roots with a medial ऋ *ṛi* retain that vowel; as, from स्पृह् 'to desire,' स्पृहय *spṛihaya*.

289. Observe—Every Sanskṛit root may have a causal form, and all causal verbs follow the 10th conjugation; but there are a considerable number of active primitive verbs, not causal in their signification, which belong to this conjugation. In these verbs, therefore, the causal form will be identical with the primitive verb. Hence there will often be a difficulty in determining whether a verb be a primitive verb of the 10th conjugation, or a causal verb; and the consideration of the 10th conjugation must to a great extent be mixed up with that of the causal form of the root (see 479).

a. Observe also, that all verbs, whether primitive or causal, which belong to the 10th conjugation, have this great peculiarity, viz. that the conjugational *ay* is carried throughout all the tenses of the verb, non-conjugational as well as conjugational, excepting only the 3d preterite and the benedictive, Parasmai-pada (compare 254). For this reason the formation of the base of the non-conjugational tenses of verbs of the 10th conjugation will not be explained under the general head of the non-conjugational tenses (at 363), but will fall under causal verbs.

FORMATION OF THE BASE IN THE 2D, 3D, 7TH, 5TH, 8TH, AND 9TH CLASSES OF VERBS.

290. Before entering upon the formation of the base in the last two groups of conjugations, observe that they take the regular terminations of the memorial scheme at 246, without any substitutions, excepting in the 3d plur. present and imperative, Átmane-pada, where the nasal is rejected in all six classes (see scheme at 247).

a. The 3d class, however, owing to the burden occasioned by reduplication, rejects the nasal from the 3d plur. of the Parasmai-pada, as well as from the Átmane-pada, in these two tenses, and takes *us* for *an* in the 3d pl. 1st preterite.

b. Two roots, moreover, in the 2d class (*jaksh*, 'to eat,' and *śás*, 'to rule'), and roots of more than one syllable (very few in number), resemble the 3d class in rejecting the nasal from the 3d pl. Parasmai, and taking *us* for *an* in the 1st preterite*.

291. Observe also, that roots *ending in consonants*, of the 2d, 3d, and 7th classes, and the root हु *hu* of the 3d, take *dhi* (the Greek θι) for *hi* in the 2d sing. imperative† (see 247); and that roots *ending in vowels*, of the 5th and 8th classes, resemble the first group of classes at 259, in rejecting this termination altogether.

292. Again, roots ending in consonants will reject the terminations *s* and *t* of the 2d and 3d sing. 1st preterite by 43. *a*, changing the final of the root, if a soft consonant, to an unaspirated hard, by 42. *a*; and in other respects changing a final consonant, as indicated at 43. But in the 2d sing. the termination *s* is sometimes *optionally* retained, and the final letter of the root rejected.

a. If a root end in ह् *h*, this final *h* becomes *k*, in the 2d and 3d sing. 1st pret., by 43. *c*: but if the root begin with *d* or *g*, the aspirate is thrown back on these letters, which become *dh*, *gh*.

b. If a root end in स् *s*, it may change this *s* to *t* in the 2d sing.

293. Although comparatively few verbs fall under the last two groups of conjugations, yet some of these are among the most useful in the language. Their formation presents more difficulties than that of the 1st, 4th, 6th, and 10th conjugations. In these latter the verbal base, although varying slightly in each conjugation, preserves the same form before all the terminations of every tense; but in the last two groups of conjugations the base is liable to variation before

---

* A few other roots of the 2d class (as, विद्, द्विष्, पा, या) optionally take *us* for *an* in the 1st preterite. *Śás* probably follows the analogy of reduplicated verbs, on account of its double sibilant.

† *Dhi* was originally the only form. Hence in the Vedas श्रुधि (κλῦθι); and in the Mahábhárata अपाकृधि. *Dhi* then passed into *hi*, as *dhita* passed into *hita*, and *bhúmi* into the Latin *humus*.

the different terminations of each tense, such variation being denoted by the letter P and other indicatory letters of the memorial scheme at 246, which, be it remembered, are significant only in reference to the second and third groups, and not to the first.

a. In the 2d preterite, however, being a non-conjugational tense, the P is equally significant for verbs of all conjugations. Observe—This P, which usually indicates that in those persons of the tense where it occurs, the root must be guṇated or vṛiddhied, is generally to be found after light terminations. The 1st, 2d, and 3d sing. Parasmai of the present, 1st preterite, and 2d preterite are manifestly light terminations. The 3d sing. Parasmai of the imperative is also clearly light; and the 1st sing. du. and pl. Parasmai and Átmane of this tense must have been originally light, as these also have a P affixed. The object, therefore, of the P is to show, that fulness of form or weight is to be imparted to the root or base before these light terminations, and these only: thus इ *i*, 2d conj., 'to go,' is in the pres. sing. *emi, eshi, eti;* in du. *ivas, ithas, itas;* in pl. *imas*, &c.: just as in Greek εἶμι, εἶς, εἶσι; ἴτον, ἴτον; ἴμεν, &c.: compare also φημί (for φᾱμι), φής, φησί, φατόν, φατόν, φαμέν, φατέ, φασί. So again, *stṛi*, 'to strew,' is in pres. sing. *stṛiṇomi, stṛiṇoshi, stṛiṇoti;* in du. *stṛiṇuvas, stṛiṇuthas, stṛiṇutas;* in pl. *stṛiṇumas*, &c.: just as in Greek στόρνῡμι, στόρνῡς, στόρνῡτι, στόρνῠτον, στόρνῠτον, στόρνῠμες, &c. Similarly, *krí*, 'to buy,' is in pres. sing. *kríṇámi, kríṇási, kríṇáti;* in du. &c. *kríṇívas, kríṇíthas, kríṇítas, kríṇímas*, &c., the *á* being heavier than *í*. Compare Greek πέρνᾱμι (πέρνημι), πέρνᾱς, πέρνᾱτι, πέρνᾰτον, πέρνᾰτον, &c. When a root is long by nature or position, no additional weight is necessary, and no Guṇa is then possible (see 28. *b*); but in place of Guṇa, the root or base sometimes remains unmutilated before the light terminations, while mutilation takes place before the heavy. Thus *dá* and *dhá* suppress their final vowels before the heavy terminations, and preserve them before the light; see 335, 336. Similarly, *as*, 'to be,' which by 28. *b*. cannot be guṇated, drops its initial vowel before the heavy terminations, retaining it before the light; see 322, and compare 320. Observe, that since Guṇa takes place before all the terminations of the 2d future indiscriminately, the P affixed to the singular terminations of this tense can have no significance, unless it be to show that the terminations of this tense are taken from the present, with *sya* prefixed.

294. Another source of difficulty is, that in the second group (viz. the 2d, 3d, and 7th) the verbal base will generally end in a consonant, there being no provision for the interposition of a vowel between the root and the terminations. Hence the combination of the final consonant of a base with the initial *t*, *th*, or *s*, of a termination in the conjugational tenses of these three classes requires a knowledge of the laws of Sandhi already propounded, as well as of the following additional rules.

a. Observe, however, that as regards the initial *m* or *v* of a termination, a hard consonant at the end of a root is not made soft before these letters, as might be expected by 41, but remains unchanged: thus, *vach + mi = vachmi*, and *chekshep + mi = chekshepmi*.

295. The following rules will also apply in forming the base of the non-conjugational tenses of *all* the conjugations excepting the 10th, and in some of the participles; for although in most roots ending in consonants provision is made for the insertion of the vowel इ *i* (see terminations of 1st future &c. at p. 107) before the terminations of these tenses, yet there are a large class of common roots which reject this inserted vowel, leaving the final of the base to coalesce with the initial consonant of the termination. It will be convenient, therefore, in the following pages to introduce by anticipation a few examples from the non-conjugational tenses and participles.

Combination of final च् ch *and* ज् j *with* त t, थ th, *and* स s.

296. Final च् *ch* and ज् *j*, before त *t*, थ *th*, and स *s*, are changed to क् *k* (compare 43. *d*), the *k* blending with *s* into क्ष् *ksh* by 70: thus, *vach + ti = vakti; vach + thas = vakthas; vach + si = vakshi; moch + syámi = mokshyámi; much + ta = mukta; tyaj + ta = tyakta; tyaj + syámi = tyakshyámi.*

297. But a final palatal is sometimes changed to ष् *sh* before त *t*, थ *th*; and त *t*, थ *th*, then become ट्, ठ्: thus, मार्ज् + *ti* = मार्ष्टि; मृज् + *thas* = मृष्ठस्; मृज् + *ta* = मृष्ट; प्रच्छ् + *ta* = प्रष्ट.

Combination of final ध् dh *and* भ् bh *with* त t, थ th, *and* स s.

298. Final ध् *dh* and भ् *bh*, before त *t* and थ *th*, are changed, the one to द् *d*, the other to ब् *b*, and both *t* and *th* then become ध *dh*: thus, *rundh* with *tas* or *thas* becomes equally रुन्द्धस् *runddhas*; *labh + táhe* = लब्धाहे *labdháhe*. But if the root begin with *d* it follows 42. *c*. See 664.

a. Observe—When final ध् *dh* is preceded by a conjunct न् *n*, as in *rundh*, then the final *dh*, which has become *d* (before *t* and *th* changed to *dh*), may optionally be rejected; so that *rundh + tas* = रुन्द्धस् or रुन्धस्; *rundh + tam* = रुन्द्धं or रुन्धं.

299. Final ध् *dh* and भ् *bh*, before स *s*, are changed by 42, the one to त् *t*, the other to प् *p*: thus, रुणध् *ruṇadh + si* becomes रुणत्सि *ruṇatsi; sedh + syámi = setsyámi; labh + sye = lapsye.*

a. And if the initial of the root be *b* or *d*, the aspirate, which has been rejected in the final, is thrown back on the initial; as, *bodh* +

sye = भोत्स्ये *bhotsye; dadh* + *swa* = धत्स्व *dhatswa.* See 42. *c*, 664; and compare θρέψω from τρέφω. Observe—The aspirate is also thrown back on the initial, when final *dh* is changed to *d*, before the terminations *dhwe* and *dhwam.* See 664.

Combination of final श् ś, ष् sh, स् s, *with* त t, थ th, स s, ध dh.

300. Final श् *ś*, before त *t* and थ *th*, is changed to ष् *sh;* and the *t*, *th*, take the cerebral form ट्, ठ्: thus, ईश् + *te* = ईष्टे; and ऐश् + *thás* = ऐष्ठास्.

301. Similarly, final ष् *sh*, before त *t* and थ *th*, requires the change of *t*, *th*, to ट्, ठ्: thus, द्वेष् + *ti* = द्वेष्टि; and द्विष् + *thas* = द्विष्ठस्.

302. Final श् *ś* or ष् *sh*, before स *s*, is changed to क् *k* by 43. *e*, the *s* then becoming ष *sh* by 70: thus, वश् + *si* = वक्षि; द्वेष् + *si* = द्वेक्षि; दृश् + *syámi* = द्रक्ष्यामि.

303. Final श् *ś* or ष् *sh*, before ध *dh*, is changed to ड् *ḍ*, the ध *dh* becoming ढ *ḍh* by 51: thus, द्विष् + *dhi* = द्विड्ढि. Similarly, द्विष् + *dhwam* = द्विड्ढ्वं. A final ज् *j* may also follow this rule; see 632, 651.

304. Final स् *s*, before ध *dh*, is either dropped or changed to द् *d*: thus, *chakás* + *dhi* = either चकाधि *chakádhi* or चकाद्धि *chakáddhi;* शास् + *dhi* = शाधि; हिंस् + *dhi* = हिंद्धि.

a. Before स *s* it is changed to त् *t;* as, *vas* + *syámi* = *vatsyámi.* So in the 2d sing. 1st pret. of *śás*, *aśás* + *s* = *aśáts* = *aśát* by 43. *a.*

Combination of final ह् h *with* त t, थ th, स s, ध dh.

305. In roots beginning with द् *d*, like दुह् *duh*, 'to milk,' final ह् *h* is changed to ग् *g* before त *t* and थ *th*, and both *t* and *th* then become ध *dh:* thus, दुह् *duh* + *tas* or *thas* becomes equally दुग्धस् *dugdhas;* दह् *dah* + *tásmi* = *dagdhásmi.* In the root नह् the final *h* becomes *dh*, and blends with *t* and *th* into द्ध *ddh.* See 624.

a. But if the root begin with any other letter than द् *d* or न *n*, then its final ह् *h* is dropped, and both the त *t* and थ *th* of the termination become ढ *ḍh.* Moreover, to compensate for the rejection of the final *h*, the radical vowel, if not guṇated, is lengthened, and in the roots *sah* and *vah* changed to *o;* as, मुह् + *ta* = मूढ; रुह् + *ta* = रूढ; लेह् *leh* + *ti* = लेढि *leḍhi;* रोह् + *tásmi* = रोढास्मि; *sah* + *tá* = सोढा; *vah* + *tá* = वोढा.

306. Final ह् *h*, before स् *s*, follows the analogy of final श् *ś* and ष् *sh*, and is changed to क् *k*, which blends with स *s* into क्ष *ksh:*

thus, लेह् *leh* with *si* becomes लेक्षि; रोह् + *syámi* = रोक्ष्यामि. Similarly, in Latin, final *h* becomes *k* before *s*; as, *veksit* (*vexit*) from *veho*.

a. And if the initial of the root be द् *d* or ग *g*, the final ह् *h* is still changed to क् *k* before *s*; but the initial द् *d* then becomes ध *dh*, and ग *g* becomes घ *gh*: thus, दोह् *doh* + *si* = धोक्षि; दह् *dah* + *syámi* = धक्ष्यामि; अगुह् *aguh* + *sam* = अघुक्षं. Compare 42. *c*.

b. In the root नह् *nah* final *h* becomes ध् *dh*, and then त् *t*, before *s*. Compare 182. *e*, and see 624.

c. In roots beginning with द् *d*, like दुह् *duh* and दिह्, final ह् *h* becomes ग *g* before *dh*; i. e. before the *dhi* of the 2d sing. imperative, and before the terminations *dhwe* and *dhwam*: thus, दुह् *duh* + *dhi* = दुग्धि *dugdhi*. And in a root beginning with *n*, like *nah*, final *h* becomes *dh*, and then *d*, before these terminations. But if the root begin with any other letter than *d* or *n*, then final *h* is dropped, and the ध *dh* of the termination becomes ढ *ḍh*, the radical vowel being lengthened: thus, लिह् *lih* + *dhi* = लीढि; *lih* + *dhwam* = लीढ्वं.

d. Again, in roots beginning with द् *d* or ग *g* these letters become respectively ध *dh* and घ *gh*, when final ह् *h* becomes *g* or is dropped before *dhwe* and *dhwam*; but not before the *dhi* of the imperative: thus, *duh* + *dhwe* = धुग्ध्वे *dhugdhwe*; and *aguh* + *dhwam* = अघूढ्वं *aghúḍhwam*.

FORMATION OF THE BASE IN THE 2D, 3D, AND 7TH CLASSES OF VERBS.

Second class (2d conjugation), containing 70 primitive verbs.

307. Rule for the formation of the base in the four conjugational tenses. Guṇate the vowel of the root (except when debarred by 28. *b*) before those terminations only which are marked with P in the memorial scheme at 246. Before all the other terminations the original vowel of the root must be retained by 293. *a*. Remember, that no vowel is interposed between the root and the terminations, as in Greek verbs like εἶμι, φημί, &c. See 258. *a*, 294.

308. Thus, from विद् *vid*, 'to know' (Greek εἴδω, ἴδον, Lat. *video*), is formed the base of the singular present *ved* (1. *ved* + *mi* = वेद्मि *vedmi*, &c.), and the base of the dual and plural *vid* (Du. 1. *vid* + *vas* = विद्वस् *vidwas*, &c.; Pl. 1. *vid* + *mas* = विद्मस् *vidmas*, &c.). So also the base of the potential *vid* (1. *vid* + *yám* = विद्यां *vidyám*, &c.); the base of the imperative *ved* and *vid* (1. *ved* + *áni* = *vedáni*, 2. *vid* +

dhi = *viddhi* 291, *ved* + *tu* = *vettu*; Du. 1. *ved* + *áva* = *vedáva*, &c.*); and the base of the 1st pret. *aved* and *avid* (1. *aved* + *am* = *avedam*, 2. *aved* + *s* = *avet* or *aves* by 43. *a.* and 292). See the table at 583.

a. A contracted form of the 2d preterite of *vid* (365) is sometimes used for the present: thus, Sing. *veda, vettha, veda;* Du. *vidwa, vidathus, vidatus;* Pl. *vidma, vida, vidus;* see 168. *a.* Compare the Greek οἶδα or Ϝοῖδα from the root Ϝιδ (εἴδω), also used with a present signification; and the Latin *vidi, vidisti,* &c. Cf. also the present *vidmas* with ἴδμεν (ἴσμεν), *vittha* with ἴστε, and *viddhi* with ἴσθι.

309. Similarly, from द्विष्, 'to hate,' come the bases *dwesh* and *dwish* (Pres. 1. द्वेष्मि; Du. 1. द्विष्वस्, &c.; see 657).

310. So also, from इ *i*, 'to go,' will come the bases *e* and *i* (Pres. 1. एमि *emi*, cf. εἶμι, 2. एषि by 70, 3. एति; Pl. 1. इमस्, cf. ἴμεν, see 645); from जागृ 'to awake,' the bases जागर् *jágar* and जागृ *jágṛi* (Pres. 1. जागर्मि, &c.; Du. 1. जागृवस्; Pl. 3. जाग्रति by 290. *b*).

311. The preposition अधि *adhi*, 'over,' prefixed to the root इ *i*, 'to go,' gives the sense of 'to read' (Átmane-pada only): इ then becomes *iy* (compare 123), and blends with *adhi* into अधीय् *adhíy* before the vowel-terminations of the pres. pot. and 1st pret. Before the consonantal-terminations it becomes अधी *adhí*. (Hence the Pres. 1. अधीये, 2. अधीषे, 3. अधीते; Du. 1. अधीवहे, &c.; Pot. 1. अधीयीय, &c.; Imp. 1. *adhi* + *e* + *ai* = अध्ययै by 36. *a*, 2. अधीष्व, &c.; 1st Pret. 1. *adhi* + *a* + *iy* + *i* = अध्यैयि by 260. *a*, 2. अध्यैथास्, 3. अध्यैत; Du. 1. अध्यैवहि, 2. अध्यैयाथां, &c.)

a. The preposition आ *á* is prefixed to the root इ *i*, according to the usual rules of Sandhi, and gives the sense of 'to come:' thus, Pres. ऐमि, ऐषि, ऐति; एवस्, &c.; Pot. इयां, एयास्, &c.; Imp. आयानि, एहि, ऐतु, &c.; 1st Pret. आयं, ऐस्, &c. Again, the prep. अप *apa* prefixed gives the sense of 'to go away:' thus, Pres. अपैमि, &c.

312. Other roots in ई *í* and उ *u* or ऊ *ú* change these vowels to *iy* and *uv* (compare 123 and 125. *a*) before the vowel-terminations; as, from वी *ví*, 'to go,' come the bases *ve*, *ví*, and *viy* (Pres. 1. वेमि, &c.; Du. 1. वीव; Pl. 3. वियन्ति). Similarly, सू, 'to bring forth' (Átmane only), makes in Pres. S. Du. Pl. 3. सूते, सुवाते, सुवते; and in Imp. S. Du. Pl. 1. सुवै, सुवावहै, सुवामहै, Guṇa being suppressed†.

313. स्तु *stu* and नु *nu*, 'to praise;' यु *yu*, 'to join,' 'to mix;' and रु *ru*, 'to sound'—follow 312, and take Vṛiddhi instead of Guṇa before the consonantal P terminations‡. Hence the bases स्तौ *stau*, स्तु *stu*, and स्तुव् *stuv;* see 648. Before the

---

* The imperative of *vid* is optionally formed with the syllable *ám* and the auxiliary verb *kṛi* (compare 384): thus, s. 3. विदांकरोतु or विदाङ्करोतु. Páṇini III. 1. 41.

† See Páṇini VII. 3. 88.

‡ That is, the terminations marked with P, which begin with consonants.

vowel P terminations both Vṛiddhi and Guṇa are generally (but not always) suppressed, and *uv* substituted, as in सू at 312. Note, that these roots may optionally insert an ई *í* before the consonantal P terminations; and before this vowel Guṇa, not Vṛiddhi, is required. According to some authorities, however, *í* is inserted before *all* the consonantal-terminations; and, according to others, before all the consonants, excepting *y*, *v*, or *m*, not followed by an indicatory P.

314. ब्रू, 'to speak,' can never take Vṛiddhi, like the roots at 313; but inserts an ई *í* after Guṇa in the places where those roots optionally insert it, viz. before the consonantal P terminations. Hence the bases *bravī́*, *brū́*, *bruv*. See 649.

a. Before the vowel P terminations Guṇa is not suppressed, excepting in the 1st pret. 1st sing.

315. शी, 'to lie down,' 'to sleep' (Átmane only), guṇates the radical vowel before *all* the terminations, and inserts *r* in the 3d pl. pres., 1st pret., and imperative, after the analogy of the 3d pl. potential. See 646.

316. ऊर्णु, 'to cover,' takes either Vṛiddhi or Guṇa of the final *u* before the consonantal P terminations, excepting before the 2d and 3d sing. of the 1st pret., where Guṇa only is admissible. Before the vowel-terminations it follows 312, but Guṇa is retained before the vowel P terminations, excepting in the 1st pret. 1st sing. Hence the bases *urnau*, *urno*, *urnu*, and *urnuv* (Pres. 1. ऊर्णौमि or ऊर्णोमि; Du. 1. ऊर्णुवस्; Pl. 3. ऊर्णुवन्ति, see 290. *b*; Pot. 1. ऊर्णुयां; Imp. s. 1. ऊर्णवानि, 3. ऊर्णौतु or ऊर्णोतु; 1st Pret. 1. और्णुवं by 260. *a*, 2. और्णोस्, &c.).

317. Roots like या 'to go,' पा 'to protect,' अद् 'to eat' (*edo*), आस् 'to sit,' Átm., having *a* or *á* for their vowels, cannot be guṇated, but are themselves bases (Pres. 1. *yá* + *mi* = *yámi*, see 644, *ad* + *mi* = *admi*, 2. *ad* + *si* = *atsi*, 3. *ad* + *ti* = *atti*; Du. 3. *ad* + *tas* = *attas*, &c., see 652. Similarly, *ás* + *e* = *áse*, *ás* + *se* = *ásse*, *ás* + *te* = *áste*, &c.). With *atti* compare Lat. *edit*.

a. Before the terminations of the 2d and 3d sing. 1st preterite of अद्, 'to eat,' the vowel अ *a* is inserted by special rule; and some others of these roots require peculiar changes, as follows:—

318. हन् *han*, 'to kill,' makes its base ह *ha* before *t* or *th* (by 57. *a*); घ्न् *ghn* before *anti*, *an*, *antu*; and ज *ja* before हि. The last change is to avoid the proximity of two aspirates. See 654, and compare 331. *b*.

319. वच् *vach*, 'to speak,' changes its final palatal to a guttural before all the hard consonantal-terminations, in conformity with 176; but not before the soft, by 294. *a*. It is defective in the 3d pl. present and imperative, where its place must be supplied by ब्रू at 314, 649. Hence the bases *vach* and *vak*. See 650.

320. वश् *vaś*, 'to desire,' 'to choose,' suppresses the *a*, and changes *v* to *u* before the terminations which have no P (see 293. *a*); and उश् *uś* becomes उष् *ush* before *t* and *th* by 300. See 656.

321. चक्ष् *chaksh*, 'to speak' (Átmane-pada only), drops the penultimate *k* before all consonantal-terminations, excepting those beginning with *m* or *v* (Pres. 1. चक्षे, 2. चष् + से = चक्षे by 292, 3. चष्टे, &c.).

322. अस् *as*, 'to be' (Parasmai-pada only), a very useful auxiliary verb, follows

293. *a*, and rejects its initial *a*, excepting before the P terminations. The 2d pers. sing. of the pres. is असि for अस्सि. The 1st pret. has the character of a 3d pret., and retains the initial *a* throughout, and inserts ई *í* before the *s* and *t* of the 2d and 3d sing.; see 584. This root is never found in the Átmane-pada, excepting with the prepositions *vi* and *ati*, when the Present is Sing. व्यतिहे, -षे, -स्ते; Du. -स्वहे, -साथे, -साते, -स्महे, -ध्वे, -सते; Pot. S. 1. व्यतिषीय, &c.

323. शास् *śás*, 'to rule,' changes its vowel to इ *i* before *t*, *th*, and *y*; and, after *i*, स् becomes ष् by 70. Hence the bases शास् and शिष्. See 658.

324. मृज् *mṛij*, 'to cleanse,' is vṛiddhied before the P terminations, and optionally before the vowel-terminations having no P. Hence the bases *márj* and *mṛij*. See 651.

325. The roots ईश् *íś*, 'to rule' (Átm.), and ईड् *íḍ*, 'to praise' (Átm.), not guṇated by 28. *b*, insert the vowel इ *i* between the root and the terminations of the 2d person से, स्व, ध्वे, and ध्वं (ईड्—Pres. 1. ईडे, 2. ईडिषे, 3. ईट्टे; Du. 1. ईड्वहे, &c.; Pot. 1. ईडीय, &c.; Imp. 1. ईडै, 2. ईडिष्व, 3. ईट्टां; 1st Pret. 3. ऐट्ट, &c. ईश्—Pres. 1. ईशे, 2. ईशिषे, 3. ईष्टे by 300; Imp. 3. ईष्टां, &c.; 1st Pret. 3. ऐष्ट, &c.).

326. रुद् *rud*, 'to weep,' besides the usual Guṇa change before the P terminations, inserts the vowel इ *i* before all the consonantal-terminations except *y*, and optionally *a* or *i* in the 2d and 3d sing. 1st pret. Hence the three bases *rodi*, *rudi*, *rud*; see 653. Similarly, but without Guṇa, the roots स्वप् 'to sleep,' श्वस् and अन् 'to breathe,' and जक्ष् 'to eat.' The last obeys 290. *b*.

327. दुह् *duh*, 'to milk,' and लिह् *lih*, 'to lick,' form their bases as explained at 305, 306. They are conjugated at 660, 661.

328. दरिद्रा *daridrá*, 'to be poor' (Parasmai-pada), follows 293. *a*, making its base *daridri* before the consonantal-terminations not marked with P, and *daridr* before *ati*, *us*, *atu* (Pres. S. Du. Pl. 3. दरिद्राति, दरिद्रितस्, दरिद्रति; see 290. *b*).

329. दीधी *dídhí*, 'to shine' (Átm.), changes its final to *y*, and not to *iy*, before the vowel-terminations (compare 312); but in the potential the final *í* coalesces with the *í* of the terminations (Pres. Pl. 3. दीध्यते; Pot. 1. दीधीय, &c.).

Third class (3d conjugation), containing about 20 primitive verbs.

330. Rule for the formation of the base in the four conjugational tenses. Reduplicate the initial consonant and vowel of the root, and guṇate the vowel of the *radical syllable* before the P terminations only, as in the 2d conjugation, by 293. *a*. Note, that this conjugation resembles the 2d in interposing no vowel between the root and the terminations. It is the only conjugation that rejects the nasal in the 3d plur. Parasmai-pada, by 290. *a*, and takes *us* for *an* in the 3d plur. 1st pret., before which *us* Guṇa is generally required.

331. In reduplication the following rules are observed. 1st, As to consonants.

a. A corresponding unaspirated letter is substituted for an aspirate: thus, *d* for *dh*. So in Greek τ is repeated for θ; as, θύω, τέθυκα, &c.

b. The palatal च *ch* is substituted for the gutturals क *k* or ख *kh*; and the palatal ज *j* for the gutturals ग *g*, घ *gh*, or ह *h*.

c. If a root begin with a double consonant, the first consonant only is reduplicated; but if with a double consonant, whose first is a sibilant and whose second is hard, the second is reduplicated: thus, च *ch* for क्ष *ksh*; त *t* for स्थ *sth*; ज *j* for ह्र *hr*; क *k* for स्क *sk*.

d. 2dly, As to vowels. अ *a* is the reduplicated vowel for आ *á*; इ *i* for ई *í* or ऋ *ṛi*; उ *u* for ऊ *ú*. In certain cases इ *i* is also repeated for *a* and *á*, as being a lighter vowel.

e. Observe—As a general rule, the reduplicated syllable has a tendency to lighten the weight of the radical syllable.

332. Thus, from भृ *bhṛi*, 'to bear' (φέρω, *fero*), is formed the base of the present singular बिभर् *bibhar* (1. *bibhar* + *mi* = बिभर्मि), and the base of the dual and plural बिभृ *bibhṛi* (Du. 1. *bibhṛi* + *vas* = बिभृवस्; Pl. 1. *bibhṛi* + *mas* = बिभृमस्; Pl. 3. *bibhṛi* + *ati* = बिभ्रति by 34 and 290). See the table at 583.

a. Note, that *bibharti* bears the same relation to *bibhṛimas* that *fert* does to *ferimus*, and *vult* to *volumus*.

333. Similarly, from भी *bhí*, 'to fear,' come the two bases *bibhe* and *bibhí*; from हु *hu*, 'to sacrifice,' the two bases *juho* and *juhu*. The former of these roots may optionally shorten the radical vowel before a consonant, when not guṇated. See 667. The latter may optionally reject its final before *vas* and *mas*, and is the only root ending in a vowel which takes *dhi* for *hi* in the 2d sing. imperative. See 662.

a. ह्री, 'to be ashamed,' is like भी, but changes its final ई to इय् *iy* before the vowel-terminations, in conformity with 123. *a*. See 668.

334. ऋ *ṛi*, 'to go,' is the only verb in this conjugation that begins with a vowel. It substitutes *iy* for *ṛi* in the reduplication, and makes its bases इयर् *iyar* and इयृ *iyṛi* (Pres. S. Du. Pl. 3. इयर्ति, इयृतस्, इय्रति; 1st Pret. S. 1. ऐयरं, 2. ऐयर्, 3. ऐयर्, &c.).

335. दा *dá*, 'to give' (δίδωμι, *do*), drops its final *á* before all excepting the P terminations. Hence the bases *dadá* and *dad*. It becomes दे *de* before the *hi* of the imperative. See 663.

336. Similarly, the root धा *dhá*, 'to place' (τίθημι). Hence the bases *dadhá* and *dadh*; but *dadh* becomes धत् before *t*, *th*, and *s*, by 42. *c*; and *dhe* before the *hi* of the imperative. See 664.

337. हा *há*, 'to abandon,' changes its final *á* to ई *í* before the consonantal-terminations not marked with P, and drops the final altogether before the vowel-terminations, and before *y* of the potential. Hence the bases *jahá*, *jahí*, *jah*. Before *hi* of the imperative the base is optionally *jahi*, *jahí*, or *jahá*; and, according

to some authorities, जही may be shortened into जहि in the present, imperative, and 1st preterite. See 666.

338. मा *má*, 'to measure' (Átm.), and हा *há*, 'to go' (Átm.), make their bases मिमी *mimí* and जिही *jihí* before the consonantal-terminations not marked with P. Before the vowel-terminations their bases are *mim* and *jih*. According to some authorities, *mimí* and *jihí* may be optionally shortened into *mimi* and *jihi*. See 665.

339. जन् *jan*, 'to produce' (Parasmai-pada), rejects the final nasal (see 57. *a*), and lengthens the radical *a* before *t* and *th* and *hi*, and, according to some, optionally before *y*. Before the vowel-terminations not marked with P it rejects the radical *a* (compare the declension of *rájan* at 149). Hence the three bases *jajan*, *jajá*, and *jaju*. The 2d sing. pres. is either जजंसि or जज्ञनिषि. See 667. *b*.

340. भस् *bhas*, 'to shine,' like *jan*, rejects the radical *a* before the vowel-terminations not marked with P; and *bh* coalescing with *s* becomes *p* by 42 (Pres. S. Du. Pl. 3. बभस्ति, बभस्तस्, बप्सति).

341. The roots निज् 'to purify,' विज् 'to separate,' and विष् 'to divide,' gunate the reduplicated syllable before *all* the terminations, and forbid the usual Guṇa of the radical syllable in the 1st pers. sing. du. pl., imperative (Pres. 1. नेनेज्मि, 2. नेनेक्षि, 3. नेनेक्ति; Du. 1. नेनिज्वस्, &c.; Pl. 1. नेनिज्मस्, 3. नेनिजति; Imp. 1. नेनिजानि; Du. 1. नेनिजाव; Pl. 1. नेनिजाम; 1st Pret. 1. अनेनेजं, 2. अनेनेक्, &c.; Pl. 3. अनेनिजुस्, &c.).

Seventh class (7th conjugation), containing about 24 primitive verbs.

342. Rule for the formation of the base in the four conjugational tenses. Insert न *na* (changeable to ण *ṇa* after *ṛi* &c. by 58) *between* the vowel and final consonant* of the root before the P terminations, and न् *n* (changeable to ङ, ञ, or Anuswára, according to the consonant immediately succeeding) before all the other terminations by 293. *a*. Note, that this conjugation resembles the 2d and 3d in interposing no vowel between the final consonant of the root and the terminations.

a. Similarly, *n* is inserted in certain Greek and Latin roots; as, μαθ, μανθάνω; λαβ, λαμβάνω; θιγ, θιγγάνω; *scid*, *scindo*; *fid*, *findo*; *tag*, *tango*; *liq*, *linquo*, &c. See 258. *a*.

343. Thus, from भिद् *bhid*, 'to divide,' 'to break,' is formed the base of the present tense singular भिनद् *bhinad*, and the base of the dual and plural भिन्द् *bhind*, changeable to *bhinat* and *bhint* by 46 (1. *bhinad* + *mi* = भिनद्मि, 3. *bhinad* + *ti* = भिनत्ति; Du. 1. *bhind* + *vas* = भिन्द्वस्, 3. *bhind* + *tas* = भिन्त्तस् or भिन्तस्; Pl. 3. *bhind* + *anti* = भिन्दन्ति). See the table at 583.

* All the roots in this conjugation end in consonants.

344. Similarly, from रुध् *rudh*, 'to hinder,' the two bases रुणध् *ruṇadh* and रुन्ध् *rundh*, changeable to *ruṇat*, *ruṇad*, and *rund* (1. *ruṇadh* + *mi* = रुणध्मि, 2. *ruṇadh* + *si* = रुणत्सि, 3. *ruṇadh* + *ti* = रुणद्धि; Du. 3. *rundh* + *tas* = रुन्द्धस्). See 671.

345. Observe—Roots ending in त् *t* and द् *d* may reject these letters before *th*, *t*, and *dhi*, when *n* immediately precedes: hence भिन्तस् may be written for भिन्त्तस्; भिन्धि for भिन्द्धि. Similarly, रुन्धस् may be written for रुन्द्धस्, see 298. *a;* and on the same principle तृण्ढस् is written for तृण्ढ्ढस् from तृह्, see 674.

346. The roots भुज् 'to eat,' युज् 'to join,' विच् 'to distinguish,' conform to 296. Hence, from *bhuj* come *bhunaj* and *bhuñj*, changeable to *bhunak* and *bhun·k*.

347. The roots भञ्ज् 'to break,' अञ्ज् 'to anoint,' उन्द् 'to moisten,' and इन्ध् 'to kindle,' are placed under this class; but the nasal belonging to the root takes the place of the conjugational nasal. Hence, from *bhañj* come the two bases *bhanaj* and *bhañj*, changeable to *bhanak* and *bhan·k*.

348. The root तृह्, 'to strike,' 'to kill,' inserts णे instead of ण before all the P terminations, excepting the 1st sing. du. pl. imperative and 1st pret. See 674.

FORMATION OF THE BASE IN THE 5TH, 8TH, AND 9TH CLASSES OF VERBS.

Fifth class (5th conjugation,) containing about 30 primitive verbs.

349. Rule for the formation of the base in the four conjugational tenses. Add नु *nu* to the root, which must be guṇated into नो *no* before the P terminations by 293. *a*. Note, that roots ending in consonants add *nuv*, instead of *nu*, to the root before the vowel-terminations. Roots ending in vowels may drop the *u* of *nu* before initial *v* and *m* (not marked with P), and always reject the termination *hi* of the imperative. See 291 and 259 with note.

a. This change of *nu* to *no* is supplied in the corresponding Greek affix νυ, by lengthening the υ, as in ζεύγνῡμι, ζεύγνυμεν; δείκνῡμι, δείκνυμεν. See 258. *a*.

350. Thus, from चि *chi*, 'to gather,' are formed the bases *chino* and *chinu* (Pres. 1. *chino* + *mi* = चिनोमि, *chino* + *si* = चिनोषि by 70; Du. 1. *chinu* + *vas* = चिनुवस् or चिन्वस्; Pl. 1. *chinu* + *mas* = चिनुमस् or चिन्मस्, 3. *chinu* + *anti* = चिन्वन्ति by 34; Imp. 1. *chino* + *áni* = चिनवानि by 36. *b*, 2. *chinu* by 291). See the table at 583.

351. Similarly, from आप् *áp*, 'to obtain,' come *ápno* and *ápnu*. See 681.

352. श्रु *śru*, 'to hear' (sometimes placed under the 1st class), substitutes शृ *śṛi* for the root, and makes its bases *śṛiṇo* and *śṛiṇu*. See 677.

Eighth class (8th conjugation), containing 10 primitive verbs.

353. Rule for the formation of the base in the four conjugational

tenses. Add उ *u* to the root, which must be guṇated into ओ *o* before the P terminations by 293. *a*.

a. Observe—There are only ten roots in this conjugation, and nine of these end either in न् *n* or ण् *ṇ*: hence the addition of *u* and *o* will have the same apparent effect as the addition of *nu* and *no* in the 5th conjugation.

354. Thus, from तन् *tan*, 'to stretch,' 'to extend,' are formed the bases *tano* and *tanu* (Pres. 1. *tano* + *mi* = तनोमि, 2. *tano* + *si* = तनोषि by 70; Du. 1. *tanu* + *vas* = तनुवस् or तन्वस्; Pl. 1. *tanu* + *mas* = तनुमस् or तन्मस्; Imp. 1. *tano* + *áni* = तनवानि by 36. *b*). Compare the Greek τάνυμι, τάνυμες.

a. The root सन् *san*, 'to give,' optionally rejects its *n*, and lengthens the radical *a* before the *y* of the potential: thus, सन्यां *sanyám* or सायां *sáyám*, &c.

355. The tenth root in this class is कृ *kṛi*, 'to do,' by far the most common and useful root in the language. This root guṇates the radical vowel *ṛi*, as well as the conjugational *u*, before the P terminations. Before the other terminations it changes the radical *ṛi* to *ur*. Before initial *m* (not marked with P), *v*, and *y*, it rejects the conjugational *u*. Hence the three bases *karo*, *kuru*, and *kur*. See 682.

Ninth class (9th conjugation), containing about 52 primitive verbs.

356. Rule for the formation of the base in the four conjugational tenses. Add ना *ná* to the root before the P terminations; नी *ní* before all the others, excepting those beginning with vowels, where only न् *n* is added, by 293. *a*. Observe—ना, नी, and न्, are changeable to णा, णी, and ण्, by 58.

357. Thus, from यु *yu*, 'to join,' are formed the three bases *yuná*, *yuní*, and *yun* (Pres. 1. *yuná* + *mi* = युनामि; Du. 1. *yuní* + *vas* = युनीवस्; Pl. 1. *yuní* + *mas* = युनीमस्, 3. *yun* + *anti* = युनन्ति. Pres. Átm. 1. *yun* + *e* = युने; Imp. 1. *yuná* + *áni* = युनानि, 2. *yuní* + *hi* = युनीहि, &c.).

a. Observe—Roots ending in consonants substitute *ána* for *níhi* in the 2d sing. imperative: so, अशान 'eat thou,' from अश् 'to eat;' पुषाण 'nourish thou,' from पुष्, &c. See 696, 698.

358. The roots री, ली, भी, व्री, ब्ली, धू, पू, लू, स्तॄ, कॄ, गॄ, जॄ, दॄ, नॄ, पॄ, भॄ, वॄ, शॄ, स्तॄ, shorten the radical vowel in forming their bases: thus, from पू, 'to purify,' come the bases *puná*, *puní*, and *pun*. See the table at 583.

359. ग्रह्, 'to take,' becomes गृह्, 'and makes its bases गृह्णा, गृह्णी, and गृह्ण्. See 699.

360. ज्ञा, 'to know,' becomes जा, and makes its bases *janá, janí,* and *jáu*. See 688.

361. ज्या, 'to grow old,' becomes जि, and makes its bases *jiná, jiní,* and *jin*.

362. The roots बन्ध्, ग्रन्थ्, मन्थ्, श्रन्थ्, and कुन्थ्, reject the radical nasal in favour of the conjugational: thus, from *bandh* are formed the three bases *badhná, badhní,* and *bandh*. See 692.

PRIMITIVE VERBS OF THE FIRST NINE CLASSES IN THE SIX NON-CONJUGATIONAL TENSES.

363. Observe—The general rules for the formation of the base in the 2d preterite, 1st and 2d futures, 3d preterite, benedictive, and conditional, apply to all verbs of the first nine classes indiscriminately; see 250. *a*. The 10th class alone carries its conjugational characteristic into most of the non-conjugational tenses; and for this reason the consideration of its five last tenses falls most conveniently under causal verbs. Compare 289. *a*.

Second preterite (Greek perfect).

364. Rule for the formation of the base in verbs of the first nine classes. In the first place, if a root begin with a consonant, reduplicate the initial consonant, according to the rules given at 331, with its vowel (*a* being reduplicated for *a, á, ṛi, ṛí; i* for *i, í, e; u* for *u, ú, o*): thus, from बुध् *budh*, 1st c.*, 'to know,' comes the base बुबुध् *bubudh;* from नृत् *nṛit*, 4th c., 'to dance,' ननृत् *nanṛit;* from याच् *yách*, 1st c., 'to ask,' ययाच् *yayách;* from कृ *kṛi*, 8th c., 'to do,' चकृ *chakṛi;* from तॄ *tṛí*, 1st c., 'to cross,' ततॄ *tatṛí;* from सिध् *sidh*, सिषिध् *sishidh* by 70; from *sev, sishev;* from *pú, pupú*.

a. And if it begin with a vowel, double the initial vowel: thus, from अस् *as*, 'to be,' आस् *ás*.

b. In the second place, if the root end in a consonant, guṇate † the vowel of the radical syllable, except when debarred by 28. *b*, in the 1st, 2d, and 3d *singular*, Parasmai-pada (as *bubodh* for *bubudh*); but leave the vowel unchanged before all the other terminations, Parasmai and Átmane-pada. See 293. *a*.

c. And if the root end in a vowel, vṛiddhi the vowel of the radical syllable in the 1st and 3d *singular*, Parasmai ‡ (as *chakár* for *chakṛi*),

---

* 1st c. means 1st class or conjugation.

† The guṇation of the vowel is indicated by the P of णप्, थप्, णप्, in the singular terminations. See scheme at 246.

‡ Grammarians assert, that there is optionally Guṇa in the 1st singular. Vṛiddhi is indicated by the ण of णप् *ṇaP*. See scheme at 246.

and guṇate it in the 2d *singular* (as *chakar* for *chakṛi*, see 293. *a*); but before all the other terminations, Parasmai and A'tmane-pada, it must revert to its original form, and then suffer the usual change required by the rules of Sandhi.

365. Thus, from बुध् *budh*, 1st c., comes the base of the singular Parasm. बुबोध् *bubodh*, and the base of the rest of the tense बुबुध् *bubudh* (1. *bubodh* + *a* = बुबोध *bubodha*, 2. *bubodh* + *itha* = बुबोधिथ *bubodhitha*, 3. *bubodh* + *a* = *bubodha*; Du. 1. *bubudh* + *iva* = बुबुधिव, 2. *bubudh* + *athus* = *bubudhathus*, &c. A'tm. 1. *bubudh* + *e* = बुबुधे, &c.). Similarly, from विद् *vid*, 2d c., 'to know,' come the two bases *vived* and *vivid* (1. 3. *viveda*; Du. 1. *vividiva*; Pl. 1. *vividima*, &c.) *.

a. Greek affords many examples of verbs which suffer a kind of Guṇa or Vṛiddhi change in the perfect; but this change is not confined to the singular, as in Sanskṛit. Compare λέλοιπα (from λείπω, ἔλιπον), πέποιθα (from πείθω, ἔπιθον), τέτροφα (from τρέφω), τέθεικα (from τίθημι), &c. There is one Greek root, however, which agrees very remarkably with the Sanskṛit in restricting Guṇa to the singular, viz. Ϝιδ (εἴδω), 'to know,' answering to the Sanskṛit *vid* above: thus, οἶδα, οἶσθα, οἶδε; ἴστον, ἴστον; ἴσμεν, ἴστε, ἴσασι. The root *vid* has a contracted form of its 2d pret. used for the present, which agrees exactly with οἶδα: thus, *veda*, *vettha*, &c. See 308. *a*.

366. Again, from कृ *kṛi*, 8th c., 'to do' (see 684), comes the base of the 1st and 3d singular Parasm. चकार् *chakár* (331. *b*), the base of the 2d sing. चकर् *chakar*, and the base of the rest of the tense चकृ *chakṛi* (1. *chakár* + *a* = चकार, 2. *chakar* + *tha* = चकर्थ, 3. *chakár* + *a* = चकार; Du. 1. *chakṛi* + *va* = चकृव 267. *a*, 2. *chakṛi* + *athus* = चक्रथुस् by 34; Pl. 1. *chakṛi* + *ma* = चकृम, &c. A'tm. 1. *chakṛi* + *e* = चक्रे by 34; Pl. 2. *chakṛi* + *ḍhwe* = चकृढ्वे. See scheme at 247).

a. Observe—In the 2d preterite the 1st and 3d sing. Parasmai and A'tmane have the same termination, and are identical in form.

367. Note, that if a root end in इ *i* or ई *í* this vowel does not blend with the initial *i* of the terminations in the du. pl. Parasmai, sing. du. pl. A'tmane-pada, but is changed to *y*, violating 31: thus, from चि *chi*, 5th c., 'to collect' (see the table at 583), come the bases *chichai*, *chiche*, and *chichi*, changeable to *chicháy*, *chichay*, and *chichy* (1. 3. चिचाय, 2. चिचयिथ or चिचेथ; Du. 1. चिच्यिव, 2. चिच्यथुस् by 34. A'tm. 1. 3. चिच्ये, &c.). Similarly, नी *ní*, 1st c., 'to lead' (Du. 1. निन्यिव, &c.; A'tm. 1. निन्ये, &c.). Observe, *chi* has also an anomalous form of the 2d pret. चिकाय.

* There is a contracted form of the 2d preterite of *vid* sometimes used for the present. See 308. *a*.

a. But roots ending in *i* or *í*, and having a *double* initial consonant, change इ् *i* or ई् *í* to इय् *iy* before all the terminations, excepting those of the singular, Parasmai-pada: hence, from श्रि 1st c., 'to have recourse,' come the three bases *śiśrai*, *śiśre*, and *śiśriy* (1. 3. शिश्राय, 2. शिश्रयिथ or शिश्रेथ; Du. 1. शिश्रियिव, &c.). So क्री 9th c. makes 1. 3. *chikráya*, 2. *chikrayitha* or *chikretha;* Du. 1. *chikriyiva;* Pl. *chikriyima*, &c. Átm. *chikriye*, &c.

b. And *all roots* ending in *u* or *ú* change *u* or *ú* to उव् *uv* before these terminations, excepting of course the roots श्रु, स्तु, द्रु, स्रु, in the persons marked with * at p. 107, and excepting भू *bhú*, 1st c., 'to be,' at 585, which makes its base बभूव् *babhúv* throughout sing. du. and pl. Parasmai and Átmane: thus, from धू 5th c., 'to shake,' come the bases *dudhau*, *dudho*, and *dudhuv* (1. 3. दुधाव, 2. दुधविथ or दुधोथ; Du. 1. दुधुविव. Átm. 1. 3. दुधुवे, 2. दुधुविषे). But श्रु 5th c. makes 1. 3. शुश्राव, 2. शुश्रोथ; Du. 1. शुश्रुव, 2. शुश्रुवथुस्. Átm. 1. 3. शुश्रुवे. See 676.

c. And roots ending in the vowel *ṛi*, preceded by a double consonant, and most roots in long *ṛí*, instead of retaining this vowel, and changing it to *r* by 364. *c.* before the terminations of the du. and pl. Parasmai, sing. du. and pl. Átmane, guṇate it into *ar*, as in the 2d sing., before all these terminations: thus, from स्मृ *smṛi*, 'to remember,' 1. 3. *sasmára*, 2. *sasmaritha;* Du. 1. *sasmariva*. Átm. 1. 3. *sasmare*. But पॄ 'to fill,' शॄ 'to dissolve,' and दॄ 'to rend,' may optionally retain *ṛi*, changeable to *r:* thus, Du. पपरिव or पप्रिव.

368. By referring back to the scheme at p. 107, it will be seen that all the terminations of this tense begin with vowels. Those which begin with *i* are distinguished by the mark *, because eight roots, and only eight roots in the language (viz. कृ 'to do,' भृ 'to bear,' सृ 'to go,' वृ 'to surround,' श्रु 'to hear,' स्तु 'to praise,' द्रु 'to run,' स्रु 'to drop'), reject the *i* from these terminations.

a. Most roots, however, ending in vowels, and most of those in consonants which absolutely reject the initial *i* from the terminations of the futures (see 394), are allowed the option of rejecting it in the 2d sing. Parasmai of the 2d preterite; but in these *itha* as well as *tha* is generally admissible †.

b. Since, therefore, only eight roots reject the initial *i* from the 1st dual &c.‡, and these all end in vowels, it follows that the final consonants of roots can never in this tense coalesce with the initial consonants of terminations, excepting sometimes optionally in the 2d

† Nevertheless, six of the eight roots at 368 and p. 107, and a few others ending in vowels, take *tha* only. स्रु, वृ, and many roots assuming *i*, take *itha* only.

‡ It is said, however, that some roots ending in consonants optionally reject the *i* in the 1st du. and plur.: thus, the 1st du. of the 2d pret. of *sidh* is said to be either सिषिध्व or सिषिधिव.

singular; in which case the rules of Sandhi propounded at 296 &c. are observed *: see also 388. *c*. Its formation, therefore, is not attended with many difficulties of consonantal combination. Nevertheless, there are numerous anomalies, as follows.

ANOMALOUS REDUPLICATION OF AN INITIAL VOWEL.

369. We have already seen at 364. *a*, that if a root ending in a single consonant begin with अ *a*, इ *i*, or उ *u*, these vowels are repeated, and the two similar vowels blend into one long one by 31: thus, from अस् *as*, 'to be,' comes *a as*, or *ás* (1. 3. *ás* + *a* = आस *ása*). So from आप् *áp*, 'to obtain,' comes *a áp*, or *áp*. See 681.

370. But when an initial *i* or *u* is guṇated (as in the sing. Parasm.), then the reduplicated *i* becomes *iy* before *e*, and the reduplicated *u* becomes *uv* before *o*: thus, from इष् *ish*, 6th c., 'to wish,' come the two bases *iyesh* and *ísh*, see 637 (1. 3. इयेष, &c.; Du. 1. ईषिव, &c.); and from उख् *ukh*, 1st c., 'to move,' the two bases *uvokh* and *úkh* (1. 3. उवोख, &c.; Du. 1. ऊखिव).

371. And if a root begin with अ *a* and end in a *double* consonant, or begin with ऋ *ṛi* and end in a single consonant, the reduplicated syllable is *án*: thus, from अर्च् *arch*, 1st c., 'to worship,' comes the base आनर्च् *ánarch* (1. 3. आनर्च); from ऋध् *ṛidh*, 5th c., 'to flourish,' comes आनर्ध् *ánardh* (1. 3. आनर्ध; Du. 1. आनृधिव, &c.).

a. अश् 5th c. Átm., 'to pervade,' although ending in श्, follows 371 (1. 3. आनशे).

372. इ *i*, 2d c., 'to go,' is vṛiddhied in 1st and 3d sing., and the reduplicated syllable is इय् *iy*, in accordance with 370. In the du. and pl. the base is ईय् *íy* (1. 3. इयाय, 2. इययिथ or इयेथ; Du. 1. ईयिव, &c.). See 645.

a. Observe—When the preposition *adhi* is prefixed to the root *i*, it is then Átmane only, and the 2d preterite is formed as if from *gá*: thus, 1. 3. *adhijage*, &c.

ANOMALOUS MODES OF FORMING THE BASE OF THE SECOND PRETERITE.

373. Roots ending in आ *á* (as, दा *dá*, 3d c., 'to give;' धा *dhá*, 3d c., 'to place;' या *yá*, 2d c., 'to go;' स्था *sthá*, 1st c., 'to stand,' &c.) drop the *á* before all the terminations, excepting the *tha* of the 2d sing., and substitute औ *au* for the terminations of the 1st and 3d sing. Parasmai. Hence, from *dá* comes the base *dad*, see 663 (1. 3. ददौ, 2. ददिथ or ददाथ; Du. 1. ददिव. Átm. 1. 3. ददे, 2. ददिषे, &c.).

374. Roots ending in the diphthongs ए *e* (except व्हे &c. at 379), ऐ *ai*, औ *au*, follow 373, and form their 2d preterite as if they ended in *á*: thus, धे 1st c., 'to drink,' makes in 1st and 3d sing. दधौ, 2d दधिथ or दधाथ, Du. 1. दधिव; गै 1st c., 'to sing,' makes जगौ; म्लै 1st c., 'to fade,' मम्लौ; शो 4th c., 'to sharpen,' शशौ.

375. Roots beginning with any consonant, and ending with a single consonant, and enclosing a short अ *a*, lengthen the *a* in the 1st † and 3d sing.; as, from

* Thus, from *pach*, 'to cook,' 2d sing. *papaktha*; from *dṛiś*, 'to see,' 2d sing. *dadrashṭha*. See 388. *c*.

† The lengthening of *a* is said to be optional in 1st sing.: thus, *pach* makes in sing. 1. either *papácha* or *papacha*.

पच् *pach*, 1st c., 'to cook,' पपाच् *papách;* from *tyaj*, 1st c., 'to quit,' *tatyáj* (1. 3. *tatyája*, 2. *tatyajitha;* Du. 1. *tatyajiva*, &c.).

a. Moreover, before *itha* and in the dual and plur. Parasmai, and all the persons of the Átmane, if the initial as well as the final consonant of the root be single, the अ *a* is changed to ए *e*, and, to compensate for this, the reduplication suppressed*: thus, from *pach* come the two bases पपाच् *papách* and पेच् *pech* (1. 3. *papácha*, 2. *pechitha* or *papaktha* 296; Du. 1. *pechiva*. Átm. 1. 3. *peche*, &c.). Similarly, from लभ् *labh*, 1st c. Átm., 'to obtain' (cf. λαμβάνω, ἔλαβον), the base लेभ् *lebh* throughout (*lebhe, lebhishe, lebhe, lebhivahe*, &c.). So *nah*, 4th c., 'to bind,' makes 1. 3. *nanáha*, 2. *nehitha* or *nanaddha* by 305; Du. 1. *nehiva*, &c. Átm. *nehe*, &c. Similarly, *naś*, 4th c., 'to perish,' 1. 3. *nanáśa*, 2. *neśitha* or *nananshṭha* (ननंष्ठ), &c.: compare 388. *d*.

b. Roots of this last kind, that require a substituted consonant in the reduplication, are excepted from the rule (but not भज् *bhaj* and फल् *phal*).

c. So also the roots वच्, वद्, वप्, वश्, वस्, वह्, beginning with *v*, are excepted. These require that the reduplicated syllable be उ *u*, or the corresponding vowel of the semivowel, and also change *va* of the root to उ *u* before every termination, except those of the sing. Parasmai, the two *u*'s blending into one long ऊ *ú:* thus, from वच् *vach*, 2d c., 'to speak,' come the two bases उवाच् *uvách* and ऊच् *úch* (1. 3. *uvácha*, 2. *uvachitha* or *uvaktha;* Du. 3. *úchatus;* Pl. 3. *úchus*). The root वह् *vah*, 1st c., 'to carry,' changes the radical vowel to ओ *o* before *tha* (see 305. *a*), optionally substituted for *itha* (1. 3. उवाह, 2. उवहिथ or उवोढ). Compare 424.

d. Observe—The root वम् *vam*, 1st c., 'to vomit,' usually follows 375 (Páṇ. VII. 2. 5), but may also follow 375. *a*.

e. A similar rule is applied in यज् *yaj*, 1st c., 'to sacrifice' (1. 3. *iyája;* Du. 3. *íjatus;* Pl. 3. *íjus*); and the 2d sing. of this root will be either इयजिथ or इयष्ठ by 297, or येजिथ by 375. *a*. The Átmane is 1. 3. ईजे, 2. ईजिषे, &c. See 597.

f. The roots ग्रन्थ् 9th and 1st c., श्रन्थ् 9th c., स्वन् 1st c., भ्रम् 4th c., राज् 1st c., भ्राज् 1st c. Átm., भ्राश् 1st and 4th c., may optionally follow 375. *a*, although not answering its conditions, and त्रप् 1st c. Átm. necessarily: thus, *granth* makes sing. du. pl. 3. either *jagrantha, jagranthatus, jagranthus* or *jagrantha, grethatus, grethus;* *bhram* makes *babhráma, babhramatus, babhramus*, by 375, or *babhráma, bhrematus, bhremus;* and *trap* makes *trepe, trepáte, trepire*.

Similarly, राध् 4th and 5th c., but not when *á* is prefixed.

g. तॄ 1st c., 'to pass,' also follows 375. *a* (as if it were *tar*): thus, 1. 3. *tatára*, 2. *teritha;* Du. 1. *teriva*, &c. जॄ 4th c., 'to grow old,' may optionally follow 367. *c* or 375. *a* (3. *jajára;* Du. 3. *jajaratus* or *jeratus*, &c.).

376. गम् *gam*, 1st c., 'to go,' जन् *jan*, 4th c., 'to be born,' खन् *khan*, 1st c., 'to dig,' and हन् *han*, 2d c., 'to kill' (which last forms its 2d pret. as if from घन् *ghan*), drop the medial *a* before all the terminations, except those of the sing. Parasm.

---

* Bopp deduces forms like *pechiva*, from *papachiva*, by supposing that the second *p* is suppressed, the two *a*'s combined into *á*, and *á* weakened into *e*.

(compare the declension of *rájan* at 146, 149). Hence, *gam* makes in sing. du. pl. 3. *jagáma, jagmatus, jagmus; jan* makes *jajána, jajñatus, jajñus; khan* makes *chakhána, chakhnatus, chakhnus;* and *han* makes *jagħána, jaghnatus, jaghnus.*

377. घस् *ghas*, 1st c., 'to eat,' is analogous, making *jaghása, jakshatus, jakshus.* See 42 and 70.

378. जि *ji*, 1st c., 'to conquer,' forms its 2d pret. as if from गि *gi*, see 590 (1. and 3. जिगाय; Du. 1. जिगियिव, &c.); हि *hi*, 5th c., 'to send,' as if from घि (1. 3. जिघाय); ऋ *ṛi*, 1st c., 'to go,' makes its base आर् *ár* throughout *.

379. ह्वे *hwe*, 1st c., 'to call,' forms its 2d pret. as if from हु or हू, see 595 (1. 3. जुहाव; Du. 1. जुहुविव); दे *de*, 1st c., 'to pity,' 'to protect,' makes its base *digi* (1. 3. Átm. दिग्ये, 2. दिग्यिषे, &c.); व्ये *vye*, 1st c., 'to cover,' makes its bases *vivyáy, vivyay*, and *vivy* (1. विव्याय, 2. विव्ययिथ; Du. 1. विव्यिव or विव्ययिव); वे *ve*, 1st c., 'to weave,' forms its 2d pret. as if from *vá* or *vav* or *vay* (1. 3. ववौ or उवाय, 2. ववाथ or वविथ or उवयिथ; Du. 1. ववव or ऊविव or ऊयिव, &c.).

380. ग्रह् *grah*, 9th c., 'to take,' makes its base जग्राह् and जगृह् (S. Du. Pl. 3. जग्राह, जगृहतुस्, जगृहुस्). See 699.

381. प्रच्छ् *prachchh*, 6th c., 'to ask,' makes its base पप्रच्छ् † throughout; see 631. भ्रज्ज् *bhrajj*, 6th c., 'to fry,' makes either बभर्ज्ज् or बभ्रज्ज् throughout. See 632.

382. स्वप् *swap*, 2d c., 'to sleep,' makes its bases सुष्वाप् and सुषुप्. See 655 and 70.

383. व्यध 4th c. 'to pierce,' व्यच् 6th c. 'to deceive,' व्यथ् 1st c. 'to be pained,' and व्यय् 1st c. 'to spend,' make their reduplicated syllable *vi;* and the first two roots change *vya* to *vi* before all the terminations, excepting the sing. Parasmai: thus, from *vyadh* comes sing. du. pl. 3. विव्याध, विविधतुस्, विविधुस्; Átm. विविधे, &c. See 615 and 629.

384. अह् *ah*, 'to say,' is only used in the 2d pret., and is defective in sing. du. pl. 1. and pl. 2, forming 2d sing. from अत् (2. आत्थ, 3. आह; Du. 2. आहथुस्, 3. आहतुस्; Pl. 3. आहुस्).

385. Roots which begin with a vowel, long by nature or position (except *áp*, 5th c., 'to obtain;' *áñchh*, 1st c., 'to stretch;' and except roots having an initial *a* before two consonants), and all roots of more than one syllable (excepting *úrnu*, 2d c., 'to cover'), form their 2d preterites by adding आम् *ám* to the base, and affixing the 2d preterite of some one of the auxiliary verbs, अस् *as*, 'to be;' भू *bhú*, 'to be;' कृ *kṛi*, 'to do.' (Observe—आम् with चकार becomes आञ्चकार by 59.) Thus, from ईश् 2d c., 'to rule,' comes 1st and 3d sing. 2d pret. ईशामास or ईशाम्बभूव or ईशाञ्चकार 59; from चकास् 2d c., 'to shine,' comes चकासाञ्चकार. When the Átmane-pada inflection has to be employed, कृ only is used: thus, ईड् 2d c. Átm., 'to praise,' makes 1st and 3d sing. 2d pret. ईडाञ्चक्रे. The root ऊर्णु 2d c.,

---

* Pánini VII. 4. 11. VII. 2. 66.

† This rests on Siddhánta Kaum. 134. Some grammarians make the base in du. and pl. &c. पपृच्छ्.

'to cover,' is anomalous, and makes sing. du. pl. 1. ऊर्णुनाव, ऊर्णुनुविव, ऊर्णुनुविम; Átm. ऊर्णुनुवे, &c.

a. Observe—Roots of the 10th class form their 2d pret. according to 385, the syllable *ám* being added to the base: thus, from *chur*, 10th c., 'to steal,' 2d pret. sing. 1. 3. *chorayámása*. See under Causals, 471.

b. Also according to 385 is formed the 2d preterite of all derivative verbs, such as causals, desideratives, and frequentatives.

c. Also of the roots अय् *ay*, 1st c., 'to go;' दय् *day*, 1st c., 'to pity;' and कास् *kás*, 1st c., 'to shine' (कासाञ्चक्रे) *: and optionally of the roots भी *bhí*, 3d c., 'to fear' (बिभाय or बिभयाञ्चकार); ह्री *hrí*, 3d c., 'to be ashamed' (जिह्राय or जिह्रयाञ्चकार); भृ *bhṛi*, 3d c., 'to bear' (बिभार or बिभराञ्चकार); हु *hu*, 3d c., 'to sacrifice' (जुहाव or जुहवाञ्चकार); विद् *vid*, 2d c., 'to know;' उष् *ush*, 1st c., 'to burn' (उवोष or ओषाञ्चकार).

d. Some polysyllabic roots also take both forms of the 2d preterite: thus, *daridrá*, 2d c., 'to be poor,' makes दरिद्राञ्चकार and ददरिद्रौ; *jágṛi*, 2d c., 'to awake,' makes जागराञ्चकार and जजागार.

First and second future.

386. Observe—The first future results from the union of the nom. case of the noun of agency (formed with the affix तृ *tṛi*, see 83. I) with the present tense of the verb अस् *as*, 'to be:' thus, taking दातृ *dátṛi*, 'a giver' (declined at 127), and combining its nom. case with अस्मि *asmi* and हे *he*, we have *dátásmi* and *dátáhe*, 'I am a giver,' identical with the 1st pers. sing. Parasmai and Átmane of the 1st fut., 'I will give.' So also *dátási* and *dátáse*, 'thou art a giver,' or 'thou wilt give.' In the 1st and 2d persons dual and plur. the sing. of the noun is joined with the dual and plur. of the auxiliary. In the 3d person the auxiliary is omitted, and the 3d sing. dual and plur. of the 1st future in both voices is then identical with the nom. case sing. dual and plur. of the noun of agency: thus, *dátá*, 'a giver,' or 'he will give;' *dátárau*, 'two givers,' or 'they two will give,' &c. †

387. Observe also—The second future, in its terminations, resembles the present tense, the chief difference being that *sya* is prefixed.

388. Rule for the formation of the base in verbs of the first nine classes. Guṇate the vowel of the root (except when debarred by 28. *b*, and except in certain uncommon roots of the 6th class) throughout all the persons of both first and second future. See 293. *a*. at the end.

a. Note, that in all roots ending in consonants, excepting those included in the list at 400, and in a few ending in vowels, enu-

* Páṇini III. 1. 37. 35.

† The future signification inherent in the noun of agency *dátá*, seems implied in Latin by the relation of *dator* to *daturus*.

merated at 397, 399, the vowel इ *i* must be inserted between the root so guṇated, and the terminations.

b. The roots of the 6th class not guṇated are कुच्, गुज्, कुट्, घुट्, चुट्, छुट्, तुट्, त्रुट्, पुट्, मुट्, स्फुट्, कुड्, क्रुड्, कृड्, गुड्, घुड्, चुड्, जुड्, तुड्, थुड्, नुड्, पुड्, बुड्, भुड्, व्रुड्, मुड्, लुड्, हुड्, डिप्, छुर्, स्फुर्, ध्रुव्.

c. Roots containing the vowel *ṛi* are generally guṇated, but they may optionally change *ṛi* to *ra*, when *i* is not inserted: thus, *tṛip* becomes either *tarp* or *trap*. The root *mṛij* is vṛiddhied into *márj* (compare 324). Note, that when the change of *ṛi* to *ra* is allowed in the futures, it is admitted also in the 3d preterite and conditional, and before *tha* in the 2d singular of the 2d preterite.

d. One or two roots, like *majj*, *naś*, insert a nasal in the two futures and some of the other non-conjugational tenses. See 403, 410.

389. Thus, from जि *ji*, 1st c., 'to conquer,' comes the base जे *je* (1st Fut. *je* + *tásmi* = जेतास्मि, &c.; A'tm. *je* + *táhe* = जेताहे. 2d Fut. *je* + *syámi* = जेष्यामि, &c.; A'tm. *je* + *sye* = जेष्ये, by 70). Similarly, from श्रु *śru*, 5th c., 'to hear,' comes the base श्रो *śro* (1st Fut. *śro* + *tásmi* = श्रोतास्मि, &c.; 2d Fut. *śro* + *syámi* = श्रोष्यामि, &c., by 70).

390. So also, from बुध् *budh*, 1st c., 'to know,' comes the base बोधि *bodhi* (1st Fut. *bodhi* + *tásmi* = बोधितास्मि, &c.; A'tm. *bodhi* + *táhe* = बोधिताहे. 2d Fut. *bodhi* + *syámi* = बोधिष्यामि, &c.; A'tm. *bodhi* + *sye* = बोधिष्ये).

391. This insertion of *i*, the manifest object of which is to prevent the coalition of consonants, is unfortunately forbidden in one hundred and three roots ending in consonants, some of which are of very common occurrence; and the combination of the final consonant of the root with the initial *t* and *s* of the terminations, will require an acquaintance with the rules already laid down at 296, &c. When these rules are known, there will be no difficulty in the formation of these tenses. The only question is, how are we to ascertain whether a root inserts *i*, or whether it rejects it? The lists about to be given at 394 and 400 will determine this point.

392. It is of the utmost importance that the attention of the student be directed towards these lists, as the assumption or rejection of this inserted vowel is not confined to the two futures, but extends to many other parts of the verb; insomuch, that if the first future reject इ *i*, it is, as a necessary consequence, rejected in the third preterite, the A'tmane-pada of the benedictive, the conditional, the infinitive mood, the passive past participle, the indeclinable past participle, the future participle formed with the affix *tavya*, and the noun of agency formed with the affix *tṛi*; and is, moreover, optionally rejected in the 2d pers. sing. of the 2d

preterite, and decides the formation of the desiderative form of the root by *s* instead of *ish*. So that the learner, if he know the first future, will pass on with great ease to the formation of these other parts of the verb, and should always look to this tense as his guide. For example, taking the root *kship*, 'to throw,' and finding the 1st future to be *ksheptásmi*, he knows that *i* is rejected. Therefore he knows the 2d future to be *kshepsyámi;* the 3d pret. to be *akshaipsam;* the Átmane of the benedictive, *kshipsíya;* the conditional, *akshepsyam;* the infinitive, *ksheptum;* the passive past participle, *kshipta;* the indeclinable participle, *kshiptwá;* the future participle, *ksheptavya;* the noun of agency, *ksheptṛi;* the 2d pers. sing. of the 2d pret. optionally *chikshepṭha;* the desiderative, *chikshipsámi*. On the other hand, taking the root *yách*, 'to ask,' and finding the 1st future to be *yáchitá*, he knows that *i* is inserted, and therefore the same parts of the verb will be *yáchishyámi, ayáchisham, yáchishíya, ayáchishyam, yáchitum, yáchita, yáchitwá, yáchitavya, yáchitṛi, yayáchitha, yayáchishámi,* respectively.

393. It is evident that roots ending in vowels do not require *i;* and it may be taken as a general rule that they all reject it, excepting roots ending in ऊ *ú* and ॠ *ṛí;* and excepting a few roots ending in the other vowels.

Observe—In the following lists the 3d pers. sing. of the 1st and 2d future is given after each root. The roots are arranged in the order of their radical vowels.

ROOTS ENDING IN VOWELS, REJECTING OR INSERTING इ *i* IN THE LAST FIVE TENSES.

394. All roots in आ *á*, as दा 3d c. (दाता, दास्यति, δώσει), reject *i*.

395. All roots in इ *i* and ई *í*, as जि 1st c. (जेता, जेष्यति), नी 1st c. (नेता, नेष्यति), reject *i*.

a. Except श्रि (श्रयिता, श्रयिष्यति), श्वि 1st c. (श्वयिता, श्वयिष्यति), डी 1st and 4th c. (डयिता, डयिष्यति), and शी 2d c. (शयिता, शयिष्यति).

396. All roots in उ *u*, as श्रु 5th c. (श्रोता, श्रोष्यति), reject *i*.

a. Except the roots क्षु, क्ष्णु, नु, यु, रु, स्नु (क्षविता, क्षविष्यति, &c.).

b. The root सु 2d c. Átm. optionally inserts *i* (सोता or सविता, सोष्यते or सविष्यते).

397. Roots in ऊ *ú* insert इ *i*, as भू 1st c. (भविता, भविष्यति); but धू 5th c. optionally rejects it (धविता or धोता, धविष्यति or धोष्यति).

398. All roots in ऋ *ṛi* reject *i* in the 1st future, but not in the 2d, as कृ 8th c. (कर्त्ता, करिष्यति).

a. Except the root वृ 5th c., which optionally lengthens the *i* (वरिता or वरीता, वरिष्यति or वरीष्यति).

b. The roots स्तृ 9th c. and स्तृ 1st c. have three forms of the 1st future (स्तर्त्ता, स्तरिता or स्तरीता &c., स्तर्त्ता &c.).

399. Roots in ॠ *rí* long, insert इ *i*, as तॄ (तरिता, तरिष्यति).

a. They may optionally lengthen the *i* (तरीता, तरीष्यति).

b. Roots in ए *e*, ऐ *ai*, ओ *o*, reject *i*; but change their final diphthongs to आ *á* before the terminations of the futures; thus सो 4th c. (साता, सास्यति). The root प्यै 1st c. may optionally insert *i* (प्याता or प्यायिता, &c.).

ROOTS ENDING IN CONSONANTS, REJECTING इ *i* IN THE LAST FIVE TENSES.

Observe—The roots marked * optionally reject *i* or insert it.

400. One in क् *k*.

शक्, शक्ता, शक्ष्यति, see 296.

401. Six in च् *ch*, and one optionally.

पच् 1st c., पक्ता, पक्ष्यति 296.
वच् 2d c., वक्ता, वक्ष्यति.
रिच् 7th c., रेक्ता, रेक्ष्यति.
विच् 7th and 3d c., वेक्ता, वेक्ष्यति.
सिच् 6th c., सेक्ता, सेक्ष्यति.
मुच् 6th c., मोक्ता, मोक्ष्यति.
*व्रश्च् 6th c., व्रष्टा or व्रश्चिता, व्रक्ष्यति or व्रश्चिष्यति.

402. One in छ् *chh*.

प्रच्छ् 6th c., प्रष्टा, प्रक्ष्यति 297.

403. Fifteen in ज् *j*, and two optionally.

त्यज् 1st c., त्यक्ता, त्यक्ष्यति 296.
भज् 1st c., भक्ता, भक्ष्यति.
यज् 1st c., यष्टा 297, यक्ष्यति.
भ्रस्ज् 6th c., भ्रष्टा, भर्ष्टा, भ्रक्ष्यति, भर्क्ष्यति.
मस्ज् 6th c., मंक्ता, मंक्ष्यति 388. *c.*
भञ्ज् 7th c., भंक्ता, भंक्ष्यति.
रञ्ज् 1st and 4th c., रंक्ता, रंक्ष्यति.
सञ्ज् 1st c., संक्ता, संक्ष्यति.
स्वञ्ज् 1st c., स्वंक्ता, स्वंक्ष्यते.
निज् 3d c., नेक्ता, नेक्ष्यति.
विज् 3d c.†, वेक्ता, &c., like विच्.
भुज् 7th c., भोक्ता, भोक्ष्यति.
युज् 7th c., योक्ता, योक्ष्यति.
रुज् 6th c., रोक्ता, रोक्ष्यति.
सृज् 6th c., स्रष्टा 297, स्रक्ष्यति.
*अञ्ज् 7th c., अंक्ता or अञ्जिता, अंक्ष्यति or अञ्जिष्यति.
*मृज् 2d c., मार्ष्टा or मार्जिता, मार्क्ष्यति or मार्जिष्यति 388. *b.*

404. Fourteen in द् *d*.

अद् 2d c., अत्ता, अत्स्यति, see 46.
पद् 4th c., पत्ता, पत्स्यते.
शद् 1st and 6th c., शत्ता, शत्स्यति.
सद् 1st and 6th c., सत्ता, सत्स्यति.
स्कन्द् 1st c., स्कन्ता, स्कन्त्स्यति.
हद् 1st c., हत्ता, हत्स्यते.
खिद् 6th c., खेत्ता, खेत्स्यति.
छिद् 7th c., छेत्ता, छेत्स्यति.
भिद् 7th c., भेत्ता, भेत्स्यति.
विद् 6th c., वेत्ता, वेत्स्यति.
स्विद् 4th c., स्वेत्ता, स्वेत्स्यति.
क्षुद् 7th c., क्षोत्ता, क्षोत्स्यति.
तुद् 6th c., तोत्ता, तोत्स्यति.
नुद् 6th c., नोत्ता, नोत्स्यति.

† When विज् belongs to the 7th c., it takes *i*: thus, विजिता, विजिष्यति.

405. Eleven in ध् *dh*.

बन्ध् 9th c., बन्द्धा, भन्त्स्यति 299. *a*.
व्यध् 4th c., व्यद्धा, व्यत्स्यति.
राध् 5th c., राद्धा, रात्स्यति.
साध् 4th and 5th c., साद्धा, सात्स्यति.
सिध् 4th c.†, सेद्धा, सेत्स्यति.
क्रुध् 4th c., क्रोद्धा, क्रोत्स्यति.
क्षुध् 4th c., क्षोद्धा 298, क्षोत्स्यति 299.
बुध् 4th c.†, बोद्धा 298, भोत्स्यते 299. *a*.
युध् 4th c., योद्धा, योत्स्यते.
रुध् 7th c., रोद्धा, रोत्स्यति.
शुध् 4th c., शोद्धा, शोत्स्यति.

406. Two in न् *n*.

मन् 4th c., मन्ता, मंस्यते 6. *b*.
हन् 2d c., हन्ता, but हनिष्यति.

407. Eleven in प् *p*, and three optionally.

तप् 1st c., तप्ता, तप्स्यति.
वप् 1st c., वप्ता, वप्स्यति.
शप् 1st c., शप्ता, शप्स्यति.
स्वप् 2d c., स्वप्ता, स्वप्स्यति.
आप् 5th c., आप्ता, आप्स्यति.
क्षिप् 6th c., क्षेप्ता, क्षेप्स्यति.
तिप् 1st c., तेप्ता, तेप्स्यति.
लिप् 6th c., लेप्ता, लेप्स्यति.
लुप् 6th c., लोप्ता, लोप्स्यति.
लुप् 6th c., लोप्ता, लोप्स्यति.
*कॢप् 1st c., कल्प्ता or कल्पिता, कल्प्स्यति or कल्पिष्यते.
*तृप् 4th c., तर्प्ता or तर्पिता, तर्प्स्यति or तर्पिष्यति ‡.
*दृप् 4th c., दर्प्ता or दर्पिता, दर्प्स्यति or दर्पिष्यति ‡.
सृप् 1st c., सर्प्ता, सर्प्स्यति ‡.

408. Three in भ् *bh*, and one optionally.

यभ् 1st c., यब्धा, यप्स्यति.
रभ् 1st c., रब्धा, रप्स्यते.
लभ् 1st c., लब्धा 298, लप्स्यते 299.
*लुभ् 4th c., लोब्धा or लोभिता, but लोभिष्यति.

409. Four in म् *m*, and one optionally.

गम् 1st c., गन्ता 59, but गमिष्यति.
नम् 1st c., नन्ता, नंस्यति.
यम् 1st c., यन्ता, यंस्यति.
रम् 1st c., रन्ता 59, रंस्यते 6. *b*.
*क्रम् 1st c. Átm., क्रन्ता or क्रमिता, क्रंस्यते or क्रमिष्यति.

410. Ten in श् *ś*, and two optionally.

दंश् 1st c., दंष्टा 300, दंक्ष्यति 302.
दिश् 6th c., देष्टा, देक्ष्यति (δείξει).
विश् 6th c., वेष्टा 300, वेक्ष्यति 302.
रिश् 6th c., रेष्टा, रेक्ष्यति.
लिश् 4th c., लेष्टा, लेक्ष्यते.
क्रुश् 1st c., क्रोष्टा, क्रोक्ष्यति.
रुश् 6th c., रोष्टा, रोक्ष्यति.
दृश् 1st c., द्रष्टा, द्रक्ष्यति.
मृश् 6th c., मर्ष्टा, मर्क्ष्यति ‡.
स्पृश् 6th c., स्पर्ष्टा, स्पर्क्ष्यति ‡.
*नश् 4th c., नंष्टा or नशिता, नंक्ष्यति or नशिष्यति.

† When सिध् and बुध् belong to the 1st c., they take *i*: thus, सेधिता, बोधिता, &c.
‡ These may optionally change the radical vowel *ṛi* to *ra* instead of *ar*: thus, *sarptá* or *sraptá*, &c. See 388. *c*.

*क्लिश् 9th c., क्लेष्टा or क्लेशिता, क्लेक्ष्यति or क्लेशिष्यति.

411. Eleven in ष् *sh*, and six optionally.

त्विष् 1st c., त्वेष्टा, त्वेक्ष्यति.
द्विष् 2d c., द्वेष्टा 301, द्वेक्ष्यति 302.
पिष् 7th c., पेष्टा, पेक्ष्यति.
विष् 3d c., वेष्टा, वेक्ष्यति.
शिष् 7th c., शेष्टा, शेक्ष्यति.
श्लिष् 4th c., श्लेष्टा 301, श्लेक्ष्यति 302.
तुष् 4th c., तोष्टा, तोक्ष्यति.
दुष् 4th c., दोष्टा, दोक्ष्यति.
पुष् 4th c.†, पोष्टा, पोक्ष्यति.
शुष् 4th c., शोष्टा, शोक्ष्यति.
कृष् 1st and 6th c., कर्ष्टा, कर्क्ष्यति‡.
*तक्ष् 1st and 5th c., तष्टा or तक्षिता, तक्ष्यति or तक्षिष्यति.
*त्वक्ष् 1st c., त्वष्टा or त्वक्षिता, &c.
*इष् 6th c., एष्टा or एषिता, but एषिष्यति.
*रिष् 1st and 4th c., रेष्टा or रेषिता, but रेषिष्यति.
*कुष् (with निस्) 9th c., -कोष्टा or -कोषिता, -कोक्ष्यति or -कोषिष्यति.
*रुष् 1st and 4th c., रोष्टा or रोषिता, but रोषिष्यति.

412. Two in स् *s*.

घस् 1st c., घस्ता, घत्स्यति 304. *a*.
वस् 1st c., वस्ता, वत्स्यति 304. *a*.

413. Eight in ह् *h*, and seven optionally.

दह् 1st c., दग्धा 305, धक्ष्यति 306. *a*.
नह् 4th c., नद्धा 305, नत्स्यति 306. *b*.
वह् 1st c., वोढा 305. *a*, वक्ष्यति 306.
दिह् 2d c., देग्धा 305, धेक्ष्यति 306. *a*.
मिह् 1st c., मेढा 305. *a*, मेक्ष्यति 306.
लिह् 2d c., लेढा 305. *a*, लेक्ष्यति 306.
दुह् 2d c., दोग्धा 305, धोक्ष्यति 306. *a*.
रुह् 1st c., रोढा 305. *a*, रोक्ष्यति 306.
*सह् 1st c., सोढा 305. *a*. or सहिता, सहिष्यते.
*गाह् 1st c., गाढा or गाहिता, घाक्ष्यते 306. *a*. or गाहिष्यते.
*स्निह् 4th c., स्नेग्धा or स्नेढा or स्नेहिता, स्नेक्ष्यति or स्नेहिष्यति.
*गुह् 1st c., गोढा or गूहिता, घोक्ष्यति 306. *a*. or गूहिष्यति.
*द्रुह् 4th c., द्रोग्धा or द्रोढा or द्रोहिता, ध्रोक्ष्यति 306. *a*. or द्रोहिष्यति.
*मुह् 4th c., मोग्धा or मोढा or मोहिता, मोक्ष्यति or मोहिष्यति.
*तृह् 7th c., तर्ढा or तर्हिता, तर्हिष्यति or तर्क्ष्यति.

414. All roots, without exception, ending in ख् *kh*, ग् *g*, घ् *gh*, झ् *jh*, ट् *ṭ*, ठ् *ṭh*, ड् *ḍ*, ढ् *ḍh*, ण् *ṇ*, त् *t*, थ् *th*, फ् *ph*, ब् *b*, य् *y*, र् *r*, ल् *l*, व् *v*, take the inserted इ *i* in the last five tenses.

a. The root ग्रह् 9th c., 'to take,' lengthens the inserted *i* in every tense except the 2d preterite: thus, ग्रहीता, ग्रहीष्यति, &c. See 699.

† When *push* belongs to the 9th c., it takes *i*.

‡ *Kṛish* may optionally change *ṛi* to *ra*; as, *krashṭá*, &c.

Third preterite (Greek aorist, Latin perfect).

415. This complex and multiform tense, the most troublesome and intricate in the whole Sanskṛit verb, is not so much one tense, as an aggregation of several tenses, all more or less allied to each other, all bearing a manifest resemblance to the first preterite, but none of them exactly assignable to that tense, and none of them so distinct in its character or so universal in its application as to admit of segregation from the general group, under any separate title of its own.

Fortunately, however, the third preterite occurs but rarely in the better specimens of Hindú composition; so that the student may satisfy himself with a cursory survey of its character and functions.

416. Although grammarians assert that there are seven different varieties of this tense, four of which correspond more or less to the Greek 1st aorist, and three to the 2d aorist, yet we shall endeavour to show that all these varieties may be included under the two distinct forms of terminations given in the table at 247, p. 107. The first form of terminations corresponds to those of the memorial scheme at 246, and belongs both to roots which reject *i* and to roots which assume it (see 394): but in the latter case the initial *s* of the 2d and 3d sing. is rejected, and the *i* blends with the *í*, which then becomes the initial of those terminations. Moreover, in the case of roots which assume *i* the base is formed according to rules different to those which apply in the case of roots which reject *i*. The 2d form of terminations resembles those of the first preterite, and belongs, in the first place, to certain roots, whose bases in the *first* preterite present some important variation from the root; in the second, to certain roots ending in श् *ś*, ष् *sh*, or ह् *h*, which have *i*, *u*, or *ṛi*, for their radical vowel; and, in the third, to verbs of the 10th class and causals.

417. Observe also—In all the modifications of the third preterite, the first step in the formation of the base is the prefixing of the augment अ *a*, a further indication of the community of character which this tense presents to the first preterite.

a. It will appear, however, in the Syntax, that when the third preterite is used as a prohibitive imperative, the particle मा *má* being prefixed, the augment *a* is then rejected.

b. When a root begins with the vowels इ *i*, उ *u*, or ऋ *ṛi*, short or long, the augment is prefixed in accordance with 260. *a*.

Form I.

418. The terminations are here repeated from 247, p. 107.

1. *sam*	*swa*	*sma*	*si*	*swahi*	*smahi*
2. *sís*	*stam* or *tam*	*sta* or *ta*	*sthás* or *thás*	*sáthám*	*dhwam* or *ḍhwam*
3. *sít*	*stám* or *tám*	*sus*	*sta* or *ta*	*sátám*	*sata*

419. Observe, that when *i* is not inserted before the above terminations, the initial *s* may be discarded from those terminations in which it is compounded with *t* and *th*, if the base ends in any consonant excepting *n*, or in any *short* vowel. Observe also, that ढ्वं *ḍhwam* takes the place of ध्वं *dhwam*, when the base ends in any other vowel than *á*.

420. Rule for the formation of the base for those verbs of the first nine classes, at 395, 396, 398, 400, &c., which reject इ *i*. In the Parasmai, if a root end in either a vowel or a consonant, vṛiddhi the radical vowel before *all* the terminations. In the Átmane, if a root end in इ *i*, ई *í*, उ *u*, or ऊ *ú*, guṇate the radical vowel; and if in ऋ *ṛi* or any consonant, leave the vowel unchanged before *all* the terminations. Observe—The augment अ *a* must always be prefixed, as in the 1st preterite. See 260.

421. Thus, from नी 1st c., 'to lead,' come the two bases *anai* for Parasmai and *ane* for Átmane (*anai* + *sam* = अनैषं by 70; Átm. *ane* + *si* = अनेषि, *ane* + *sthás* = अनेष्ठास्, &c.); and from कृ 8th c., 'to make,' come the two bases *akár* for Parasmai and *akṛi* for Átmane (*akár* + *sam* = अकार्षं by 70, &c.; Átm. *akṛi* + *si* = अकृषि by 70, *akṛi* + *thás* = अकृथास् by 419, *akṛi* + *ta* = अकृत, &c.). See 682. Similarly, भृ 3d c., 'to bear.' See the table at 583.

422. So from युज् 7th c., 'to join,' come the two bases *ayauj* for Parasmai and *ayuj* for Átmane (Parasmai *ayauj* + *sam* = अयौक्षं by 296, *ayauj* + *swa* = अयौक्ष्व, *ayauj* + *tam* = अयौक्तं by 419; Átm. *ayuj* + *si* = अयुक्षि by 296, *ayuj* + *thás* = अयुक्थास्, *ayuj* + *ta* = अयुक्त); and from रुध् 7th c., 'to hinder,' the bases *araudh* and *arudh* (Parasmai *araudh* + *sam* = अरौत्सं by 299, Du. *araudh* + *swa* = अरौत्स्व, *araudh* + *tam* = अरौद्धं; Átm. *arudh* + *si* = अरुत्सि, *arudh* + *thás* = अरुद्धास्, &c.).

423. Similarly, from पच् 1st c., 'to cook,' come the bases *apách* and *apach* (*apách* + *sam* = अपाक्षं by 296; Átm. *apach* + *si* = अपक्षि, *apach* + *thás* = अपक्थास्, &c.); and from दह् 1st c., 'to burn' (601), the bases *adáh* and *adah* (*adáh* + *sam* =

अधाक्षं by 306. *a*, *adáh+tam*=अदाग्धं by 305; Átm. *adah+si*=अधक्षि by 306. *a*, *adah+thás*=अदग्धास्, &c.).

424. The root वह् 1st c., 'to carry' (611), changes the radical vowel to ओ *o* before those terminations which reject an initial *s* (see 419, 305. *a*): thus, *avâksham*, *avákshís*, *avákshít*, *avákshwa*, *avoḍham*, &c.; Átm. *avakshi*, *avoḍhás*, *avoḍha*, &c.: compare 375. *c*. सह् 1st c. Átm., 'to bear,' generally follows 427 (*asahishi*, &c.), though the form *asoḍha* is given for the 3d sing. With *avákshít* compare the Latin *vexit*, and with *avakshi* compare *vexi*.

425. नह् 4th c., 'to tie,' 'to fasten,' makes *anátsam*, *anátsís*, *anátsít*, *anátswa*, *anáddham*, &c.; and Átm. *anatsi*, *anaddhás*, &c., by 306. *b* (compare 182. *e*). Similarly, वस् 1st c., 'to dwell' (607), makes *avátsam*, &c., by 304. *a*.

426. मज्ज् 6th c., 'to be immersed,' and सञ्ज् 1st c., 'to adhere,' make *amán-ksham* &c., *asán-ksham* &c. See 633, 597. *a*.

a. The root इ 2d c., 'to go,' with *adhi* prefixed, signifying 'to go over,' 'to read,' Átmane-pada only, substitutes गी *gí* in the 3d pret.: thus, अध्यगीषि, अध्यगीष्ठास्, अध्यगीष्ट, &c.

b. Roots ending in न् or ण् rarely reject the sibilant from some of the terminations in the Átmane, as indicated at 418, dropping the final nasal where *s* is rejected: thus, तन् 8th c. makes in Átmane 2d and 3d sing. अतथास्, अतत (compare 57). Similarly, क्षण् 8th c. makes अक्षथास्, अक्षत. And the roots सन् 8th c., जन् 4th c., खन् 1st c., may lengthen the *a* when *n* is dropped: thus, असाथास्, असात, &c.; compare 354. *a*, 339. But the above roots generally follow 427, and prefix *i* to all the terminations; so that अतनिष्ठास्, अतनिष्ट, is more usual than अतथास्, अतत. The root मन् 4th and 8th c. makes 3d sing. अमंस्त or अमनिष्ट or अमत.

The same form with इ i *prefixed.*

427. Those verbs which assume इ *i* (see 388. *a*, 397, 399, 414) reject the initial sibilant from the terminations of the 2d and 3d sing., and the *i* then blends with the initial *i* of those terminations. In the other terminations the *i* causes the change of *s* to *sh* by 70: thus,

1. *isham*	*ishwa*	*ishma*	*ishi*	*ishwahi*	*ishmahi*
2. *ís*	*ishṭam*	*ishṭa*	*ishṭhás*	*isháthám*	*idhwam* or *iḍhwam*
3. *ít*	*ishṭám*	*ishus*	*ishṭa*	*ishátám*	*ishata*

Verbs which assume *i*, and take the above terminations, require a different rule for the formation of their base, as follows:—

428. Rule for the formation of the base for those verbs of the first nine classes which assume इ *i* before the terminations, as above.

a. If a root end in the vowels इ *i*, ई *í*, उ *u*, ऊ *ú*, ऋ *ṛi*, ॠ *ṛí*, vṛiddhi those vowels in the Parasmai before *all* the terminations, and guṇate them in the Átmane.

Observe—Roots ending in any other vowel than *ú* and *ṛí* rarely follow 427, as they generally reject *i*, and follow 418* (see 394, &c.).

b. If a root end in a single consonant, guṇate the radical vowel in both Parasmai and Átmane (except when debarred by 28. *b*, and except in the roots enumerated at 388. *b*). Of course the augment अ *a* must in every case be prefixed. See 260.

429. Thus, from पू 9th c., 'to purify,' come the two bases *apau* for Parasmai and *apo* for Átmane (*apau* + *i* + *sam* = अपाविषं by 37, *apau* + *i* + *ís* = अपावीस्, *apau* + *i* + *ít* = अपावीत्, &c.; Átm. *apo* + *i* + *si* = अपविषि, &c., by 36), see 583; and from तॄ 1st c., 'to cross,' comes the base *atár* for Parasmai (*atár* + *i* + *sam* = *atárisham*, &c.).

a. Observe—Roots in ॠ *ṛí*, and the root वृ *vṛi*, may optionally lengthen the inserted *i* in the Átmane: thus, अकरिषि or अकरीषि.

430. Similarly, बुध् *budh*, 1st c., 'to know,' makes *abodhisham*, &c., see 583; and वृत् *vṛit*, 1st c., 'to be,' makes *avartishi*, &c.; and एध् *edh*, 1st c., 'to increase,' makes *aidhishi*, &c. (260. *b*), see 600.

431. A medial अ *a* is sometimes lengthened: thus, वद् *vad*, 1st c., makes अवादिषं, &c. See 598.

432. The roots कू, गू, धू, ध्रू, नू, all of the 6th c., may either follow 429 or make अधुविषं *adhuvisham*, &c.

a. हन् 2d c., 'to kill,' forms its 3d preterite from वध्: thus, अवधिषं, &c. See 654.

433. Many roots in आ *á*, ए *e*, ओ *o*, and ऐ *ai*, with three in म् *m*, viz. यम् *yam*, रम् *ram*, नम् *nam*, assume *i*, but insert *s* before it; the final *e*, *o*, and *ai*, being changed to आ *á*: thus, from या 2d c., 'to go,' comes अयासिषं, &c. (see 644); from शो 4th c., 'to sharpen,' अशासिषं, &c.; from यम् 1st c., 'to restrain,' अयंसिषं, &c. दरिद्रा 2d c., 'to be poor,' makes *adaridrisham* or *adaridrásisham*, &c.

a. In the Átmane these roots reject the *i* and the *s* which precedes it, and follow 418: thus, from मा 3d c., 'to measure,' comes अमासि, &c. (see 665); from रम् 1st c., 'to sport,' अरंसि, अरंस्थास्, अरंस्त, &c.

434. Some Átmane-pada verbs of the 4th class form the 3d person sing. of the 3d preterite by rejecting the termination *sta*, and leaving *i*, as in the passive (475. *a*): thus, पद् 4th c., 'to go,' makes 3d pret. 3d sing. अपादि; जन् 4th c., 'to be born,' makes अजनि; and बुध् 4th c., 'to know,' makes अबोधि. Compare 253. *a*.

---

* Except जागृ, ऊर्णु, and श्वि, which follow 427, and are guṇated, instead of taking Vṛiddhi: thus, अजागरिषं, और्णविषं, अश्वयिषं.

Form II.

435. Resembling the first preterite.

1. *am*	*áva* or *va*	*áma* or *ma*	*e* or *i*	*ávahi*	*ámahi*
2. *as* or *s*	*atam* or *tam*	*ata* or *ta*	*athás*	*ethám* or *áthám*	*adhwam*
3. *at* or *t*	*atám* or *tám*	*an* or *us*	*ata*	*etám* or *átám*	*anta*

Note, that this form corresponds to the Greek 2d aorist (compare *asthám, asthás, asthát*, with ἔστην, ἔστης, ἔστη), and that the first form is more or less analogous to the 1st aorist. The substitution of *i* for *e*, and *áthám, átám*, for *ethám, etám*, in the Átmane of form II, is confined to a class of roots mentioned at 439.

436. Rule for the formation of the base in verbs of the first nine classes. In general the terminations are attached directly to the root: thus, गम् 1st c., 'to go,' makes अगमं *agamam*, &c., see 602; भिद् 7th c., 'to break,' अभिदं; नश् 4th c., 'to perish,' अनशं (or अनेशं, see 441). But दृश् 1st c., 'to see,' is guṇated, and makes *adarśam*, see 604. Observe—Sometimes roots which follow this form in the Parasmai, follow form I. (418) in the Átmane.

437. No confusion can arise from this apparent identity with the 1st preterite, as in all cases where these terminations are used for the 3d preterite, the 1st preterite presents some difference in the form of its base; as in *agachchham* (270), *abhinadam* (343). So again, the sixth conjugation, which alone can ever show a perfect identity of root and base, never makes use of this form for its 3d preterite, unless by some special rule the base of its 1st preterite is made to differ from the root: thus, *lip*, 'to smear' (cf. ἀλείφω), which is *alipam* in the 3d preterite, is *alimpam* in the first (281). So in Greek, compare the imperfect ἔλειπον with the 2d aor. ἔλιπον; and similarly, ἐλάμβανον with ἔλαβον; ἐδάμνην with ἔδαμον, &c.

a. One or two roots in आ *á* and इ *i* reject their finals; and one or two in ऋ *ṛi* and ॠ *ṛí* change these vowels to *ar* before the above terminations: thus, ख्या 2d c., 'to tell,' makes अख्यं; श्वि 1st c., 'to swell,' makes अश्वं; सृ 1st c., 'to go,' makes असरं; जॄ 4th c., 'to grow old,' अजरं.

438. Certain roots ending in long vowels reject the initial vowel from the terminations of the Parasmai, as indicated in the table at 435: thus, दा 3d c., 'to give,' makes *adám, adás, adát, adáva*, &c.; 3d pl. *adus*, see 663. So also, धा 3d c., 'to place,' makes *adhám*, &c., 664; and स्था 1st c., 'to stand,' makes *asthám*, &c., 587. Similarly, भू 1st c., 'to be,' excepting in 1st sing. and 3d pl. (अभूवं, अभूस्, अभूत्, अभूव, &c.; 3d pl. अभूवन्), see 585.

a. Observe, however, that some roots in *á*, like *yá*, 2d c., 'to go,' follow 434.

b. Some roots in ए *e* and ओ *o*, which follow 434, optionally follow 438; in which case *e* and *o* are changed as before to *á*: thus, धे *dhe*, 1st c., 'to drink,' makes either *adhásisham* &c., or *adhám* &c.; सो *so*, 4th c., 'to come to an end,' makes either *asásisham* or *asám*, see 613: धे also makes अदधं, see 440. *a*.

c. But ह्वे 1st c., 'to call,' drops the final *e*, and retains the initial vowel of the terminations: thus, *ahwam, ahwas, ahwat*, &c. See 595.

d. In the Átmane-pada, roots like दा, धा, स्था, &c., at 438, follow form I. at 418; but drop the final *á*, and assume *i* in its place: thus, *adishi, adithás, adita, adishwahi*, &c.; 2d pl. अदिढ्वं. See 663.

e. इ 2d c., 'to go,' makes its 3d preterite from a root गा: thus, *agám, agás*, &c.

f. The classical scholar will observe, that *adadám*, the 1st preterite of the root *dá*, 'to give,' bears the same relation to its 3d preterite *adám* that ἐδίδων does to ἔδων. So also the relation of *adhám* (3d pret. of *dhá*, 'to place') to *adadhám* (1st pret.) corresponds to that of ἔθην to ἐτίθην. Compare also *abhavas* and *abhús* with ἔφυες and ἔφυς.

439. Certain roots ending in श् *ś*, ष् *sh*, ह् *h*, enclosing a medial *i*, *u*, or *ri*, form their 3d preterites according to form II. at 435; but whenever confusion is likely to arise between the 1st and 3d preterites, *s* is prefixed to the terminations, before which sibilant the final of the root becomes *k* by 302 and 306.

a. Thus, दिश् 6th c., 'to point out,' the 1st pret. of which is *adiśam*, makes *adiksham* &c. in 3d pret. (compare the Greek 1st aorist ἔδειξα). Similarly, द्विष् 2d c., 'to hate,' makes *adwiksham* &c. 657; दुह् 2d c., 'to milk,' makes *adhuksham* &c. by 306. *a*. See 660.

b. This class of roots substitutes *i* for *e*, and *áthám, átám*, for *ethám, etám*, in the Átmane terminations: thus, *adikshi, adikshathás, adikshata, adikshávahi, adikshá-thám*, &c.

c. A few roots of this kind optionally follow 418 in the Átmane: thus, लिह् 2d c. may make अलिह्वि, अलीढास्, अलीढ, &c., 661; and दुह् 2d c., 'to milk,' may make अधुह्वि, अदुग्धास्, &c. See 660.

440. Causal verbs make use of form II, but the base assumes a peculiar reduplication (analogous to the Greek pluperfect), to be explained at 492: thus, from बुध् 1st c., 'to know,' comes अबूबुधं, &c.

a. A few primitive verbs take a reduplicated 3d preterite, analogous to causals: thus, श्रि 1st c., 'to have recourse,' makes अशिश्रियं, &c.; श्वि 1st c., 'to swell,' makes either अश्वं or अश्वयिषं or अशिश्वियं; द्रु 1st c., 'to run,' अदुद्रुवं; स्रु 1st c., 'to flow,' असुस्रुवं; धे 1st c., 'to drink,' अदधं; कम् 1st c., 'to love,' अचकमे, &c. This last is defective when it belongs to the 1st c., having no conjugational tenses; but when it belongs to the 10th c. (Pres. कामये, &c.) its 3d preterite is अचीकमे.

441. The following primitive verbs take a contracted form of reduplicated 3d preterite: वच् 2d c., 'to speak,' makes अवोचं *avocham*

(from अवउचं for अववचं 650); पत् 1st c., 'to fall,' अपप्तं (from अपपतं; compare Greek ἔπιπτον); शास् 2d c., 'to rule,' अशिषं (from अशिशसं. The Átmane follows 427; see 658); अस् 4th c., 'to throw,' आस्थं (from आससं, contracted into आस्सं for आत्सं 304. *a*, whence by transposition आस्थं); नश् 4th c., 'to perish,' अनेशं (from अनश्पं for अननिशं 620, 436).

Benedictive or *precative.*

442. Observe, that the terminations of this tense resemble those of the potential in the memorial scheme at p. 105. In the 2d and 3d singular they are identical. In the other persons of the Parasmai a sibilant is inserted, and in some of the Átmane both prefixed and inserted. The only difference between the potential and benedictive of verbs of the 2d and 3d groups, at 290, will often be that the potential will have the conjugational characteristic: thus, *bhid*, 7th c., 'to break,' will be *bhindyát* in the potential, and *bhidyát* in the benedictive. Compare the optative of the Greek aorist δοίην with the optative of the present διδοίην.

443. Rule for the formation of the base in verbs of the first nine classes. In the Parasmai, as a general rule, leave the root unchanged before the terminations, and never insert *i;* but in the Átmane prefix *i* to the terminations in those roots ending in consonants or vowels which take the inserted *i* in the futures (388. *a*, 414), and before this *i* guṇate the radical vowel. It is also guṇated in the Átmane in some roots ending in vowels which reject *i:* but if a root end in a *consonant,* and reject *i*, the radical vowel is left unchanged in the Átmane, as well as Parasmai.

444. Thus, from भू 1st c., 'to be,' come the base of the Parasmai *bhú*, and the base of the Átmane *bhavi*, by 36. *b* (*bhú* + *yásam* = भूयासं &c., *bhavi* + *síya* = भविषीय by 70).

445. Frequently, however, before the *y* of the Parasmai terminations, the root is liable to changes analogous to those which take place before the *y* of the 4th conjugation at 272, and the *y* of passive verbs at 465; and not unfrequently it undergoes changes similar to those of the 2d preterite at 373, &c., as follows:—

446. A final आ *á* is changed to ए *e* in the Parasmai, but remains unchanged in the Átmane: thus, दा 3d c., 'to give,' makes देयासं &c. for Parasmai; दासीय &c. for Átmane-pada.

447. Final इ *i* and उ *u* are lengthened in Parasmai, and guṇated in Átmane: thus, चि 5th c., 'to gather,' makes चीयासं &c., चेषीय &c.; and हु 3d c., 'to sacrifice,' makes हूयासं &c., होषीय &c.

448. Final ऋ *ṛi* is changed to रि *ri* in Parasmai, but retained in Átmane: thus, कृ 8th c., 'to do,' makes क्रियासं &c., and कृषीय &c. After a double consonant *ṛi* is guṇated in Parasmai, as well as before inserted *i:* thus, स्तृ 5th and 9th c., 'to spread,' makes स्तर्यासं &c., स्तृषीय &c., or स्तरिषीय &c.

a. वृ, 'to cover,' 'to choose,' makes either व्रियासं or वूर्यासं, वृषीय or वरिषीय or वूर्षीय.

449. Final ॠ *ṛí* is changed to ईर् *ír* in both voices, but is guṇated before inserted *i* in Átmane: thus, तॄ 1st c., 'to cross,' makes तीर्यासं &c., तीर्षीय &c., or तरिषीय &c., or तरीषीय &c.

a. One root, पॄ 10th c., 'to fill,' makes पूर्यासं &c. Compare 448. *a.*

450. Of roots in ए *e*, धे 1st c., 'to drink,' makes धेयासं &c.; but ह्वे 1st c., 'to call,' makes हूयासं &c., and ह्वासीय &c.; व्ये 1st c., 'to cover,' makes वीयासं &c., and व्यासीय &c.; and वे 1st c., 'to weave,' makes ऊयासं &c., and वासीय &c.

451. Final ऐ *ai* and ओ *o* are treated like final *á* at 446: thus, गै 1st c., 'to sing,' makes गेयासं &c.; त्रै 1st c., 'to preserve,' makes त्रासीय &c.

452. If a root end in a consonant, there is no change in Parasmai; and there are no changes in Átmane, excepting those of Sandhi, unless the root take *i*, when the radical vowel is guṇated: thus, दुह् 2d c., 'to milk,' makes दुह्यासं &c., and धुक्षीय &c., by 306. *a*; द्विष् 2d c., 'to hate,' makes द्विष्यासं &c., and द्विक्षीय &c., by 302; and बुध् 1st c., 'to know,' makes बुध्यासं &c., and बोधिषीय &c.

a. Roots of the 10th class, however, retain Guṇa in the Parasmai, as well as in the Átmane, rejecting the conjugational *aya* in the Parasmai only; see under Causals (460).

b. And if a root end in a double consonant, of which the first member is a nasal, the latter is generally rejected: thus, *bhañj*, 7th c., makes *bhajyásam*, &c.

453. ग्रह् 9th c., 'to take,' makes in Parasmai गृह्यासं &c.; प्रच्छ् 6th c., 'to ask,' makes पृच्छ्यासं &c. Similarly, भ्रज्ज् 6th c., 'to fry,' and व्रश्च् 6th c., 'to cut.' In the Átmane they are regular.

454. वच् 2d c. 'to speak,' वद् 1st c. 'to say,' वप् 1st c. 'to sow,' वश् 2d c. 'to wish,' वह् 1st c. 'to carry,' and स्वप् 2d c. 'to sleep,' substitute उ *u* for व *v* in the Parasmai: thus, उच्यासं &c., सुप्यासं &c. In the Átmane they are regular; as, वक्षीय from वह्.

Conditional.

455. Note, that this tense bears the same relation to the 2d future that the 1st preterite does to the present. In its formation it lies half-way between a first preterite and a second future. It resembles the first preterite in prefixing the augment अ *a* to the base (see 260), and in the latter part of its terminations: it resembles the second future in guṇating the radical vowel, in inserting इ *i* in exactly those roots in which the future inserts *i*, and in the *sy* of its terminations. See the scheme at 246, p. 105.

456. Rule for the formation of the base in verbs of the first nine classes. Prefix the augment अ *a*, guṇate the radical vowel, except when debarred by 28. *b*, and insert *i* before the terminations if the futures insert *i*. When *i* is rejected, as in all the roots at 400 &c., the rules of Sandhi must be observed.

457. Thus, बुध् 1st c., 'to know,' makes अबोधिष्यं &c.; दुह् 2d c.,

'to milk,' makes अधोक्ष्यं &c., by 306. *a*; द्विष् 2d c., 'to hate,' makes अद्वेक्ष्यं &c., by 302.

Infinitive.

458. The termination of the infinitive is तुं *tum*, like the *um* of the Latin *supine*.

459. Rule for the formation of the base in verbs of the ten classes. The base of the infinitive is identical with the base of the first future, and where one inserts इ *i*, the other does also: thus, *budh*, 1st c., 'to know,' makes बोधितुं *bodhitum*; *kship*, 6th c., 'to throw,' makes क्षेप्तुं *ksheptum*. Moreover, all the rules for the change of the final consonant of a root before the *t* of the future terminations apply equally before the *t* of the infinitive. Hence, by substituting *um* for the final *á* of the 3d pers. sing. of the 1st future, the infinitive is at once obtained: thus, *śaktá*, *śaktum*; *tyaktá*, *tyaktum*; प्रष्टा, प्रष्टुं; सोढा, सोढुं, &c. See 400, &c.

a. The following examples will show how remarkably the Sanskṛit infinitive answers to the Latin *supine*. S. स्थातुं 'to stand,' L. *statum*; S. दातुं 'to give,' L. *datum*; S. पातुं 'to drink,' L. *potum*; S. एतुं 'to go,' L. *itum*; S. स्तर्तुं 'to strew,' L. *stratum*; S. अंक्तुं 'to anoint,' L. *unctum*; S. जनितुं 'to beget,' L. *genitum*; S. स्वनितुं 'to sound,' L. *sonitum*; S. सर्प्तुं 'to go,' L. *serptum*; S. वमितुं 'to vomit,' L. *vomitum*. Prof. Bopp considers that the infinitive affix *tum* is the accusative of an affix *tu*, of which the affix *twá* of the indeclinable participle (see 555. *a*) is the instrumental case.

DERIVATIVE VERBS.

460. Having explained the formation of the verbal base in the ten classes of primitive verbs, we come next to the four kinds of derivative verbs, viz. passives, causals, desideratives, and frequentatives.

PASSIVE VERBS.

461. Every root in every one of the ten classes may take a passive form*, which is conjugated as an Átmane-pada verb of the 4th class.

a. It is a form, however, not very commonly used, except in the 3d singular and plural of the present and imperative; for although a passive construction is exceedingly common in Sanskṛit syntax, yet almost all the tenses of the passive verb are expressed by participles.

462. Observe—Passive verbs take the regular Átmane-pada terminations* at 247, making use of the substitutions required in the

* See 253, and 253. *a*. *b*. There are occasional instances in the Mahábhárata of passive verbs conjugated in the Parasmai.

4th class. In the 3d preterite they take either of the forms at 418 and 427, according as the root may admit the inserted इ *i* or not; but they require that in the 3d singular of both forms the termination be इ *i* in place of *sta* and *ishṭa*.

Conjugational tenses.

463. Rule for the formation of the base in the four conjugational tenses, Átmane-pada, of roots of the first nine classes. The rule is the same as in the 4th class at 272, viz. affix य *ya**—lengthened to या *yá* before initial *m* or *v*—to the root, the vowel of which is not guṇated, and generally remains unchanged.

464. Thus, from भू 1st c., 'to be,' comes the base भूय *bhúya* (Pres. *bhúya* + *i* = भूये, *bhúya* + *se* = भूयसे, &c.; Pot. *bhúya* + *íya* = भूयेय, &c.; Imp. *bhúya* + *ai* = भूयै, &c.; 1st Pret. *abhúya* + *i* = अभूये, &c.); from तुद् 6th c., 'to strike,' comes *tudya* (Pres. *tudya* + *i* = तुद्ये, &c.).

465. A final vowel, however, often undergoes changes, some of which are different from, and some analogous to, those of the 4th class, as follows:—

Six roots in आ *á*, and one or two in ए *e*, ऐ *ai*, and ओ *o*, change their final vowels to ई *í*: thus, दा 3d c., 'to give,' makes Pres. दीये, दीयसे, दीयते, &c. So also, धा, स्था, मा, पा, 1st c. 'to drink;' हा 3d c. 'to quit;' धे 1st c. 'to drink' (3d sing. धीयते, &c.); गै 1st c. 'to sing' (गीयते); सो 4th c. 'to be destroyed' (सीयते).

a. But other roots in *á* remain unchanged; and most others in *ai* and *o* are changed to *á*: thus, ख्या 2d c., 'to tell,' makes 3d sing. ख्यायते; and ज्ञा 9th c., 'to know,' ज्ञायते; पा 2d c., 'to protect,' पायते; ध्यै 1st c., 'to meditate,' ध्यायते; शो 4th c., 'to sharpen,' शायते. But दरिद्रा 2d c. makes दरिद्र्यते.

b. ह्वे 1st c. 'to call,' व्ये 1st c. 'to cover,' वे 1st c. 'to weave,' make their bases *húya*, *víya*, and *úya* (3d sing. हूयते).

466. Final इ *i* or उ *u* are lengthened, as also *i* or *u* before *v* or *r*: thus, from जि 1st c., हु 3d c., दिव् 4th c., come the three bases जीय, हूय, दीव्य.

a. But श्वि 1st c., 'to swell,' makes शूयते; and शी 2d c., 'to sleep,' शय्यते.

467. Final ऋ *ri* becomes रि *ri*, but if preceded by a double consonant is guṇated: thus, कृ 8th c., 'to do,' makes क्रियते; but स्मृ 1st c., स्मर्यते. The roots ऋ and जागृ are also guṇated.

468. Final ॠ *rí* becomes ईर् *ír*: thus, कॄ 6th c., 'to scatter,' makes कीर्यते; but पॄ, 'to fill,' पूर्यते.

469. Roots ending in two consonants, of which the first is a nasal, usually reject the nasal; as, from बन्ध्, स्तम्भ्, सञ्ज्, come the bases *badhya*, &c. (बध्यते, &c.).

---

* Bopp considers that this *ya* is derived from *yá*, 'to go,' just as the causal *aya* is derived from *i*, 'to go.' It is certain that in Bengálí and Hindí the passive is formed with the root *yá*. Compare the Latin *amatum iri*, &c. See 481.

470. जन् 4th c., खन् 1st c., तन् 8th c., may optionally reject the final nasal, and lengthen the preceding *a*: thus, जायते or जन्यते, &c.

471. वच् 2d c., वह् 1st c., वप् 1st c., वस् 1st c., वश् 2d c. 'to wish,' वह् 1st c., स्वप् 2d c., यज् 1st c., make their bases उच्य, उह्य, उप्य, उष्य, उश्य, उह्य, सुप्य, इज्य (उच्यते, &c.).

472. ग्रह्, प्रच्छ्, भ्रज्ज्, व्यच्, व्यध्, व्रश्च्, शास्, make their bases गृह्य, पृच्छ्य, भृज्ज्य, विच्य, विध्य, वृश्च्य, शिष्य, respectively (गृह्यते, &c.).

Non-conjugational tenses.—Second preterite of passives.

473. The base of this tense in the passive verb is identical with that of all primitive verbs, in all ten conjugations. The bases, therefore, as formed at 364, will serve equally well for the 2d preterite of the passive, provided only that they be restricted to the A'tmane-pada inflection.

a. According to some grammarians, however, the root भू may make बुभूवे *bubhúve*, as well as बभूवे *babhúve*, in the passive 2d preterite.

First and second future of passives.

474. In these and the remaining tenses no variation can occur from the bases of the same tenses in the primitive, unless the root end in a vowel. In that case the insertion of इ *i* may take place in the passive, although prohibited in the primitive, provided the final vowel of the root be first vṛiddhied: thus, from चि *chi*, 5th c., 'to gather,' may come the base of the 1st and 2d fut. pass. *cháyi* (*cháyitáhe* &c., *cháyishye* &c.), although the base of the same tenses in the primitive is *che* (*chetáhe* &c., *cheshye* &c.). Similarly, from हु *hu* and कृ *kṛi* may come *hávi* and *kári* (*hávitáhe, káritáhe*), although the bases in the primitive are *ho* and *kar*.

a. In like manner इ *i* may be inserted when the root ends in long आ *á*, or in ए *e* changeable to *á*, provided that, instead of Vṛiddhi (which is impossible), *y* be interposed between the final *á* and inserted *i*: thus, from *dá*, 'to give,' may come the base of the fut. pass. *dáyi* (*dáyitáhe* &c.), although the base of the same tenses in the primitive is *dá* (*dátáhe* &c.); from *hwe*, 'to call,' may come *hwáyi* (ह्वायिताहे &c.), although the base in the primitive is *hwá*. But in all these cases it is permitted to take the base of the primitive for that of the passive, and *chetáhe* or *cháyitáhe* may equally stand for the 1st fut. pass.*

b. In the case of roots ending in consonants, the base of the two futures in the passive will be identical with that of the same tenses in the primitive verb †, the inflection being that of the A'tmane.

c. In verbs of the 10th conjugation deviation from the A'tmane form of the primitive may take place in these and the succeeding tenses. See 496.

---

* This explanation of the passive rests on the authority of Páṇini (VI. 4. 62), and the Siddhánta Kaumudí.

† The root दृश् 1st c., 'to see,' however, in the passive, may be दर्शिताहे, दर्शिष्ये, as well as द्रष्टाहे, द्रक्ष्ये; and हन् may be घानिताहे, घानिष्ये, as well as हन्ताहे, हनिष्ये; and ग्रह् may be ग्राहिताहे, ग्राहिष्ये, as well as ग्रहीताहे, ग्रहीष्ये.

Third preterite of passives.

475. In this tense, also, variation from the primitive may occur when the root ends in a vowel. For in that case the insertion of इ *i* may take place, although forbidden in the primitive verb, provided the final of the root be vṛiddhied: thus, from चि *chi* may come the base of the 3d pret. pass. *acháyi* (*acháyishi* &c., 427), although the base in the A'tmane of the primitive is *ache* (*acheshi* &c., 418). So also, from हु *hu* and कृ *kṛi* may come *ahávi* and *akári* (*ahávishi, akárishi*, 427), although the bases in the A'tmane of the primitive are *aho* and *akṛi* (*ahoshi, akṛishi*, 418). Again, *i* may be inserted when the root ends in long आ *á*, provided that *y* be interposed between final *á* and inserted *i*: thus, from *dá*, 'to give,' may come *adáyi* (*adáyishi* &c.), although the base in the A'tmane of the primitive is *adi* (*adishi* &c.). But in all these cases it is permitted to take the base of the primitive for that of the passive (so that the passive of *chi* may be either *acháyishi* or *acheshi*), except in the 3d pers. sing., where the terminations *ishṭa* and *sta* being rejected, the base, as formed by Vṛiddhi and the inserted *i*, must stand alone: thus, *acháyi*, 'it was gathered;' *ahávi*, 'it was sacrificed;' *akári*, 'it was done;' *adáyi*, 'it was given.' Sometimes, however, the regular form of the 3d sing. A'tmane is admissible, as well as the mutilated form.

a. If the root end in a consonant, the base of the 3d pret. pass. will always be identical with that of the 3d pret. A'tmane of the primitive, except in the 3d pers. sing., where इ *i* being substituted for the terminations *ishṭa* and *sta* of the 1st form, requires before it the lengthening of a medial *a*, and the *Guṇa* of any other short medial vowel*. Hence, in *tan*, 8th c., 'to stretch,' the form of the 1st, 2d, and 3d sing. 3d pret. will be *atanishi, atanishṭhás, atáni*; from *kship*, 6th c., 'to throw,' *akshipsi, akshipthás, akshepi*; from *vid*, 2d c., 'to know,' *avedishi, avedishṭhás, avedi*. Observe—This 3d sing. of the 3d pret. passive is not unfrequently found, even in the simplest writings.

Benedictive and conditional of passives.

476. In these tenses the same variation is permitted in the case of roots ending in vowels as in the last; that is, the insertion of इ *i* is allowed, provided that, before it, Vṛiddhi take place in a final vowel capable of such a change, and *y* be interposed after final *á*: thus, from *chi* may come the bases *cháyi* and *acháyi* (*cháyishíya, acháyishye*); from *hu*, *hávi* and *ahávi*; from *kṛi*, *kári* and *akári*; from *dá*, *dáyi* and *adáyi*. But *cheshíya, acheshye, hoshíya, ahoshye*, &c., the forms belonging to the A'tmane of the primitive verb, are equally admissible in the passive.

---

* A medial vowel, long by nature or position, remains unchanged (by 28. *b*), and in one or two cases a short; as, *aśami* for *aśámi*. The above explanation of the 3d preterite rests on the authority of Páṇini, the Siddhánta Kaumudí, and the Bhaṭṭi Kávya (15. 64, 65).

Passive infinitive mood.

477. There is no passive infinitive mood in Sanskṛit distinct in form from the active. But although the affix *tum* has generally an active, it is capable of a passive sense, when joined with certain verbs, especially with शक् *śak*, 4th c., 'to be able.' It is also used passively, in connection with the participles *árabdha*, *nirúpita*, *yukta*, &c. See Syntax.

Passive verbs from roots of the 10th class.

478. In forming a passive verb from roots of the 10th class, although the conjugational अय is rejected in the first four tenses, yet the other conjugational changes of the root are retained before the affix *ya:* thus, from चुर् 10th c., 'to steal,' comes the base *chorya* (चोर्यते). In the 2d pret. अय is retained (see 473), and in the other non-conjugational tenses the base may deviate from the Átmane form of the primitive by the optional rejection or assumption of अय, especially in the 3d preterite. See Causal Passives at 496.

CAUSAL VERBS.

479. Every root in every one of the ten classes may take a causal form, which is conjugated as a verb of the 10th class; and which is not only employed to give a causal sense to a primitive verb, but also an active sense to a neuter verb; see 289, 254: thus the primitive verb *bodhati*, 'he knows' (from the root *budh*, 1st c.), becomes in the causal बोधयति *bodhayati*, 'he causes to know,' 'he informs;' and the neuter verb *kshubhyati*, 'he is shaken' (from *kshubh*, 4th c.), becomes क्षोभयति 'he shakes.'

a. This form may rarely imply 'allowing,' 'permitting:' thus, *hárayati*, 'he allows to take;' *náśayati*, 'he suffers to perish.'

480. As to the terminations of causal verbs, they are the same as those of the scheme at 247, p. 106; and the same substitutions are required in the first four tenses as in the 1st, 4th, 6th, and 10th classes.

Conjugational tenses.

481. Rule for the formation of the base in the four conjugational tenses of roots of the ten classes. If a root end in a vowel, vṛiddhi that vowel; if in a consonant, guṇate the radical vowel before *all* the terminations, and affix अय *aya* * (changeable to *ayá* before initial *m* or *v*) to the root so vṛiddhied or guṇated.

---

* Derived from the root इ *i*, 'to go,' just as the passive *ya* is derived from *yá*. See 463.

482. Thus, from नी 1st c., 'to lead,' comes the base नायय by 37 (Pres. *náyayá* + *mi* = नाययामि, *náyaya* + *si* = नाययसि &c.; Pot. *náyaya* + *iyam* = नाययेयं &c.; Imp. *náyaya* + *áni* = नाययानि &c.; 1st Pret. *anáyaya* + *m* = अनाययं &c. A'tm. Pres. *náyaya* + *i* = नायये &c.). Similarly, from भू *bhú*, 1st c., 'to be,' comes the base भावय *bhávaya;* and from कृ 8th c., 'to do,' the base कारय *káraya.* But from बुध् 1st and 4th c., 'to know,' comes the guṇated बोधय *bodhaya;* and from सृप् 1st c., 'to creep,' the guṇated सर्पय *sarpaya.*

483. Roots ending in आ *á*, or in ए *e*, ऐ *ai*, ओ *o*, changeable to आ *á*, cannot be vṛiddhied, but generally insert प् *p* between the root and the affix *aya:* thus, दा 1st c., 'to give,' makes दापयामि *dápayámi*, &c.; धे 1st c., 'to drink,' धापयामि *dhápayámi*, &c.; गै 1st c., 'to sing,' गापयामि *gápayámi*, &c.

a. All other roots in *á* insert *p*, excepting पा 1st c., 'to drink,' which inserts य् *y*, making पाययामि &c.; and पा 2d c., 'to preserve,' which inserts ल् *l*, making पालयामि &c.

b. All other roots in *ai* insert *p*, but most other roots in *e* and *o* insert *y:* thus, ह्वे 1st c., 'to call,' makes ह्वाययामि &c.; and शो 4th c., 'to sharpen,' makes शाययामि &c.

484. ज्ञा 9th c. 'to know,' श्रा 2d c. 'to cook,' स्ना 2d c. 'to bathe,' and ग्लै 1st c. 'to languish,' may optionally shorten the *á*, the last two only when not joined with prepositions: thus, ज्ञापयामि &c., or ज्ञपयामि &c.; ग्लापयामि &c., or ग्लपयामि &c.

485. Some roots in *i*, *í*, *ṛi*, also insert *p*, after changing the final vowel to *á:* thus, जि 1st c., 'to conquer,' makes जापयामि &c.; स्मि 1st c., 'to smile,' makes स्माययामि &c., and स्मापये &c.; चि 5th c., 'to collect,' has four forms; 1. चापयामि &c., 2. चपयामि &c., 3. चाययामि &c., 4. चययामि &c.; भी 3d c., 'to fear,' has three forms; 1. भाययामि &c., 2. भापये &c., A'tm. only, 3. भीषये &c.; इ 2d c., 'to go,' makes आपयामि &c., especially with the preposition अधि 'over,' अध्यापयामि 'I cause to go over,' 'I teach.'

a. Three roots insert *n;* ली 4th c., 'to embrace,' 'to adhere,' making (with prep. वि) -लीनयामि &c., as well as -लापयामि, -लाययामि, and -लालयामि &c.; प्री 9th c., 'to please,' making प्रीणयामि; and धू 5th and 9th c., 'to shake,' धूनयामि.

486. ह्री 3d c. 'to be ashamed' and ऋ 1st c. 'to go' insert *p* after guṇation: thus, ह्रेपयामि &c., अर्पयामि &c.

487. Roots ending in consonants, enclosing a medial अ *a*, generally, but not always, lengthen the *a:* thus, पच् 1st c., 'to cook,' makes पाचयामि &c.

a. Note, that few roots in *m* lengthen the *a:* thus, गम् 1st c., 'to go,' makes गमयामि &c. Some, however, optionally do so.

488. Anomalies.—रुह् 1st c., 'to grow,' changes *h* to *p*, making रोपयामि &c.; दुष् 4th c., 'to be corrupt,' makes दूषयामि &c., 'I corrupt;' हन् 2d c., 'to kill,' घातयामि &c.; शद् 1st and 6th c., 'to perish,' शातयामि &c.; स्फुर् 6th c., 'to quiver,' स्फारयामि &c.; स्फाय् 1st c., 'to increase,' स्फावयामि &c.

Non-conjugational tenses.

489. The changes of the root required to form the base of the conjugational tenses are continued in the non-conjugational. Moreover, *aya* is retained in all these tenses, excepting in the 3d preterite and benedictive, Parasmai; but the last *a* of *aya* is dropped before the inserted इ् *i*, which is invariably assumed.

Second preterite of causals.

490. This tense is formed by adding आं *ám* to the base of the conjugational tenses, and affixing the 2d preterite of one of the three auxiliary verbs, अस् 'to be,' भू 'to be,' or कृ 'to do:' thus, बुध् 1st c., 'to know,' makes बोधयामास or बोधयाम्बभूव * or बोधयाञ्चकार. See 385.

First and second future of causals.

491. In these tenses the inserted इ् *i* is invariably assumed between the base, as formed in the conjugational tenses, and the usual terminations: thus, *budh* makes *bodhayitásmi* &c., *bodhayishyámi* &c.

Third preterite of causals (Greek pluperfect).

492. The terminations are those of form II; see 435. In the formation of the base of this tense, the affix *ay* is rejected; but any other change that may take place in the conjugational tenses, such as the insertion of *p* or *y*, is preserved. The base is a reduplicated form of this change, and to this reduplication the augment अ *a* is prefixed: thus, taking the bases *bodhay* and *jápay* (causal bases of *budh*, 'to know,' and *ji*, 'to conquer'), and rejecting *ay*, we have *bodh* and *jáp*; and from these are formed the bases of the 3d pret. *abúbudh* and *ajíjap* (अबूबुधं *abúbudham* &c., अबूबुधे *abúbudhe* &c., अजीजपं *ajíjapam* &c., अजीजपे *ajíjape* &c., cf. the Greek pluperfect).

493. The rule for this reduplication is as follows:—The initial consonant of the root, with its vowel, is reduplicated, and the reduplicated consonant follows the rules given at 331; but the reduplication of the vowel is peculiar.

Rules for the reduplication of the vowel of the initial consonant.

a. Causal bases, after rejecting *ay*, will end either in *áy*, *áv*, *ár*, or a consonant preceded by *a*, *á*, *e*, *o*, or *ar*. The usual reduplicated vowel for all these vowels, except *o*, is *i*. But *u* is reduplicated for *o*, and sometimes also for *áv*. The rule is, that either the reduplicated syllable or the base syllable must be long either by

* It may, however, be questioned whether भू is often found added to causals.

nature or position; and in general the reduplicated vowel is made long, and, to compensate for this, the long vowel of the causal base shortened, or, if it be Guṇa, changed to its cognate short vowel: thus, the causal base *náy* (from *ní*, rejecting *ay*) makes the base of the 3d pret. *anínay* (अनीनयं *anínayam* &c.); the causal base *bháv* (from *bhú*) makes *abíbhav* (अबीभवं &c.); the causal base *kár* (form *kṛi*), *achíkar; gam* (from *gam*), *ajígam; pách* (from *pach*), *apípach; pál* (from *pá*), *apípal; ved* (from *vid*), *avívid; vart* (from *vṛit*), *avívṛit*. But *bodh* (from *budh*), *abúbudh;* and *sáv* (from *su*), *asúshav*. Sometimes the reduplicated vowel is only long by position before two consonants, the radical vowel being still made short; as, *śráv* (from *śru*) makes *aśuśrav; dráv* from (*dru*), *adudrav; bhráj, abibhraj*. Sometimes the reduplicated vowel remains short, whilst the vowel of the causal base, which must be long either by nature or position, remains unchanged: thus, the causal base *jív* (from *jív*) may make *ajijív; chint, achichint; kalp, achikalp*. In such cases *a* may be reduplicated for *a* or *á;* as, *laksh* makes *alalaksh; yách, ayayách; vart* (from *vṛit*), *avavart*, &c.

b. The following are anomalous: from *páy* (*pá*, 'to drink'), अपीप्यं &c.*; from *stháp* (*sthá*, 'to stand'), अतिष्ठिपं &c.; from *ghráp* (*ghrá*, 'to smell'), अजिघ्रिपं &c., and अजिघ्रपं &c.; from *adhyáp* (*i*, 'to go,' with *adhi*), अध्यजीगपं &c.

Reduplication of an initial vowel in causal third preterites.

494. Roots beginning with vowels, and ending with single consonants, form their causal third preterites by a peculiar reduplication of the root (after rejecting अय). The rule is that not only the initial vowel, as in the 2d pret. at 364. *a*, but the final consonant also be reduplicated. In fact, the whole root is doubled, as it would be if it began with a consonant, and ended with a vowel; but the consonant is reduplicated according to the rules at 331, and the reduplicated vowel is always *i*. This *i*, however, takes the place of the radical vowel, instead of beginning the reduplicated syllable; and the vowel of the root then becomes the initial of the reduplicated syllable, combining with the augment अ *a*, according to 260. *a:* thus, ऋध् 5th c., 'to prosper,' which ought to be reduplicated into इऋध् by 331. *a*, becomes, by transposition of the vowels, ऋदिध्; and with अ prefixed, आर्दिध् by 260. *a* (आर्दिधं 'I caused to prosper,' &c.). Similarly, ऊह् 1st c., 'to infer,' which ought to be इजूह् *ijúh*, becomes ऊजिह् *újih;* and with अ prefixed, औजिह् (औजिहं 'I caused to infer'). So also, आप् 5th c., 'to obtain,' makes आपिपं 'I caused to obtain;' ईड् 2d c., 'to praise,' makes ऐडिडं 'I caused to praise.' Compare the Greek 2d aorist ἤγαγον from ἄγω, and ὤρορον from ὄρω.

a. If a root end in a compound consonant, the first member of the compound is rejected from the final, but not from the reduplicated letter: thus, अर्ह् 1st c., 'to be worthy,' makes आर्जिहं 'I caused to be worthy,' 'I honoured;' उन्द् 7th c., 'to moisten,' makes औन्दिदं 'I caused to moisten.'

b. Note, that क्ष् *ksh* is treated as a single consonant, and च् *ch* is reduplicated for it by 331. *c:* thus, ईक्ष् 1st c., 'to see,' makes ऐचिक्षं *aichiksham*, 'I caused to see.'

* Páṇini VII. 4. 4.

c. Roots consisting of a single vowel, form their causal 3d preterite from the causal base (after rejecting *aya*): thus, the root ऋ, 'to go,' makes its causal base *arp*, 'to deliver over;' and its causal 3d pret. आर्पिपं 'I caused to deliver.'

d. ऊर्णु 2d c., 'to cover,' makes और्णुनुवं.

Benedictive and conditional of causals.

495. The base of the benedictive, Átmane, and of the conditional in both voices, does not differ from that of the non-conjugational tenses; but the last *a* of *aya* is dropped before the inserted इ *i*, which is always assumed. In the Parasmai of the benedictive both *ay* and *i* are rejected, but any other change of the root is retained: thus, बुध् 1st c., 'to know,' makes in benedictive *bodhyásam* &c., *bodhayishíya* &c.; in conditional, *abodhayishyam* &c., *abodhayishye* &c.

Passive form of causals.

496. In forming a passive verb from a causal base, the causal affix अय is rejected, but the other causal changes of the root are retained before the passive affix *ya*: thus, from the causal base पातय *pátaya* (from पत् 1st c., 'to fall') comes the passive *pátya*, making 3d sing. पात्यते 'he is made to fall.' Similarly, स्था 1st c., 'to stand,' makes स्थापयति 'he causes to stand,' स्थाप्यते 'he is made to stand;' and ज्ञा 9th c., 'to know,' makes ज्ञपयति 'he causes to know,' and ज्ञप्यते 'he is caused to know,' 'he is informed.'

a. In the non-conjugational tenses, the base of all the tenses, excepting the 2d preterite, may vary from the Átmane form by the optional rejection of the conjugation अय. But in the 2d preterite, the Átmane of the usual form with *ám* and the auxiliaries (490, 385) is admitted for the passive. In the 3d preterite, the usual reduplicated form (492) gives place to the Átmane form which belongs to those verbs of the first nine classes which assume *i*: thus, from भावय, the causal base of भू 'to be,' come the passive 2d pret. भावयाञ्चक्रे; 1st fut. भावयिताहे or भाविताहे; 2d fut. भावयिष्ये or भाविष्ये; 3d pret. अभावयिषि or अभाविषि, 3d sing. अभावि; bened. भावयिषीय or भाविषीय; cond. अभावयिष्ये or अभाविष्ये. So also, from शमय, the causal base of शम् 'to cease,' come the passive 2d pret. शमयाञ्चक्रे or शमयामासे; 1st fut. शमयिताहे or शमिताहे; 2d fut. शमयिष्ये or शमिष्ये; 3d pret. अशमयिषि or अशमिषि, 3d sing. अशमि; bened. शमयिषीय &c.; and the radical *a* may in every case be optionally lengthened: thus, 1st fut. शमयिताहे or शामयिताहे &c.

Desiderative form of causals.

497. Causals may take a desiderative form (498): thus, from *pátayámi*, 'I cause to fall,' *pipátayishámi*, 'I desire to cause to fall;' from *swápayámi*, 'I cause to sleep,' *sushwápayishámi*, 'I desire to cause to sleep.'

DESIDERATIVE VERBS.

498. Every root in the ten classes may take a desiderative form.

a. Although this form of the root rarely appears in its character of a verb, yet nouns and participles derived from the desiderative base are not uncommon (see 80. XXII, and 82. III). Moreover, there are certain roots which take a desiderative form, without yielding a volitive signification; and these, as being equivalent to primitive verbs (amongst which they are sometimes classed), may occur in the best writers. For example, *jugups*, 'to blame,' from the root गुप् *gup; chikits*, 'to cure,' from कित् *kit; titiksh*, 'to bear,' from तिज् *tij; mímáns*, 'to reason,' from मन् *man; bíbhats*, 'to abhor,' from बाध् *bádh*.

499. Note, that desideratives take the terminations of the scheme at 247, with the substitutions required in the 1st, 4th, 6th, and 10th classes; and their inflection, either in the Parasmai or A'tmane, is determined by the practice of the primitive verb: thus, the root बुध् *budh*, 1st c., 'to know,' taking both inflections in the primitive, may take both in the desiderative (*bubodhishámi* &c., or *bubodhishe* &c., 'I desire to know'); and लभ् *labh*, 'to take,' taking only the A'tmane in the primitive, may take only the A'tmane in the desiderative (*lipse* &c., 'I desire to take').

500. Rule for the formation of the base in the four conjugational tenses. Reduplicate the initial consonant and vowel of the root, and if the primitive verb inserts इ *i* (see 388. *a*), affix इष् *ish;* if it rejects *i*, then simply स् *s*, changeable to ष् *sh*, to the root so reduplicated: the vowel *a* is then added to form the base, as in the 1st, 4th, 6th, and 10th classes; and, according to the rule in those classes, this *a* is lengthened before *m* and *v*.

a. Thus, from क्षिप् *kship*, 6th c., 'to throw,' comes the base *chikshipsa* (*chiksipsá* + *mi* = चिक्षिप्सामि *chikshipsámi* &c., 'I desire to throw'); but from विद् *vid*, 2d c., 'to know,' taking inserted *i*, comes *vividisha* (*vividishá* + *mi* = विविदिषामि *vividishámi* &c.).

b. The reduplication of the consonant is strictly in conformity with the rules laid down at 331, and that of the vowel of the initial consonant follows the analogy of causal third preterites at 493; that is, the vowel इ *i* (generally, however, short) is reduplicated for *a, á, i, í, ṛi, ṛí, e,* or *ai;* but the vowel उ *u* for *u, ú,* and *o.* Observe—The final consonant of a root rejecting *i* will unite with the *s* of *sa,* in accordance with the rules at 296: thus, from पच् 1st c. comes the base *pipaksha* by 296; from याच् 1st c. comes *yiyáchisha;* from जीव् 1st c., *jijívisha;* from दृश् 1st c., *didṛiksha;* from सेव् 1st c., *siserisha* (in this and in some other roots beginning with *s,* the *i* of the reduplicated syllable does not influence the following *s,* as might be expected from rule 70); from गै 1st c., *jigás;* from ज्ञा, *jijńás* (γιγνώσκω): but from युज् 7th c. comes *yuyuksha;* from पू 9th c., *pupúsha;* from बुध् 4th c., बुभुत्स *bubhutsa,* see 299. *a* (पिपक्षामि &c., यियाचिषामि &c.).

c. And if the root begin with a vowel the reduplication still follows the analogy of the same tense: thus, from अश् comes अशिश्; and with *isha* added, अशिशिष. Similarly, from अर्ह् comes *arjihisha;* from ऊह्, *újihisha;* from ईक्ष्, *íchikshisha;* from उन्द्, *undidisha:* see 494. The vowel *i* is reduplicated for *a,* as being lighter; see 331. *e.*

501. When a root takes the inserted *i,* and consequently forms its desiderative with *isha,* the radical vowel may in general be optionally guṇated: thus, मुद् 1st c., 'to rejoice,' makes either *mumodisha* or *mumudisha.*

502. When स *sa* is affixed to roots ending in vowels, it has the effect of lengthening a final इ *i* or उ *u;* of changing ए *e,* ऐ *ai,* ओ *o,* to आ *á;* ऋ *ṛi* or ॠ *ṛí* to ईर् *ír,* or after a labial to ऊर् *úr:* thus, from चि 5th c. comes *chichísha;* from श्रु 5th c., *śuśrúsha;* from कृ 8th c., *chikírsha;* from गै 1st c., *jigása;* from तॄ, *titírsha;* from पॄ, *pupúrsha;* from भृ, *bubhúrsha;* from मृ, *mumúrsha.*

a. When it is affixed to roots ending in consonants, the radical vowel remains unchanged, but the final consonant combines with the initial sibilant, in accordance with the rules laid down at 296; as, from युध् 4th c. comes *yuyutsa* (299); from दह् 1st c. comes *didhaksha* (306. *a*); from दुह् 2d c., *dudhuksha;* from भुज् 7th c., *bubhuksha.*

503. The following roots form their desiderative bases anomalously: from दा 3d c., 'to give,' comes *ditsa* (*ditsámi,* 'I wish to give'); from मा, 'to measure,' *mitsa;* from आप् 5th c., 'to obtain,' comes *ípsa;* from धा, 'to place,' *dhitsa:* so also, from धे, 'to drink,' *dhitsa;* from जि, 'to conquer,' *jigísha;* from चि, 'to gather,' *chikísha,* as well as *chichísha;* from हन्, 'to kill,' जिघांस; from ग्रह्, जिघृक्ष; from प्रच्छ्, पिपृच्छिष; from स्वप्, सुषुप्स; from शक्, 'to be able,' शिक्ष; from लभ्, 'to obtain,' लिप्स; from राध्, रित्स; from रभ्, रिप्स; from पत्, पित्स; from ऋध्, ईर्त्स, or regularly अर्दिधिष; from दिव्, दुद्यूष, or regularly दिदेविष; from ह्वे, जुहूष; from दरिद्रा, दिदरिद्रिष; from अद्, जिघत्स, substituted from घस् 304. *a.*

504. When causals and verbs of the 10th class take a desiderative form, they retain *ay,* and are all formed with *isha:* thus, चुर् makes *chuchorayishámi* &c. The causal *adhyápayati,* 'he causes to go over,' 'he teaches,' makes अध्यापिपयिषति or अधिजिगापयिषति &c., 'he desires to teach.'

Non-conjugational tenses of desideratives.

505. The second preterite is formed by affixing *ám* to the desiderative base, as already formed, and adding the second preterite of either one of the auxiliaries *kṛi* or *bhú* (see 385. *b*): thus, from *pach* comes the 2d preterite *pipakshánchakára*, 'I wished to cook.' In all the remaining tenses it is an universal rule, that inserted *i* be assumed after the desiderative base, whether formed by *sa* or *isha*, except in the bened. Parasmai: thus, from *pach* comes 1st fut. 1st sing. *pipakshitásmi* &c.; 2d fut. *pipakshishyámi* &c; 3d pret. *apipakshisham* &c. (form II. at 427); bened. Parasmai *pipakshyásam* &c.; A'tmane *pipakshishíya* &c.; cond. *apipakshishyam* &c. So also, taking *vividish* (formed with *ish* from *vid*), the 1st fut. is *vividishitásmi;* 2d fut. *vividishishyámi;* 3d pret. *avividishisham* &c.

Causal form of desideratives.

506. Desiderative verbs may sometimes take a causal form: thus, *div*, 'to play,' makes Pres. *dudyúshámi*, 'I desire to play;' *dudyúshayámi*, 'I cause to desire to play.'

FREQUENTATIVE OR INTENSIVE VERBS.

507. Every one of the roots in the ten classes may take a frequentative form.

a. This form is even less used than the desiderative. In the present participle, however, and in a few nouns, it may sometimes appear (see 80. XXII). It either expresses repetition or gives intensity to the radical idea, especially in the case of roots signifying 'to shine,' 'to be beautiful,' or 'to lament:' thus, from दीप्, 'to shine,' comes the frequentative base *dedípya* (Pres. 3d sing. *dedípyate*, 'it shines brightly'), and the present participle *dedípyamána*, 'shining brightly:' so also, from शुभ्, 'to be beautiful,' comes *śośubhya* and *śośubhyamána;* from रुद्, 'to weep,' *rorudya* and *rorudyamána*.

508. There are two kinds of frequentative verb, the one a reduplicated A'tmane-pada verb, conforming, like neuter and passive verbs, to the conjugation of the 4th class, and usually, though not always, yielding a neuter signification; the other a reduplicated Parasmai-pada verb, following the conjugation of the 3d class of verbs. This last is rarely used *.

a. Observe—There is no frequentative form for roots of the 10th class, or for polysyllabic roots †, or for most roots beginning with

---

* Intensive or frequentative forms are found in Greek, such as παιπάλλω, δαιδάλλω, μαιμάζω or μαιμάω, παμφαίνω, ἀλαλάζω.

† ऊर्णु 'to cover' excepted, which has for its first form ऊर्णोनूय, and for its second ऊर्णोनु.

vowels. Some roots beginning with vowels take the Átmane form of frequentative; see 511, 682.

b. The terminations for the first form of frequentative will be those of the Átmane at 247, with the usual substitutions required for the 4th class of verbs. For the second form they will be the regular Parasmai-pada terminations of the memorial scheme at 246.

ÁTMANE-PADA FREQUENTATIVES.

509. Rule for the formation of the base in the four conjugational tenses. Reduplicate the initial consonant and vowel of the passive base according to the rules for reduplicating consonants at 331, and guṇate the reduplicated vowel (if capable of Guṇa), whether it be long or short: thus, from the passive base दीय (of *dá*, 'to give') comes the frequentative base *dedíya* (Pres. 1. *dedíya* + *i* = देदीये, 2. *dedíya* + *se* = देदीयसे &c.); from हीय (passive of *há*, 'to quit') comes *jehíya* (*jehíye* &c.); from *stírya* comes *testírya*; from *púya*, *popúya*; from *vidya*, *vevidya*; from *budhya*, *bobudhya* (Pres. बोबुध्ये, बोबुध्यसे, बोबुध्यते, &c.). The conjugation of all four tenses will correspond exactly with that of the passive.

510. If the passive base contain a medial अ *a*, long *á* is substituted in the reduplication; as, *pápachya* from *pachya*; *sásmarya* from *smarya*: if a medial *á*, *e*, or *o*, the same are reduplicated; as, *yáyáchya* from *yáchya*; *seshevya* from *sevya*; *lolochya* from *lochya*: if a medial ऋ *ṛi*, then अरी *arí** is substituted in the reduplication; as, दरीदृश्य from *dṛiśya*; परीस्पृश्य from *spṛiśya*, &c.

511. If a passive base contain रि *ri*, this becomes री *rí* in the frequentative base; as, चेक्रीय from क्रिय (passive of कृ 'to do'). If the base begin with अ *a*, as in अट्य *aṭya* (from अट् 'to wander'), the initial *aṭ* is repeated, and the radical *á* lengthened: thus, अटाट्य *aṭáṭya* (3d sing. अटाट्यते).

512. If the passive base contain a nasal after short *a*, this nasal is often repeated; as, from *gam*, 'to go,' comes जङ्गम्य (जङ्गम्ये &c.), 'to walk crookedly;' from *bhram*, *bambhramya*.

a. The passive bases जप्य, जल्प्य, दश्य, भज्य, and some others, may insert nasals, instead of lengthening the vowel in the reduplication: thus, जञ्जप्ये &c.

b. *Padya* (from *pad*) inserts नी *ní*: thus, *panípadya* †; from *charya* is formed चञ्चूर्ये; from *hanya*, passive of *han*, 'to kill,' जेघ्नीय; from *ghráya*, जेघ्रीय; from *dhmáya*, देध्मीय (देध्मीये &c.).

---

* This supports the idea that the original Guṇa of *ṛi* is *aṛi*. See 29. *b*.

† Similarly, the roots भ्रंश्, स्रंस्, ध्वंस्, स्कन्द्, वञ्च् (बनीभ्रश्य &c.).

Non-conjugational tenses of Átmane-pada frequentatives.

513. In these tenses frequentatives follow the analogy of passives, and reject the affix *ya*. Since, however, the base of the second preterite is formed by affixing *ám* (as usual in all polysyllabic forms, see 385. *b*), and since, in all the other tenses, inserted *i* is assumed, a coalition of vowels might arise were it not allowed to retain *y* in all cases in which a vowel immediately precedes that letter *: thus, from *dedípya* is formed the 2d preterite (1st sing.) *dedípáñchakre* &c., rejecting *ya*; but from *dedíya*, *dedíyáñchakre* &c., retaining *y*. Similarly in the other tenses: 1st fut. *dedípitáhe* &c., *dedíyitáhe* &c.; 2d fut. *dedípishye* &c., *dedíyishye* &c.; 3d pret. *adedípishi* &c., *adedíyishi* &c.; bened. *dedípishíya* &c., *dedíyishíya* &c.; cond. *adedípishye* &c., *adedíyishye* &c. In the 3d sing. 3d preterite *i* is not allowed to take the place of the regular terminations, as in the passive form.

PARASMAI-PADA FREQUENTATIVES.

514. Rule for the formation of the base in the four conjugational tenses. The base is here also formed by a reduplication similar to that of Átmane-pada frequentatives; not, however, from the passive, but from the root: thus, from the root *pach* comes *pápach*; from *vid*, *vevid*; from दृश्, *darídriś*; from कृ, *charíkri* †. Moreover, in accordance with the rules for the 2d and 3d conjugation (307, 330), the radical vowel is guṇated before the P terminations of the scheme at 246. Hence come the two bases *veved* and *vevid* (Pres. *vevedmi*, *vevetsi*, *vevetti*; Du. *vevidwas*, &c.; 1st Pret. *avevedam*, *avevet*, *avevet*, *avevidwa*, &c.; Pot. *vevidyám*, &c.; Imp. *vevedáni*, *veviddhi*, *vevettu*, *vevedáva*, *vevittam*, &c.). Again, the base will vary in accordance with the rules of combination at 296 &c., as in *budh* (Pres. *bobodhmi*, *bobhotsi*, *boboddhi*, *bobudhwas*, &c.). And in further analogy to the 2d conjugation (313, 314) long *í* is often optionally inserted before the consonantal P terminations (Pres. *vevedími*, *vevedíshi*, *vevedíti*; Du. *vevidwas*, &c.; 1st Pret. *avevedam*, *avevedís*, *avevedít*, *avevidwa*, &c.; Imp. *vevedáni*, *veviddhi*, *vevedítu*).

515. Lastly, when the root ends in a vowel, the usual changes take place of *i* and *í* to *y* or *iy*; of *u* and *ú* to *uv*; and of *ri* to *r* (see 312): as in the roots *bhí*, *bhú*, *kri* (Pres. 1st sing. *bebhemi*, *bobhomi*, *charkarmi*; 3d plur. *bebhyati*, *bobhuvati*, *charkrati*).

a. Observe—Roots in ॠ *rí* substitute *á* in the reduplicated syllable: thus, from कॄ, चाकॄ; from स्तॄ, तास्तॄ; from पॄ, पापॄ, &c.

Non-conjugational tenses of Parasmai-pada frequentatives.

516. The second preterite follows the usual rule for polysyllabic bases (385. *b*),

---

* In passives this coalition of vowels is avoided by the change of a final vowel to Vriddhi, as of *chi* to *cháy*, of *hu* to *háv*, and of *kri* to *kár*; and by the change of final *á* to *áy*, as of *dá* to *dáy*; see 473.

† In the Parasmai form of frequentative, *ari* and *ar* as well as *arí* may be reduplicated for the vowel ऋ *ri*; so that दृश् may make दरीदृश् or दरिदृश् or दर्दृश्; and कृ, चरीकृ or चरिकृ or चर्कृ.

and affixes *ám* with the auxiliaries: thus, from *vid*, 'to know,' comes 1st sing. *vevidámása;* from *bhí*, *bebhyámása*. In the other tenses, excepting the benedictive, inserted *i* is invariably assumed; and before this inserted *i* roots ending in vowels forbid the usual Guṇa change in the futures, but admit Vṛiddhi in the 3d preterite: thus, 1st fut. 1st sing. *veveditásmi* &c., *bebhyitásmi* &c. (367); 2d fut. *vevedishyámi* &c., *bebhyishyámi* &c.; 3d pret. *avevedisham* &c., *abebháyisham* &c.; bened. *vevidyásam* &c., *bebhíyásam;* cond. *avevedishyam*, *abebhyishyam*. This rejection of Guṇa, however, admits of question, especially in the case of roots in *u* or *ú*.

Causal, desiderative, and desiderative causal form of frequentatives.

517. Frequentatives are said to be capable of these forms: thus, from the frequentative base *totud*, 'to strike often,' come *totudayámi*, 'I cause to strike often;' *totudishámi*, 'I desire to strike often;' *totudayishami*, 'I desire to cause to strike often.'

NOMINAL VERBS, OR VERBS DERIVED FROM NOUNS.

518. These are formed by adding certain affixes to the crude base of nouns. They are not in very common use, but, theoretically, there is no limit to their formation. They might be classed under three heads, according to their meaning; viz. 1st, transitive nominals, yielding the sense of performing, practising, making or using the thing or quality expressed by the noun; 2d, intransitive nominals, giving a sense of behaving like, becoming like, acting like the person or thing expressed by the noun; 3d, desiderative nominals, yielding the sense of wishing for the thing expressed by the noun. It will be more convenient, however, to arrange them according to the affixes by which they are formed, as follows:—

Observe—The terminations of nominals will be those of the scheme at 247, making use of the substitutions required by the 1st, 4th, 6th, and 10th classes.

519. 1st, Those formed by affixing अ *a* (changeable to *á* before *m* and *v*) to a nominal base, the final of the base being guṇated (if capable of Guṇa). When the base ends in *a*, this vowel takes the place of the affix *a*. A final *á* absorbs the affix.

a. Thus, from कृष्ण 'Krishṇa,' Pres. 1. कृष्णामि 'I act like Krishṇa,' 2. कृष्णसि, 3. कृष्णति, &c. So from कवि 'a poet,' Pres. 1. कवयामि 'I act the poet,' 2. कवयसि, &c.; and from पितृ 'a father,' Pres. 1. पितरामि 'I act like a father,' 2. पितरसि, 3. पितरति. Átm. Pres. 1. पितरे, &c.; from माला 'a garland,' Pres. 1. मालामि, 2. मालासि, 3. मालाति; 1st Pret. 1. अमालां, 2. अमालास्, &c.; Pot. मालेयं, &c.; from स्व 'own,' Pres. 3. स्वति 'he acts like himself.' Sometimes a final *i* or *u* is not guṇated; as, from चञ्चु 'a beak,' Pres. चञ्चुामि, चञ्चुसि, चञ्चुति, 'he uses his beak,' &c.; from कवि 'a poet,' कव्यामि, कव्यसि, &c. Words ending in nasals preserve the nasals, and lengthen the preceding vowels; as, राजानति 'he acts like a king,' पथीनति 'it serves as a road,' इदामति 'he acts like this.'

520. 2dly, Those formed by affixing य *ya* to a nominal base.

a. If it is intended to express 'wish' or 'desire,' then a final अ *a* or आ *á* must be changed to ई *í*; a final इ *i* or उ *u* must be lengthened; a final ऋ *ṛi* changed to री *ṛí*; and a final न् *n* dropped, before य *ya* is affixed.

b. Thus, from पुत्र 'a son,' Pres. 1. पुत्रीयामि 'I desire a son,' 2. पुत्रीयसि, &c.; from पति 'a husband,' Pres. 1. पतीयामि 'I desire a husband,' &c. So also, from मातृ comes मात्रीयामि, &c.; from राजन्, Pres. राजीयामि, &c.; Pot. राजीयेयं, &c. If a word end in a consonant, *ya* is generally affixed without change; as, from वाच् 'a word,' वाच्यति 'he wishes for words.'

c. This form of nominal has not always a desiderative meaning. The following are examples of other meanings, some of which properly belong to the next form: प्रसादीयति 'he fancies himself in a palace;' कवीयति 'he acts like a poet;' कण्डूयति or -ते 'he scratches;' मन्तूयति or -ते 'he sins' or 'he is angry;' मित्रीयते 'he acts the part of a friend;' तपस्यति 'he performs penance' (from *tapas*, 'penance'); तिरस्यति 'he vanishes;' गव्यति 'he seeks cows' (from गो 'a cow').

d. If it is intended to express 'behaving like,' 'acting like,' a final अ *a* must be lengthened, a final आ *á* retained, and a final न् *n*, स् *s*, or त् *t*, may be dropped: thus, from पण्डित 'a wise man,' Pres. 1. पण्डिताये 'I act the part of a wise man,' 2. पण्डितायसे, 3. पण्डितायते, &c.; from द्रुम 'a tree,' Pres. 1. द्रुमाये, &c.; from राजन् 'a king,' Pres. 1. राजाये, &c.; from उन्मनस् 'sorrowful,' Pres. उन्मनाये, &c.; from वृहत् 'great,' Pres. वृहाये, &c.

e. This nominal is sometimes found with an active sense, especially when derived from nouns expressive of colour; as, from कृष्ण 'black,' कृष्णायते or -ति 'he blackens:' and sometimes in the Parasmai with a neuter sense; as, from जिह्म 'crooked,' जिह्मायति 'it is crooked;' from दास 'a slave,' दासायति 'he is a slave.' It corresponds to Greek desiderative denominatives in ιάω, as θανατιάω &c.

521. 3dly, Those formed by affixing अय *aya* to a nominal base. This form is similar to that of causals and verbs of the 10th class, with which it is sometimes confounded. Like them it has generally an active sense. A final vowel must be dropped before *aya*; and if the nominal base have more than one syllable, and end in a consonant, both the consonant and its preceding vowel must be dropped.

a. Thus, from वस्त्र 'cloth,' Pres. 1. वस्त्रयामि 'I clothe,' 2. वस्त्रयसि, 3. वस्त्रयति, &c.; from वर्मन् 'armour,' Pres. 1. वर्मयामि 'I put on armour,' &c.; from प्रमाण 'authority,' प्रमाणयामि 'I propose as authority;' from स्रज् 'a garland,' स्रजयामि 'I crown,' &c.

b. In further analogy to causals, a प् *p* is sometimes inserted between the base and *aya*, especially if the noun be monosyllabic, and end in *a*. Before this प् *p*, Vṛiddhi is required: thus, from स्व 'own,' Pres. स्वापयामि 'I make my own.' There are one or two examples of dissyllabic nouns: thus, from सत्य 'true,' सत्यापयामि, &c.*

c. If the base be monosyllabic, and end in a consonant, Guṇa may take place; as, from क्षुध् 'hunger,' क्षोधयामि.

d. Whatever modifications adjectives undergo before the affixes *íyas* and *ishṭha* at 194, the same take place before *aya*: thus, from दीर्घ 'long,' द्राघयामि, द्राघयसि, &c.; from अन्तिक 'near,' नेदयामि 'I make near,' &c.

e. This form of nominal is rarely neuter, as चिरयति 'he delays' (from चिर 'long'). According to Prof. Bopp, Greek denominatives in αζω, αω, εω, οω, ιζω, correspond to this form; as, ὀνομ-άζω, γυναικ-ίζω, πολεμ-όω.

522. 4thly, Those formed by affixing स्य *sya* or अस्य *asya* to a nominal base, giving it the form of a future tense, generally with the sense of 'desiring,' 'longing for.'

a. Thus, from क्षीर 'milk,' Pres. 1. क्षीरस्यामि 'I desire milk,' 2. क्षीरस्यसि, &c.; from वृष 'a bull,' वृषस्यति '(the cow) desires the bull;' from दधि 'curds,' दध्यस्यामि 'I desire curds,' &c. Compare Greek desideratives in σείω.

523. 5thly, Those formed by affixing काम्य *kámya* (derived from *kam*, 'to desire') to a nominal base; as, from पुत्र 'a son,' Pres. 1. पुत्रकाम्यामि 'I desire a son,' 2. पुत्रकाम्यसि, 3. पुत्रकाम्यति, &c.

PARTICIPLES.

PRESENT PARTICIPLES; PARASMAI-PADA.—FORMATION OF THE BASE.

524. These are the only participles that have any affinity with the conjugational structure of the verb. The base in the Parasmai is formed by substituting त् *t* for *nti*, and अत् *at* for *anti* and *ati*, the terminations of the 3d plural present; so that the peculiarities of conjugation necessarily appear in the participle: thus, from पचन्ति *pachanti*, 'they cook' (3d pl. pres. of पच्, 1st c.), comes पचत् *pachat*, 'cooking;' from घ्नन्ति *ghnanti* (3d pl. of *han*, 2d c.) comes *ghnat*; from सन्ति (3d pl. of *as*, 2d c., 'to be') comes *sat*; from यन्ति 'they go' (3d pl. of इ, 2d c.), यत् 'going;' from यान्ति (3d pl. of या, 2d c.), यात्; from जुह्वति *juhwati* (3d pl. of *hu*, 3d c.), जुह्वत् *juhwat*; from नृत्यन्ति *nṛityanti*, 4th c., *nṛityat*; from चिन्वन्ति *chinwanti*, 5th c., चिन्वत् *chinwat*; from *ápnuvanti*, 5th c., *ápnuvat*; from *rundhanti*, 7th c., *rundhat*; from *kurvanti*, 8th c., *kurvat*; from *punanti*, 9th c., *punat*.

* Similarly, अर्थ, 'substance,' makes अर्थापयामि, &c.

525. So again, from the causal बोधयन्ति, 'they cause to know' (479), comes *bodhayat*, 'causing to know;' from the desiderative बुबोधिषन्ति, 'they desire to know' (499), comes *bubodhishat*, 'desiring to know;' from *ditsanti*, 'they desire to give' (503), comes *ditsat*, 'desiring to give.'

a. It has been remarked at 253. *b*, that the passive verb may sometimes assume a Parasmai-pada inflection; and that all the neuter verbs placed under the 4th conjugation may be considered as so many examples of this form of the passive. This theory is corroborated by the fact of the existence of a Parasmai-pada present participle derivable from a passive base: thus, from the passive base दृश्य *dṛiśya* comes दृश्यत् 'being seen;' from चीय *chíya* (passive base of *chi*) comes चीयत् 'being gathered.'

b. The inflection of Parasmai-pada present participles is explained at 141. In the first five inflections a nasal is inserted, proving that the base of this participle properly ends in *ant*. In the cognate languages the *n* is preserved throughout.

c. Thus, compare Sanskṛit *bharan, bharantam* (from *bhṛi*), with φέρων, φέροντα, *ferentem*; also, *bharantau* (Ved. *bharantá*) with φέροντε; *bharantas* with φέροντες, *ferentes*; *bharatas* with φέροντας; gen. sing. *bharatas* with φέροντος, *ferentis*. So also, Sanskṛit *vahan, vahantam*, with *vehens, vehentem*; and *san, santam* (from *as*, 'to be'), with the *sens* of *ab-sens, præ-sens*. Compare also the base *stṛinwant* with στορνυντ.

PRESENT PARTICIPLES; ÁTMANE-PADA.—FORMATION OF THE BASE.

526. The base is formed by substituting मान *mána* for *nte*, the termination of the 3d plur. pres. of verbs of the 1st, 4th, and 6th conjugations, and passives; and by substituting आन *ána* for *ate*, the termination of the 3d plur. pres. of verbs of the other conjugations; see 247, p. 106: thus, from पचन्ते *pachante* (1st conj.) comes पचमान *pachamána*, 'cooking;' from तिष्ठन्ते (*sthá*, 1st conj.), तिष्ठमान 'standing;' from नृत्यन्ते (4th conj.), नृत्यमान; from लिम्पन्ते (*lip*, 6th conj.), लिम्पमान.

a. But from ब्रुवते *bruvate* (ब्रू 2d conj.), ब्रुवाण *bruváṇa* (see 58); from निघ्नते (हन् with नि 2d conj.), निघ्नान; from दधते (*dhá*, 3d conj.), दधान; from चिन्वते (5th conj.), चिन्वान; from युञ्जते (7th conj.), युञ्जान; from कुर्वते (8th conj.), कुर्वाण; from पुनते (9th conj.), पुनान. The root आस् 2d c., 'to sit,' makes आसीन for आसान; and शी 2d c. is शेरते in 3d pl. (see 315), but शयान in the pres. participle.

b. Observe—The real affix for the Átmane-pada pres. participle is *mána*, of which *ána* is probably an abbreviation. Compare the Greek μενο: भरमाण (58) = φερόμενος.

527. Verbs of the 10th conjugation and causals may substitute either *mána* or *ána*, but more frequently the latter: thus, from *bodhayante* comes *bodhayamána* and *bodhayána*; from *darśayante*, *darśayána*; from *vedayante*, *vedayána*. The affix *ána* is probably preferred on account of the greater fulness of form of verbs of the 10th class.

528. Passives and other derivative verbs always substitute *mána*: thus, from क्रियन्ते, 'they are made,' comes क्रियमाण, 'being made' (58); from दीयन्ते, 'they are given,' दीयमान, 'being given;' from the desiderative दित्सन्ते, 'they desire to give,' दित्समान, 'desiring to give;' from जिघांसन्ते, 'they desire to kill,' जिघांसमान, 'desiring to kill.'

529. The inflection of Átmane-pada pres. participles follows that of the 1st class of nouns at 103: thus, N. masc. sing. पचमानस्; fem. पचमाना; neut. पचमानं.

PAST PARTICIPLES.

PAST PASSIVE PARTICIPLES.—FORMATION OF THE BASE.

530. These participles may be regarded as falling under four heads: 1st, as derived from roots; 2dly, as derived from causal bases; 3dly, as derived from desiderative bases; 4thly, as derived from nominal bases.

1. *Derived from roots.*

531. In general the base is formed by adding त *ta* directly to the root; as, from क्षिप् *kship*, 'to throw,' क्षिप्त *kshipta*, 'thrown.'

a. But if the root end in ॠ *ṛí*, by adding न *na*; as, from कॄ *kṛí*, 'to scatter,' कीर्ण *kírṇa*, 'scattered.' Some roots in आ *á*, ई *í*, and ऊ *ú*, some in ऐ *ai* preceded by two consonants, with some of those in द् *d*, र् *r*, ज् *j*, one in ग् *g*, and one in च् *ch*, rejecting inserted *i* (see the lists at 394) from the participle, also take *na* instead of *ta*.

532. Roots ending in vowels do not admit inserted इ *i* in this participle, although they may admit it in the futures* (395. *a*, 396. *b*, 397, &c.), but attach *ta* or *na* directly to the root; as, from या *yá*, यात *yáta*, 'gone;' from जि, जित 'conquered;' from नी, नीत *níta*;

* शी, however, makes शयित: and पू may be पवित as well as पूत.

from श्रु, श्रुत; from भू, भूत; from कृ, कृत; from घ्रा, घ्राण (58); from ली, लीन; from ह्री, ह्रीण; from लू, लून; from श्वि, शून.

533. But in certain cases the final vowel of the root is changed: thus, some roots in आ *á* change *á* to *i* before *ta;* as, from स्था *sthá*, स्थित *sthita;* from मा, मित; from दरिद्रा, दरिद्रित. धा, 'to place,' becomes हित; दा, 'to give,' दत्त*; पा, 'to drink,' पीत. हा, 'to quit,' becomes ही before *na* (हीन). Some roots in *á* take both *na* and *ta;* as, from घ्रा, घ्राण and घ्रात; from वा, with the preposition निर्, निर्वाण and निर्वात.

534. Roots in ॠ *rí* change *rí* to *ír* before *na*, which passes into ण *ṇa* by 58; as, from तॄ, 'to pass,' तीर्ण, 'passed.' But from पॄ, पूर्ण 'full,' 'filled.'

535. The root धे *dhe*, 'to suck,' becomes धी before *ta* (धीत); ह्वे *hwe*, 'to call,' *hú* (हूत); वे *ve*, 'to weave,' *u* (उत); व्ये *vye*, 'to cover,' वी *ví* (वीत).

536. Roots in ऐ *ai* generally change *ai* to *á* before *na* or *ta;* as, from म्लै *mlai*, 'to fade,' म्लान *mlána;* from ध्यै, 'to meditate,' ध्यात; from दै, 'to purify,' दात; from त्रै, 'to rescue,' त्राण or त्रात. But from गै, 'to sing,' गीत; from क्षै, 'to waste,' क्षाम.

537. Roots in ओ *o* change *o* to *i;* as, from सो, सित; from शो, शित.

538. Those roots ending in consonants which take the inserted *i* in the last five tenses (388. *a*), generally take this vowel also in the past passive participle, but not invariably (see 542). Whenever *i* is assumed, *ta* is affixed, and not *na;* as, from पत् *pat*, 'to fall,' पतित *patita*, 'fallen;' and if उ *u* or ऋ *ṛi* precede the final consonant of the root, these vowels may take Guṇa; as, from द्युत् *dyut*, द्योतित *dyotita;* from मृष्, मर्षित. ग्रह्, 'to take,' lengthens the inserted *i* (गृहीत 'taken').

539. Roots ending in consonants which reject the inserted *i* in the last five tenses (400), generally reject it in the past passive participle. They must be combined with *ta*, agreeably to the rules at 296, &c. Whatever form, therefore, the final consonant assumes before the termination *tá* of the 1st future (see the lists at 400), the same form will generally, though not invariably, be preserved before the *ta* of the past participle; so that, in many cases, this participle may be derived from the 3d sing. of the 1st future by shortening the final *á*, and, if necessary, restoring the radical vowel to its original state: thus, taking some of the examples at 400; शक्ता

* When prepositions are prefixed to *datta*, the initial *da* may be rejected: thus, *átta* for *ádatta*, 'taken;' *pratta* for *pradatta*, 'bestowed;' *vyátta* for *vyádatta*, 'expanded;' *parítta* for *paridatta;* *sútta* for *sudatta*, the *i* and *u* being lengthened.

śaktá, 'he will be able,' gives शक्त *śakta*, 'able;' सेक्ता *sektá*, 'he will sprinkle,' सिक्त *sikta*, 'sprinkled;' मोक्ता *moktá*, मुक्त *mukta*; प्रष्टा, पृष्ट; त्यक्ता, त्यक्त; योक्ता, युक्त; स्रष्टा, सृष्ट; मार्ष्टा, मृष्ट; सेद्धा, सिद्ध; बोद्धा, बुद्ध; योद्धा, युद्ध; क्षेप्ता, क्षिप्त; लोप्ता, लुप्त; सर्प्ता, सृप्त; कल्प्ता, क्लृप्त; लब्धा, लब्ध; लोब्धा, लुब्ध; वेष्टा, विष्ट; द्रष्टा, दृष्ट; क्रोष्टा, क्रुष्ट; द्वेष्टा, द्विष्ट; दोष्टा, दुष्ट; क्रष्टा, कृष्ट; तष्टा, तष्ट; त्वष्टा, त्वष्ट; यष्टा, इष्ट; दग्धा, दग्ध; सोढा, सोढ; नद्धा, नद्ध; गाढा, गाढ; लेढा, लीढ (305. *a*); देग्धा, दिग्ध; स्नेग्धा, स्निग्ध; रोढा, रूढ (305. *a*); मोढा, मूढ; or मोग्धा, मुग्ध; दोग्धा, दुग्ध; गोढा, गूढ: but भ्रज्ज् 'to fry,' which is भ्रष्टा in the 1st future, is भृष्ट in the participle.

540. Most roots ending in द् *d*, forbidding the inserted इ *i* (404), take *na* instead of *ta*, and are combined with *na*, agreeably to 47; as, from पद्, पन्न; from भिद्, भिन्न; from सद्, with the preposition वि, विषण्ण (70 and 58); from अद् 'to eat,' अन्न (unless जग्ध is substituted, from *jaksh* at 542).

541. Those roots ending in ज् *j*, which take *na*, change *j* to *g* before *na*; as, from विज् *vij*, विग्न *vigna*; from रुज् *ruj*, रुग्न *rugna*. So from मज्ज्, rejecting one *j*, मग्न; from लज्ज् 'to be ashamed,' लग्न (as well as लज्जित). लग्, 'to adhere,' also makes लग्न; and व्रश्च्, 'to cut,' makes वृक्ण or वृक्त (see 58).

542. Some roots which admit *i* in the futures, reject it in this participle; as, धृष्, 1st fut. धर्षिता, but pass. part. धृष्ट; so अर्द्, अर्दिता, but अर्त्त (with आ *á* prefixed, आर्त्त 'pained'); दृह्, दर्हिता, but दृढ; मद्, मदिता, but मत्त; जक्ष् 'to eat,' जक्षिता, but जग्ध; दीप् 'to shine,' दीपिता, but दीप्त; नश् 'to perish,' नशिता, but नष्ट; मूर्छ् 'to faint,' मूर्छिता, but मूर्त्त as well as मूर्छित; म्लेच्छ् 'to speak barbarously,' म्लेच्छिता, but म्लिष्ट as well as म्लेच्छित; नृत् 'to dance,' नर्तिता, but नृत्त as well as नर्तित.

543. If in forming the passive base (471), or in the 2d preterite (375. c. *d*), the *v* or *y* contained in a root is changed to its semivowel *u* or *i*, the same change takes place in the past passive participle: thus, from वच् *vach*, 'to say,' उक्त *ukta*; from वप् *vap*, उप्त *upta*; from वह्, ऊढ; from स्वप्, सुप्त; from यज्, इष्ट. Similarly, from दिव्, द्यून or द्यूत; from त्वर्, तूर्ण.

544. Some other changes which take place in forming the passive base (472) are preserved before *ta*: thus, from शास्, शिष्ट; from व्यध्, विद्ध. And when the root ends in two conjunct consonants, of which the first is a nasal, this nasal is rejected; as, from बन्ध्, बद्ध; from भ्रंश्, भ्रष्ट; from स्रंस्? —

545. Roots ending in म् *m* or न् *n* reject these nasals before *ta*; as, from गम् *gam*, 'to go,' गत *gata*; from यम् *yam*, यत *yata*; from रम्, रत; from तन्, तत; from हन्, हत: but retain them if इ *i* is inserted; as, from स्वन्, स्वनित. From जन्, 'to be born,' is formed जात; from खन्, खात; the *a* being lengthened.

546. Those roots ending in म् *m*, of the 4th conjugation, which lengthen a

medial *a* before the conjugational affix *y*, also lengthen it before *ta*, and change *m* to *n* as in the futures: thus, from क्रम्, क्रान्त; from भ्रम्, भ्रान्त; from शम्, शान्त; from दम्, दान्त; from क्षम्, क्षान्त; from क्लम्, क्लान्त. Similarly, from वम्, वान्त; from कम्, कान्त.

547. From स्फाय्, 'to swell,' is formed स्फीत or स्फात; from पूय्, 'to be putrid,' पूत; from प्याय् or प्यै, 'to be fat,' 'to increase,' पीन or प्यान; from ज्या, 'to grow old,' जीन; from मुर्व्, 'to bind,' मूर्ण.

548. The following are quite anomalous: from पच् *pach*, 'to cook,' पक्व *pakwa;* from शुष्, 'to dry,' शुष्क; from क्षीव्, 'to be drunk,' क्षीव.

2. *Derived from causal bases.*

549. In forming the past passive participles from these, the causal affix अय *aya* is rejected, but the inserted इ *i* is always assumed: thus, from कारय, causal of कृ 'to make,' comes कारित *kárita*, 'caused to be made;' from स्थापय, causal of स्था 'to stand,' comes स्थापित *sthápita*, 'placed.'

3. *Derived from desiderative bases.*

550. In adding त *ta* to a desiderative base, the inserted इ *i* is invariably assumed; as, from पिपास, 'to desire to drink,' comes पिपासित; from चिकीर्ष, चिकीर्षित; from ईप्स, ईप्सित, &c.

4. *Derived from nominal bases.*

551. There are in Sanskṛit certain participles, which are said to be formed by adding इत *ita* to nouns: thus, from शिथिल, 'loose,' शिथिलित, 'loosened;' from जिह्म, 'crooked,' जिह्मित, 'curved.' These may be regarded as the passive participles of the transitive nominal verbs शिथिलयति, जिह्मयति (521); and whenever this kind of participial adjective is found, it may indicate that a nominal verb is in use, whence the participle is derived.

a. Moreover, as *na* sometimes takes the place of *ta*, so *ina* is added to some nouns instead of *ita:* thus, *malina*, 'soiled,' from *mala;* *śṛingiṇa*, 'horned,' from *śṛinga*.

b. Corresponding forms in Latin are *barbatus, alatus, cordatus, turritus,* &c.; and in Greek, ὀμφαλωτός, κροκωτός, αὐλωτός, &c. See Bopp's Comp. Gr.

552. The inflection of past passive participles follows that of the first class of nouns at 103; thus exhibiting a perfect similarity to the declension of Latin participles in *tus:* thus, कृत *kṛita*, nom. sing. masc. fem. neut. कृतस्, कृता, कृतं.

a. The perfect identity between Sanskṛit passive participles in *ta*, Latin participles in *tu-s*, and Greek verbals in το-ς, will be evident from the following examples: Sanskṛit *jńátas* = (*g*)*notus* (*ignotus*), γνωτός; *dattas* = *datus*, δοτός; *śrutas* = *clutus*, κλυτός; *bhútas* = φυτός; *yuktas* = *junctus*, ζευκτός; *labdhas* = ληπτός; *pítas* = πότος; *bhṛitas* = *fertus*, φερτός; *dishṭas* = *dictus*, δεικτός. And, like Sanskṛit, Latin often inserts an *i*, as in *domitus* (= Sanskṛit *damitas*), *monitus*, &c. In Greek, ε is inserted in forms like μενετός, ἑρπετός. There are also examples of Latin and Greek formations in *nu-s* and νο-ς, corresponding to the Sanskṛit participle in *na*: thus, *plenus* (= *púrṇa*), *magnus* (from Sanskṛit root *mah*), *dignus* (from Sanskṛit *diś*, *dik*, Greek δεικ); and στυγνό-ς, στεγνό-ς, σεμνό-ς, &c. See Eastwick's Bopp's Comp. Gr. 1117.

PAST ACTIVE PARTICIPLES.

These are of two kinds: 1st, those derived from the past passive participle; 2dly, those derived from the second preterite. These latter rarely occur. The former are much used to supply the place of a perfect tense active.

PAST ACTIVE PARTICIPLES DERIVED FROM PAST PASSIVE PARTICIPLES.—FORMATION OF THE BASE.

553. The base of these participles is easily formed by adding वत् *vat* to that of the past passive participle: thus, from कृत 'made,' कृतवत् 'who made;' from दग्ध 'burnt,' दग्धवत् 'who burnt;' from उक्त 'said,' उक्तवत् 'who addressed;' from भिन्न 'broken,' भिन्नवत् 'who broke;' from स्थापित 'placed,' स्थापितवत् 'who placed,' &c.

a. These participles are declined at 140. *a. b.*

Participles of the second preterite.

554. In the case of participles derived from the 2d preterite, either वस् *vas* or इवस् *ivas* is added to the base of that tense, as formed in the dual and plural. *Vas*, when the base in the dual and plural consists of more than one syllable; as, from *vivid* (365), *vividwas*; from *chichi* (367), *chichivas*; from *nanṛit* (364, compare 45. *a*), *nanṛitwas*; from *sasmar* (367. *c*), *sasmarvas*. But *ivas*, when the base in the dual and plural consists of one syllable only; as, from *ten* (375. *a*), *tenivas*; from *jagm* (376), *jagmivas*; from *jaksh* (377), *jakshivas*. Roots which take *ám* in the 2d preterite (385. *a. b. c. d*) form the participles of this tense by adding the 2d preterite participles of *kṛi*, *bhú*, and *as*, to *ám*: thus, from *chur*, 10th c., *chorayámbabhúvas*, *chorayáńchakṛivas*, *chorayámásivas*. Those roots which insert a *y* or *v* in the base of the 2d preterite (see 367. *a. b*), reject it in the participle: thus, *śri*, 'to have recourse,' makes its participle *śiśrivas*; and *bhú*, 'to be,' makes *babhúvas*, not *babhúvvas*, &c.

a. There is an Átmane-pada participle of the 2d preterite formed by adding *ána* to the base of the dual and plural: thus, *vividána, chichyána, jagmána.* See 526. *a:* and compare the Greek perfect participle in μενο: तुतुपान = τετυμμένος.

b. The participles of the 2d preterite are inflected at 168. Those of the Átmane-pada follow the inflection of the first class of nouns at 103.

c. Observe—Sanskṛit has no past participles derived from the 1st or 3d preterite, corresponding to the participles of the Greek aorists.

PAST INDECLINABLE PARTICIPLES.

555. These may be classed under two heads: 1st, as formed by affixing त्वा *twá* to uncompounded roots; as, from भू *bhú,* 'to be,' भूत्वा *bhútwá,* 'having been:' 2dly, as formed by affixing य *ya* to roots compounded with prepositions or other adverbial prefixes; as, from अनुभू *anubhú,* 'to perceive,' अनुभूय *anubhúya,* 'having perceived;' from सज्जीभू *sajjíbhú,* 'to become ready,' सज्जीभूय *sajjíbhúya,* 'having become ready.' The sense involved in them is generally expressed by the English 'when,' 'after,' 'having,' or 'by:' thus, तत् कृत्वा *tat kṛitwá,* 'when he had done that,' 'after he had done that,' 'having done that,' 'by doing that.' See the chapter on Syntax.

a. Prof. Bopp considers the affix *twá* of this participle to be the instrumental case of an affix *tu,* of which the infinitive affix *tum* is the accusative. There can be little doubt that the indeclinable participle has about it much of the character of an instrumental case (see Syntax); but the form of its base varies considerably from that of the infinitive: thus, *vaktum, uktwá,* from *vach; yashṭum, ishṭwá,* from *yaj,* &c.

Indeclinable participles formed from uncompounded roots.

556. When the root stands alone and uncompounded, the indeclinable participle is formed with त्वा *twá* *.

This affix is closely allied to the त *ta* of the past passive participle at 531, insomuch that the rules for the annexation of त *ta* to the root apply equally to the indeclinable affix त्वा *twá.* The formation, therefore, of one participle generally involves that of the other: thus, from क्षिप्त *kshipta,* 'thrown,' क्षिप्त्वा *kshiptwá,* 'having thrown;' from कृत, 'done,' कृत्वा, 'having done;' so from स्थित, स्थित्वा; from दृष्ट, दृष्ट्वा; from दत्त, दत्त्वा; from पीत, पीत्वा; from क्रान्त, क्रान्त्वा; from गृहीत, गृहीत्वा; from उषित, उषित्वा; from उक्त, उक्त्वा; from बुद्ध, बुद्ध्वा; from ऊढ, ऊढ्वा; from हित (root धा), हित्वा; from जग्ध, जग्ध्वा. And where *i* is inserted, there is often an optional change of the radical

* There are one or two instances in which an uncompounded root takes य; as, अर्च्य 'having reverenced.' Manu VII. 145. I. 4. Mahábh. 3. 8017.

vowel to Guṇa, as in the passive participle at 538: thus, द्युतित्वा *dyutitwá* or द्योतित्वा *dyotitwá* from द्युत्; मृषित्वा or मर्षित्वा from मृष्.

a. When there are two forms of the passive participle, there is often only one of the indeclinable: thus, नृत् makes नृत्त and नर्तित, but only नर्तित्वा; लज्ज् makes लग्न and लज्जित, but only लज्जित्वा; and, *vice versa*, वस्, 'to dwell,' makes only उषित, but उषित्वा and उष्ट्वा; and सह्, 'to bear,' makes only सोढ, but सहित्वा and सोढ्वा.

b. The penultimate nasal, which is rejected before *ta* (544), is often only optionally rejected before *twá*: thus, from रञ्ज्, रक्त, but रंक्त्वा or रक्त्वा.

557. The only important variation from the passive participle occurs in those roots, at 531. *a*, which take *na* for *ta*. In such roots no corresponding change takes place of *twá* to *nwá*: thus, from जॄ, जीर्ण, but जरित्वा (or जरीत्वा); from तॄ, तीर्ण, but तीर्त्वा; from छिद्, छिन्न, but छित्त्वा; from भञ्ज्, भग्न, but भंक्त्वा or भक्त्वा; from रुज्, रुग्न, but रुक्त्वा; from हा, हीन, but हित्वा, 'having quitted' (not distinguishable from हित्वा, 'having placed,' from धा).

558. Observe, moreover, that verbs of the 10th class and causals, which reject the characteristic अय before the *ita* of the past passive participle, retain *ay* before *itwá*: thus, स्थापित 'made to stand' (from the causal base स्थापय), but स्थापयित्वा 'having made to stand;' चिन्तित 'thought' (from चिन्त् 10th c., 'to think'), but चिन्तयित्वा 'having thought.'

Indeclinable participles formed from compounded roots.

559. When a root is compounded with a preposition or any indeclinable prefix (excepting अ *a*, 'not'), the indeclinable participle cannot be formed with *twá* *. The affix य *ya* is then used, and the rules which regulate its annexation to the root are some of them analogous to those which prevail in other cases in which *ya* is affixed; see the rules for the formation of the fourth conjugation at 272, of passives at 461, and of the benedictive at 443.

560. But if a root end in a short vowel, instead of any lengthening of this vowel, त् *t* is interposed; as, from आश्रि *áśri*, 'to take refuge' (root श्रि), आश्रित्य *áśritya*, 'having taken refuge;' from निश्रि, निश्रित्य; from उत्प्लु, उत्प्लुत्य; from संस्कृ, संस्कृत्य; from निःसृ, निःसृत्य. The lengthening of the radical vowel by coalition does not prevent this rule; as, from अती *atí* (*ati* with *i*), अतीत्य *atítya*.

561. If a root end in long आ *á*, ई *í*, or ऊ *ú*, no change takes

* There are one or two instances of compounded roots formed with *twá*: thus, अनुध्यात्वा (from ध्यै), Rámáyana I. 2. 20. Especially in the case of causals; as, निवर्त्तयित्वा. When अ *a*, 'not,' is prefixed, *twá* is always used; as, अकृत्वा 'not having done,' 'without having done;' अदत्त्वा 'not having given.'

place; as, from विहा, विहाय; from उपक्री, उपक्रीय; from विधू, विधूय: but if in long ॠ *rí*, this vowel becomes *ír*; as, from अवकॄ, अवकीर्य 'having scattered.' आपॄ (from पॄ 'to fill') makes आपूर्य (compare 534).

562. Final diphthongs pass into आ *á*; as, from परिव्ये, परिव्याय (also परिवीय); from अभिध्यै, अभिध्याय; from अवसो, अवसाय.

a. But from सो with व्यव comes व्यवस्य; and from ह्वे with आ, आहूय.

563. A penultimate nasal is generally rejected; as, from समासञ्ज् *samásañj*, समासज्य *samásajya*; from प्रमन्थ्, प्रमथ्य (used adverbially, 'violently').

a. But not always; as, from आशङ्क्, आशङ्क्य; from आलिङ्ग्, आलिङ्ग्य.

564. If a root end in a consonant the general rule is, that no change takes place; as, from निक्षिप् *nikship*, निक्षिप्य *nikshipya*; from प्राप् (*pra* and *áp*), प्राप्य; from वीक्ष् (*vi* and *íksh*), वीक्ष्य.

a. But some roots ending in *am* and *an* may optionally reject the nasal, and interpose *t* between the final short *a* and *ya*; as, from निर्गम् *nirgam*, निर्गत्य *nirgatya* or निर्गम्य *nirgamya*; from निहन्, निहत्य. जन् and खन्, instead of interposing *t*, lengthen the final *a*; as, from उत्खन्, उत्खाय.

565. The changes which take place in certain roots before the *ya* of the passive (471, 472) are preserved before *ya*; as, from निवप्, न्युप्य; from विवस्, व्युष्य; from विग्रह्, विगृह्य; from आप्रछ्, आपृछ्य; from आव्यध्, आविध्य. स्फुर् lengthens its vowel before य; as, विस्फूर्य.

566. In affixing य *ya* to the bases of causals and verbs of the 10th class the characteristic अय is generally rejected; as, from प्रबोधय *prabodhaya*, प्रबोध्य *prabodhya*; from प्रसारय, प्रसार्य; from सन्दर्शय, सन्दर्श्य.

a. It is, however, retained in some few instances; as, विगणय्य, 'having calculated,' from गण्; आकलय्य, 'having imagined,' from कल्; सङ्कथय्य, 'having narrated,' from कथ्.

Adverbial indeclinable participle.

567. There is another indeclinable participle yielding the same sense as those formed with *twá* and *ya*, but of rare occurrence. It is equivalent to the accusative case of a noun derived from a root, used adverbially; and is formed by adding अम् *am* to the root, before which affix changes of the radical vowel take place, similar to those required before the causal affix अय (481): thus, from नी *ní*, 'to lead,' नायं *náyam*, 'having led;' from पा, 'to drink,' पायं, 'having drunk;' from ह्वे, ह्वायं; from पच्, पाचं; from क्षिप्, क्षेपं; from हन्, 'to kill,' घातं. It often occupies the last place in a compound; as in the expression समूलघातं, 'having totally exterminated;' and in the following passage from Bhaṭṭi:

लतानुपातं कुसुमान्यगृह्णात् स नद्यवस्कन्दमुपास्पृशच्च ।
कुतूहलाचारुशिलोपवेशं काकुत्स्थ ईषत्स्मयमान आस्त ॥

'The descendant of Kakutstha, smiling softly, repeatedly bending down the creepers, would pluck the blossoms; descending to the streams, would sip (the waters); seating himself on some variegated rock, would recline in admiration (of the scene).' Compare also the passage at the end of Act V. of S'akuntalá; बाहूत्क्षेपं क्रन्दितुं प्रवृत्ता 'repeatedly throwing up her arms she began to weep.'

a. These participles generally imply repetition of the action, as in the passage above, and in this sense are themselves often repeated; as, *dáyam, dáyam,* 'having repeatedly given.'

FUTURE PASSIVE PARTICIPLES.

568. These are amongst the most common and useful of all participles, and may be classed under three heads: 1st, as formed with the affix तव्य *tavya;* 2dly, as formed with अनीय *aníya;* 3dly, as formed with य *ya.* These affixes yield a sense corresponding to the Latin future passive participle in *dus*, and the English *able* and *ible*, and most commonly denote 'obligation' or 'propriety' and 'fitness.'

a. Although these participles agree in signification with the Latin participles in *dus*, yet Prof. Bopp considers that the affix *tavya* corresponds in form to the Latin *tivus*, and in sense as well as form to the Greek *τεος*. In some of the Latin formations with *tivus*, the passive sense is preserved, as in *captivus, nativus, coctivus.* Compare Sanskrit *dátavya* with *dativus* (*dandus*), δοτέος; *yoktavya* with (*con*)*junctivus* (*jungendus*); *janitavya* with *genitivus* (*gignendus*); *dhátavya* with θετέος, &c.

Future passive participles formed with तव्य tavya.

569. These are formed by substituting तव्य *tavya* for ता *tá*, the termination of the 3d pers. sing. of the 1st future: thus, from क्षेप्ता *ksheptá*, 'he will throw,' क्षेप्तव्य *ksheptavya*, 'to be thrown;' कर्त्ता, 'he will do,' कर्त्तव्य, 'to be done;' from भविता, 'he will be,' भवितव्य, 'about to be.' And in the case of roots ending in consonants rejecting *i*, whatever changes take place before *tá*, the same take place before *tavya* (see 400): thus, त्यक्ता, त्यक्तव्य (*relinquendus*); प्रष्टा, प्रष्टव्य; द्रष्टा, द्रष्टव्य; वोढा, वोढव्य; दग्धा, दग्धव्य; सोढा, सोढव्य; and from the causal कारयिता, कारयितव्य, &c.

Future passive participles formed with अनीय aníya.

570. This affix is added directly to the root, without any other change than the Guṇa of the radical vowel: thus, from चि *chi*, 'to gather,' चयनीय *chayaníya*, 'to be gathered;' from भू, भवनीय; from कृ, करणीय (58); from लिख्, लेखनीय; from शुध्, शोधनीय; from स्पृश्, स्पर्शनीय; from कृप्, कर्पणीय (58). A final diphthong is changed to आ *á;* as, from ध्यै, ध्यानीय; from गै, गानीय.

Future passive participles formed with य ya.

571. Before this affix, as before all others beginning with *y*, certain changes of final vowels become necessary.

a. If a root end in आ *á*, or in ए *e*, ऐ *ai*, ओ *o*, changeable to आ *á*, this vowel becomes ए *e* (compare 446); as, from मा *má*, 'to measure,' मेय *meya*, 'to be measured,' 'measurable;' from हा *há*, हेय *heya*; from ध्यै *dhyai*, ध्येय *dhyeya*; from ग्लै, ग्लेय, &c.

b. If in इ *i*, ई *í*, उ *u*, or ऊ *ú*, these vowels are guṇated; as, from चि *chi*, चेय *cheya*. But the Guṇa ओ *o* is changed to *av*, and sometimes the Guṇa ए *e* to *ay*, before *ya* (as if before a vowel): thus, from भू, भव्य; from जि, 'to conquer,' जय्य *jayya*. The Guṇa ओ *o*, however, oftener passes into *áv* before *y*; as, from श्रु, श्राव्य; from प्लु, प्लाव्य; from भू, भाव्य.

c. If in ऋ *ṛi* or ॠ *ṛí*, these vowels are vṛiddhied; as, from कृ, कार्य्य.

572. Sometimes if a root end in a short vowel no change takes place, but *t* is interposed, after the analogy of the indeclinable participle formed with *ya* at 560; so that the crude base of the future participle is often not distinguishable from the indeclinable: thus, from जि *ji*, 'to conquer,' जित्य *jitya*, 'conquerable;' from स्तु *stu*, 'to praise,' स्तुत्य *stutya*, 'laudable;' from कृ *kṛi*, 'to do,' कृत्य *kṛitya*, 'practicable;' from इ 'to go,' इत्य 'to be gone;' from आदृ 'to honour,' आदृत्य 'to be honoured.'

573. If a root end in a single consonant with a medial *a*, the latter may be vṛiddhied; as, from ग्रह् *grah*, ग्राह्य *gráhya*: but not always; as, from शक्, शक्य; from सह्, सह्य; from बध्, बध्य *badhya*: and rarely if the final is a labial; as, from गम्, गम्य; from लभ्, लभ्य.

a. If with a medial इ *i* or उ *u*, these are generally guṇated; as, from भुज्, भोज्य; from लिह्, लेह्य.

b. If with a medial ऋ *ṛi*, no change takes place; as, from स्पृश्, स्पृश्य; from दृश्, दृश्य.

574. A final च् *ch* may sometimes optionally be changed to क् *k*, and ज् *j* to ग् *g*; and other changes may take place, some of which are similar to those before the *ya* of passives; as, from पच् *pach*, पाक्य *pákya* and पाच्य *páchya*; from वच्, वाक्य and वाच्य; from भुज्, भोग्य and भोज्य; from ग्रह्, गृह्य as well as ग्राह्य *gráhya*; from वद्, उद्य (471); from यज्, इज्य; from शास्, शिष्य (472); from खन्, खेय.

575. Many of these participles are used as substantives: thus, वाक्य n. 'speech;' भोज्य n. 'food;' भोग्या f. 'a harlot;' इज्या f. 'sacrifice;' खेय n. 'a ditch;' भार्य्या f. 'a wife,' from भृ 'to support,' &c.

576. The affix *ya* may occasionally be added to nouns or nominal bases: thus, from मुसल 'a pestle,' मुसल्य 'to be pounded with a pestle.'

577. The inflection of future passive participles follows that of the first class of nouns at 103: thus, कर्तव्य 'to be done;' N. sing. m. f. n. *kartavyas, kartavyá, kartavyam.* Similarly, *karaṇíyas, karaṇíyá, karaṇíyam;* and *káryas, káryá, káryam.*

PARTICIPLES OF THE SECOND FUTURE.—FORMATION OF THE BASE.

578. These are not common. They are of two kinds, either Parasmai-pada or Átmane-pada; the former being formed by changing अन्ति *anti,* the termination of the 3d plur. of the 2d future, into अत् *at;* the latter, by changing अन्ते *ante* into अमान *amána:* thus, from करिष्यन्ति *karishyanti* and करिष्यन्ते *karishyante,* 'they will do,' come करिष्यत् *karishyat* and करिष्यमाण *karishyamáṇa* (58), 'about to do;' from the passive 2d fut. वक्ष्यन्ते, 'they will be said,' comes वक्ष्यमाण, 'about to be said.'

a. In the mode of their formation from the 3d person plural, by the affixes *at* and *amána,* and in their inflection, they resemble present participles at 524 and 526.

b. Observe—The future participle in *mána* may be compared with the Greek in μενο: *dásyamána* = δωσόμενος.

PARTICIPIAL NOUNS OF AGENCY.

579. These have been already incidentally noticed at 80, 83, 85. As, however, they partake of the nature of participles, and are of great practical utility, some further mention of them is necessary. They may be classed under three heads: 1st, as formed from the root; 2dly, as formed from the 1st future; 3dly, as formed from the causal base.

580. The base of the first class (see 80. II) is formed from the root by affixing अ *a,* before which Guṇa, and rarely Vṛiddhi, of a final vowel is required; as, from जि *ji,* 'to conquer,' जय *jaya,* 'conquering.' Medial vowels are generally unchanged; as, from वद् *vad,* 'to say,' वद *vada,* 'saying;' from तुद् *tud,* 'to vex,' तुद *tuda,* 'vexing:' and final आ *á,* अम् *am,* or अन् *an,* are dropped; as, from दा *dá,* 'to give,' द *da,* 'giving;' from गम् *gam,* 'to go,' ग *ga,* 'going;' from जन् *jan,* 'to be born,' ज *ja,* 'being born.' Their declension follows the first class of nouns at 103.

581. The base of the second class (see 83) is formed from the 3d pers. sing. of the 1st future of primitive verbs, by substituting the vowel ऋ *ṛi* for the final vowel *á,* the nominative case being therefore *identical* with the 3d pers. sing. of that tense (see 386): thus, from भोक्ता *bhoktá,* 'he will eat,' भोक्तृ *bhoktṛi*, 'an eater;' from योद्धा, 'he will fight,' योद्धृ, 'a fighter;' from याचिता, याचितृ; from मोढा, मोढृ, &c. They are inflected at 127.

582. The base of the third class is formed in three ways.

a. By adding इन् *in* to the root (see 85. V), before which affix changes take place similar to those required before the causal affix *aya* (481, 482, 483); as, from कृ, कारिन् *kárin*, 'a doer;' from हन् (488), घातिन् *ghátin*, 'a killer;' from शी, शायिन्, 'a sleeper:' *y* being inserted after roots in *á* (483); as, from पा, पायिन्, 'a drinker;' from दा, दायिन् *dáyin*, 'a giver.' They are inflected at 159.

b. By adding अक *aka* to the root (see 80. IV), before which affix changes take place analogous to those before the causal *aya* (481, 482, 483); as, from कृ, कारक *káraka*, 'a doer,' 'doing;' from नी, नायक *náyaka*, 'a leader,' 'leading;' from ग्रह्, ग्राहक *gráhaka;* from सिध्, साधक; from हन्, घातक; from दुष्, दूषक; from क्रम्, क्रमक; from नन्द्, नन्दक; from स्था, स्थापक.

c. By adding अन *ana* to some few roots ending in consonants (see 80. V), after changes similar to those required before the causal affix; as, from नन्द्, नन्दन *nandana*, 'rejoicing;' from दुष्, दूषण, 'vitiating;' from शुध्, शोधन, 'cleansing.'

Observe—The inflection of the last two follows that of the first class of nouns at 103.

EXAMPLES OF PRIMITIVE VERBS IN THE TEN CLASSES, AND OF DERIVATIVE VERBS INFLECTED AT FULL.

583. We begin by giving a synopsis of the inflection of the primitive forms of the ten roots: बुध् *budh*, 'to know,' 1st c.; नृत् *nṛit*, 'to dance,' 4th c.; दिश् *diś*, 'to point out,' 6th c.; युज् *yuj*, 'to unite,' 10th c.; विद् *vid*, 'to know,' 2d c.; भृ *bhṛi*, 'to bear,' 3d c.; भिद् *bhid*, 'to break,' 7th c.; चि *chi*, 'to gather,' 5th c.; तन् *tan*, 'to stretch,' 8th c.; पू *pú*, 'to purify,' 9th c.: grouping together, first, the 1st, 4th, 6th, and 10th classes; then the 2d, 3d, and 7th; and lastly, the 5th, 7th, and 9th, for the reasons stated at 257. In the next place, the passive forms of these ten roots will be synoptically exhibited, followed by the present tense of the causal desiderative and frequentative forms, and the participles. Examples will then be given of primitive verbs of all the ten classes (according to the grouping at 257), *inflected at full;* and under every verb the derivative forms and participles will be indicated. Lastly, a full example will be given of each of the four kinds of derivative verbs, passives, causals, desideratives, and frequentatives.

INFLECTION OF THE BASE OF PRIMITIVE VERBS OF THE TEN CLASSES OR CONJUGATIONS.

PRESENT.

	Parasmai-pada.									Átmane-pada.								
ROOT.	SING.			DUAL.			PLURAL.			SING.			DUAL.			PLURAL.		
1. *Budh*	*bodhá*	*bodha*	*bodha*	*bodhá*	*bodha*	*bodha*	*bodhá*	*bodha*	*bodha*	*bodha*	*bodha*	*bodha*	*bodhá*	*bodha*	*bodha*	*bodhá*	*bodha*	*bodha*
4. *Nṛit*	*nṛityá*	*nṛitya*	*nṛitya*	*nṛityá*	*nṛitya*	*nṛitya*	*nṛityá*	*nṛitya*	*nṛitya*	*nṛitya*	*nṛitya*	*nṛitya*	*nṛityá*	*nṛitya*	*nṛitya*	*nṛityá*	*nṛitya*	*nṛitya*
6. *Diś*	*diśá*	*diśa*	*diśa*	*diśá*	*diśa*	*diśa*	*diśá*	*diśa*	*diśa*	*diśa*	*diśa*	*diśa*	*diśá*	*diśa*	*diśa*	*diśá*	*diśa*	*diśa*
10. *Yuj*	*yojayá*	*yojaya*	*yojaya*	*yojayá*	*yojaya*	*yojaya*	*yojayá*	*yojaya*	*yojaya*	*yojaya*	*yojaya*	*yojaya*	*yojayá*	*yojaya*	*yojaya*	*yojayá*	*yojaya*	*yojaya*
2. *Vid*	*ved*	*vet**	*vet*	*vid*	*vit*	*vit*	*vid*	*vit*	*vid*	*vid*	*vit**	*vit*	*vid*	*vid*	*vid*	*vid*	*vid*	*vid*
3. *Bhṛi*	*bibhar*	*bibhar*	*bibhar*	*bibhṛi*	*bibhṛi*	*bibhṛi*	*bibhṛi*	*bibhṛi*	*bibhr*	*bibhr*	*bibhṛi*	*bibhṛi*	*bibhṛi*	*bibhr*	*bibhr*	*bibhṛi*	*bibhṛi*	*bibhr*
7. *Bhid*	*bhinad*	*bhinat**	*bhinat*	*bhind*	*bhint*	*bhint*	*bhind*	*bhint*	*bhind*	*bhind*	*bhint**	*bhint*	*bhind*	*bhind*	*bhind*	*bhind*	*bhind*	*bhind*
5. *Chi*	*chino*	*chino*	*chino*	*chinu*	*chinu*	*chinu*	*chinu*	*chinu*	*chinw*	*chinw*	*chinu*	*chinu*	*chinu*	*chinw*	*chinw*	*chinu*	*chinu*	*chinw*
8. *Tan*	*tano*	*tano*	*tano*	*tanu*	*tanu*	*tanu*	*tanu*	*tanu*	*tanw*	*tanw*	*tanu*	*tanu*	*tanu*	*tanw*	*tanw*	*tanu*	*tanu*	*tanw*
9. *Pú*	*puná*	*puná**	*puná*	*puní*	*puní*	*puní*	*puní*	*puní*	*pun*	*pun*	*puní*	*puní*	*puní*	*pun*	*pun*	*puní*	*puní*	*pun*
1. 4. 6. 10.		** si*							*nti*	*i*	** se*			*ithe*	*ite*			*nte*
	mi		*ti*	*vas*	*thas*	*tas*	*mas*	*tha*				*te*	*vahe*			*mahe*	*dhwe*	
2. 3. 7. 5. 8. 9.		*shi*							*anti*	*e*	*she*			*áthe*	*áte*			*ate*

Observe—The base is to be united with the terminations: thus, 1st sing. Pres. Parasmai, *bodhá*+*mi*=*bodhámi*, 2d sing. *bodha*+*si*=*bodhasi*, 3d sing. *bodha*+*ti*=*bodhati*; 1st dual, *bodhá*+*vas*=*bodhávas*, &c. Átmane, *bodha*+*i*=*bodhe*, *bodha*+*se*=*bodhase*, &c. Observe also, that whenever the terminations of the 1st, 4th, 6th, and 10th classes differ from those of the others, they are placed in the upper line. *Bhṛi* will make *bibhrati*, not *bibhranti*, in 3d pl.

POTENTIAL.

	Parasmai-pada.									Átmane-pada.								
ROOT.	SING.			DUAL.			PLURAL.			SING.			DUAL.			PLURAL.		
1. *Budh*	*bodha*	*bodha*	*bodha*	*bodha*	*bodha*	*bodha*	*bodha*	*bodha*	*bodha*	*bodha*	*bodha*	*bodha*	*bodha*	*bodha*	*bodha*	*bodha*	*bodha*	*bodha*
4. *Nṛit*	*nṛitya*	*nṛitya*	*nṛitya*	*nṛitya*	*nṛitya*	*nṛitya*	*nṛitya*	*nṛitya*	*nṛitya*	*nṛitya*	*nṛitya*	*nṛitya*	*nṛitya*	*nṛitya*	*nṛitya*	*nṛitya*	*nṛitya*	*nṛitya*
6. *Diś*	*diśa*	*diśa*	*diśa*	*diśa*	*diśa*	*diśa*	*diśa*	*diśa*	*diśa*	*diśa*	*diśa*	*diśa*	*diśa*	*diśa*	*diśa*	*diśa*	*diśa*	*diśa*
10. *Yuj*	*yojaya*	*yojaya*	*yojaya*	*yojaya*	*yojaya*	*yojaya*	*yojaya*	*yojaya*	*yojaya*	*yojaya*	*yojaya*	*yojaya*	*yojaya*	*yojaya*	*yojaya*	*yojaya*	*yojaya*	*yojaya*
2. *Vid*	*vid*	*vid*	*vid*	*vid*	*vid*	*vid*	*vid*	*vid*	*vid*	*vid*	*vid*	*vid*	*vid*	*vid*	*vid*	*vid*	*vid*	*vid*
3. *Bhṛi*	*bibhṛi*	*bibhṛi*	*bibhṛi*	*bibhṛi*	*bibhṛi*	*bibhṛi*	*bibhṛi*	*bibhṛi*	*bibhṛi*	*bibhr*	*bibhr*	*bibhr*	*bibhr*	*bibhr*	*bibhr*	*bibhr*	*bibhr*	*bibhr*
7. *Bhid*	*bhind*	*bhind*	*bhind*	*bhind*	*bhind*	*bhind*	*bhind*	*bhind*	*bhind*	*bhind*	*bhind*	*bhind*	*bhind*	*bhind*	*bhind*	*bhind*	*bhind*	*bhind*
5. *Chi*	*chinu*	*chinu*	*chinu*	*chinu*	*chinu*	*chinu*	*chinu*	*chinu*	*chinu*	*chinw*	*chinw*	*chinw*	*chinw*	*chinw*	*chinw*	*chinw*	*chinw*	*chinw*
8. *Tan*	*tanu*	*tanu*	*tanu*	*tanu*	*tanu*	*tanu*	*tanu*	*tanu*	*tanu*	*tanw*	*tanw*	*tanw*	*tanw*	*tanw*	*tanw*	*tanw*	*tanw*	*tanw*
9. *Pú*	*puní*	*puní*	*puní*	*puní*	*puní*	*puní*	*puní*	*puní*	*puní*	*pun*	*pun*	*pun*	*pun*	*pun*	*pun*	*pun*	*pun*	*pun*
1. 4. 6. 10.	*iyam*	*is*	*it*	*iva*	*itam*	*itám*	*ima*	*ita*	*iyus*	*íya*	*íthás*	*íta*	*ívahi*	*íyáthám*	*íyátám*	*ímahi*	*ídhwam*	*íran*
2. 3. 7. 5. 8. 9.	*yám*	*yás*	*yát*	*yáva*	*yátam*	*yátám*	*yáma*	*yáta*	*yus*									

Observe—As the base in the 1st group of conjugations ends in *a*, and the terminations begin with *i*, these two vowels will blend into *e* by 32: thus, *bodha*+*iyam*=*bodheyam*, *bodha*+*is*=*bodhes*, &c.; Átmane, *bodha*+*íya*=*bodheya*.

IMPERATIVE.

Root.	Parasmai-pada. Sing.			Dual.			Plural.			Átmane-pada. Sing.			Dual.			Plural.		
1. *Budh*	*bodha*	*bodha*	*bodha*	*bodha*	*bodha*	*bodha*	*bodha*	*bodha*	*bodha*	*bodha*	*bodha*	*bodha*	*bodha*	*bodha*	*bodha*	*bodha*	*bodha*	*bodha*
4. *Nṛit*	*nṛitya*	*nṛitya*	*nṛitya*	*nṛitya*	*nṛitya*	*nṛitya*	*nṛitya*	*nṛitya*	*nṛitya*	*nṛitya*	*nṛitya*	*nṛitya*	*nṛitya*	*nṛitya*	*nṛitya*	*nṛitya*	*nṛitya*	*nṛitya*
6. *Diś*	*diśa*	*diśa*	*diśa*	*diśa*	*diśa*	*diśa*	*diśa*	*diśa*	*diśa*	*diśa*	*diśa*	*diśa*	*diśa*	*diśa*	*diśa*	*diśa*	*diśa*	*diśa*
10. *Yuj*	*yojaya*	*yojaya*	*yojaya*	*yojaya*	*yojaya*	*yojaya*	*yojaya*	*yojaya*	*yojaya*	*yojaya*	*yojaya*	*yojaya*	*yojaya*	*yojaya*	*yojaya*	*yojaya*	*yojaya*	*yojaya*
2. *Vid*	*ved*	*vid*†	*vet*	*ved*	*vit*	*vit*	*ved*	*vit*	*vid*	*ved*	*vit**	*vit*	*ved*	*vid*	*vid*	*ved*	*vid*	*vid*
3. *Bhṛi*	*bibhar*	*bibhṛi*	*bibhar*	*bibhar*	*bibhṛi*	*bibhṛi*	*bibhar*	*bibhṛi*	*bibhr**	*bibhar*	*bibhṛi*	*bibhṛi*	*bibhar*	*bibhr*	*bibhr*	*bibhar*	*bibhṛi*	*bibhr*
7. *Bhid*	*bhinad*	*bhind*†	*bhinat*	*bhinad*	*bhint*	*bhint*	*bhinad*	*bhint*	*bhind*	*bhinad*	*bhint**	*bhint*	*bhinad*	*bhind*	*bhind*	*bhinad*	*bhind*	*bhind*
5. *Chi*	*chinav*	*chinu**	*chino*	*chinav*	*chinu*	*chinu*	*chinav*	*chinu*	*chinw*	*chinav*	*chinu*	*chinu*	*chinav*	*chinw*	*chinw*	*chinav*	*chinu*	*chinw*
8. *Tan*	*tanav*	*tanu**	*tano*	*tanav*	*tanu*	*tanu*	*tanav*	*tanu*	*tanw*	*tanav*	*tanu*	*tanu*	*tanav*	*tanw*	*tanw*	*tanav*	*tanu*	*tanw*
9. *Pú*	*puná*	*puní*	*puná*	*puná*	*puní*	*puní*	*puná*	*puní*	*pun*	*pun*	*puní*	*puní*	*puná*	*pun*	*pun*	*puná*	*puní*	*pun*
1. 4. 6. 10.		*—							*ntu*		**swa*			*ithám*	*itám*			*ntám*
	áni		*tu*	*áva*	*tam*	*tám*	*áma*	*ta*		*ai*		*tám*	*ávahai*			*ámahai*	*dhwam*	
2.3.7.5.8.9.		*hi* †*dhi*							*antu* **atu*		*shwa*			*áthám*	*átám*			*atám*

Observe—In the 2d sing., Parasmai, the roots of the 5th and 8th conj. are like those of the 1st group, and make *chinu, tanu*, rejecting the termination. The 2d and 7th take *dhi* for *hi* by 291, and make *viddhi, bhinddhi*. *Bhṛi* makes *bibhratu* for *bibhrantu* in 3d pl. In the A'tmane, *bodha+ai=bodhai* by 33, *bodha+ithám=bodhethám* by 32.

FIRST PRETERITE.

ROOT.	Parasmai-pada. Sing.			Dual.			Plural.			Átmane-pada. Sing.			Dual.			Plural.		
1. *Budh*	*abodha*	*abodha*	*abodha*	*abodhá*	*abodha*	*abodha*	*abodhá*	*abodha*	*abodha*	*abodha*	*abodha*	*abodha*	*abodhá*	*abodha*	*abodha*	*abodhá*	*abodha*	*abodha*
4. *Nṛit*	*anṛitya*	*anṛitya*	*anṛitya*	*anṛityá*	*anṛitya*	*anṛitya*	*anṛityá*	*anṛitya*	*anṛitya*	*anṛitya*	*anṛitya*	*anṛitya*	*anṛityá*	*anṛitya*	*anṛitya*	*anṛityá*	*anṛitya*	*anṛitya*
6. *Diś*	*adiśa*	*adiśa*	*adiśa*	*adiśá*	*adiśa*	*adiśa*	*adiśá*	*adiśa*	*adiśa*	*adiśa*	*adiśa*	*adiśa*	*adiśá*	*adiśa*	*adiśa*	*adiśá*	*adiśa*	*adiśa*
10. *Yuj*	*ayojaya*	*ayojaya*	*ayojaya*	*ayojayá*	*ayojaya*	*ayojaya*	*ayojayá*	*ayojaya*	*ayojaya*	*ayojaya*	*ayojaya*	*ayojaya*	*ayojayá*	*ayojaya*	*ayojaya*	*ayojayá*	*ayojaya*	*ayojaya*
2. *Vid*	*aved*	*avet*	*avet*	*avid*	*avit*	*avit*	*avid*	*avit*	*avid**	*avid*	*avit*	*avit*	*avid*	*avid*	*avid*	*avid*	*avid*	*avid*
3. *Bhṛi*	*abibhar*	*abibhar*	*abibhar*	*abibhṛi*	*abibhṛi*	*abibhṛi*	*abibhṛi*	*abibhṛi*	*abibhar**	*abibhr*	*abibhṛi*	*abibhṛi*	*abibhṛi*	*abibhr*	*abibhr*	*abibhṛi*	*abibhṛi*	*abibhr*
7. *Bhid*	*abhinad*	*abhinat*	*abhinat*	*abhind*	*abhint*	*abhint*	*abhind*	*abhint*	*abhind*	*abhind*	*abhint*	*abhint*	*abhind*	*abhind*	*abhind*	*abhind*	*abhind*	*abhind*
5. *Chi*	*achinav*	*achino*	*achino*	*achinu*	*achinu*	*achinu*	*achinu*	*achinu*	*achinw*	*achinw*	*achinu*	*achinu*	*achinu*	*achinw*	*achinw*	*achinu*	*achinu*	*achinw*
8. *Tan*	*atanav*	*atano*	*atano*	*atanu*	*atanu*	*atanu*	*atanu*	*atanu*	*atanw*	*atanw*	*atanu*	*atanu*	*atanu*	*atanw*	*atanw*	*atanu*	*atanu*	*atanw*
9. *Pú*	*apuná*	*apuná*	*apuná*	*apuní*	*apuní*	*apuní*	*apuní*	*apuní*	*apun*	*apun*	*apuní*	*apuní*	*apuní*	*apun*	*apun*	*apuní*	*apuní*	*apun*
1. 4. 6. 10.	*m*								*n*					*ithám*	*itám*			*nta*
		s	*t*	*va*	*tam*	*tám*	*ma*	*ta*		*i*	*thás*	*ta*	*vahi*			*mahi*	*dhwam*	
2. 3. 7. 5. 8. 9.	*am*								*an* *us					*áthám*	*átám*			*ata*

Observe—In the 2d and 3d sing., Parasmai, the roots of the 2d group reject the terminations by 292: thus, 2d and 3d sing., *avet, abibhar, abhinat.* In the Átmane the final *a* of the bases of the roots of the 1st group will blend with the initial *i* of a termination into *e* by 32.

SECOND PRETERITE.

ROOT.	Parasmai-pada. Sing.			Dual.			Plural.			Átmane-pada. Sing.			Dual.			Plural.		
1. *Budh*	*bubodh*	*bubodh*	*bubodh*	*bubudh*	*bubudh*	*bubudh*	*bubudh*	*bubudh*	*bubudh*	*bubudh*	*bubudh*	*bubudh*	*bubudh*	*bubudh*	*bubudh*	*bubudh*	*bubudh*	*bubudh*
4. *Nṛit*	*nanart*	*nanart*	*nanart*	*nanṛit*	*nanṛit*	*nanṛit*	*nanṛit*	*nanṛit*	*nanṛit*	*nanṛit*	*nanṛit*	*nanṛit*	*nanṛit*	*nanṛit*	*nanṛit*	*nanṛit*	*nanṛit*	*nanṛit*
6. *Diś*	*dideś*	*dideś*	*dideś*	*didiś*	*didiś*	*didiś*	*didiś*	*didiś*	*didiś*	*didiś*	*didiś*	*didiś*	*didiś*	*didiś*	*didiś*	*didiś*	*didiś*	*didiś*
10. *Yuj*	*yojay*†	*yojay*†	*yojay*†	*yojay*†	*yojay*†	*yojay*†	*yojay*†	*yojay*†	*yojay*†	*yojay*†	*yojay*†	*yojay*†	*yojay*†	*yojay*†	*yojay*†	*yojay*†	*yojay*†	*yojay*†
2. *Vid*	*vived*	*vived*	*vived*	*vivid*	*vivid*	*vivid*	*vivid*	*vivid*	*vivid*	*vivid*	*vivid*	*vivid*	*vivid*	*vivid*	*vivid*	*vivid*	*vivid*	*vivid*
3. *Bhṛi**	*babhár*	*babhar**	*babhár*	*babhṛi**	*babhr*	*babhr*	*babhṛi**	*babhr*	*babhr*	*babhr*	*babhṛi**	*babhr*	*babhṛi**	*babhr*	*babhr*	*babhṛi**	*babhṛi**	*babhr*
7. *Bhid*	*bibhed*	*bibhed*	*bibhed*	*bibhid*	*bibhid*	*bibhid*	*bibhid*	*bibhid*	*bibhid*	*bibhid*	*bibhid*	*bibhid*	*bibhid*	*bibhid*	*bibhid*	*bibhid*	*bibhid*	*bibhid*
5. *Chi*	*chicháy*	*chichay*	*chicháy*	*chichy*	*chichy*	*chichy*	*chichy*	*chichy*	*chichy*	*chichy*	*chichy*	*chichy*	*chichy*	*chichy*	*chichy*	*chichy*	*chichy*	*chichy*
8. *Tan*	*tatán*	*ten*	*tatán*	*ten*	*ten*	*ten*	*ten*	*ten*	*ten*	*ten*	*ten*	*ten*	*ten*	*ten*	*ten*	*ten*	*ten*	*ten*
9. *Pú*	*pupáv*	*pupav*	*pupáv*	*pupuv*	*pupuv*	*pupuv*	*pupuv*	*pupuv*	*pupuv*	*pupuv*	*pupuv*	*pupuv*	*pupuv*	*pupuv*	*pupuv*	*pupuv*	*pupuv*	*pupuv*
	a	*itha* * *tha*	*a*	*iva* * *va*	*athus*	*atus*	*ima* * *ma*	*a*	*us*	*e*	*ishe* * *she*	*e*	*ivahe* * *vahe*	*áthe*	*áte*	*imahe* * *mahe*	*idhwe* * *dhwe*	*ire*

† The syllable *ám* must be added to *yojay* throughout; and the base of the second preterites of *as*, *bhú*, or *kṛi*, must be affixed to *yojayám*: thus, 1st sing. *yojayámás*+*a* or *yojayámbabhúv*+*a* or *yojayánchakár*+*a*; see 385. *a*. Some of the above roots may optionally take *tha* as well as *itha* in the 2d sing.: thus, *diś* makes *dideśitha* or *dideshṭha*; *bhid* makes *bibheditha* or *bibhettha*; *chi* makes *chichayitha* or *chichetha*: but *bhṛi* makes only *babhartha*, see p. 107.

FIRST FUTURE.

ROOT.	BASE.	PAR. TERM.	ÁTM. TERM.
1. *Budh*	*bodhi**	*túsmi*	*táhe*
4. *Nṛit*	*narti*	*tási*	*táse*
6. *Diś*	*desh*	*tá*	*tá*
10. *Yuj*	*yojayi*	———	———
		táswas	*táswahe*
2. *Vid*	*vedi*	*tásthas*	*tásáthe*
3. *Bhṛi*	*bhar*	*tárau*	*tárau*
7. *Bhid*	*bhet*	———	———
		tásmas	*tásmahe*
5. *Chi*	*che*	*tástha*	*tádhwe*
8. *Tan*	*tani*	*táraṣ*	*táraṣ*
9. *Pú*	*pavi*		

* Note, that *budh* also forms *boddháhe* &c. in Átm. by 405. After *desh* the *t* of the terminations will become *ṭ* by 300.

SECOND FUTURE.

ROOT.	BASE.	PAR. TERM.	ÁTM. TERM.
1. *Budh*	*bodhi**	*shyámi*	*shye*
4. *Nṛit*	*narti*	*shyasi*	*shyase*
6. *Diś*	*dek*	*shyati*	*shyate*
10. *Yuj*	*yojayi*	———	———
		shyávas	*shyávahe*
2. *Vid*	*vedi*	*shyathas*	*shyethe*
3. *Bhṛi*	*bhari*	*shyatas*	*shyete*
7. *Bhid*	*bhet**	———	———
		shyámas	*shyámahe*
5. *Chi*	*che*	*shyatha*	*shyadhwe*
8. *Tan*	*tani*	*shyanti*	*shyante*
9. *Pú*	*pavi*		

* Note, that *budh* also forms *bhotsye* &c. in Átm. (see 405); and that after *bhet* the terminations will be *syámi* &c.

THIRD PRETERITE.

Form I.				Form II.			
ROOT.	BASE.	PAR. TERM.	ÁTM. TERM.	ROOT.	BASE.	PAR. TERM.	ÁTM. TERM.
1. *Budh*	*abodhi* †	*sham*	*shi*	6. *Diś*	*adiksh*	*am*	*i* or * *e*
		shís or † *ís*	*shṭhás* or * *thás*			*as*	*athás*
4. *Nṛit*	*anarti* †	*shít* or † *ít*	*shṭa* or * *ta*	10. *Yuj*	*ayúyuj* *	*at*	*ata*
		shwa	*shwahi*	7. *Bhid* follows this form in Parasm., but not in Átm.	*abhid*	*áva*	*ávahi*
2. *Vid*	*avedi* †	*shṭam*	*sháthám*			*atam*	*áthám* or * *etham*
		shṭám	*shátám*			*atám*	*átám* or * *etám*
3. *Bhṛi*	Par. *abhár* Átm. *abhṛi* *	*shma*	*shmahi*			*áma*	*ámahi*
5. *Chi*	Par. *achai* Átm. *ache*	*shṭa*	*dhwam* or * *ḍhwam*			*ata*	*adhwam*
		shus	*shata*			*an*	*anta*
8. *Tan*	Par. *atáni* † Átm. *atani*	Note, that *bhid*, 7th c., follows this form in Átmane, and makes *abhitsi*, *abhitthás*, *abhitta*, &c., by 419. *Tan* may make *atathás*, &c., as well as *atanishṭhás*. See 426. *b*.				Note, that *bhid* follows form I. in Átmane.	
9. *Pú*	Par. *apávi* † Átm. *apavi*						

BENEDICTIVE.

ROOT.	BASE.	PAR. TERM.	BASE.	ÁTM. TERM.
1. *Budh*	*budh*	*yásam*	*bodhi*	*shíya*
4. *Nṛit*	*nṛit*	*yás*	*narti*	*shíshṭhás*
6. *Diś*	*diś*	*yát*	*dik*	*shíshṭa*
10. *Yuj*	*yuj*	*yáswa*	*yojayi*	*shívahi*
2. *Vid*	*vid*	*yástam*	*vedi*	*shíyásthám*
3. *Bhṛi*	*bhri*	*yástám*	*bhṛi*	*shíyástám*
7. *Bhid*	*bhid*	*yásma*	*bhit* *	*shímahi*
		yásta		*shídhwam*
5. *Chi*	*chí*	*yásus*	*che*	*shíran*
8. *Tan*	*tan*		*tani*	
9. *Pú*	*pú*		*pavi*	

* Note, that after *bhit* the terminations will be *síya* &c.

CONDITIONAL.

ROOT.	BASE.	PAR. TERM.	ÁTM. TERM.
1. *Budh*	*abodhi*	*shyam*	*shye*
4. *Nṛit*	*anarti*	*shyas*	*shyathás*
6. *Diś*	*adek*	*shyat*	*shyata*
10. *Yuj*	*ayojayi*	*shyáva*	*shyávahi*
2. *Vid*	*avedi*	*shyatam*	*shyethám*
3. *Bhṛi*	*abhari*	*shyatám*	*shyetám*
7. *Bhid*	*abhet**	*shyáma*	*shyámahi*
		shyata	*shyadhwam*
5. *Chi*	*ache*	*shyan*	*shyanta*
8. *Tan*	*atani*		
9. *Pú*	*apavi*		

* Note, that after *abhet* the terminations will be *syam* &c.

INFINITIVE.

ROOT.	BASE.	TERM.
1. *Budh*	*bodhi*	*tum* or * *ṭum* after *desh* by 300.
4. *Nṛit*	*narti*	
6. *Diś*	*desh**	
10. *Yuj*	*yojayi*	
2. *Vid*	*vedi*	
3. *Bhṛi*	*bhar*	
7. *Bhid*	*bhet*	
5. *Chi*	*che*	
8. *Tan*	*tani*	
9. *Pú*	*pavi*	

INFLECTION OF THE BASE OF PASSIVE VERBS FROM THE SAME TEN ROOTS.

PRESENT.

ROOT.	BASE.	TERM.
1. *Budh*	*budhya* / *budhyá**	*i*
4. *Nṛit*	*nṛitya* / *nṛityá**	*se*
6. *Diś*	*diśya* / *diśyá**	*te*
10. *Yuj*	*yojya* / *yojyá**	—— **vahe*
2. *Vid*	*vidya* / *vidyá**	*ithe*
3. *Bhṛi*	*bhriya* / *bhriyá**	*ite*
7. *Bhid*	*bhidya* / *bhidyá**	——
5. *Chi*	*chíya* / *chíyá**	**mahe*
8. *Tan*	*tanya* / *tanyá**	*dhwe*
9. *Pú*	*púya* / *púyá**	*nte*

POTENTIAL.

ROOT.	BASE.	TERM.
1. *Budh*	*budhya*	*íya*
4. *Nṛit*	*nṛitya*	*íthás*
6. *Diś*	*diśya*	*íta*
10. *Yuj*	*yojya*	—— *ívahi*
2. *Vid*	*vidya*	*íyáthám*
3. *Bhṛi*	*bhriya*	*íyátám*
7. *Bhid*	*bhidya*	——
5. *Chi*	*chíya*	*ímahi*
8. *Tan*	*tanya*	*ídhwam*
9. *Pú*	*púya*	*íran*

IMPERATIVE.

ROOT.	BASE.	TERM.
1. *Budh*	*budhya*	*ai*
4. *Nṛit*	*nṛitya*	*swa*
6. *Diś*	*diśya*	*tám*
10. *Yuj*	*yojya*	—— *ávahai*
2. *Vid*	*vidya*	*ithám*
3. *Bhṛi*	*bhriya*	*itám*
7. *Bhid*	*bhidya*	——
5. *Chi*	*chíya*	*ámahai*
8. *Tan*	*tanya*	*dhwam*
9. *Pú*	*púya*	*ntám*

FIRST PRETERITE.

ROOT.	BASE.	TERM.
1. *Budh*	*abudhya* / *abudhyá**	*i*
4. *Nṛit*	*anṛitya* / *anṛityá**	*thás*
6. *Diś*	*adiśya* / *adiśyá**	*ta*
10. *Yuj*	*ayojya* / *ayojyá**	—— **vahi*
2. *Vid*	*avidya* / *avidyá**	*ithám*
3. *Bhṛi*	*abhriya* / *abhriyá**	*itám*
7. *Bhid*	*abhidya* / *abhidyá**	——
5. *Chi*	*achíya* / *achíyá**	**mahi*
8. *Tan*	*atanya* / *atanyá**	*dhwam*
9. *Pú*	*apúya* / *apúyá**	*nta*

SECOND PRETERITE.

ROOT.	BASE.	TERM.
1. *Budh*	*bubudh*	*e*
4. *Nṛit*	*nanṛit*	*ishe*
6. *Diś*	*didiś*	*e*
10. *Yuj*	*yojayámás*	
		ivahe
2. *Vid*	*vivid*	
		áthe
3. *Bhṛi*	*babhr*	
		áte
7. *Bhid*	*bibhid*	
		imahe
5. *Chi*	*chichy*	
		idhwe
8. *Tan*	*ten*	
		ire
9. *Pú*	*pupuv*	

FIRST FUTURE.

ROOT.	BASE.	TERM.
1. *Budh*	*bodhi*	*táhe*
4. *Nṛit*	*narti*	*táse*
6. *Diś*	*desh* (300)	*tá*
10. *Yuj*	*yojayi* or *yoji*	
		táswahe
2. *Vid*	*vedi*	
		tásáthe
3. *Bhṛi*	*bhári* or *bhar*	
		tárau
7. *Bhid*	*bhet*	
		tásmahe
5. *Chi*	*cháyi* or *che*	
		tádhwe
8. *Tan*	*tani*	
		táras
9. *Pú*	*pávi* or *pavi*	

SECOND FUTURE.

ROOT.	BASE.	TERM.
1. *Budh*	*bodhi*	*shye*
4. *Nṛit*	*narti*	*shyase*
6. *Diś*	*dek* (302)	*shyate*
10. *Yuj*	*yojayi* or *yoji*	
		shyávahe
2. *Vid*	*vedi*	
		shyethe
3. *Bhṛi*	*bhári* or *bhari*	
		shyete
7. *Bhid*	*bhet*	
		shyámahe
5. *Chi*	*cháyi* or *che*	
		shyadhwe
8. *Tan*	*tani*	
		shyante
9. *Pú*	*pávi* or *pavi*	

THIRD PRETERITE.

ROOT.	BASE.	TERM.	BASE OF 3D SING.	TERM.
1. *Budh*	*abodhi*	*shi*	*abodh*	*i*
4. *Nṛit*	*anarti*	*shṭhás*	*anart*	
6. *Diś*	*adik* *		*adeś*	
10. *Yuj*	*ayojayi* (496. *b*) or *ayoji*	—— *shwahi*	*ayoj*	
2. *Vid*	*avedi*	*sháthám*	*aved*	
3. *Bhṛi*	*abhári* or *abhṛi* (421)	*shátám*	*abhár*	
7. *Bhid*	*abhit* *	—— *shmahi*	*abhed*	
5. *Chi*	*acháyi* or *ache*	*dhwam*	*acháy*	
8. *Tan*	*atani*	*shata*	*atán*	
9. *Pú*	*apávi* or *apavi*		*apáv*	

* Observe—After *abhit* the initial *sh* of the termination takes the dental form *s*, in this and the following tenses. Again, *adik* and *abhit* reject the sibilant from *shṭhás*, and become *adig* and *abhid* before *dhwam*: thus, *adikshi*, *adikthás*, *adeśi*, *adikshwahi*, *adiksháthám*, *adikshátám*, *adikshmahi*, *adigdhwam*, *adikshata*. So also, *abhitsi*, *abhitthás*, *abhedi*, *abhitswahi*, &c. (419, 475. *a*).

BENEDICTIVE.

ROOT.	BASE.	TERM.
1. *Budh*	*bodhi*	*shíya*
4. *Nṛit*	*narti*	*shíshṭhás*
6. *Diś*	*dik*	*shíshṭa*
10. *Yuj*	*yojayi* or *yoji*	—— *shívahi*
2. *Vid*	*vedi*	*shíyásthám*
3. *Bhṛi*	*bhári* or *bhṛi*	*shíyástám*
7. *Bhid*	*bhit*	—— *shímahi*
5. *Chi*	*cháyi* or *che*	*shídhwam*
8. *Tan*	*tani*	*shíran*
9. *Pú*	*pávi* or *pavi*	

CONDITIONAL.

ROOT.	BASE.	TERM.
1. *Budh*	*abodhi*	*shye*
4. *Nṛit*	*anarti*	*shyathás*
6. *Diś*	*adek*	*shyata*
10. *Yuj*	*ayojayi* or *ayoji*	—— *shyávahi*
2. *Vid*	*avedi*	*shyethám*
3. *Bhṛi*	*abhári* or *abhari*	*shyetám*
7. *Bhid*	*abhet*	—— *shyámahi*
5. *Chi*	*acháyi* or *ache*	*shyadhwam*
8. *Tan*	*atani*	*shyanta*
9. *Pú*	*apávi* or *apavi*	

CAUSAL FORM. PRESENT TENSE.

ROOT.	BASE.	PAR. TERM.	ÁTM. TERM.
1. Budh	bodhaya / bodhayá*	*mi	i
4. Nṛit	nartaya / nartayá*	si	se
6. Diś	deśaya / deśayá*	ti	te
10. Yuj	yojaya / yojayá*	*vas	*vahe
2. Vid	vedaya / vedayá*	thas	ithe
3. Bhṛi	bháraya / bhárayá*	tas	ite
7. Bhid	bhedaya / bhedayá*	*mas	*mahe
5. Chi	chápaya / chápayá*	tha	dhwe
8. Tan	tánaya / tánayá*	nti	nte
9. Pú	pávaya / pávayá*		

DESIDERATIVE FORM. PRESENT TENSE.

ROOT.	BASE.	PAR. TERM.	ÁTM. TERM.
1. Budh	bubodhisha / bubodhishá*	*mi	i
4. Nṛit	ninartisha / ninartishá*	si	se
6. Diś	didiksha / didikshá*	ti	te
10. Yuj	yuyojayisha / yuyojayishá*	*vas	*vahe
2. Vid	vividisha / vividishá*	thas	ithe
3. Bhṛi	bibharisha / bibharishá*	tas	ite
7. Bhid	bibhitsa / bibhitsá*	*mas	*mahe
5. Chi	chichísha / chichíshá*	tha	dhwe
8. Tan	titanisha / titanishá*	nti	nte
9. Pú	pipavisha / pipavishá*		

Observe—Nṛit also makes its base ninṛitsa; bhṛi, bubhúrsha; chi, chikísha; tan, tatansa or tatánsa; pú, pupúsha—in both Átmane and Parasmai: and budh and vid may respectively make their bases bubhutsa (299. a) and vivitsa, but in Átmane only.

FREQUENTATIVE FORM. PRESENT ÁTMANE.

ROOT.	BASE.	TERM.
1. Budh	bobudhya / bobudhyá*	i
4. Nṛit	naríṇṛitya / naríṇṛityá*	se
6. Diś	dediśya / dediśyá*	te
10. Yuj†		*vahe
2. Vid	vevidya / vevidyá*	ithe
3. Bhṛi	bebhríya / bebhríyá*	ite
7. Bhid	bebhidya / bebhidyá*	*mahe
5. Chi	chechíya / chechíyá*	dhwe
8. Tan	tantanya / tantanyá*	nte
9. Pú	popúya / popúyá*	

† Observe—The 10th class has no frequentative form.

PARTICIPLES.

ROOT.	PRES. PARASM.	PRES. ÁTMANE.	PRES. PASSIVE.	PAST PASSIVE.	PAST ACTIVE.	2D PRET. PARASMAI.	2D PRET. ÁTMANE.	PAST INDECL.	FUTURE PASS. I.	FUTURE PASS. 2.	FUTURE PASS. 3.	2D FUT. PARASMAI.	2D FUT. ÁTMANE OR PASSIVE.
1. *Budh*	*bodhat*	*bodhamána*	*budhyamána*	*buddha*	*buddhavat*	*bubudhwas*	*bubudháṇa*	*buddhwá*	*boddhavya*	*bodhaníya*	*bodhya*	*bodhishyat*	*bodhishyamáṇa*
4. *Nṛit*	*nṛityat*	*nṛityamána*	*nṛityamána*	*nṛitta* or *nartita*	*nṛittavat* or *nartitavat*	*nanṛitwas*	*nanṛitána*	*nartitwá*	*nartitavya*	*nartaníya*	*nṛitya*	*nartishyat*	*nartishyamáṇa*
6. *Diś*	*diśat*	*diśamána*	*diśyamána*	*dishṭa*	*dishṭavat*	*didiśwas*	*didiśána*	*dishṭwá*	*deshṭavya*	*deśaníya*	*deśya*	*dekshyat*	*dekshyamáṇa*
10. *Yuj*	*yojayat*	*yojayána*	*yojyamána*	*yojita*	*yojitavat*	*yojayáñ* †	*yojayáñ* †	*yojayitwá*	*yojayitavya*	*yojaníya*	*yojya*	*yojayishyat*	*yojayishyamáṇa*
2. *Vid*	*vidat*	*vidána*	*vidyamána*	*vidita*	*viditavat*	*vividwas*	*vividána*	*viditwá*	*veditavya*	*vedaníya*	*vedya*	*vedishyat*	*vedishyamáṇa*
3. *Bhṛi*	*bibhrat*	*bibhráṇa*	*bhriyamáṇa*	*bhṛita*	*bhṛitavat*	*babhrivas*	*babhráṇa*	*bhṛitwá*	*bhartavya*	*bharaṇíya*	*bhárya*	*bharishyat*	*bharishyamáṇa*
7. *Bhid*	*bhindat*	*bhindána*	*bhidyamána*	*bhinna*	*bhinnavat*	*bibhidwas*	*bibhidána*	*bhittwá*	*bhettavya*	*bhedaníya*	*bhedya*	*bhetsyat*	*bhetsyamáṇa*
5. *Chi*	*chinwat*	*chinwána*	*chíyamána*	*chita*	*chitavat*	*chichivas*	*chichyána*	*chitwá*	*chetavya*	*chayaníya*	*cheya*	*cheshyat*	*cheshyamána*
8. *Tan*	*tanwat*	*tanwána*	*tanyamána*	*tata*	*tatavat*	*tenivas*	*tenána*	*tanitwá*	*tanitavya*	*tananíya*	*tánya*	*tanishyat*	*tanishyamáṇa*
9. *Pú*	*punat*	*punána*	*púyamána*	*púta*	*pútavat*	*pupúvas*	*pupuvána*	*pútwá*	*pavitavya*	*pavaníya*	*pávya*	*pavishyat*	*pavishyamáṇa*

† *Chakṛivas* must be added to *yojayáñ* for the participle of the 2d pret. Parasmai, and *chakráṇa* for that of the 2d pret. Átmane.

584. Root अस् *as*, 'to be' (see 322). PARASMAI-PADA.

Note, that although this root belongs to the 2d class, its inflection is exhibited here, both because it is sometimes used as an auxiliary, and because it is desirable that the student should study its inflection at the same time with that of the other substantive verb *bhú*, 'to be,' which will follow at 585, and which supplies many of the defective tenses of *as*. It may be remarked, that all the cognate languages have two roots similar to the Sanskrit for the substantive verb 'to be.' Compare φῡ and ασ (εσ) in Greek, *es* (*sum*) and *fu* (*fui*) in Latin; and observe how the different parts of the Sanskrit verbs correspond to the Greek and Latin: thus, *asmi, asi, asti;* ἐμμί, ἐσσί, ἐστί; *sum, es, est.* Compare also *santi* with *sunt; ástam, ástám*, with ἦστον, ἤστην; *ásma, ásta*, with ἦσμεν, ἦστε, &c. Two other roots in Sanskrit are sometimes employed as substantive verbs, with the sense 'to be,' viz. *sthá*, 1st c., 'to stand' (see 269, 587), and *ás*, 2d c., 'to sit' (see 317). Indeed, the root *as*, here inflected, is probably only an abbreviation of *ás*.

Present, 'I am.' | *First preterite*, 'I was.'

PERS.	SING.	DUAL.	PLURAL.	SING.	DUAL.	PLURAL.
1st,	अस्मि *asmi*	स्वस् *swas*	स्मस् *smas*	आसं *ásam*	आस्व *áswa*	आस्म *ásma*
2d,	असि *asi*	स्थस् *sthas*	स्थ *stha*	आसीस् *ásís*	आस्तं *ástam*	आस्त *ásta*
3d,	अस्ति *asti*	स्तस् *stas*	सन्ति *santi*	आसीत् *ásít*	आस्तां *ástám*	आसन् *ásan*

Potential, 'I may be,' &c. | *Imperative*, 'Let me be.'

स्यां *syám*	स्याव *syáva*	स्याम *syáma*	असानि *asáni*	असाव *asáva*	असाम *asáma*
स्यास् *syás*	स्यातं *syátam*	स्यात *syáta*	एधि *edhi*	स्तं *stam*	स्त *sta*
स्यात् *syát*	स्यातां *syátám*	स्युस् *syus*	अस्तु *astu*	स्तां *stám*	सन्तु *santu*

*Second preterite**, 'I was,' &c.

PARASMAI.			ÁTMANE.		
आस *ása*	आसिव *ásiva*	आसिम *ásima*	आसे *áse*	आसिवहे *ásivahe*	आसिमहे *ásimahe*
आसिथ *ásitha*	आसथुस् *ásathus*	आस *ása*	आसिषे *ásishe*	आसाथे *ásáthe*	आसिध्वे (द्वे) *ásidhwe*
आस *ása*	आसतुस् *ásatus*	आसुस् *ásus*	आसे *áse*	आसाते *ásáte*	आसिरे *ásire*

Observe—The root *as*, 'to be,' has no derivative forms, and only two participles, viz. those of the present, Parasmai and Átmane, सत् *sat*, सान *sána* (see 524, 526). The conjugational tenses have an Átmane-pada, which is not used unless the root is compounded with prepositions. In this Pada ह् *h* is substituted for the root in the 1st sing. pres., and स् *s* is changed to *d* before *dh* in the 2d plur.: thus, Pres. *he, se, ste; swahe, sáthe, sáte; smahe, ddhwe, sate:* see 322.

* The 2d preterite of *as* is never used by itself, but is employed in forming the 2d preterite of causals and some other verbs, see 385, 490; in which case the Átmane may be used. The other tenses of *as* are wanting, and are supplied from *bhú* at 585.

EXAMPLES OF PRIMITIVE VERBS OF THE FIRST CONJUGATION, EXPLAINED AT 261.

585. Root भू *bhú*. Infin. भवितुं *bhavitum*, 'to be' or 'become.'

PARASMAI-PADA. *Present tense*, 'I am' or 'I become.'

PERS. SING.	DUAL.	PLURAL.
1st, भवामि *bhavámi*	भवावस् *bhavávas*	भवामस् *bhavámas*
2d, भवसि *bhavasi*	भवथस् *bhavathas*	भवथ *bhavatha*
3d, भवति *bhavati*	भवतस् *bhavatas*	भवन्ति *bhavanti*

Potential, 'I may be.'

भवेयं *bhaveyam*	भवेव *bhaveva*	भवेम *bhavema*
भवेस् *bhaves*	भवेतं *bhavetam*	भवेत *bhaveta*
भवेत् *bhavet*	भवेतां *bhavetám*	भवेयुस् *bhaveyus*

Imperative, 'Let me be.'

भवानि *bhaváni*	भवाव *bhaváva*	भवाम *bhaváma*
भव *bhava*	भवतं *bhavatam*	भवत *bhavata*
भवतु *bhavatu*	भवतां *bhavatám*	भवन्तु *bhavantu*

First preterite, 'I was.'

अभवं *abhavam*	अभवाव *abhaváva*	अभवाम *abhaváma*
अभवस् *abhavas*	अभवतं *abhavatam*	अभवत *abhavata*
अभवत् *abhavat*	अभवतां *abhavatám*	अभवन् *abhavan*

Second preterite, 'I was.'

बभूव *babhúva*	बभूविव *babhúviva*	बभूविम *babhúvima*
बभूविथ *babhúvitha*	बभूवथुस् *babhúvathus*	बभूव *babhúva*
बभूव *babhúva*	बभूवतुस् *babhúvatus*	बभूवुस् *babhúvus*

First future, 'I will be.'

भवितास्मि *bhavitásmi*	भवितास्वस् *bhavitáswas*	भवितास्मस् *bhavitásmas*
भवितासि *bhavitási*	भवितास्थस् *bhavitásthas*	भवितास्थ *bhavitástha*
भविता *bhavitá*	भवितारौ *bhavitárau*	भवितारस् *bhavitáras*

Second future, 'I shall be.'

भविष्यामि *bhavishyámi*	भविष्यावस् *bhavishyávas*	भविष्यामस् *bhavishyámas*
भविष्यसि *bhavishyasi*	भविष्यथस् *bhavishyathas*	भविष्यथ *bhavishyatha*
भविष्यति *bhavishyati*	भविष्यतस् *bhavishyatas*	भविष्यन्ति *bhavishyanti*

Third preterite, 'I was' or 'had been,' &c.

अभूवं *abhúvam*	अभूव *abhúva*	अभूम *abhúma*
अभूस् *abhús*	अभूतं *abhútam*	अभूत *abhúta*
अभूत् *abhút*	अभूतां *abhútám*	अभूवन् *abhúvan*

Benedictive, 'May I be.'

भूयासं *bhúyásam*	भूयास्व *bhúyáswa*	भूयास्म *bhúyásma*
भूयास् *bhúyás*	भूयास्तं *bhúyástam*	भूयास्त *bhúyásta*
भूयात् *bhúyát*	भूयास्तां *bhúyástám*	भूयासुस् *bhúyásus*

Conditional, (If) 'I should be.'

अभविष्यं *abhavishyam*	अभविष्याव *abhavishyáva*	अभविष्याम *abhavishyáma*
अभविष्यस् *abhavishyas*	अभविष्यतं *abhavishyatam*	अभविष्यत *abhavishyata*
अभविष्यत् *abhavishyat*	अभविष्यतां *abhavishyatám*	अभविष्यन् *abhavishyan*

586. ÁTMANE-PADA. *Present tense,* 'I am,' &c.

भवे *bhave*	भवावहे *bhavávahe*	भवामहे *bhavámahe*
भवसे *bhavase*	भवेथे *bhavethe*	भवध्वे *bhavadhwe*
भवते *bhavate*	भवेते *bhavete*	भवन्ते *bhavante*

Potential, 'I may be,' &c.

भवेय *bhaveya*	भवेवहि *bhavevahi*	भवेमहि *bhavemahi*
भवेथास् *bhavethás*	भवेयाथां *bhaveyáthám*	भवेध्वं *bhavedhwam*
भवेत *bhaveta*	भवेयातां *bhaveyátám*	भवेरन् *bhaveran*

Imperative, 'Let me be.'

भवै *bhavai*	भवावहै *bhavávahai*	भवामहै *bhavámahai*
भवस्व *bhavaswa*	भवेथां *bhavethám*	भवध्वं *bhavadhwam*
भवतां *bhavatám*	भवेतां *bhavetám*	भवन्तां *bhavantám*

First preterite, 'I was.'

अभवे *abhave*	अभवावहि *abhavávahi*	अभवामहि *abhavámahi*
अभवथास् *abhavathás*	अभवेथां *abhavethám*	अभवध्वं *abhavadhwam*
अभवत *abhavata*	अभवेतां *abhavetám*	अभवन्त *abhavanta*

Second preterite, 'I was,' &c.

बभूवे *babhúve*	बभूविवहे *babhúvivahe*	बभूविमहे *babhúvimahe*
बभूविषे *babhúvishe*	बभूवाथे *babhúváthe*	बभूविध्वे (ढ्वे) *babhúvidhwe*
बभूवे *babhúve*	बभूवाते *babhúváte*	बभूविरे *babhúvire*

First future, 'I will be,' &c.

भविताहे *bhavitáhe*	भवितास्वहे *bhavitáswahe*	भवितास्महे *bhavitásmahe*
भवितासे *bhavitáse*	भवितासाथे *bhavitásáthe*	भविताध्वे *bhavitádhwe*
भविता *bhavitá*	भवितारौ *bhavitárau*	भवितारस् *bhavitáras*

Second future, 'I shall be,' &c.

भविष्ये *bhavishye*	भविष्यावहे *bhavishyávahe*	भविष्यामहे *bhavishyámahe*
भविष्यसे *bhavishyase*	भविष्येथे *bhavishyethe*	भविष्यध्वे *bhavishyadhwe*
भविष्यते *bhavishyate*	भविष्येते *bhavishyete*	भविष्यन्ते *bhavishyante*

Third preterite, 'I was' or 'had been,' &c.

अभविषि *abhavishi*	अभविष्वहि *abhavishwahi*	अभविष्महि *abhavishmahi*
अभविष्ठास् *abhavishṭhás*	अभविषाथां *abhavisháthám*	अभविध्वं (ढ्वं) *abhavidhwam*
अभविष्ट *abhavishṭa*	अभविषातां *abhavishátám*	अभविषत *abhavishata*

Benedictive, 'I wish I may be.'

भविषीय *bhavishíya*	भविषीवहि *bhavishívahi*	भविषीमहि *bhavishímahi*
भविषीष्ठास् *bhavishíshṭhás*	भविषीयास्थां *bhavishíyásthám*	भविषीध्वं (ढ्वं) *bhavishídhwam*
भविषीष्ट *bhavishíshṭa*	भविषीयास्तां *bhavishíyástám*	भविषीरन् *bhavishíran*

Conditional, (If) 'I should be,' &c.

अभविष्ये *abhavishye*	अभविष्यावहि *abhavishyávahi*	अभविष्यामहि *abhavishyámahi*
अभविष्यथास् *abhavishyathás*	अभविष्येथां *abhavishyethám*	अभविष्यध्वं *abhavishyadhwam*
अभविष्यत *abhavishyata*	अभविष्येतां *abhavishyetám*	अभविष्यन्त *abhavishyanta*

Passive (461), Pres. भूये, भूयसे, &c.; 3d Pret. 3d sing. (475) अभावि. *Causal* (479), Pres. भावयामि, भावयसि, &c.; 3d Pret. (492) अबीभवं, &c. *Desiderative* (498), Pres. बुभूषामि, बुभूषसि, &c. Desiderative form of Causal (497) बिभावयिषामि, &c. *Frequentative* (507), Pres. बोभूये, बोभोमि or बोभवीमि*. *Participles,* Pres. भवत् (524); Past pass. भूत (531); Past indecl. भूत्वा (556), -भूय (559); Fut. pass. भवितव्य (569), भवनीय (570), भाव्य or भव्य (571).

EXAMPLES OF OTHER VERBS OF THE FIRST CONJUGATION IN THE ORDER OF THEIR FINAL LETTERS.

587. Root स्था. Inf. स्थातुं 'to stand' (269, 269. *a*). Parasmai and Átmane. Pres. तिष्ठामि, तिष्ठसि, तिष्ठति; तिष्ठावस्, तिष्ठथस्, तिष्ठतस्; तिष्ठामस्,

* These derivative verbs will be inflected at full at the end of the examples of primitive verbs. See 706, 707.

तिष्ठथ, तिष्ठन्ति. Átm. तिष्ठे, तिष्ठसे, तिष्ठते; तिष्ठावहे, तिष्ठेथे, तिष्ठेते; तिष्ठामहे, तिष्ठध्वे, तिष्ठन्ते. Pot. तिष्ठेयं, तिष्ठेस्, तिष्ठेत्; तिष्ठेव, &c. Átm. तिष्ठेय, तिष्ठेथास्, तिष्ठेत; तिष्ठेवहि, तिष्ठेयाथां, &c. Imp. तिष्ठानि, तिष्ठ, तिष्ठतु; तिष्ठाव, &c. Átm. तिष्ठै, तिष्ठस्व, तिष्ठतां; तिष्ठावहै, &c. 2d Pret. तस्थौ (373), तस्थिथ or तस्थाथ, तस्थौ; तस्थिव, तस्थथुस्, तस्थतुस्; तस्थिम, तस्थ, तस्थुस्. Átm. तस्थे, तस्थिषे, तस्थे; तस्थिवहे, तस्थाथे, तस्थाते; तस्थिमहे, तस्थिध्वे, तस्थिरे. 1st Fut. स्थातास्मि, स्थातासि, &c. Átm. स्थाताहे, स्थातासे, &c. 2d Fut. स्थास्यामि, स्थास्यसि, स्थास्यति, &c. Átm. स्थास्ये, स्थास्यसे, स्थास्यते, &c. 3d Pret. (438) अस्थां, अस्थास्, अस्थात्; अस्थाव, अस्थातं, अस्थातां; अस्थाम, अस्थात, अस्थुस्. Átm. (438. *c*, 419) अस्थिषि, अस्थिथास्, अस्थित; अस्थिष्वहि, अस्थिषाथां, अस्थिषातां; अस्थिष्महि, अस्थिढ्वं, अस्थिषत. Bened. स्थेयासं, स्थेयास्, &c. Átm. स्थासीय, स्थासीष्ठास्, &c. Cond. अस्थास्यं, अस्थास्यस्, &c. Átm. अस्थास्ये, अस्थास्यथास्, &c. *Passive*, Pres. स्थीये (465); 3d Pret. 3d sing. अस्थायि. *Causal*, Pres. स्थापयामि, -ये; 3d Pret. अतिष्ठिपं, अतिष्ठिपे. *Des.* तिष्ठासामि, &c. *Freq.* तेष्ठीये or तास्थेमि or तास्थामि. *Participles*, Pres. तिष्ठत्; Past pass. स्थित; Past indecl. स्थित्वा, -स्थाय, -ष्ठाय; Fut. pass. स्थातव्य, स्थानीय, स्थेय.

588. Root घ्रा. Inf. घ्रातुं 'to smell' (269). Parasmai. Pres. जिघ्रामि, जिघ्रसि, &c. Pot. जिघ्रेयं, जिघ्रेस्, &c. Imp. जिघ्राणि (58), जिघ्र, &c. 1st Pret. अजिघ्रं, अजिघ्रस्, &c. 2d Pret. जघ्रौ (373), जघ्रिथ or जघ्राथ, जघ्रौ; जघ्रिव, जघ्रथुस्, जघ्रतुस्; जघ्रिम, जघ्र, जघ्रुस्. 1st Fut. घ्रातास्मि, घ्रातासि, &c. 2d Fut. घ्रास्यामि, घ्रास्यसि, &c. 3d Pret. (438) अघ्रां, अघ्रास्, अघ्रात्; अघ्राव, अघ्रातं, अघ्रातां; अघ्राम, अघ्रात, अघ्रुस्. Or by 433, अघ्रासिषं, अघ्रासीस्, अघ्रासीत्; अघ्रासिष्व, अघ्रासिष्टं, अघ्रासिष्टां; अघ्रासिष्म, अघ्रासिष्ट, अघ्रासिषुस्. Bened. घ्रायासं, घ्रायास्, &c. Or घ्रेयासं, &c. Cond. अघ्रास्यं, अघ्रास्यस्, &c. *Passive*, Pres. घ्राये (465. *a*); 3d Pret. 3d sing. अघ्रायि. *Causal*, Pres. घ्रापयामि; 3d Pret. अजिघ्रपं or अजिघ्रिपं. *Des.* जिघ्रासामि. *Freq.* जेघ्रीये, जाघ्रामि or जाघ्रेमि. *Participles*, Pres. जिघ्रत्; Past pass. घ्रात or घ्राण; Past indecl. घ्रात्वा, -घ्राय; Fut. pass. घ्रातव्य, घ्राणीय, घ्रेय.

589. Root पा. Inf. पातुं 'to drink' (269). Parasmai. Pres. पिबामि, पिबसि, &c. Pot. पिबेयं, पिबेस्, &c. Imp. पिबानि, पिब, &c. 1st Pret. अपिबं, अपिबस्, &c. 2d Pret. (373) पपौ, पपिथ or पपाथ, पपौ; पपिव, पपथुस्, पपतुस्; पपिम, पप, पपुस्. 1st Fut. पातास्मि, पातासि, &c. 2d Fut. पास्यामि, पास्यसि, &c. 3d Pret. (438) अपां, अपास्, अपात्; अपाव, अपातं, अपातां; अपाम, अपात, अपुस्. Bened. पेयासं, पेयास्, &c. Cond. अपास्यं, अपास्यस्, &c. *Passive*, Pres. पीये (465); 3d Pret. 3d sing. अपायि. *Causal*, Pres. पाययामि, -ये; 3d Pret. अपीप्यं (475). *Des.* पिपासामि.

Freq. पेपीये, पापेमि or पापामि. *Participles*, Pres. पिबत्; Past pass. पीत (533); Past indecl. पीत्वा, -पाय; Fut. pass. पातव्य, पानीय, पेय.

590. Root जि. Inf. जेतुं 'to conquer.' Parasmai *. Pres. जयामि, जयसि, जयति; जयावस्, जयथस्, जयतस्; जयामस्, जयथ, जयन्ति. Pot. जयेयं, जयेस्, जयेत्; जयेव, जयेतं, जयेतां; जयेम, जयेत, जयेयुस्. Imp. जयानि, जय, जयतु; जयाव, जयतं, जयतां; जयाम, जयत, जयन्तु. 1st Pret. अजयं, अजयस्, अजयत्; अजयाव, अजयतं, अजयतां; अजयाम, अजयत, अजयन्. 2d Pret. जिगाय (378), जिगयिथ or जिगेथ, जिगाय; जिग्यिव (367), जिग्यथुस्, जिग्यतुस्; जिग्यिम, जिग्य, जिग्युस्. 1st Fut. जेतास्मि, जेतासि, जेता; जेतास्वस्, जेतास्थस्, जेतारौ; जेतास्मस्, जेतास्थ, जेतारस्. 2d Fut. जेष्यामि, जेष्यसि, जेष्यति; जेष्यावस्, जेष्यथस्, जेष्यतस्; जेष्यामस्, जेष्यथ, जेष्यन्ति. 3d Pret. अजैषं (420), अजैषीस्, अजैषीत्; अजैष्व, अजैष्टं, अजैष्टां; अजैष्म, अजैष्ट, अजैषुस्. Bened. जीयासं, जीयास्, जीयात्; जीयास्व, जीयास्तं, जीयास्तां; जीयास्म, जीयास्त, जीयासुस्. Cond. अजेष्यं, अजेष्यस्, अजेष्यत्; अजेष्याव, अजेष्यतं, अजेष्यतां; अजेष्याम, अजेष्यत, अजेष्यन्. *Passive*, Pres. जीये, &c.; 3d Pret. 3d sing. अजायि. *Causal*, Pres. जापयामि; 3d Pret. अजीजपं. *Des.* जिगीषामि. *Freq.* जेजीये, जेजेमि or जेजयीमि. *Participles*, Pres. जयत्; Past pass. जित; Past indecl. जित्वा, -जित्य; Fut. pass. जेतव्य, जयनीय, जेय or जित्य or जय्य (571, 572).

a. In the same manner may be conjugated नी. Inf. नेतुं 'to lead.'

591. Root स्मि. Inf. स्मेतुं 'to smile.' A'tmane. Pres. स्मये, स्मयसे, &c. Pot. स्मयेय, स्मयेथास्, &c. Imp. स्मयै, स्मयस्व, &c. 1st Pret. अस्मये, अस्मयथास्, &c. 2d Pret. (367. *a*) सिष्मिये, सिष्मियिषे, सिष्मिये; सिष्मियिवहे, सिष्मियाथे, सिष्मियाते; सिष्मियिमहे, सिष्मियिध्वे, सिष्मियिरे. 1st Fut. स्मेताहे, स्मेतासे, &c. 2d Fut. स्मेष्ये, स्मेष्यसे, &c. 3d Pret. अस्मेषि, अस्मेष्ठास्, अस्मेष्ट; अस्मेष्वहि, अस्मेषाथां, अस्मेषातां; अस्मेष्महि, अस्मेढ्वं, अस्मेषत. Bened. स्मेषीय, &c. Cond. अस्मेष्ये, &c. *Passive*, स्मीये, &c.; 3d Pret. 3d sing. अस्मायि. *Causal*, Pres. स्माययामि or स्मापयामि; 3d Pret. असिष्मयं or असिष्मपं. *Des.* सिस्मयिषे. *Freq.* सेष्मीये, सेष्मेमि or सेष्मयीमि. *Participles*, Pres. स्मयमान; Past pass. स्मित; Past indecl. स्मित्वा, -स्मित्य; Fut. pass. स्मेतव्य, स्मयनीय, स्मेय.

592. Root द्रु. Inf. द्रोतुं 'to run.' Parasmai. Pres. द्रवामि, द्रवसि, द्रवति; द्रवावस्, द्रवथस्, द्रवतस्; द्रवामस्, द्रवथ, द्रवन्ति. Pot. द्रवेयं, द्रवेस्, &c. Imp. द्रवाणि (58), द्रव, &c. 1st Pret. अद्रवं, अद्रवस्, &c. 2d Pret. दुद्राव, दुद्रोथ, दुद्राव; दुद्रुव (368), दुद्रुवथुस् (367. *b*), दुद्रुवतुस्; दुद्रुम,

---

* जि is not generally used in the A'tmane, excepting with the prepositions *vi* or *pará*.

दुद्रुव, दुद्रुवुस्. 1st Fut. द्रोतास्मि, द्रोतासि, &c. 2d Fut. द्रोष्यामि, द्रोष्यसि, &c. 3d Pret. अदुद्रुवं (440. *a*), अदुद्रुवस्, अदुद्रुवत्; अदुद्रुवाव, अदुद्रुवतं, अदुद्रुवतां; अदुद्रुवाम, अदुद्रुवत, अदुद्रुवन्. Bened. द्रूयासं, द्रूयास्, &c. Cond. अद्रोष्यं, अद्रोष्यस्, &c. *Passive*, Pres. द्रूये; 3d Pret. 3d sing. अद्रावि. *Causal*, Pres. द्रावयामि; 3d Pret. अदुद्रवं or अदिद्रवं. *Des.* दुद्रूषामि. *Freq.* दोद्रूये, दोद्रोमि or दोद्रवीमि. *Participles*, Pres. द्रवत्; Past pass. द्रुत; Past indecl. द्रुत्वा, -द्रुत्य; Fut. pass. द्रोतव्य, द्रवणीय, द्राव्य or द्रव्य.

593. Root हृ. Inf. हर्तुं 'to seize,' 'to take.' Parasmai and Átmane. Pres. हरामि, हरसि, हरति; हरावस्, &c. Átm. हरे, हरसे, हरते; हरावहे, &c. Pot. हरेयं, हरेस्, &c. Átm. हरेय, हरेथास्, &c. Imp. हराणि (58), हर, &c. Átm. हरै, हरस्व, &c. 1st Pret. अहरं, अहरस्, अहरत्; अहराव, &c. Átm. अहरे, अहरथास्, अहरत; अहरावहि, &c. 2d Pret. जहार, जहर्थ or जहर्थ, जहार; जह्रिव, जह्रथुस्, जह्रतुस्; जह्रिम, जह्र, जह्रुस्. Átm. जह्रे, जह्रिषे, जह्रे; जह्रिवहे, जह्राथे, जह्राते; जह्रिमहे, जह्रिढ्वे, जह्रिरे. 1st Fut. हर्तास्मि, हर्तासि, &c. Átm. हर्ताहे, हर्तासे, &c. 2d Fut. हरिष्यामि, हरिष्यसि, &c. Átm. हरिष्ये, हरिष्यसे, &c. 3d Pret. अहार्षं, अहार्षीस्, अहार्षीत्; अहार्ष्व, अहार्ष्टं, अहार्ष्टां; अहार्ष्म, अहार्ष्ट, अहार्षुस्. Átm. अहृषि, अहृथास्, अहृत; अहृष्वहि, अहृषाथां, अहृषातां; अहृष्महि, अहृढ्वं, अहृषत. Bened. ह्रियासं, ह्रियास्, &c. Átm. हृषीय, हृषीष्ठास्, &c. Cond. अहरिष्यं, अहरिष्यस्, &c. Átm. अहरिष्ये, अहरिष्यथास्, &c. *Passive*, Pres. ह्रिये; 3d Pret. 3d sing. अहारि. *Causal*, Pres. हारयामि, -ये; 3d Pret. अजीहरं. *Des.* जिहीर्षामि, -र्षे. *Freq.* जेह्रीये, जर्हरीमि or जरीहरीमि or जरिहरीमि or जरीहर्मि or जरि- or जर्हर्मि. *Participles*, Pres. हरत्; Pass. ह्रियमाण; Past pass. हृत; Past indecl. हृत्वा, -हृत्य; Fut. pass. हर्तव्य, हरणीय, हार्य.

594. Root स्मृ. Inf. स्मर्तुं 'to remember.' Parasmai and Átmane. Pres. स्मरामि, स्मरसि, &c. Átm. स्मरे. Pot. स्मरेयं, स्मरेस्, &c. Átm. स्मरेय, &c. Imp. स्मराणि (58), स्मर, &c. Átm. स्मरै, &c. 1st Pret. अस्मरं, अस्मरस्, &c. Átm. अस्मरे. 2d Pret. (367. *c*) सस्मार, सस्मरिथ, सस्मार; सस्मरिव, सस्मरथुस्, सस्मरतुस्; सस्मरिम, सस्मर, सस्मरुस्. Átm. सस्मरे, सस्मरिषे, सस्मरे; सस्मरिवहे, सस्मराथे, सस्मराते; सस्मरिमहे, सस्मरिढ्वे, सस्मरिरे. 1st Fut. स्मर्तास्मि, &c. Átm. स्मर्ताहे, &c. 2d Fut. स्मरिष्यामि, &c. Átm. स्मरिष्ये, &c. 3d Pret. अस्मार्षं, &c. (see हृ at 593). Átm. अस्मृषि, अस्मृथास्, &c. (see हृ at 593). Bened. स्मर्यासं, &c. Átm. स्मृषीय &c., or स्मरिषीय &c. Cond. अस्मरिष्यं, &c. Átm. अस्मरिष्ये, &c. *Passive*, Pres. स्मर्ये; 3d Pret. 3d sing. अस्मारि. *Causal*, Pres. स्मारयामि, -ये; 3d Pret. असस्मरं. *Des.* सुस्मूर्षे. *Freq.* सास्मर्ये, सास्मर्मि or सास्मरीमि.

Participles, Pres. स्मरत्; Past pass. स्मृत; Past indecl. स्मृत्वा, -स्मृत्य; Fut. pass. स्मर्त्तव्य, स्मरणीय, स्मार्य्य.

595. Root ह्वे. Inf. ह्वातुं 'to call.' Parasmai and Átmane. Pres. ह्वयामि, &c. Átm. ह्वये, &c. Pot. ह्वयेयं, &c. Átm. ह्वयेय, &c. Imp. ह्वयानि, &c. Átm. ह्वयै, &c. 1st Pret. अह्वयं, &c. Átm. अह्वये. 2d Pret. (379) जुहाव, जुहविथ or जुहोथ, जुहाव; जुहुविव, जुहुवथुस्, जुहुवतुस्; जुहुविम, जुहुव, जुहुवुस्. Átm. जुहुवे, जुहुविषे, जुहुवे; जुहुविवहे, जुहुवाथे, जुहुवाते; जुहुविमहे, जुहुविढ्वे, जुहुविरे. 1st Fut. ह्वातास्मि, &c. Átm. ह्वाताहे, &c. 2d Fut. ह्वास्यामि, &c. Átm. ह्वास्ये, &c. 3d Pret. (438. *c*) अह्वं, अह्वस्, अह्वत्; अह्वाव, अह्वतं, अह्वतां; अह्वाम, अह्वत, अह्वन्. Átm. अह्वे, अह्वथास्, अह्वत; अह्वावहि, अह्वेथां, अह्वेतां; अह्वामहि, अह्वध्वं, अह्वन्त. Or अह्वासि (433. *a*), अह्वास्थास्, अह्वास्त; अह्वास्वहि, अह्वासाथां, अह्वासातां; अह्वास्महि, अह्वाध्वं, अह्वासत. Bened. हूयासं, &c. Átm. ह्वासीय. Cond. अह्वास्यं, &c. Átm. अह्वास्ये, &c. *Passive*, हूयते (465. *b*); 3d Pret. 3d sing. अह्वायि or अह्वायिष्ट or अह्वत or अह्वास्त. 2d Fut. ह्वास्यते or ह्वायिष्यते (474. *a*). *Causal*, Pres. ह्वाययामि (483); 3d Pret. अजूहवं. *Des.* जुहूषामि, जुहूषे. *Freq.* जोहूये, जोहोमि or जोहवीमि. *Participles*, Pres. ह्वयत्; Pass. हूयमान; Past pass. हूत; Past indecl. हूत्वा, -हूय; Fut. pass. ह्वातव्य, ह्वानीय, ह्वेय.

a. The root गै (268), Inf. गातुं 'to sing,' follows the analogy of *hwe*, the final diphthong being changed to *á* before all terminations beginning with *t* or *s*. Pres. गायामि, &c. Pot. गायेयं, &c. Imp. गायानि, &c. 1st Pret. अगायं, &c. 2d Pret. (374) जगौ, जगिथ or जगाथ, जगौ; जगिव, जगथुस्, जगतुस्; जगिम, जग, जगुस्. 1st Fut. गातास्मि, &c. 2d Fut. गास्यामि, &c. 3d Pret. (433) अगासिषं, अगासीस्, अगासीत्; अगासिष्व, अगासिष्टं, अगासिष्टां; अगासिष्म, अगासिष्ट, अगासिषुस्. Bened. गेयासं, &c. (451). Cond. अगास्यं, &c. *Passive*, गीयते (465); 3d Pret. 3d sing. अगायि. *Causal*, Pres. गापयामि (483); 3d Pret. अजीगपं. *Des.* जिगासामि. *Freq.* जेगीये, जागेमि or जागामि. *Participles*, Pres. गायत्; Pass. गीयमान; Past pass. गीत; Past indecl. गीत्वा, -गाय; Fut. pass. गातव्य, गानीय, गेय.

b. After गै may be conjugated ग्लै 'to be weary;' ध्यै 'to meditate;' म्लै 'to fade;' and all other roots in *ai*.

596. Root त्यज्. Inf. त्यक्तुं 'to abandon,' 'to quit.' Parasmai. Pres. त्यजामि, त्यजसि, &c. Pot. त्यजेयं, त्यजेस्, &c. Imp. त्यजानि, त्यज, &c. 1st Pret. अत्यजं, अत्यजस्, &c. 2d Pret. तत्याज, तत्यजिथ or तत्यक्थ (368. *a*), तत्याज; तत्यजिव, तत्यजथुस्, तत्यजतुस्; तत्यजिम, तत्यज, तत्यजुस्.

1st Fut. त्यक्तास्मि, त्यक्तासि, &c. 2d Fut. त्यक्ष्यामि, त्यक्ष्यसि, &c. 3d Pret. (423, 296) अत्याक्षं, अत्याक्षीस्, अत्याक्षीत्; अत्याक्ष्व, अत्याक्तं, अत्याक्तां; अत्याक्ष्म, अत्याक्त, अत्याक्षुस्. Bened. त्यज्यासं, त्यज्यास्, &c. Cond. अत्यक्ष्यं, अत्यक्ष्यस्, &c. *Passive,* Pres. त्यज्ये; 3d Pret. 3d sing. अत्याजि. *Causal,* Pres. त्याजयामि; 3d Pret. अतित्यजं. *Des.* तित्यक्षामि. *Freq.* तात्यज्ये, तात्यज्मि or तात्यजीमि. *Participles,* Pres. त्यजत्; Past pass. त्यक्त; Past indecl. त्यक्त्वा, -त्यज्य; Fut. pass. त्यक्तव्य, त्यजनीय, त्याज्य (573).

597. Root यज्. Inf. यष्टुं 'to sacrifice,' 'to worship.' Parasmai and Átmane. Pres. यजामि, यजसि, &c. Átm. यजे, &c. Pot. यजेयं, यजेस्, &c. Átm. यजेय, &c. Imp. यजानि, यज, &c. Átm. यजै, &c. 1st Pret. अयजं, अयजस्, &c. Átm. अयजे, &c. 2d Pret. (375. *e*) इयाज, इयजिथ or येजिथ or इयष्ठ (297), इयाज; ईजिव, ईजथुस्, ईजतुस्; ईजिम, ईज, ईजुस्. Átm. ईजे, ईजिषे, ईजे; ईजिवहे, ईजाथे, ईजाते; ईजिमहे, ईजिढ्वे, ईजिरे. 1st Fut. यष्टास्मि, यष्टासि, &c. (403). Átm. यष्टाहे, &c. 2d Fut. यक्ष्यामि, यक्ष्यसि, &c. (403). Átm. यक्ष्ये, &c. 3d Pret. (423) अयाक्षं, अयाक्षीस्, अयाक्षीत्; अयाक्ष्व, अयाष्टं, अयाष्टां; अयाक्ष्म, अयाष्ट, अयाक्षुस्. Átm. अयक्षि, अयष्ठास्, अयष्ट; अयक्ष्वहि, अयक्षाथां, अयक्षातां; अयक्ष्महि, अयग्ध्वं, अयक्षत. Bened. इज्यासं, इज्यास्, &c. Átm. यक्षीय, &c. Cond. अयक्ष्यं, अयक्ष्यस्, &c. Átm. अयक्ष्ये, &c. *Passive,* Pres. इज्ये (471); 1st Pret. ऐज्ये (260. *a*); 3d Pret. 3d sing. अयाजि. *Causal,* Pres. याजयामि, -ये; 3d Pret. अयीयजं. *Des.* यियक्षामि, -क्षे. *Freq.* यायज्ये, यायज्मि or यायजीमि. *Participles,* Pres. यजत्; Átm. यजमान; Pass. इज्यमान; Past pass. इष्ट; Past indecl. इष्ट्वा, -इज्य; Fut. pass. यष्टव्य, यजनीय, याज्य or यज्य.

a. Root सञ्ज्*. Inf. संक्तुं 'to adhere,' 'to embrace.' Parasmai. Pres. सजामि*, &c. Pot. सजेयं, &c. Imp. सजानि, &c. 1st Pret. असजं, &c. 2d Pret. ससञ्ज, ससञ्जिथ or ससंक्थ, ससञ्ज; ससञ्जिव, ससञ्जथुस्, ससञ्जतुस्; ससञ्जिम, ससञ्ज, ससञ्जुस्. 1st Fut. संक्तास्मि, &c. 2d Fut. संक्ष्यामि, &c. 3d Pret. असांक्षं, -क्षीस्, -क्षीत्; असांक्ष्व, असांक्तं, -क्तां; असांक्ष्म, असांक्त, असांक्षुस्. Bened. सज्यासं, &c. Cond. असंक्ष्यं, &c. *Passive,* Pres. सज्ये. *Causal,* Pres. सञ्जयामि; 3d Pret. अससञ्जं. *Des.* सिसंक्षामि, &c. *Freq.* सासज्ये, सासञ्ज्मि. *Participles,* Pres. सजत् or

---

* This root rejects its nasal in the conjugational tenses, and sometimes doubles the final *j* in those tenses (Pres. सज्जामि, सज्जसि, सज्जति, &c.). It is not, however, to be confounded with an uncommon root सज्ज् or सस्ज्, meaning 'to go,' 'to move,' which also belongs to the 1st c., and makes सज्जामि &c. in the present tense.

सञ्जत्; Pass. सज्यमान; Past pass. सक्त; Past indecl. सक्त्वा or संक्त्वा, -सज्य; Fut. pass. संक्तव्य, सञ्जनीय, संग्य or संज्य.

b. Root द्युत्. Inf. द्योतितुं 'to shine.' Átmane, and optionally Parasmai in 3d preterite. Pres. द्योते, &c. Pot. द्योतेय, &c. Imp. द्योतै, &c. 1st Pret. अद्योते, &c. 2d Pret. दिद्युते*, दिद्युतिषे, दिद्युते; दिद्युतिवहे, दिद्युताथे, दिद्युताते; दिद्युतिमहे, दिद्युतिध्वे or -ढ्वे, दिद्युतिरे. 1st Fut. द्योतिताहे, &c. 2d Fut. द्योतिष्ये, &c. 3d Pret. अद्योतिषि, अद्योतिष्ठास्, अद्योतिष्ट; अद्योतिष्वहि, -तिषाथां, -तिषातां; -तिष्महि, -तिध्वं, -तिषत. Par. अद्युतं, -तस्, -तत्; -ताव, -ततं, -ततां; -ताम, -तत, -तन्. Bened. द्योतिषीय. Cond. अद्योतिष्ये, &c. *Passive,* Pres. द्युत्ये; 3d Pret. 3d sing. अद्योति. *Causal,* Pres. द्योतयामि; 3d Pret. अदिद्युतं. *Des.* दिद्युतिषे or दिद्योतिषे. *Freq.* देद्युत्ये, देद्योत्मि or देद्योतीमि. *Participles,* Pres. द्योतमान; Past pass. द्युतित or द्योतित; Past indecl. द्युतित्वा or द्योतित्वा, -द्युत्य; Fut. pass. द्योतितव्य, द्योतनीय, द्योत्य.

598. Root वृत्. Inf. वर्तितुं or वर्त्तितुं (73) 'to be,' 'to exist.' Átmane, and optionally Parasmai in the 2d future, 3d preterite, and conditional, when it rejects *i.* Pres. वर्ते, &c. Pot. वर्तेय, &c. Imp. वर्तै, &c. 1st Pret. अवर्ते, &c. 2d Pret. ववृते, ववृतिषे, ववृते; ववृतिवहे, ववृताथे, ववृताते; ववृतिमहे, ववृतिध्वे or -ढ्वे, ववृतिरे. 1st Fut. वर्तिताहे, &c. 2d Fut. वर्तिष्ये or वर्त्स्यामि, &c. 3d Pret. अवर्तिषि, अवर्तिष्ठास्, अवर्तिष्ट; अवर्तिष्वहि, -तिषाथां, -तिषातां; -तिष्महि, -तिध्वं, -तिषत. Par. अवृतं, -तस्, -तत्; -ताव, -ततं, -ततां; -ताम, -तत, -तन्. Bened. वर्तिषीय, &c. Cond. अवर्तिष्ये or अवर्त्स्यं, &c. *Passive,* Pres. वृत्ये. *Causal,* Pres. वर्तयामि; 3d Pret. अवीवृतं or अववर्तं. *Des.* विवर्तिषे or विवृत्सामि. *Freq.* वरीवृत्ये, वरिवर्त्मि or वरिवृतीमि or वरीवृतीमि. *Participles,* Pres. वर्तमान; Past pass. वृत्त; Past indecl. वर्तित्वा or वृत्त्वा, -वृत्य; Fut. pass. वर्तितव्य, वर्तनीय, वृत्य.

599. Root वद्. Inf. वदितुं 'to speak.' Parasmai. Pres. वदामि, वदसि, &c. Pot. वदेयं, वदेस्, &c. Imp. वदानि, वद, &c. 1st Pret. अवदं, अवदस्, &c. 2d Pret. (375. *c*) उवाद, उवदिथ, उवाद; ऊदिव, ऊदथुस्, ऊदतुस्; ऊदिम, ऊद, ऊदुस्. 1st Fut. वदितास्मि, वदितासि, &c. 2d Fut. वदिष्यामि, वदिष्यसि, &c. 3d Pret. (431) अवादिषं, अवादीस्, अवादीत्; अवादिष्व, अवादिष्टं, अवादिष्टां; अवादिष्म, अवादिष्ट, अवादिषुस्. Bened. उद्यासं, उद्यास्, &c. Cond. अवदिष्यं, अवदिष्यस्, &c. *Passive,* Pres. उद्ये (471);

* The root द्युत् violates 331. *d.* by making its reduplicated syllable *di* for *du* in the 2d preterite, &c. Similarly, the reduplicated syllable of the frequentative is *de.* Páṇini VII. 4. 67.

3d Pret. 3d sing. अवादि. *Causal,* Pres. वादयामि; 3d Pret. अवीवदं. *Des.* विवदिषामि, -षे. *Freq.* वावद्ये, वावद्मि or वावदीमि. *Participles,* Pres. वदत्; Past pass. उदित (543); Past indecl. उदित्वा, -उद्य; Fut. pass. वदितव्य, वदनीय, वाद्य or उद्य.

a. Root सद् (270). Inf. सत्तुं 'to sink.' Parasmai. Pres. सीदामि, सीदसि, &c. Pot. सीदेयं, सीदेस्, &c Imp. सीदानि, सीद, &c. 1st Pret. असीदं, असीदस्, &c. 2d Pret. ससाद, सेदिथ (375. *a*) or ससत्थ, ससाद; सेदिव, सेदथुस्, सेदतुस्; सेदिम, सेद, सेदुस्. 1st Fut. सत्तास्मि, सत्तासि, &c. 2d Fut. सत्स्यामि, सत्स्यसि. 3d Pret. असदं (436, 437), असदस्, असदत्; असदाव, असदतं, असदतां; असदाम, असदत, असदन्. Bened. सद्यासं, सद्यास्, &c. Cond. असत्स्यं, असत्स्यस्, &c. *Passive,* Pres. सद्ये; 3d Pret. 3d sing. असादि. *Causal,* Pres. सादयामि; 3d Pret. असीषदं. *Des.* सिषत्सामि. *Freq.* सासद्ये, सासद्मि or सासदीमि. *Participles,* Pres. सीदत्; Past pass. सन्न (540); Past indecl. सत्त्वा, -सद्य; Fut. pass. सत्तव्य, सदनीय, साद्य.

600. Root एध्. Inf. एधितुं 'to increase,' 'to flourish.' Átmane. Pres. एधे, एधसे, &c. Pot. एधेय, एधेथास्, &c. Imp. एधै, एधस्व, &c. 1st Pret. ऐधे (260), ऐधथास्, &c. 2d Pret. (385) एधाञ्चक्रे, एधाञ्चकृषे, एधाञ्चक्रे; एधाञ्चकृवहे, एधाञ्चक्राथे, एधाञ्चक्राते; एधाञ्चकृमहे, एधाञ्चकृढ्वे, एधाञ्चक्रिरे. 1st Fut. एधिताहे, &c. 2d Fut. एधिष्ये, &c. 3d Pret. ऐधिषि (430, 260. *b*), ऐधिष्ठास्, ऐधिष्ट; ऐधिष्वहि, ऐधिषाथां, ऐधिषातां; ऐधिष्महि, ऐधिढ्वं, ऐधिषत. Bened. एधिषीय, &c. Cond. ऐधिष्ये, &c. (260. *b*). *Passive,* एध्ये, &c.; 3d Pret. 3d sing. ऐधि. *Causal,* Pres. एधयामि; 3d Pret. ऐदिधं (494). *Des.* एदिधिषे (500. *b*). *Participles,* Pres. एधमान; Past pass. एधित; Past indecl. एधित्वा, -एध्य; Fut. pass. एधितव्य, एधनीय, एध्य.

601. Root लभ्. Inf. लब्धुं 'to take.' Átmane. Pres. लभे, लभसे, लभते; लभावहे, लभेथे, लभेते; लभामहे, लभध्वे, लभन्ते. Pot. लभेय, लभेथास्, लभेत; लभेवहि, लभेयाथां, लभेयातां; लभेमहि, लभेध्वं, लभेरन्. Imp. लभै, लभस्व, लभतां; लभावहै, लभेथां, लभेतां; लभामहै, लभध्वं, लभन्तां. 1st Pret. अलभे, अलभथास्, अलभत; अलभावहि, अलभेथां, अलभेतां; अलभामहि, अलभध्वं, अलभन्त. 2d Pret. लेभे (375. *a*), लेभिषे, लेभे; लेभिवहे, लेभाथे, लेभाते; लेभिमहे, लेभिध्वे, लेभिरे. 1st Fut. लब्धाहे (408), लब्धासे, लब्धा; लब्धास्वहे, लब्धासाथे, लब्धारौ; लब्धास्महे, लब्धाध्वे, लब्धारस्. 2d Fut. लप्स्ये (299), लप्स्यसे, लप्स्यते; लप्स्यावहे, लप्स्येथे, लप्स्येते; लप्स्यामहे, लप्स्यध्वे, लप्स्यन्ते. 3d Pret. अलप्सि (420, 299), अलब्धास् (298), अलब्ध; अलप्स्वहि, अलप्साथां, अलप्सातां; अलप्स्महि, अलब्ध्वं, अलप्सत. Bened. लप्सीय, लप्सीष्ठास्, लप्सीष्ट; लप्सीवहि, लप्सीयास्थां, लप्सीयास्तां; लप्सीमहि, लप्सीध्वं, लप्सीरन्. Cond. अलप्स्ये, अलप्स्यथास्, अलप्स्यत; अलप्स्यावहि, अलप्स्येथां, अलप्स्येतां; अलप्स्या-

महि, अलप्स्यध्वं, अलप्स्यन्त. *Passive*, Pres. लभ्ये; 3d Pret. अलम्भि, अलब्धास्, अलाभि (475) or अलम्भि, &c. *Causal*, Pres. लम्भयामि, &c.; 3d Pret. अललम्भं. *Des.* लिप्से (503). *Freq.* लालभ्ये. *Participles*, Pres. लभमान; Past pass. लब्ध; Past indecl. लब्ध्वा, -लभ्य; Fut. pass. लब्धव्य, लभनीय, लभ्य.

a. In the same manner may be conjugated रभ् (with prep. आ *á*), आरब्धुं 'to begin.'

602. Root गम् (270). Inf. गन्तुं 'to go.' Parasmai. Pres. गच्छामि, गच्छसि, गच्छति; गच्छावस्, गच्छथस्, गच्छतस्; गच्छामस्, गच्छथ, गच्छन्ति. Pot. गच्छेयं, गच्छेस्, &c. Imp. गच्छानि, गच्छ, &c. 1st Pret. अगच्छं, अगच्छस्, &c. 2d Pret. (375) जगाम, जगमिथ or जगन्थ, जगाम; जग्मिव (376), जग्मथुस्, जग्मतुस्; जग्मिम, जग्म, जग्मुस्. 1st Fut. गन्तास्मि, गन्तासि, &c. 2d Fut. गमिष्यामि, गमिष्यसि, गमिष्यति; गमिष्यावस्, गमिष्यथस्, गमिष्यतस्; गमिष्यामस्, गमिष्यथ, गमिष्यन्ति. 3d Pret. (436) अगमं, अगमस्, अगमत्; अगमाव, अगमतं, अगमतां; अगमाम, अगमत, अगमन्. Bened. गम्यासं, गम्यास्, &c. Cond. अगमिष्यं, अगमिष्यस्, &c. *Passive*, Pres. गम्ये; 3d Pret. 3d sing. अगामि. *Causal*, Pres. गमयामि; 3d Pret. अजीगमं. *Des.* जिगमिषामि. *Freq.* जङ्गम्ये, जङ्गन्मि or जङ्गमीमि; see 709. *Participles*, Pres. गच्छत्; Past pass. गत; Past indecl. गत्वा, -गम्य, -गत्य (563. *a*, 560); Fut. pass. गन्तव्य, गमनीय, गम्य.

603. Root जीव्. Inf. जीवितुं 'to live.' Parasmai. Pres. जीवामि, जीवसि, &c. Pot. जीवेयं, जीवेस्, &c. Imp. जीवानि, जीव, &c. 1st Pret. अजीवं, अजीवस्, &c. 2d Pret. जिजीव, जिजीविथ, जिजीव; जिजीविव (28. *b*), जिजीवथुस्, जिजीवतुस्; जिजीविम, जिजीव, जजीवुस्. 1st Fut. जीवितास्मि, &c. 2d Fut. जीविष्यामि, &c. 3d Pret. अजीविषं, अजीवीस्, अजीवीत्; अजीविष्व, अजीविष्टं, अजीविष्टां; अजीविष्म, अजीविष्ट, अजीविषुस्. Bened. जीव्यासं, &c. Cond. अजीविष्यं, &c. *Passive*, Pres. जीव्ये; 3d Pret. 3d sing. अजीवि. *Causal*, Pres. जीवयामि; 3d Pret. अजिजीवं or अजीजिवं. *Des.* जिजीविषामि. *Freq.* जेजीव्ये. *Participles*, Pres. जीवत्; Past pass. जीवित; Past indecl. जीवित्वा, -जीव्य; Fut. pass. जीवितव्य, जीवनीय, जीव्य.

604. Root दृश् (270). Inf. द्रष्टुं 'to see.' Parasmai. Pres. पश्यामि, पश्यसि, पश्यति; पश्यावस्, पश्यथस्, पश्यतस्; पश्यामस्, पश्यथ, पश्यन्ति. Pot. पश्येयं, पश्येस्, पश्येत्; पश्येव, &c. Imp. पश्यानि, पश्य, पश्यतु; पश्याव, &c. 1st Pret. अपश्यं, अपश्यस्, अपश्यत्; अपश्याव, &c. 2d Pret. ददर्श, ददर्शिथ or दद्रष्ठ (368. *a*. *b*, 388. *c*), ददर्श; ददृशिव, ददृशथुस्, ददृशतुस्; ददृशिम, ददृश, ददृशुस्. 1st Fut. द्रष्टास्मि, द्रष्टासि, &c. 2d Fut. द्रक्ष्यामि, द्रक्ष्यसि, &c. 3d Pret. (436) अदर्शं, अदर्शस्, अदर्शत्; अदर्शाव, अदर्शतं, अदर्शतां; अदर्शाम, अदर्शत, अदर्शन्. Or अद्राक्षं (420, 388. *c*),

अद्राक्षीस्, अद्राक्षीत्; अद्राक्ष्व, अद्राष्टं, अद्राष्टां; अद्राक्ष्म, अद्राष्ट, अद्राक्षुस्. Bened. दृश्यासं, दृश्यास्, &c. Cond. अद्रक्ष्यं, अद्रक्ष्यस्, &c. *Passive*, Pres. दृश्ये; 3d Pret. 3d sing. अदर्शि. *Causal*, Pres. दर्शयामि; 3d Pret. अदीदृशं or अददर्शं; see 703. *Des.* दिदृक्षे. *Freq.* दरिदृश्ये or दरी-, दरिदृशीमि or दर्दर्श्मि. *Participles*, Pres. पश्यत्; Past pass. दृष्ट; Past indecl. दृष्ट्वा, -दृश्य; Fut. pass. द्रष्टव्य, दर्शनीय, दृश्य.

605. Root ईक्ष्. Inf. ईक्षितुं 'to see.' Átmane. Pres. ईक्षे, &c. Pot. ईक्षेय, &c. Imp. ईक्षै, &c. 1st Pret. ऐक्षे, &c. (260. *a*). 2d Pret. ईक्षाञ्चक्रे, &c. (385, and compare एध् at 600). 1st Fut. ईक्षिताहे, &c. 2d Fut. ईक्षिष्ये, &c. 3d Pret. ऐक्षिषि (260. *b*), ऐक्षिष्ठास्, ऐक्षिष्ट; ऐक्षिष्वहि, ऐक्षिषाथां, ऐक्षिषातां; ऐक्षिष्महि, ऐक्षिढ्वं, ऐक्षिषत. Bened. ईक्षिषीय, &c. Cond. ऐक्षिष्ये, &c. *Passive*, ईक्ष्ये, &c.; 3d Pret. 3d sing. ऐक्षि. *Causal*, Pres. ईक्षयामि; 3d Pret. ऐचिक्षं (494). *Des.* ईचिक्षिषे (500. *b*). *Participles*, Pres. ईक्षमाण; Past pass. ईक्षित; Past indecl. ईक्षित्वा, -ईक्ष्य; Fut. pass. ईक्षितव्य, ईक्षणीय, ईक्ष्य.

606. Root कृष्*. Inf. कर्ष्टुं or क्रष्टुं 'to draw,' 'to drag.' Parasmai and Átmane. Pres. कर्षामि, &c. Átm. कर्षे. Pot. कर्षेयं &c., कर्षेय &c. Imp. कर्षाणि &c., कर्षै &c. 1st Pret. अकर्षं, &c. Átm. अकर्षे, &c. 2d Pret. चकर्ष, चकर्षिथ, चकर्ष; चकृषिव, चकृषथुस्, चकृषतुस्; चकृषिम, चकृष, चकृषुस्. Átm. चकृषे, चकृषिषे, चकृषे; चकृषिवहे, चकृषाथे, चकृषाते; चकृषिमहे, चकृषिढ्वे, चकृषिरे. 1st Fut. कर्ष्टास्मि or क्रष्टास्मि, &c. Átm. कर्ष्टाहे &c. or क्रष्टाहे &c. 2d Fut. कर्क्ष्यामि or क्रक्ष्यामि, &c. Átm. कर्क्ष्ये or क्रक्ष्ये, &c. 3d Pret. अकार्क्षं, अकार्क्षीस्, अकार्क्षीत्; अकार्क्ष्व, अकार्ष्टं, अकार्ष्टां; अकार्क्ष्म, अकार्ष्ट, अकार्क्षुस्. Or अक्राक्षं, अक्राक्षीस्, &c. Or अकृक्षं, अकृक्षस्, अकृक्षत्; अकृक्षाव, अकृक्षतं, अकृक्षतां; अकृक्षाम, अकृक्षत, अकृक्षन्. Átm. अकृक्षि, अकृक्षथास् or अकृष्ठास्, अकृक्षत or अकृष्ट; अकृक्षावहि or अकृक्ष्वहि, अकृक्षाथां, अकृक्षातां; अकृक्षामहि or अकृक्ष्महि, अकृक्षध्वं or अकृड्ढ्वं, अकृक्षन्त or अकृक्षत. Bened. कृष्यासं, &c. Átm. कृक्षीय, &c. Cond. अकर्क्ष्यं or अक्रक्ष्यं, &c. Átm. अकर्क्ष्ये or अक्रक्ष्ये, &c. *Passive*, Pres. कृष्ये; 3d Pret. 3d sing. अकर्षि. *Causal*, Pres. कर्षयामि; 3d Pret. अचकर्षं or अचीकृषं. *Des.* चिकृक्षामि, -क्षे. *Freq.* चरीकृष्ये, चरीकर्ष्मि or चरीक्रष्मि. *Participles*, Pres. कर्षत्; Past pass. कृष्ट; Past indecl. कृष्ट्वा, -कृष्य; Fut. pass. कर्ष्टव्य or क्रष्टव्य, कर्षणीय, कृष्य.

607. Root वस्. Inf. वस्तुं 'to dwell.' Parasmai. Pres. वसामि, वससि, &c. Pot. वसेयं, वसेम्, &c. Imp. वसानि, वस, &c. 1st Pret. अवसं, अवसस्, &c. 2d Pret. उवास, उवसिथ or उवस्थ, उवास; ऊषिव,

---

* This root is also conjugated in the 6th conj. Pres. कृषामि, &c.; Pot. कृषेयं, &c.

ऊषथुस्, ऊषतुस्; ऊषिम, ऊष, ऊषुस्. 1st Fut. वस्तास्मि, वस्तासि, &c. 2d Fut. वत्स्यामि, वत्स्यसि, &c. (304. *a*). 3d Pret. अवात्सं (304. *a*, 425), अवात्सीस्, अवात्सीत्; अवात्स्व, अवात्तं, अवात्तां; अवात्स्म, अवात्त, अवात्सुस्. Bened. उष्यासं, उष्यास्, &c. Cond. अवत्स्यं (304. *a*), अवत्स्यस्, &c. *Passive,* Pres. उष्ये (471); 3d Pret. 3d sing. अवासि. *Causal,* Pres. वासयामि, -ये; 3d Pret. अवीवसं. *Des.* विवत्सामि (304. *a*). *Freq.* वावस्ये, वावस्मि or वावसीमि. *Participles,* Pres. वसत्; Past pass. उषित; Past indecl. उषित्वा, -उष्य (565); Fut. pass. वस्तव्य, वसनीय, वास्य.

608. Root अर्ह्. Inf. अर्हितुं 'to deserve.' Parasmai. Pres. अर्हामि, &c. Pot. अर्हेयं, &c. Imp. अर्हाणि, &c. (58). 1st Pret. आर्हं, &c. (260). 2d Pret. (371) आनर्ह, आनर्हिथ, आनर्ह; आनर्हिव, आनर्हथुस्, आनर्हतुस्; आनर्हिम, आनर्ह, आनर्हुस्. 1st Fut. अर्हितास्मि, &c. 2d Fut. अर्हिष्यामि, &c. 3d Pret. आर्हिषं, आर्हीस्, आर्हीत्; आर्हिष्व, आर्हिष्टं, आर्हिष्टां; आर्हिष्म, आर्हिष्ट, आर्हिषुस्. Bened. अर्ह्यासं, &c. Cond. आर्हिष्यं, &c. *Passive,* अर्ह्ये, &c.; 3d Pret. 3d sing. आर्हि. *Causal,* Pres. अर्हयामि, -ये; 3d Pret. आर्जिहं (494). *Des.* अर्जिहिषामि, &c. (500. *b*). *Participles,* Pres. अर्हत्; Past pass. अर्हित; Past indecl. अर्हित्वा, -अर्ह्य; Fut. pass. अर्हितव्य, अर्हणीय, अर्ह्य.

609. Root गुह् (271). Inf. गूहितुं or गोढुं 'to hide.' Parasmai and Ātmane. Pres. गूहामि, &c. Ātm. गूहे, &c. Pot. गूहेयं &c., गूहेय &c. Imp. गूहानि &c., गूहै &c. 1st Pret. अगूहं &c., अगूहे &c. 2d Pret. जुगूह (28. *b*), जुगूहिथ or जुगोढ (305. *a*), जुगूह; जुगुहिव or जुगुह्व (see note to 368. *b*), जुगुहथुस्, जुगुहतुस्; जुगुहिम or जुगुह्म, जुगुह, जुगुहुस्. Ātm. जुगुहे, जुगुहिषे, जुगुहे, &c. 1st Fut. (413) गूहितास्मि or गोढास्मि, &c. (305. *a*). Ātm. गूहिताहे or गोढाहे, &c. 2d Fut. (413) गूहिष्यामि or घोक्ष्यामि, &c. Ātm. गूहिष्ये or घोक्ष्ये, &c. 3d Pret. अगूहिषं, अगूहीस्, अगूहीत्; अगूहिष्व, अगूहिष्टं, अगूहिष्टां; अगूहिष्म, अगूहिष्ट, अगूहिषुस्. Or अघुक्षं (306. *a*), अघुक्षस्, अघुक्षत्; अघुक्षाव, अघुक्षतं, अघुक्षतां; अघुक्षाम, अघुक्षत, अघुक्षन्. Ātm. अगूहिषि, अगूहिष्ठास्, अगूहिष्ट, &c. Or अघुक्षि, अगूढास् (305. *a*), अगूढ; अघुक्ष्वहि, अघुक्षाथां, अघुक्षातां; अघुक्ष्महि, अघूढ्वं (306. *c. d*), अघुक्षत. Or अघुक्षि (439), अघुक्षथास्, अघुक्षत; अघुक्षावहि, अघुक्षाथां, अघुक्षातां; अघुक्षामहि, अघुक्षध्वं, अघुक्षन्त. Bened. गुह्यासं, &c. Ātm. गूहिषीय &c. or घुक्षीय &c. (306. *a*). Cond. अगूहिष्यं or अघोक्ष्यं &c., अगूहिष्ये or अघोक्ष्ये &c. *Passive,* Pres. गुह्ये, &c.; 3d Pret. 3d sing. अगूहि. *Causal,* Pres. गूहयामि; 3d Pret. अजूगुहं. *Des.* जुघुक्षामि, -क्षे. *Freq.* जोगुह्ये, जोगोह्मि (3d sing. जोगोढि 305. *a*) or जोगुहीमि. *Participles,* Pres. गूहत्; Past pass. गूढ (305. *a*); Past indecl. गूहित्वा or गूढ्वा or गुहित्वा, -गुह्य; Fut. pass. गूहितव्य or गोढव्य, गूहनीय, गुह्य or गोह्य.

610. Root दह्. Inf. दग्धुं 'to burn.' Parasmai. Pres. दहामि, दहसि, &c. Pot. दहेयं, दहेस्, &c. Imp. दहानि, दह, &c. 1st Pret. अदहं, अदहस्, &c. 2d Pret. ददाह, देहिथ (375. *a*) or ददग्ध (305), ददाह; देहिव, देहथुस्, देहतुस्; देहिम, देह, देहुस्. 1st Fut. दग्धास्मि, दग्धासि, &c. (305). 2d Fut. धक्ष्यामि, धक्ष्यसि, &c. (306. *a*). 3d Pret. अधाक्षं (423), अधाक्षीस्, अधाक्षीत्; अधाक्ष्व, अदाग्धं, अदाग्धां; अधाक्ष्म, अदाग्ध, अधाक्षुस्. Bened. दह्यासं, दह्यास्, &c. Cond. अधक्ष्यं, अधक्ष्यस् (306. *a*). *Passive*, Pres. दह्ये, &c.; 3d Pret. 3d sing. अदाहि. *Causal*, Pres. दाहयामि, -ये; 3d Pret. अदीदहं. *Des.* दिधक्षामि (306. *a*). *Freq.* दंदह्ये, दंदह्मि or दंदहीमि; 3d sing. दंदग्धि. *Participles*, Pres. दहत्; Past pass. दग्ध; Past indecl. दग्ध्वा, -दह्य; Fut. pass. दग्धव्य, दहनीय, दाह्य.

611. Root वह्. Inf. वोढुं 'to carry.' Parasmai and A'tmane. Pres. वहामि, वहसि, &c. A'tm. वहे, &c. Pot. वहेयं, वहेस्, &c. Imp. वहानि, वह, &c. A'tm. वहै, &c. 1st Pret. अवहं, अवहस्, &c. A'tm. अवहे, &c. 2d Pret. (375. *c*) उवाह, उवहिथ or उवोढ (375. *c*), उवाह; ऊहिव, ऊहथुस्, ऊहतुस्; ऊहिम, ऊह, ऊहुस्. A'tm. ऊहे, ऊहिषे, ऊहे; ऊहिवहे, ऊहाथे, ऊहाते; ऊहिमहे, ऊहिढ्वे, ऊहिरे. 1st Fut. वोढास्मि, वोढासि, &c. A'tm. वोढाहे, &c. 2d Fut. वक्ष्यामि, वक्ष्यसि, &c. A'tm. वक्ष्ये, वक्ष्यसे, &c. 3d Pret. (424) अवाक्षं, अवाक्षीस्, अवाक्षीत्; अवाक्ष्व, अवोढं, अवोढां; अवाक्ष्म, अवोढ, अवाक्षुस्. A'tm. अवक्षि, अवोढास् (424), अवोढ; अवक्ष्वहि, अवक्षाथां, अवक्षातां; अवक्ष्महि, अवोढ्वं, अवक्षत. Bened. उह्यासं, उह्यास्, &c. A'tm. वक्षीय, &c. Cond. अवक्ष्यं, अवक्ष्यस्, &c. A'tm. अवक्ष्ये, &c. *Passive*, Pres. (471) उह्ये; 1st Pret. औह्ये (260. *a*); 3d Pret. 3d sing. अवाहि. *Causal*, Pres. वाहयामि, -ये; 3d Pret. अवीवहं. *Des.* विवक्षामि, -क्षे. *Freq.* वावह्ये, वावह्मि; 3d sing. वावोढि (compare 424). *Participles*, Pres. वहत्; A'tm. वहमान; Pass. उह्यमान; Past pass. ऊढ; Past indecl. ऊढ्वा, -उह्य (565); Fut. pass. वोढव्य, वहनीय, वाह्य.

a. The root सह्, Inf. सोढुं 'to bear,' is A'tmane only, and follows *vah* in making सोढाहे &c. in 1st Fut.: but in this tense it optionally, and in the other non-conjugational tenses it necessarily inserts *i*; thus, 1st Fut. सहिताहे; 2d Fut. सहिष्ये; 3d Pret. असहिषि; Bened. सहिषीय; Cond. असहिष्ये. The 2d Pret. is सेहे (375. *a*), सेहिषे, सेहे; सेहिवहे, &c. The other tenses are like the A'tmane of *vah*; thus, Pres. सहे, &c.

EXAMPLES OF PRIMITIVE VERBS OF THE FOURTH CONJUGATION, EXPLAINED AT 272.

612. Root मुह् *muh*. Infin. मोहितुं *mohitum*, 'to be troubled.'

PARASMAI-PADA. *Present tense*, 'I am troubled.'

मुह्यामि *muhyámi*	मुह्यावस् *muhyávas*	मुह्यामस् *muhyámas*
मुह्यसि *muhyasi*	मुह्यथस् *muhyathas*	मुह्यथ *muhyatha*
मुह्यति *muhyati*	मुह्यतस् *muhyatas*	मुह्यन्ति *muhyanti*

Potential, 'I may be troubled.'

मुह्येयं *muhyeyam*	मुह्येव *muhyeva*	मुह्येम *muhyema*
मुह्येस् *muhyes*	मुह्येतं *muhyetam*	मुह्येत *muhyeta*
मुह्येत् *muhyet*	मुह्येतां *muhyetám*	मुह्येयुस् *muhyeyus*

Imperative, 'Let me be troubled.'

मुह्यानि *muhyáni*	मुह्याव *muhyáva*	मुह्याम *muhyáma*
मुह्य *muhya*	मुह्यतं *muhyatam*	मुह्यत *muhyata*
मुह्यतु *muhyatu*	मुह्यतां *muhyatám*	मुह्यन्तु *muhyantu*

First preterite, 'I was troubled.'

अमुह्यं *amuhyam*	अमुह्याव *amuhyáva*	अमुह्याम *amuhyáma*
अमुह्यस् *amuhyas*	अमुह्यतं *amuhyatam*	अमुह्यत *amuhyata*
अमुह्यत् *amuhyat*	अमुह्यतां *amuhyatám*	अमुह्यन् *amuhyan*

Second preterite, 'I became troubled.'

मुमोह *mumoha*	मुमुहिव *mumuhiva*	मुमुहिम *mumuhima*
मुमोहिथ *mumohitha* *	मुमुहथुस् *mumuhathus*	मुमुह *mumuha*
मुमोह *mumoha*	मुमुहतुस् *mumuhatus*	मुमुहुस् *mumuhus*

First future †, 'I will be troubled.'

मोहितास्मि *mohitásmi*	मोहितास्वस् *mohitáswas*	मोहितास्मस् *mohitásmas*
मोहितासि *mohitási*	मोहितास्थस् *mohitásthas*	मोहितास्थ *mohitástha*
मोहिता *mohitá*	मोहितारौ *mohitárau*	मोहितारस् *mohitáras*

Second future †, 'I shall be troubled.'

मोहिष्यामि *mohishyámi*	मोहिष्यावस् *mohishyávas*	मोहिष्यामस् *mohishyámas*
मोहिष्यसि *mohishyasi*	मोहिष्यथस् *mohishyathas*	मोहिष्यथ *mohishyatha*
मोहिष्यति *mohishyati*	मोहिष्यतस् *mohishyatas*	मोहिष्यन्ति *mohishyanti*

* Or मुमोढ (305. *a*) or मुमोग्ध (305).

† The 1st and 2d futures may optionally reject the inserted *i*; see under 412.

Third preterite (435), 'I became troubled.'

अमुहं *amuham*	अमुहाव *amuháva*	अमुहाम *amuháma*
अमुहस् *amuhas*	अमुहतं *amuhatam*	अमुहत *amuhata*
अमुहत् *amuhat*	अमुहतां *amuhatám*	अमुहन् *amuhan*

Benedictive, 'May I be troubled.'

मुह्यासं *muhyásam*	मुह्यास्व *muhyáswa*	मुह्यास्म *muhyásma*
मुह्यास् *muhyás*	मुह्यास्तं *muhyástam*	मुह्यास्त *muhyásta*
मुह्यात् *muhyát*	मुह्यास्तां *muhyástám*	मुह्यासुस् *muhyásus*

Conditional, 'I should be troubled.'

अमोहिष्यं *amohishyam*	अमोहिष्याव *amohishyáva*	अमोहिष्याम *amohishyáma*
अमोहिष्यस् *amohishyas*	अमोहिष्यतं *amohishyatam*	अमोहिष्यत *amohishyata*
अमोहिष्यत् *amohishyat*	अमोहिष्यतां *amohishyatám*	अमोहिष्यन् *amohishyan*

Passive, Pres. मुह्ये; 3d Pret. 3d sing. अमोहि. *Causal,* Pres. मोहयामि; 3d Pret. अमूमुहं. *Des.* मुमोहिषामि or मुमुहिषामि or मुमुक्षामि. *Freq.* मोमुह्ये, मोमोह्मि; 3d sing. मोमोढि or मोमोग्धि (305). *Participles,* Pres. मुह्यत्; Past pass. मूढ (305) or मुग्ध; Past indecl. मोहित्वा or मुहित्वा or मुग्ध्वा or मूढ्वा, -मुह्य; Fut. pass. मोहितव्य or मोग्धव्य, मोहनीय, मोह्य.

EXAMPLES OF OTHER VERBS OF THE FOURTH CONJUGATION IN THE ORDER OF THEIR FINAL LETTERS.

613. Root सो (276. *a*). Inf. सातुं 'to destroy' (with prepositions *vi* and *ava*, 'to determine,' 'to strive'). Parasmai. Pres. स्यामि, &c. Pot. स्येयं, &c. Imp. स्यानि, &c. 1st Pret. अस्यं, &c. 2d Pret. (374) ससौ, ससिथ or ससाथ, ससौ; ससिव, ससथुस्, ससतुस्; ससिम, सस, ससुस्. 1st Fut. सातास्मि, &c. 2d Fut. सास्यामि, &c. 3d Pret. (438. *b*) असां, असास्, असात्; असाव, असातं, असातां; असाम, असात, असुस्. Or असासिषं (433), असासीस्, असासीत्; असासिष्व, असासिष्टं, असासिष्टां; असासिष्म, असासिष्ट, असासिषुस्. Bened. सेयासं, &c. Cond. असास्यं, &c. *Passive,* Pres. सीये; 3d Pret. 3d sing. असायि. *Causal,* साययामि; 3d Pret. असीषयं. *Des.* सिषासामि. *Freq.* सेषीये, सासेमि, सासामि. *Participles,* Pres. स्यत्; Past pass. सित; Past indecl. सित्वा, -साय; Fut. pass. सातव्य, सानीय, सेय.

614. Root बुध्. Inf. बोद्धुं 'to know'*. Átmane. Pres. बुध्ये, &c. Pot. बुध्येय, &c. Imp. बुध्यै, &c. 1st Pret. अबुध्ये, &c. 2d Pret. बुबुधे;

* This verb is also of the 1st conjugation. See the tables at 583.

see the tables at 583. 1st Fut. बोद्धाहे, &c. 2d Fut. भोत्स्ये, &c. (299. *a*). 3d Pret. (420, 299. *a*) अभुत्सि, अबुद्धास्, अबुद्ध or अबोधि (434); अभुत्स्वहि, अभुत्साथां, अभुत्सातां; अभुत्स्महि, अबुद्धं, अभुत्सत. Bened. भुत्सीय, &c. Cond. अभोत्स्ये, &c. For the other forms, see बुध् at 583.

615. Root व्यध् (277). Inf. व्यद्धुं 'to pierce.' Parasmai. Pres. विध्यामि, &c. Pot. विध्येयं, &c. Imp. विध्यानि, &c. 1st Pret. अविध्यं, &c. 2d Pret. (383) विव्याध, विव्यधिथ or विव्यद्ध, विव्याध; विविधिव, विविधथुस्, विविधतुस्; विविधिम, विविध, विविधुस्. 1st Fut. व्यद्धास्मि, &c. (298). 2d Fut. व्यत्स्यामि, &c. (299). 3d Pret. (420) अव्यात्सं, अव्यात्सीस्, अव्यात्सीत्; अव्यात्स्व, अव्याद्धं (419), अव्याद्धां; अव्यात्स्म, अव्याद्ध, अव्यात्सुस्. Bened. विध्यासं, &c. Cond. अव्यत्स्यं. *Passive,* Pres. विध्ये, &c.; 3d Pret. 3d sing. अव्याधि. *Causal,* व्याधयामि; 3d Pret. अविव्यधं. *Des.* विव्यत्सामि. *Freq.* वेविध्ये, वाव्यध्मि. *Participles,* Pres. विध्यत्; Past pass. विद्ध; Past indecl. विद्ध्वा, -विध्य; Fut. pass. व्यद्धव्य, व्यधनीय, वेध्य or व्याध्य.

616. Root सिध् (273). Inf. सेद्धुं 'to succeed.' Parasmai. Pres. सिध्यामि, &c. Pot. सिध्येयं, &c. Imp. सिध्यानि, &c. 1st Pret. असिध्यं, &c. 2d Pret. सिषेध, सिषेधिथ or सिषेद्ध, सिषेध; सिषिधिव or सिषिध्व (see note to 368. *b*), सिषिधथुस्, सिषिधतुस्; सिषिधिम or सिषिध्म, सिषिध, सिषिधुस्. 1st Fut. सेद्धास्मि, &c. (298). 2d Fut. सेत्स्यामि, &c. (299). 3d Pret. *असिधं, असिधस्, असिधत्; असिधाव, असिधतं, असिधतां; असिधाम, असिधत, असिधन्. Bened. सिध्यासं, &c. Cond. असेत्स्यं, &c. *Passive,* सिध्ये, &c.; 3d Pret. 3d sing. असेधि. *Causal,* Pres. सेधयामि or साधयामि; 3d Pret. असीषिधं. *Des.* सिषित्सामि. *Freq.* सेषिध्ये, सेषेध्मि. *Participles,* Pres. सिध्यत्; Past pass. सिद्ध; Past indecl. सिद्ध्वा or सेधित्वा or सिधित्वा, -सिध्य; Fut. pass. सेद्धव्य, सेधनीय, सेध्य.

617. Root मन् †. Inf. मन्तुं 'to think,' 'to imagine.' Átmane. Pres. मन्ये, &c. Pot. मन्येय, &c. Imp. मन्यै, &c. 1st Pret. अमन्ये, &c. 2d Pret. मेने (375. *a*), मेनिषे, मेने; मेनिवहे, मेनाथे, मेनाते; मेनिमहे, मेनिध्वे, मेनिरे. 1st Fut. मन्ताहे. 2d Fut. मंस्ये, &c. 3d Pret. (418) † अमंसि, अमंस्थास्, अमंस्त; अमंस्वहि, अमंसाथां, अमंसातां; अमंस्महि, अमन्ध्वं, अमंसत. Bened. मंसीय, &c. Cond. अमंस्ये. *Passive,* Pres. मन्ये; 3d Pret. 3d sing. अमानि. *Causal,* Pres. मानयामि; 3d Pret. अमीमनं. *Des.* मिमंसे or मीमांसे or मिमनिषे. *Freq.* मन्मन्ये, मन्मन्मि. *Participles,* Pres. मन्यमान;

* When सिध् is of the 1st c., it makes its 3d preterite असेधिषं &c. or असैत्सं &c.

† The root मन् is rarely conjugated in the 8th c. Átmane (see 684), when the 3d preterite is अमनिषि, अमनिष्ठास् or अमथास्, अमनिष्ट or अमत, &c. See 426. *b*.

Past pass. मत; Past indecl. मत्वा or मनित्वा, -मत्य; Fut. pass. मन्तव्य, मननीय, मान्य.

a. The root जन्, Inf. जनितुं 'to be born,' makes Pres. जाये, &c.; Pot. जायेय, &c.; Imp. जायै, &c.; 1st Pret. अजाये, &c. But these may be regarded as coming from the Passive of *jan*, 3d conj. See 667.

618. Root तृप्. Inf. तर्प्तुं or त्रप्तुं or तर्पितुं 'to be satisfied.' Parasmai. Pres. तृप्यामि, &c. Pot. तृप्येयं, &c. Imp. तृप्याणि, &c. 1st Pret. अतृप्यं, &c. 2d Pret. ततर्प, ततर्पिथ or ततर्प्थ or तत्रप्थ, ततर्प; ततृपिव or ततृप्व, ततृपथुस्, ततृपतुस्; ततृपिम or ततृप्म, ततृप, ततृपुस्. 1st Fut. (388. *c*) तर्प्तास्मि or त्रप्तास्मि or तर्पितास्मि, &c. 2d Fut. तर्प्स्यामि or त्रप्स्यामि or तर्पिष्यामि, &c. 3d Pret. (420) अतार्प्सं, अतार्प्सीस्, अतार्प्सीत्; अतार्प्स्व, अतार्प्तं, अतार्प्तां; अतार्प्स्म, अतार्प्त, अतार्प्सुस्. Or अत्राप्सं, अत्राप्सीस्, अत्राप्सीत् (388. *c*), &c. Or अतर्पिषं, अतर्पीस्, अतर्पीत्, &c. Or अतृपं, अतृपस्, अतृपत्; अतृपाव, अतृपतं, अतृपतां; अतृपाम, अतृपत, अतृपन्. Bened. तृप्यासं, &c. Cond. अतर्प्स्यं or अत्रप्स्यं or अतर्पिष्यं, &c. *Passive,* Pres. तृप्ये, &c.; 3d Pret. 3d sing. अतर्पि. *Causal,* Pres. तर्पयामि; 3d Pret. अतीतृपं or अततर्पं. *Des.* तितृप्सामि or तित्रप्सामि or तितर्पिषामि. *Freq.* तरीतृप्ये, तरीतर्प्मि or तरीत्रप्मि. *Participles,* Pres. तृप्यत्; Past pass. तृप्त; Past indecl. तृप्त्वा, -तृप्य; Fut. pass. तर्प्तव्य, तर्पणीय, तृप्य.

619. Root शम् (275). Inf. शमितुं 'to be appeased.' Parasmai. Pres. शाम्यामि, &c. Pot. शाम्येयं, &c. Imp. शाम्यानि, &c. 1st Pret. अशाम्यं, &c. 2d Pret. शशाम, शेमिथ (375. *a*), शशाम; शेमिव, शेमथुस्, शेमतुस्; शेमिम, शेम, शेमुस्. 1st Fut. शमितास्मि, &c. 2d Fut. शमिष्यामि, &c. 3d Pret. अशमं, अशमस्, अशमत्; अशमाव, अशमतं, अशमतां; अशमाम, अशमत, अशमन्. Or अशमिषं, अशमीस्, अशमीत्; अशमिष्व, &c. Bened. शम्यासं, &c. Cond. अशमिष्यं, &c. *Passive,* Pres. शम्ये, &c.; 3d Pret. 3d sing. अशमि. *Causal,* Pres. शमयामि; 3d Pret. अशीशमं, &c. *Des.* शिशमिषामि. *Freq.* शंशम्ये, शंशन्मि; 3d sing. शंशन्ति. *Participles,* Pres. शाम्यत्; Past pass. शान्त; Past indecl. शान्त्वा or शमित्वा, -शम्य; Fut. pass. शमितव्य, शमनीय, शम्य.

620. Root नश्. Inf. नशितुं or नंष्टुं 'to perish.' Parasmai. Pres. नश्यामि, &c. Pot. नश्येयं, &c. Imp. नश्यानि, &c. 1st Pret. अनश्यं, &c. 2d Pret. (375. *a*) ननाश or ननश, नेशिथ or ननंष्ठ (388. *d*, 375. *a*), ननाश; नेशिव or नेश्व, नेशथुस्, नेशतुस्; नेशिम, नेश, नेशुस्. 1st Fut. नशितास्मि or नंष्टास्मि (388. *d*), &c. 2d Fut. नशिष्यामि or नंक्ष्यामि, &c. 3d Pret. (436) अनशं, अनशस्, अनशत्; अनशाव, अनशतं, अनशतां; अनशाम, अनशत, अनशन्. Or अनेशं, &c. (436, 441). Bened. नश्यासं, &c. Cond.

अनशिष्यं &c. or अनंक्ष्यं &c. *Passive*, Pres. नश्ये; 3d Pret. 3d sing. अनाशि. *Causal*, Pres. नाशयामि; 3d Pret. अनीनशं. *Des.* निनशिषामि, निनंक्षामि. *Freq.* नानश्ये, नानश्मि; 3d sing. नानष्टि or नानंष्टि. *Participles*, Pres. नश्यत्; Past pass. नष्ट; Past indecl. नष्ट्वा or नंष्ट्वा, -नश्य; Fut. pass. नशितव्य, नशनीय, नाश्य.

621. Root पुष्*. Inf. पोष्टुं 'to be nourished,' 'to grow fat.' Parasmai. Pres. पुष्यामि, &c. Pot. पुष्येयं, &c. Imp. पुष्याणि, &c. 1st Pret. अपुष्यं, &c. 2d Pret. पुपोष, पुपोषिथ, पुपोष; पुपुषिव, पुपुषथुस्, पुपुषतुस्; पुपुषिम, पुपुष, पुपुषुस्. 1st Fut. पोष्टास्मि, &c. 2d Fut. पोक्ष्यामि, &c. 3d Pret. (436) अपुषं, अपुषस्, अपुषत्; अपुषाव, अपुषतं, अपुषतां; अपुषाम, अपुषत, अपुषन्. Bened. पुष्यासं, &c. Cond. अपोक्ष्यं, &c. *Passive*, Pres. पुष्ये; 3d Pret. 3d sing. अपोषि. *Causal*, Pres. पोषयामि; 3d Pret. अपूपुषं. *Des.* पुपोषिषामि or पुपुषिषामि or पुपुक्षामि. *Freq.* पोपुष्ये, पोपोष्मि. *Participles*, Pres. पुष्यत्; Past pass. पुष्ट; Past indecl. पुष्ट्वा, -पुष्य; Fut. pass. पोष्टव्य, पोषणीय, पोष्य.

622. Root अस्. Inf. असितुं 'to throw.' Parasmai. Pres. अस्यामि, &c. Pot. अस्येयं, &c. Imp. अस्यानि, &c. 1st Pret. आस्यं, &c. 2d Pret. आस, आसिथ, आस; आसिव, आसथुस्, आसतुस्; आसिम, आस, आसुस्. 1st Fut. असितास्मि, &c. 2d Fut. असिष्यामि, &c. 3d Pret. (441) आस्थं, आस्थस्, आस्थत्; आस्थाव, आस्थतं, आस्थतां; आस्थाम, आस्थत, आस्थन्. Bened. अस्यासं, &c. Cond. आसिष्यं. *Passive*, Pres. अस्ये; 3d Pret. 3d sing. आसि. *Causal*, Pres. आसयामि; 3d Pret. आसिसं. *Des.* असिसिषामि. *Participles*, Pres. अस्यत्; Past pass. अस्त; Past indecl. असित्वा or अस्त्वा, -अस्य; Fut. pass. असितव्य, असनीय, आस्य.

623. Root द्रुह्. Inf. द्रोग्धुं or द्रोहितुं 'to injure,' 'to bear malice.' Parasmai. Pres. द्रुह्यामि, &c. Pot. द्रुह्येयं, &c. Imp. द्रुह्याणि, &c. 1st Pret. अद्रुह्यं, &c. 2d Pret. दुद्रोह, दुद्रोहिथ or दुद्रोग्ध or दुद्रोढ, दुद्रोह; दुद्रुहिव, दुद्रुहथुस्, दुद्रुहतुस्; दुद्रुहिम, दुद्रुह, दुद्रुहुस्. 1st Fut. (413) द्रोग्धास्मि or द्रोढास्मि or द्रोहितास्मि, &c. 2d Fut. ध्रोक्ष्यामि (306. *a*) or द्रोहिष्यामि, &c. 3d Pret. अद्रुहं, अद्रुहस्, अद्रुहत्; अद्रुहाव, अद्रुहतं, अद्रुहतां; अद्रुहाम, अद्रुहत, अद्रुहन्. Bened. द्रुह्यासं, &c. Cond. अध्रोक्ष्यं (306. *a*) or अद्रोहिष्यं, &c. *Passive*, Pres. द्रुह्ये; 3d Pret. 3d sing. अद्रोहि. *Causal*, Pres. द्रोहयामि; 3d Pret. अदुद्रुहं. *Des.* दुद्रोहिषामि or दुद्रुहिषामि or दुध्रुक्षामि (306. *a*). *Freq.* दोद्रुह्ये, दोद्रोह्मि (3d sing. दोद्रोग्धि or दोद्रोढि). *Participles*, Pres. द्रुह्यत्; Past pass. द्रुग्ध or द्रुढ; Past indecl. द्रुग्ध्वा or द्रुहित्वा or द्रोहित्वा, -द्रुह्य; Fut. pass. द्रोग्धव्य, द्रोहणीय, द्रोह्य.

* This root is also conjugated in the 9th conj. See 698.

624. Root नह्. Inf. नद्धुं 'to tie,' 'to bind,' 'to fasten.' Parasmai and Átmane. Pres. नह्यामि, &c. Átm. नह्ये, &c. Pot. नह्येयं, &c. Átm. नह्येय. Imp. नह्यानि, &c. Átm. नह्यै, &c. 1st Pret. अनह्यं, &c. Átm. अनह्ये, &c. 2d Pret. ननाह or ननह, नेहिथ or ननद्ध, ननाह; नेहिव, नेहथुस्, नेहतुस्; नेहिम, नेह, नेहुस्. Átm. नेहे, नेहिषे, नेहे; नेहिवहे, नेहाथे, नेहाते; नेहिमहे, नेहिढ्वे, नेहिरे. 1st Fut. नद्धास्मि, &c. Átm. नद्धाहे, &c. 2d Fut. (306. b) नत्स्यामि, &c. Átm. नत्स्ये, &c. 3d Pret. (425) अनात्सं, अनात्सीस्, अनात्सीत्; अनात्स्व, अनाद्धं, अनाद्धां; अनात्स्म, अनाद्ध, अनात्सुस्. Átm. अनत्सि, अनद्धास्, अनद्ध; अनत्स्वहि, अनत्साथां, अनत्सातां; अनत्स्महि, अनद्धुं, अनत्सत. Bened. नह्यासं, &c. Átm. नत्सीय, &c. Cond. अनत्स्यं, &c. Átm. अनत्स्ये, &c. *Passive*, Pres. नह्ये, &c.; 3d Pret. 3d sing. अनाहि. *Causal*, नाहयामि; 3d Pret. अनीनहं. *Des.* निनत्सामि, -त्से (306. b). *Freq.* नानह्ये, नानह्मि (3d sing. नानद्धि). *Participles*, Pres. नह्यत्; Past pass. नद्ध; Past indecl. नद्धा, -नह्य; Fut. pass. नद्धव्य, नहनीय, नाह्य.

EXAMPLES OF PRIMITIVE VERBS OF THE SIXTH CONJUGATION, EXPLAINED AT 278.

625. Root सृज् *srij.* Infin. स्रष्टुं *srashṭum*, 'to create' or 'let go.'

PARASMAI-PADA only.

Present tense, 'I create.'

सृजामि *srijámi*	सृजावस् *srijávas*	सृजामस् *srijámas*
सृजसि *srijasi*	सृजथस् *srijathas*	सृजथ *srijatha*
सृजति *srijati*	सृजतस् *srijatas*	सृजन्ति *srijanti*

Potential, 'I may create.'

सृजेयं *srijeyam*	सृजेव *srijeva*	सृजेम *srijema*
सृजेस् *srijes*	सृजेतं *srijetam*	सृजेत *srijeta*
सृजेत् *srijet*	सृजेतां *srijetám*	सृजेयुस् *srijeyus*

Imperative, 'Let me create.'

सृजानि *srijáni*	सृजाव *srijáva*	सृजाम *srijáma*
सृज *srija*	सृजतं *srijatam*	सृजत *srijata*
सृजतु *srijatu*	सृजतां *srijatám*	सृजन्तु *srijantu*

First preterite, 'I was creating.'

असृजं *asrijam*	असृजाव *asrijáva*	असृजाम *asrijáma*
असृजस् *asrijas*	असृजतं *asrijatam*	असृजत *asrijata*
असृजत् *asrijat*	असृजतां *asrijatám*	असृजन् *asrijan*

Second preterite, 'I created.'

ससर्ज *sasarja*	ससृजिव *sasṛijiva*	ससृजिम *sasṛijima*
ससर्जिथ *sasarjitha* *	ससृजथुस् *sasṛijathus*	ससृज *sasṛija*
ससर्ज *sasarja*	ससृजतुस् *sasṛijatus*	ससृजुस् *sasṛijus*

First future, 'I will create.'

स्रष्टास्मि *srashṭásmi* (388. *c*)	स्रष्टास्वस् *srashṭáswas*	स्रष्टास्मस् *srashṭásmas*
स्रष्टासि *srashṭási*	स्रष्टास्थस् *srashṭásthas*	स्रष्टास्थ *srashṭástha*
स्रष्टा *srashṭá*	स्रष्टारौ *srashṭárau*	स्रष्टारस् *srashṭáras*

Second future, 'I shall create.'

स्रक्ष्यामि *srakshyámi*	स्रक्ष्यावस् *srakshyávas*	स्रक्ष्यामस् *srakshyámas*
स्रक्ष्यसि *srakshyasi*	स्रक्ष्यथस् *srakshyathas*	स्रक्ष्यथ *srakshyatha*
स्रक्ष्यति *srakshyati*	स्रक्ष्यतस् *srakshyatas*	स्रक्ष्यन्ति *srakshyanti*

Third preterite, 'I created.'

अस्राक्षं *asráksham*	अस्राक्ष्व *asrákshwa*	अस्राक्ष्म *asrákshma*
अस्राक्षीस् *asrákshís*	अस्राष्टं *asráshṭam*	अस्राष्ट *asráshṭa*
अस्राक्षीत् *asrákshít*	अस्राष्टां *asráshṭám*	अस्राक्षुस् *asrákshus*

Benedictive, 'May I create.'

सृज्यासं *sṛijyásam*	सृज्यास्व *sṛijyáswa*	सृज्यास्म *sṛijyásma*
सृज्यास् *sṛijyás*	सृज्यास्तं *sṛijyástam*	सृज्यास्त *sṛijyásta*
सृज्यात् *sṛijyát*	सृज्यास्तां *sṛijyástám*	सृज्यासुस् *sṛijyásus*

Conditional, 'I should create.'

अस्रक्ष्यं *asrakshyam*	अस्रक्ष्याव *asrakshyáva*	अस्रक्ष्याम *asrakshyáma*
अस्रक्ष्यस् *asrakshyas*	अस्रक्ष्यतं *asrakshyatam*	अस्रक्ष्यत *asrakshyata*
अस्रक्ष्यत् *asrakshyat*	अस्रक्ष्यतां *asrakshyatám*	अस्रक्ष्यन् *asrakshyan*

Passive, Pres. सृज्ये; 3d Pret. 3d sing. असर्जि. *Causal*, Pres. सर्जयामि; 3d Pret. अससर्जं or असीसृजं. *Des.* सिसृक्षामि, -क्षे. *Freq.* सरीसृज्ये or सरीसृज्मि (3d sing. सरीसृष्टि). *Participles*, Pres. सृजत्; Past pass. सृष्ट (297); Past indecl. सृष्ट्वा, -सृज्य; Fut. pass. स्रष्टव्य, सर्जनीय, सृज्य.

EXAMPLES OF OTHER VERBS OF THE SIXTH CONJUGATION IN THE ORDER OF THEIR FINAL LETTERS.

626. Root मृ (280). Inf. मर्तुं 'to die.' Átmane only in conj. tenses. Pres. म्रिये, &c. Pot. म्रियेय, &c. Imp. म्रियै, &c. 1st Pret. अम्रिये, &c. 2d Pret. ममार, ममरिथ or ममर्थ, ममार; मम्रिव, मम्रथुस्, मम्रतुस्;

* Or सस्रष्ठ *sasrashṭha*. See 297 and 388. *c*.

मम्रिम, मम्र, मम्रुस्. Átm. मम्रे, मम्रिषे, मम्रे; मम्रिवहे, मम्राथे, मम्राते; मम्रिमहे, मम्रिद्वे, मम्रिरे. 1st Fut. मर्त्तास्मि, &c. 2d Fut. मरिष्यामि, &c. 3d Pret. Átm. अमृषि, अमृथास्, अमृत; अमृष्वहि, अमृषाथां, अमृषातां; अमृष्महि, अमृढ्वं, अमृषत. Bened. Átm. मृषीय, &c. Cond. अमरिष्यं, &c. *Passive,* Pres. म्रियये; 3d Pret. 3d sing. अमारि. *Causal,* Pres. मारयामि; 3d Pret. अमीमरं. *Des.* मुमूर्षामि (502). *Freq.* मेम्रीये, मामर्मि. *Participles,* Pres. म्रियमाण; Past pass. मृत; Past indecl. मृत्वा, -मृत्य; Fut. pass. मर्त्तव्य, मरणीय, मार्य्य.

627. Root कॄ (280). Inf. करितुं or करीतुं 'to scatter.' Parasmai. Pres. किरामि, &c. Pot. किरेयं, &c. Imp. किराणि, &c. 1st Pret. अकिरं, &c. 2d Pret. (367. *c*) चकार, चकरिथ, चकार; चकरिव, चकरथुस्, चकरतुस्; चकरिम, चकर, चकरुस्. 1st Fut. (399) करितास्मि or करीतास्मि, &c. 2d Fut. (399) करिष्यामि or करीष्यामि, &c. 3d Pret. अकारिषं, अकारीस्, अकारीत्; अकारिष्व, अकारिष्टं, अकारिष्टां; अकारिष्म, अकारिष्ट, अकारिषुस्. Bened. कीर्यासं, &c. Cond. अकरिष्यं or अकरीष्यं. *Passive,* Pres. कीर्ये; 3d Pret. 3d sing. अकारि. *Causal,* Pres. कारयामि; 3d Pret. अचीकरं. *Des.* चिकरिषामि or चिकरीषामि. *Freq.* चेकीर्ये, चाकर्मि. *Participles,* Pres. किरत्; Past pass. कीर्ण (531. *a*); Past indecl. कीर्त्वा, -कीर्य; Fut. pass. करितव्य or करीतव्य, करणीय, कार्य्य.

628. Root मुच् (281). Inf. मोक्तुं 'to loose,' 'to let go.' Parasmai and Átmane. Pres. मुञ्चामि, &c. Átm. मुञ्चे, &c. Pot. मुञ्चेयं, &c. Átm. मुञ्चेय, &c. Imp. मुञ्चानि, &c. Átm. मुञ्चै, &c. 1st Pret. अमुञ्चं, &c. Átm. अमुञ्चे, &c. 2d Pret. मुमोच, मुमोचिथ, मुमोच; मुमुचिव, मुमुचथुस्, मुमुचतुस्; मुमुचिम, मुमुच, मुमुचुस्. Átm. मुमुचे, मुमुचिषे, मुमुचे; मुमुचिवहे, मुमुचाथे, मुमुचाते; मुमुचिमहे, मुमुचिध्वे, मुमुचिरे. 1st Fut. मोक्तास्मि, &c. Átm. मोक्ताहे, &c. 2d Fut. मोक्ष्यामि, &c. Átm. मोक्ष्ये, &c. 3d Pret. अमुचं, अमुचस्, अमुचत्; अमुचाव, अमुचतं, अमुचतां; अमुचाम, अमुचत, अमुचन्. Átm. अमुक्षि, अमुक्थास्, अमुक्त; अमुक्ष्वहि, अमुक्षाथां, अमुक्षातां; अमुक्ष्महि, अमुग्ध्वं, अमुक्षत. Bened. मुच्यासं, &c. Átm. मुक्षीय, &c. (452). Cond. अमोक्ष्यं, &c. Átm. अमोक्ष्ये, &c. *Passive,* Pres. मुच्ये; 3d Pret. 3d sing. अमोचि. *Causal,* Pres. मोचयामि; 3d Pret. अमूमुचं. *Des.* मुमुक्षामि, -क्षे. *Freq.* मोमुच्ये, मोमोच्मि (3d sing. मोमोक्ति). *Participles,* Pres. मुञ्चत्; Past pass. मुक्त; Past indecl. मुक्त्वा, -मुच्य; Fut. pass. मोक्तव्य, मोचनीय, मोच्य. For the other verbs of this class which insert a nasal, see 281.

629. Root व्यच् (282). Inf. व्यचितुं 'to deceive.' Parasmai. Pres. विचामि, &c. Pot. विचेयं, &c. Imp. विचानि, &c. 1st Pret. अविचं, &c. 2d Pret. (383) विव्याच, विव्यचिथ, विव्याच; विविचिव, विविचथुस्, विविचतुस्;

विविचिम, विविच, विविचुस्. 1st Fut. व्यचितास्मि, &c. 2d Fut. व्यचिष्यामि. 3d Pret. अव्याचिषं, अव्याचीस्, &c. Or अव्यचिषं, अव्यचीस्, &c.; see 427. Bened. विच्यासं, &c. Cond. अव्यचिष्यं, &c. *Passive*, Pres. विच्ये; 3d Pret. 3d sing. अव्याचि. *Causal*, Pres. व्याचयामि; 3d Pret. अविव्यचं. *Des.* विविचिषामि or विव्यचिषामि. *Freq.* वेविच्ये, वाव्यच्मि or वाव्यचीमि. *Participles*, Pres. विचत्; Past pass. विचित; Past indecl. विचित्वा, -विच्य; Fut. pass. व्यचितव्य, विचनीय, व्याच्य.

630. Root व्रश्च् (282). Inf. व्रश्चितुं 'to cut.' Parasmai. Pres. वृश्चामि, &c. Pot. वृश्चेयं. Imp. वृश्चानि. 1st Pret. अवृश्चं, &c. 2d Pret. वव्रश्च, वव्रश्चिथ or वव्रष्ठ, वव्रश्च; वव्रश्चिव, वव्रश्चथुस्, वव्रश्चतुस्; वव्रश्चिम, वव्रश्च, वव्रश्चुस्. 1st Fut. (401) व्रश्चितास्मि or व्रष्टास्मि, &c. 2d Fut. व्रश्चिष्यामि or व्रक्ष्यामि, &c. 3d Pret. अव्रश्चिषं, अव्रश्चीस्, अव्रश्चीत्; अव्रश्चिष्व, &c., see 427. Or अव्राक्षं (418, 419), अव्राक्षीस्, अव्राक्षीत्; अव्राक्ष्व, अव्राष्टं (297), अव्राष्टां; अव्राक्ष्म, अव्राष्ट, अव्राक्षुस्. Bened. वृश्च्यासं, &c. Cond. अव्रश्चिष्यं or अव्रक्ष्यं, &c. *Passive*, Pres. वृश्च्ये (472); 3d Pret. 3d sing. अव्रश्चि (475. *a*, note). *Causal*, Pres. व्रश्चयामि; 3d Pret. अविव्रश्चं. *Des.* विव्रश्चिषामि or विव्रक्षामि. *Freq.* वरीवृश्च्ये, वरीवृश्चीमि. *Participles*, Pres. वृश्चत्; Past pass. वृक्ण or वृक्त (541, 58); Past indecl. व्रश्चित्वा, -वृश्च्य (565); Fut. pass. व्रश्चितव्य or व्रष्टव्य, व्रश्चनीय, व्रश्च्य.

631. Root प्रछ् or प्रच्छ् (282). Inf. प्रष्टुं 'to ask.' Parasmai. Pres. पृच्छामि, &c. Pot. पृच्छेयं, &c. Imp. पृच्छानि, &c. 1st Pret. अपृच्छं, &c. 2d Pret. (381) पप्रच्छ, पप्रच्छिथ or पप्रष्ठ, पप्रच्छ; पप्रच्छिव, पप्रच्छथुस्, पप्रच्छतुस्; पप्रच्छिम, पप्रच्छ, पप्रच्छुस्. 1st Fut. प्रष्टास्मि, &c. 2d Fut. प्रक्ष्यामि, &c. 3d Pret. अप्राक्षं, अप्राक्षीस्, अप्राक्षीत्; अप्राक्ष्व, अप्राष्टं, अप्राष्टां; अप्राक्ष्म, अप्राष्ट, अप्राक्षुस्. Bened. पृच्छ्यासं, &c. Cond. अप्रक्ष्यं, &c. *Passive*, Pres. पृच्छ्ये (472); 3d Pret. 3d sing. अप्रच्छि. *Causal*, प्रच्छयामि; 3d Pret. अपप्रच्छं. *Des.* पिपृच्छिषामि. *Freq.* परीपृच्छ्ये, पाप्रच्छ्मि. *Participles*, Pres. पृच्छत्; Past pass. पृष्ट; Past indecl. पृष्ट्वा, -पृच्छ्य (565); Fut. pass. प्रष्टव्य, प्रच्छनीय, प्रच्छ्य.

632. Root भ्रज्ज् or भ्रस्ज्. Inf. भ्रष्टुं or भर्ष्टुं 'to fry.' Parasmai and Átmane. Pres. भृज्जामि, &c. Átm. भृज्जे, &c. Pot. भृज्जेयं, &c. Átm. भृज्जेय, &c. Imp. भृज्जानि, &c. Átm. भृज्जै, &c. 1st Pret. अभृज्जं, &c. Átm. अभृज्जे, &c. 2d Pret. (381) बभ्रज्ज, बभ्रज्जिथ or बभ्रष्ठ, बभ्रज्ज; बभ्रज्जिव, बभ्रज्जथुस्, बभ्रज्जतुस्; बभ्रज्जिम, बभ्रज्ज, बभ्रज्जुस्. Or बभर्ज्ज, बभर्ज्जिथ or बभर्ष्ठ, बभर्ज्ज; बभर्ज्जिव, &c. Átm. बभ्रज्जे, बभ्रज्जिषे, &c. Or बभर्ज्जे, बभर्ज्जिषे, &c. 1st Fut. भ्रष्टास्मि or भर्ष्टास्मि, &c. Átm. भ्रष्टाहे or भर्ष्टाहे, &c. 2d Fut. भ्रक्ष्यामि or भर्क्ष्यामि &c., भ्रक्ष्ये or भर्क्ष्ये &c. 3d Pret. अभ्राक्षं, अभ्राक्षीस्, अभ्राक्षीत्; अभ्राक्ष्व, अभ्राष्टं, अभ्राष्टां; अभ्राक्ष्म, अभ्राष्ट, अभ्राक्षुस्. Or अभार्क्षं, &c.

Átm. अभक्षि, अभक्षास्, अभक्षत; अभक्ष्वहि, अभक्षाथां, अभक्षातां; अभक्ष्महि, अभड्ढ्वं, अभक्षत. Or अभर्क्षि, अभर्ष्ठास्, अभर्ष्ट; अभर्क्ष्वहि, अभर्क्षाथां, अभर्क्षातां; अभर्क्ष्महि, अभर्ड्ढ्वं, अभर्क्षत. Bened. भृज्ज्यासं, &c. Átm. भक्षीय &c. or भर्क्षीय &c. Cond. अभ्रक्ष्यं &c. or अभर्क्ष्यं &c. Átm. अभ्रक्ष्ये &c. or अभर्क्ष्ये &c. *Passive,* Pres. भृज्ज्ये. *Causal,* Pres. भ्रज्जयामि; 3d Pret. अबभ्रज्जं or अबभर्ज्जं. *Des.* बिभ्रक्षामि, -क्षे, or बिभर्क्षामि, -क्षे; or बिभ्रज्जिषामि, -षे, or बिभर्ज्जिषामि, -षे, &c. *Freq.* बरीभृज्ज्ये, बाभ्रज्ज्मि (3d sing. बाभ्रष्टि). *Participles,* Pres. भृज्जत्; Past pass. भृष्ट; Past indecl. भृष्ट्वा, -भृज्ज्य; Fut. pass. भ्रष्टव्य or भर्ष्टव्य, भर्जनीय, भर्ग्य.

633. Root मज्ज् or मस्ज्. Inf. मंक्तुं 'to be immersed,' 'to sink.' Parasmai. Pres. मज्जामि, &c. Pot. मज्जेयं, &c. Imp. मज्जानि, &c. 1st Pret. अमज्जं, &c. 2d Pret. ममज्ज, ममज्जिथ or ममंक्थ, ममज्ज; ममज्जिव, ममज्जथुस्, ममज्जतुस्; ममज्जिम, ममज्ज, ममज्जुस्. 1st Fut. मंक्तास्मि, &c. 2d Fut. मंक्ष्यामि, &c. 3d Pret. (426) अमांक्षं, अमांक्षीस्, अमांक्षीत्; अमांक्ष्व, अमांक्तं, अमांक्तां; अमांक्ष्म, अमांक्त, अमांक्षुस्. Bened. मज्ज्यासं, &c. Cond. अमंक्ष्यं, &c. *Passive,* Pres. मज्ज्ये. *Causal,* Pres. मज्जयामि; 3d Pret. अममज्जं. *Des.* मिमंक्षामि. *Freq.* मामज्ज्ये, मामज्ज्मि (3d sing. मामंक्ति). *Participles,* Pres. मज्जत्; Past pass. मग्न; Past indecl. मंक्त्वा, मक्त्वा, -मज्ज्य; Fut. pass. मंक्तव्य, मज्जनीय, मज्ज्य.

634. Root तुद्. Inf. तोत्तुं 'to strike,' 'to hurt.' Parasmai and Átmane. Pres. तुदामि, &c. Átm. तुदे, &c. Pot. तुदेयं, &c. Átm. तुदेय, &c. Imp. तुदानि, &c. Átm. तुदै, &c. 1st Pret. अतुदं, &c. Átm. अतुदे, &c. 2d Pret. तुतोद, तुतोदिथ, तुतोद; तुतुदिव, तुतुदथुस्, तुतुदतुस्; तुतुदिम, तुतुद, तुतुदुस्. Átm. तुतुदे, तुतुदिषे, तुतुदे; तुतुदिवहे, तुतुदाथे, तुतुदाते; तुतुदिमहे, तुतुदिध्वे (ढ्वे), तुतुदिरे. 1st Fut. तोत्तास्मि, &c. Átm. तोत्ताहे, &c. 2d Fut. तोत्स्यामि, &c. Átm. तोत्स्ये, &c. 3d Pret. अतौत्सं, अतौत्सीस्, अतौत्सीत्; अतौत्स्व, अतौत्तं, अतौत्तां; अतौत्स्म, अतौत्त, अतौत्सुस्. Átm. अतुत्सि, अतुत्थास्, अतुत्त; अतुत्स्वहि, अतुत्साथां, अतुत्सातां; अतुत्स्महि, अतुद्ध्वं, अतुत्सत. Bened. तुद्यासं &c., तुत्सीय &c. (452). Cond. अतोत्स्यं &c., अतोत्स्ये &c. *Passive,* Pres. तुद्ये; 3d Pret. 3d sing. अतोदि. *Causal,* Pres. तोदयामि; 3d Pret. अतूतुदं. *Des.* तुतुत्सामि, -त्से. *Freq.* तोतुद्ये, तोतोद्मि (3d sing. तोतोत्ति). *Participles,* Pres. तुदत्; Past pass. तुन्न; Past indecl. तुत्त्वा, -तुद्य; Fut. pass. तोत्तव्य, तोदनीय, तोद्य.

635. Root क्षिप्. Inf. क्षेप्तुं 'to throw.' Parasmai and Átmane. Pres. क्षिपामि, &c. Átm. क्षिपे, &c. Pot. क्षिपेयं, &c. Átm. क्षिपेय, &c. Imp. क्षिपाणि, &c. Átm. क्षिपै, &c. 1st Pret. अक्षिपं, &c. Átm. अक्षिपे, &c. 2d Pret. चिक्षेप, चिक्षेपिथ, चिक्षेप; चिक्षिपिव, चिक्षिपथुस्,

चिक्षिपतुस्; चिक्षिपिम, चिक्षिप, चिक्षिपुस्. A'tm. चिक्षिपे, चिक्षिपिषे, चिक्षिपे; चिक्षिपिवहे, चिक्षिपाथे, चिक्षिपाते; चिक्षिपिमहे, चिक्षिपिध्वे or -ढ्वे, चिक्षिपिरे. 1st Fut. क्षेप्तास्मि, &c. A'tm. क्षेप्ताहे. 2d Fut. क्षेप्स्यामि. A'tm. क्षेप्स्ये. 3d Pret. अक्षैप्सं, अक्षैप्सीस्, अक्षैप्सीत्; अक्षैप्स्व, अक्षैप्तं, अक्षैप्तां; अक्षैप्स्म, अक्षैप्त, अक्षैप्सुस्. A'tm. अक्षिप्सि, अक्षिप्थास्, अक्षिप्त; अक्षिप्स्वहि, अक्षिप्साथां, अक्षिप्सातां; अक्षिप्स्महि, अक्षिब्ध्वं, अक्षिप्सत. Bened. क्षिप्यासं, &c. A'tm. क्षिप्सीय, &c. Cond. अक्षेप्स्यं, &c. A'tm. अक्षेप्स्ये, &c. *Passive,* क्षिप्ये; 3d Pret. 3d sing. अक्षेपि. *Causal,* Pres. क्षेपयामि; 3d Pret. अचिक्षिपं. *Des.* चिक्षिप्सामि, -प्से. *Freq.* चेक्षिप्ये, चेक्षेप्मि (710, 294. *a*). *Participles,* Pres. क्षिपत्; Past pass. क्षिप्त; Past indecl. क्षिप्त्वा, -क्षिप्य; Fut. pass. क्षेप्तव्य, क्षेपणीय, क्षेप्य.

636. Root स्पृश्. Inf. स्पर्ष्टुं or स्प्रष्टुं 'to touch.' Parasmai. Pres. स्पृशामि, &c. Pot. स्पृशेयं, &c. Imp. स्पृशानि, &c. 1st Pret. अस्पृशं, &c. 2d Pret. पस्पर्श, पस्पर्शिथ, पस्पर्श; पस्पृशिव, पस्पृशथुस्, पस्पृशतुस्; पस्पृशिम, पस्पृश, पस्पृशुस्. 1st Fut. स्पर्ष्टास्मि or स्प्रष्टास्मि. 2d Fut. स्पर्क्ष्यामि or स्प्रक्ष्यामि. 3d Pret. अस्पार्क्षं, अस्पार्क्षीस्, अस्पार्क्षीत्; अस्पार्क्ष्व, अस्पार्ष्टं, अस्पार्ष्टां; अस्पार्क्ष्म, अस्पार्ष्ट, अस्पार्क्षुस्. Or अस्प्राक्षं, अस्प्राक्षीस्, &c. Or अस्पृक्षं, अस्पृक्षस्, अस्पृक्षत्; अस्पृक्षाव, अस्पृक्षतं, अस्पृक्षतां; अस्पृक्षाम, अस्पृक्षत, अस्पृक्षन्. Bened. स्पृश्यासं. Cond. अस्पर्क्ष्यं or अस्प्रक्ष्यं. *Passive,* Pres. स्पृश्ये; 3d Pret. 3d sing. अस्पर्शि. *Causal,* Pres. स्पर्शयामि; 3d Pret. अपस्पर्शं or अपिस्पृशं. *Des.* पिस्पृक्षामि. *Freq.* परीस्पृश्ये, परीस्पर्श्मि or परीस्प्रश्मि. *Participles,* Pres. स्पृशत्; Past pass. स्पृष्ट; Past indecl. स्पृष्ट्वा, -स्पृश्य; Fut. pass. स्पर्ष्टव्य or स्प्रष्टव्य, स्पर्शनीय, स्पृश्य.

637. Root इष् (282). Inf. एषितुं or एष्टुं 'to wish.' Parasmai. Pres. इच्छामि, &c. Pot. इच्छेयं. Imp. इच्छानि. 1st Pret. ऐच्छं. 2d Pret. (370) इयेष, इयेषिथ, इयेष; ईषिव, ईषथुस्, ईषतुस्; ईषिम, ईष, ईषुस्. 1st Fut. एषितास्मि or एष्टास्मि, &c. 2d Fut. एषिष्यामि, &c. 3d Pret. ऐषिषं, ऐषीस्, ऐषीत्; ऐषिष्व, ऐषिष्टं, ऐषिष्टां; ऐषिष्म, ऐषिष्ट, ऐषिषुस्. Bened. इष्यासं, &c. Cond. ऐषिष्यं, &c. *Passive,* Pres. इष्ये; 3d Pret. 3d sing. ऐषि. *Causal,* Pres. एषयामि; 3d Pret. ऐषिषं. *Des.* एषिषिषामि. *Participles,* Pres. इच्छत्; Past pass. इष्ट; Past indecl. इष्ट्वा or इषित्वा, -इष्य; Fut. pass. एष्टव्य or एषितव्य, एषणीय, एष्य.

EXAMPLES OF PRIMITIVE VERBS OF THE TENTH CONJUGATION, EXPLAINED AT 283.

638. Root चुर् *chur*. Infin. चोरयितुं *chorayitum*, 'to steal.'

PARASMAI-PADA. *Present tense*, 'I steal.'

चोरयामि *chorayámi*	चोरयावस् *chorayávas*	चोरयामस् *chorayámas*
चोरयसि *chorayasi*	चोरयथस् *chorayathas*	चोरयथ *chorayatha*
चोरयति *chorayati*	चोरयतस् *chorayatas*	चोरयन्ति *chorayanti*

Potential, 'I may steal,' &c.

चोरयेयम् *chorayeyam*	चोरयेव *chorayeva*	चोरयेम *chorayema*
चोरयेस् *chorayes*	चोरयेतं *chorayetam*	चोरयेत *chorayeta*
चोरयेत् *chorayet*	चोरयेतां *chorayetám*	चोरयेयुस् *chorayeyus*

Imperative, 'Let me steal,' &c.

चोरयाणि *chorayáṇi*	चोरयाव *chorayáva*	चोरयाम *chorayáma*
चोरय *choraya*	चोरयतं *chorayatam*	चोरयत *chorayata*
चोरयतु *chorayatu*	चोरयतां *chorayatám*	चोरयन्तु *chorayantu*

First preterite, 'I was stealing,' &c.

अचोरयम् *achorayam*	अचोरयाव *achorayáva*	अचोरयाम *achorayáma*
अचोरयस् *achorayas*	अचोरयतं *achorayatam*	अचोरयत *achorayata*
अचोरयत् *achorayat*	अचोरयतां *achorayatám*	अचोरयन् *achorayan*

Second preterite, 'I stole.'

चोरयामास *chorayámása*	चोरयामासिव *chorayámásiva*	चोरयामासिम *chorayámásima*
चोरयामासिथ *chorayámásitha*	चोरयामासथुस् *chorayámásathus*	चोरयामास *chorayámása*
चोरयामास *chorayámása*	चोरयामासतुस् *chorayámásatus*	चोरयामासुस् *chorayámásus*

First future, 'I will steal,' &c.

चोरयितास्मि *chorayitásmi*	चोरयितास्वस् *chorayitáswas*	चोरयितास्मस् *chorayitásmas*
चोरयितासि *chorayitási*	चोरयितास्थस् *chorayitásthas*	चोरयितास्थ *chorayitástha*
चोरयिता *chorayitá*	चोरयितारौ *chorayitárau*	चोरयितारस् *chorayitáras*

Second future, 'I shall steal,' &c.

चोरयिष्यामि *chorayishyámi*	चोरयिष्यावस् *chorayishyávas*	चोरयिष्यामस् *chorayishyámas*
चोरयिष्यसि *chorayishyasi*	चोरयिष्यथस् *chorayishyathas*	चोरयिष्यथ *chorayishyatha*
चोरयिष्यति *chorayishyati*	चोरयिष्यतस् *chorayishyatas*	चोरयिष्यन्ति *chorayishyanti*

Third preterite, 'I stole,' &c.

अचूचुरम् *achúchuram*	अचूचुराव *achúchuráva*	अचूचुराम *achúchuráma*
अचूचुरस् *achúchuras*	अचूचुरतं *achúchuratam*	अचूचुरत *achúchurata*
अचूचुरत् *achúchurat*	अचूचुरतां *achúchuratám*	अचूचुरन् *achúchuran*

Benedictive, 'May I steal,' &c.

चोर्यासं *choryásam*	चोर्यास्व *choryáswa*	चोर्यास्म *choryásma*
चोर्यास् *choryás*	चोर्यास्तं *choryástam*	चोर्यास्त *choryásta*
चोर्यात् *choryát*	चोर्यास्तां *choryástám*	चोर्यासुस् *choryásus*

Conditional, 'I should steal.'

अचोरयिष्यं *achorayishyam*	अचोरयिष्याव *achorayishyáva*	अचोरयिष्याम *achorayishyáma*
अचोरयिष्यस् *achorayishyas*	अचोरयिष्यतं *achorayishyatam*	अचोरयिष्यत *achorayishyata*
अचोरयिष्यत् *achorayishyat*	अचोरयिष्यतां *achorayishyatám*	अचोरयिष्यन् *achorayishyan*

639. ÁTMANE-PADA. *Present tense*, 'I steal.'

चोरये *choraye*	चोरयावहे *chorayávahe*	चोरयामहे *chorayámahe*
चोरयसे *chorayase*	चोरयेथे *chorayethe*	चोरयध्वे *chorayadhwe*
चोरयते *chorayate*	चोरयेते *chorayete*	चोरयन्ते *chorayante*

Potential, 'I may steal,' &c.

चोरयेय *chorayeya*	चोरयेवहि *chorayevahi*	चोरयेमहि *chorayemahi*
चोरयेथास् *chorayethás*	चोरयेयाथां *chorayeyáthám*	चोरयेध्वं *chorayedhwam*
चोरयेत *chorayeta*	चोरयेयातां *chorayeyátám*	चोरयेरन् *chorayeran*

Imperative, 'Let me steal,' &c.

चोरयै *chorayai*	चोरयावहै *chorayávahai*	चोरयामहै *chorayámahai*
चोरयस्व *chorayaswa*	चोरयेथां *chorayethám*	चोरयध्वं *chorayadhwam*
चोरयतां *chorayatám*	चोरयेतां *chorayetám*	चोरयन्तां *chorayantám*

First preterite, 'I was stealing,' &c.

अचोरये *achoraye*	अचोरयावहि *achorayávahi*	अचोरयामहि *achorayámahi*
अचोरयथास् *achorayathás*	अचोरयेथां *achorayethám*	अचोरयध्वं *achorayadhwam*
अचोरयत *achorayata*	अचोरयेतां *achorayetám*	अचोरयन्त *achorayanta*

Second preterite, 'I stole.'

चोरयाञ्चक्रे *chorayáñchakre*	-चकृवहे *chorayáñchakṛivahe*	-चकृमहे *chorayáñchakṛimahe*
चोरयाञ्चकृषे *chorayáñchakṛishe*	-चक्राथे *chorayáñchakráthe*	-चकृढ्वे *chorayáñchakṛiḍhwe*
चोरयाञ्चक्रे *chorayáñchakre*	-चक्राते *chorayáñchakráte*	-चक्रिरे *chorayáñchakrire*

First future, 'I shall steal.'

चोरयिताहे *chorayitáhe*	चोरयितास्वहे *chorayitáswahe*	चोरयितास्महे *chorayitásmahe*
चोरयितासे *chorayitáse*	चोरयितासाथे *chorayitásáthe*	चोरयिताध्वे *chorayitádhwe*
चोरयिता *chorayitá*	चोरयितारौ *chorayitárau*	चोरयितारस् *chorayitáras*

Second future, 'I will steal.'

चोरयिष्ये *chorayishye*	चोरयिष्यावहे *chorayishyávahe*	चोरयिष्यामहे *chorayishyámahe*
चोरयिष्यसे *chorayishyase*	चोरयिष्येथे *chorayishyethe*	चोरयिष्यध्वे *chorayishyadhwe*
चोरयिष्यते *chorayishyate*	चोरयिष्येते *chorayishyete*	चोरयिष्यन्ते *chorayishyante*

Third preterite, 'I stole,' &c.

अचूचुरे *achúchure*	अचूचुरावहि *achúchurávahi*	अचूचुरामहि *achúchurámahi*
अचूचुरथास् *achúchurathás*	अचूचुरेथां *achúchurethám*	अचूचुरध्वं *achúchuradhwam*
अचूचुरत *achúchurata*	अचूचुरेतां *achúchuretám*	अचूचुरन्त *achúchuranta*

Benedictive, 'May I steal.'

चोरयिषीय *chorayishíya*	-यिषीवहि *chorayishívahi*	-यिषीमहि *chorayishímahi*
चोरयिषीष्ठास् *chorayishíshṭhás*	-यिषीयास्थां *chorayishíyásthám*	-यिषीध्वं *chorayishídhwam*
चोरयिषीष्ट *chorayishíshṭa*	-यिषीयास्तां *chorayishíyástám*	-यिषीरन् *chorayishíran*

Conditional, 'I should steal.'

अचोरयिष्ये *achorayishye*	-यिष्यावहि *achorayishyávahi*	-यिष्यामहि *achorayishyámahi*
अचोरयिष्यथास् *achorayishyathás*	-यिष्येथां *achorayishyethám*	-यिष्यध्वं *achorayishyadhwam*
अचोरयिष्यत *achorayishyata*	-यिष्येतां *achorayishyetám*	-यिष्यन्त *achorayishyanta*

Passive, Pres. चोर्ये; 3d Pret. 3d sing. अचोरि. *Causal*, same as the Primitive verb. *Des.* चुचोरयिषामि. *Participles*, Pres. चोरयत्; Past pass. चुरित or चोरित; Past indecl. चोरयित्वा; Fut. pass. चोरयितव्य, चोरणीय, चोर्य्य.

EXAMPLES OF OTHER VERBS OF THE TENTH CONJUGATION IN THE ORDER OF THEIR FINAL LETTERS.

640. Root पॄ (285). Inf. पूरयितुं 'to fill*.' Parasmai. Pres. पूरयामि, &c. Pot. पूरयेयं, &c. Imp. पूरयाणि, &c. 1st Pret. अपूरयं, &c. 2d Pret. पूरयामास, &c. 1st Fut. पूरयितास्मि, &c. 2d Fut. पूरयिष्यामि, &c. 3d Pret. अपूपुरं, &c. Bened. पूर्यासं, &c. Cond. अपूरयिष्यं. *Passive*, Pres. पूर्ये; 3d Pret. 3d sing. अपूरि or अपूरिष्ट. *Causal*, like the Primitive. *Des.* पुपूरयिषामि. *Participles*, Pres. पूरयत्; Past pass. पूर्ण or पूरित or पूर्त्त; Past indecl. पूरयित्वा or पूर्त्वा, -पूर्य; Fut. pass. पूरयितव्य, पूरणीय, पूर्य्य.

641. Root चिन्त्. Inf. चिन्तयितुं 'to think.' Parasmai. Pres. चिन्तयामि, &c. Pot. चिन्तयेयं, &c. Imp. चिन्तयानि, &c. 1st Pret. अचिन्तयं, &c. 2d Pret. चिन्तयामास, &c. 1st Fut. चिन्तयितास्मि, &c. 2d Fut. चिन्तयिष्यामि, &c. 3d Pret. अचिचिन्तं, &c. Bened. चिन्त्यासं. Cond. अचिन्तयिष्यं. *Passive*, Pres. चिन्त्ये. *Causal*, like the Primitive. *Des.* चिचिन्तयिषामि, &c. *Participles*, Pres. चिन्तयत्; Átm. चिन्तयान (527);

* This root makes its base पारय *páraya* as well as पूरय *púraya*, but its meaning is then rather 'to fulfil,' 'to accomplish,' 'to get through.'

Past pass. चिन्तित; Past indecl. चिन्तयित्वा, -चिन्त्य; Fut. pass. चिन्तयितव्य, चिन्तनीय, चिन्त्य.

642. Root अर्थ्. Inf. अर्थयितुं (with prep. प्र, प्रार्थ्, प्रार्थयितुं) 'to ask,' 'to seek.' Átmane. Pres. अर्थये, &c. Pot. अर्थयेय, &c. Imp. अर्थयानि, &c. 1st Pret. आर्थये, &c. 2d Pret. अर्थयाञ्चक्रे, &c. 1st Fut. अर्थयिताहे, &c. 2d Fut. अर्थयिष्ये, &c. 3d Pret. आर्तिथे, आर्तिथथास्, &c. Bened. अर्थयिषीय. Cond. आर्थयिष्ये. *Passive,* Pres. अर्थ्ये. *Causal,* like the Primitive. *Des.* अर्तिथयिषामि, -षे. *Participles,* Pres. अर्थयान (527); Past pass. अर्थित; Past indecl. अर्थयित्वा, -अर्थ्य; Fut. pass. अर्थयितव्य, अर्थनीय, अर्थ्य.

643. Root कथ्. Inf. कथयितुं 'to say,' 'to tell.' Parasmai. Pres. कथयामि, &c. Pot. कथयेयं, &c. Imp. कथयानि, &c. 1st Pret. अकथयं, &c. 2d Pret. कथयामास, &c. 1st Fut. कथयितास्मि, &c. 2d Fut. कथयिष्यामि, &c. 3d Pret. अचकथं &c. or अचीकथं &c. Bened. कथ्यासं, &c. Cond. अकथयिष्यं, &c. *Passive,* कथ्ये, &c. *Causal,* like the Primitive. *Des.* चिकथयिषामि, &c. *Participles,* Pres. कथयत्; Past pass. कथित; Past indecl. कथयित्वा, -कथय्य (566. *a*); Fut. pass. कथयितव्य, कथनीय, कथ्य.

a. Root घुष्. Inf. घोषयितुं 'to proclaim.' Parasmai. Pres. घोषयामि, &c. Pot. घोषयेयं, &c. Imp. घोषयाणि, &c. (58). 1st Pret. अघोषयं, &c. 2d Pret. घोषयाञ्चकार, &c. 1st Fut. घोषयितास्मि, &c. 2d Fut. घोषयिष्यामि, &c. 3d Pret. अजूघुषं, &c. Bened. घोष्यासं, &c. Cond. अघोषयिष्यं, &c. *Passive,* Pres. घोष्ये; 3d Pret. 3d sing. अघोषि. *Causal,* like the Primitive. *Des.* जुघोषयिषामि. *Participles,* Pres. घोषयत्; Past pass. घोषित; Past indecl. घोषयित्वा, -घोष्य; Fut. pass. घोषयितव्य, घोषणीय, घोष्य.

b. Root भक्ष्. Inf. भक्षयितुं 'to eat,' 'to devour.' Parasmai. Pres. भक्षयामि, &c. Pot. भक्षयेयं, &c. Imp. भक्षयाणि, &c. 1st Pret. अभक्षयं, &c. 2d Pret. भक्षयामास, &c. 1st Fut. भक्षयितास्मि, &c. 2d Fut. भक्षयिष्यामि, &c. 3d Pret. अबभक्षं, &c. Bened. भक्ष्यासं. Cond. अभक्षयिष्यं. *Passive,* भक्ष्ये, &c. *Des.* बिभक्षयिषामि. *Participles,* Pres. भक्षयत्; Past pass. भक्षित; Past indecl. भक्षयित्वा, -भक्ष्य; Fut. pass. भक्षयितव्य, भक्षणीय, भक्ष्य.

EXAMPLES OF PRIMITIVE VERBS OF THE SECOND CONJUGATION, EXPLAINED AT 307.

644. Root या *yá*. Infin. यातुं *yátum*, 'to go.'

PARASMAI-PADA only.

Present, 'I go.'

यामि *yámi*	यावस् *yávas*	यामस् *yámas*
यासि *yási*	याथस् *yáthas*	याथ *yátha*
याति *yáti*	यातस् *yátas*	यान्ति *yánti*

Potential, 'I may go.'

यायां *yáyám*	यायाव *yáyáva*	यायाम *yáyáma*
यायास् *yáyás*	यायातं *yáyátam*	यायात *yáyáta*
यायात् *yáyát*	यायातां *yáyátám*	यायुस् *yáyus*

Imperative, 'Let me go.'

यानि *yáni*	याव *yáva*	याम *yáma*
याहि *yáhi*	यातं *yátam*	यात *yáta*
यातु *yátu*	यातां *yátám*	यान्तु *yántu*

First preterite, 'I was going.'

अयां *ayám*	अयाव *ayáva*	अयाम *ayáma*
अयास् *ayás*	अयातं *ayátam*	अयात *ayáta*
अयात् *ayát*	अयातां *ayátám*	अयान् *ayán**

2d Pret. ययौ (373),ययिथ, ययौ; ययिव, ययथुस्, ययतुस्; ययिम, यय, ययुस्. 1st Fut. यातास्मि, यातासि, याता, &c. 2d Fut. यास्यामि, यास्यसि, यास्यति; यास्यावस्, &c. 3d Pret. अयासिषं (433), अयासीस्, अयासीत्; अयासिष्व, अयासिष्टं, अयासिष्टां; अयासिष्म, अयासिष्ट, अयासिषुस्. Bened. यायासं, यायास्, यायात्; यायास्व, &c. Cond. अयास्यं, अयास्यस्, अयास्यत्, &c. *Passive*, Pres. याये, &c.; 3d Pret. 3d sing.

645. Root इ *i* (310). Infin. एतुं *etum*, 'to go.'

For इ with *adhi*, *á*, &c., see 311.

Present, 'I go.'

एमि *emi* †	इवस् *ivas*	इमस् *imas*
एषि *eshi*	इथस् *ithas*	इथ *itha*
एति *eti*	इतस् *itas*	यन्ति *yanti* (34)

Potential, 'I may go.'

इयां *iyám*	इयाव *iyáva*	इयाम *iyáma*
इयास् *iyás*	इयातं *iyátam*	इयात *iyáta*
इयात् *iyát*	इयातां *iyátám*	इयुस् *iyus*

Imperative, 'Let me go.'

अयानि *ayáni*	अयाव *ayáva*	अयाम *ayáma*
इहि *ihi*	इतं *itam*	इत *ita*
एतु *etu*	इतां *itám*	यन्तु *yantu*

First preterite, 'I was going.'

आयं *áyam* (37)	ऐव *aiva* (260. *a*)	ऐम *aima*
ऐस् *ais* (33)	ऐतं *aitam*	ऐत *aita*
ऐत् *ait*	ऐतां *aitám*	आयन् *áyan* ‡

2d Pret. इयाय (372), इययिथ or इयेथ, इयाय; ईयिव, ईयथुस्, ईयतुस्; ईयिम, ईय, ईयुस्. 1st Fut. एतास्मि, &c. 2d Fut. एष्यामि, &c. 3d Pret. (438. *e*) अगां, अगास्, अगात्; अगाव, अगातं, अगातां; अगाम, अगात, अगुस्. Bened. ईयासं, &c. (the initial ई may be shortened when a prep. is prefixed; as, निरियासं 'may I go forth?'). Cond. ऐष्यं, &c. (260. *a*). *Passive*, Pres. ईये; 1st Fut. एताहे or आयिताहे (474); 2d Fut. एष्ये

* Or अयुस् *ayus* by 290. *b*, note.

† This root is also of the 1st conjugation, making अयामि, अयसि, &c., in Pres. tense.

‡ Foster gives अयन्, which might here be expected; but in the 3d pl. *ay* is substituted for the root, making आयन्. See Páṇini (VI. 4. 81), and compare Lagh. Kaum. 608.

अयायि. *Causal*, Pres. यापयामि, &c.; 3d Pret. अयीयपं, &c. *Des.* यियासामि. *Freq.* यायाये, यायामि or यायेमि (3d sing. यायाति or यायेति). *Participles*, Pres. यात् (Nom. case यान्); Past pass. यात; Past indecl. यात्वा, -याय; Fut. pass. यातव्य, यानीय, येय.

or आयिष्ये; 3d Pret. 3d sing. अगायि or अगासत or आयिषत. *Causal*, गमयामि (substituted from गम् at 602) or आययामि or आपयामि; 3d Pret. अजीगमं or आयियं or आपिपं (with *adhi* prefixed, अध्यजीगपं 493.*b*). *Des.* जिगमिषामि (substituted from गम् at 602) or ईयिषामि, -षे. *Participles*, Pres. यत् (Nom. case यन्); Past pass. इत; Past indecl. इत्वा, -इत्य; Fut. pass. एतव्य, अयनीय, इत्य or एय.

EXAMPLES OF OTHER VERBS OF THE SECOND CONJUGATION IN THE ORDER OF THEIR FINAL LETTERS.

646. Root शी (315). Inf. शयितुं 'to lie down,' 'to sleep.' Ātmane. Pres. शये, शेषे, शेते (κεῖται); शेवहे, शयाथे, शयाते; शेमहे (κείμεθα), शेध्वे, शेरते. Pot. शयीय, शयीथास्, शयीत; शयीवहि, शयीयाथां, शयीयातां; शयीमहि, शयीध्वं, शयीरन्. Imp. शयै, शेष्व, शेतां; शयावहै, शयाथां, शयातां; शयामहै, शेध्वं, शेरतां. 1st Pret. अशयि, अशेथास्, अशेत; अशेवहि, अशयाथां, अशयातां; अशेमहि, अशेध्वं, अशेरत. 2d Pret. शिश्ये, शिश्यिषे, शिश्ये; शिश्यिवहे, शिश्याथे, शिश्याते; शिश्यिमहे, शिश्यिध्वे or -श्यिढ्वे, शिश्यिरे. 1st Fut. शयिताहे, &c. 2d Fut. शयिष्ये, &c. 3d Pret. अशयिषि, अशयिष्ठास्, अशयिष्ट; अशयिष्वहि, अशयिषाथां, अशयिषातां; अशयिष्महि, अशयिध्वं or -यिढ्वं, अशयिषत. Bened. शयिषीय, &c. Cond. अशयिष्ये. *Passive*, Pres. शय्ये, &c.; 3d Pret. 3d sing. अशायि. *Causal*, Pres. शाययामि; 3d Pret. अशीशयं. *Des.* शिशयिषे or शिशीषे. *Freq.* शाशय्ये, शेशेमि or शेशयीमि. *Participles*, Pres. शयान (526. *a*); Past pass. शयित; Past indecl. शयित्वा, -शय्य; Fut. pass. शयितव्य, शयनीय, शेय.

647. Root सू or सु (312). Inf. सोतुं or सवितुं 'to bring forth.' Ātmane. Pres. सुवे, सूषे, सूते; सूवहे, सुवाथे, सुवाते; सूमहे, सूध्वे, सुवते. Pot. सुवीय, &c. Imp. सुवै (Pāṇini VII. 3, 88), सूष्व, सूतां; सुवावहै, सुवाथां, सुवातां; सुवामहै, सूध्वं, सुवतां. 1st Pret. असुवि, असूथास्, असूत; असूवहि, असुवाथां, असुवातां; असूमहि, असूध्वं, असुवत. 2d Pret. सुषुवे, सुषुविषे, सुषुवे; सुषुविवहे, सुषुवाथे, सुषुवाते; सुषुविमहे, सुषुविढ्वे, सुषुविरे. 1st Fut. सोताहे or सविताहे. 2d Fut. सोष्ये or सविष्ये. 3d Pret. असविषि, असविष्ठास्, असविष्ट; असविष्वहि, असविषाथां, असविषातां; असविष्महि, असविध्वं or -ढ्वं, असविषत. Or असोषि, असोष्ठास्, असोष्ट; असोष्वहि, असोषाथां, असोषातां; असोष्महि, असोढ्वं, असोषत. Bened. सोषीय or सविषीय, &c. Cond. असोष्ये or असविष्ये, &c. *Passive*, Pres. सूये; 3d Pret. 3d sing. असावि.

Causal, Pres. सावयामि; 3d Pret. असूषवं. *Des.* सुसूषामि, -षे. *Freq.* सोषूये, सोषोमि or सोषवीमि. *Participles*, Pres. सुवान; Past pass. सुत or सूत or सून; Past indecl. सूत्वा or सुत्वा, -सूय; Fut. pass. सोतव्य or सवितव्य, सवनीय, साव्य or सव्य.

648. Root स्तु (313). Inf. स्तोतुं 'to praise.' Parasmai and Átmane. Pres. स्तौमि or स्तवीमि, स्तौषि or स्तवीषि, स्तौति or स्तवीति; स्तुवस् or स्तुवीवस्*, स्तुथस् or स्तुवीथस्*, स्तुतम् or स्तुवीतस्; स्तुमस् or स्तुवीमस्*, स्तुथ or स्तुवीथ*, स्तुवन्ति. Átm. स्तुवे, स्तुषे or स्तुवीषे*, स्तुते or स्तुवीते; स्तुवहे or स्तुवीवहे, स्तुवाथे, स्तुवाते; स्तुमहे or स्तुवीमहे*, स्तुध्वे or स्तुवीध्वे*, स्तुवते. Pot. स्तुयां or स्तुवीयां*, &c. Átm. स्तुवीय, &c. Imp. स्तुवानि or स्तवानि, स्तुहि or स्तुवीहि*, स्तौतु or स्तवीतु; स्तवाव, स्तुतं or स्तुवीतं, स्तुतां or स्तुवीतां; स्तवाम, स्तुत or स्तुवीत, स्तुवन्तु. Átm. स्तवै, स्तुष्व or स्तुवीष्व*, स्तुतां or स्तुवीतां; स्तवावहै, स्तुवाथां, स्तुवातां; स्तवामहै, स्तुध्वं or स्तुवीध्वं*, स्तुवतां. 1st Pret. अस्तुवं or अस्तवं, अस्तौस् or अस्तवीस्, अस्तौत् or अस्तवीत्; अस्तुव or अस्तुवीव*, अस्तुतं or अस्तुवीतं, अस्तुतां or अस्तुवीतां; अस्तुम or अस्तुवीम*, अस्तुत or अस्तुवीत, अस्तुवन्. Átm. अस्तुवि, अस्तुथास् or अस्तुवीथास्, अस्तुत or अस्तुवीत; अस्तुवहि or अस्तुवीवहि*, अस्तुवाथां, अस्तुवातां; अस्तुमहि or अस्तुवीमहि*, अस्तुध्वं or अस्तुवीध्वं*, अस्तुवत. 2d Pret. (368) तुष्टाव, तुष्टोथ, तुष्टाव; तुष्टुव, तुष्टुवथुस्, तुष्टुवतुस्; तुष्टुम, तुष्टुव, तुष्टुवुस्. Átm. तुष्टुवे, तुष्टुषे, तुष्टुवे; तुष्टुवहे, तुष्टुवाथे, तुष्टुवाते; तुष्टुमहे, तुष्टुढ्वे, तुष्टुविरे. 1st Fut. स्तोतास्मि, &c. Átm. स्तोताहे, &c. 2d Fut. स्तोष्यामि, &c. Átm. स्तोष्ये, &c. 3d Pret. (428. *a*) अस्ताविषं, अस्तावीस्, अस्तावीत्; अस्ताविष्व, अस्ताविष्टं, अस्ताविष्टां; अस्ताविष्म, अस्ताविष्ट, अस्ताविषुस्. Átm. अस्तोषि, अस्तोष्ठास्, अस्तोष्ट; अस्तोष्वहि, अस्तोषाथां, अस्तोषातां; अस्तोष्महि, अस्तोढ्वं, अस्तोषत. Bened. स्तूयासं, &c. Átm. स्तोषीय, &c. Cond. अस्तोष्यं, &c. Átm. अस्तोष्ये, &c. *Passive*, Pres. स्तूये; 3d Pret. 3d sing. अस्तावि. *Causal*, Pres. स्तावयामि; 3d Pret. अतुष्टवं. *Des.* तुष्टूषामि, -षे. *Freq.* तोष्टूये, तोष्टोमि. *Participles*, Pres. स्तुवत्; Past pass. स्तुत; Past indecl. स्तुत्वा, -स्तुत्य; Fut. pass. स्तोतव्य, स्तवनीय, स्तुत्य or स्ताव्य or स्तव्य.

649. Root ब्रू (314). Inf. वक्तुं (borrowed from वच् at 650) 'to say,' 'to speak.' Parasmai and Átmane. Pres. ब्रवीमि, ब्रवीषि †, ब्रवीति †; ब्रूवस्, ब्रूथस् †, ब्रूतस् †; ब्रूमस्, ब्रूथ, ब्रुवन्ति †. Átm. ब्रुवे, ब्रूषे, ब्रूते; ब्रूवहे, ब्रुवाथे, ब्रुवाते; ब्रूमहे, ब्रूध्वे, ब्रुवते. Pot. ब्रूयां, ब्रूयास्, &c. Átm. ब्रुवीय,

---

* Some authorities reject these forms.

† For these forms are sometimes substituted 2d sing. आत्थ, 3d sing. आह; 2d du. आहथुस्, 3d du. आहतुस्; 3d pl. आहुस्; all from the 2d preterite of a defective root अह्, with a present signification.

ब्रुवीथास्, &c. Imp. ब्रवाणि (58), ब्रूहि, ब्रवीतु; ब्रवाव, ब्रूतं, ब्रूतां; ब्रवाम, ब्रूत, ब्रुवन्तु. Átm. ब्रवै, ब्रूष्व, ब्रूतां; ब्रवावहै, ब्रुवाथां, ब्रुवातां; ब्रवामहै, ब्रूध्वं, ब्रुवतां. 1st Pret. अब्रुवं (314. *a*), अब्रवीस्, अब्रवीत्; अब्रूव, अब्रूतं, अब्रूतां; अब्रूम, अब्रूत, अब्रुवन्. Átm. अब्रुवि, अब्रूथास्, अब्रूत; अब्रूवहि, अब्रुवाथां, अब्रुवातां; अब्रूमहि, अब्रूध्वं, अब्रुवत. The other tenses and forms are borrowed from वच्; as, 2d Pret. उवाच, &c.; 1st Fut. वक्तास्मि, &c.; see वच् at 650. But the Pres. participles are ब्रुवत् and ब्रुवाण.

650. Root वच् (319). Inf. वक्तुं 'to say,' 'to speak.' Parasmai. In the conjugational tenses Átmane also. Pres. वच्मि, वक्षि, वक्ति; वच्वस्, वक्थस्, वक्तस्; वच्मस्, वक्थ, ब्रुवन्ति (borrowed from ब्रू at 649). Pot. वच्यां, वच्यास्, &c. Imp. वचानि, वग्धि, वक्तु; वचाव, वक्तं, वक्तां; वचाम, वक्त, ब्रुवन्तु (borrowed from ब्रू). 1st Pret. अवचं, अवक् or अवग् (43. *a*), अवक् or अवग् (43. *a*); अवच्व, अवक्तं, अवक्तां; अवच्म, अवक्त, अवचन्*. 2d Pret. (375. *c*) उवाच, उवचिथ or उवक्थ, उवाच; ऊचिव, ऊचथुस्, ऊचतुस्; ऊचिम, ऊच, ऊचुस्. Átm. ऊचे, ऊचिषे, ऊचे; ऊचिवहे, ऊचाथे, ऊचाते; ऊचिमहे, ऊचिध्वे or -ढ्वे, ऊचिरे. 1st Fut. वक्तास्मि, &c. Átm. वक्ताहे, &c. 2d Fut. वक्ष्यामि, &c. Átm. वक्ष्ये, &c. 3d Pret. (441) अवोचं, अवोचस्, अवोचत्; अवोचाव, अवोचतं, अवोचतां; अवोचाम, अवोचत, अवोचन्. Átm. अवोचे, अवोचथास्, अवोचत; अवोचावहि, अवोचेथां, अवोचेतां; अवोचामहि, अवोचध्वं, अवोचन्त. Bened. उच्यासं, &c. Átm. वक्षीय, &c. Cond. अवक्ष्यं. Átm. अवक्ष्ये, &c. *Passive*, Pres. उच्ये (471); 3d Pret. 3d sing. अवाचि. *Causal*, Pres. वाचयामि; 3d Pret. अवीवचं. *Des.* विवक्षामि, -क्षे. *Freq.* वावच्ये, वावच्मि. *Participles*, Pres. ब्रुवत्; Átm. ब्रुवाण (borrowed from ब्रू at 649); Past pass. उक्त; Past indecl. उक्त्वा, -उच्य; Fut. pass. वक्तव्य, वचनीय, वाच्य or वाक्य.

651. Root मृज् (324). Inf. मार्ष्टुं or मार्जितुं 'to wipe,' 'to rub,' 'to clean.' Parasmai. Pres. मार्ज्मि, मार्क्षि (296), मार्ष्टि (297); मृज्वस्, मृष्ठस् (297), मृष्टस्; मृज्मस्, मृष्ठ, मार्जन्ति or मृजन्ति. Pot. मृज्यां, मृज्यास्, &c. Imp. मार्जानि, मृड्ढि (303), मार्ष्टु; मार्जाव, मृष्टं, मृष्टां; मार्जाम, मृष्ट, मार्जन्तु or मृजन्तु. 1st Pret. अमार्जं, अमार्ट् or अमार्ड् (292), अमार्ट् or अमार्ड्; अमृज्व, अमृष्टं, अमृष्टां; अमृज्म, अमृष्ट, अमार्जन् or अमृजन्. 2d Pret. ममार्ज, ममार्जिथ or ममार्ष्ठ (297), ममार्ज; ममृजिव or ममार्जिव, ममृजथुस् or ममार्जथुस्, ममृजतुस् or ममार्जतुस्; ममृजिम or ममार्जिम, ममृज or ममार्ज, ममृजुस् or ममार्जुस्. 1st Fut. मार्ष्टास्मि or मार्जितास्मि, &c. 2d Fut. मार्क्ष्यामि or मार्जिष्यामि, &c. 3d Pret. अमार्क्षं, अमार्क्षीस्, अमार्क्षीत्; अमार्क्ष्व, अमार्ष्टं, अमार्ष्टां; अमार्क्ष्म, अमार्ष्ट, अमार्क्षुस्. Or अमार्जिषं, अमार्जीस्, अमार्जीत्; अमार्जिष्व, &c. Bened. मृज्यासं, &c.

* According to some, the 3d pl. of the 1st preterite is also wanting.

Cond. अमार्क्ष्यं or अमार्जिष्यं. *Passive*, Pres. मृज्ये, &c.; 3d Pret. 3d sing. अमार्जि. *Causal*, Pres. मार्जयामि; 3d Pret. अममार्जं or अमीमृजं. *Des.* मिमार्क्षामि or मिमृक्षामि or मिमार्जिषामि. *Freq.* मरीमृज्ये or मरिमृज्ये, मरीमार्ज्मि (3d sing. मरीमार्ष्टि). *Participles*, Pres. मार्जत्; Past pass. मृष्ट; Past indecl. मृष्ट्वा or मार्जित्वा, -मृज्य; Fut. pass. मार्ष्टव्य or मार्जितव्य, मार्जनीय, मार्ग्य or मृज्य.

652. Root अद् (317). Inf. अत्तुं 'to eat.' Parasmai. Pres. अद्मि, अत्सि, अत्ति; अद्वस्, अत्थस्, अत्तस्; अद्मस्, अत्थ, अदन्ति. Pot. अद्यां, &c. Imp. अदानि, अद्धि, अत्तु; अदाव, अत्तं, अत्तां; अदाम, अत्त, अदन्तु. 1st Pret. आदं, आदस् (317. *a*), आदत्; आद्व, आत्तं, आत्तां; आद्म, आत्त, आदन्. 2d Pret. आद, आदिथ, आद; आदिव, आदथुस्, आदतुस्; आदिम, आद, आदुस्. 1st Fut. अत्तास्मि, &c. 2d Fut. अत्स्यामि, &c. 3d Pret. अघसं (borrowed from root घस्), अघसस्, अघसत्; अघसाव, अघसतं, अघसतां; अघसाम, अघसत, अघसन्. Bened. अद्यासं, &c. Cond. आत्स्यं, &c. *Passive*, Pres. अद्ये; 3d Pret. 3d sing. आदि. *Causal*, Pres. आदयामि; 3d Pret. आदिदं. *Des.* जिघत्सामि (borrowed from घस्). *Participles*, Pres. अदत्; Past pass. जग्ध; Past indecl. जग्ध्वा; Fut. pass. अत्तव्य, अदनीय, आद्य.

653. Root रुद् (326). Inf. रोदितुं 'to weep.' Parasmai. Pres. रोदिमि, रोदिषि, रोदिति; रुदिवस्, रुदिथस्, रुदितस्; रुदिमस्, रुदिथ, रुदन्ति. Pot. रुद्यां, &c. Imp. रोदानि, रुदिहि, रोदितु; रोदाव, रुदितं, रुदितां; रोदाम, रुदित, रुदन्तु. 1st Pret. अरोदं, अरोदस् or अरोदीस्, अरोदत् or अरोदीत् (Páṇini VII. 3. 98, 99); अरुदिव, अरुदितं, अरुदितां; अरुदिम, अरुदित, अरुदन्. 2d Pret. रुरोद, रुरोदिथ, रुरोद; रुरुदिव, रुरुदथुस्, रुरुदतुस्; रुरुदिम, रुरुद, रुरुदुस्. 1st Fut. रोदितास्मि, &c. 2d Fut. रोदिष्यामि, &c. 3d Pret. अरुदं, अरुदस्, अरुदत्; अरुदाव, अरुदतं, अरुदतां; अरुदाम, अरुदत, अरुदन्. Or अरोदिषं, अरोदीस्, अरोदीत्; अरोदिष्व, अरोदिष्टं, अरोदिष्टां; अरोदिष्म, अरोदिष्ट, अरोदिषुस्. Bened. रुद्यासं, &c. Cond. अरोदिष्यं, &c. *Passive*, Pres. रुद्ये; 3d Pret. 3d sing. अरोदि. *Causal*, Pres. रोदयामि; 3d Pret. अरूरुदं. *Des.* रुरुदिषामि. *Freq.* रोरुद्ये, रोरोद्मि (3d sing. रोरोत्ति) or रोरुदीमि. *Participles*, Pres. रुदत्; Past pass. रुदित; Past indecl. रुदित्वा, -रुद्य; Fut. pass. रोदितव्य, रोदनीय, रोद्य.

654. Root हन् (318). Inf. हन्तुं 'to kill,' 'to strike.' Parasmai. Pres. हन्मि, हंसि, हन्ति; हन्वस्, हथस्, हतस्; हन्मस्, हथ, घ्नन्ति. Pot. हन्यां, &c. Imp. हनानि, जहि, हन्तु; हनाव, हतं, हतां; हनाम, हत, घ्नन्तु. 1st Pret. अहनं, अहन्, अहन् (292); अहन्व, अहतं, अहतां; अहन्म, अहत, अघ्नन्. 2d Pret. जघान (376), जघनिथ or जघन्थ, जघान; जघ्निव (376), जघ्नथुस्, जघ्नतुस्; जघ्निम, जघ्न, जघ्नुस्. 1st Fut. हन्तास्मि, &c. 2d Fut. हनिष्यामि,

&c. 3d Pret. (432. *a*) अवधिषं, अवधीस्, अवधीत्; अवधिष्व, अवधिष्टं, अवधिष्टां; अवधिष्म, अवधिष्ट, अवधिषुस्. Bened. वध्यासं, &c. Cond. अहनिष्यं, &c. *Passive*, Pres. हन्ये; 2d Pret. जघ्ने (473); 3d Pret. अहंसि, अहथास् (426. *b*), अघानि (or अवधि, borrowed from वध्); अहंस्वहि, अहंसाथां, अहंसातां; अहंस्महि, &c.; 1st Fut. हन्ताहे or घानिताहे, &c.; 2d Fut. हनिष्ये or घानिष्ये, &c. *Causal*, Pres. घातयामि; 3d Pret. अजीघतं. *Des.* जिघांसामि. *Freq.* जेघ्नीये, जङ्घन्मि or जंहन्मि or जङ्घनीमि; see 708. *Participles*, Pres. घ्नत्; Past pass. हत; Past indecl. हत्वा, -हत्य; Fut. pass. हन्तव्य, हननीय, घात्य.

655. Root स्वप् (326). Inf. स्वप्तुं 'to sleep.' Parasmai. Pres. स्वपिमि, स्वपिषि, स्वपिति; स्वपिवस्, स्वपिथस्, स्वपितस्; स्वपिमस्, स्वपिथ, स्वपन्ति. Pot. स्वप्यां, &c. Imp. स्वपानि, स्वपिहि, स्वपितु; स्वपाव, स्वपितं, स्वपितां; स्वपाम, स्वपित, स्वपन्तु. 1st Pret. अस्वपं, अस्वपस् or अस्वपीस्, अस्वपत् or अस्वपीत्; अस्वपिव, &c.; see रुद् at 653. 2d Pret. (382) सुष्वाप, सुष्वपिथ or सुष्वप्थ, सुष्वाप; सुषुपिव, सुषुपथुस्, सुषुपतुस्; सुषुपिम, सुषुप, सुषुपुस्. 1st Fut. स्वप्तास्मि, &c. 2d Fut. स्वप्स्यामि, &c. 3d Pret. अस्वाप्सं, अस्वाप्सीस्, अस्वाप्सीत्; अस्वाप्स्व, अस्वाप्तं, अस्वाप्तां; अस्वाप्स्म, अस्वाप्त, अस्वाप्सुस्. Bened. सुप्यासं, &c. Cond. अस्वप्स्यं, &c. *Passive*, Pres. सुप्ये (471); 3d Pret. 3d sing. अस्वापि. *Causal*, Pres. स्वापयामि; 3d Pret. असूषुपं, &c. *Des.* सुषुप्सामि. *Freq.* सोषुप्ये, सास्वप्मि or सास्वपीमि. *Participles*, Pres. स्वपत्; Past pass. सुप्त; Past indecl. सुप्त्वा, -सुप्य; Fut. pass. स्वप्तव्य, स्वपनीय, स्वाप्य.

656. Root वश् (320). Inf. वशितुं 'to desire,' 'to wish.' Parasmai. Pres. वश्मि, वक्षि (302), वष्टि (300); उश्वस्, उष्ठस्, उष्टस्; उश्मस्, उष्ठ, उशन्ति. Pot. उश्यां, &c. Imp. वशानि, उड्ढि (303), वष्टु; वशाव, उष्टं, उष्टां; वशाम, उष्ट, उशन्तु. 1st Pret. अवशं, अवट् or अवड् (292), अवट् or अवड्; औश्व (260. *a*), औष्टं, औष्टां; औश्म, औष्ट, औशन्. 2d Pret. (375. *c*) उवाश, उवशिथ, उवाश; ऊशिव, ऊशथुस्, ऊशतुस्; ऊशिम, ऊश, ऊशुस्. 1st Fut. वशितास्मि, &c. 2d Fut. वशिष्यामि, &c. 3d Pret. अवाशिषं, अवाशीस्, अवाशीत्, &c.; or अवशिषं, -शीस्, -शीत्, &c.; see 427. Bened. उश्यासं, &c. Cond. अवशिष्यं. *Passive*, उश्ये (471); 3d Pret. 3d sing. अवाशि or अवशि. *Causal*, Pres. वाशयामि; 3d Pret. अवीवशं. *Des.* विवशिषामि. *Freq.* वावश्ये, वावश्मि or वावशीमि. *Participles*, Pres. उशत्; Past pass. उशित; Past indecl. वशित्वा, -उश्य; Fut. pass. वशितव्य, वशनीय, वाश्य.

657. Root द्विष् (309). Inf. द्वेष्टुं 'to hate.' Parasmai and Ātmane. Pres. द्वेष्मि, द्वेक्षि (302), द्वेष्टि (301); द्विष्वस्, द्विष्ठस्, द्विष्टस्; द्विष्मस्, द्विष्ठ, द्विषन्ति. Ātm. द्विषे, द्विक्षे, द्विष्टे; द्विष्वहे, द्विषाथे, द्विषाते; द्विष्महे, द्विड्ढ्वे,

द्विषते. Pot. द्विष्यां, &c. Átm. द्विषीय, &c. Imp. द्वेषाणि, द्विड्ढि, द्वेष्टु; द्वेषाव, द्विष्टं, द्विष्टां; द्वेषाम, द्विष्ट, द्विषन्तु. Átm. द्वेषै, द्विक्ष्व, द्विष्टां; द्वेषावहै, द्विषाथां, द्विषातां; द्वेषामहै, द्विड्ढ्वं, द्विषतां. 1st Pret. अद्वेषं, अद्वेट् (292), अद्वेट्; अद्विष्व, अद्विष्टं, अद्विष्टां; अद्विष्म, अद्विष्ट, अद्विषन् or अद्विषुस्. Átm. अद्विषि, अद्विष्ठास्, अद्विष्ट; अद्विष्वहि, अद्विषाथां, अद्विषातां; अद्विष्महि, अद्विड्ढ्वं, अद्विषत. 2d Pret. दिद्वेष, दिद्वेषिथ, दिद्वेष; दिद्विषिव, दिद्विषथुस्, दिद्विषतुस्; दिद्विषिम, दिद्विष, दिद्विषुस्. Átm. दिद्विषे, दिद्विषिषे, दिद्विषे; दिद्विषिवहे, दिद्विषाथे, दिद्विषाते; दिद्विषिमहे, दिद्विषिध्वे or -षिढ्वे, दिद्विषिरे. 1st Fut. द्वेष्टास्मि, &c. Átm. द्वेष्टाहे, &c. 2d Fut. द्वेक्ष्यामि, &c. Átm. द्वेक्ष्ये, &c. 3d Pret. (439. *a*) अद्विक्षं, -क्षस्, -क्षत्; -क्षाव, -क्षतं, -क्षतां; -क्षाम, -क्षत, -क्षन्. Átm. (439. *c*) अद्विक्षि, -क्षथास्, -क्षत; -क्षावहि, -क्षाथां, -क्षातां; -क्षामहि, -क्षध्वं, -क्षन्त. Bened. द्विष्यासं, &c. Átm. द्विक्षीय, &c. Cond. अद्वेक्ष्यं. Átm. अद्वेक्ष्ये. *Passive*, Pres. द्विष्ये, &c.; 3d Pret. 3d sing. अद्वेषि. *Causal*, Pres. द्वेषयामि; 3d Pret. अदिद्विषं. *Des*. दिद्विक्षामि, -क्षे. *Freq*. देद्विष्ये, देद्वेष्मि or देद्विषीमि. *Participles*, Pres. द्विषत्; Past pass. द्विष्ट; Past indecl. द्विष्ट्वा, -द्विष्य; Fut. pass. द्वेष्टव्य, द्वेषणीय, द्वेष्य.

658. Root शास् (323). Inf. शासितुं 'to rule,' 'to punish.' Parasmai. (With आ 'to bless,' Átmane.) Pres. शास्मि, शास्सि, शास्ति; शास्वस्, शिष्ठस्, शिष्टस्; शास्मस्, शिष्ठ, शासति (290. *b*). Átm. शासे, शास्से, शास्ते; शास्वहे, शासाथे, शासाते; शास्महे, शाद्ध्वे or शाध्वे (304), शासते. Pot. शिष्यां, शिष्यास्, &c. Átm. शासीय, &c. Imp. शासानि, शाद्धि or शाधि (304), शास्तु; शासाव, शिष्टं, शिष्टां; शासाम, शिष्ट, शासतु. Átm. शासै, &c. 1st Pret. अशासं, अशात् or अशास् (292, 304. *a*), अशात्; अशास्व, अशिष्टं, अशिष्टां; अशास्म, अशिष्ट, अशासुस्. Átm. अशासि, &c. 2d Pret. शशास, शशासिथ, शशास; शशासिव, शशासथुस्, शशासतुस्; शशासिम, शशास, शशासुस्. Átm. शशासे, शशासिषे, &c. 1st Fut. शासितास्मि. Átm. शासिताहे, &c. 2d Fut. शासिष्यामि. Átm. शासिष्ये, &c. 3d Pret. (441) अशिषं, अशिषस्, अशिषत्; अशिषाव, अशिषतं, अशिषतां; अशिषाम, अशिषत, अशिषन्. Átm. अशासिषि, अशासिष्ठास्, अशासिष्ट; अशासिष्वहि, अशासिषाथां, अशासिषातां; अशासिष्महि, अशासिढ्वं, अशासिषत. Bened. शिष्यासं, &c. Átm. शासिषीय, &c. Cond. अशासिष्यं, &c. Átm. अशासिष्ये, &c. *Passive*, Pres. शिष्ये, &c.; 3d Pret. 3d sing. अशासि. *Causal*, शासयामि, &c.; 3d Pret. अशशासं. *Des*. शिशासिषामि. *Freq*. शेशिष्ये, शाशास्मि or शाशासीमि. *Participles*, Pres. शासत् (141. *a*); Past pass. शिष्ट; Past indecl. शासित्वा or शिष्ट्वा, -शिष्य; Fut. pass. शासितव्य, शासनीय, शिष्य.

659. Root दिह्. Inf. देग्धुं 'to anoint,' 'to smear.' Parasmai and Átmane. Pres. देह्मि, धेक्षि (306. *a*), देग्धि (305); दिह्वस्, दिग्धस् (305), दिग्धस्; दिह्मस्, दिग्ध, दिहन्ति. Átm. दिहे, धिक्षे, दिग्धे; दिह्वहे, दिहाथे,

दिहाते; दिह्महे, धिग्ध्वे (306. *d*), दिहते. Pot. दिह्यां, &c. Átm. दिहीय, &c. Imp. देहानि, दिग्धि, देग्धु; देहाव, दिग्धं, दिग्धां; देहाम, दिग्ध, दिहन्तु. Átm. देहै, धिक्ष्व, दिग्धां; देहावहै, दिहाथां, दिहातां; देहामहै, धिग्ध्वं, दिहतां. 1st Pret. अदेहं, अधेक् or अधेग् (292. *a*), अधेक् or अधेग्; अदिह्व, अदिग्धं, अदिग्धां; अदिह्म, अदिग्ध, अदिहन्. Átm. अदिहि, अदिग्धास्, अदिग्ध; अदिह्वहि, अदिहाथां, अदिहातां; अदिह्महि, अधिग्ध्वं, अदिहत. 2d Pret. दिदेह, दिदेहिथ, दिदेह; दिदिहिव, दिदिहथुस्, दिदिहतुस्; दिदिहिम, दिदिह, दिदिहुस्. Átm. दिदिहे, दिदिहिषे, दिदिहे; दिदिहिवहे, दिदिहाथे, दिदिहाते; दिदिहिमहे, दिदिहिध्वे or -ढ्वे, दिदिहिरे. 1st Fut. देग्धास्मि. Átm. देग्धाहे, &c. 2d Fut. धेक्ष्यामि. Átm. धेक्ष्ये, &c. 3d Pret. (439) अधिक्षं, अधिक्षस्, अधिक्षत्; अधिक्षाव, अधिक्षतं, अधिक्षतां; अधिक्षाम, अधिक्षत, अधिक्षन्. Átm. अधिक्षि, अधिक्षथास् or अदिग्धास्, अधिक्षत or अदिग्ध; अधिक्षावहि, अधिक्षाथां, अधिक्षातां; अधिक्षामहि, अधिक्षध्वं or अधिग्ध्वं, अधिक्षन्त. Bened. दिह्यासं. Átm. धिक्षीय, &c. Cond. अधेक्ष्यं. Átm. अधेक्ष्ये. *Passive,* Pres. दिह्ये; 3d Pret. 3d sing. अदेहि. *Causal,* Pres. देहयामि; 3d Pret. अदीदिहं. *Des.* दिधिक्षामि, -क्षे. *Freq.* देदिह्ये, देदेह्मि (3d sing. देदेग्धि). *Participles,* Pres. दिहत्; Átm. दिहान; Past pass. दिग्ध; Past indecl. दिग्ध्वा, -दिह्य; Fut. pass. देग्धव्य, देहनीय, देह्य.

660. Root दुह्. Inf. दोग्धुं 'to milk.' Parasmai and Átmane. Pres. दोह्मि, धोक्षि (306. *a*), दोग्धि (305); दुह्वस्, दुग्धस्, दुग्धस्; दुह्मस्, दुग्ध, दुहन्ति. Átm. दुहे, धुक्षे, दुग्धे; दुह्वहे, दुहाथे, दुहाते; दुह्महे, धुग्ध्वे (306. *d*), दुहते. Pot. दुह्यां, &c. Átm. दुहीय, &c. Imp. दोहानि, दुग्धि (306. *c*), दोग्धु; दोहाव, दुग्धं, दुग्धां; दोहाम, दुग्ध, दुहन्तु. Átm. दोहै, धुक्ष्व, दुग्धां; दोहावहै, दुहाथां, दुहातां; दोहामहै, धुग्ध्वं (306. *d*), दुहतां. 1st Pret. अदोहं, अधोक् or अधोग् (292. *a*), अधोक् or अधोग्; अदुह्व, अदुग्धं, अदुग्धां; अदुह्म, अदुग्ध, अदुहन्. Átm. अदुहि, अदुग्धास्, अदुग्ध; अदुह्वहि, अदुहाथां, अदुहातां; अदुह्महि, अधुग्ध्वं, अदुहत. 2d Pret. दुदोह, दुदोहिथ, दुदोह; दुदुहिव, दुदुहथुस्, दुदुहतुस्; दुदुहिम, दुदुह, दुदुहुस्. Átm. दुदुहे, दुदुहिषे, दुदुहे; दुदुहिवहे, दुदुहाथे, दुदुहाते; दुदुहिमहे, दुदुहिध्वे or -ढ्वे, दुदुहिरे. 1st Fut. दोग्धास्मि. Átm. दोग्धाहे, &c. 2d Fut. धोक्ष्यामि. Átm. धोक्ष्ये, &c. 3d Pret. (439. *a*) अधुक्षं, अधुक्षस्, अधुक्षत्; अधुक्षाव, अधुक्षतं, अधुक्षतां; अधुक्षाम, अधुक्षत, अधुक्षन्. Átm. (439. *c*) अधुक्षि, अधुक्षथास् or अदुग्धास्, अधुक्षत or अदुग्ध; अधुक्षावहि, अधुक्षाथां, अधुक्षातां; अधुक्षामहि, अधुक्षध्वं or अधुग्ध्वं, अधुक्षन्त. Bened. दुह्यासं. Átm. धुक्षीय, &c. Cond. अधोक्ष्यं. Átm. अधोक्ष्ये, &c. *Passive,* Pres. दुह्ये; 3d Pret. 3d sing. अदोहि. *Causal,* Pres. दोहयामि; 3d Pret. अदूदुहं. *Des.* दुधुक्षामि, -क्षे. *Freq.* दोदुह्ये, दोदोह्मि (3d sing. दोदोग्धि). *Participles,* Pres. दुहत्, दुहान; Past pass. दुग्ध; Past indecl. दुग्ध्वा, -दुह्य; Fut. pass. दोग्धव्य, दोहनीय, दोह्य.

661. Root लिह्. Inf. लेढुं 'to lick.' Parasmai and Átmane. Pres. लेह्मि, लेक्षि (306), लेढि (305. *a*); लिह्वस्, लीढस् (305. *a*), लीढस्; लिह्मस्, लीढ, लिहन्ति. Átm. लिहे, लिक्षे, लीढे; लिह्वहे, लिहाथे, लिहाते; लिह्महे, लीढ्वे, लिहते. Pot. लिह्यां. Átm. लिहीय, &c. Imp. लेहानि, लीढि (306. *c*), लेढु; लेहाव, लीढं, लीढां; लेहाम, लीढ, लिहन्तु. Átm. लेहै, लिक्ष्व, लीढां; लेहावहै, लिहाथां, लिहातां; लेहामहै, लीढ्वं (306. *c*), लिहतां. 1st Pret. अलेहं, अलेट् or अलेड् (292. *a*), अलेट् or अलेड्; अलिह्व, अलीढं, अलीढां; अलिह्म, अलीढ, अलिहन्. Átm. अलिहि, अलीढास्, अलीढ; अलिह्वहि, अलिहाथां, अलिहातां; अलिह्महि, अलीढ्वं, अलिहत. 2d Pret. लिलेह, लिलेहिथ, लिलेह; लिलिहिव, लिलिहथुस्, लिलिहतुस्; लिलिहिम, लिलिह, लिलिहुस्. Átm. लिलिहे, लिलिहिषे, &c. 1st Fut. लेढास्मि. Átm. लेढाहे, &c. 2d Fut. लेक्ष्यामि. Átm. लेक्ष्ये, &c. 3d Pret. (439. *a*) अलिक्षं, -क्षस्, -क्षत्; -क्षाव, -क्षतं, -क्षतां; -क्षाम, -क्षत, -क्षन्. Átm. (439. *c*) अलिक्षि, अलिक्षथास् or अलीढास्, अलिक्षत or अलीढ; अलिक्षावहि, -क्षाथां, -क्षातां; अलिक्षामहि, अलिक्षध्वं or अलीढ्वं, अलिक्षन्त. Bened. लिह्यासं. Átm. लिक्षीय, &c. Cond. अलेक्ष्यं. Átm. अलेक्ष्ये, &c. *Passive*, Pres. लिह्ये; 3d Pret. 3d sing. अलेहि. *Causal*, Pres. लेहयामि; 3d Pret. अलीलिहं. *Des.* लिलिक्षामि, -क्षे. *Freq.* लेलिह्ये, लेलेह्मि (3d sing. लेलेढि). *Participles*, Pres. लिहत्; Átm. लिहान; Past pass. लीढ; Past indecl. लीढ्वा, -लिह्य; Fut. pass. लेढव्य, लेहनीय, लेह्य.

EXAMPLES OF PRIMITIVE VERBS OF THE THIRD CONJUGATION, EXPLAINED AT 330.

662. Root हु *hu*. Infin. होतुं *hotum*, 'to sacrifice.'

PARASMAI-PADA. *Present tense*, 'I sacrifice.'

जुहोमि *juhomi*	जुहुवस् *juhuvas* *	जुहुमस् *juhumas* †
जुहोषि *juhoshi*	जुहुथस् *juhuthas*	जुहुथ *juhutha*
जुहोति *juhoti*	जुहुतस् *juhutas*	जुह्वति *juhwati*

Potential, 'I may sacrifice.'

जुहुयाम् *juhuyám*	जुहुयाव *juhuyáva*	जुहुयाम *juhuyáma*
जुहुयास् *juhuyás*	जुहुयातं *juhuyátam*	जुहुयात *juhuyáta*
जुहुयात् *juhuyát*	जुहुयातां *juhuyátám*	जुहुयुस् *juhuyus*

Imperative, 'Let me sacrifice.'

जुहवानि *juhaváni*	जुहवाव *juhaváva*	जुहवाम *juhaváma*
जुहुधि *juhudhi* (291)	जुहुतं *juhutam*	जुहुत *juhuta*
जुहोतु *juhotu*	जुहुतां *juhutám*	जुह्वतु *juhwatu*

* Or जुह्वस् *juhwas*. † Or जुह्मस् *juhmas*.

First preterite, 'I was sacrificing.'

अजुहवं *ajuhavam*	अजुहुव *ajuhuva*	अजुहुम *ajuhuma*
अजुहोस् *ajuhos*	अजुहुतं *ajuhutam*	अजुहुत *ajuhuta*
अजुहोत् *ajuhot*	अजुहुतां *ajuhutám*	अजुहवुस् *ajuhavus* (330)

2d Pret. (367. *b*) जुहाव, जुहविथ or जुहोथ, जुहाव; जुहुविव, जुहुवथुस्, जुहुवतुस्; जुहुविम, जुहुव, जुहुवुस्. Or जुहवाञ्चकार, &c.; see 385. *c*. 1st Fut. होतास्मि, &c. 2d Fut. होष्यामि, &c. 3d Pret. अहौषं, अहौषीस्, अहौषीत्; अहौष्व, अहौष्टं, अहौष्टां; अहौष्म, अहौष्ट, अहौषुस्. Bened. हूयासं, &c. Cond. अहोष्यं, &c. *Passive,* Pres. हूये; 3d Pret. 3d sing. अहावि, *Causal,* Pres. हावयामि; 3d Pret. अजूहवं. *Des.* जुहूषामि. *Freq.* जोहूये, जोहोमि or जोहवीमि. *Participles,* Pres. जुह्वत्; Past pass. हुत; Past indecl. हुत्वा, -हुत्य; Fut. pass. होतव्य, हवनीय, हव्य or हाव्य.

EXAMPLES OF OTHER VERBS OF THE THIRD CONJUGATION IN THE ORDER OF THEIR FINAL LETTERS.

663. Root दा (335). Inf. दातुं 'to give.' Parasmai and Átmane. Pres. ददामि, ददासि, ददाति; दद्वस्, दत्थस्, दत्तस्; दद्मस्, दत्थ, ददति. Átm. ददे, दत्से, दत्ते; दद्वहे, ददाथे, ददाते; दद्महे, दद्ध्वे, ददते. Pot. दद्यां, दद्यास्, &c. Átm. ददीय, &c. Imp. ददानि, देहि, ददातु; ददाव, दत्तं, दत्तां; ददाम, दत्त, ददतु. Átm. ददै, दत्स्व, दत्तां; ददावहै, ददाथां, ददातां; ददामहै, दद्ध्वं, ददतां. 1st Pret. अददां, अददास्, अददात्; अदद्व, अदत्तं, अदत्तां; अदद्म, अदत्त, अददुस् (330). Átm. अददि, अदत्थास्, अदत्त; अदद्वहि, अददाथां, अददातां; अदद्महि, अदद्ध्वं, अददत. 2d Pret. (373) ददौ, ददिथ or ददाथ, ददौ; ददिव, ददथुस्, ददतुस्; ददिम, दद, ददुस्. Átm. ददे, ददिषे, ददे; ददिवहे, ददाथे, ददाते; ददिमहे, ददिध्वे or -ढ्वे, ददिरे. 1st Fut. दातास्मि. Átm. दाताहे, &c. 2d Fut. दास्यामि. Átm. दास्ये, &c. 3d Pret. (438) अदां, अदास्, अदात्; अदाव, अदातं, अदातां; अदाम, अदात, अदुस्. Átm. (438. *d*) अदिषि, अदिथास्, अदित; अदिष्वहि, अदिषाथां, अदिषातां; अदिष्महि, अदिढ्वं or -ढ्वं, अदिषत. Bened. देयासं. Átm. दासीय, &c. Cond. अदास्यं. Átm. अदास्ये, &c. *Passive,* Pres. दीये, &c.; 3d Pret. 3d sing. अदायि, see 700. *Causal,* Pres. दापयामि (483); 3d Pret. अदीदपं. *Des.* (503) दित्सामि, दित्से. *Freq.* देदीये, दादामि or दादेमि. *Participles,* Pres. ददत् (141. *a*); Past pass. दत्त; Past indecl. दत्त्वा, -दाय; Fut. pass. दातव्य, दानीय, देय.

664. Root धा (336). Inf. धातुं 'to place.' Parasmai and Átmane. Pres. दधामि, दधासि, दधाति; दध्वस्, धत्थस् (42. *c*) *, धत्तस् (42. *c*); दध्मस्,

* The root being practically दध् is amenable to 42. *c*.

धत्थ, दधति. Átm. दधे, धत्से, धत्ते; दध्वहे, दधाथे, दधाते; दध्महे, धद्ध्वे *, दधते. Pot. दध्यां, दध्यास्, &c. Átm. दधीय, दधीथास्, &c. Imp. दधानि, धेहि, दधातु; दधाव, धत्तं, धत्तां; दधाम, धत्त, दधतु. Átm. दधै, धत्स्व, धत्तां; दधावहै, दधाथां, दधातां; दधामहै, धद्ध्वं, दधतां. 1st Pret. अदधां, अदधास्, अदधात्; अदध्व, अधत्तं, अधत्तां; अदध्म, अधत्त, अदधुस्. Átm. अदधि, अधत्थास्, अधत्त; अदध्वहि, अदधाथां, अदधातां; अदध्महि, अधद्ध्वं, अदधत. 2d Pret. (373) दधौ, दधिथ or दधाथ, दधौ; दधिव, दधथुस्, दधतुस्; दधिम, दध, दधुस्. Átm. दधे, दधिषे, &c.; see दा at 663. 1st Fut. धातास्मि. Átm. धाताहे, &c. 2d Fut. धास्यामि. Átm. धास्ये, &c. 3d Pret. (438) अधां, अधास्, अधात्; अधाव, अधातं, अधातां; अधाम, अधात, अधुस्. Átm. (438. *d*) अधिषि, अधिथास्, अधित; अधिष्वहि, अधिषाथां, अधिषातां; अधिष्महि, अधिध्वं or -ढ्वं, अधिषत. Bened. धेयासं. Átm. धासीय, &c. Cond. अधास्यं. Átm. अधास्ये, &c. *Passive*, Pres. धीये; 1st Fut. धायिताहे or धाताहे; 3d Pret. 3d sing. अधायि. *Causal*, धापयामि; 3d Pret. अदीधपं. *Des.* धित्सामि (503). *Freq.* देधीये, दाधामि or दाधेमि. *Participles*, Pres. दधत् (141. *a*); Átm. दधान; Past pass. हित; Past indecl. हित्वा, -धाय; Fut. pass. धातव्य, धानीय, धेय.

a. Root मा (338). Inf. मातुं 'to measure.' Átmane. Pres. मिमे, मिमीषे or मिमिषे †, मिमीते or मिमिते; मिमीवहे or मिमिवहे †, मिमाथे, मिमाते; मिमीमहे or मिमिमहे †, मिमीध्वे or मिमिध्वे †, मिमते. Pot. मिमीय, मिमीथास्, मिमीत, &c. Imp. मिमै, मिमीष्व or मिमिष्व †, मिमीतां or मिमितां †; मिमावहै, मिमाथां, मिमातां; मिमामहै, मिमीध्वं or मिमिध्वं †, मिमतां. 1st Pret. अमिमि, अमिमीथास् or अमिमिथास् †, अमिमीत or अमिमित †; अमिमीवहि or अमिमिवहि, अमिमाथां, अमिमातां; अमिमीमहि or अमिमिमहि †, अमिमीध्वं or अमिमिध्वं †, अमिमत. 2d Pret. ममे, ममिषे, ममे; ममिवहे, ममाथे, ममाते; ममिमहे, ममिध्वे or -ढ्वे, ममिरे. 1st Fut. माताहे, &c. 2d Fut. मास्ये, &c. 3d Pret. (433. *a*) अमासि, अमास्थास्, अमास्त; अमास्वहि, अमासाथां, अमासातां; अमास्महि, अमाध्वं, अमासत. Bened. मासीय, &c. Cond. अमास्ये, &c. *Passive*, Pres. मीये; 3d Pret. 3d sing. अमायि. *Causal*, मापयामि; 3d Pret. अमीमपं. *Des.* मित्सामि, -त्से (503). *Freq.* मेमीये, मामामि or मामेमि. *Participles*, Pres. मिमान; Past pass. मित; Past indecl. मित्वा, -माय, -मीय; Fut. pass. मातव्य, मानीय, मेय.

665. Root हा (337). Inf. हातुं 'to quit.' Parasmai. Pres. जहामि, जहासि, जहाति; जहीवस् or जहिवस् †, जहीथस् or जहिथस् †, जहीतस् or

---

* The aspirate is thrown back on the initial of the root, both before terminations beginning with *s* and *t*, and before *dhwe* and *dhwam*, as in roots ending in ह् *h*. Compare 306. *d*.

† According to some authorities. See Foster.

जहितस्*; जहीमस् or जहिमस्*, जहीथ or जहिथ*, जहति. Pot. जह्यां, जह्यास्, &c. Imp. जहानि, जहीहि or जहिहि or जहाहि, जहातु; जहाव, जहीतं or जहितं*, जहीतां or जहितां*; जहाम, जहीत or जहित*, जहतु. 1st Pret. अजहां, अजहास्, अजहात्; अजहीव or अजहिव*, अजहीतं or अजहितं*, अजहीतां or अजहितां*; अजहीम or अजहिम*, अजहीत or अजहित*, अजहुस्. 2d Pret. जहौ, जहिथ or जहाथ, जहौ; जहिव, जहथुस्, जहतुस्; जहिम, जह, जहुस्. 1st Fut. हातास्मि, &c. 2d Fut. हास्यामि, &c. 3d Pret. (433) अहासिषं, अहासीस्, अहासीत्; अहासिष्व, अहासिष्टं, अहासिष्टां; अहासिष्म, अहासिष्ट, अहासिषुस्. Bened. हेयासं, &c. Cond. अहास्यं. *Passive,* Pres. हीये; 3d Pret. 3d sing. अहायि. *Causal,* Pres. हापयामि; 3d Pret. अजीहपं. *Des.* जिहासामि. *Freq.* जेहीये, जाहामि or जाहेमि. *Participles,* Pres. जहत् (141. *a*); Past pass. हीन; Past indecl. हित्वा, -हाय; Fut. pass. हातव्य, हानीय, हेय.

666. Root भी (333). Inf. भेतुं 'to fear.' Parasmai. Pres. बिभेमि, बिभेषि, बिभेति; बिभीवस् or बिभिवस्, बिभीथस् or बिभिथस्, बिभीतस् or बिभितस्; बिभीमस् or बिभिमस्, बिभीथ or बिभिथ, बिभ्यति (34). Pot. बिभीयां or बिभियां, &c. Imp. बिभयानि, बिभीहि or बिभिहि, बिभेतु; बिभयाव, बिभीतं or बिभितं, बिभीतां or बिभितां; बिभयाम, बिभीत or बिभित, बिभ्यतु (34). 1st Pret. अबिभयं, अबिभेस्, अबिभेत्; अबिभीव or अबिभिव, अबिभीतं or अबिभितं, अबिभीतां or अबिभितां; अबिभीम or अबिभिम, अबिभीत or अबिभित, अबिभयुस् (330). Or बिभयाञ्चकार (385. *c*). 2d Pret. (367) बिभाय, बिभयिथ or बिभेथ, बिभाय; बिभ्यिव, बिभ्यथुस्, बिभ्यतुस्; बिभ्यिम, बिभ्य, बिभ्युस्. 1st Fut. भेतास्मि, &c. 2d Fut. भेष्यामि, &c. 3d Pret. अभैषं, अभैषीस्, अभैषीत्; अभैष्व, अभैष्टं, अभैष्टां; अभैष्म, अभैष्ट, अभैषुस्. Bened. भीयासं. Cond. अभेष्यं. *Passive,* Pres. भीये; 3d Pret. 3d sing. अभायि. *Causal,* Pres. भाययामि or -ये, or भापये or भीषये; 3d Pret. अबीभयं or अबीभपं or अबीभिषं. *Des.* बिभीषामि. *Freq.* बेभीये or बेभेमि or बेभयीमि. *Participles,* Pres. बिभ्यत् (141. *a*); Past pass. भीत; Past indecl. भीत्वा, -भीय; Fut. pass. भेतव्य, भयनीय, भेय.

a. Root ह्री. Inf. ह्रेतुं 'to be ashamed.' Parasmai. Pres. जिह्रेमि, जिह्रेषि, जिह्रेति; जिह्रीवस्, जिह्रीथस्, जिह्रीतस्; जिह्रीमस्, जिह्रीथ, जिह्रियति (123. *a*). Pot. जिह्रीयां, &c. Imp. जिह्रयाणि, जिह्रीहि, जिह्रेतु; जिह्रयाव, जिह्रीतं, जिह्रीतां; जिह्रयाम, जिह्रीत, जिह्रियतु. 1st Pret. अजिह्रयं, अजिह्रेस्, अजिह्रेत्; अजिह्रीव, अजिह्रीतं, अजिह्रीतां; अजिह्रीम, अजिह्रीत, अजिह्रयुस् (330). 2d Pret. जिह्राय, जिह्रयिथ or जिह्रेथ, जिह्राय; जिह्रियिव (367. *a*), जिह्रियथुस्, जिह्रियतुस्; जिह्रियिम, जिह्रिय, जिह्रियुस्. 1st Fut. ह्रेतास्मि, &c. 2d Fut.

* According to some authorities. See Foster.

ह्रेष्यामि, &c. 3d Pret. अह्रैषं, अह्रैषीस्, अह्रैषीत्; अह्रैष्व, -ष्टं, -ष्टां; अह्रैष्म, -ष्ट, -षुस्. Bened. ह्रीयासं. Cond. अह्रेष्यं. *Passive*, Pres. ह्रीये; 3d Pret. 3d sing. अह्रायि. *Causal*, Pres. ह्रेपयामि; 3d Pret. अजिह्रिपं*. *Des.* जिह्रीषामि. *Freq.* जेह्रीये, जेह्रेमि or जेह्रयीमि. *Participles*, Pres. जिह्रियत् (141. *a*); Past pass. ह्रीण or ह्रीत; Past indecl. ह्रीत्वा; Fut. pass. ह्रेतव्य, ह्रयणीय, ह्रेय.

b. Root जन्. Inf. जनितुं 'to produce.' Parasmai. Pres. जजन्मि, जजंसि or जजनिषि, जजन्ति; जजन्वस्, जजाथस्, जजातस्; जजन्मस्, जजाथ, जज्ञति. Pot. जजन्यां or जजायां, &c. Imp. जजनानि, जजाहि, जजन्तु; जजनाव, जजातं, जजातां; जजनाम, जजात, जज्ञतु. 1st Pret. अजजनं, अजजन् (292. *a*), अजजन्; अजजन्व, अजजातं, अजजातां; अजजन्म, अजजात, अजज्ञुस्. 2d Pret. जजान or जजन, जजनिथ, जजान; जज्ञिव, जज्ञथुस्, जज्ञतुस्; जज्ञिम, जज्ञ, जज्ञुस्. 1st Fut. जनितास्मि, &c. 2d Fut. जनिष्यामि, &c. 3d Pret. अजानिषं, अजानीस्, अजानीत्; अजानिष्व, &c. Or अजनिषं, &c.; see 427. Bened. जन्यासं or जायासं, &c. Cond. अजनिष्यं, &c. *Passive*, Pres. जाये (compare 617. *a*) or जन्ये; 3d Pret. 3d sing. अजनि. *Causal*, Pres. जनयामि; 3d Pret. अजीजनं. *Des.* जिजनिषे. *Freq.* जाजाये or जञ्जन्ये, जञ्जन्मि. *Participles*, Pres. जज्ञत् (141. *a*); Past pass. जात, जनित; Past indecl. जनित्वा, -जन्य, -जाय; Fut. pass. जनितव्य, जननीय, जन्य.

EXAMPLES OF PRIMITIVE VERBS OF THE SEVENTH CONJUGATION, EXPLAINED AT 342.

667. Root छिद् *chhid*. Infin. छेत्तुं *chhettum*, 'to cut.'

PARASMAI-PADA. *Present tense*, 'I cut.'

छिनद्मि *chhinadmi*	छिन्द्वस् *chhindwas*	छिन्द्मस् *chhindmas*
छिनत्सि *chhinatsi*	छिन्थस् *chhinthas* (345)	छिन्थ *chhintha* (345)
छिनत्ति *chhinatti*	छिन्तस् *chhintas* (345)	छिन्दन्ति *chhindanti*

Potential, 'I may cut.'

छिन्द्यां *chhindyám*	छिन्द्याव *chhindyáva*	छिन्द्याम *chhindyáma*
छिन्द्यास् *chhindyás*	छिन्द्यातं *chhindyátam*	छिन्द्यात *chhindyáta*
छिन्द्यात् *chhindyát*	छिन्द्यातां *chhindyátám*	छिन्द्युस् *chhindyus*

Imperative, 'Let me cut.'

छिनदानि *chhinadáni*	छिनदाव *chhinadáva*	छिनदाम *chhinadáma*
छिन्द्धि *chhinddhi* †	छिन्तं *chhintam* (345)	छिन्त *chhinta* (345)
छिनत्तु *chhinattu*	छिन्तां *chhintám* (345)	छिन्दन्तु *chhindantu*

* So Foster. Westergaard gives अजिह्रीपं.

† Or छिन्धि *chhindhi*, see 345.

First preterite, 'I was cutting.'

अछिनदं *achhinadam*	अछिन्द्व *achhindwa*	अछिन्द्म *achhindma*
अछिनत् *achhinat* (292)	अछिन्तं *achhintam*	अछिन्त *achhinta*
अछिनत् *achhinat* (292)	अछिन्तां *achhintám*	अछिन्दन् *achhindan*

2d Pret. चिच्छेद (48. *b*), चिच्छेदिथ, चिच्छेद; चिच्छिदिव, चिच्छिदथुस्, चिच्छिदतुस्; चिच्छिदिम, चिच्छिद, चिच्छिदुस्. 1st Fut. छेत्तास्मि, &c. 2d Fut. छेत्स्यामि, &c. 3d Pret. अछिदं, अछिदस्, अछिदत्; अछिदाव, अछिदतं, अछिदतां; अछिदाम, अछिदत, अछिदन्. Or अछैत्सं, अछैत्सीस्, अछैत्सीत्; अछैत्स्व, अछैत्तं, अछैत्तां; अछैत्स्म, अछैत्त, अछैत्सुस्. Bened. छिद्यासं, &c. Cond. अछेत्स्यं, &c.

ÁTMANE-PADA. *Present tense*, 'I cut.'

छिन्दे *chhinde*	छिन्द्वहे *chhindwahe*	छिन्द्महे *chhindmahe*
छिन्त्से *chhintse*	छिन्दाथे *chhindáthe*	छिन्द्ध्वे *chhinddhwe*
छिन्ते *chhinte* (345)	छिन्दाते *chhindáte*	छिन्दते *chhindate*

Potential, 'I may cut.'

छिन्दीय *chhindíya*	छिन्दीवहि *chhindívahi*	छिन्दीमहि *chhindímahi*
छिन्दीथास् *chhindíthás*	छिन्दीयाथां *chhindíyáthám*	छिन्दीध्वं *chhindídhwam*
छिन्दीत *chhindíta*	छिन्दीयातां *chhindíyátám*	छिन्दीरन् *chhindíran*

Imperative, 'Let me cut.'

छिनदै *chhinadai*	छिनदावहै *chhinadávahai*	छिनदामहै *chhinadámahai*
छिन्त्स्व *chhintswa*	छिन्दाथां *chhindáthám*	छिन्द्ध्वं *chhinddhwam*
छिन्तां *chhintám*	छिन्दातां *chhindátám*	छिन्दतां *chhindatám*

First preterite.

अछिन्दि *achhindi*	अछिन्द्वहि *achhindwahi*	अछिन्द्महि *achhindmahi*
अछिन्थास् *achhinthás*	अछिन्दाथां *achhindáthám*	अछिन्द्ध्वं *achhinddhwam*
अछिन्त *achhinta*	अछिन्दातां *achhindátám*	अछिन्दत *achhindata*

2d Pret. चिच्छिदे, चिच्छिदिषे, चिच्छिदे; चिच्छिदिवहे, चिच्छिदाथे, चिच्छिदाते; चिच्छिदिमहे, चिच्छिदिध्वे, चिच्छिदिरे. 1st Fut. छेत्ताहे, &c. 2d Fut. छेत्स्ये, &c. 3d Pret. अछित्सि, अछित्थास्, अछित्त; अछित्स्वहि, अछित्साथां, अछित्सातां; अछित्स्महि, अछिद्ध्वं, अछित्सत. Bened. छित्सीय, &c. Cond. अछेत्स्ये. *Passive*, Pres. छिद्ये, &c.; 3d Pret. 3d sing. अछेदि. *Causal*, Pres. छेदयामि; 3d Pret. अचिच्छिदं. *Des.* चिच्छित्सामि, -त्से. *Freq.* चेच्छिद्ये, चेच्छेद्मि. *Participles*, Pres. छिन्दत्; Átm. छिन्दान; Past pass. छिन्न; Past indecl. छित्त्वा, -छिद्य; Fut. pass. छेत्तव्य, छेदनीय, छेद्य.

EXAMPLES OF OTHER VERBS OF THE SEVENTH CONJUGATION IN THE ORDER OF THEIR FINAL LETTERS.

668. Root अञ्ज्. Inf. अंक्तुं 'to anoint,' 'to make clear.' Parasmai. Pres. अनज्मि, अनक्षि (296), अनक्ति; अंज्वस्, अंक्थस्, अंक्तस्; अंज्मस्, अंक्थ, अञ्जन्ति. Pot. अंज्यां, &c. Imp. अनजानि, अंग्धि, अनक्तु; अनजाव, अंक्तं, अंक्तां; अनजाम, अंक्त, अञ्जन्तु. 1st Pret. आनजं, आनक् (292), आनक्; आंज्व, आंक्तं, आंक्तां; आंज्म, आंक्त, आञ्जन्. 2d Pret. आनञ्ज, आनञ्जिथ or आनंक्थ, आनञ्ज; आनञ्जिव, आनञ्जथुस्, आनञ्जतुस्; आनञ्जिम, आनञ्ज, आनञ्जुस्. 1st Fut. अंक्तास्मि or अञ्जितास्मि, &c. 2d Fut. अंक्ष्यामि or अञ्जिष्यामि, &c. 3d Pret. आञ्जिषं, आञ्जीस्, आञ्जीत्; आञ्जिष्व, &c., see 427. Bened. अज्यासं (452. *b*). Cond. आंक्ष्यं or आञ्जिष्यं. *Passive*, Pres. अज्ये (469); 3d Pret. 3d sing. आञ्जि. *Causal*, Pres. अञ्जयामि; 3d Pret. आञ्जिजं. *Des.* अञ्जिजिषामि. *Participles*, Pres. अञ्जत्; Past pass. अक्त; Past indecl. अञ्जित्वा or अंक्त्वा or अक्त्वा, -अज्य; Fut. pass. अंक्तव्य or अञ्जितव्य, अञ्जनीय, अंज्य or अंग्य.

a. Root भुज् (346). Inf. भोक्तुं 'to eat,' 'to enjoy.' Parasmai and Átmane. Pres. भुनज्मि, भुनक्षि, भुनक्ति; भुंज्वस्, भुंक्थस्, भुंक्तस्; भुंज्मस्, भुंक्थ, भुञ्जन्ति. Átm. भुञ्जे, भुंक्षे, भुंक्ते; भुंज्वहे, भुञ्जाथे, भुञ्जाते; भुंज्महे, भुंग्ध्वे, भुञ्जते. Pot. भुंज्यां, &c. Átm. भुञ्जीय, &c. Imp. भुनजानि, भुंग्धि, भुनक्तु; भुनजाव, भुंक्तं, भुंक्तां; भुनजाम, भुंक्त, भुञ्जन्तु. Átm. भुनजै, भुंक्ष्व, भुंक्तां; भुनजावहै, भुञ्जाथां, भुञ्जातां; भुनजामहै, भुंग्ध्वं, भुञ्जतां. 1st Pret. अभुनजं, अभुनक् (292), अभुनक्; अभुंज्व, अभुंक्तं, अभुंक्तां; अभुंज्म, अभुंक्त, अभुञ्जन्. Átm. अभुञ्जि, अभुंक्थास्, अभुंक्त; अभुंज्वहि, अभुञ्जाथां, अभुञ्जातां; अभुंज्महि, अभुंग्ध्वं, अभुञ्जत. 2d Pret. बुभोज, बुभोजिथ, बुभोज; बुभुजिव, बुभुजथुस्, बुभुजतुस्; बुभुजिम, बुभुज, बुभुजुस्. Átm. बुभुजे, बुभुजिषे, बुभुजे; -जिवहे, -जाथे, -जाते; -जिमहे, -जिध्वे, -जिरे. 1st Fut. भोक्तास्मि. Átm. भोक्ताहे, &c. 2d Fut. भोक्ष्यामि. Átm. भोक्ष्ये, &c. 3d Pret. अभौक्षं, -क्षीस्, क्षीत्; अभौक्ष्व, अभौक्तं, -क्तां; अभौक्ष्म, अभौक्त, अभौक्षुस्. Átm. अभुक्षि, अभुक्थास्, अभुक्त; अभुक्ष्वहि, अभुक्षाथां, अभुक्षातां; अभुक्ष्महि, अभुग्ध्वं, अभुक्षत. Bened. भुज्यासं, &c. Átm. भुक्षीय, &c. Cond. अभोक्ष्यं, &c. Átm. अभोक्ष्ये, &c. *Passive*, Pres. भुज्ये; 3d Pret. 3d sing. अभोजि. *Causal*, Pres. भोजयामि, -ये; 3d Pret. अबूभुजं. *Des.* बुभुक्षामि, -क्षे. *Freq.* बोभुज्ये, बोभोज्मि. *Participles*, Pres. भुञ्जत्; Átm. भुञ्जान; Past pass. भुक्त; Past indecl. भुक्त्वा, -भुज्य; Fut. pass. भोक्तव्य, भोजनीय, भोज्य or भोग्य.

669. Root भञ्ज् (347). Inf. भंक्तुं 'to break.' Parasmai. Pres. भनज्मि, भनक्षि, भनक्ति; भंज्वस्, भंक्थस्, भंक्तस्; भंज्मस्, भंक्थ, भञ्जन्ति. Pot. भंज्यां, &c. Imp. भनजानि, भंग्धि, भनक्तु; भनजाव, भंक्तं, भंक्तां; भनजाम, भंक्त, भञ्जन्तु. 1st Pret. अभनजं, अभनक् (292), अभनक्; अभंज्व, अभंक्तं, अभंक्तां;

अभंज्म, अभंक्त, अभञ्जन्. 2d Pret. बभञ्ज, बभञ्जिथ or बभंक्थ, बभञ्ज; बभञ्जिव, बभञ्जथुस्, बभञ्जतुस्; बभञ्जिम, बभञ्ज, बभञ्जुस्. 1st Fut. भंक्तास्मि, &c. 2d Fut. भंक्ष्यामि, &c. 3d Pret. अभांक्षं, -क्षीस्, -क्षीत्; अभांक्ष्व, अभांक्तं, -क्तां; अभांक्ष्म, अभांक्त, अभांक्षुस्. Bened. भज्यासं, &c. (452. *b*). Cond. अभंक्ष्यं, &c. *Passive*, Pres. भज्ये (469); 3d Pret. 3d sing. अभाजि. *Causal*, Pres. भञ्जयामि; 3d Pret. अबभञ्जं. *Des.* बिभंक्षामि. *Freq.* बंभज्ये, बंभज्मि. *Participles*, Pres. भञ्जत्; Past pass. भग्न; Past indecl. भंक्त्वा or भक्त्वा, -भज्य; Fut. pass. भंक्तव्य, भञ्जनीय, भंज्य.

670. Root युज्. Inf. योक्तुं 'to join,' 'to unite.' Parasmai and Átmane. Pres. युनज्मि, युनक्षि, &c.; see भुज् at 668. *a*. Átm. युञ्जे, युंक्षे, &c.; see 668. *a*. Pot. युंज्यां, &c. Átm. युञ्जीय, &c. Imp. युनजानि, युंग्धि, युनक्तु; युनजाव, &c.; see 668. *a*. Átm. युनजै, युंक्ष्व, युंक्तां, &c. 1st Pret. अयुनजं, अयुनक् (292), अयुनक्; अयुंज्व, &c.; see 668. *a*. Átm. अयुञ्जि, अयुंक्थास्, &c. 2d Pret. युयोज, युयोजिथ, युयोज; युयुजिव, &c.; see भुज् at 668. *a*. Átm. युयुजे, &c. 1st Fut. योक्तास्मि, &c. Átm. योक्ताहे, &c. 2d Fut. योक्ष्यामि, &c. Átm. योक्ष्ये, &c. 3d Pret. अयुजं, -जस्, -जत्; -जाव, -जतं, -जतां; -जाम, -जत, -जन्. Or अयौक्षं, -क्षीस्, -क्षीत्; अयौक्ष्व, &c.; see 668. *a*. Átm. अयुक्षि, अयुक्थास्, अयुक्त; अयुक्ष्वहि, &c. Bened. युज्यासं, &c. Átm. युक्षीय. Cond. अयोक्ष्यं. Átm. अयोक्ष्ये. *Passive*, Pres. युज्ये; 3d Pret. 3d sing. अयोजि, see 702. *Causal*, Pres. योजयामि; 3d Pret. अयूयुजं. *Des.* युयुक्षामि, -क्षे. *Freq.* योयुज्ये, योयोज्मि. *Participles*, Pres. युञ्जत्; Átm. युञ्जान; Past pass. युक्त; Past indecl. युक्त्वा, -युज्य; Fut. pass. योक्तव्य, योजनीय, योग्य or योज्य.

671. Root रुध्. Inf. रोद्धुं 'to hinder.' Parasmai and Átmane. Pres. रुणध्मि, रुणत्सि, रुणद्धि; रुन्ध्वस्, रुन्द्धस्*, रुन्द्धस्*; रुन्ध्मस्, रुन्द्ध*, रुन्धन्ति. Átm. रुन्धे, रुन्त्से, रुन्द्धे*; रुन्ध्वहे, रुन्धाथे, रुन्धाते; रुन्ध्महे, रुन्द्ध्वे, रुन्धते. Pot. रुन्ध्यां, &c. Átm. रुन्धीय, &c. Imp. रुणधानि, रुन्द्धि, रुणद्धु; रुणधाव, रुन्द्धं*, रुन्द्धां*; रुणधाम, रुन्द्ध*, रुन्धन्तु. Átm. रुणधै, रुन्त्स्व, रुन्द्धां; रुणधावहै, रुन्धाथां, रुन्धातां; रुणधामहै, रुन्द्ध्वं, रुन्धतां. 1st Pret. अरुणधं, अरुणत् or अरुणद् or अरुणस् (292), अरुणत् or अरुणद्; अरुन्ध्व, अरुन्द्धं, अरुन्द्धां; अरुन्ध्म, अरुन्द्ध, अरुन्धन्. Átm. अरुन्धि, अरुन्द्धास्, अरुन्द्ध; अरुन्ध्वहि, अरुन्धाथां, अरुन्धातां; अरुन्ध्महि, अरुन्द्ध्वं, अरुन्धत. 2d Pret. रुरोध, रुरोधिथ, रुरोध; रुरुधिव, रुरुधथुस्, रुरुधतुस्; रुरुधिम, रुरुध, रुरुधुस्. Átm. रुरुधे, रुरुधिषे, रुरुधे; रुरुधिवहे, रुरुधाथे, रुरुधाते; रुरुधिमहे, रुरुधिध्वे, रुरुधिरे. 1st Fut. रोद्धास्मि, &c. Átm. रोद्धाहे, &c. 2d Fut. रोत्स्यामि.

* रुन्धस् may be written for रुन्द्धस्. Similarly, रुन्ध for रुन्द्ध, रुन्धे for रुन्द्धे, &c. See 298. *a*.

Átm. रोत्स्ये. 3d Pret. अरुधं, -धस्, -धत्; -धाव, -धतं, -धतां; -धाम, -धत, -धन्. Or अरौत्सं, अरौत्सीस्, अरौत्सीत्; अरौत्स्व, अरौद्धं, अरौद्धां; अरौत्स्म, अरौद्ध, अरौत्सुस्. Átm. अरुत्सि, अरुद्धास्, अरुद्ध; अरुत्स्वहि, अरुत्साथां, अरुत्सातां; अरुत्स्महि, अरुद्धं, अरुत्सत. Bened. रुध्यासं, &c. Átm. रुत्सीय, &c. Cond. अरोत्स्यं, &c. Átm. अरोत्स्ये, &c. *Passive*, Pres. रुध्ये; 3d Pret. 3d sing. अरोधि. *Causal*, Pres. रोधयामि; 3d Pret. अरूरुधं. *Des.* रुरुत्सामि, -त्से. *Freq.* रोरुध्ये, रोरोध्मि. *Participles*, Pres. रुन्धत्; Átm. रुन्धान; Past pass. रुद्ध; Past indecl. रुद्ध्वा, -रुध्य; Fut. pass. रोद्धव्य, रोधनीय, रोध्य.

672. Root शिष्. Inf. शेष्टुं 'to distinguish,' 'to separate,' 'to leave.' Parasmai. Pres. शिनष्मि, शिनक्षि, शिनष्टि; शिंष्वस्, शिंष्ठस्, शिंष्टस्; शिंष्मस्, शिंष्ठ, शिंषन्ति. Pot. शिंष्यां, &c. Imp. शिनषाणि, शिंड्ढि or शिण्ढि (see 303, and compare 345), शिनष्टु; शिनषाव, शिंष्टं, शिंष्टां; शिनषाम, शिंष्ट, शिंषन्तु. 1st Pret. अशिनषं, अशिनट् (292, 43. *e*), अशिनट्; अशिंष्व, अशिंष्टं, अशिंष्टां; अशिंष्म, अशिंष्ट, अशिंषन्. 2d Pret. शिशेष, शिशेषिथ, शिशेष; शिशिषिव, शिशिषथुस्, शिशिषतुस्; शिशिषिम, शिशिष, शिशिषुस्. 1st Fut. शेष्टास्मि, &c. 2d Fut. शेक्ष्यामि, &c. 3d Pret. अशिषं, -षस्, -षत्; -षाव, -षतं, -षतां; -षाम, -षत, -षन्. Bened. शिष्यासं, &c. Cond. अशेक्ष्यं, &c. *Passive*, Pres. शिष्ये; 3d Pret. 3d sing. अशेषि. *Causal*, Pres. शेषयामि; 3d Pret. अशीशिषं. *Des.* शिशिक्षामि. *Freq.* शेशिष्ये, शेशेष्मि. *Participles*, Pres. शिंषत्; Past pass. शिष्ट; Past indecl. शिष्ट्वा, -शिष्य; Fut. pass. शेष्टव्य, शेषणीय, शेष्य.

673. Root हिंस्. Inf. हिंसितुं 'to injure.' Parasmai. Pres. हिनस्मि, हिनस्सि, हिनस्ति; हिंस्वस्, हिंस्थस्, हिंस्तस्; हिंस्मस्, हिंस्थ, हिंसन्ति. Pot. हिंस्यां, &c. Imp. हिनसानि, हिन्द्धि or हिन्धि (304), हिनस्तु; हिनसाव, हिंस्तं, हिंस्तां; हिनसाम, हिंस्त, हिंसन्तु. 1st Pret. अहिनसं, अहिनत् or अहिनस् (292, 304. *a*), अहिनत्; अहिंस्व, अहिंस्तं, अहिंस्तां; अहिंस्म, अहिंस्त, अहिंसन्. 2d Pret. जिहिंस, जिहिंसिथ, जिहिंस; जिहिंसिव, जिहिंसथुस्, जिहिंसतुस्; जिहिंसिम, जिहिंस, जिहिंसुस्. 1st Fut. हिंसितास्मि, &c. 2d Fut. हिंसिष्यामि, &c. 3d Pret. अहिंसिषं, अहिंसीस्, अहिंसीत्; अहिंसिष्व, अहिंसिष्टं, अहिंसिष्टां; अहिंसिष्म, अहिंसिष्ट, अहिंसिषुस्. Bened. हिंस्यासं, &c. Cond. अहिंसिष्यं. *Passive*, Pres. हिंस्ये; 3d Pret. 3d sing. अहिंसि. *Causal*, Pres. हिंसयामि; 3d Pret. अजिहिंसं. *Des.* जिहिंसिषामि. *Freq.* जेहिंस्ये, जेहिंस्मि. *Participles*, Pres. हिंसत्; Past pass. हिंसित; Past indecl. हिंसित्वा, -हिंस्य; Fut. pass. हिंसितव्य, हिंसनीय, हिंस्य.

674. Root तृह्. Inf. तर्हितुं or तर्ढुं 'to injure,' 'to kill.' Parasmai. Pres. तृणेह्मि, तृणेक्षि (306), तृणेढि (305); तृंह्वस्, तृण्ढस् (345), तृण्ढस्; तृंह्मस्, तृण्ढ, तृंहन्ति. Pot. तृंह्यां, &c. Imp. तृणहानि, तृण्ढि (see 306. *c*), तृणेढु; तृणहाव,

तृण्ढं, तृण्ढां; तृणहाम, तृण्ढ, तृंहन्तु. 1st Pret. अतृणहं, अतृणेट् or अतृणेड् (292), अतृणेट् or अतृणेड्; अतृंह्व, अतृण्ढं, अतृण्ढां; अतृंह्म, अतृण्ढ, अतृंहन्. 2d Pret. ततर्ह, ततर्हिथ or ततर्ढ, ततर्ह; ततृहिव, ततृहथुस्, ततृहतुस्; ततृहिम, ततृह, ततृहुस्. 1st Fut. तर्हितास्मि or तर्ढास्मि, &c. 2d Fut. तर्हिष्यामि or तर्क्ष्यामि, &c. 3d Pret. अतर्हिषं, -हीस्, -हीत्; -र्हिष्व, -र्हिष्टं, -र्हिष्टां; -र्हिष्म, -र्हिष्ट, -र्हिषुस्. Or अतृक्षं, -क्षस्, -क्षत्; -क्षाव, -क्षतं, -क्षतां; -क्षाम, -क्षत, -क्षन्. Bened. तृह्यासं, &c. Cond. अतर्हिष्यं or अतर्क्ष्यं, &c. *Passive*, Pres. तृह्ये; 3d Pret. 3d sing. अतर्हि. *Causal*, Pres. तर्हयामि; 3d Pret. अततर्हं or अतीतृहं. *Des.* तितर्हिषामि or तितृक्षामि. *Freq.* तरीतृह्ये, तरीतर्ह्मि (3d sing. तरीतर्ढि). *Participles*, Pres. तृंहत्; Past pass. तृढ; Past indecl. तर्हित्वा or तृढ्वा, -तृह्य; Fut. pass. तर्हितव्य or तर्ढव्य, तर्हणीय, तृह्य.

EXAMPLES OF PRIMITIVE VERBS OF THE FIFTH CONJUGATION, EXPLAINED AT 349.

675. Root वृ *vri*. Infin. वरितुं *varitum* or वरीतुं *varítum*, 'to cover,' 'to enclose,' 'to choose *.'

Note, that the conjugational नु *nu* becomes णु *ṇu* after वृ *vri* by 58.

PARASMAI-PADA. *Present tense*, 'I cover,' &c.

वृणोमि *vriṇomi*	वृणुवस् *vriṇuvas* †	वृणुमस् *vriṇumas* ‡
वृणोषि *vriṇoshi*	वृणुथस् *vriṇuthas*	वृणुथ *vriṇutha*
वृणोति *vriṇoti*	वृणुतस् *vriṇutas*	वृण्वन्ति *vriṇwanti*

Potential, 'I may cover,' &c.

वृणुयां *vriṇuyám*	वृणुयाव *vriṇuyáva*	वृणुयाम *vriṇuyáma*
वृणुयास् *vriṇuyás*	वृणुयातं *vriṇuyátam*	वृणुयात *vriṇuyáta*
वृणुयात् *vriṇuyát*	वृणुयातां *vriṇuyátám*	वृणुयुस् *vriṇuyus*

Imperative, 'Let me cover,' &c.

वृणवानि *vriṇaváni*	वृणवाव *vriṇaváva*	वृणवाम *vriṇaváma*
वृणु *vriṇu*	वृणुतं *vriṇutam*	वृणुत *vriṇuta*
वृणोतु *vriṇotu*	वृणुतां *vriṇutám*	वृण्वन्तु *vriṇwantu*

First preterite, 'I was covering,' &c.

अवृणवं *avriṇavam*	अवृणुव *avriṇuva* §	अवृणुम *avriṇuma* ‖
अवृणोस् *avriṇos*	अवृणुतं *avriṇutam*	अवृणुत *avriṇuta*
अवृणोत् *avriṇot*	अवृणुतां *avriṇutám*	अवृण्वन् *avriṇwan*

* In the sense of 'to choose,' this root generally follows the 9th conjugation; thus, Pres. वृणामि, वृणासि, वृणाति; वृणीवस्, &c. See 686.

† Or वृण्वस् *vriṇwas*. ‡ Or वृण्मस् *vriṇmas*. § Or अवृण्व *avriṇwa*. ‖ Or अवृण्म *avriṇma*.

2d Pret. (368) ववार, ववरिथ, ववार; ववृव or ववरिव, वव्रथुस्, वव्रतुस्; ववृम or ववरिम, वव्र, वव्रुस् or ववरुस् (367. *c*). 1st Fut. (399) वरितास्मि or वरीतास्मि. 2d Fut. (399) वरिष्यामि or वरीष्यामि. 3d Pret. अवारिषं, अवारीस्, अवारीत्; अवारिष्व, अवारिष्टं, अवारिष्टां; अवारिष्म, अवारिष्ट, अवारिषुस्. Bened. व्रियासं or वूर्यासं, &c. (448. *a*). Cond. अवरिष्यं or अवरीष्यं, &c.

ÁTMANE-PADA. *Present tense*, 'I cover,' &c.

वृण्वे *vriṇwe*	वृणुवहे *vriṇuvahe* *	वृणुमहे *vriṇumahe* †
वृणुषे *vriṇushe*	वृण्वाथे *vriṇwáthe*	वृणुध्वे *vriṇudhwe*
वृणुते *vriṇute*	वृण्वाते *vriṇwáte*	वृण्वते *vriṇwate*

Potential, 'I may cover,' &c.

वृण्वीय *vriṇwíya*	वृण्वीवहि *vriṇwívahi*	वृण्वीमहि *vriṇwímahi*
वृण्वीथास् *vriṇwíthás*	वृण्वीयाथां *vriṇwíyáthám*	वृण्वीध्वं *vriṇwídhwam*
वृण्वीत *vriṇwíta*	वृण्वीयातां *vriṇwíyátám*	वृण्वीरन् *vriṇwíran*

Imperative, 'Let me cover,' &c.

वृणवै *vriṇavai*	वृणवावहै *vriṇavávahai*	वृणवामहै *vriṇavámahai*
वृणुष्व *vriṇushwa*	वृण्वाथां *vriṇwáthám*	वृणुध्वं *vriṇudhwam*
वृणुतां *vriṇutám*	वृण्वातां *vriṇwátám*	वृण्वतां *vriṇwatám*

First preterite.

अवृण्वि *avriṇwi*	अवृणुवहि *avriṇuvahi* ‡	अवृणुमहि *avriṇumahi* §
अवृणुथास् *avriṇuthás*	अवृण्वाथां *avriṇwáthám*	अवृणुध्वं *avriṇudhwam*
अवृणुत *avriṇuta*	अवृण्वातां *avriṇwátám*	अवृण्वत *avriṇwata*

2d Pret. वव्रे (34) or ववरे (367. *c*), ववृषे, वव्रे or ववरे; ववृवहे, वव्राथे, वव्राते; ववृमहे, ववृढ्वे, वव्रिरे. 1st Fut. वरिताहे or वरीताहे, &c. 2d Fut. वरिष्ये or वरीष्ये, &c. 3d Pret. अवरिषि, अवरिष्ठास्, अवरिष्ट; अवरिष्वहि, अवरिषाथां, अवरिषातां; अवरिष्महि, अवरिध्वं or -रिढ्वं, अवरिषत. Or अवरीषि, अवरीष्ठास्, &c. Or अवृषि, अवृथास्, अवृत; अवृष्वहि, अवृषाथां, अवृषातां; अवृष्महि, अवृढ्वं, अवृषत. Or अवूर्षि, अवूर्ष्ठास्, अवूर्ष्ट; अवूर्ष्वहि, अवूर्षाथां, अवूर्षातां; अवूर्ष्महि, अवूर्ढ्वं, अवूर्षत. Bened. वरिषीय or वृषीय or वूर्षीय (448. *a*). Cond. अवरिष्ये or अवरीष्ये. *Passive*, व्रियै; 3d Pret. 3d sing. अवारि. *Causal*, Pres. वरयामि or -ये, or वारयामि or -ये; 3d Pret. अवीवरं. *Des.* विवरिषामि or -षे, विवरीषामि or -षे, वुवूर्षामि or -षे (502). *Freq.* वेव्रीये (511) or वोवूर्ये, वर्वर्मि. *Participles*, Pres. वृण्वत्; Átm. वृण्वान; Past pass. वृत; Past indecl. वृत्वा, -वृत्य; Fut. pass. वरितव्य or वरीतव्य, वरणीय, वार्य्य.

* Or वृण्वहे *vriṇwahe*. † Or वृण्महे *vriṇmahe*. ‡ Or अवृण्वहि *avriṇwahi*. § Or अवृण्महि *avriṇmahi*.

EXAMPLES OF OTHER VERBS OF THE FIFTH CONJUGATION IN THE ORDER OF THEIR FINAL LETTERS.

676. Root श्रु*. Inf. श्रोतुं 'to hear.' Parasmai. Pres. शृणोमि, शृणोषि, शृणोति; शृणुवस् or शृण्वस्, शृणुथस्, शृणुतस्; शृणुमस् or शृण्मस्, शृणुथ, शृण्वन्ति. Pot. शृणुयां, &c. Imp. शृणवानि, शृणु, शृणोतु; शृणवाव, शृणुतं, शृणुतां; शृणवाम, शृणुत, शृण्वन्तु. 1st Pret. अशृणवं, अशृणोस्, अशृणोत्; अशृणुव or अशृण्व, अशृणुतं, अशृणुतां; अशृणुम or अशृण्म, अशृणुत, अशृण्वन्. 2d Pret. (368) शुश्राव, शुश्रोथ, शुश्राव; शुश्रुव, शुश्रुवथुस्, शुश्रुवतुस्; शुश्रुम, शुश्रुव, शुश्रुवुस्. 1st Fut. श्रोतास्मि, &c. 2d Fut. श्रोष्यामि, &c. 3d Pret. अश्रौषं, अश्रौषीस्, अश्रौषीत्; अश्रौष्व, अश्रौष्टं, -ष्टां; अश्रौष्म, अश्रौष्ट, अश्रौषुस्. Bened. श्रूयासं, &c. Cond. अश्रोष्यं, &c. *Passive*, Pres. श्रूये; 3d Pret. 3d sing. अश्रावि. *Causal*, Pres. श्रावयामि; 3d Pret. अशिश्रवं or अशुश्रवं. *Des.* शुश्रूषे. *Freq.* शोश्रूये, शोश्रोमि or शोश्रवीमि. *Participles*, Pres. शृण्वत्; Past pass. श्रुत; Past indecl. श्रुत्वा, -श्रुत्य; Fut. pass. श्रोतव्य, श्रवणीय, श्राव्य.

677. Root धू†. Inf. धवितुं or धोतुं 'to shake,' 'to agitate.' Parasmai and Átmane. Pres. धूनोमि, धूनोषि, धूनोति; धूनुवस् or धून्वस्, धूनुथस्, धूनुतस्; धूनुमस् or धून्मस्, धूनुथ, धून्वन्ति. Átm. धून्वे, धूनुषे, धूनुते; धूनुवहे or धून्वहे, धून्वाथे, धून्वाते; धूनुमहे or धून्महे, धूनुध्वे, धून्वते. Pot. धूनुयां, &c. Átm. धून्वीय, &c. Imp. धूनवानि, धूनु, धूनोतु; धूनवाव, धूनुतं, धूनुतां; धूनवाम, धूनुत, धून्वन्तु. Átm. धूनवै, धूनुष्व, धूनुतां; धूनवावहै, धून्वाथां, धून्वातां; धूनवामहै, धूनुध्वं, धून्वतां. 1st Pret. अधूनवं, अधूनोस्, अधूनोत्; अधूनुव or अधून्व, अधूनुतं, अधूनुतां; अधूनुम or अधून्म, अधूनुत, अधून्वन्. Átm. अधून्वि, अधूनुथास्, अधूनुत; अधूनुवहि or अधून्वहि, अधून्वाथां, अधून्वातां; अधूनुमहि, अधूनुध्वं, अधून्वत. 2d Pret. (367. *b*) दुधाव, दुधविथ or दुधोथ, दुधाव; दुधुविव, दुधुवथुस्, दुधुवतुस्; दुधुविम, दुधुव, दुधुवुस्. Átm. दुधुवे, दुधुविषे, दुधुवे; दुधुविवहे, दुधुवाथे, दुधुवाते; दुधुविमहे, दुधुविध्वे or -ढ्वे, दुधुविरे. 1st Fut. धवितास्मि or धोतास्मि, &c. Átm. धविताहे or धोताहे, &c. 2d Fut. धविष्यामि or धोष्यामि. Átm. धविष्ये or धोष्ये. 3d Pret.† अधाविषं, अधावीस्, अधावीत्; अधाविष्व, अधाविष्टं, अधाविष्टां; अधाविष्म, अधाविष्ट, अधाविषुस्. Or अधौषं, -षीस्, -षीत्; अधौष्व, अधौष्टं, -ष्टां; अधौष्म, अधौष्ट, अधौषुस्. Átm. अधविषि, अधविष्ठास्, अधविष्ट; अधविष्वहि, अधविषाथां, -षातां; अधविष्महि,

---

* This root, although manifestly following the 5th conjugation, is placed by Indian grammarians under the 1st class.

† This root may also be conjugated in the 9th conjugation; thus, Pres. धुनामि, धुनासि, धुनाति; धुनीवस्, &c.; see 686: and in the 6th (धुवामि 280). In the latter case the 3d Pret. is अधुविषं, &c.; see 432.

अधविध्वं (-ढ्वं), अधविषत. Or अधोषि, अधोष्टास्, अधोष्ट; अधोष्वहि, अधोषाथां, -षातां; अधोष्महि, अधोढ्वं (-ढ्वं), अधोषत. Bened. धूयासं. Átm. धविषीय or धोषीय, &c. Cond. अधविष्यं or अधोष्यं, &c. Átm. अधविष्ये &c. or अधोष्ये &c. *Passive*, Pres. धूये, &c.; 3d Pret. 3d sing. अधावि. *Causal*, Pres. धूनयामि or धावयामि; 3d Pret. अदूधुनं or अदूधवं. *Des.* दुधूषामि, -षे. *Freq.* दोधूये, दोधोमि or दोधवीमि. *Participles*, Pres. धून्वत्; Átm. धून्वान; Past pass. धूत or धून; Past indecl. धूत्वा, -धूय; Fut. pass. धवितव्य or धोतव्य, धवनीय, धाव्य or धव्य.

a. After धू may be conjugated the root सु ‘to press out the juice of the Asclepias plant,’ which in native grammars is the model of the 5th conjugation; thus, Pres. सुनोमि, सुनोषि, &c. The two futures reject *i*; thus, 1st Fut. सोतास्मि, &c.

678. Root स्तृ or स्तॄ*. Inf. स्तरितुं or स्तरीतुं or स्तर्तुं ‘to spread,’ ‘to cover.’ Parasmai and Átmane. Pres. स्तृणोमि, &c.; see वृ at 675. Átm. स्तृण्वे, स्तृणुषे, &c. Pot. स्तृणुयां, स्तृणुयास्, &c. Átm. स्तृण्वीय, &c. Imp. स्तृणवानि, &c. Átm. स्तृणवै, &c. 1st Pret. अस्तृणवं, &c. Átm. अस्तृण्वि, &c.; see 675. 2d Pret. (331. *c*) तस्तार, तस्तर्थ, तस्तार; तस्तरिव, तस्तरथुस्, तस्तरतुस्; तस्तरिम, तस्तर, तस्तरुस्. Átm. तस्तरे, तस्तरिषे, तस्तरे; तस्तरिवहे, तस्तराथे, तस्तराते; तस्तरिमहे, तस्तरिध्वे or -ढ्वे, तस्तरिरे. 1st Fut. स्तरितास्मि or स्तरीतास्मि or स्तर्तास्मि, &c. Átm. स्तरिताहे or स्तरीताहे or स्तर्ताहे, &c. 2d Fut. स्तरिष्यामि or स्तरीष्यामि. Átm. स्तरिष्ये or स्तरीष्ये, &c. 3d Pret. अस्तारिषं, -रीस्, -रीत्; अस्तारिष्व, &c.; see 675. Or अस्तार्षं, -र्षीस्, -र्षीत्; अस्तार्ष्व, -ष्टं, -ष्टां; अस्तार्ष्म, -ष्ट, -र्षुस्. Átm. अस्तरिषि &c. or अस्तरीषि &c. or अस्तृषि &c. or अस्तीर्षि &c.; see 3d Pret. of वृ at 675. Bened. स्तर्यासं &c. or स्तीर्यासं &c. Átm. स्तृषीय or स्तरिषीय or स्तीर्षीय, &c. Cond. अस्तरिष्यं or अस्तरीष्यं, &c. Átm. अस्तरिष्ये or अस्तरीष्ये, &c. *Passive*, Pres. (467) स्तर्ये; 3d Pret. 3d sing. अस्तारि. *Causal*, Pres. स्तारयामि; 3d Pret. अतिस्तरं or अतस्तरं. *Des.* तिस्तरिषामि or -षे, or तिस्तरीषामि or -षे, or तिस्तीर्षामि or -र्षे. *Freq.* तास्तर्ये or तेस्तीर्ये, तास्तर्मि or तरीस्तर्मि. *Participles*, Pres. स्तृण्वत्; Átm. स्तृण्वान; Past pass. स्तृत or स्तीर्ण (534); Past indecl. स्तृत्वा, -स्तीर्य, -स्तृत्य; Fut. pass. स्तरितव्य or स्तरीतव्य or स्तर्तव्य, स्तरणीय, स्तार्य.

679. Root शक्†. Inf. शक्तुं ‘to be able.’ Parasmai. Pres. शक्नोमि,

---

* This root may also be conjugated in the 9th conjugation; thus, Pres. स्तृणामि, स्तृणासि, स्तृणाति; स्तृणीवस्, &c. See 686.

† शक् is also conjugated in the 4th conjugation, Parasmai and Átmane (Pres. शक्यामि &c., शक्ये); but it may then be regarded as a passive verb. See 253. *b*.

शक्नोषि, शक्नोति; शक्नुवस्, शक्नुथस्, शक्नुतस्; शक्नुमस्, शक्नुथ, शक्नुवन्ति. Pot. शक्नुयां, &c. Imp. शक्नवानि, शक्नुहि (291), शक्नोतु; शक्नवाव, शक्नुतं, शक्नुतां; शक्नवाम, शक्नुत, शक्नुवन्तु. 1st Pret. अशक्नवं, अशक्नोस्, अशक्नोत्; अशक्नुव, अशक्नुतं, अशक्नुतां; अशक्नुम, अशक्नुत, अशक्नुवन्. 2d Pret. शशाक, शेकिथ or शशक्थ, शशाक; शेकिव, शेकथुस्, शेकतुस्; शेकिम, शेक, शेकुस्. 1st Fut. शक्तास्मि, &c. 2d Fut. शक्ष्यामि, &c. 3d Pret. अशकं, -कस्, -कत्; -काव, -कतं, -कतां; -काम, -कत, -कन्. Or अशकिषं, -कीस्, -कीत्; अशकिष्व, -किष्टं, -ष्टं; अशकिष्म, -किष्ट, -किषुस्. Bened. शक्यासं, &c. Cond. अशक्ष्यं, &c. *Passive,* Pres. शक्ये; 3d Pret. 3d sing. अशाकि. *Causal,* Pres. शाकयामि; 3d Pret. अशीशकं. *Des.* शिशकिषामि or शिक्षामि or -क्षे* (503). *Freq.* शाशक्ये, शाशक्मि or शाशकीमि. *Participles,* Pres. शक्नुवत्; Ātm. शक्नुवान; Past pass. शक्त; Past indecl. शक्त्वा, -शक्य; Fut. pass. शक्तव्य, शकनीय, शक्य.

680. Root ऋध्. Inf. अर्धितुं 'to prosper,' 'to flourish,' 'to increase.' Parasmai. Pres. ऋध्नोमि, ऋध्नोषि, ऋध्नोति; ऋध्नुवस्, ऋध्नुथस्, ऋध्नुतस्; ऋध्नुमस्, ऋध्नुथ, ऋध्नुवन्ति. Pot. ऋध्नुयां, &c. Imp. ऋध्नवानि, ऋध्नुहि, ऋध्नोतु; ऋध्नवाव, ऋध्नुतं, -तां; ऋध्नवाम, ऋध्नुत, ऋध्नुवन्तु. 1st Pret. (260. *a*) आर्ध्नवं, आर्ध्नोस्, आर्ध्नोत्; आर्ध्नुव, आर्ध्नुतं, आर्ध्नुतां; आर्ध्नुम, आर्ध्नुत, आर्ध्नुवन्. 2d Pret. आनर्ध, आनर्धिथ, आनर्ध; आनर्धिव, आनर्धथुस्, आनर्धतुस्; आनर्धिम, आनर्ध, आनर्धुस्. 1st Fut. अर्धितास्मि, &c. 2d Fut. अर्धिष्यामि, &c. 3d Pret. आर्धिषं, आर्धीस्, आर्धीत्; आर्धिष्व, आर्धिष्टं, -ष्टां; आर्धिष्म, आर्धिष्ट, आर्धिषुस्. Or आर्धं, -र्धस्, -र्धत्; -र्धाव, &c. Bened. ऋध्यासं, &c. Cond. आर्धिष्यं, &c. *Passive,* Pres. ऋध्ये; 3d Pret. 3d sing. आर्धि. *Causal,* अर्धयामि; 3d Pret. आर्दिधं. *Des.* अर्दिधिषामि or ईर्त्सामि (503). *Participles,* Pres. ऋध्नुवत्; Past pass. ऋद्ध; Past indecl. अर्धित्वा or ऋद्ध्वा, -ऋध्य; Fut. pass. अर्धितव्य, अर्धनीय, ऋध्य.

681. Root आप्. Inf. आप्तुं 'to obtain.' Parasmai. Pres. आप्नोमि, आप्नोषि, आप्नोति; आप्नुवस्, आप्नुथस्, आप्नुतस्; आप्नुमस्, आप्नुथ, आप्नुवन्ति. Pot. आप्नुयां, &c. Imp. आप्नवानि, आप्नुहि, आप्नोतु; आप्नवाव, आप्नुतं, -तां; आप्नवाम, आप्नुत, आप्नुवन्तु. 1st Pret. आप्नवं, आप्नोस्, आप्नोत्; आप्नुव, आप्नुतं, -तां; आप्नुम, आप्नुत, आप्नुवन्. 2d Pret. आप, आपिथ, आप; आपिव, आपथुस्, आपतुस्; आपिम, आप, आपुस्. 1st Fut. आप्तास्मि, &c. 2d Fut. आप्स्यामि, &c. 3d Pret. आपं, आपस्, आपत्; आपाव, आपतं, -तां; आपाम, आपत, आपन्. Bened. आप्यासं, &c. Cond. आप्स्यं, &c. *Passive,* Pres. आप्ये; 3d Pret. 3d sing. आपि. *Causal,* Pres. आपयामि; 3d Pret.

* This form of the Des. generally means 'to learn,' and is said by some to come from a root शिक्ष्.

आपिपं. *Des.* (503) ईप्सामि. *Participles,* Pres. आप्नुवत्; Past pass. आप्त; Past indecl. आप्त्वा, -आप्य; Fut. pass. आप्तव्य, आपनीय, आप्य.

a. Root अश्. Inf. अशितुं or अष्टुं 'to obtain,' 'to enjoy,' 'to pervade.' Átmane. Pres. अश्नुवे, अश्नुषे, अश्नुते; अश्नुवहे, अश्नुवाथे, अश्नुवाते; अश्नुमहे, अश्नुध्वे, अश्नुवते. Pot. अश्नुवीय, अश्नुवीथास्, &c. Imp. अश्नवै, अश्नुष्व, अश्नुतां; अश्नवावहै, अश्नुवाथां, अश्नुवातां; अश्नवामहै, अश्नुध्वं, अश्नुवतां. 1st Pret. आश्नुवि, आश्नुथास्, आश्नुत; आश्नुवहि, आश्नुवाथां, आश्नुवातां; आश्नुमहि, आश्नुध्वं, आश्नुवत. 2d Pret. (371. *a*) आनशे, आनशिषे or आनक्षे*, आनशे; आनशिवहे, आनशाथे, आनशाते; आनशिमहे, आनशिध्वे or आनड्ढ्वे*, आनशिरे. 1st Fut. अशिताहे or अष्टाहे. 2d Fut. अशिष्ये or अक्ष्ये. 3d Pret. आक्षि, आष्ठास्, आष्ट; आक्ष्वहि, आक्षाथां, आक्षातां; आक्ष्महि, आड्ढ्वं, आक्षत. Or आशिषि, आशिष्ठास्, आशिष्ट; आशिष्वहि, आशिषाथां, आशिषातां; आशिष्महि, आशिढ्वं, आशिषत. Bened. अशिषीय or अक्षीय. Cond. आशिष्ये or आक्ष्ये. *Passive,* Pres. अश्ये; 3d Pret. 3d sing. आशि. *Causal,* Pres. आशयामि; 3d Pret. आशिशं. *Des.* अशिशिषे. *Freq.* अशाश्ये (508. *a*). *Participles,* Pres. अश्नुवान; Past pass. अशित or अष्ट; Past indecl. अशित्वा or अष्ट्वा, -अश्य; Fut. pass. अशितव्य or अष्टव्य, अशनीय, आश्य.

EXAMPLES OF PRIMITIVE VERBS OF THE EIGHTH CONJUGATION, EXPLAINED AT 353.

682. Root कृ *kri.* Infin. कर्त्तुं *karttum* or कर्तुं *kartum,* 'to do' (355).

PARASMAI-PADA. *Present tense,* 'I do.'

करोमि *karomi*	कुर्व्वस् † *kurvas*	कुर्म्मस् † *kurmas*
करोषि *karoshi*	कुरुथस् *kuruthas*	कुरुथ *kurutha*
करोति *karoti*	कुरुतस् *kurutas*	कुर्व्वन्ति † *kurvanti*

Potential, 'I may do,' &c.

कुर्य्यां † *kuryám*	कुर्य्याव *kuryáva*	कुर्य्याम *kuryáma*
कुर्य्यास् *kuryás*	कुर्य्यातं *kuryátam*	कुर्य्यात *kuryáta*
कुर्य्यात् *kuryát*	कुर्य्यातां *kuryátám*	कुर्य्युस् *kuryus*

Imperative, 'Let me do,' &c.

करवाणि *karaváṇi*	करवाव *karaváva*	करवाम *karaváma*
कुरु *kuru*	कुरुतं *kurutam*	कुरुत *kuruta*
करोतु *karotu*	कुरुतां *kurutám*	कुर्व्वन्तु † *kurvantu*

* So Westergaard under this root.

† कुर्वस्, कुर्मस्, कुर्यां, &c., would be equally correct; see 73.

First preterite, 'I was doing,' &c.

अकरवं *akaravam*	अकुर्व्व *akurva* (73)	अकुर्म्म *akurma* (73)
अकरोस् *akaros*	अकुरुतं *akurutam*	अकुरुत *akuruta*
अकरोत् *akarot*	अकुरुतां *akurutám*	अकुर्व्वन् *akurvan*

Second preterite, 'I did,' &c.

चकार *chakára*	चकृव *chakṛiva*	चकृम *chakṛima*
चकर्थ *chakartha*	चक्रथुस् *chakrathus*	चक्र *chakra*
चकार *chakára*	चक्रतुस् *chakratus*	चक्रुस् *chakrus*

First future, 'I will do,' &c.

कर्त्तास्मि *karttásmi*	कर्त्तास्वस् *karttáswas*	कर्त्तास्मस् *karttásmas*
कर्त्तासि *karttási*	कर्त्तास्थस् *karttásthas*	कर्त्तास्थ *karttástha*
कर्त्ता *karttá*	कर्त्तारौ *karttárau*	कर्त्तारस् *karttáras*

Second future, 'I shall do,' &c.

करिष्यामि *karishyámi*	करिष्यावस् *karishyávas*	करिष्यामस् *karishyámas*
करिष्यसि *karishyasi*	करिष्यथस् *karishyathas*	करिष्यथ *karishyatha*
करिष्यति *karishyati*	करिष्यतस् *karishyatas*	करिष्यन्ति *karishyanti*

Third preterite, 'I did,' &c.

अकार्षं *akársham*	अकार्ष्व *akárshwa*	अकार्ष्म *akárshma*
अकार्षीस् *akárshís*	अकार्ष्टं *akárshṭam*	अकार्ष्ट *akárshṭa*
अकार्षीत् *akárshít*	अकार्ष्टां *akárshṭám*	अकार्षुस् *akárshus*

Benedictive, 'May I do,' &c.

क्रियासम् *kriyásam*	क्रियास्व *kriyáswa*	क्रियास्म *kriyásma*
क्रियास् *kriyás*	क्रियास्तं *kriyástam*	क्रियास्त *kriyásta*
क्रियात् *kriyát*	क्रियास्तां *kriyástám*	क्रियासुस् *kriyásus*

Conditional, 'I should do,' &c.

अकरिष्यम् *akarishyam*	अकरिष्याव *akarishyáva*	अकरिष्याम *akarishyáma*
अकरिष्यस् *akarishyas*	अकरिष्यतं *akarishyatam*	अकरिष्यत *akarishyata*
अकरिष्यत् *akarishyat*	अकरिष्यतां *akarishyatám*	अकरिष्यन् *akarishyan*

683. ÁTMANE-PADA. *Present tense*, 'I do,' &c.

कुर्व्वे *kurve* (73)	कुर्व्वहे *kurvahe*	कुर्म्महे *kurmahe*
कुरुषे *kurushe*	कुर्व्वाथे *kurváthe*	कुरुध्वे *kurudhwe*
कुरुते *kurute*	कुर्व्वाते *kurváte*	कुर्व्वते *kurvate*

Potential, 'I may do,' &c.

कुर्व्वीय *kurvíya*	कुर्व्वीवहि *kurvívahi*	कुर्व्वीमहि *kurvímahi*
कुर्व्वीथास् *kurvíthás*	कुर्व्वीयाथां *kurvíyáthám*	कुर्व्वीध्वं *kurvídhwam*
कुर्व्वीत *kurvíta*	कुर्व्वीयातां *kurvíyátám*	कुर्व्वीरन् *kurvíran*

Imperative, 'Let me do,' &c.

करवै *karavai*	करवावहै *karavávahai*	करवामहै *karavámahai*
कुरुष्व *kurushwa*	कुर्वाथां *kurvátháṃ*	कुरुध्वं *kurudhwam*
कुरुतां *kurutám*	कुर्वातां *kurvátám*	कुर्वतां *kurvatám*

First preterite, 'I was doing,' &c.

अकुर्वि *akurvi* (73)	अकुर्वहि *akurvahi*	अकुर्महि *akurmahi*
अकुरुथास् *akuruthás*	अकुर्वाथां *akurváthám*	अकुरुध्वं *akurudhwam*
अकुरुत *akuruta*	अकुर्वातां *akurvátám*	अकुर्वत *akurvata*

Second preterite, 'I did,' &c.

चक्रे *chakre*	चकृवहे *chakṛivahe*	चकृमहे *chakṛimahe*
चकृषे *chakṛishe*	चक्राथे *chakráthe*	चकृध्वे *chakṛidhwe* or -ढ्वे -ḍhwe
चक्रे *chakre*	चक्राते *chakráte*	चक्रिरे *chakrire*

First future, 'I will do,' &c.

कर्त्ताहे *karttáhe*	कर्त्तास्वहे *karttáswahe*	कर्त्तास्महे *karttásmahe*
कर्त्तासे *karttáse*	कर्त्तासाथे *karttásáthe*	कर्त्ताध्वे *karttádhwe*
कर्त्ता *karttá*	कर्त्तारौ *karttárau*	कर्त्तारस् *karttáras*

Second future, 'I shall do,' &c.

करिष्ये *karishye*	करिष्यावहे *karishyávahe*	करिष्यामहे *karishyámahe*
करिष्यसे *karishyase*	करिष्येथे *karishyethe*	करिष्यध्वे *karishyadhwe*
करिष्यते *karishyate*	करिष्येते *karishyete*	करिष्यन्ते *karishyante*

Third preterite, 'I did,' &c.

अकृषि *akṛishi*	अकृष्वहि *akṛishwahi*	अकृष्महि *akṛishmahi*
अकृथास् *akṛithás*	अकृषाथां *akṛisháthám*	अकृध्वं *akṛidhwam* or -ढ्वं -ḍhwam
अकृत *akṛita*	अकृषातां *akṛishátám*	अकृषत *akṛishata*

Benedictive, 'May I do,' &c.

कृषीय *kṛishíya*	कृषीवहि *kṛishívahi*	कृषीमहि *kṛishímahi*
कृषीष्ठास् *kṛishíshṭhás*	कृषीयास्थां *kṛishíyásthám*	कृषीध्वं *kṛishídhwam*
कृषीष्ट *kṛishíshṭa*	कृषीयास्तां *kṛishíyástám*	कृषीरन् *kṛishíran*

Conditional, 'I should do,' &c.

अकरिष्ये *akarishye*	अकरिष्यावहि *akarishyávahi*	अकरिष्यामहि *akarishyámahi*
अकरिष्यथास् *akarishyathás*	अकरिष्येथां *akarishyethám*	अकरिष्यध्वं *akarishyadhwam*
अकरिष्यत *akarishyata*	अकरिष्येतां *akarishyetám*	अकरिष्यन्त *akarishyanta*

Passive, Pres. क्रिये; 3d Pret. 3d sing. अकारि, see 701. *Causal*, Pres. कारयामि; 3d Pret. अचीकरं. *Des.* चिकीर्षामि, -षे (502). *Freq.* चेक्रीये, चर्कर्मि or चरिकर्मि or चरीकर्मि or चर्करीमि or चरिकरीमि or चरीकरीमि.

Participles, Pres. कुर्वत्; A'tm. कुर्वाण; Past pass. कृत; Past indecl. कृत्वा, -कृत्य; Fut. pass. कर्त्तव्य, करणीय, कार्य्य.

684. There are only nine other roots in this class. Of these the commonest is तन् 'to stretch,' conjugated in the table at 583. The others are, ऋण् 'to go,' क्षण् 'to kill' or 'to hurt,' क्षिण् 'to kill' or 'to hurt,' घृण् 'to shine,' तृण् 'to eat grass,' मन् 'to imagine,' A'tm.; वन् 'to ask,' सन् 'to give.' As these all end in nasals, their conjugation will resemble that of verbs of the 5th class at 675; thus—

685. Root क्षण्. Inf. क्षणितुं 'to kill,' 'to hurt.' Parasmai and A'tmane. Pres. क्षणोमि, क्षणोषि, क्षणोति; क्षणुवस्, &c. A'tm. क्षण्वे, क्षणुषे, &c. Pot. क्षणुयां, &c. A'tm. क्षण्वीय, &c. Imp. क्षणवानि, &c. A'tm. क्षणवै, &c. 1st Pret. अक्षणवं, अक्षणोस्, &c. A'tm. अक्षण्वि, &c. 2d Pret. चक्षाण, चक्षणिथ, चक्षाण; चक्षणिव, चक्षणथुस्, चक्षणतुस्; चक्षणिम, चक्षण, चक्षणुस्. A'tm. चक्षणे, चक्षणिषे, चक्षणे; चक्षणिवहे, चक्षणाथे, चक्षणाते; चक्षणिमहे, चक्षणिध्वे, चक्षणिरे. 1st Fut. क्षणितास्मि, &c. A'tm. क्षणिताहे, &c. 2d Fut. क्षणिष्यामि, &c. A'tm. क्षणिष्ये, &c. 3d Pret. अक्षणिषं, -णीस्, -णीत्; अक्षणिष्व, -णिष्टं, -ष्टां; अक्षणिष्म, -णिष्ट, -णिषुस्. A'tm. अक्षणिषि, अक्षणिष्ठास् or अक्षथास् (426. *b*), अक्षणिष्ट or अक्षत (426. *b*); अक्षणिष्वहि, -णिषाथां, -णिषातां; अक्षणिष्महि, -णिध्वं, -णिषत. Bened. क्षण्यासं. A'tm. क्षणिषीय. Cond. अक्षणिष्यं. A'tm. अक्षणिष्ये. *Passive*, Pres. क्षण्ये; 3d Pret. 3d sing. अक्षाणि. *Causal*, Pres. क्षाणयामि; 3d Pret. अचिक्षणं. *Des.* चिक्षणिषामि, -षे. *Freq.* चंक्षण्ये, चंक्षण्मि. *Participles*, Pres. क्षण्वत्; A'tm. क्षण्वान; Past pass. क्षत; Past indecl. क्षत्वा or क्षणित्वा, -क्षत्य; Fut. pass. क्षणितव्य, क्षणनीय, क्षाण्य.

EXAMPLES OF PRIMITIVE VERBS OF THE NINTH CONJUGATION, EXPLAINED AT 356.

686. Root यु *yu*. Infin. यवितुं *yavitum*, 'to join,' 'to mix.'

PARASMAI-PADA. *Present tense*, 'I join.'

युनामि *yunámi*	युनीवस् *yunívas*	युनीमस् *yunímas*
युनासि *yunási*	युनीथस् *yuníthas*	युनीथ *yunítha*
युनाति *yunáti*	युनीतस् *yunítas*	युनन्ति *yunanti*

Potential, 'I may join.'

युनीयां *yuníyám*	युनीयाव *yuníyáva*	युनीयाम *yuníyáma*
युनीयास् *yuníyás*	युनीयातं *yuníyátam*	युनीयात *yuníyáta*
युनीयात् *yuníyát*	युनीयातां *yuníyátám*	युनीयुस् *yuníyus*

Imperative, 'Let me join.'

युनानि *yunáni*	युनाव *yunáva*	युनाम *yunáma*
युनीहि *yuníhi*	युनीतं *yunítam*	युनीत *yuníta*
युनातु *yunátu*	युनीतां *yunítám*	युनन्तु *yunantu*

First preterite, 'I was joining.'

अयुनां *ayunám*	अयुनीव *ayunìva*	अयुनीम *ayuníma*
अयुनास् *ayunás*	अयुनीतं *ayunítam*	अयुनीत *ayuníta*
अयुनात् *ayunát*	अयुनीतां *ayunítám*	अयुनन् *ayunan*

2d Pret. युयाव, युयविथ or युयोथ, युयाव; युयुविव, युयुवथुस्, युयुवतुस्; युयुविम, युयुव, युयुवुस्. 1st Fut. यवितास्मि or योतास्मि*, &c. 2d Fut. यविष्यामि, &c. 3d Pret. अयाविषं, -वीस्, -वीत्; अयाविष्व, -विष्टं, -विष्टां; अयाविष्म, -विष्ट, -विषुस्. Bened. यूयासं, &c. Cond. अयविष्यं, &c.

687. ÁTMANE-PADA. *Present tense*, 'I join.'

युने *yune*	युनीवहे *yunívahe*	युनीमहे *yunímahe*
युनीषे *yuníshe*	युनाथे *yunáthe*	युनीध्वे *yunídhwe*
युनीते *yuníte*	युनाते *yunáte*	युनते *yunate*

Potential, 'I may join.'

युनीय *yuníya*	युनीवहि *yunívahi*	युनीमहि *yunímahi*
युनीथास् *yuníthás*	युनीयाथां *yuníyáthám*	युनीध्वं *yunídhwam*
युनीत *yuníta*	युनीयातां *yuníyátám*	युनीरन् *yuníran*

Imperative, 'Let me join.'

युनै *yunai*	युनावहै *yunávahai*	युनामहै *yunámahai*
युनीष्व *yuníshwa*	युनाथां *yunáthám*	युनीध्वं *yunídhwam*
युनीतां *yunítám*	युनातां *yunátám*	युनतां *yunatám*

First preterite, 'I joined.'

अयुनि *ayuni*	अयुनीवहि *ayunívahi*	अयुनीमहि *ayunímahi*
अयुनीथास् *ayuníthás*	अयुनाथां *ayunáthám*	अयुनीध्वं *ayunídhwam*
अयुनीत *ayuníta*	अयुनातां *ayunátám*	अयुनत *ayunata*

2d Pret. युयुवे, युयुविषे, युयुवे; युयुविवहे, युयुवाथे, युयुवाते; युयुविमहे, युयुविध्वे or -ढ्वे, युयुविरे. 1st Fut. यविताहे, &c. 2d Fut. यविष्ये, &c. 3d Pret. अयविषि, -विष्ठास्, -विष्ट; अयविष्वहि, अयविषाथां, -षातां; अयविष्महि, -विध्वं, -विषत. Bened. यविषीय, &c. Cond. अयविष्ये, &c. *Passive*, Pres. यूये; 1st Fut. याविताहे; 3d Pret. 3d sing. अयावि or अयाविषत. *Causal*, Pres. यावयामि; 3d Pret. अयीयवं. *Des.* युयूषामि or यियविषामि.

* Some authorities give योतास्मि &c. as the only form. See Laghu Kaum. 724.

Freq. योयूये, योयोमि or योयवीमि. *Participles,* Pres. युनत्; Átm. युनान; Past pass. युत; Past indecl. युत्वा, -युत्य; Fut. pass. यवितव्य, यवनीय, याव्य or यव्य.

688. Root ज्ञा (360). Inf. ज्ञातुं 'to know.' Parasmai and Átmane. Pres. जानामि, जानासि, जानाति; जानीवस्, जानीथस्, जानीतस्; जानीमस्, जानीथ, जानन्ति. Átm. जाने, जानीषे, जानीते; जानीवहे, जानाथे, जानाते; जानीमहे, जानीध्वे, जानते. Pot. जानीयां, &c. Átm. जानीय, &c. Imp. जानानि, जानीहि, जानातु; जानाव, जानीतं, जानीतां; जानाम, जानीत, जानन्तु. Átm. जानै, जानीष्व, जानीतां; जानावहै, जानाथां, जानातां; जानामहै, जानीध्वं, जानतां. 1st Pret. अजानां, अजानास्, अजानात्; अजानीव, अजानीतं, अजानीतां; अजानीम, अजानीत, अजानन्. Átm. अजानि, अजानीथास्, अजानीत; अजानीवहि, अजानाथां, अजानातां; अजानीमहि, अजानीध्वं, अजानत. 2d Pret. (373) जज्ञौ, जज्ञिथ, जज्ञौ; जज्ञिव, जज्ञथुस्, जज्ञतुस्; जज्ञिम, जज्ञ, जज्ञुस्. Átm. जज्ञे, जज्ञिषे, जज्ञे; जज्ञिवहे, जज्ञाथे, जज्ञाते; जज्ञिमहे, जज्ञिध्वे or -ढ्वे, जज्ञिरे. 1st Fut. ज्ञातास्मि, &c. 2d Fut. ज्ञास्यामि, &c. 3d Pret. (433) अज्ञासिषं, अज्ञासीस्, अज्ञासीत्; अज्ञासिष्व, अज्ञासिष्टं, -ष्टां; अज्ञासिष्म, अज्ञासिष्ट, अज्ञासिषुस्. Átm. अज्ञासि, अज्ञास्थास्, अज्ञास्त; अज्ञास्वहि, अज्ञासाथां, अज्ञासातां; अज्ञास्महि, अज्ञाध्वं, अज्ञासत. Bened. ज्ञेयासं or ज्ञायासं. Átm. ज्ञासीय, &c. Cond. अज्ञास्यं, &c. Átm. अज्ञास्ये, &c. *Passive,* Pres. (465. *a*) ज्ञाये; 2d Pret. जज्ञे (473); 1st Fut. ज्ञाताहे or ज्ञायिताहे (474); 2d Fut. ज्ञास्ये or ज्ञायिष्ये; 3d Pret. 3d sing. अज्ञायि. *Causal,* Pres. ज्ञापयामि or ज्ञपयामि; 3d Pret. अजिज्ञपं. *Des.* जिज्ञासे. *Freq.* जाज्ञाये, जाज्ञामि or जाज्ञेमि. *Participles,* Pres. जानत्; Átm. जानान; Past pass. ज्ञात; Past indecl. ज्ञात्वा, -ज्ञाय; Fut. pass. ज्ञातव्य, ज्ञानीय, ज्ञेय.

689. Root क्री. Inf. क्रेतुं 'to buy.' Parasmai and Átmane. Pres. क्रीणामि, क्रीणासि, क्रीणाति; क्रीणीवस्, क्रीणीथस्, क्रीणीतस्; क्रीणीमस्, क्रीणीथ, क्रीणन्ति. Átm. क्रीणे, क्रीणीषे, क्रीणीते; क्रीणीवहे, क्रीणाथे, क्रीणाते; क्रीणीमहे, क्रीणीध्वे, क्रीणते. Pot. क्रीणीयां, &c. Átm. क्रीणीय, &c. Imp. क्रीणानि, क्रीणीहि, क्रीणातु; क्रीणाव, क्रीणीतं, क्रीणीतां; क्रीणाम, क्रीणीत, क्रीणन्तु. Átm. क्रीणै, क्रीणीष्व, क्रीणीतां; क्रीणावहै, क्रीणाथां, क्रीणातां; क्रीणामहै, क्रीणीध्वं, क्रीणतां. 1st Pret. अक्रीणां, अक्रीणास्, अक्रीणात्; अक्रीणीव, अक्रीणीतं, अक्रीणीतां; अक्रीणीम, अक्रीणीत, अक्रीणन्. Átm. अक्रीणि, अक्रीणीथास्, अक्रीणीत; अक्रीणीवहि, अक्रीणाथां, अक्रीणातां; अक्रीणीमहि, अक्रीणीध्वं, अक्रीणत. 2d Pret. (367. *a*) चिक्राय, चिक्रयिथ or चिक्रेथ, चिक्राय; चिक्रियिव, चिक्रियथुस्, चिक्रियतुस्; चिक्रियिम, चिक्रिय, चिक्रियुस्. Átm. चिक्रिये, चिक्रियिषे, चिक्रिये; चिक्रियिवहे, चिक्रियाथे, चिक्रियाते; चिक्रियिमहे, चिक्रियिध्वे or -ढ्वे, चिक्रियिरे. 1st Fut. क्रेतास्मि, &c. Átm. क्रेताहे, &c. 2d Fut. क्रेष्यामि, &c. Átm. क्रेष्ये, &c. 3d Pret. अक्रैषं, -षीस्, -षीत्;

अक्रैष्व, -ष्टं, -ष्टां; अक्रैष्म, -ष्ट, -षुस्. Átm. अक्रेषि, -ष्ठास्, -ष्ट; अक्रेष्वहि, -षाथां, -षातां; अक्रेष्महि, अक्रेढ्वं or -ढ्ढुं, अक्रेषत. Bened. क्रीयासं, &c. Átm. क्रेषीय, &c. Cond. अक्रेष्यं, &c. Átm. अक्रेष्ये, &c. *Passive*, Pres. क्रीये, &c.; 3d Pret. 3d sing. अक्रायि. *Causal*, Pres. क्रापयामि; 3d Pret. अचिक्रपं. *Des.* चिक्रीषामि, -षे. *Freq.* चेक्रीये, चेक्रेमि or चेक्रयीमि. *Participles*, Pres. क्रीणत्; Átm. क्रीणान; Past pass. क्रीत; Past indecl. क्रीत्वा, -क्रीय; Fut. pass. क्रेतव्य, क्रयणीय, क्रेय.

690. After क्री may be conjugated प्री 'to please;' thus, Pres. प्रीणामि, &c.; Átm. प्रीणे, &c. The *Causal* is प्रीणयामि or प्राययामि; 3d Pret. अपिप्रणं* or अपिप्रीणं*. *Des.* पिप्रीषामि, &c. *Freq.* पेप्रीये, &c.

691. The root लू, 'to cut,' follows the conjugation of पू, 'to purify,' in the table at 583; thus, Pres. लुनामि, &c.; Átm. लुने, &c.; Pot. लुनीयां, &c.; Átm. लुनीय, &c.; 2d Pret. लुलाव, &c.; Átm. लुलुवे, &c.; 1st Fut. लवितास्मि, &c.; 2d Fut. लविष्यामि, &c.; 3d Pret. अलाविषं, &c.

692. Root बन्ध्. Inf. बन्द्धुं 'to bind.' Parasmai. Pres. बध्नामि, बध्नासि, बध्नाति; बध्नीवस्, बध्नीथस्, बध्नीतस्; बध्नीमस्, बध्नीथ, बध्नन्ति. Pot. बध्नीयां, &c. Imp. बध्नानि, बधान (357. *a*), बध्नातु; बध्नाव, बध्नीतं, -तां; बध्नाम, बध्नीत, बध्नन्तु. 1st Pret. अबध्नां, अबध्नास्, अबध्नात्; अबध्नीव, अबध्नीतं, -तां; अबध्नीम, अबध्नीत, अबध्नन्. 2d Pret. बबन्ध, बबन्धिथ or बबन्द्ध (298) or बबन्थ (298. *a*), बबन्ध; बबन्धिव, बबन्धथुस्, बबन्धतुस्; बबन्धिम, बबन्ध, बबन्धुस्. 1st Fut. बन्द्धास्मि (298), &c. 2d Fut. भन्त्स्यामि (299. *a*), &c. 3d Pret. अभान्त्सं (299. *a*), अभान्त्सीस्, अभान्त्सीत्; अभान्त्स्व, अबान्द्धं, अबान्द्धां; अभान्त्स्म, अबान्द्ध, अभान्त्सुस्. Bened. बध्यासं. Cond. अभन्त्स्यं. *Passive*, Pres. (469) बध्ये. *Causal*, Pres. बन्धयामि; 3d Pret. अबबन्धं. *Des.* बिभन्त्सामि (299. *a*). *Freq.* बाबध्ये, बाबन्ध्मि, बाबन्धीमि. *Participles*, Pres. बध्नत्; Past pass. बद्ध; Past indecl. बद्ध्वा, -बध्य; Fut. pass. बन्द्धव्य, बन्धनीय, बन्ध्य.

693. Root ग्रन्थ्. Inf. ग्रन्थितुं 'to connect,' 'to tie,' 'to fasten together.' Parasmai. Pres. ग्रथ्नामि, ग्रथ्नासि, ग्रथ्नाति; ग्रथ्नीवस्, ग्रथ्नीथस्, ग्रथ्नीतस्; ग्रथ्नीमस्, ग्रथ्नीथ, ग्रथ्नन्ति. Pot. ग्रथ्नीयां, &c. Imp. ग्रथ्नानि, ग्रथान†, ग्रथ्नातु; ग्रथ्नाव, ग्रथ्नीतं, -तां; ग्रथ्नाम, ग्रथ्नीत, ग्रथ्नन्तु. 1st Pret. अग्रथ्नां, अग्रथ्नास्, अग्रथ्नात्; अग्रथ्नीव, अग्रथ्नीतं, -तां; अग्रथ्नीम, अग्रथ्नीत, अग्रथ्नन्. 2d Pret. (375. *f*) जग्रन्थ†, जग्रन्थिथ or ग्रेथिथ, जग्रन्थ†; जग्रन्थिव or ग्रेथिव,

* Foster gives अपिप्रणं; Westergaard, अपिप्रीणं.

† Some authorities give ग्रन्थान in 2d sing. Imp.; and the option of जग्राथ in the 1st and 3d of the 2d Pret. Compare 339.

जग्रन्थथुस् or ग्रेथथुस्, जग्रन्थतुस् or ग्रेथतुस्; जग्रन्थिम or ग्रेथिम, जग्रन्थ or ग्रेथ, जग्रन्थुस् or ग्रेथुस्. 1st Fut. ग्रन्थितास्मि, &c. 2d Fut. ग्रन्थिष्यामि, &c. 3d Pret. अग्रन्थिषं, -न्थीस्, -न्थीत्, &c.; see 427. Bened. ग्रथ्यासं, &c. Cond. अग्रन्थिष्यं, &c. *Passive,* Pres. (469) ग्रथ्ये, &c. *Causal,* Pres. ग्रन्थयामि; 3d Pret. अजग्रन्थं. *Des.* जिग्रन्थिषामि. *Freq.* जाग्रथ्ये, जंग्रन्थ्मि, जंग्रन्थीमि. *Participles,* Pres. ग्रथ्नत्; Past pass. ग्रथित; Past indecl. ग्रथित्वा or ग्रन्थित्वा, -ग्रथ्य; Fut. pass. ग्रन्थितव्य, ग्रन्थनीय, ग्रन्थ्य.

a. After ग्रन्थ् may be conjugated श्रन्थ् 'to loosen,' मन्थ् 'to churn,' &c.

694. Root क्षुभ्*. Inf. क्षोभितुं 'to agitate,' 'to shake.' Parasmai. Pres. क्षुभ्नामि, क्षुभ्नासि, क्षुभ्नाति; क्षुभ्नीवस्, क्षुभ्नीथस्, क्षुभ्नीतस्; क्षुभ्नीमस्, क्षुभ्नीथ, क्षुभ्नन्ति. Pot. क्षुभ्नीयां, &c. Imp. क्षुभ्नानि, क्षुभाण (357. *a*, 58), क्षुभ्नातु; क्षुभ्नाव, क्षुभ्नीतं, -तां; क्षुभ्नाम, क्षुभ्नीत, क्षुभ्नन्तु. 1st Pret. अक्षुभ्नां, अक्षुभ्नास्, अक्षुभ्नात्; अक्षुभ्नीव, अक्षुभ्नीतं, -तां; अक्षुभ्नीम, अक्षुभ्नीत, अक्षुभ्नन्. 2d Pret. चुक्षोभ, चुक्षोभिथ, चुक्षोभ; चुक्षुभिव, चुक्षुभथुस्, चुक्षुभतुस्; चुक्षुभिम, चुक्षुभ, चुक्षुभुस्. 1st Fut. क्षोभितास्मि, &c. 2d Fut. क्षोभिष्यामि, &c. 3d Pret. अक्षोभिषं, -भीस्, -भीत्, &c.; see 427. Or अक्षुभं, -भस्, -भत्; -भाव, -भतं, -भतां; -भाम, -भत, -भन्. Bened. क्षुभ्यासं, &c. Cond. अक्षोभिष्यं, &c. *Passive,* Pres. क्षुभ्ये; 3d Pret. 3d sing. अक्षोभि. *Causal,* Pres. क्षोभयामि; 3d Pret. अचुक्षुभं. *Des.* चुक्षोभिषामि or चुक्षुभिषामि. *Freq.* चोक्षुभ्ये, चोक्षोभ्मि (3d sing. चोक्षोब्धि). *Participles,* Pres. क्षुभ्नत्; Past pass. क्षुब्ध or क्षुभित; Past indecl. क्षुब्ध्वा or क्षुभित्वा, -क्षुभ्य; Fut. pass. क्षोभितव्य, क्षोभणीय (58), क्षोभ्य.

695. Root स्तम्भ्†. Inf. स्तम्भितुं 'to stop,' 'to stay,' 'to support.' Parasmai. Pres. स्तभ्नामि, &c.; see क्षुभ् at 694. Pot. स्तभ्नीयां, &c. Imp. स्तभ्नानि, स्तभान (357. *a*), स्तभ्नातु; स्तभ्नाव, स्तभ्नीतं, -तां; स्तभ्नाम, स्तभ्नीत, स्तभ्नन्तु. 1st Pret. अस्तभ्नां, &c. 2d Pret. तस्तम्भ, तस्तम्भिथ, तस्तम्भ; तस्तम्भिव, तस्तम्भथुस्, तस्तम्भतुस्; तस्तम्भिम, तस्तम्भ, तस्तम्भुस्. 1st Fut. स्तम्भितास्मि, &c. 2d Fut. स्तम्भिष्यामि, &c. 3d Pret. अस्तम्भिषं, -म्भीस्, -म्भीत्, &c.; see 427. Or अस्तभं, -भस्, -भत्; -भाव, -भतं, -भतां; -भाम, -भत, -भन्. Bened. स्तभ्यासं. Cond. अस्तम्भिष्यं. *Passive,* Pres. स्तभ्ये. *Causal,* Pres. स्तम्भयामि; 3d Pret. अतस्तम्भं. *Des.* तिस्तम्भिषामि. *Freq.* तास्तभ्ये, तास्तम्भ्मि or तास्तम्भीमि. *Participles,* Pres. स्तभ्नत्; Past pass. स्तब्ध; Past indecl. स्तब्ध्वा or स्तम्भित्वा; Fut. pass. स्तम्भितव्य, स्तम्भनीय, स्तम्भ्य.

---

* This root is also conjugated in the 4th conjugation, when it is neuter, and signifies 'to be agitated;' thus, Pres. क्षुभ्यामि, &c. See 612.

† This root also follows the 5th conjugation; thus, Pres. स्तभ्नोमि, &c. See 675.

696. Root अश्*. Inf. अशितुं 'to eat.' Parasmai. Pres. अश्नामि, अश्नासि, अश्नाति; अश्नीवस्, अश्नीथस्, अश्नीतस्; अश्नीमस्, अश्नीथ, अश्नन्ति. Pot. अश्नीयां, &c. Imp. अश्नानि, अशान (357. *a*), अश्नातु; अश्नाव, अश्नीतं, -तां; अश्नाम, अश्नीत, अश्नन्तु. 1st Pret. आश्नां, आश्नास्, आश्नात्; आश्नीव, आश्नीतं, -तां; आश्नीम, आश्नीत, आश्नन्. 2d Pret. आश, आशिथ, आश; आशिव, आशथुस्, आशतुस्; आशिम, आश, आशुस्. 1st Fut. अशितास्मि, &c. 2d Fut. अशिष्यामि, &c. 3d Pret. आशिषं, आशीस्, आशीत्; आशिष्व, आशिष्टं, आशिष्टां; आशिष्म, आशिष्ट, आशिषुस्. Bened. अश्यासं, &c. Cond. आशिष्यं, &c. *Passive*, Pres. अश्ये. *Causal*, Pres. आशयामि; 3d Pret. आशिशं. *Des.* अशिशिषामि. *Freq.* अशाश्ये (508. *a*). *Participles*, Pres. अश्नत्; Past pass. अशित; Past indecl. अशित्वा, -अश्य; Fut. pass. अशितव्य, अशनीय, आश्य.

697. Root क्लिश्. Inf. क्लेशितुं or क्लेष्टुं 'to harass,' 'to vex,' 'to distress.' Parasmai. Pres. क्लिश्नामि, &c.; see अश् at 696. Pot. क्लिश्नीयां, &c. Imp. क्लिश्नानि, क्लिशान (357. *a*), &c. 1st Pret. अक्लिश्नां, अक्लिश्नास्, अक्लिश्नात्; अक्लिश्नीव, अक्लिश्नीतं, -तां; अक्लिश्नीम, अक्लिश्नीत, अक्लिश्नन्. 2d Pret. चिक्लेश, चिक्लेशिथ or चिक्लेष्ठ, चिक्लेश; चिक्लिशिव, चिक्लिशथुस्, चिक्लिशतुस्; चिक्लिशिम, चिक्लिश, चिक्लिशुस्. 1st Fut. क्लेशितास्मि or क्लेष्टास्मि, &c. 2d Fut. क्लेशिष्यामि or क्लेक्ष्यामि, &c. 3d Pret. अक्लेशिषं, -शीस्, -शीत्; अक्लेशिष्व, -शिष्टं, -शिष्टां; अक्लेशिष्म, -शिष्ट, -शिषुस्. Or अक्लिक्षं, -क्षस्, -क्षत्; -क्षाव, -क्षतं, -क्षतां; -क्षाम, -क्षत, -क्षन् (see 439). Bened. क्लिश्यासं, &c. Cond. अक्लेशिष्यं or अक्लेक्ष्यं. *Passive*, Pres. क्लिश्ये; 3d Pret. 3d sing. अक्लेशि. *Causal*, Pres. क्लेशयामि; 3d Pret. अचिक्लिशं. *Des.* चिक्लिशिषामि or चिक्लेशिषामि or चिक्लिक्षामि. *Freq.* चेक्लिश्ये, चेक्लेश्मि. *Participles*, Pres. क्लिश्नत्; Past pass. क्लिष्ट or क्लिशित; Past indecl. क्लिष्ट्वा or क्लिशित्वा, -क्लिश्य; Fut. pass. क्लेशितव्य or क्लेष्टव्य, क्लेशनीय, क्लेश्य.

698. Root पुष् (357. *a*). Inf. पोषितुं 'to nourish.' Parasmai. Pres. पुष्णामि, पुष्णासि, पुष्णाति; पुष्णीवस्, पुष्णीथस्, पुष्णीतस्; पुष्णीमस्, पुष्णीथ, पुष्णन्ति. Pot. पुष्णीयां, &c. Imp. पुष्णानि, पुषाण, पुष्णातु; पुष्णाव, पुष्णीतं, -तां; पुष्णाम, पुष्णीत, पुष्णन्तु. 1st Pret. अपुष्णां, अपुष्णास्, अपुष्णात्; अपुष्णीव, अपुष्णीतं, -तां; अपुष्णीम, अपुष्णीत, अपुष्णन्. For the other tenses and forms, see पुष् 4th c. at 621.

699. Root ग्रह् (359). Inf. ग्रहीतुं 'to take' (414. *a*). Parasmai and Átmane. Pres. गृह्णामि, गृह्णासि, गृह्णाति; गृह्णीवस्, गृह्णीथस्, गृह्णीतस्; गृह्णीमस्, गृह्णीथ, गृह्णन्ति. Átm. गृह्णे, गृह्णीषे, गृह्णीते; गृह्णीवहे, गृह्णाथे, गृह्णाते; गृह्णीमहे, गृह्णीध्वे, गृह्णते. Pot. गृह्णीयां. Átm. गृह्णीय, &c.

* This is a different root from अश् 5th conjugation. See 682.

Imp. गृह्णानि, गृहाण, गृह्णातु; गृह्णाव, गृह्णीतं, गृह्णीतां; गृह्णाम, गृह्णीत, गृह्णन्तु. A'tm. गृह्णै, गृह्णीष्व, गृह्णीतां; गृह्णावहै, गृह्णाथां, गृह्णातां; गृह्णामहै, गृह्णीध्वं, गृह्णतां. 1st Pret. अगृह्णां, अगृह्णास्, अगृह्णात्; अगृह्णीव, अगृह्णीतं, अगृह्णीतां; अगृह्णीम, अगृह्णीत, अगृह्णन्. A'tm. अगृह्णि, अगृह्णीथास्, अगृह्णीत; अगृह्णीवहि, अगृह्णाथां, अगृह्णातां; अगृह्णीमहि, अगृह्णीध्वं, अगृह्णत. 2d Pret. (380) जग्राह, जग्रहिथ, जग्राह; जगृहिव, जगृहथुस्, जगृहतुस्; जगृहिम, जगृह, जगृहुस्. A'tm. जगृहे, जगृहिषे, जगृहे; जगृहिवहे, जगृहाथे, जगृहाते; जगृहिमहे, जगृहिध्वे or -ढ्वे, जगृहिरे. 1st Fut. ग्रहीतास्मि, &c. (414. *a*). A'tm. ग्रहीताहे, &c. 2d Fut. ग्रहीष्यामि. A'tm. ग्रहीष्ये, &c. 3d Pret. अग्रहीषं, अग्रहीस्, अग्रहीत्; अग्रहीष्व, अग्रहीष्टं, अग्रहीष्टां; अग्रहीष्म, अग्रहीष्ट, अग्रहीषुस्. A'tm. अग्रहीषि, अग्रहीष्ठास्, अग्रहीष्ट; अग्रहीष्वहि, अग्रहीषाथां, अग्रहीषातां; अग्रहीष्महि, अग्रहीध्वं, अग्रहीषत. Bened. गृह्यासं, &c. A'tm. ग्रहीषीय. Cond. अग्रहीष्यं. A'tm. अग्रहीष्ये. *Passive*, Pres. गृह्ये; 2d Pret. जगृहे; 1st Fut. ग्रहीताहे or ग्राहिताहे; 2d Fut. ग्रहीष्ये or ग्राहिष्ये; 3d Pret. 3d sing. अग्राहि, 3d pl. अग्रहीषत or अग्राहिषत. *Causal*, Pres. ग्राहयामि; 3d Pret. अजिग्रहं. *Des.* जिघृक्षामि, -क्षे (503). *Freq.* जरीगृह्ये, जाग्रह्मि (3d sing. जाग्राढि) or जाग्रहीमि; see 711. *Participles*, Pres. गृह्णत्; A'tm. गृह्णान; Past pass. गृहीत; Past indecl. गृहीत्वा, -गृह्य; Fut. pass. ग्रहीतव्य, ग्रहणीय, ग्राह्य.

EXAMPLES OF PASSIVE VERBS, EXPLAINED AT 461.

700. Root दा *dá* (465). Infin. दातुं *dátum*, 'to be given.'

Present, 'I am given.'

दीये *díye*	दीयावहे *díyávahe*	दीयामहे *díyámahe*
दीयसे *díyase*	दीयेथे *díyethe*	दीयध्वे *díyadhwe*
दीयते *díyate*	दीयेते *díyete*	दीयन्ते *díyante*

Potential, 'I may be given.'

दीयेय *díyeya*	दीयेवहि *díyevahi*	दीयेमहि *díyemahi*
दीयेथास् *díyethás*	दीयेयाथां *díyeyáthám*	दीयेध्वं *díyedhwam*
दीयेत *díyeta*	दीयेयातां *díyeyátám*	दीयेरन् *díyeran*

Imperative, 'Let me be given.'

दीयै *díyai*	दीयावहै *díyávahai*	दीयामहै *díyámahai*
दीयस्व *díyaswa*	दीयेथां *díyethám*	दीयध्वं *díyadhwam*
दीयतां *díyatám*	दीयेतां *díyetám*	दीयन्तां *díyantám*

First preterite, 'I was given.'

अदीये *adíye*	अदीयावहि *adíyávahi*	अदीयामहि *adíyámahi*
अदीयथास् *adíyathás*	अदीयेथां *adíyethám*	अदीयध्वं *adíyadhwam*
अदीयत *adíyata*	अदीयेतां *adíyetám*	अदीयन्त *adíyanta*

Second preterite, 'I have been given.'

ददे *dade*	ददिवहे *dadivahe*	ददिमहे *dadimahe*
ददिषे *dadishe*	ददाथे *dadáthe*	ददिध्वे *dadidhwe* or -ढ्वे -*ḍhwe*
ददे *dade*	ददाते *dadáte*	ददिरे *dadire*

First future, 'I shall be given.'

दाताहे *dátáhe* or	दातास्वहे *dátáswahe*	दातास्महे *dátásmahe,* &c.
दायिताहे *dáyitáhe*	दायितास्वहे *dáyitáswahe*	दायितास्महे *dáyitásmahe,* &c.

Second future, 'I shall be given.'

दास्ये *dásye* or	दास्यावहे *dásyávahe*	दास्यामहे *dásyámahe,* &c.
दायिष्ये *dáyishye*	दायिष्यावहे *dáyishyávahe*	दायिष्यामहे *dáyishyámahe,* &c.

Third preterite, 'I was given.'

अदिषि *adishi* or	अदिष्वहि *adishwahi*	अदिष्महि *adishmahi*
अदायिषि *adáyishi*	अदायिष्वहि *adáyishwahi*	अदायिष्महि *adáyishmahi*
अदिथास् *adithás* or	अदिषाथां *adisháthám*	अदिढ्वं *adiḍhwam*
अदायिष्ठास् *adáyishṭhás*	अदायिषाथां *adáyisháthám*	अदायिध्वं *adáyidhwam*
अदायि *adáyi,* 'it was given,'	अदिषातां *adishátám*	अदिषत *adishata*
	अदायिषातां *adáyishátám*	अदायिषत *adáyishata*

Bened. दासीय or दायिषीय, &c. Cond. अदास्ये or अदायिष्ये.

701. Root कृ *kṛi* (467). Infin. कर्त्तुं *karttum,* 'to be made' or 'done.'

Present, 'I am made.'

क्रिये	क्रियावहे	क्रियामहे
क्रियसे	क्रियेथे	क्रियध्वे
क्रियते	क्रियेते	क्रियन्ते

Potential, 'I may be made.'

क्रियेय	क्रियेवहि	क्रियेमहि
क्रियेथास्	क्रियेयाथां	क्रियेध्वं
क्रियेत	क्रियेयातां	क्रियेरन्

Imperative, 'Let me be made.'

क्रियै	क्रियावहै	क्रियामहै
क्रियस्व	क्रियेथां	क्रियध्वं
क्रियतां	क्रियेतां	क्रियन्तां

First preterite, 'I was made.'

अक्रिये	अक्रियावहि	अक्रियामहि
अक्रियथास्	अक्रियेथां	अक्रियध्वं
अक्रियत	अक्रियेतां	अक्रियन्त

Second preterite.

चक्रे	चकृवहे	चकृमहे
चकृषे	चक्राथे	चकृढ्वे
चक्रे	चक्राते	चक्रिरे

First future.

कर्त्ताहे	कर्त्तास्वहे	कर्त्तास्महे, &c.
or कारिताहे	कारितास्वहे	कारितास्महे, &c.

Second fut. करिष्ये or कारिष्ये, &c.

Third preterite.

SING.	DUAL.	PLURAL.
अकृषि or अकारिषि	अकृष्वहि or अकारिष्वहि	अकृष्महि or अकारिष्महि
अकृथास् or अकारिष्ठास्	अकृषाथां or अकारिषाथां	अकृढ्वं or अकारिध्वं
अकारि 'it was done'	अकृषातां or अकारिषातां	अकृषत or अकारिषत

Bened. कृषीय or कारिषीय. Cond. अकरिष्ये or अकारिष्ये.

702. The following is an example of a passive verb from a root ending in a consonant:

Root युज् *yuj*. Infin. योक्तुं *yoktum*, 'to be fitting.'

Pres. युज्ये 'I am fitting,' युज्यसे, युज्यते, &c. Pot. युज्येय, &c. Imp. युज्यै, युज्यस्व, युज्यतां, &c. 1st Pret. अयुज्ये, अयुज्यथास्, अयुज्यत, &c. 2d Pret. युयुजे, युयुजिषे, युयुजे, &c. 1st Fut. योक्ताहे, योक्तासे, योक्ता, &c. 2d Fut. योक्ष्ये, योक्ष्यसे, योक्ष्यते, &c. 3d Pret. अयुक्षि, अयुक्थास्, अयोजि; अयुक्ष्वहि, अयुक्षाथां, &c. Bened. युक्षीय, &c. Cond. अयोक्ष्ये, &c.

EXAMPLES OF CAUSAL VERBS, EXPLAINED AT 479.

703. Root भू *bhú*. Infin. भावयितुं *bhávayitum*, 'to cause to be.'

PARASMAI-PADA. ÁTMANE-PADA.

Present, 'I cause to be,' &c.

भावयामि	भावयावस्	भावयामस्	भावये	भावयावहे	भावयामहे
भावयसि	भावयथस्	भावयथ	भावयसे	भावयेथे	भावयध्वे
भावयति	भावयतस्	भावयन्ति	भावयते	भावयेते	भावयन्ते

Potential, 'I may cause to be,' &c.

भावयेयं	भावयेव	भावयेम	भावयेय	भावयेवहि	भावयेमहि
भावयेस्	भावयेतं	भावयेत	भावयेथास्	भावयेयाथां	भावयेध्वं
भावयेत्	भावयेतां	भावयेयुस्	भवयेत	भावयेयातां	भावयेरन्

Imperative, 'Let me cause to be,' &c.

भावयानि	भावयाव	भावयाम	भावयै	भावयावहै	भावयामहै
भावय	भावयतं	भावयत	भावयस्व	भावयेथां	भावयध्वं
भावयतु	भावयतां	भावयन्तु	भावयतां	भावयेतां	भावयन्तां

First preterite, 'I was causing to be,' &c.

अभावयम्	अभावयाव	अभावयाम	अभावये	अभावयावहि	अभावयामहि
अभावयस्	अभावयतं	अभावयत	अभावयथास्	अभावयेथां	अभावयध्वं
अभावयत्	अभावयतां	अभावयन्	अभावयत	अभावयेतां	अभावयन्त

Second preterite, 'I caused to be,' &c.

भावयाञ्चकार	भावयाञ्चकृव	भावयाञ्चकृम	भावयाञ्चक्रे	भावयाञ्चकृवहे	भावयाञ्चकृमहे
भावयाञ्चकर्थ	भावयाञ्चक्रथुस्	भावयाञ्चक्र	भावयाञ्चकृषे	भावयाञ्चक्राथे	भावयाञ्चकृढ्वे
भावयाञ्चकार	भावयाञ्चक्रतुस्	भावयाञ्चक्रुस्	भावयाञ्चक्रे	भावयाञ्चक्राते	भावयाञ्चक्रिरे

First future, 'I will cause to be,' &c.

भावयितास्मि	भावयितास्वस्	भावयितास्मस्	भावयिताहे	भावयितास्वहे	भावयितास्महे
भावयितासि	भावयितास्थस्	भावयितास्थ	भावयितासे	भावयितासाथे	भावयिताध्वे
भावयिता	भावयितारौ	भावयितारस्	भावयिता	भावयितारौ	भावयितारस्

Second future, 'I shall or will cause to be,' &c.

भावयिष्यामि	भावयिष्यावस्	भावयिष्यामस्	भावयिष्ये	भावयिष्यावहे	भावयिष्यामहे
भावयिष्यसि	भावयिष्यथस्	भावयिष्यथ	भावयिष्यसे	भावयिष्येथे	भावयिष्यध्वे
भावयिष्यति	भावयिष्यतस्	भावयिष्यन्ति	भावयिष्यते	भावयिष्येते	भावयिष्यन्ते

Third preterite, 'I caused to be,' &c.

अबीभवम्	अबीभवाव	अबीभवाम	अबीभवे	अबीभवावहि	अबीभवामहि
अबीभवस्	अबीभवतं	अबीभवत	अबीभवथास्	अबीभवेथां	अबीभवध्वं
अबीभवत्	अबीभवतां	अबीभवन्	अबीभवत	अबीभवेतां	अबीभवन्त

Benedictive or *optative*, 'May I cause to be,' &c.

भाव्यासम्	भाव्यास्व	भाव्यास्म	भावयिषीय	भावयिषीवहि	भावयिषीमहि
भाव्यास्	भाव्यास्तं	भाव्यास्त	भावयिषीष्ठास्	भावयिषीयास्थां	भावयिषीध्वं
भाव्यात्	भाव्यास्तां	भाव्यासुस्	भावयिषीष्ट	भावयिषीयास्तां	भावयिषीरन्

Conditional, 'I should cause to be,' &c.

अभावयिष्यम्	अभावयिष्याव	अभावयिष्याम	अभावयिष्ये	अभावयिष्यावहि	अभावयिष्यामहि
अभावयिष्यस्	अभावयिष्यतं	अभावयिष्यत	अभावयिष्यथास्	अभावयिष्येथां	अभावयिष्यध्वं
अभावयिष्यत्	अभावयिष्यतां	अभावयिष्यन्	अभावयिष्यत	अभावयिष्येतां	अभावयिष्यन्त

704. Root दृश् *driś*. Infin. दर्शयितुं *darśayitum*, 'to cause to see.'

PARASMAI-PADA. *Present*, 'I cause to see.'

दर्शयामि *darśayámi*	दर्शयावस् *darśayávas*	दर्शयामस् *darśayámas*
दर्शयसि *darśayasi*	दर्शयथस् *darśayathas*	दर्शयथ *darśayatha*
दर्शयति *darśayati*	दर्शयतस् *darśayatas*	दर्शयन्ति *darśayanti*

Potential, 'I may cause to see.'

दर्शयेयं *darśayeyam*	दर्शयेव *darśayeva*	दर्शयेम *darśayema*
दर्शयेस् *darśayes*	दर्शयेतं *darśayetam*	दर्शयेत *darśayeta*
दर्शयेत् *darśayet*	दर्शयेतां *darśayetám*	दर्शयेयुस् *darśayeyus*

Imperative, 'Let me cause to see.'

दर्शयानि *darśayáni*	दर्शयाव *darśayáva*	दर्शयाम *darśayáma*
दर्शय *darśaya*	दर्शयतं *darśayatam*	दर्शयत *darśayata*
दर्शयतु *darśayatu*	दर्शयतां *darśayatám*	दर्शयन्तु *darśayantu*

First preterite, 'I was causing to see.'

अदर्शयं *adarśayam*	अदर्शयाव *adarśayáva*	अदर्शयाम *adarśayáma*
अदर्शयस् *adarśayas*	अदर्शयतं *adarśayatam*	अदर्शयत *adarśayata*
अदर्शयत् *adarśayat*	अदर्शयतां *adarśayatám*	अदर्शयन् *adarśayan*

Second preterite, 'I caused to see.'

दर्शयामास *darśayámása* *	दर्शयामासिव *darśayámásiva*	दर्शयामासिम *darśayámásima*
दर्शयामासिथ *darśayámásitha*	दर्शयामासथुस् *darśayámásathus*	दर्शयामास *darśayámása*
दर्शयामास *darśayámása*	दर्शयामासतुस् *darśayámásatus*	दर्शयामासुस् *darśayámásus*

First future, 'I will cause to see.'

दर्शयितास्मि *darśayitásmi*	दर्शयितास्वस् *darśayitáswas*	दर्शयितास्मस् *darśayitásmas*
दर्शयितासि *darśayitási*	दर्शयितास्थस् *darśayitásthas*	दर्शयितास्थ *darśayitástha*
दर्शयिता *darśayitá*	दर्शयितारौ *darśayitárau*	दर्शयितारस् *darśayitáras*

Second future, 'I will cause to see.'

दर्शयिष्यामि *darśayishyámi*	दर्शयिष्यावस् *darśayishyávas*	दर्शयिष्यामस् *darśayishyámas*
दर्शयिष्यसि *darśayishyasi*	दर्शयिष्यथस् *darśayishyathas*	दर्शयिष्यथ *darśayishyatha*
दर्शयिष्यति *darśayishyati*	दर्शयिष्यतस् *darśayishyatas*	दर्शयिष्यन्ति *darśayishyanti*

3d Pret. अदीदृशं or अददर्शं, &c.; see 638. Bened. दश्यासं, &c. Cond. अदर्शयिष्यं. Átm. Pres. दर्शये, दर्शयसे, दर्शयते, &c. Pot. दर्शयेय. Imp. दर्शयै, दर्शयस्व, &c. 1st Pret. अदर्शये. 2d Pret. दर्शयाञ्चक्रे. 1st Fut. दर्शयिताहे. 2d Fut. दर्शयिष्ये. 3d Pret. अदीदृशे, अदीदृशयास्, &c. Bened. दर्शयिषीय. Cond. अदर्शयिष्ये.

After these models, and after the model of primitive verbs of the 10th class at 638, may be conjugated all causal verbs.

EXAMPLES OF DESIDERATIVE VERBS, EXPLAINED AT 498.

705. Root भू *bhú*. Infin. बुभूषितुं *bubhúshitum*, 'to wish to be.'

Present, 'I wish to be,' &c.

Parasmai-pada.			Átmane-pada.		
बुभूषामि	बुभूषावस्	बुभूषामस्	बुभूषे	बुभूषावहे	बुभूषामहे
बुभूषसि	बुभूषथस्	बुभूषथ	बुभूषसे	बुभूषेथे	बुभूषध्वे
बुभूषति	बुभूषतस्	बुभूषन्ति	बुभूषते	बुभूषेते	बुभूषन्ते

* Or दर्शयाञ्चकार *darśayáñchakára*; see 490.

Potential, 'I may wish to be,' &c.

बुभूषेयं	बुभूषेव	बुभूषेम	बुभूषेय	बुभूषेवहि	बुभूषेमहि
बुभूषेस्	बुभूषेतं	बुभूषेत	बुभूषेथास्	बुभूषेयाथां	बुभूषेध्वं
बुभूषेत्	बुभूषेतां	बुभूषेयुस्	बुभूषेत	बुभूषेयातां	बुभूषेरन्

Imperative, 'Let me wish to be,' &c.

बुभूषाणि	बुभूषाव	बुभूषाम	बुभूषै	बुभूषावहै	बुभूषामहै
बुभूष	बुभूषतं	बुभूषत	बुभूषस्व	बुभूषेथां	बुभूषध्वं
बुभूषतु	बुभूषतां	बुभूषन्तु	बुभूषतां	बुभूषेतां	बुभूषन्तां

First preterite, 'I was wishing to be,' &c.

अबुभूषम्	अबुभूषाव	अबुभूषाम	अबुभूषे	अबुभूषावहि	अबुभूषामहि
अबुभूषस्	अबुभूषतं	अबुभूषत	अबुभूषथास्	अबुभूषेथां	अबुभूषध्वं
अबुभूषत्	अबुभूषतां	अबुभूषन्	अबुभूषत	अबुभूषेतां	अबुभूषन्त

Second preterite, 'I wished to be,' &c.

बुभूषाञ्चकार*	बुभूषाञ्चकृव	बुभूषाञ्चकृम	बुभूषाञ्चक्रे	बुभूषाञ्चकृवहे	बुभूषाञ्चकृमहे
बुभूषाञ्चकर्थ	बुभूषाञ्चक्रथुस्	बुभूषाञ्चक्र	बुभूषाञ्चकृषे	बुभूषाञ्चक्राथे	बुभूषाञ्चकृढ्वे
बुभूषाञ्चकार	बुभूषाञ्चक्रतुस्	बुभूषाञ्चक्रुस्	बुभूषाञ्चक्रे	बुभूषाञ्चक्राते	बुभूषाञ्चक्रिरे

First future, 'I will wish to be,' &c.

बुभूषितास्मि	बुभूषितास्वस्	बुभूषितास्मस्	बुभूषिताहे	बुभूषितास्वहे	बुभूषितास्महे
बुभूषितासि	बुभूषितास्थस्	बुभूषितास्थ	बुभूषितासे	बुभूषितासाथे	बुभूषिताध्वे
बुभूषिता	बुभूषितारौ	बुभूषितारस्	बुभूषिता	बुभूषितारौ	बुभूषितारस्

Second future, 'I will or shall wish to be,' &c.

बुभूषिष्यामि	बुभूषिष्यावस्	बुभूषिष्यामस्	बुभूषिष्ये	बुभूषिष्यावहे	बुभूषिष्यामहे
बुभूषिष्यसि	बुभूषिष्यथस्	बुभूषिष्यथ	बुभूषिष्यसे	बुभूषिष्येथे	बुभूषिष्यध्वे
बुभूषिष्यति	बुभूषिष्यतस्	बुभूषिष्यन्ति	बुभूषिष्यते	बुभूषिष्येते	बुभूषिष्यन्ते

Third preterite, 'I wished to be,' &c.

अबुभूषिषम्	अबुभूषिष्व	अबुभूषिष्म	अबुभूषिषि	अबुभूषिष्वहि	अबुभूषिष्महि
अबुभूषीस्	अबुभूषिष्टं	अबुभूषिष्ट	अबुभूषिष्ठास्	अबुभूषिषाथां	अबुभूषिढ्वं
अबुभूषीत्	अबुभूषिष्टां	अबुभूषिषुस्	अबुभूषिष्ट	अबुभूषिषातां	अबुभूषिषत

Benedictive, 'May I wish to be,' &c.

बुभूष्यासम्	बुभूष्यास्व	बुभूष्यास्म	बुभूषिषीय	बुभूषिषीवहि	बुभूषिषीमहि
बुभूष्यास्	बुभूष्यास्तं	बुभूष्यास्त	बुभूषिषीष्ठास्	बुभूषिषीयास्थां	बुभूषिषीध्वं
बुभूष्यात्	बुभूष्यास्तां	बुभूष्यासुस्	बुभूषिषीष्ट	बुभूषिषीयास्तां	बुभूषिषीरन्

Conditional, 'I should wish to be,' &c.

अबुभूषिष्यम्	अबुभूषिष्याव	अबुभूषिष्याम	अबुभूषिष्ये	अबुभूषिष्यावहि	अबुभूषिष्यामहि
अबुभूषिष्यस्	अबुभूषिष्यतं	अबुभूषिष्यत	अबुभूषिष्यथास्	अबुभूषिष्येथां	अबुभूषिष्यध्वं
अबुभूषिष्यत्	अबुभूषिष्यतां	अबुभूषिष्यन्	अबुभूषिष्यत	अबुभूषिष्येतां	अबुभूषिष्यन्त

* Or बुभूषाञ्चकर.

EXAMPLES OF FREQUENTATIVE OR INTENSIVE VERBS, EXPLAINED AT 507.

706. Root भू *bhú*. Infin. बोभवितुं *bobhavitum* or बोभूयितुं *bobhúyitum*, 'to be repeatedly' 'or frequently.'

ÁTMANE-PADA FORM (509).

Present, 'I am repeatedly,' &c.

बोभूये	बोभूयावहे	बोभूयामहे
बोभूयसे	बोभूयेथे	बोभूयध्वे
बोभूयते	बोभूयेते	बोभूयन्ते

Potential, 'I may be frequently,' &c.

बोभूयेय	बोभूयेवहि	बोभूयेमहि
बोभूयेथास्	बोभूयेयाथां	बोभूयेध्वं
बोभूयेत	बोभूयेयातां	बोभूयेरन्

Imperative, 'Let me be frequently,' &c.

बोभूयै	बोभूयावहै	बोभूयामहै
बोभूयस्व	बोभूयेथां	बोभूयध्वं
बोभूयतां	बोभूयेतां	बोभूयन्तां

First preterite, 'I was frequently,' &c.

अबोभूये	अबोभूयावहि	अबोभूयामहि
अबोभूयथास्	अबोभूयेथां	अबोभूयध्वं
अबोभूयत	अबोभूयेतां	अबोभूयन्त

Second preterite, 'I was frequently,' &c.

बोभूयाञ्चक्रे	बोभूयाञ्चकृवहे	बोभूयाञ्चकृमहे
बोभूयाञ्चकृषे	बोभूयाञ्चक्राथे	बोभूयाञ्चकृढ्वे
बोभूयाञ्चक्रे	बोभूयाञ्चक्राते	बोभूयाञ्चक्रिरे

First future, 'I will be frequently,' &c.

बोभूयिताहे	बोभूयितास्वहे	बोभूयितास्महे
बोभूयितासे	बोभूयितासाथे	बोभूयिताध्वे
बोभूयिता	बोभूयितारौ	बोभूयितारस्

Second future, 'I will or shall be frequently,' &c.

बोभूयिष्ये	बोभूयिष्यावहे	बोभूयिष्यामहे
बोभूयिष्यसे	बोभूयिष्येथे	बोभूयिष्यध्वे
बोभूयिष्यते	बोभूयिष्येते	बोभूयिष्यन्ते

Third preterite, 'I was frequently,' &c.

अबोभूयिषि	अबोभूयिष्वहि	अबोभूयिष्महि
अबोभूयिष्ठास्	अबोभूयिषाथां	अबोभूयिध्वं or -ढ्वं
अबोभूयिष्ट	अबोभूयिषातां	अबोभूयिषत

Benedictive, 'May I be frequently,' &c.

बोभूयिषीय	बोभूयिषीवहि	बोभूयिषीमहि
बोभूयिषीष्ठास्	बोभूयिषीयास्थां	बोभूयिषीध्वं or -ढ्वं
बोभूयिषीष्ट	बोभूयिषीयास्तां	बोभूयिषीरन्

Conditional, 'I should be frequently.'

अबोभूयिष्ये	अबोभूयिष्यावहि	अबोभूयिष्यामहि
अबोभूयिष्यथास्	अबोभूयिष्येथां	अबोभूयिष्यध्वं or -ढ्वं
अबोभूयिष्यत	अबोभूयिष्येतां	अबोभूयिष्यन्त

707. PARASMAI-PADA FORM (514).

Present, 'I am frequently,' &c.

बोभवीमि or बोभोमि	बोभूवस्	बोभूमस्
बोभवीषि or बोभोषि	बोभूथस्	बोभूथ
बोभवीति or बोभोति	बोभूतस्	बोभुवति

Potential, 'I may be frequently,' &c.

बोभूयां	बोभूयाव	बोभूयाम
बोभूयास्	बोभूयातं	बोभूयात
बोभूयात्	बोभूयातां	बोभूयुस्

Imperative, 'May I be frequently,' &c.

बोभवानि	बोभवाव	बोभवाम
बोभूहि	बोभूतं	बोभूत
बोभवीतु or बोभोतु	बोभूतां	बोभुवतु

First preterite, 'I was frequently,' &c.

अबोभवम्	अबोभूव	अबोभूम
अबोभवीस् or अबोभोस्	अबोभूतं	अबोभूत
अबोभवीत् or अबोभोत्	अबोभूतां	अबोभवुस्

Second preterite, 'I was frequently,' &c.

बोभुवाञ्चभूव, &c.	बोभुवाञ्चभूविव, &c.	बोभुवाञ्चभूविम, &c.
or	or	or
बोभाव or बोभूव	बोभुविव or बोभूविव	बोभुविम or बोभूविम
बोभूविथ	बोभुवथुस् or बोभूवथुम्	बोभुव or बोभूव
बोभाव or बोभूव	बोभुवतुस् or बोभूवतुस्	बोभुवुस् or बोभूवुस्

First future, 'I will be frequently,' &c.

बोभवितास्मि	बोभवितास्वस्	बोभवितास्मस्
बोभवितासि	बोभवितास्थस्	बोभवितास्थ
बोभविता	बोभवितारौ	बोभवितारस्

Second future, 'I will or shall be frequently,' &c.

बोभविष्यामि   बोभविष्यावस्   बोभविष्यामस्
बोभविष्यसि   बोभविष्यथस्   बोभविष्यथ
बोभविष्यति   बोभविष्यतस्   बोभविष्यन्ति

Third preterite, 'I was frequently,' &c.

अबोभूवम्   अबोभूव   अबोभूम
अबोभूस्   अबोभूतं   अबोभूत
अबोभूत्   अबोभूतां   अबोभूवन्
or   or   or
अबोभाविषम्   अबोभाविष्व   अबोभाविष्म
अबोभावीस्   अबोभाविष्टं   अबोभाविष्ट
अबोभावीत्   अबोभाविष्टां   अबोभाविषुस्

Benedictive, 'May I be frequently,' &c.

बोभूयासं   बोभूयास्व   बोभूयास्म
बोभूयास्   बोभूयास्तं   बोभूयास्त
बोभूयात्   बोभूयास्तां   बोभूयासुस्

Conditional, 'I should be frequently,' &c.

अबोभविष्यम्   अबोभविष्याव   अबोभविष्याम
अबोभविष्यस्   अबोभविष्यतं   अबोभविष्यत
अबोभविष्यत्   अबोभविष्यतां   अबोभविष्यन्

708. Root हन् 'to kill' (318, 654). Parasmai form of Frequentative. Pres. जङ्घन्मि or जङ्घनीमि, जङ्घंसि or जङ्घनीषि, जङ्घन्ति or जङ्घनीति; जङ्घन्वस्, जङ्घघस्, जङ्घतस्; जङ्घन्मस्, जङ्घथ, जङ्घनति or जंघ्नति. Pot. जङ्घन्यां, &c. Imp. जङ्घनानि, जंघहि, जङ्घन्तु or जङ्घनीतु; जङ्घनाव, जङ्घतं, -तां; जङ्घनाम, जङ्घत, जङ्घनतु or जंघ्नतु. 1st Pret. अजङ्घनं, अजङ्घन् or अजङ्घनीस्, अजङ्घन् or अजङ्घनीत्; अजङ्घन्व, अजङ्घतं, -तां; अजङ्घन्म, अजङ्घत, अजङ्घनुस् or अजंघ्नुस्. 2d Pret. जङ्घनाम्बभूव or जङ्घनाञ्चकार, &c. &c.

709. Root गम् 'to go' (602, 270). Parasmai form of Frequentative. Pres. जङ्गन्मि or जङ्गमीमि, जङ्गंसि or जङ्गमीषि, जङ्गन्ति or जङ्गमीति; जङ्गन्वस्, जङ्गथस्, जङ्गतस्; जङ्गन्मस्, जङ्गथ, जङ्गमति or जंग्मति. Pot. जङ्गम्यां, &c. Imp. जङ्गमानि, जङ्गहि, जङ्गन्तु or जङ्गमीतु; जङ्गमाव, जङ्गतं, जङ्गतां; जङ्गमाम, जङ्गत, जङ्गमतु or जंग्मतु. 1st Pret. अजङ्गमं, अजङ्गन् or अजङ्गमीस्, अजङ्गन् or अजङ्गमीत्; अजङ्गन्व, अजङ्गतं, -तां; अजङ्गन्म, अजङ्गत, अजङ्गमुस् or अजंग्मुस्. 2d Pret. जङ्गमाम्बभूव or जङ्गमाञ्चकार, &c. &c.

710. Root क्षिप् 'to throw' (635). Parasmai form of Frequentative. Pres. चेक्षेप्मि or चेक्षिपीमि, चेक्षेप्सि or चेक्षिपीषि, चेक्षेप्ति or चेक्षिपीति;

चेक्षिप्वस्, चेक्षिप्थस्, चेक्षिप्तस्; चेक्षिप्मस्, चेक्षिप्थ, चेक्षिपति. Pot. चेक्षिप्यां, &c. Imp. चेक्षेपाणि, चेक्षिब्धि, चेक्षेप्तु or चेक्षिपीतु; चेक्षेपाव, चेक्षिप्तं, -प्तां; चेक्षेपाम, चेक्षिप्त, चेक्षिपतु. 1st Pret. अचेक्षेपं, अचेक्षेप् or अचेक्षिपीस्, अचेक्षेप् or अचेक्षिपीत्; अचेक्षिप्व, अचेक्षिप्तं, -प्तां; अचेक्षिप्म, अचेक्षिप्त, अचेक्षिपुस्. 2d Pret. चेक्षिपाम्बभूव or चेक्षिपाञ्चकार, &c. &c.

711. Root ग्रह् 'to take' (699, 359). Parasmai form of Frequentative. Pres. जाग्रह्मि or जाग्रहीमि, जाघ्रक्षि (306. *a*) or जाग्रहीषि, जाग्राढि (305. *a*) or जाग्रहीति; जागृह्वस्, जागृढस्, जागृढस्; जागृह्मस्, जागृढ, जागृहति. Pot. जागृह्यां. Imp. जाग्रहाणि, जागृढि, जाग्राढु or जाग्रहीतु; जाग्रहाव, जागृढं, -ढां; जाग्रहाम, जागृढ, जागृहतु. 1st Pret. अजाग्रहं, अजाघ्रट् (292. *a*, 43. *c*) or अजाग्रहीस्, अजाघ्रट् or अजाग्रहीत्; अजागृह्व, अजागृढं, -ढां; अजागृह्म, अजागृढ, अजागर्हुस् (330), &c.

CHAPTER VII.

INDECLINABLE WORDS.

ADVERBS.

712. ADVERBS, like nouns and verbs, may be divided into simple and compound. The latter are treated of in the next Chapter on Compound Words.

Simple adverbs may be classed under four heads; 1st, as formed from the cases of nouns; 2dly, adverbs of less obvious derivation; 3dly, adverbial affixes; 4thly, adverbial prefixes.

Adverbs formed from the Cases of Nouns.

The following cases of nouns are used adverbially:

713. The nominative or accusative neuter of any adjective.

As, सत्यं 'truly;' बहु 'much;' शीघ्रं, क्षिप्रं, 'quickly;' युक्तं 'fitly;' समीपं 'near;' लघु 'lightly;' निर्भरं, अत्यन्तं, गाढं, भृशं, 'exceedingly;' अवश्यं 'certainly;' नित्यं 'constantly;' चिरं 'for a long while;' बलवत् 'strongly;' भूयस् 'again,' 'repeatedly' (194); केवलं 'only,' 'merely.'

a. The nom. or acc. neuter of certain pronouns; as, तत् 'therefore,' 'then;' यत् 'wherefore,' 'when;' तावत् 'so long,' 'so soon;' यावत् 'as long as,' 'as soon as;' किम् 'why?'

b. The nom. or acc. neuter of certain substantives and obsolete words; as, रहस् 'secretly;' कामं 'willingly;' स्वयं 'of one's own accord,' 'of one's self,' 'spontaneously;' नाम 'by name,' 'that is to say;' वारं वारं 'repeatedly;' चिरं 'long ago;' सुखं 'pleasantly;' साम्प्रतं 'now;' नक्तं 'by night' (*noctu*).

714. The instrumental case of nouns and pronouns.

As, धर्म्मेण 'virtuously;' दक्षिणेन 'southwards' or 'to the right;' उत्तरेण 'northwards;' व्यतिरेकेण 'without;' उच्चैस् 'above;' नीचैस् 'below;' शनैस् 'slowly;' तेन 'therefore;' येन 'wherefore.' The instr. case of certain obsolete nouns; as, चिरेण 'for a long time;' अचिरेण 'in a short time;' दिवा 'by day;' दिष्ट्या 'fortunately;' सहसा, अञ्जसा, 'quickly;' अधुना 'now.'

715. The ablative case of nouns and pronouns.

As, बलात् 'forcibly;' हर्षात् 'joyfully;' दूरात् 'at a distance;' तस्मात् 'therefore;' कस्मात् 'wherefore?' अकस्मात् 'without cause,' 'unexpectedly;' उत्तरात् 'from the north:' and of a few obsolete nouns; as, चिरात् 'for a long time;' पश्चात् 'afterwards;' तत्क्षणात् 'at that instant.'

716. The locative case of a few nouns and obsolete words.

As, रात्रौ 'at night;' दूरे 'far off;' प्रभाते 'in the morning;' प्राह्णे 'in the forenoon;' स्थाने 'suitably;' अग्रे 'in front;' एकपदे 'at once;' सपदि 'instantly;' अन्तरे 'within.'

Adverbs of less obvious Derivation.

717. Of *affirmation*.—नूनं, खलु, किल, एव, 'indeed;' अपि 'even.'

a. Of *negation*.—न, नो, नहि, 'not.' मा, मास्म, are prohibitive; as, मा कुरु, मा कार्षीस्, 'do not.' See 889.

b. Of *interrogation*.—किम्, किन्नु, कच्चित्, नु, ननु, किमुत, 'whether?'

c. Of *comparison*.—इव 'like;' एव, एवं, 'so;' किम्पुनर् 'how much rather;' तथैव (तथा + एव) 'in like manner.'

d. Of *quantity*.—अतीव 'exceedingly;' ईषत् 'a little;' सकृत् 'once;' असकृत्, पुनः पुनर्, मुहुस्, 'repeatedly.'

e. Of *manner*.—इति, एवं, 'so,' 'thus;' पुनर् 'again;' प्रायस् 'for the most part;' नाना 'variously;' पृथक् 'separately;' मिथ्या 'falsely;' वृथा, मुधा, 'in vain;' अलं 'enough;' झटिति, आशु (cf. ὠκύς), 'quickly;' तूष्णीं 'silently;' मिथस् 'reciprocally,' 'together.'

f. Of *time*.—अद्य 'to-day,' 'now;' इदानीं, सम्प्रति, 'now;' तदानीं, तर्हि, 'then;' पुरा 'formerly;' पुरस्, पुरस्तात्, प्राक्, 'before;' युगपत् 'at once;' सद्यस् 'instantly;' प्रेत्य 'after death;' परं 'afterwards;' जातु 'ever;' न जातु 'never;' अन्येद्युस्, परेद्युस्, 'another day,' 'next day.'

g. Of *place*.—इह 'here;' क्व 'where?' बहिस् 'without.'

h. Of *doubt*.—किंस्वित्, अपिनाम, 'perhaps.'

Adverbial Affixes.

718. चित् *chit*, अपि *api*, and चन *chana*, may form *indefinite* adverbs of time and place, when affixed to interrogative adverbs.

As, from कदा 'when?' कदाचित्, कदापि, and कदाचन, 'sometimes;' from कुत्र and क्व 'where?' कुत्रचित्, कुत्रापि, क्वचित्, क्वापि, 'somewhere;' from कुतस् 'whence?' कुतश्चित् and कुतश्चन 'from somewhere;' from कति 'how many?' कतिचित् 'a few;' from कर्हि 'when?' कर्हिचित् 'at some time;' from कथं 'how?' कथमपि, कथञ्चन, 'somehow or other,' 'with some difficulty.' Compare 228, 230.

719. तस् *tas* (changeable to तः or तो by 63, 64) may be added to any noun, and to some pronouns, to form adverbs.

As, from यत्न, यत्नतस् 'with effort;' from आदि, आदितस् 'from the beginning;' from त (the proper base of the pronoun तद्), ततस् 'thence,' 'then,' 'thereupon,' 'therefore:' similarly, यतस् 'whence,' 'since,' 'because;' अतस्, इतस् 'hence,' 'hereupon.'

a. This affix usually gives the sense of the prepositions *with* and *from*, and is often equivalent to the ablative case; as in मत्तस् 'from me;' त्वत्तस् 'from thee *;' पितृतस् 'from the father;' शत्रुतस् 'from an enemy.'

b. But it is sometimes vaguely employed to express other relations; as, पृष्ठतस् 'behind the back;' अन्यतस् 'to another place,' 'elsewhere;' प्रथमतस् 'in the first place;' इतस्ततस् 'here and there,' 'hither and thither;' समन्ततस् 'on all sides;' पुरतस्, अग्रतस्, 'in front;' अभितस् 'near to;' विभवतस् 'in pomp or state.'

720. त्र *tra*, forming adverbs of *place*.

As, अत्र 'here;' तत्र 'there;' कुत्र 'where?' यत्र 'where;' सर्व्वत्र 'every where;' अन्यत्र 'in another place;' एकत्र 'in one place;' बहुत्र 'in many places;' अमुत्र 'there,' 'in the next world.'

721. था *thá* and थं *tham*, forming adverbs of *manner*.

As, तथा 'so,' 'in like manner;' यथा 'as;' सर्व्वथा 'in every way,' 'by all means;' अन्यथा 'otherwise;' कथं 'how?' इत्थं 'thus.'

722. दा *dá*, forming adverbs of *time* from pronouns, &c.

As, तदा 'then;' यदा 'when;' कदा 'when?' एकदा 'once;' नित्यदा 'constantly;' सर्व्वदा, सदा, 'always.'

723. धा *dhá*, forming adverbs of *distribution* from numerals.

As, एकधा 'in one way;' द्विधा 'in two ways;' षोधा 'in six ways;' शतधा 'in a hundred ways;' सहस्रधा 'in a thousand ways;' बहुधा or अनेकधा 'in many ways.'

---

* In fact, these are the forms generally used for the ablative case of the personal pronouns, the proper ablative cases मत्, त्वत्, being rarely used, except as substitutes for the crude base, in compound words.

724. वत् *vat* may be added to any noun to form adverbs of *comparison* or *similitude*.

As, from सूर्य्य, सूर्य्यवत् 'like the sun;' from पूर्व्व, पूर्व्ववत् 'as before.' It may be used in connexion with a word in the accusative case. See 918.

a. This affix sometimes expresses 'according to;' as, विधिवत् 'according to rule;' प्रयोजनवत् 'according to need.'

725. शस् *śas*, forming adverbs of *quantity*.

As, बहुशस् 'abundantly;' अल्पशस् 'in small quantities;' एकशस् 'singly;' शतसहस्रशस् 'by hundreds and thousands;' क्रमशस् 'by degrees.'

Adverbial Prefixes.

726. अ *a*, prefixed to nouns and even to participles with a privative or negative force, corresponding to the Greek α, the Latin *in*, and the English 'in,' 'im,' 'un;' as, from शक्य 'possible,' अशक्य 'impossible;' from स्पृशत् 'touching' (pres. part.), अस्पृशत् 'not touching;' from कृत्वा 'having done' (indecl. part.), अकृत्वा 'not having done.' When a word begins with a vowel, अन् is euphonically substituted; as, अन्त 'end;' अनन्त 'endless.'

a. अति *ati*, 'excessively,' 'very;' as, अतिमहत् 'very great.'

b. आ *á*, prefixed to imply 'diminution;' as, आपाण्डु 'somewhat pale.' ईषत् is prefixed with the same sense.

c. का *ká* or कु *ku*, prefixed to words to imply 'disparagement;' as, कापुरुष 'a coward;' कुरूप 'deformed.'

d. दुर् *dur*, prefixed to imply 'badly' or 'with difficulty;' as, दुष्कृत 'badly done' (see 72); दुर्भेद्य 'not easily broken.' It is opposed to सु, and corresponds to the Greek δυσ.

e. निर् *nir* and वि *vi* are prefixed to nouns like अ *a* with a privative or negative sense; as, निर्बल 'powerless;' निष्फल 'without fruit' (see 72); विशस्त्र 'unarmed:' but not to participles.

f. सु *su*, prefixed to imply 'well,' 'easily;' as, सुकृत 'well done;' सुभेद्य 'easily broken.' In this sense it is opposed to दुर्, and corresponds to the Greek εὖ. It is also used for अति, to imply 'very,' 'excessively;' as, सुमहत् 'very great.'

CONJUNCTIONS.

Copulative.

727. च *cha*, 'and,' 'also,' corresponding to the Latin *que* and not to *et*. It can never, therefore, stand as the *first word* in a sentence, but follows the word of which it is the copulative.

a. तथा 'so,' 'in like manner' (see 721), is not unfrequently used for च, as a kind of copulative conjunction; and like च is generally placed after the word which it connects with another.

b. हि 'for,' like च, is always placed after its word, and never admitted to the first place in a sentence. यदि, चेत्, 'if;' ततस् 'upon that,' 'then' (see 719). अन्यच्च, किञ्च, अपरञ्च, परञ्च, अपिच, 'again,' 'moreover,' used very commonly before quotations. चैव 'also.'

c. अथ 'then,' 'now,' is used as an inceptive particle at the commencement of sentences or narratives. It is opposed to इति, which marks the close of a story or chapter.

Disjunctive.

728. वा *vá*, 'or,' corresponds to the Latin *ve*, and is always placed after its word, being never admitted to the first place in a sentence.

a. तु, किन्तु, 'but;' the former is placed after its word.

b. यद्यपि 'although;' तथापि 'nevertheless,' 'yet,' sometimes used as a correlative to the last; अथवा, किम्वा, 'or else;' नवा 'or not;' यदिवा 'whether,' 'whether or no.'

c. अथवा may also be used to correct or qualify a previous thought, when it is equivalent to 'but,' 'yet,' 'however.'

d. स्म, ह, तु, वै, are expletives, often used in poetry to fill up the verse.

PREPOSITIONS.

729. There are a great many prepositions in Sanskṛit, but they are generally found as inseparable prefixes, qualifying the sense of roots, and the nouns and verbs derived from roots; see 783. Only three, out of the list of prepositions at 783, are commonly used in government with nouns; viz. आ *á*, प्रति *prati*, and अनु *anu;* and of these the two last are rarely so used, except as *postpositions.*

730. आ *á*, generally signifying 'as far as,' 'up to,' 'until,' with an ablative case; as, आसमुद्रात् 'as far as the ocean;' आमनोस् 'up to Manu:' and rarely with an accusative; as, शतम् आजातीस् 'for a hundred births.'

a. आ *á* may sometimes express 'from;' as, आमूलात् 'from the beginning;' आप्रथमदर्शनात् 'from the first sight.'

b. प्रति *prati*, generally signifying 'at,' 'about,' 'with regard to,' 'to,' 'towards,' 'against,' with an accusative; as, गङ्गां प्रति 'at the Ganges;' धर्मं प्रति 'with regard to justice;' शत्रुं प्रति 'against an enemy.' It sometimes has the force of *apud;* as, मां प्रति, '*apud me*,' 'as far as regards me.'

c. अनु *anu*, 'after,' with an accusative; as, तदनु 'after that.'

d. प्रति, and more rarely अनु, may be used distributively to signify 'each,' 'every.' They are then prefixed; thus, प्रतिवत्सरं or अनुवत्सरं 'every year,' 'year by year.'

e. Observe—The preposition आ is generally not separated from the word which it governs, and may be regarded as forming with it a kind of adverbial compound. Instances are not uncommon of other prepositions united in composition with the neuter form or accusative case of nouns; as, प्रतिस्कन्धं 'upon the shoulders;' प्रतिमुखं 'face to face;' अधिवृक्षं 'upon the tree;' अनुगङ्गं 'along the Ganges.' See 760. *b.*

ADVERBS USED AS PREPOSITIONS IN GOVERNMENT WITH NOUNS.

731. There are certain adverbs used as prepositions in government with nouns, but generally placed after the nouns which they govern.

a. These are, ऋते 'besides,' with the accusative and sometimes ablative case. यावत् 'up to,' 'as far as,' sometimes found with the accusative. सह, सार्द्धं, 'with,' 'along with,' with the instrumental. विना 'without,' with the instrumental or accusative, or sometimes the ablative. वहिर् 'out;' प्रभृति, '*inde a*,' 'from a particular time,' with the ablative, or placed after the crude base. अर्थं, अर्थे, हेतोस्, हेतौ, कृते, निमित्ते, 'on account of,' 'for the sake of,' 'for,' with the genitive, or usually placed after the crude base*; उपरि, ऊर्द्धं, 'above,' 'over,' 'upon' (cf. ὑπέρ, *super*), with the genitive: so अधस् or अधस्तात् 'below;' अनन्तरं 'after,' 'afterwards;' समीपं, सकाशं, 'near;' सकाशात् 'from;' अग्रे, पुरतस्, समक्षं, साक्षात्, 'before the eyes,' 'in the presence of;' पश्चात् 'after:' all with the genitive. प्राक्, पूर्वं, 'before,' with ablative or genitive; परं, अर्वाक्, ऊर्द्धं, 'after,' with the ablative; अन्तरेण 'without,' 'except,' 'with regard to,' with the genitive or accusative; अन्तर् 'within,' with the genitive. All the above may be placed after the crude base. उपरि and अधस् are sometimes doubled; thus, उपर्युपरि, अधोऽधस्.

b. Some of the adverbs enumerated at 714, 715, may be used in government with the cases of nouns; thus, दक्षिणेन, 'to the south' or 'to the right,' may govern a genitive case; व्यतिरेकेण, 'without,' is placed after the crude base.

---

* अर्थं is almost always found in composition with a crude base, and may even be compounded adjectively to agree with another noun; as, द्विजार्थः सूपस् 'broth for the Bráhman;' द्विजार्थं पयस् 'milk for the Bráhman.' See 760.

INTERJECTIONS.

732. भोस्, भो, हे, are vocative; रे, अरे, less respectfully vocative, or sometimes expressive of 'contempt.' धिक् expresses 'contempt,' 'abhorrence;' आस्, अहो, अहह, 'surprise,' 'alarm;' हा, हाहा, अहो, अहोबत्, 'grief;' साधु, सुष्ठु, 'approbation;' स्वस्ति, 'salutation.'

CHAPTER VIII.

COMPOUND WORDS.

733. Compounds abound in Sanskṛit to a degree wholly unequalled in any other language, and it becomes necessary to study the principles on which they are constructed, before the learner can hope to understand the simplest sentence in the most elementary book. In the foregoing chapters we have treated of simple nouns, simple verbs, and simple adverbs. We have now to treat of compound nouns, compound verbs, and compound adverbs.

a. Observe, that in this chapter the nom. case, and not the base, of a substantive terminating a compound will be given; and in the instance of an adjective forming the last member of a compound, the nom. case masc., fem., and neut. The examples are chiefly taken from the Hitopadeśa, and sometimes the oblique cases in which they are there found have been retained. A dot placed underneath marks the division of the words in a compound.

SECTION I.

COMPOUND NOUNS.

734. The student has now arrived at that portion of the subject in which the use of the base of the noun becomes most strikingly apparent. This use has been already noticed at 77, p. 42; and its formation explained at pp. 44—53. In all compound nouns (with some few exceptions) the last word alone admits of declension, and the preceding word or words require to be placed in the crude form or base, to which a plural as well as singular signification may be attributed.

a. It may here be noted, that while Sanskṛit generally exhibits the first member or members of a compound in the crude base with the final letter unchanged, excepting by the laws of euphony, Latin frequently and Greek less frequently change the final vowel of the base into the light vowel *i;* and both

Greek and Latin often make use of a vowel of conjunction, which in Greek is generally *o*, but occasionally *ι*: thus, *cœli-cola* for *cœlu-cola* or *cœlo-cola; lani-ger* for *lana-ger; χαλκί-ναος, ἰχθυ-ο-φάγος, fœder-i-fragus*. Both Greek and Latin, however, possess many compounds which are completely analogous to Sanskṛit formations. In English we have occasional examples of the use of a vowel of conjunction, as in 'handicraft' for 'hand-craft.'

735. Native grammarians class compound nouns under six heads: the 1st they call TAT-PURUSHA*, or those composed of two nouns, the first of which (being in the crude base) would be, if uncompounded, in a case different from, or dependent on, the last; as, चन्द्र.प्रभा 'moon-light' (for चन्द्रस्य प्रभा 'the light of the moon'); शस्त्र.कुशलम्, -ला, -लं, 'skilled in arms' (for शस्त्रेषु कुशलम्); मणि.भूषितम्, -ता, -तं, 'adorned with gems' (for मणिभिर् भूषितम्). The 2d, DWANDWA, or those formed by the aggregation into one compound of two or more nouns (the last word being, according to circumstances, either in the dual, plural, or neuter singular, and the preceding word or words being in the crude base), when, if uncompounded, they would all be in the same case, connected by a copulative conjunction; as, गुरु.शिष्यौ 'master and pupil' (for गुरुः शिष्यश्च); मरण.व्याधि.शोकास् 'death, sickness, and sorrow' (for मरणं व्याधिः शोकश्च); पाणि.पादं 'hand and foot' (for पाणिः पादश्च). The 3d, KARMA-DHÁRAYA, or those composed of an adjective or participle and substantive, the adjective or participle being placed first in its crude base, when, if uncompounded, it would be in grammatical concord with the substantive; as, साधु.शीलम् 'a good disposition' (for साधुः शीलम्); सर्व्व.द्रव्याणि 'all things' (for सर्व्वाणि द्रव्याणि). The 4th, DWIGU, or those in which a numeral in its crude base is compounded with a noun, either so as to form a singular collective noun, or an adjective; as, त्रि.गुणं 'three qualities' (for त्रयो गुणास्); त्रि.गुणस्, -णा, -णं, 'possessing the three qualities.' The 5th, BAHU-VRÍHI, or those formed of any number

* These names either furnish examples of the several kinds of compounds, or give some sort of definition of them: thus, तत्पुरुषः, 'his servant,' is an example of the 1st kind (for तस्य पुरुषः); द्वन्द्वः is a definition of the 2d kind, meaning 'conjunction;' कर्म्मधारयः is a definition of the 3d kind, i. e. 'containing the object' (कर्म्म); द्विगुः is an example of the 4th kind, meaning 'any thing to the value of two cows;' बहुव्रीहिः is an example of the 5th kind, meaning 'possessed of much rice.' The 6th class, अव्ययीभावः *avyayíbhávah*, means 'the indeclinable state.'

of words associated to form an epithet to a noun; as, चन्द्र.प्रभस्, -भा, -भं, 'brilliant as the moon;' मरण.व्याधि.शोकस्, -का, -कं, 'liable to death, sickness, and sorrow;' साधु.शीलस्, -ला, -लं, 'well-disposed.' The 6th, AVYAYÍ-BHÁVA, or those resulting from the combination of a preposition or adverbial prefix with a noun; the latter, whatever may be its gender, always taking the form of an accusative neuter.

736. Such then, in brief, is the native division of compound words, a division leading to some confusion, from the incompleteness and want of sufficient comprehensiveness in the definitions, and the absence of sufficient distinctness and opposition between the several parts or members of the division. For it is plain, from the examples given, that the 5th class of compounds may often be regarded as another name for the first three, when they take the form of adjectives declinable in three genders; and that the second species of the 4th class is for this reason referrible to the 5th. The student, moreover, finds it difficult to understand why, if the definition of the 5th class of compounds be, that they are epithets of other nouns, such compounds as शस्त्र.कुशल and मणि.भूषित should not be comprehended under it. And further, he is often at a loss to refer a compound to its proper head *, from the inadequacy of the definitions to express all the cases included under each class.

In the following pages the subject is discussed according to a different method, although it has been thought desirable to keep the native arrangement in view.

737. Compound nouns may be regarded either as *simply* or *complexly* compounded. The latter have reference to a class of compounds within compounds, very prevalent in poetry, involving two or three species of simple compounds under one head.

SIMPLY COMPOUNDED NOUNS.

738. These will be divided into, 1st, Dependent compounds or compounds dependent in case (corresponding to *Tat-purusha*); 2d, Aggregative (*Dwandwa*); 3d, Descriptive † (*Karma-dháraya*); 4th, Collective (*Dwigu*); 5th, Indeclinable or Adverbial (*Avyayí-bháva*);

* Ex. gr. such a compound as कृष्णशुक्लस्, -क्ला, -क्लं, 'any thing black and white.'

† As being composed of an adjective or participle preceding a substantive, and always descriptive of the substantive. Prof. Bopp calls them 'Determinativa,' a word of similar import.

6th, Relative (*Bahu-vrīhi*). This last consists of, *a*. Relative form of absolute Dependent compounds, terminated by substantives; *b*. Relative form of Aggregative compounds; *c*. Relative form of Descriptive compounds; *d*. Relative form of Collective compounds; *e*. Relative form of Adverbial compounds.

DEPENDENT COMPOUNDS (TAT-PURUSHA).

Accusatively Dependent.

739. These comprehend all those compounds in which the relation of the first word (being in the crude base) to the last is equivalent to that of an accusative case. They are generally composed of a noun in the first member, and a participle or noun of agency in the last; as, स्वर्ग-प्राप्तस्, -प्ता, -प्तं, 'one who has obtained heaven' (equivalent to स्वर्गं प्राप्तस्); प्रिय-वादी 'one who speaks kind words;' बहु-दस् 'one who gives much;' शस्त्र-भृत् 'one who bears arms;' पत्र-गतस्, -ता, -तं, 'committed to a leaf,' 'committed to paper' (as 'writing'); चित्र-गतस्, -ता, -तं, 'committed to painting.'

a. Observe—गत 'gone' (past pass. part. of गम् 'to go') is used loosely at the end of compounds of this description to express relationship and connexion, without any necessary implication of motion. In the above compound, and in many others (such as शिला-भेद-गतो मणिस् 'a jewel lying in the cleft of a rock;' हस्त-तल-गतस्, -ता, -तं, 'lying in the palm of the hand'), it has the sense of स्थ 'staying:' but it may often have other senses; as, गोष्ठी-गतस्, -ता, -तं, 'engaged in conversation;' सखी-गतं किञ्चित् 'something relating to a friend.' In theatrical language आत्म-गतं and स्वगतं (lit. 'gone to one's self') mean 'spoken to one's self,' 'aside.'

b. Before the nouns of agency the accusative case is often retained, especially in poetry; as, अरिन्दमस्, -मा, -मं, 'enemy-subduing;' हृदयङ्गमस्, -मा, -मं, 'heart-touching;' भयङ्करस्, -रा, -रं, 'fear-inspiring' (see 580).

Instrumentally Dependent,

740. Or those in which the relation of the first word (being in the crude base) to the last is equivalent to that of an instrumental case. These are very common, and are, for the most part, composed of a substantive in the first member, and a passive participle in the last; as, लोभ-मोहितस्, -ता, -तं, 'beguiled by avarice' (for लोभेन मोहित); वस्त्र-वेष्टितस्, -ता, -तं, 'covered with clothes;' राज-पूजितस्, -ता, -तं, 'honoured by kings;' विद्या-हीनस्, -ना, -नं, 'deserted by (i. e. destitute of) learning;' बुद्धि-रहितस्, -ता, -तं, 'destitute of intelligence;'

दुःखार्त्तस्, -र्त्ता, -र्त्तं, 'pained with grief;' आत्म-कृतस्, -ता, -तं, 'done by one's self;' आदित्य-सदृशस्, -शी, -शं, 'like the sun' (for आदित्येन सदृशस्, see 826); अस्मदुपार्जितस्, -ता, -तं, 'acquired by us.'

a. Sometimes, but rarely, this kind of compound contains a substantive or noun of agency in the last member; as, विद्या-धनं 'money acquired by science;' शस्त्रोपजीवी 'one who lives by arms.'

Datively Dependent,

741. Or those in which the relation of the first word to the last is equivalent to that of a dative; as, परिधान-वल्कलं 'bark for clothing;' पादोदकं 'water for the feet;' यूप-दारुस् 'wood for a stake;' शरणागतस्, -ता, -तं, 'come for protection' (for शरणाय आगत). This kind of compound is rare, and is generally supplied by the use of अर्थं (731. *a*); as, शरणार्थम् आगतस्.

Ablatively Dependent,

742. Or those in which the relation of the first word to the last is equivalent to that of an ablative; as, पितृ-प्राप्तस्, -प्ता, -प्तं, 'received from a father;' राज्य-भ्रष्टस्, -ष्टा, -ष्टं, 'fallen from the kingdom' (for राज्याद् भ्रष्टस्); तरङ्ग-चञ्चलतरस्, -रा, -रं, 'more changeable than a wave;' भवदन्यस् 'other than you' (for भवतोऽन्यस्); भवद्भयं 'fear of you' (814. *d*); शास्त्र-पराङ्मुखस्, -खी, -खं, 'turning the face from books,' 'averse to study.'

Genitively Dependent,

743. Or those in which the relation of the first word to the last is equivalent to that of a genitive. These are the most common of all dependent compounds, and may generally be expressed by a similar compound in English. They are for the most part composed of two substantives; as, समुद्रतीरं 'sea-shore' (for समुद्रस्य तीरं 'shore of the sea').

a. Other examples are, अश्व-पृष्ठं 'horse-back;' धनुर्गुणस् 'bow-string;' इष्टिका-गृहं 'brick-house;' गिरि-नदी 'mountain-torrent;' जल-तीरं 'water's edge;' अर्थागमस् or अर्थोपार्जना 'acquisition of wealth;' विपद्दशा 'state of misfortune;' सुहृद्भेदस् 'separation of friends;' यन्मूर्ध्नि 'on whose brow' (loc. c.); तद्वचस् 'his words;' जन्म-स्थानं or जन्मभूमिस् 'birth-place;' मूर्ख-शतैस् 'with hundreds of fools' (instrum. c. plur.); श्लोक-द्वयं 'a couple of S'lokas;' भू-तलं 'the surface of the earth;' पृथिवी-पतिस् 'lord of the earth;' तज्जीवनाय 'for his support' (dat. c.); ब्राह्मण-पुत्रास् 'the sons of a Bráhman;' अस्मत्पुत्रास् 'our sons;' त्वत्कर्म 'thy deed;' पितृ-वचनं 'a father's speech;' मृत्यु-द्वारं 'the gate of death;' इच्छा-सम्पत् 'fulfilment of wishes;' मातृानन्दस् 'a mother's joy;' जलाशयम् 'a receptacle of water,' 'a lake;' विद्यार्थी 'seeker of knowledge,' 'a scholar.'

b. Sometimes an adjective in the superlative degree, used substantively, occupies the last place in the compound; as, नर्श्रेष्ठस् or पुरुषोत्तमस् 'the best of men.'

c. In a few instances the genitive case is retained; as, विशाम्पतिस् 'lord of men;' दिवस्पतिस् 'lord of the sky.'

Locatively Dependent,

744. Or those in which the relation of the first word to the last is equivalent to that of a locative case; as, पङ्कमग्नस्, -ग्ना, -ग्नं, 'sunk in the mud' (for पङ्के मग्न); गगणविहारी 'sporting in the sky;' जलक्रीडा 'sport in the water;' ग्रामवासी 'a dweller in a village;' जलचरस् 'going in the water;' जलजस् 'born in the water;' शिरोरत्नं 'gem on the head.'

a. It is not unusual to retain the locative case, especially before nouns of agency; as, ग्रामेवासी 'a villager;' जलेचरस् 'going in the water;' उरसिभूषितस्, -ता, -तं, 'ornamented on the breast.'

Dependent in more than one Case.

745. Dependent compounds do not always consist of two words. They may be composed of almost any number of nouns, all depending upon each other, in the manner that one case depends upon another in a sentence; thus, चक्षुर्विषयातिक्रान्तस्, -न्ता, -न्तं, 'passed beyond the range of the eye' (for चक्षुषो विषयम् अतिक्रान्तम्); रथमध्यस्थस् 'standing in the middle of the chariot;' भीतपरित्राणवस्तूपालम्भपण्डितस् 'skilful in censuring the means of rescuing those in danger.'

a. There is an anomalous form of Tat-purusha compound, which is really the result of the elision of the second or middle member (*uttara-pada-lopa, madhyama-pada-lopa*) of a complex compound; thus, अभिज्ञानशकुन्तला 'token-S'akuntalá' for अभिज्ञानस्मृतशकुन्तला 'S'akuntalá (recognised) by the token.'

b. Dependent compounds abound in all the cognate languages. The following are examples from Greek and Latin; *οἰνο-θήκη, οἰκο-φύλαξ, λιθό-στρωτος, γυναικο-κήρυκτος, ἀνθρωπο-δίδακτος, θεό-δοτος, θεό-τρεπτος, χειρο-ποίητος, auri-fodina, manu-pretium, parri-cida* for *patri-cida, parri-cidium, matri-cidium, marti-cultor, mus-cerda.* English furnishes innumerable examples of dependent compounds, ex. gr. 'ink-stand,' 'snow-drift,' 'moth-eaten,' 'priest-ridden,' 'door-mat,' 'writing-master,' &c.

AGGREGATIVE COMPOUNDS (DWANDWA).

746. This class of compounds has no exact parallel in other languages.

When two or more persons or things are enumerated together, it is usual in Sanskṛit, instead of connecting them by a copulative, to aggregate them into one compound word. No syntactical dependence of one case upon another subsists between the members of Dwandwa compounds, since they must always consist of words which, if uncompounded, would be in the *same* case; and no other grammatical connexion exists than that which would ordinarily be expressed by the use of the copulative conjunction *and* in English, or च in Sanskṛit. In fact, the difference between this class and the last turns upon this dependence *in case* of the words compounded on each other; insomuch that the existence or absence of such dependence, as deducible from the context, is, in some cases, the only guide by which the student is enabled to refer the compound to the one head or to the other: thus, गुरुशिष्यसेवकास् may either be a Dependent compound, and mean 'the servants of the pupils of the Guru,' or an Aggregative, 'the Guru, and the pupil, and the servant.' And मांसशोणितं may either be Dependent, 'the blood of the flesh,' or Aggregative, 'flesh and blood.' This ambiguity, however, can never occur in aggregatives inflected in the dual, and rarely occasions any practical difficulty.

747. There are three kinds of Aggregative compounds: 1st, inflected in the plural; 2d, inflected in the dual; 3d, inflected in the singular. In the first two cases the final letter of the base of the word terminating the compound determines the declension, and its gender the particular form of declension; in the third case it seems to be a law that this kind of compound cannot be formed unless the last word ends in अ *a*, or in a vowel changeable to अ *a*, or in a consonant to which अ *a* may be subjoined; and the gender is invariably neuter, whatever may be the gender of the final word.

Inflected in the Plural.

748. When *more than two* animate objects are enumerated, the last is inflected in the plural; as, इन्द्रानिलयमार्कास् 'Indra, Anila, Yama, and Arka' (for इन्द्रस्, अनिलस्, यमस्, अर्कश्च); रामलक्ष्मणभरतास्, 'Ráma, Lakshmaṇa, and Bharata;' मृगव्याधसर्पशूकरास् 'the deer, the hunter, the serpent, and the hog.' The learner will observe, that although the last member of the compound is inflected in the plural, each of the members has here a singular acceptation. But a plural signification may often be inherent in some or all of the words

constituting the compound; thus, ब्राह्मण-क्षत्रिय-वैश्य-शूद्रास् 'Bráhmaṇs, Kshatriyas, Vaiśyas, and Śúdras;' मित्रोदासीन-शत्रवस् 'friends, neutrals, and foes' (for मित्राणि, उदासीनास्, शत्रवश्च); ऋषि-देव-पितृ-अतिथि-भूतानि 'sages, gods, ancestors, guests, and spirits' (for ऋषयस्, देवास्, पितरस्, अतिथयस्, भूतानि च); सिंह-व्याघ्र-महोरगास् 'lions, tigers, and serpents;' श्व-गृध्र-कङ्क-काकोल-भास-गोमायु-वायसास् 'dogs, vultures, herons, ravens, kites, jackals, and crows.'

749. So also when *more than two* inanimate objects are enumerated, the last may be inflected in the plural; as, धर्मार्थ-काम-मोक्षास् 'virtue, wealth, enjoyment, and beatitude' (for धर्मस्, अर्थस्, कामस्, मोक्षश्च); इज्याध्ययन-दानानि 'sacrifice, study, and liberality' (for इज्या, अध्ययनं, दानं च). In some of the following a plural signification is inherent; as, पुष्प-मूल-फलानि 'flowers, roots, and fruits;' अजात-मृत-मूर्खाणां 'of the unborn, the dead, and the foolish' (for अजातानां, मृतानां, मूर्खाणां च); नेत्र-मनः-स्वभावास् 'eyes, mind, and disposition;' रोग-शोक-परिताप-बन्धन-व्यसनानि 'sickness, sorrow, anguish, bonds, and afflictions;' काष्ठ-जल-फल-मूल-मधूनि 'wood, water, fruit, roots, and honey.'

750. So also when *only two* animate or inanimate objects are enumerated, in which a *plural* signification is inherent, the last is inflected in the plural; as, देव-मनुष्यास् 'gods and men;' पुत्र-पौत्रास् 'sons and grandsons;' पातोत्पातास् 'falls and rises;' प्राकार-परिखास् 'ramparts and trenches;' सुख-दुःखेषु 'in pleasures and pains' (for सुखेषु, दुःखेषु च); पाप-पुण्यानि 'sins and virtues.'

Inflected in the Dual.

751. When *only two* animate objects are enumerated, in each of which a *singular* signification is inherent, the last is inflected in the dual; as, राम-लक्ष्मणौ 'Ráma and Lakshmaṇa' (for रामस्, लक्ष्मणश्च); चन्द्र-सूर्यौ 'the moon and sun;' मृग-काकौ 'a deer and a crow;' भार्या-पती 'wife and husband.'

752. So also when *only two* inanimate objects are enumerated, in each of which a *singular* signification is inherent, the last is inflected in the dual; as, आरम्भावसाने 'beginning and end' (for आरम्भस्, अवसानं च); अनुरागापरागौ 'affection and enmity' (for अनुरागस्, अपरागश्च); हर्ष-विषादौ 'joy and sorrow;' क्षुत्पिपासे 'hunger and thirst' (for क्षुत् पिपासा च); क्षुद्व्याधी 'hunger and sickness;' स्थानासनाभ्यां 'by standing and sitting' (for स्थानेन, आसनेन च); मधु-सर्पिषी 'honey and ghee;' सुख-दुःखे 'pleasure and pain;' उलूखल-मुसले 'mortar and pestle;'

प्रत्युत्थाना.भिवादाभ्यां 'by rising and saluting;' मृद्वारिभ्यां 'by earth and water.'

Inflected in the Singular Neuter.

753. When two or more *inanimate* objects are enumerated, whether singular or plural in their signification, the last may either be inflected as above (748, 749, 750, 751), or in the singular number, neut. gender; as, पुष्प.मूल.फलं 'flowers, roots, and fruits' (for पुष्पाणि, मूलानि, फलानि च); यवसा.न्नो.दके.न्धनं 'grass, food, water, and fuel' (for यवसम्, अन्नं, उदकं, इन्धनं च); अहो.रात्रं 'a day and night' (for अहस्, रात्रिश्च); दिग्.देशं 'quarters and countries' (for दिशस्, देशाश्च); द्यु.निशं 'day and night;' शिरो.ग्रीवं 'head and neck;' चर्म.मांस.रुधिरं 'skin, flesh, and blood.'

a. Sometimes two or more animate objects are thus compounded; as, पुत्र.पौत्रं 'sons and grandsons;' हस्त्य.श्वं 'elephants and horses:' especially inferior objects; as, श्व.चाण्डालं 'a dog and an outcast.'

754. In enumerating two qualities the opposite of each other, it is common to form a Dwandwa compound of this kind, by doubling an adjective or participle, and interposing the negative अ *a;* as, चराचरं 'moveable and immoveable' (for चरम् अचरं च); शुभाशुभं 'good and evil;' प्रियाप्रिये 'in agreeable and disagreeable' (for प्रिये अप्रिये च); दृष्टादृष्टं 'seen and not seen;' कृताकृतं 'done and not done;' मृदुक्रूरं 'gentle and cruel.'

a. In the Dwandwas which occur in the Vedas the first member of the compound, as well as the last, may sometimes take a dual termination; thus, मित्रा.वरुणौ (see 97. *a*), इन्द्रा.विष्णू, पितरा.मातरौ; and some of the anomalous Dwandwas used in more modern Sanskṛit are probably Vaidik in their character; thus, द्यावा.पृथिवी 'heaven and earth;' माता.पितरौ 'mother and father,' &c.

b. Greek and Latin furnish examples of complex compounds involving Dwandwas; thus, *βατραχο-μυο-μαχία*, 'frog-mouse war;' *su-ovi-taurilia*, 'pig-sheep-bull sacrifice;' *ζωό-φυτον*, 'animal-plant.' *Zoophyte* is also a kind of Dwandwa. In English, compounds like 'plano-convex,' 'convexo-concave,' are examples of the relative form of Dwandwa explained at 765.

DESCRIPTIVE COMPOUNDS (KARMA-DHÁRAYA).

755. In describing, qualifying, or defining a substantive by means of an adjective or participle, it is common in Sanskṛit to compound the two words together, placing the adjective or participle in the first member of the compound in its crude base; as, साधु.जनस् 'a good man' (for साधुर् जनस्); चिर.मित्रं 'an old friend' (for चिरं मित्रं); प्रिय.भार्य्या* 'a dear wife' (for प्रिया भार्य्या); रूपवद्भार्य्या* 'a beautiful wife'

* The feminine bases of adjectives rarely appear in compounds; so that प्रियाभार्य्या and रूपवतीभार्य्या are not found; although there can be no question that

(for रूपवती भार्या); क्षुब्धार्णवः 'a troubled ocean;' पुण्यकर्म्म 'a holy act;' अनन्तात्मा 'the infinite soul;' संस्कृतोक्तिस् 'polished speech;' पुण्यकर्म्माणि 'holy acts' (for पुण्यानि कर्म्माणि); उत्तमनराणां 'of the best men' (for उत्तमानां नराणां); महापातकं 'a great crime' (see 778); महाराजस् 'a great king' (see 778); प्रियसखस् 'a dear friend' (see 778); दीर्घरात्रं 'a long night' (see 778).

a. An indeclinable word or prefix may sometimes take the place of an adjective in this kind of compound; thus, सुपथः 'a good road;' सुदिनं 'a fine day;' सुभाषितं 'good speech;' दुश्चरितं 'bad conduct;' अभयं 'not fear,' &c.; बहिःशौचं 'external cleanliness' (from *vahis*, 'externally,' and *śaucha*, 'purity'); अन्तःशौचं 'internal purity.'

756. Numerals in their crude state are sometimes found occupying the place of adjectives in the first member of a compound of this class; as, चतुर्वर्णास् 'the four castes;' पञ्चबाणास् 'five arrows.'

757. Adjectives, used substantively, sometimes occupy the last place in Descriptive compounds; as, परमधार्म्मिकस् 'a very just man;' परमाद्भुतं 'a very wonderful thing.'

a. In the same manner, substantives, used adjectively, may occupy the first place; as, मलद्रव्याणि 'impure substances.'

758. Compounds expressing 'excellence' are said to fall under this class, and are composed of two substantives, one of which is used as an adjective to describe or define the other, and is placed last, being generally the name of an animal denoting 'superiority;' as, पुरुषपुङ्गवः 'man-bull,' पुरुषसिंहः 'man-lion,' पुरुषर्षभः 'man-bull,' equivalent to 'an illustrious man.'

a. The following are examples of Greek and Latin compounds falling under this class; *μεγαλο-μήτηρ, ἰσό-πεδον, μεγαλό-νοια, ἡμι-κύων, sacri-portus, meri-dies* (for *medi-dies*), *decem-viri, semi-deus.* Parallel compounds in English are, 'good-will,' 'good-sense,' 'ill-nature,' &c.

COLLECTIVE COMPOUNDS (DWIGU).

759. A numeral is often compounded with a substantive to form a collective noun of the neuter gender; thus, चतुर्युगं 'the four ages' (for चत्वारि युगानि); चतुर्दिशं 'the four quarters;' त्रिदिनं 'three days' (*triduum*); त्रिरात्रं 'three nights' (रात्र being substituted for रात्रि, see 778); त्र्यब्दं 'three years' (*triennium*); पञ्चाग्नि 'the five fires.'

a. Compare Greek and Latin compounds like *τετραόδιον, τριννύκτιον, τέθριππον, triduum, triennium, trinoctium, quadrivium, quinquertium.*

प्रिया and रूपवती are the proper bases of the feminine form of the adjectives. There are, however, a few examples of feminine adjective bases in compounds of this kind, as कामिनीजनस्, where कामिनी is used substantively. See also 766. *a*, note.

b. Sometimes the final vowel of the substantive is changed to ई; as, त्रिलोकी 'the three worlds.'

INDECLINABLE OR ADVERBIAL COMPOUNDS (AVYAYÍ-BHÁVA).

760. In this class of compounds the first member must be either a preposition (such as अनु, प्रति, &c.) or an adverbial prefix (such as यथा 'as,' अ or अन् 'not,' सह 'with'). The last member is a substantive which always takes the form of an accusative case neuter, whatever may be the termination of its crude base; thus, यथाश्रद्धं 'according to faith,' 'proportioned to faith' (from यथा and श्रद्धा).

a. The majority of these compounds are formed with the adverbial preposition सह, contracted into स; thus, सकोपं 'with anger' (from स and कोप); सादरं 'with respect' (from स and आदर); साष्टाङ्गपातं 'with prostration of eight parts of the body.'

b. The following are examples of indeclinable compounds formed with other prefixes; अनुज्येष्ठं 'according to seniority;' प्रत्यङ्गं 'over every limb' (compare 730. *d*); प्रतिमासं 'every month' (730. *d*); यथाविधि 'according to rule;' यथाशक्ति or यावच्छक्यं (49) 'according to one's ability;' यथासुखं 'happily;' अनुक्षणं 'every moment;' समक्षं 'before the eyes' (see 778); प्रतिस्कन्धं 'upon the shoulders;' अधिवृक्षं 'upon the tree;' असंशयं 'without doubt;' निर्विशेषं 'without distinction.'

c. Analogous indeclinable compounds are found in Latin and Greek, such as *admodum, obviam, affatim, ἀντιβίην, ἀντίβιον, ὑπέρμορον, παράχρημα.* In these, however, the original gender is retained, whereas, according to the Sanskṛit rule, *obvium* would be written for *obviam*, and *affate* for *affatim*. In Greek compounds like *σήμερον*, the feminine *ἡμέρα* appends a neuter form, as in Sanskṛit.

d. The neuter word अर्थं 'for the sake of,' 'on account of' (see 731. *a*), is often used at the end of compounds; thus, स्वप्नार्थं 'for the sake of sleep;' कर्म्मानुष्ठानार्थं 'for the sake of the performance of business.' See, however, 731, note.

RELATIVE COMPOUNDS (BAHU-VRÍHI).

761. The greater number of compounds in the preceding four divisions are terminated by substantives, the sense of each being in that case absolute and complete in itself. All such compounds may be used *relatively*, that is, as epithets of other words, the final substantive becoming susceptible of three genders, like an adjective (see 108, 119, 130, 134. *a*): and it cannot be too forcibly impressed upon the memory that the terms *Relative* and *Bahu-vríhi* have reference to the adjective use of those compounds only which have a substantive in the last member. This is not to be regarded,

therefore, as a distinct division of the subject of compound words, so much as a distinct view of the *same* subject; the object of which is to show that all compounds, which are in themselves absolute and complete in sense, and are *terminated by substantives*, may be used adjectively, and in the relation of an epithet to some other word in the sentence. We have given the name *relative* to compounds when thus used, not only for the obvious reason of their being relatively and not absolutely employed, but also because they usually involve a relative pronoun, and are sometimes translated into English by the aid of this pronoun, and are, moreover, resolved by native commentators into their equivalent uncompounded words by the aid of the genitive case of the relative (यस्य). Thus, महाधनं is a Descriptive compound, meaning 'great wealth,' and may be used adjectively in relation to पुरुषस्, as महाधनः पुरुषः 'a man *who* has great wealth;' or to स्त्री, as महाधना स्त्री 'a woman *who* has great wealth;' and would be resolved by commentators into यस्य or यस्या महद् धनं. In English we have similar compounds, as 'high-minded,' 'left-handed,' and the like, where the substantive terminating the compound is converted into an adjective.

Relative form of Dependent Compounds.

762. Many Dependent compounds (especially those that are instrumentally dependent at 740) are already *in their own nature* relative, and cannot be used except in connexion with some other word in the sentence. But, on the other hand, many others, and especially those which are genitively dependent, constituting by far the largest number of this class of compounds, are in their nature absolute, and yield a sense complete in itself. These may be made relative by declining the final substantive after the manner of an adjective; thus, चन्द्राकृतिस्, -तिस्, -ति, 'moon-shaped' (see 119), from the absolute compound चन्द्राकृतिस् 'the shape of the moon.'

a. Other examples are, देवरूपस्, -पी, -पं, 'whose form is godlike' (see 108); सूर्यप्रभावस्, -वा, -वं, 'splendid as the sun' (108); हस्तिपादस्, -दा, -दं*, 'elephant-footed' (see 57); सागरान्तस्, -न्ता, -न्तं, 'ending at the sea;' मरणान्तस्, -न्ता, -न्तं, 'terminated by death;' कर्णपुरोगमस्, -मा, -मं, or कर्णमुखस्, -खा, -खं, 'headed by Karṇa;' विष्णुशर्मनामा, -मा, -म, 'named Vishṇuśarma' (see 154);

* पाद् may be substituted for पाद in compounds of this kind, but not after हस्तिन्. See 778.

पुण्डरीकाक्षस्, -क्षी, -क्षं, 'lotus-eyed' (see 778); नारायणाख्यस्, -ख्या, -ख्यं, 'called Náráyana;' धनमूलस्, -ला, -लं, 'founded on wealth;' लक्षसंख्यानि (agreeing with धनानि), 'money to the amount of a lac;' गदाहस्तस्, -स्ता, -स्तं, 'having a club in the hand,' or 'club in hand;' शस्त्रपाणिस्, -णिस्, -णि, 'arms in hand;' जालहस्तस्, -स्ता, -स्तं, 'net in hand;, पुष्पविषयस्, -या, -यं, 'on the subject of flowers,' 'relating to flowers.' These examples are not distinguishable from absolute dependent compounds, except by declension in three genders.

763. Many of them, however, are not found, except as relatives; and if used absolutely would yield a different sense; thus, कर्णमुखं means 'the face of Karṇa,' but when used relatively to राजानस्, 'the kings headed by Karṇa.' So also चारचक्षुस् signifies 'the eye of the spy,' but when used relatively to राजा, 'a king who sees by means of his spies,' the nom. case masc. being then चारचक्षूस्. See 166. *a.*

764. The substantive आदि, 'a beginning,' when it occurs in the last member of a compound of this nature, is always used relatively to some word expressed or understood, and yields a sense equivalent to *et cetera.* It is generally found either in the plural or neuter singular; as, इन्द्रादयस् 'Indra and the others' (agreeing with the nom. case सुरास् expressed or understood, 'the gods commencing with Indra'); अग्न्यादीनां 'of Agni and the others' (agreeing with पूर्वोक्तानां understood, 'of those above-named things of which Agni was the first'); चक्षुरादीनि 'the eyes, &c.' (agreeing with इन्द्रियाणि 'the senses commencing with the eyes'). When used in the neut. sing. it either agrees with पूर्वोक्तं, 'the aforesaid,' understood, or with a number of things taken collectively, and the adverb *iti* * may be prefixed; as, देवानित्यादि 'the word *deván*, &c.' (agreeing with पूर्वोक्तं understood, 'the aforesaid sentence of which *deván* is the first word'); दानादिना 'by liberality, &c.' (agreeing with some class of things understood, 'by that class of things of which liberality is the first').

a. It may occasionally be used in the masc. sing.; as, मार्जन्यादिस् 'brooms, &c.' (agreeing with उपस्करस् 'furniture').

b. Sometimes आदिक is used for आदि; as, दानादिकं 'gifts, &c.:' and sometimes आद्य; as, इन्द्राद्याः सुरास् 'the gods of whom Indra is the first.'

c. The feminine substantive प्रभृति 'manner,' 'kind,' may be used in the same way; thus, इन्द्रप्रभृतयः सुरास् 'the gods, Indra and the others;' तेषां ग्रामनिवासिप्रभृतीनां 'of those villagers, &c.'

d. Observe—The neuter of आदि may optionally take the terminations of the masculine in all but the nom. and accus. cases; thus, हस्त्यश्वादेस् 'of elephants, horses, &c.' (agreeing with बलस्य gen. neut. of बल 'an army').

---

* Sometimes *evam* is prefixed; as, एवमादीनि प्रलापानि 'lamentations beginning thus.'

Relative form of Aggregative Compounds.

765. Aggregative compounds are sometimes used relatively; as, मरण-व्याधि-शोकस्, -का, -कं, 'that which is liable to sorrow, sickness, and death:' especially in the case of adjectives or participles; as, कृष्ण-शुक्लस्, -क्ला, -क्लं, 'black and white;' स्नातानुलिप्तस्, -प्ता, -प्तं, 'bathed and anointed;' पौर-जानपदस्, -दा, -दं, 'city and country;' कृतापकृतस्, -ता, -तं, 'done and done badly;' शुभाशुभस्, -भा, -भं, 'good and evil' (754); सान्द्र-स्निग्धस्, -ग्धा, -ग्धं, 'thick and unctuous;' गृहीत-प्रतिमुक्तस्य 'of him taken and let loose.' Compare Greek compounds like λευκο-μέλας, 'white and black.' Examples are still more common under the head of Complex Compounds.

Relative form of Descriptive Compounds.

766. A greater number of compound words may be referred to this head than to any other. Every style of writing abounds with them; thus, अल्प-शक्तिस्, -क्तिस्, -क्ति, 'whose strength is small' (119).

a. Other examples are, महा-बलस्, -ला, -लं, 'whose strength is great' (108, see also 778); महा-तेजास्, -जास्, -जस्, 'whose glory is great' (164. *a*); अल्पधनस्, -ना, -नं, 'whose wealth is small;' महात्मा, -त्मा, -त्म, 'high-minded' (151); उदार-चरितस्, -ता, -तं, 'of noble demeanour;' बहु-मत्स्यस्, -त्स्या, -त्स्यं, 'having many fish;' स्वल्प-सलिलस्, -ला, -लं, 'having very little water;' पण्डित-बुद्धिस्, -द्धिस्, -द्धि, 'of wise intellect' (119); प्रियभार्य्यस्, -र्य्या, -र्य्यं, 'having a dear wife*;' अशक्य-सन्धानस्, -ना, -नं, 'not to be reconciled;' संवृतसंवार्य्यस्, agreeing with राजा, 'a king who conceals what ought to be concealed.'

767. Although a passive participle is not often prefixed to a noun in an absolute sense, this kind of combination prevails most extensively in the formation of relative compounds; as, प्राप्त-कालस्, -ला, -लं, 'whose time has arrived.'

a. Other examples are, जितेन्द्रियस्, -या, -यं, 'whose passions are subdued;' शान्त-चेतास्, -तास्, -तस्, 'whose mind is composed;' संहृष्ट-मनास्, -नास्, -नस्, 'whose mind is rejoiced' (see 164); भग्नाशस्, -शा, -शं, 'whose hopes are broken;' हृत-राज्यस्, -ज्या, -ज्यं, 'whose kingdom is taken away;' अमित-तेजास्, -जास्, -जस्, 'whose glory is boundless;' आसन्न-मृत्युस्, -त्युस्, -त्यु, 'whose death is near;' कृत-कामस्, -मा, -मं, 'whose desire is accomplished,' i. e. 'successful;' कृत-भोजनस्, -ना, -नं, 'one who has finished eating;' अनधिगत-शास्त्रस्, -स्त्रा, -स्त्रं, 'one

---

* Occasionally the feminine of the adjective appears in the compound; as, षष्ठीभार्य्यस् 'having a sixth wife.' Compare 755, note.

by whom the S'ástras have not been read;' भिन्न.हृदयस्, -या, -यं, 'whose heart is pierced.'

b. Examples of Greek and Latin compounds of this kind are, *μεγαλο-κέφαλος, μεγαλό-μητις, λευκό-πτερος, πολύ-χρυσος, χρυσεο-στέφανος, ἡδύ-γλωσσος, ἐρημό-πολις, magn-animus, longi-manus, multi-comus, albi-comus, multi-vius, atri-color.*

c. In English compounds of this kind abound; ex. gr. 'blue-eyed,' 'narrow-minded,' 'good-tempered,' 'pale-faced,' &c.

Relative form of Collective Compounds.

768. Collective or Dwigu compounds may be used relatively; as, द्वि.पर्णस्, -र्णी, -र्णं, 'two-leaved;' त्रि.लोचनस्, -नी, -नं, 'tri-ocular.'

a. Other examples are, त्रि.मूर्द्धस्, -र्द्धी, -र्द्धं, 'three-headed' (मूर्द्ध being substituted for मूर्द्धन्, see 778); चतु.र्मुखस्, -खी, -खं, 'four-faced;' चतुष्.कोणस्, -णा, -णं, 'quadrangular;' शत.द्वारस्, -रा, -रं, 'hundred-gated;' चतुर्.विद्यस्, -द्या, -द्यं, 'possessed of the four sciences;' सहस्रा.क्षस्, -क्षी, -क्षं, 'thousand-eyed' (see 778); पञ्च.गव.धनस्, -ना, -नं, 'having the wealth of five bullocks.'

Relative form of Adverbial or Avyayí-bháva Compounds.

769. The adverbial compounds most frequently employed relatively as adjectives are those formed with the adverbial preposition सह 'with,' contracted into स; thus, स.क्रोधस्, -धा, -धं, 'angry' (lit. 'with-anger,' 'having anger'); स.फलस्, -ला, -लं, 'fruitful' (108); स.बन्धुस्, -न्धुस्, -न्धु, 'possessed of kindred' (119); स.यत्नस्, -त्ना, -त्नं, 'energetic;' सजीवस्, -वा, -वं, 'possessed of life,' 'living;' सा.नन्दस्, -न्दा, -न्दं, 'joyful;' स.सचिवस्, -वा, -वं, 'accompanied by ministers;' स.भार्यस् 'accompanied by a wife,' 'having a wife;' स.ज्यस्, -ज्या, -ज्यं, 'strung' (as a bow, lit. 'with-bowstring').

a. Sometimes the affix क *ka* is pleonastically added; as, स.श्रीकस्, -का, -कं, 'possessed of fortune;' स.स्त्रीकस्, -का, -कं, 'accompanied by women.' Compare 80. XVII.

b. The following are examples of other nouns combined with adverbial prefixes, so as to form relative compounds: उद्.आयुधस्, -धा, -धं, 'with uplifted weapon;' नाना.प्रकारस्, -रा, -रं, 'of various shapes;' सामि.भुक्तस्, -क्ता, -क्तं, 'half-eaten;' क्व.निवासस्, -सा, -सं, 'where dwelling?' क्व.जन्मा, -न्मा, -न्म, 'where born?' निरपराधस्, -धा, -धं, 'without fault;' निराहारस्, -रा, -रं, 'having no food;' अप.भीस्, -भीस्, -भि, 'fearless' (123. *b*); अज्ञातस्, -ता, -तं, 'unknown;' तथा.विधस्, -धा, -धं, 'of that kind,' 'in such a state;' दुर्बुद्धिस्, -द्धिस्, -द्धि, 'weak-minded;' दुष्प्रकृतिस्, -तिस्, -ति, 'ill-natured' (see 72); सुमुखस्, -खी, -खं, 'handsome-faced;' सुबुद्धिस्, -द्धिस्, -द्धि, 'of good understanding.' Some of the above may be regarded as the relative form of Descriptive compounds, formed with indeclinable prefixes; see 755. *a*. Similar compounds in Greek and Latin are, ἄ-γνωτος, ἀν-ήμερος, εὔ-δηλος, *in-imicus*, *in-felix*, *dis-similis*, *semi-plenus*.

c. Observe—The adverbial prefixes दुर् and सु (726. *d*. *f*) impart a passive sense to participial nouns of agency, just as δυσ and εὖ in Greek; thus, दुष्कर 'difficult to be done,' सुकर 'easy to be done;' दुर्लभ 'difficult to be obtained,' सुलभ 'easy to be attained;' दुस्तर 'difficult to be crossed.' Compare the Greek εὔφορος, 'easy to be borne;' δύσπορος, 'difficult to be passed,' &c.

d. स॒नाथस्, -था, -थं, 'possessed of a master,' is sometimes used at the end of compounds to denote simply 'possessed of,' 'furnished with;' thus, वितान॒सनाथं शिलातलं 'a stone-seat furnished with a canopy;' शिलापट्ट॒सनाथो मण्डपः 'an arbour having a marble-slab as its master,' i. e. 'furnished with,' 'provided with,' &c. Similarly, बहु॒बक॒सनाथो वट॒पादपः 'a fig-tree occupied by a number of cranes.'

e. Observe—The relative form of a compound would be marked in the Veda by the accent; thus in *mahá-báhus*, 'great arm,' the accent would be on the last syllable; but in *mahá-báhus*, 'great armed,' on the ante-penultimate.

f. Note, that आत्मक and रूप are used at the end of relative compounds to denote 'composed of,' 'consisting of;' but are more frequently found at the end of complex relatives; see 774.

COMPLEX COMPOUND NOUNS.

770. We have now to speak of those complex compound words, or compounds within compounds, which form the most remarkable feature in Sanskṛit composition. Instances might be given of twenty or thirty words thus compounded together; but these are the productions of the vitiated taste of more modern times, and are only curious as showing that the power of compounding words may often be extravagantly abused. But even in the best specimens of Sanskṛit composition, and in the simplest prose writings, four, five, or even six words are commonly compounded together, involving two or three forms under one head. It will be easy, however, to determine the character of the forms involved, by the rules propounded in the preceding pages; in proof of which the student has only to study attentively the following examples.

Instances of absolute complex compounds, whose sense is complete and unconnected, are not rare.

a. The following are examples: काला॒न्तरा॒वृत्ति॒शुभा॒शुभानि 'good and evil (occurring) in the revolutions of the interval of time,' the whole being a dependent, involving a dependent and an aggregative; सेना॒पति॒बला॒ध्यक्षौ 'the general of the army and the overseer of the forces,' the whole being an aggregative, involving two dependents; शोकारातिभयत्राणं 'the protection from sorrow, enemies, and perils,' the whole being a dependent, involving an aggregative; अवधीरितसुहृद्वाक्यं 'the disregarded words of a friend,' the whole being a descriptive, involving a dependent; शुक्लाम्बरमाल्यदाम 'a white robe and a string of garlands,' the whole being an aggregative, involving a descriptive and dependent; सर्वशास्त्रपारगस् 'one who has gone to the opposite bank (*pára*) of all the S'ástras,' i. e. 'one who has read them through;' मृतसिंहास्थीनि 'the bones of a dead lion.'

771. The greater number of complex compounds are used as adjectives, or relatively, as epithets of some other word in the sentence; thus, गलितनखनयनस्, -नी, -नं, 'whose teeth and eyes were decayed,' the whole being the relative form of descriptive, involving an aggregative; क्षुत्क्षामकण्ठस् 'having a throat emaciated with hunger,' the whole being the relative form of descriptive, involving a dependent.

a. Other examples are, शुक्लमाल्यानुलेपनस्, -ना, -नं, 'having a white garland and unguents,' the whole being the relative form of aggregative, involving a descriptive; पूर्वजन्मकृतस्, -ता, -तं, 'done in a former birth,' the whole being a dependent, involving a descriptive; विद्यावयोवृद्धस्, -द्धा, -द्धं, 'advanced in learning and age,' the whole being a dependent, involving an aggregative; हृषितस्रग्रजोहीनस्, -ना, -नं, 'having fresh garlands, and being free from dust,' the whole being the relative form of aggregative, involving a descriptive and dependent; अभिषेकार्द्रशिरास्, -रास्, -रस्, 'whose head was moist with unction;' यथेप्सितमुखस्, -खा, -खं, 'having the face turned in any direction one likes;' शूलमुद्गरहस्तस्, -स्ता, -स्तं, 'spear and club in hand;' एकरात्रनिर्वाहोचितस्, -ता, -तं, 'sufficient for support during one night' (see 778); ऋग्यजुःसामाख्यत्रयग्रन्थार्थाभिज्ञास् 'acquainted with the meaning of the three Vedas, called Rig, Yajur, and Sáma' (agreeing with विदुषस्); सन्दष्टदन्तच्छदताम्रनेत्रास् 'biting their lips and having red eyes' (agreeing with राजानस्); परद्रोहकर्म्मधीस् 'injuring another by action or by intention.'

772. The substantive आदि, 'a beginning,' often occurs in complex relative compounds, with the force of *et cetera*, as in simple relatives at 764; thus, शुकसारिकादयस् 'parrots, starlings, &c.' (agreeing with पक्षिगणस् 'birds beginning with parrots and starlings'), the whole being the relative form of dependent, involving an aggregative; सन्धिविग्रहादि 'peace, war, &c.' (agreeing with पूर्वोक्तं understood); गृहदेवागारादियुक्तस्, -क्ता, -क्तं, 'possessed of houses, temples, &c.;' करितुरगकोषादिपरिच्छदयुक्तस्, -क्ता, -क्तं, 'possessed of elephants, horses, treasuries, and other property.'

a. Similarly, आद्य in the example उत्तमगन्धाद्यास् (agreeing with स्रजस् 'garlands possessing the best odour and other qualities').

773. Long complex compounds may be generally translated by beginning at the last word and proceeding regularly backwards, as in the following; मत्तमधुकरनिकरमुक्तझङ्कारमिलितकोकिलालापसङ्गीतकसुखावहः, -हा, -हं, 'causing pleasure by the music of the voice of the cuckoo, blended with the hum emitted by the swarms of joyous bees.'

774. आत्मक or रूप, as occupying the last place in a complex relative, denote 'composed of;' thus, हस्त्यश्वरथपदातिकर्म्मकरात्मकं बलं 'a force consisting of elephants, horses, chariots, infantry, and servants;' प्राग्जन्मसुकृतदुष्कृतरूपे कर्म्मणी 'the two actions consisting of the good and evil done in a former birth.'

775. Complex compounds may sometimes have their second or middle member elided or omitted; thus, अभिज्ञानशकुन्तला is really a complex compound, the whole being a descriptive, involving a dependent; but the middle member स्मृत is elided: see 745. *a*. Similarly, शाकपार्थिवस् 'the era-king' is for शाकप्रियपार्थिवस् 'the king (beloved) by the era.'

a. Sometimes the substantive verb 'to be' may be inherent in a relative compound; as, प्रारम्भसदृशोदयस् 'his success was proportionate to his undertakings;' पीताम्भसि 'on his drinking water,' for तेन अम्भसि पीते सति.

776. Complex compound adverbs, or indeclinable compounds, involving other compounds, are sometimes found; as, स्वगृहनिर्विशेषेण 'not differently from one's own house;' शब्दोच्चारणानन्तरं 'after uttering a sound;' स्तनभरविनमन्मध्यभङ्गानपेक्षं 'regardlessly of the curving of her waist bending under the weight of her bosom;' यथादृष्टश्रुतं 'as seen and heard.'

ANOMALOUS COMPOUNDS.

777. There are certain compounds which are too anomalous in their formation to admit of ready classification under any one of the preceding heads. Amongst these may be placed those compounds expressive of 'comparison' or 'resemblance,' usually included under the Karma-dháraya or Descriptive class. In these the adjective is placed last; as, छायाचञ्चलस्, -ला, -लं, 'fickle as a shadow;' वज्रपातसदृशस्, -शी, -शं, 'like a clap of thunder;' फेनोपमस्, -मा, -मं, 'like foam;' अम्बुदश्यामस्, -मा, -मं, 'dark as a cloud;' भूधरविस्तीर्णस्, -र्णा, -र्णं, 'spread out like a mountain;' जलविन्दुलोलचपलस्, -ला, -लं, 'unsteady as a trembling drop of water;' नलिनीदलतोयतरलस्, -ला, -लं, 'tremulous as water on the leaf of a lotus:' the last two examples are complex.

a. कल्प, देशीय, दघ्न, द्वयस, मात्र, affixed to crude bases, form anomalous compounds; see 80. XX. XXI. and 919.

b. There is a common anomalous compound formed by placing अन्तर after a crude base, to express 'another,' 'other;' as, स्थानान्तरं or देशान्तरं 'another place;' राजान्तरेण सह 'along with another king;' जन्मान्तराणि 'other births.' The following examples, also, are not readily assignable to any class: त्यक्तजीवितयोधी

'a fighter who abandons all idea of life;' सारसद्वितीयस्, -या, -यं, 'accompanied by the Sárasa *;' अदृष्टपूर्व्वस्, -र्व्वा, -र्व्वं, 'never before seen.'

c. पूर्व्व or पूर्व्वक or पुरःसर (meaning literally 'preceded by') may be added to crude bases to form a kind of anomalous compound, as in the following example; पूजापूर्व्वकम् अन्नं ददौ 'he gave food with reverence.' See 792.

CHANGES UNDERGONE BY CERTAIN WORDS AT THE END OF COMPOUNDS.

778. The following is an alphabetical list of the substitutions or changes which take place in the final syllables of certain words, when used at the end of compounds. Observe—The most common substitution is that of अ *a* for the final vowel or final consonant and vowel of a word.

अक्ष m. for अक्षि n. 'the eye.'—अङ्गुल m. in a few compounds for अङ्गुलि f. 'the finger.'—अञ्जल m. in a few compounds for अञ्जलि m. 'joining the hands in reverence.'—अध्व m. joined with a few inseparable prepositions for अध्वन् m. 'a road.'—अनस in Karma-dháraya compounds for अनस् n. 'a cart,' 'a carriage.'—अयस in Karma-dhárayas for अयस् n. 'iron.'—अश्म in Karma-dhárayas for अश्मन् m. 'a stone.'—अष्ठीव in Dwandwas for अष्ठीवत् m. n. 'the knee.'—अस्र for अस्रि f. 'an angle.'—अह for अहन् n. 'a day.'—अहर् in the first member of a compound for अहन् n. 'a day.'—अह्न at the end of a few compounds for अहन् n.—ईप for अप् f. 'water.'—उक्ष in a few Karma-dhárayas for उक्षन् m. 'an ox.'—उषासा in the beginning of Dwandwas for उषस् n. f. 'the dawn.'—ऊधन् (fem. ऊध्नी) for ऊधस् n. 'an udder.'—काकुद् in a few Bahu-vríhis for काकुद m. 'the palate.'—कुक्ष for कुक्षि m. 'the belly.'—गन्धि in Karma-dhárayas for गन्ध m. 'smell.'—गव in Dwigus for गो m. f. 'an ox.'—जानि for जाया f. 'a wife.'—ज्ञ and ज्ञु in Bahu-vríhis for जानु n. 'the knee.'—तमस in Karma-dhárayas (preceded by सं, अव, or अन्ध) for तमस् n. 'darkness.'—दत् in a few Bahu-vríhis for दन्त m. 'a tooth;' the feminine may be दती.—दिवा in the beginning of a few compounds for दिवन् m. 'the day.'—दुघ at the end of a few compounds for दुह् 'yielding milk.'—द्यावा as the first member of a compound for दिव् f. 'heaven.'—धन्वन् for धनुस् n. 'a bow.'—धर्म्मन् for धर्म्म m. 'virtue,' 'duty.'—धुर for धुर् f. 'a load.'—नाभ for नाभि f. 'the navel.'—नाव for नौ f. 'a ship.'—पथ for पथिन् m. 'a road.'—पाद् for पाद m. 'a foot;' the feminine may be पदी.—पृत् for पृतना f. 'an army.'—प्रजस् at the end of Bahu-vríhis (preceded by अ, सु, or दुर्) for प्रजा f.—ब्रह्म at the end of Karma-dhárayas for ब्रह्मन् m. 'a Bráhmaṇ.'—भूम for भूमि f. 'the earth.'—भ्रुव in a few Dwandwas for भ्रू f. 'the eye-brow.'—मनस in Dwandwas

* So छायाद्वितीयः in Nala, translated by Bopp *umbra geminatus*.

for मनस् n. 'the mind *.'—मूर्द्ध at the end of Bahu-vríhis (preceded by द्वि and त्रि) for मूर्द्धन् m. 'the head.'—मह and मही at the end of anomalous compounds (preceded by पिता, माता, &c., see 754. *a*) for महत् m. f. n. 'great.'—महा at the beginning of Karma-dháraya and Bahu-vríhi compounds for महत् m. f. n. 'great †.'—मेधस् at the end of Bahu-vríhis (preceded by अ, सु, दुर्, अल्प, मन्द) for मेधा f. 'intellect.'—राज at the end of Karma-dhárayas for राजन् m. 'a king;' see 151. *a*.—रात्र in Dwigus, Karma-dhárayas, and Dwandwas, for रात्रि f. 'night.'—वर्चस in Karma-dhárayas for वर्चस् n. 'splendour.'—श्रेयस in Karma-dhárayas and Bahu-vríhis for श्रेयस् n. 'felicity.'—श्व for श्वन् m. 'a dog.'—स in Avyayí-bhávas and Bahu-vríhis for सह 'with.'—सक्थ in Karma-dhárayas and Bahu-vríhis for सक्थि n. 'the thigh.'—सख in Karma-dhárayas and Dwigus for सखि m. 'a friend.'—सरस in Karma-dhárayas for सरस् n. 'a lake.'—हृद् for हृदय n. 'the heart.'

779. अहं is found in the beginning of certain anomalous compounds (such as अहङ्कार, अहम्पूर्विका, &c.) for मत् or अस्मत् 'I.'

780. Numerals, when preceded by particles, prepositions, or other numerals, may change their finals to अ *a*; or if their final letter be a consonant, may either drop that consonant or add अ *a* to it; thus, द्वित्र (nom. -त्रास्, -त्रास्, -त्राणि) 'two or three;' पञ्चष (nom. -षास्, -षास्, -षाणि) 'five or six;' उपचतुर (nom. -रास्) 'nearly four.'

Compound Nouns formed from roots combined with Prepositions.

781. In the next section it will be shown that the combination of roots with prepositions prevails most extensively in Sanskṛit. From roots thus combined nouns of the most various significations may be formed; thus, from हृ 'to seize,' with वि and अव, is formed व्यवहार 'practice;' from कृ 'to do,' with अनु, अनुकार 'imitation.' Hardly a line can occur in any book that does not afford an example of this kind of compound.

SECTION II.

COMPOUND VERBS.

782. The learner might look over the list of 2000 simple roots, and well imagine that in some of these would be contained every possible variety of idea, and that the aid of prepositions and adverbial prefixes to expand and modify the sense of each root would be unnecessary. But in real fact there are comparatively very few

* वाङ्मनसे 'speech and heart,' which is the example given by Páṇini (V. 4. 77), occurs in Manu II. 160.

† As महाकुलं 'a great family;' see also 755. In Tat-purusha or dependent compounds महत् is retained; thus, महदाश्रयः 'recourse to the great.'

Sanskṛit roots in common use; and whilst those that are so appear in a multitude of different forms by the prefixing of one or two or even three prepositions, the remainder are almost useless for any practical purposes, except the formation of nouns. Hence it is that compound verbs are of more frequent occurrence than simple ones.

They are formed in two ways: 1st, by combining roots with prepositions; 2dly, by combining the auxiliaries कृ 'to do' and भू 'to be' with adverbs, or nouns converted into adverbs.

Compound Verbs formed by combining Prepositions with roots.

783. The following list exhibits the prepositions chiefly used in combination with roots:

a. अति *ati*, 'across,' 'beyond;' as, अतिया, अती (pres. अत्येमि, &c.), अतिक्रम्, 'to pass by,' 'to pass along,' 'to transgress.'

b. अधि *adhi*, 'above,' 'upon,' 'over;' as, अधिष्ठा 'to stand over,' 'to preside' (pres. अधितिष्ठामि); अधिरुह् 'to climb upon;' अधिशी 'to lie upon;' अधिगम् 'to go over towards;' अधी 'to go over,' in the sense of 'reading.'

c. अनु *anu*, 'after;' as, अनुचर् 'to follow;' अनुष्ठा 'to follow,' in the sense of 'performing;' अनुकृ 'to imitate;' अनुमन् 'to assent.' With भू it signifies 'to experience,' 'to enjoy.'

d. अन्तर् *antar*, 'within' (Latin *inter*); as, अन्तर्धा 'to place within,' 'to conceal,' in pass. 'to vanish;' अन्तर्भू 'to be within;' अन्तश्चर् 'to walk in the midst.'

e. अप *apa*, 'off,' 'away' (ἀπό); as, अपगम्, अपसृ, अपे (from अप and इ), 'to go away;' अपनी 'to lead away;' अपकृष् 'to abstract;' अपवह् 'to bear away.' It also implies 'detraction;' as, अपवद् 'to defame.'

f. अपि *api*, 'on,' 'over,' 'up,' only used with धा and नह्; as, अपिधा 'to shut up;' अपिनह् 'to bind on.' The initial *a* is generally rejected, leaving पिधा, पिनह्.

g. अभि *abhi*, 'to,' 'towards' (ἐπί); as, अभिया, अभी, 'to go towards;' अभिधाव् 'to run towards;' अभिदृश् 'to behold;' अभिवद् or अभिधा (see धा at 664) 'to address,' 'to accost,' 'to speak to,' 'to salute.'

h. अव *ava*, 'down,' 'off;' as, अवरुह्, अवतॄ, 'to descend;' अवेक्ष् 'to look down;' अवकॄ 'to throw down,' 'to scatter;' अवकृत् 'to cut off.' It also implies 'disparagement;' as, अवज्ञा 'to despise;' अवक्षिप् 'to insult.' With धा (3d c. अवदधाति), 'to attend.'

i. आ *á*, 'to,' 'towards,' 'up' (Latin *ad*); as, आविश् 'to enter;' आक्रम् 'to go towards;' आरुह् 'to mount up.' When prefixed to गम्, या, and इ, 'to go,' and दा 'to give,' it reverses the action; thus, आगम्, आया, ए, 'to come;' आदा 'to take.' With चर्, 'to practise.'

j. उत् *ut*, 'up,' 'upwards' (opposed to नि); as, उच्चर् (48), उदि, 'to go up,' 'to rise' (pres. उदयामि, 1st conj.); उड्डी 'to fly up;' उद्धन् 'to strike up' (उत् and

हन्, 50); उद्धृ (उत् and हृ, see 50) 'to extract;' उन्मिष् and उन्मील् (47) 'to open the eyes;' उत्कृत्, उच्छिद्, 'to cut up;' उन्मूल् 'to root up;' उच्छ्रि 'to lift up' (उत् and श्रि, 49).

When prefixed to the roots स्था and स्तम्भ् it causes the elision of *s;* as, उत्था 'to stand up;' उत्तम्भ् 'to prop up.' In some cases it reverses the action; as, from पत् 'to fall,' उत्पत् 'to leap up;' from नम् 'to bend down,' उन्नम् (47) 'to raise up;' from यम् 'to keep down,' उद्यम् 'to lift up.'

k. उप *upa,* 'to,' 'towards' (ὑπό), 'near,' joined like आ and अभि to roots of motion; as, उपया 'to approach;' उपचर् 'to wait upon;' उपस्था 'to stay near,' 'to be present,' 'to arrive.' With विश् (6th c. उपविशति), 'to sit down;' with आस्, 'to sit near.'

l. नि *ni,* 'down,' 'downwards,' 'under' (opposed to उत्); as, निपत् 'to fall down;' नियम् 'to suppress;' निमिष् and निमील् 'to close the eyes;' निक्षिप्, निधा, न्यस्, 'to lay down,' 'to deposit;' निविश् 'to go within,' 'to encamp.' With वृत् it signifies 'to return,' 'to desist;' with शम्, 'to hear.' In some cases it does not alter the sense; as, निहन् 'to kill.'

m. निर् *nir,* 'out;' as, निष्क्रम् (see 72), निर्गम्, निःसृ (71. *a. c*), 'to go out,' 'to come out;' निष्कृत् 'to cut up;' निर्वृत् 'to come to an end,' 'to cease;' निश्चि (71. *b*) 'to determine.'

n. परा *pará,* 'back,' 'backwards' (παρά), combined with जि and भू in the sense of 'defeat;' as, पराजि 'to overcome' (cf. παρανικάω, Æsch. Chöe.); पराभू 'to be defeated.' When joined with इ, 2d conj., it signifies 'to retire towards' (pres. परैमि); when with इ, 1st conj. Átm., 'to run away,' 'to retreat,' *r* being changed to *l* (pres. पलाये).

o. परि *pari,* 'around' (περί, *per*); as, परिवेष्ट्, परिवृ, 'to surround;' परिचर्, परिगम्, 'to go round;' परीक्ष् 'to look round,' 'to examine;' परिवृत् 'to turn round;' परिधाव् 'to run round.' When prefixed to कृ it signifies 'to adorn,' and स् is inserted, परिष्कृ. With भू, 'to despise,' and with हृ, 'to avoid.' It sometimes merely gives intensity or completeness to the action; as, परित्यज् 'to abandon altogether;' परिज्ञा 'to ascertain completely.'

p. प्र *pra,* 'before,' 'forward' (πρό, *pro, præ*); as, प्रगम्, प्रसृप्, 'to proceed;' प्रयम् 'to set before,' 'to present;' प्रक्रम् 'to begin;' प्रवृत् 'to proceed,' 'to begin;' प्रधाव् 'to run forward;' प्रस्था 'to set out,' 'to advance;' प्रभू 'to be superior,' 'to prevail;' प्रदृश् 'to foresee.' With लभ्, 'to deceive.' Observe—In combination with verbs beginning with *e* or *o* this preposition generally drops its final *a;* as, प्रेषयामि 'I send,' from प्र and एषय, causal base of इष् 'to go.' Similarly, प्रेजते 'he trembles' (3d sing. of *ej* with *pra*).

The *r* of *pra* influences a following nasal by 58; as, प्रणम् 'to bend before,' 'to salute.' Sometimes प्र does not alter the sense of a root, as in प्राप् 'to obtain' (5th c.; see 681).

q. प्रति* *prati*, 'against,' 'towards,' 'back again;' as, प्रतियुध् 'to fight against;' प्रती 'to go towards' (pres. प्रत्येमि); प्रतिगम् 'to go towards,' 'to return;' प्रतिकृ 'to counteract;' प्रतिहन् 'to beat back,' 'to repel;' प्रतिवच् 'to answer;' प्रतिलभ् 'to recover;' प्रतिनी 'to lead back;' प्रतिनन्द् 'to re-salute.' With श्रु, 'to promise;' with पद्, 'to arrive at,' 'to obtain;' with ईक्ष्, 'to wait for,' 'to expect.' Sometimes it does not alter the sense of the root; as, प्रतिवस् 'to dwell.'

r. वि *vi*, 'apart,' implying 'separation,' 'distinction,' 'distribution,' 'dispersion' (Latin *dis*, *se*); as, विचर् 'to wander about;' विचल् 'to vacillate;' विहृ 'to roam for pleasure;' विकृ 'to dissipate;' विदृ 'to tear asunder;' विभज् 'to divide;' विविच् 'to distinguish.' Sometimes it gives a privative signification;' as, वियुज् 'to disunite;' विस्मृ 'to forget;' विक्री 'to sell.' With कृ, 'to change for the worse.' Sometimes it has no apparent influence on the root; as, विनश् 'to perish;' विचिन्त् 'to think.'

s. सम् *sam*, 'with,' 'together with' (σύν, *con*); as, सञ्चि, सङ्ग्रह्, 'to collect;' संयुज् 'to join together;' सङ्गम् 'to meet together;' सम्पद् 'to happen;' सङ्क्षिप् 'to contract.' With कृ it signifies 'to perfect,' and स् is inserted, संस्कृ. It is often prefixed without altering the sense; as, सञ्जन् 'to be produced.'

784. Two prepositions are often combined with a root; as, व्यादा 'to open' (वि, आ); व्यापद् (10th c.) 'to kill;' उपागम् 'to go under,' 'to undergo,' 'to arrive at' (उप, आ); समे 'to assemble' (सम्, आ, with root इ); प्रणिपत् 'to prostrate one's self' (प्र, नि, 58); प्रोद्धृ 'to raise up' (प्र, उत्, with root हृ): and occasionally three; as, प्रव्याहृ 'to predict' (प्र, वि, आ); प्रत्युदाहृ 'to answer' (प्रति, उत्, आ). Other combinations of three prepositions, occasionally prefixed to roots, are सं + उप + आ; अभि + वि + आ; सं + अभि + प्र; उप + सं + प्र; अनु + सं + वि.

a. Observe—Excepting in the case of प्र above, prepositions ending in vowels combine with roots beginning with vowels according to the rules of Sandhi; thus, आ with इ 'to go' becomes ए (32), and in pres. ऐमि (आ + एमि 33), &c.; in pot. एयां (आ + इयां), &c.; in imp. आयानि (आ + यानि), &c.; in 1st pret. आयं, ऐस् (645, 33), &c. Similarly, अप with एमि becomes अपैमि by 33.

785. In conjugating compound verbs formed with prepositions, the augment and reduplication do not change their position, but are inserted between the preposition and the root †; as, पर्यणयं, 1st pret.

---

* The final *i* of the prepositions प्रति, परि, नि, is optionally lengthened in forming certain nouns from compound verbs; as, प्रतीकार, परीहास, नीकार.

† There are a few exceptions to this rule in the Mahábhárata; as in अन्वसञ्चरत् (Mahábh. Selections, p. 33).

of नी, with परि; उपाविशं, 1st pret. of विश्, with उप; अन्वतिष्ठं, 1st pret. of स्था, with अनु; प्रतिजघान, 2d pret. of हन्, with प्रति; प्रोज्जहार, 2d pret. of हृ, with प्र and उत्.

786. Grammarians restrict certain roots to particular voices, when in combination with particular prepositions; as, for example, the root जि 'to conquer,' with वि, and the root विश् 'to enter,' with नि, are restricted to the A'tmane-pada; but no certain rules can be propounded on this subject: and in the two epic poems especially the choice of voice seems generally arbitrary and subservient to the purposes of metre *.

Compound Verbs formed by combining Adverbs with the roots कृ kṛi *and* भू bhú.

787. These are of two kinds; 1st, those formed by combining adverbs with कृ 'to make' and भू 'to become;' 2dly, those formed by combining nouns used adverbially with these roots.

a. Examples of the first kind are, अलङ्कृ 'to adorn;' आविष्कृ 'to make manifest' (see 72); बहिष्कृ 'to eject;' पुरस्कृ 'to place in front,' 'to follow;' विनाकृ 'to deprive;' सत्कृ 'to entertain as a guest;' नमस्कृ 'to revere;' साक्षाद्भू, प्रादुर्भू, 'to become manifest,' &c.

788. In forming the second kind, the final of a crude word, being *a* or *á*, is changed to *í*; as, from सज्ज, सज्जीकृ 'to make ready,' सज्जीभू 'to become ready;' from कृष्ण, कृष्णीकृ 'to blacken;' from परिखा 'a ditch,' परिखीकृ 'to convert into a ditch:' and sometimes *a* becomes *á*; as, प्रियाकृ from प्रिय. A final *i* or *u* is lengthened; as, from शुचि, शुचीभू 'to become pure;' from लघु, लघूकृ 'to lighten.' A final *ṛi* is changed to री *rí*; as, from मातृ, मात्रीभू 'to become a mother.' A final *as* becomes either *í* (as, from सुमनस्, सुमनीभू 'to be of good mind') or *así* (as, from शिरस्, शिरसीधा 'to place on the head').

a. But the greater number of compounds of this kind are formed from crude nouns in *a*. The following are other examples: तृणीकृ 'to esteem as a straw;' स्तम्भीकृ 'to stiffen;' एकचित्तीभू 'to fix the mind on one object;' स्वीकृ 'to make one's own,' 'to claim as one's own;' मैत्रीभू 'to become friendly.' Substantives are sometimes formed from these; as, मैत्रीभाव 'the state of being friendly,' 'friendship.'

---

* Thus, यत् 'to strive' and प्रार्थ् 'to beg for,' which are properly A'tmane-pada verbs, are found in the Parasmai. Instances of passive verbs taking Parasmai terminations have been given at 253.*b*. On the other hand, नन्द् 'to rejoice,' which is properly a Parasmai-pada verb, is found in the A'tmane.

b. Observe—This mode of compounding nouns and adverbs with *kṛi* and *bhú* is by Indian grammarians technically termed *chwí.* These compounds, however, rarely occur, excepting in the form of passive participles*; and it may be questioned whether the genius of Sanskṛit favours the combination of any other part of speech but a preposition with the tenses of verbs. In Greek and Latin, on the other hand, the composition of nouns with verbs is not unusual.

789. Sometimes सात्, placed after a crude noun, is used to form a compound verb of this kind; as, from जल 'water,' जलसात्कृ 'to reduce to liquid;' from भस्मन् 'ashes,' भस्मसात्कृ (57) 'to reduce to ashes.' These compounds, like the last, are rarely found, excepting in the form of past passive participles.

SECTION III.

COMPOUND ADVERBS.

790. Compound adverbs are formed, 1st, by combining adverbs, prepositions, and adverbial prefixes, with nouns in the nom. or accus. singular neuter; 2dly, by placing adverbs, or adjectives used as adverbs, after the crude base of nouns.

a. The first kind are identical with indeclinable compounds at 760, and the greater number are formed with the adverbial preposition सह *saha*, contracted into स *sa;* as, from कोप 'anger,' सकोपं 'angrily;' from आदर 'respect,' सादरं 'respectfully;' from अष्टाङ्गपात 'prostration of the limbs,' साष्टाङ्गपातं 'reverentially.'

b. The following may be taken as examples of compound adverbs formed with other prefixes: अनु.ज्येष्ठं 'according to seniority;' प्रत्यङ्गं 'over every limb;' प्रति.मासं 'every month;' यथा.विधि 'according to rule;' यथा.शक्ति or यावच्छक्यं 'according to one's power;' यथा.सुखं 'happily;' समक्षं 'before the eyes' (अक्ष being substituted for अक्षि, see 778); असंशयं 'undoubtedly;' निर्विशेषं 'without distinction.'

791. Most of the adverbs at 731 may be placed after the crude base of nouns; thus, बालक.समीपं 'near the child;' रक्षा.र्थं 'for the sake of protection;' किम.र्थं 'on what account?' शब्दोच्चारणा.नन्तरं 'after uttering a sound.'

792. पूर्व्वं or पूर्व्वकं or पुरःसरं (meaning literally 'preceded by') is placed after crude bases to denote 'the manner' in which any thing is done; as, क्रोध.पूर्व्वं 'with anger.' See 777. *c.*

793. A kind of compound adverb, implying 'reciprocity,' is formed

* Generally as past passive participles; thus, अलङ्कृत 'adorned;' प्रादुर्भूत 'become manifest;' सज्जीभूत 'made ready;' लघूकृत 'lightened.' The future passive participle is sometimes found so compounded; as, स्वीकरणीय 'to be agreed to.'

by doubling a noun, lengthening the final of the first word, and changing the final of the last to *i;* as, from दण्ड 'a stick,' दण्डादण्डि 'mutual striking;' अंशांशि 'share by share;' मुषलामुषलि 'club to club;' मुष्टीमुष्टि 'fist to fist.'

a. Something in the same manner, अन्य and पर, 'another,' are doubled; thus, अन्योन्यं, परस्परं, 'mutually,' 'together.'

b. The indeclinable participle आरभ्य, 'having begun,' is joined with अद्य, 'to-day' (अद्यारभ्य), in the sense of 'from this time forward;' and with the crude bases of other words to express 'beginning from;' see 925. प्रभृति is placed adverbially after words, in the same sense; as, जन्मप्रभृति 'from birth upwards.'

CHAPTER IX.

SYNTAX.

794. Sanskṛit syntax, unlike that of Greek and Latin, offers fewer difficulties to the student than any other portion of the Grammar. Indeed, compounds prevail so abundantly in this language, that the writer who has properly expounded the subject of compound words has already more than half completed his investigation into the laws which regulate syntactical combinations. We shall endeavour, in the present chapter, to collect together all the most useful rules for the connexion and collocation of uncompounded words. Much vagueness and uncertainty, however, may be expected to attach to the rules propounded, when it is remembered that Sanskṛit literature consists almost entirely of poetry, and that the laws of syntax are ever prone to yield to the necessities of metrical composition.

a. Observe—In the present chapter on Syntax, that the subject may be made as clear as possible, each word will be separated from the next, and vowels will not be allowed to coalesce, although such coalition be required by the laws of combination. When compounds are introduced into the examples, a dot, placed underneath, generally marks the division of the words.

THE ARTICLE.

795. There is no indefinite article in classical Sanskṛit; but कश्चित् (228) and in modern Sanskṛit एक (238) are sometimes used to supply the place of such an article; thus, एकस्मिन् प्रदेशे 'in a certain

country;' कश्चित् शृगालः 'a certain jackal.' The definite article may not unfrequently be expressed by the pronoun स (220); thus, स पुरुषः may mean simply 'the man,' not necessarily 'that man.'

CONCORD OF THE VERB WITH THE NOMINATIVE CASE.

796. The verb must agree with the nominative case in number and person; as, अहं करवाणि 'I must perform.'

a. Other examples are, त्वम् अवधेहि 'do thou attend;' स ददाति 'he gives;' आवां ब्रूवः 'we two say;' कपोता ऊचुः 'the pigeons said;' राजा मन्त्री च जग्मतुः 'the king and minister went;' यावच् चन्द्रार्कौ तिष्ठतः 'as long as the moon and sun remain;' युवां चिन्तयतं 'do you two reflect;' यूयम् आयात 'do ye come;' सज्जनाः पूज्यन्ते 'good men are honoured;' वाति पवनः 'the wind blows;' उदयति शशाङ्कः 'the moon rises;' स्फुटति पुष्पं 'the flower blossoms.'

b. Observe—The verb is usually, though not always, placed last in the sentence.

797. When a participle takes the place of the verb, it must agree with the nominative in number and *gender;* as, स गतः 'he went;' सा गता 'she went;' नार्य्याव् उक्तवत्यौ 'the two women spoke;' राजा हतः 'the king was killed;' बन्धनानि छिन्नानि 'the bonds were cut.'

a. Sometimes, when it is placed between two or more nominative cases, it agrees with one only; as, स्ववधूः प्रबोधिता पुत्रश्च 'his wife and son were awakened.'

b. Very often the copula, or verb which connects the subject with the predicate, is omitted; when, if an adjective stand in the place of the verb, it will follow the rules of concord in gender and number; as, धनं दुर्लभं 'wealth is difficult of attainment;' आवां कृताहारौ 'we two have finished eating.' But if a substantive stand in the place of the verb, no concord of gender or number need take place; as, सम्पदः पदम् आपदां 'successes are the road to misfortunes.'

CONCORD OF THE ADJECTIVE WITH THE SUBSTANTIVE.

798. An adjective, participle, or adjective pronoun, qualifying a substantive, when not compounded with it, must agree with the substantive in gender, number, and case; as, साधुः पुरुषः 'a good man;' महद् दुःखं 'great pain;' एतेषु पूर्व्वोक्तेषु राष्ट्रेषु 'in these before-mentioned countries;' त्रीणि मित्राणि 'three friends.'

CONCORD OF THE RELATIVE WITH THE ANTECEDENT.

799. The relative must agree with the antecedent noun in gender, number, and person; but in Sanskrit the relative pronoun generally precedes the noun to which it refers, this noun being put in the same case with the relative, and the pronoun स follows in the latter clause of the sentence; as, यस्य नरस्य बुद्धिः स बलवान् 'of whatever man there is intellect, he is strong.'

a. The noun referred to by the relative may also be joined with स, as यस्य बुद्धिः स नरो बलवान्; or may be omitted altogether, as यत् प्रतिज्ञातं तत् पालय 'what you have promised, that abide by;' येषाम् अपत्यानि खादितानि तैः (पक्षिभिः understood) जिज्ञासा समारब्धा 'by those (birds) whose young ones were devoured an inquiry was set on foot;' यः सर्वान् विषयान् प्राप्नुयाद् यश्च एतान् उपेक्षते तयोर् विषयापेक्षकः श्रेयान् 'he who would obtain all objects of sense, and he who despises them, of the two the despiser is the best.'

800. The relative sometimes stands alone, an antecedent noun or pronoun being understood, from which it takes its gender and number; as, नास्ति पुण्यवान् (तस्मात् understood) यस्य मित्रेण सम्भाषः 'there is not a happier (than that man) of whom there is conversation with a friend;' धनेन किं यो न ददाति 'What is the use of wealth (to him) who does not give?'

a. Sometimes, though rarely, the antecedent noun precedes the relative in the natural order; as, न सा भार्य्या यस्यां भर्त्ता न तुष्यति 'she is not a wife in whom the husband does not take pleasure.'

801. तावत् and यावत् stand to each other in the relation of demonstrative and relative; as, यावन्ति तस्य द्वीपस्य वस्तूनि तावन्ति अस्माकम् उपनेतव्यानि 'as many products as belong to that island, so many are to be brought to us.' See also 876.

a. Similarly, तादृश and यादृश; as, यादृशं वृत्तं तादृशं तस्मै कथितवन्तः 'as the event occurred, so they related it to him.'

SYNTAX OF SUBSTANTIVES.

802. Under this head it is proposed to explain the construction of substantives, without reference to their connexion with particular adjectives, verbs, or participles; and for this purpose it will be desirable to exhibit examples under each case.

Nominative case.

803. A substantive simply and absolutely expressed must be placed in the nominative case; as, हितोपदेशः 'the Hitopadeśa;' भट्टिकाव्यं 'the poem of Bhaṭṭi.'

a. Two nominative cases in different numbers may be placed in apposition to each other; as, तृणानि शय्या 'grass as a bed.'

Accusative case.

804. Substantives are not found in the accusative, unconnected with verbs or participles, except as expressing 'duration of time' or 'space.' See 821.

Instrumental case.

805. This case yields a variety of senses. The most usual is that of 'the instrument' or 'means' by which any thing is done; as,

मया (उक्तं) 'by me it was said;' व्याधेन (पाशो योजितः) 'by the fowler a snare was laid;' वेदाध्ययनेन 'by the study of the Vedas;' स्वचक्षुषा 'with one's own eye.'

806. It also has the force of 'with' in expressing other collateral ideas; as, बलीयसा स्पर्द्धा 'vying with the strong;' मित्रेण सम्भाषः 'conversation with a friend;' पशुभिः सामान्यं 'equality with beasts;' पितुर् गोचरेण 'with the knowledge of (his) father:' especially when 'accompaniment' is intended; as, शिष्येण गुरुः 'the master with his pupil.'

807. The other senses yielded by this case are, 'through,' 'by reason of,' 'on account of;' as, कृपया 'through compassion;' तेन अपराधेन 'on account of that transgression:' especially in the case of abstract nouns formed with ता (80. XXIII); as, मूढतया 'through infatuation.'

a. 'According to,' 'by;' as, विधिना 'according to rule;' मम सम्मतेन 'according to my opinion;' जात्या 'by birth.'

b. 'The manner' in which any thing is done, as denoted in English by the adverbial affix 'ly,' or by the prepositions 'in,' 'at;' as, बाहुल्येन 'in abundance;' धर्म्मेण 'virtuously;' यथेच्छया or स्वेच्छया 'at pleasure;' सुखेन 'at ease;' अनेन विधिना 'in this way;' महता स्नेहेन (निवसतः) 'they both dwell together in great intimacy;' (नृपः सर्व्वभूतानि अभिभवति) तेजसा 'a king surpasses all beings in glory;' मनसा (न कर्त्तव्यं) 'such a deed must not even be imagined in the mind;' मानुषरूपेण 'in human form.'

808. Substantives expressive of 'want,' 'need,' may be joined with the instrumental of the thing wanted; as, चर्च्चया न प्रयोजनं 'there is no occasion for inquiry;' मया सेवकेन न प्रयोजनं 'there is no need of me as a servant;' तृणेन कार्य्यं 'there is use for a straw.'

809. 'The price' for which any thing is done may be in the instrumental; as, पञ्चभिः पुराणैर् (याति दासत्वं) 'for five Puráṇas he becomes a slave;' बहुभिर् दत्तैर् (युध्यन्ते) 'they fight for great rewards.' Similarly, प्राणपरित्यागमूल्येन (श्रीर् न लभ्यते) 'fortune is not obtained at the price of the sacrifice of life.'

a. So also 'difference between' two things; as, त्वया समुद्रेण च महद् अन्तरं 'there is great difference between you and the ocean.'

b. The English expression 'under the idea that' is expressed by the instrumental case of the substantive बुद्धि; as, व्याघ्रबुद्ध्या 'under the idea that he was a tiger.'

Double Instrumental.

810. Sometimes when two substantives come together, expressing 'parts' of a common idea, they are both placed in the instrumental, instead of one in the genitive; as, वकुलैः पुष्पैर् वास्यते 'an odour is emitted by the bakul-plants by their flowers' (for वकुलानां पुष्पैः). Similarly, ताम् आश्वासयामास प्रेष्याभिश् चन्दनोदकैः 'he caused her to revive by her attendants by sandal-water.'

Dative case.

811. This case is of very limited applicability, and its functions, irrespectively of the influence of verbs, are restricted to the expression of 'the object,' 'motive,' or 'cause' for which any thing is done, or 'the result' to which any act tends; as, आत्म-विवृद्धये 'for self-aggrandizement;' आपत्प्रतीकाराय 'for the counteraction of calamity;' शस्त्रं च शास्त्रं च प्रतिपत्तये 'arms and books (lead) to renown.'

a. When, as in the last example, 'the result' or 'end' to which any thing leads is denoted by this case, the verb is seldom expressed, but appears to be involved in the case itself. The following are other examples: यत्र आस्ते विषसंसर्गो ऽमृतं तदपि मृत्यवे 'where there is admixture of poison, then even nectar (leads) to death;' उपदेशो मूर्खाणां प्रकोपाय न शान्तये 'advice to fools (leads) to irritation, not to conciliation;' स वृद्धपतिस् तस्याः सन्तोषाय न अभवत् 'that old husband was not to her liking.'

b. It will be seen hereafter that certain verbs of *giving* and *relating* govern the dative. Substantives derived from such verbs exercise a similar influence; as, अन्यस्मै दानं 'the *giving* to another;' अन्यस्मै कथनं 'the *telling* to another.'

c. Words expressive of 'salutation' or 'reverence' are joined with the dative; as, गणेशाय नमः 'reverence to Gaṇeśa; कुशलं ते 'health to thee.'

Ablative case.

812. The proper force of the ablative case is expressed by 'from;' as, लोभात् (क्रोधः प्रभवति) 'from avarice anger arises;' गिरेः पतनं 'falling from a mountain;' चाराणां मुखात् 'from the mouth of the spies.'

813. Hence this case passes to the expression of various correlative ideas; as, आहारात् किञ्चित् 'a portion of (from) their food:' and like the instrumental it very commonly signifies 'by reason of,' 'in consequence of;' as, गोमनुष्याणां वधात् 'on account of the slaughter of cows and men;' अनवसरप्रवेशात् (पुत्रं निन्दति) 'he blames his son for entering inopportunely;' दण्डभयात् 'through fear of punishment;' अस्मत्पुण्योदयात् 'by reason of my good fortune.'

a. 'According to;' as, मन्त्रिवचनात् 'according to the advice of the minister.' Abstract nouns in त्वं are often found in this case to express some of these ideas; as, अनवस्थितचित्तत्वात् 'by reason of the unsteadiness of his mind:' especially in the writings of commentators; as, वक्ष्यमाणत्वात् 'according to what will be said hereafter.'

814. It also expresses 'through the means' or 'instrumentality of;' as, शृगालात् पाशबद्धः 'caught in the toils through the instrumentality of the jackal;' न औषधपरिज्ञानाद् (व्याधेः शान्तिर् भवेत्) 'the alleviation of disease is not effected by the mere knowledge of the medicine.'

a. 'The manner' in which any thing is done is occasionally expressed by the ablative; as, यत्नात् 'with diligence;' बलात् 'forcibly;' कुतूहलात् 'with wonder;' मूलाद् उद्धरणं 'tearing up by the roots:' or by the ablative affix तस्; as, स्वेच्छातस् 'at one's own pleasure' (see 719. *a. b*).

b. This case also denotes 'after;' as, शरीर-विगमात् 'after separation from the body;' मुख्य-प्रतिबन्धनात् 'after the imprisonment of the Chief;' तस्य आगमनात् 'since his arrival.'

c. In reference to *time*, 'within;' as, त्रिपक्षात् 'within three fortnights.'

d. Nouns expressive of 'fear' are joined with the ablative of the thing feared; as, मृत्योर् भयं 'fear of death;' चौरतो भयं 'fear of robbers.'

Genitive case.

815. This and the locative case are of the most extensive application, and are often employed, in a vague and indeterminate manner, to express relations properly belonging to the other cases.

a. The true force of the genitive is equivalent to 'of,' and this case appears most frequently when two substantives are to be connected, so as to present one idea; as, मित्रस्य वचनं 'the speech of a friend;' भर्त्ता नार्य्याः परमं भूषणं 'the best ornament of a woman is her husband;' न नरस्य नरो दासो दासस् तु अर्थस्य 'man is not the slave of man, but the slave of wealth.'

816. 'Possession' is frequently expressed by the genitive case alone, without a verb; as, सर्व्वाः सम्पत्तयस् तस्य सन्तुष्टं यस्य मानसं 'all riches belong to him who has a contented mind;' धन्योऽहं यस्य ईदृशी भार्य्या 'happy am I in possessing such a wife.'

a. It often, however, has the force of 'to,' and is very generally used to supply the place of the dative; as, प्राणा आत्मनो ऽभीष्टाः 'one's own life is dear to one's self;' न योजन-शतं दूरं वाह्यमानस्य तृष्णया 'a hundred Yojanas is not far to one borne away by thirst (of gain);' किं प्रज्ञावताम् अविदितं 'What is unknown to the wise?' किम् अन्धस्य प्रकाशयति प्रदीपः 'What does a lamp show to a blind man?' किं मया अपकृतं राज्ञः 'What offence have I committed towards the king;' किम् अयम् अस्माकं कर्त्तुं समर्थः 'What can this man do to us?'

b. And not unfrequently of 'in' or 'on;' as, स्त्रीणां विश्वासः 'confidence in women;' मम आयत्तत्वं 'dependence on me.'

c. It is even equivalent occasionally to 'from' or 'by,' as usually expressed by the ablative or instrumental; as, न कस्यापि (उपायनं गृह्णीयात्) 'one ought not to accept a present from any one;' अस्माकं (वनं त्याज्यं) 'the wood is to be abandoned by us;' स धन्यो यस्य अर्थिनो न प्रयान्ति विमुखाः 'he is blessed from whom suppliants do not depart in disappointment.'

d. 'Difference between' two things is expressed by this case; as, सेव्य-सेवकयोर् महद् अन्तरं 'there is great difference between the master and the servant.' Compare 809. *a.*

Locative case.

817. The locative, like the genitive, expresses the most diversified relations, and frequently usurps the functions of the other cases. Properly it has the force of 'in,' 'on,' or 'at,' as expressive of many collateral and analogous ideas; thus, रात्रौ 'in the night;' ग्रामे 'in the village;' पृष्ठे 'on the back;' त्वयि विश्वासः 'confidence in you;' मरु-स्थल्यां वृष्टिः 'rain on desert ground;' प्रथम-बुभुक्षायां 'at the first desire of eating;' पृथिव्यां रोपितो वृक्षः 'a tree planted in the earth.'

818. Hence it passes into the sense 'towards;' as, क्षमा शत्रौ च मित्रे च 'leniency towards an enemy as well as a friend;' सर्व्व-भूतेषु दया 'compassion towards all creatures;' सुहृत्सु अजिह्मः 'upright towards friends;' सुकृत-शतम् असत्सु नष्टं 'a hundred good offices are thrown away upon the wicked.'

819. Words signifying 'cause,' 'motive,' or 'need,' are joined with the locative; as, सत्रपत्वे हेतुः 'the cause of his modesty;' भूपालयोर् विग्रहे भवद्वचनं निदानं 'your speech was the cause of the war between the two princes;' प्रार्थकाभावः सतीत्वे कारणं स्त्रियाः 'the absence of a suitor is the cause of a woman's chastity;' नौकायां किं प्रयोजनं 'What need of a boat?' Also words signifying 'employment' or 'occupation;' as, अर्थार्जने प्रवृत्तिः 'engaging in the acquisition of wealth.' Words derived from the root *yuj* usually require the locative; as, मम राज्य-रक्षायाम् उपयोगः 'I am of service in preserving the kingdom.'

a. This case may yield other senses equivalent to 'by reason of,' 'for,' &c.; as, मे छिद्रेषु 'through my faults;' चारः पर-राष्ट्राणाम् अवलोकने 'a spy is for the sake of examining the territory of one's enemies;' युद्धे कालोऽयं 'this is the time for battle;' तस्याम् अनुरागः 'affection for her;' उपदेशे अनादरः 'disregard for advice;' का चिन्ता मरणे रणे 'What anxiety about dying in battle!'

b. It is also used in giving the meaning of a root; as, ग्रह् उपादाने 'the root *grah* is in *taking*,' i. e. conveys the idea of 'taking.'

c. The locative case is often used absolutely; see 840.

SYNTAX OF NOUNS OF TIME.

820. When reference is made to any particular division of time, the instrumental case is usually required; as, त्रिभिर् वर्षैः 'in three years;' द्वादशभिर् मासैः 'in twelve months;' क्षणेन 'in an instant;' कियता कालेन 'In how long time?' वर्ष-शतैः 'in hundreds of years;' काल-पर्य्यायेण 'in process of time.'

821. When to duration of time, the accusative case is generally used; as, क्षणं 'for a moment;' अनेक-कालं 'for a long time;' कियन्तं कालं 'for some time;' एकं मासं 'for one month;' द्वौ मासौ 'for two months;' वर्ष-शतं 'for a hundred years;' शाश्वतीः समाः 'to all eternity;' शतं वर्षाणि 'for a hundred years;' बहूनि अहानि 'for many days.'

The instrumental, however, is sometimes used in this sense also; as, द्वादशभिर् वर्षैर् वाणिज्यं कृत्वा 'having traded for twelve years;' कतिपयदिवसैः 'for a few days.'

822. When any particular period or epoch is referred to, the locative may be employed; as, कस्मिंश्चिद् दिवसे 'on a certain day;' तृतीये दिवसे 'on the third day:' or sometimes the accusative; as, यां रात्रिं ते दूताः प्रविशन्ति स्म पुरीं तां रात्रिं भरतेन स्वप्नो दृष्टः 'on the night when the ambassadors entered the city, on that night a dream was seen by Bharata.'

NOUNS OF PLACE AND DISTANCE.

823. Nouns expressive of 'distance between two places' (according to Carey) may be in the nominative; as, कृष्णः शतं क्रोशाः सोमनाथात् 'Kṛishṇa is a hundred Kos from Somanáth.' 'Space' may also be expressed by the accusative; as, क्रोशं गिरिः 'a hill for a Kos:' or by the instrumental; as, क्रोशेन गत्वा 'having gone for a Kos.' 'The place' in which any thing is done may be in the locative; as, विदर्भेषु 'in Vidarbha.'

SYNTAX OF ADJECTIVES.

Accusative after the Adjective.

824. The only adjectives governing an accusative are those formed from desiderative bases; as, स्वगृहं जिगमिषुः 'desirous of going home;' पुत्रम् अभीप्सुः 'desirous of obtaining a son;' राजानं दिदृक्षुः 'desirous of seeing the king.'

Instrumental after the Adjective.

825. Adjectives, or participles used adjectively, expressive of 'want' or 'possession,' require this case; as, अर्थेन हीनः 'destitute of wealth;' अर्थैः समायुक्तः 'possessed of riches;' वारिणा पूर्णो घटः 'a jar full of water.'

826. So also of 'likeness' or 'equality;' as, अनेन सदृशो लोके न भूतो न भविष्यति 'there has never been, nor will there ever be, any one like him in this world;' प्रारम्भैः सदृश उदयः 'his success was equal to his undertakings;' प्राणैः समा पत्नी 'a wife as dear as life;' आदित्येन तुल्यः 'equal to the sun.' These are also joined with a genitive.

Genitive after the Adjective.

827. Adjectives signifying 'dear to,' or the reverse, are joined with the genitive; as, राज्ञां प्रियः 'dear to kings;' भर्तारः स्त्रीणां प्रियाः 'husbands are dear to women;' न कश्चित् स्त्रीणाम् अप्रियः 'women dislike nobody;' द्वेष्यो भवति मन्त्रिणां 'he is detestable to his ministers.'

a. Adjectives expressive of 'equality' often require this case as well as the instrumental; thus, सर्व्वस्य समः 'equal to all;' तस्य अनुरूपः 'like him;' चन्द्रस्य कल्पः 'like the moon;' न तस्य तुल्यः कश्चन 'nobody is equal to him.'

b. So also other adjectives; as, परोपदेशः सर्व्वेषां सुकरः नृणां 'giving advice to others is *easy* to all men;' सुखानाम् उचितः '*worthy* of happiness;' उचितः क्लेशानां '*capable* of toil.'

Locative after the Adjective.

828. Adjectives, or participles used adjectively, expressive of 'power' or 'ability,' are joined with this case; as, अध्वनि क्षमा अश्वाः 'horses able for the journey;' महति शत्रौ क्षमो राजा 'a king who is a match for a great enemy;' अशक्ता गृह॰करणे शक्ता गृह॰भञ्जने 'unable to build a house, but able to demolish one.'

a. So also other adjectives; as, शस्त्रेषु कुशलः '*skilled* in arms;' अल्पेषु प्राज्ञः '*wise* in trifles;' त्वयि अनुरक्तो विरक्तो वा स्वामी 'Is your master *attached* or *adverse* to you?' अनुजीविषु मन्दादरः '*neglectful* of his dependants.'

SYNTAX OF THE COMPARATIVE AND SUPERLATIVE DEGREE.

829. Adjectives in the comparative degree require the ablative case; as, पत्नी प्राणेभ्योऽपि गरीयसी 'a wife dearer even than one's life;' पुत्र॰स्पर्शात् सुखतरः स्पर्शो लोके न विद्यते 'there is no pleasanter touch in this world than the touch of a son;' वर्द्धनात् प्रजा॰रक्षणं श्रेयः 'the protection of one's subjects is better than aggrandizement;' न मत्तो (719.*a*) दुःखिततरः पुमान् अस्ति 'there is not a more wretched man than I;' मतिर् बलाद् बलीयसी 'mind is more powerful than strength.'

830. Sometimes they govern the instrumental; as, प्राणैः प्रियतरः 'dearer than life;' न अस्ति मया कश्चिद् अल्प॰भाग्यतरो भुवि 'there is nobody upon earth more unfortunate than I.'

a. When it is intended to express 'the better of two things' the genitive may be used; as, अनयोर् देशयोः को देशो भद्रतरः 'Of these two countries which is the better?'

831. The comparative in Sanskrit is often resolved into the expression 'better and not;' as, वरं प्राण॰परित्यागो न पुनर् ईदृशे कर्म्मणि प्रवृत्तिः 'better abandon life than (literally, and not) engage in such an action;' वरं मौनं कार्य्यं न च वचनम् उक्तं यद् अनृतं 'it is better that silence should be kept than a speech uttered which is untrue;' विद्यया सह वेदाध्यापकेन वरं मर्तव्यं न तु अध्यापन॰योग्य॰शिष्याभावे अपात्राय एतां प्रतिपादयेत् 'a teacher of the Veda should rather die with his learning than commit it to an unworthy object, in the absence of a pupil worthy to be instructed in it.'

832. The superlative degree is usually joined with the genitive; as, ब्राह्मणो द्विपदां श्रेष्ठो गौर् वरिष्ठा चतुष्पदां । गुरुर् गरीयसां श्रेष्ठः पुत्रः स्पर्शवतां वरः 'a Bráhman is the best of all bipeds, a cow of quadrupeds, a Guru of venerable things, a son of things possessed of touch:' but sometimes with the locative; as, नरेषु बलवत्तमः 'the most powerful of men:' and even with an ablative; as, धान्यानां सङ्ग्रह उत्तमः सर्व्वसङ्ग्रहात 'a store of grain is the best of all stores.'

a. A superlative degree may even take a comparative affix, and govern the genitive; as, तेषां ज्येष्ठतरस् 'the eldest of them.' See 194.

833. 'Comparison' is often expressed by an adjective in the *positive* degree, joined with a noun in the ablative case; as, नास्ति तस्मात् पुण्यवान् 'there is not a happier than he;' स मत्तो (719. *a*) महान् 'he is greater than me.'

a. In more modern Sanskṛit 'comparison' is sometimes expressed by the use of अपेक्ष्य 'regarding,' 'with reference to' (indecl. part. of the root ईक्ष् with अप), which may take the place of 'than' in English; thus, दशोपाध्यायान् अपेक्ष्य आचार्य्य आचार्य्यशतम् अपेक्ष्य पिता गौरवेण अतिरिक्ता भवति 'an A'chárya ought to be higher in estimation than ten Upádhyáyas, a father than a hundred A'cháryas.'

834. Many words have a kind of comparative influence, and require an ablative case, especially वरं, अवरं, अन्य, अन्यदा, अन्यत्र, इतर, पर, पूर्व, अधिक, ऊन, अवशिष्ट; as, प्रक्षालनात् पङ्कस्य अस्पर्शनं वरं 'it is better not to touch mud than to wash it off;' दारिद्र्यम् अवरं मरणात् 'poverty is less desirable than death;' को मां मित्राद् अन्यस् त्रातुं समर्थः 'Who is able to rescue me, other than a friend?' किन्नु दुःखम् अतः परं 'What grief is greater than this?' न श्रुताद् अन्यद् विब्रूयात् 'one ought not to speak differently from what one has heard;' तत्कालाद् अन्यदा 'at another time than the present;' नरस्य न अन्यत्र मरणाद् भयं 'there is no cause of fear to man from any other quarter than from death;' श्राद्धाहात् (731. *a*, 778) पूर्व्वदिने 'on the day before that of the S'ráddha;' योजनशताद् अधिकं 'more than a hundred Yojanas;' कान्तोदन्तः सङ्गमात् किञ्चिद् ऊनः 'intelligence of a lover is something less than a meeting;' अन्नाद् अवशिष्टं 'the remainder of the food.'

NUMERALS.

835. The syntax of numerals is explained at 206. The following examples may be added: नवतेर् नराणां 'of ninety men;' षष्टेर् नराणां 'of sixty men;' सहस्रस्य नराणां 'of a thousand men;' एषां त्रयाणां मध्याद् अन्यतमः 'one of these three.'

a. The aggregative numerals may sometimes be employed at the end of compounds for the cardinals; thus, सैन्यद्वयं 'two armies;' विवाहचतुष्टयं 'four marriages.' See 214.

b. Numerals, if used partitively, may take the genitive; as, अश्वानां शतसहस्राणि 'a hundred thousand of the horses:' and, if comparatively, the ablative; as, विवादात् द्विगुणो दमः 'a fine the double of that which is in dispute.'

SYNTAX OF PRONOUNS.

836. The chief peculiarities in the syntax of pronouns have already been noticed in Chapter V. pp. 94—101. It remains to offer one or two remarks with reference more especially to the relative and interrogative.

a. In the use of these pronouns a very peculiar *attraction* is often to be observed; that is, when either a relative or interrogative pronoun has been used, and an indefinite pronoun would naturally be expected to follow, the relative or interrogative are repeated, as in the following examples: यो यस्य (for कस्यचित्) भावः स्यात् 'whatever may be the disposition of whom (i. e. any one);' यद् रोचते यस्मै 'whatever is pleasing to any one;' यो यस्य मांसम् अश्नाति 'whoever eats the flesh of any animal;' यस्य ये गुणाः सन्ति 'whatever excellencies belong to any one;' यद् येन युज्यते 'whatever corresponds with any thing;' केषां किं शास्त्रम् अध्ययनीयं 'What book is to be read by whom? (i. e. by any one).' See Bopp's Comparative Grammar, vol. II. p. 537.

837. The relative and interrogative are sometimes used together, in an indefinite distributive sense; as, यानि कानि मित्राणि 'any friends whatever:' or more usually with चित् affixed to the interrogative; as, यस्मै कस्मैचित् 'to any one whatever.'

a. The neuter of the interrogative (किं) is often joined with the instrumental to signify 'What is the use of?' 'there is no need of;' as, श्रुतेन किं यो न धर्मम् आचरेत् किम् आत्मना यो न जितेन्द्रियो भवेत् 'Of what use is scriptural knowledge (to one) who does not practice virtue? Of what use is a soul (to one) whose passions are not kept in subjection?' किं ते अनेन प्रश्नेन 'What business have you to make this inquiry?' किं बहुना 'What need of more!' 'in short.'

b. As already shown at 761, a relative pronoun is sometimes rendered unnecessary by the use of the relative compound; thus, नगरी चन्द्रिकाधौतहर्म्या is equivalent to नगरी यस्याश् चन्द्रिकाधौतानि हर्म्याणि 'a city whose palaces were silvered by the moon-beams.'

c. The relative, when followed by a pluperfect tense, may sometimes be expressed by the indeclinable participle; thus, सिंहो व्याधं हत्वा 'a lion having killed a hunter,' or 'a lion who had killed a hunter.'

838. The following examples will illustrate the use of pronouns of quantity and pronominals: यावतः (or यत्संख्यकान्) ग्रासान् भुंक्ते तावतः (or तत्संख्यकान्) ददाति 'as many mouthfuls as he eats, so many he gives away;' यदि एतावन् मह्यं दीयते तदा एतावद् अध्यापयामि 'if so much is given to me, then I will give so much instruction;' तेषां सर्वेषां मध्याद् एकतमः 'one out of all those.' See also 801.

SYNTAX OF VERBS.

839. Nothing is more common in Sanskṛit syntax than for the verb to be omitted altogether, or supplied from the context.

a. This is more especially the case with the copula, or substantive verb; thus, यावन् मेरुस्थिता देवा यावद् गङ्गा महीतले। चन्द्रार्कौ गगने यावत् तावद् विप्रकुले

वयं 'as long as the gods have existed in Meru, as long as the Ganges upon earth, as long as the sun and moon in the sky, so long have we (existed) in the family of Brahmans;' परिच्छेदः पाण्डित्यं 'discrimination (is) wisdom.'

Locative, Genitive, and Nominative absolute.

840. The locative case is very commonly used absolutely with participles; as, तस्मिन् जीवति जीवामि मृते तस्मिन् म्रिये पुनः 'he living I live, he dying I die;' अवसन्नायां रात्रौ 'the night being ended;' ज्येष्ठे भ्रातरि अनूढे 'the elder brother being unmarried;' असति उपायान्तरे 'there being no other expedient;' तथा सति 'it being so.' Sometimes the verb is omitted; as, दूरे भये 'the danger (being) distant.' When the passive participle is thus used absolutely with a noun in the locative case, the present participle of अस्, 'to be,' is often redundantly added; as, तथा कृते सति or तथा अनुष्ठिते 'it being so done *.'

a. The genitive is less commonly used absolutely; as, आपदाम् आपतन्तीनां 'calamities impending;' पश्यतां नराणां 'the men looking on.'

b. The nominative is very rarely thus used; as, सुहृन् मे समायातः पुण्यवान् अस्मि 'my friend having arrived, I am happy.'

c. It is evident from the above examples that the locative and genitive absolute often take the place of the particles 'when,' 'while,' 'since,' 'although.'

Nominative case after the Verb.

841. Verbs signifying 'to be,' 'to become,' 'to appear,' 'to be called,' or 'to be esteemed,' and other passive verbs used denominatively, may take a nominative after them; as, राजा प्रजापालकः स्यात् 'let a king be the protector of his subjects;' सा निरानन्दा प्रतिभाति 'she appears sorrowful;' ग्रामोऽरण्यं प्रतिभाति 'the village appears like a desert;' राजा धर्म्मे अभिधीयते 'a king is called Justice.'

Accusative case after the Verb.

842. Transitive verbs generally govern this case; as, विश्वं ससर्ज वेधाः 'Brahmá *created* the universe;' पुष्पाणि चिनोति नारी 'the woman *gathers* flowers;' प्राणान् जहौ मुमूर्षुः 'the dying man *gave up* the ghost;' मधु वर्जयेत् 'one should *avoid* wine;' तत्त्वं ब्रूहि '*speak* the truth.'

843. So also verbs of *motion;* as, सरति तीर्थं मुनिः 'the holy man *goes* to the place of pilgrimage;' नद्यः समुद्रं द्रवन्ति 'rivers *run* into the ocean;' भ्रमति महीं 'he *wanders* over the earth.'

---

* Possibly the object of adding the word *sati* may be to show that the passive participle is here used as a participle, and not as a past tense. So also in commentaries सति is placed after a word like आगच्छति, to indicate the loc. c. sing. of the pres. part., as distinguished from the 3d sing. of the pres. tense.

844. Verbs of *motion* are not unfrequently used with substantives, to supply the place of other verbs; as, ख्यातिं याति 'he goes to fame,' for 'he becomes famous;' समताम् एति 'he goes to equality,' for 'he becomes equal;' तयोर् मित्रताम् आजगाम 'he came to the friendship of those two,' for 'he became a friend of those two;' पञ्चत्वं गतः 'he went to death,' for 'he died;' नृपतिं तुष्टिं नयति 'he brings the king to satisfaction,' for 'he satisfies,' &c.

a. The following are other examples: अन्येषां पीडां परिहरति 'he *avoids* paining others;' अप्राप्यम् इच्छति 'he *desires* what is unattainable;' विद्यां चिन्तयेत् 'he should *think on* wisdom;' अश्वम् आरोहति 'he *mounts* his horse;' कर्म्माणि आरेभिरे 'they *began* the business;' गतान् मा शुचः '*grieve not for* the departed;' सर्व्वलोकाधिपत्यम् अर्हति 'he *deserves* the sovereignty of the universe;' पर्व्वतकन्दरं शेते 'he *lies down* in a cave of the mountain;' गां क्षीरं पिबन्तीं न निवारयेत् 'one ought not to *prevent* a cow from drinking milk.'

845. There are certain verbs which take a redundant accusative case after them of a substantive derived from the same root; as, शपथं शेपे 'he swore an oath;' वसति वासं 'he dwells;' वर्त्तते वृत्तिं 'he conducts himself;' वाक्यं वदति 'he speaks a speech;' नदति नादं 'he raises a cry' (cf. the Greek expressions λέγω λόγον, χαίρω χαράν, &c.).

Double Accusative after the Verb.

846. Verbs of *asking* govern a double accusative; as, देवं वरं याचते 'he seeks a boon of the god;' धनं राजानं प्रार्थयते 'he begs money from the king.' Of *speaking;* as, राजानं वचनम् अब्रवीत् 'he addressed a speech to the king.' Of *leading;* as, तं गृहं नयति 'he leads him home.'

847. Causal verbs; as, अतिथिं भोजयति अन्नं 'he causes the guest to eat food;' त्वां बोधयामि यत् ते हितं 'I cause you to know what is for your interest;' शिष्यं वेदान् अध्यापयति गुरुः 'the Guru teaches his pupil the Vedas;' तां गृहं प्रवेशयति 'he causes her to enter the house;' फलपुष्पोदकं ग्राहयामास नृपात्मजं 'he presented the king's son with fruits, flowers, and water;' पुत्रम् अङ्कम् आरोपयति 'she causes her son to sit on her lap' (literally, 'her hip'); विद्या नरं नृपं सङ्गमयति 'learning causes a man to have access to a king.'

a. Other examples are, तं सेनापतिम् अभिषिषिचुः 'they *inaugurated* him general,' more usually joined with an acc. and loc.; देवं पतिं वरयति 'she *chooses* a god for her husband;' अवचिनोति कुसुमानि वृक्षान् 'she *gathers* blossoms from the trees;' तान् प्राहिणोद् यमसादनं 'he *sent* them to the abode of Yama' (Hades); स्वचेष्टितानि नरं गुरुत्वं विपरीततां वा नयन्ति 'his own acts *lead* a man to eminence or the reverse.'

Instrumental case after the Verb.

848. Any verb may be joined with the instrumental, to express 'the instrument or cause or manner' of the action; as, पुष्पं वातेन म्लायति 'the flower fades by reason of the wind;' अक्षैः क्रीडति 'he

plays with dice;' मेघोऽग्निं वर्षैर् निर्वापयति 'the cloud puts out the fire with its rain;' सुखेन जीवति 'he lives happily.'

a. In this sense many causals take an instrumental; as, तां मिष्टान्नैर् भोजयामास 'he caused her to eat sweetmeats;' पक्षिभिः पिण्डान् खादयति 'he causes the pieces to be eaten by the birds.'

849. After verbs of *motion* this case is used in reference either to *the vehicle by which*, or *the place on which*, the motion takes place; as, रथेन प्रयाति 'he goes *in a chariot;*' अश्वेन सञ्चरति 'he goes *on horseback;*' मार्गेण गच्छति 'he goes *on the road;*' शस्यक्षेत्रेण गच्छति 'he goes *through a field of corn;*' पुप्लुवे सागरं नौकया 'he navigated the ocean *in a boat.*' Similarly, सुस्राव नयनैः सलिलं 'tears flowed *through the eyes.*'

a. After verbs of *carrying, placing*, &c., it is used in reference to 'the place' on which any thing is carried or placed; as, वहति मूर्ध्ना इन्धनं 'he bears fagots *on his head;*' कुक्कुरः स्कन्धेन उह्यते 'the dog is borne *on the shoulders.*' कृ is found with this case in the sense of *placing;* as, शिरसा पुत्रम् अकरोत् 'he *placed* his son on his head.' The following are other examples: शिष्येण गच्छति गुरुः 'the master *goes in company with* the pupil;' मन्त्रयामास मन्त्रिभिः 'he *consulted with* his ministers;' but in this sense सह is usually placed after it. भर्त्ता भार्य्यया सङ्गच्छति 'the husband *meets* the wife;' संयोजयति रथं हयैः 'he *harnesses* the horses to the chariot;' देहेन वियुज्यते 'he *is separated from* the body,' more usually with the ablative. युध्यते शत्रुभिः 'he *fights* his enemies,' or शत्रुभिः सह, &c.; वैरं न केनचित् सह कुर्य्यात् 'one ought not to be at *enmity* with any one.'

850. Verbs of *boasting;* as, विद्यया विकत्थसे 'you *boast* of your learning;' परेषां यशसा श्लाघसे 'you *glory* in the fame of others.' Of *swearing;* as, धनुषा शेपे 'he *swore* by his bow.' Of *thinking, reflecting;* as, मनसा विचिन्त्य '*thinking* in his mind.'

851. Verbs denoting *liberation, freedom from*, sometimes take an instrumental after them; as, सर्वपापैः प्रमुच्यते 'he is *released from* all sins.'

852. Verbs of *buying* and *selling* take the instrumental of the price; as, सहस्रैर् अपि मूर्खाणाम् एकं क्रीणीष्व पण्डितं '*buy* one wise man even for thousands of fools;' गवां सहस्रेण गृहं विक्रीणीते 'he *sells* his house for a thousand cows.'

Dative after the Verb.

853. All verbs in which a sense of *imparting* or *communicating* any thing to any object is inherent, may take an accusative of the thing imparted, and a dative of the object to which it is imparted. (Frequently, however, they take a genitive or even a locative of the object; see 857.) पुत्राय मोदकान् ददाति 'he *gives* sweetmeats to his son;' विप्राय गां प्रतिशृणोति 'he *promises* a cow to the Bráhmaṇ;' देवदत्ताय धनं धारयति 'he *owes* money to Devadatta;' कन्यां तस्मै प्रतिपादय '*consign* the maiden to him,' more usually with the locative; see 861.

a. Other examples of the dative are, तेषां विनाशाय प्रकुरुते मनः 'he *sets his mind on* their destruction;' गमनाय मतिं दधौ 'he *set his mind on* departure,' or with the locative. तन् मह्यं रोचते 'that *is pleasing to* me;' शिष्येभ्यः प्रवक्ष्यामि तत् 'I will *declare* this to my pupils;' सर्वं राज्ञे विज्ञापयति 'he *makes known* all to the king,' these are also joined with the genitive of the person. अमृतत्वाय कल्पते 'he is *rendered fit for* immortality;' प्रभवति मम वधाय 'he *has the power* to kill me;' तान् मातुर् वधाय अचोदयत् 'he *incited* them to the murder of their mother;' पुत्राय क्रुध्यति 'he is *angry* with his son.'

Ablative after the Verb.

854. All verbs may take an ablative of 'the object' from which any thing proceeds, or arises, or is produced; as, भ्रश्यति वृक्षात् पत्रं 'the leaf *falls* from the tree;' रुधिरं स्रवति गात्रात् 'blood *flows* from the body;' आसनाद् उत्तिष्ठति 'he *rises* from his seat;' मृत्पिण्डतः (719) कर्त्ता कुरुते यद्यद् इच्छति 'from the lump of clay the artist *makes* whatever he wishes;' विनयाद् याति पात्रतां 'from education a person *attains* capacity;' निर्जगाम नगरात् 'he *went* out from the city.'

855. Verbs of *fearing* are joined with the ablative, and sometimes with the genitive; as, साधुर् न तथा मृत्योर् बिभेति यथा अनृतात् 'a good man does not *fear* death so much as falsehood;' मा शब्दाद् बिभीत 'be not *afraid* of a noise;' दण्डाद् उद्विजते जगत् 'the whole world *stands in awe* of punishment;' दक्षिणस्य ते कृतपश्चात्तापस्य बिभेमि 'I *fear* thee, a cunning penitent;' see 859.

856. Verbs which express *superiority* or *comparison* govern an ablative; as, प्रापणात् कामानां परित्यागो विशिष्यते 'the abandonment of pleasure is *superior* to (better than) the possession.'

a. Other examples of verbs followed by ablative cases are, प्रासादाद् अवरोहति 'he *descends from* the palace;' विष्णुः स्वर्गाद् अवततार 'Vishṇu *descended from* heaven;' कनकमूत्रम् अङ्गाद् अवतारयति 'he *takes off* (causes to descend) the golden bracelet from his body;' निवर्त्तते पापात् 'he *ceases from* wickedness;' वचनाद् विरराम 'he *left off* speaking;' नरकात् पितरं त्रायते पुत्रो धार्म्मिकः 'a virtuous son *saves* his father from hell;' अश्वमेधसहस्रात् सत्यम् अतिरिच्यते 'truth *is superior to* a thousand sacrifices;' स्वहितात् प्रमाद्यति 'he *neglects* his own interest;' मित्रम् अकुशलाद् निवारयति 'a friend *guards* one from evil.'

Genitive after the Verb.

857. The genitive in Sanskṛit is constantly interchangeable with the dative, locative, or even accusative*. It is more especially, however, used to supply the place of the first of these cases, so that

* This vague use of the genitive to express 'various relations' prevails also in early Greek.

almost all verbs may take a genitive as well as dative of 'the object' to which any thing is imparted. For example, दरिद्रस्य धनं ददाति 'he *gives* money to the poor.'

858. It may be used for the locative after verbs of *consigning*, as निक्षेपं मम समर्पयति 'he *deposits* a pledge with me;' or of *trusting*, as न कश्चित् स्त्रीणां श्रद्दधाति 'nobody puts *trust* in women:' and for the accusative in examples such as अचिन्तितानि दुःखानि आयान्ति देहिनां 'unexpected ills *come* upon corporeal beings.'

859. It is sometimes used after verbs of *fearing;* as, तस्य किं न भेष्यसि 'Why art thou not *afraid* of him?' see 855. Also after verbs of *longing for, desiring, envying;* as, अवमानस्य आकांक्षेत् 'he should *desire* contempt;' स्पृहयामि पुरुषाणां सचक्षुषां 'I *envy* men who possess eyes.'

a. Other examples of verbs followed by genitive cases are, अजानताम् अस्माकं ख्यापय कस्य असि भार्य्या '*tell* us, who are ignorant of it, whose wife you are;' कस्य (for कस्मात्) बिभ्यति धार्म्मिकाः 'Of whom are the righteous *afraid?*' यद् अन्यस्य प्रतिजानीते न तद् अन्यस्य दद्यात् 'one should not *give* to one what one *promises* to another;' मम न शृणोति 'he does not *hear* me' (cf. the Greek usage); मम स्मरेः '*remember* me,' or with the accusative. अस्माकं मृत्युः प्रभवति 'death *overcomes* us;' अग्निर् न तृप्यति काष्ठानां 'fire is not *satisfied with* fuel;' तेषां क्षमेथाः '*forgive* them.'

Locative after the Verb.

860. This case is very widely applicable, but, as elsewhere remarked, is frequently interchangeable with the dative and genitive. The first sense of the locative requires that it should be united with verbs in reference only to 'the place' or 'time' in which any thing is done; as, पङ्के मज्जति 'he *sinks* in the mud;' पुरे वसति 'he *dwells* in the city;' रणमूर्द्ध्नि तिष्ठति 'he *stands* in the front of the fight;' सूर्य्योदये प्रबुध्यते 'at sunrise he *awakes.*'

861. The transition from 'the place' to 'the object' or 'recipient' of any action is natural; and hence it is that verbs are found with the locative of 'the object' to which any thing is imparted or communicated, as in the following examples: मा प्रयच्छ ईश्वरे धनं '*bestow* not money on the mighty;' तस्मिन् कार्य्याणि निक्षिपामि 'I *entrust* my affairs to him;' पुत्रे अङ्गुरीयकं समर्पयति 'he *consigns* a ring to his son;' योग्ये सचिवे न्यस्यति राज्यभारं 'he *entrusts* the burden of the kingdom to a capable minister;' राज्ञि or राजकुले निवेदयति 'he *informs* the king;' प्रेतं भूमौ निदध्यात् 'one should *place* (bury) a dead man in the ground;' धर्म्मे मनो दधाति 'he *applies* his mind to virtue.'

a. In this sense कृ is used; as, पृष्ठे इन्धनम् अकरोत् 'he *placed* the wood on his back;' मतिं पापे करोति 'he *applies* his mind to sin.'

862. When दा, 'to give,' is used for 'to put,' it follows the same analogy; as,

तस्य पुच्छाग्रे हस्तं देहि '*put* your hand on the end of its tail;' भस्मचये पदं ददौ 'he *placed* his foot on a heap of ashes.' Similarly, वस्त्राञ्चले धृतोऽस्ति 'he was *held* by the skirt of his garment.' So also verbs of *seizing, striking*; as, केशेषु गृह्णाति or आकृषति 'he *seizes* or *drags* him by the hair;' सुप्ते प्रहरति 'he *strikes* a sleeping man.'

863. The locative is often put for the dative in sentences where the latter case stands for the infinitive; thus, भर्तुर् अन्वेषणे त्वरस्व '*hasten* to seek thy spouse;' नलस्य आनयने यतस्व '*strive* to bring Nala hither;' न शेकुम् तस्य धनुषो ग्रहणे 'they could not *hold* that bow.'

a. Other examples are, उग्रे तपसि वर्त्तते 'he is *engaged in* a very severe penance;' परकार्य्येषु मा व्यापृतो भूः 'do not *busy yourself* about other people's affairs;' विषयेषु सज्यते 'he is *addicted to* objects of sense;' सर्व्वलोकहिते रमते 'he *delights in* the good of all the world;' दुर्गाधिकारे नियुज्यते 'he is *appointed to* the command of the fort;' द्वौ वृषभौ धुरि नियोजयति 'he *yokes* two bulls to the pole;' सैनापत्ये अभिषिञ्च मां '*anoint* me to the generalship;' यतते पापनिग्रहे 'he *strives to* suppress evil-doers.'

b. न मद्विधे युज्यते वाक्यम् ईदृशं 'such language is not *suited* to a person like me;' प्रभुत्वं त्वयि प्रयुज्यते 'sovereignty is *suited* to you;' आसने उपाविशत् 'he *reclined* on a seat;' बृष्याम् आसस्व '*sit* thou on a cushion;' शत्रुषु विश्वसिति 'he *confides* in his enemies;' चरणयोः पतति 'it *falls* at his feet;' लुठति पादेषु 'it *rolls* at the feet.'

Change of case after the same Verb.

864. This sometimes occurs; as, विधुरो धृतराष्ट्राय कुन्ती च गान्धार्य्याः सर्व्वं न्यवेदयेतां 'Vidhura and Kuntí *announced* every thing, the one to Dhṛitaráshṭra, the other to Gándhárí' (Astraśikshá 34), where the same verb governs a dative and genitive. Similarly, in the Hitopadeśa, शृङ्गिणां विश्वासो न कर्त्तव्यः स्त्रीषु च 'confidence is not to be *placed* in horned animals or women.'

INSTRUMENTAL CASE AFTER PASSIVE VERBS.

865. The prevalence of a passive construction is the most remarkable feature in the syntax of this language. Passive verbs are joined with 'the agent, instrument, or cause,' in the instrumental case *, and agree with 'the object' in number and person; as, वातेन रज उद्धूयते 'the dust is raised by the wind;' तेन सर्व्वद्रव्याणि सज्जीक्रियन्तां 'let all things be prepared by him;' इषुभिर् आदित्योऽन्तरधीयत 'the sun was concealed by arrows.'

866. But the passive participle usually takes the place of the *past tenses* of the passive verb, and agrees with 'the object' in *gender* and *case* as well as number;

* There are a few instances of the agent in the genitive case; as, मम कृतं पापं 'a crime committed by me,' for मया.

as, नेत्राणि समाप्लुतानि वारिणा '(their) eyes were suffused with tears;' तेन उक्तं (इदं being understood) 'it was said by him.' Compare 895.

a. This instrumental construction after passive verbs is a favourite idiom in Sanskṛit prose composition, and the love for it is remarkably displayed in such phrases as the following: दुःखेन गम्यते, 'he is gone to by misery,' for दुःखं गच्छति; and आगम्यतां देवेन, 'let it be come by your majesty,' for आगच्छतु देवः; and again, अस्माभिर् एकत्र स्थीयतां, 'let it be remained by us in one spot,' for 'let us remain in one spot;' येन मार्गेण इष्टं तेन गम्यतां 'by whatever road it is desired, by that let it be gone.'

b. Active or causal verbs, which take a double accusative, will retain one accusative when constructed passively; but the other accusative passes into a nominative case: thus, instead of स मां परुषाणि उवाच, 'he addressed me in harsh words,' may be written तेन अहं परुषाणि उक्तः, 'by him I was addressed in harsh words.'

SYNTAX OF THE INFINITIVE MOOD.

867. The infinitive in Sanskṛit cannot be employed with the same latitude as in other languages. Its use is very limited, corresponding to that of the Latin *supines*, as its termination *um* indicates.

a. Let the student, therefore, accurately distinguish between the infinitive of Sanskṛit and that of Latin and Greek. In these languages we have the infinitive made the subject of a proposition; or, in other words, standing in the place of a nominative, and an accusative case often admissible before it. We have it also assuming different forms, to express present, past, or future time, and completeness or incompleteness in the progress of the action. The Sanskṛit infinitive, on the other hand, can never be made the subject or nominative case to a verb, admits of no accusative before it, and can only express indeterminate time and incomplete action. Wherever it occurs it must always be considered as the object, and never the subject, of some verb expressed or understood. And, as the object of the verb, it may be regarded as equivalent to an indeclinable substantive, in which the force of two cases, an accusative and dative *, is inherent, and which differs from other substantives in its power of governing a case. Its use as a substantive, with the force of the *accusative* case, corresponds to one use of the Latin infinitive; thus, तत् सर्वं श्रोतुम् इच्छामि 'I desire to hear all that,' '*id audire cupio*,' where श्रोतुं and *audire* are both equivalent to accusative cases, themselves also governing an accusative. Similarly, रोदितुं प्रवृत्ता 'she began to weep;' and महीं जेतुम् आरेभे 'he began to conquer the earth,' where महीजयम् आरेभे, 'he began the conquest of the earth,' would be equally correct.

---

* Bopp considers the termination of the infinitive to be the accusative of the affix तु (459. *a*); and it is certain that in the Vedas an irregular infinitive in तवे and तवै is found, which would seem to be the dative of the same affix. See Pāṇini III. 4. 9.

868. But the Sanskṛit infinitive most commonly involves a sense which belongs especially to the Sanskṛit dative, viz. that of 'the end' or 'purpose' for which any thing is done; thus, शावकान् भक्षितुम् आगच्छति 'he comes to devour the young ones;' शत्रून् योद्धुं सैन्यं प्राहिणोत् 'he sent an army to fight the enemy.'

a. In these cases it would be equally correct in Sanskṛit to substitute for the infinitive the dative case of the verbal noun, formed with the affix *ana;* thus, भक्षणाय, 'for the eating,' for भक्षितुं; योधनाय, 'for the fighting,' for योद्धुं; and in Latin the infinitive could not be used at all, but either the supine, *devoratum, pugnatum*, or, still more properly, the conjunction with the subjunctive mood, '*ut devoret*,' '*ut pugnarent*.' The following are other examples in which the infinitive has a dative force in expressing 'the purpose' of the action: पानीयं पातुं नदीम् अगमत् 'he went to the river to drink water;' मम बन्धनं छेत्तुम् उपसर्पति 'he comes to cut asunder my bonds;' मां त्रातुं समर्थः (अस्ति being understood) 'he is able to rescue me;' पाशान् संचरितुं सयत्नो बभूव 'he busied himself about collecting together the snares.'

869. The Sanskṛit infinitive, therefore, has more of the character of a supine than an infinitive; and in its character of supine is susceptible of either an active or passive signification. In its passive character, however, like the Latin *supine* in *u*, it is joined with certain words only, the most usual being the passive verbs शक् 'to be able' and युज् 'to be fitting,' and their derivatives; thus, त्यक्तुं न शक्यते 'it cannot be abandoned;' पाशो न छेत्तुं शक्यते 'the snare cannot be cut;' न शक्याः समाधातुं ते दोषाः 'those evils cannot be remedied;' श्रोतुं न युज्यते 'it is not fitting to be heard;' छेत्तुम् अयोग्यः 'unfit to be cut;' त्वया न युक्तम् अवमानम् अस्य कर्तुं 'contempt is not proper to be shown by thee for him.'

a. The following are other instances: मण्डपः कारयितुम् आरब्धः 'the shed was begun to be built;' राज्ये अभिषेक्तुं भवान् निरूपितः 'your honour has been selected to be inaugurated to the kingdom;' अर्हति कर्तुं 'it deserves to be done' (Naiśadiya V. 112); कर्तुम् अनुचितं 'improper to be done' (cf. *factu indignum* and *ποιεῖν αἰσχρόν*); सा मोचयितुं न्याय्या 'she ought to be released.'

870. The root अर्ह् 'to deserve,' when used in combination with an infinitive, is usually equivalent to 'an entreaty' or 'respectful imperative;' as, धर्मान् नो वक्तुम् अर्हसि 'deign (or simply 'be pleased') to tell us our duties.' It sometimes has the force of the Latin *debet;* as, न मादृशी त्वाम् अभिभाषुम् अर्हति 'such a person as I ought not to address you;' न एनं शोचितुम् अर्हसि 'you ought not to bewail him.'

871. The infinitive is sometimes joined with the noun काम, 'desire,' to form a kind of compound adjective, expressive of 'the wish' to do any thing, but the

final *m* is then rejected; thus, द्रष्टुकामः, -मा, -मं, 'desirous of seeing;' जेतुकामः, -मा, -मं, 'wishing to conquer.'

a. In the 2d Act of Vikramorvaśí the infinitive is joined in the same way with मनस्; thus, स द्रष्टुमनाः 'he has a mind to see.'

872. When *kim* follows the infinitive a peculiar transposition sometimes takes place, of which the 1st Act of S'akuntalá furnishes an example; thus, सखीं ते ज्ञातुम् इच्छामि किम् अनया वैखानसं व्रतं निषेवितव्यं, 'I wish to know thy friend, whether this monastic vow is to be observed by her,' for ज्ञातुम् इच्छामि किं सख्या ते &c. 'I wish to know whether this vow is to be observed by thy friend.'

USE AND CONNEXION OF THE TENSES.

873. PRESENT TENSE.—This tense, besides its proper use, is often used for the future; as, क्व गच्छामि 'Whither shall I go?' कदा त्वां पश्यामि 'When shall I see thee?' किं करोमि 'What shall I do?' and sometimes for the imperative; as, तत् कुर्मस् 'let us do that.'

874. In *narration* it is commonly used for the past tense; as, स भूमिं स्पृष्ट्वा कर्णौ स्पृशति ब्रूते च 'he, having touched the ground, touches his ears, and says.'

875. It may denote 'habitual' or 'repeated' action; as, मृगः प्रत्यहं तत्र गत्वा शस्यं खादति 'the deer going there every day was in the habit of eating the corn;' यदा स मूषिक-शब्दं शृणोति तदा विडालं संवर्द्धयति 'whenever he heard the noise of the mouse, then he would feed the cat.'

876. It is usually found after यावत् and तावत्; as, यावन् मे दन्ता न त्रुट्यन्ति तावत् तव पाशं छिनद्मि 'as long as my teeth do not break, so long will I gnaw asunder your fetters.' (Compare the use of the Latin *dum.*)

877. The present tense of the root आस्, 'to sit,' 'to remain,' is used with the present participle of another verb, to denote 'continuous' or 'simultaneous' action; as, पशूनां वधं कुर्वन् आस्ते 'he keeps making a slaughter of the beasts;' मम पश्चाद् आगच्छन् आस्ते 'he is in the act of coming after me.'

878. The particle स्म, when used with the present, gives it the force of a perfect; as, प्रविशन्ति स्म पुरीं 'they entered the city;' निवसन्ति स्म 'they dwelt.'

879. POTENTIAL.—The name of this tense is no guide to its numerous uses. Perhaps its most common force is that of 'fitness' in phrases, where in Latin we should expect to find *oportet* with the infinitive; as, आगतं भयं वीक्ष्य नरः कुर्य्याद् यथोचितं 'having beheld danger actually present, a man should act in a becoming manner.'

880. It is also employed, as might be expected, in indefinite general expressions; as, यस्य यो भावः स्यात् 'whatever may be the disposition of any one;' यदा राजा स्वयं न कुर्य्यात् कार्य्य-दर्शनं 'when the king may not himself make investigation of the case;' अप्राप्त-काल-वचनं ब्रुवन् प्राप्नुयाद् अपमानं 'by uttering unseasonable words one may meet with dishonour.'

a. Especially in conditional sentences; as, यदि राजा दण्डं न प्रणयेत् स्वाम्यं कस्मिंश्चिन् न स्यात् सर्व्वसेतवश्च भिद्येरन् 'if the king were not to inflict punishment, ownership would remain with nobody, and all barriers would be broken down.' Sometimes the conjunction is omitted; as, न भवेत् 'should it not be so;' न स्यात् पराधीनः 'were he not subject to another.'

881. The potential often occurs as a softened imperative, this language, in common with others in the East, being averse to the more abrupt form; thus, गच्छेः, 'do thou go,' for गच्छ; and अद्यात् फलानि, 'let him eat fruits,' for अत्तु.

882. IMPERATIVE.—This tense yields the usual force of 'command' or 'entreaty;' as, आश्वसिहि 'take courage;' माम् अनुस्मर 'remember me.' मा, and not न, must be used in prohibition; as, अनृतं मा ब्रूहि 'do not tell a falsehood;' मा लज्जस्व 'be not ashamed;' see 889. The first person is used to express 'necessity,' see example at 796.

a. The 3d pers. singular is sometimes used interjectionally; thus, भवतु 'Be it so!' 'Well!' यातु 'Let it go!' 'Come along!' 'Come!'

883. It is sometimes employed in conditional phrases to express 'contingency;' as, अनुजानीहि मां गच्छामि 'permit me, (and) I will go,' i.e. 'if you will permit me, I will go;' आज्ञापय हन्मि दुष्टजनं 'if you command me, I will kill the villain;' अभयवाचं मे यच्छ गच्छामि 'if you give me a promise of security, I will go.'

884. FIRST PRETERITE.—Although this tense properly has reference to 'past incomplete action' (see 242), and has been so rendered in the examples given at pp. 198—267, yet it is most commonly used to denote 'indefinite past time,' without any necessary connexion with another action; as, अर्थं ग्रहीतुं यत्नम् अकरवं 'I made an effort to collect wealth,' not necessarily 'I was making.'

885. SECOND PRETERITE.—As observed at 242, this tense is properly used to express 'an action done at some definite period of past time;' as, कौशल्यादयो नृपतिं दशरथं चक्रन्दुः 'Kauśalyá and the others bewailed king Daśaratha.' It is frequently, however, employed indeterminately.

886. FIRST FUTURE.—This tense expresses 'definite futurity;' as, तासु दिक्षु कामस्य फलं लब्धासि 'in those regions thou shalt obtain the fruit of thy desire;' but is not so frequently found as the second future.

887. SECOND FUTURE.—This tense, although properly indefinite, is employed to express 'all degrees and kinds of futurity,' immediate or remote, definite or indefinite; as, स्वादु पयः पास्यसि 'thou shalt

drink sweet water;' तत्र अवश्यं पत्नीं द्रक्ष्यति 'there certainly he will see his wife.'

a. It is sometimes used for the imperative; as, यद् देयं तद् दास्यसि 'whatever is to be given, that you will give,' (do thou give.)

888. THIRD PRETERITE.—This tense properly expresses 'time indefinitely past;' as, अभूत् नृपः 'there lived (in former times) a king;' see 242.

889. It is also employed to supply the place of the imperative, after the prohibitive particle मा or मास्म, the augment being omitted; as, मा कृथाः 'do not make;' मा त्याक्षीः समयं 'do not lose the opportunity;' मास्म अनृतं वादीः 'do not tell an untruth;' मा क्रुधः 'do not be angry;' मा शुचः 'do not grieve;' मा हिंसीः 'do not injure;' मा भैषीः 'be not afraid.'

890. BENEDICTIVE.—Only one example of this tense occurs in the Hitopadeśa: नित्यं भूयात् सकल-सुख-वसतिः 'May he constantly be the abode of all happiness!' It is chiefly used in pronouncing benedictions. Also in imprecations.

a. In the latter case a noun formed with an affix *ani* is frequently used; thus, अजीवनिस् ते भूयात् 'May there be loss of life to thee!' 'Mayst thou perish!'

891. CONDITIONAL.—This tense is even less frequent than the last. It is used in conditional propositions, as illustrated by the following example from Manu: यदि राजा दण्डं न प्रणयेत् तदा शूले मत्स्यान् इव अपक्ष्यन् दुर्बलान् बलवत्तराः 'if the king were not to inflict punishment, then the stronger would roast the weak like fish on a spit;' or, according to the Scholiast, हिंसाम् अकरिष्यन् 'would cause injury.'

SYNTAX OF PARTICIPLES.

892. Participles in Sanskṛit often discharge the functions of the tenses of verbs. They are constantly found occupying the place of past and future tenses, and more especially of passive verbs, insomuch that an instance of a passive in any other tense than the present or imperative rarely occurs.

893. Participles govern the cases of the verbs whence they are derived; as, व्याधं पश्यन् 'seeing the fowler;' अरण्ये चरन् 'walking in the forest;' तत् कृतवान् 'he did that;' शब्दम् आकर्ण्य 'having heard a noise;' पानीयम् अपीत्वा गतः 'he went away without drinking water.'

a. In the case of passive participles, as will presently appear, the agent is put in the instrumental case; and the participle agrees with the object, like an adjective.

Present Participles.

894. These are not so commonly used in Sanskṛit composition as past and future participles, but they are often idiomatically employed,

especially where in English the word 'while' or 'whilst' is introduced; thus, अहं दक्षिणारण्ये चरन् अपश्यं 'whilst walking in the southern forest, I beheld,' &c.

Past Passive Participle.

895. This most useful participle is constantly used to supply the place of a perfect tense passive, sometimes in conjunction with the auxiliary verbs *as* and *bhú*, 'to be;' thus, आदिष्टोऽस्मि 'I am commanded;' वयं विस्मिताः स्मः 'we are astonished' (compare 866). Of course the participle is made to agree adjectively with the object in gender, number, and case, as in Latin; and the agent, which in English would probably be in the nominative, and in Latin in the ablative, becomes in Sanskṛit instrumental. Thus, in Sanskṛit, the phrase 'I wrote a letter' would not be so idiomatically expressed by अहं पत्रं लिलेख, as by मया पत्रं लिखितं or मया पत्रं लिखितं आसीत् 'by me a letter was written,' '*a me epistola scripta.*' So again, तेन बन्धनानि छिन्नानि 'by him the bonds were cut' is more idiomatic than स बन्धनानि चिच्छेद 'he cut the bonds;' and तेन उक्तं 'by him it was said' is more usual than स उवाच 'he said *.'

896. But frequently the past passive participle is used as an active past participle; in which case it may sometimes govern the accusative case, like a perfect tense active; thus, स वृक्षम् आरूढः 'he ascended the tree;' स गृहं गतः or आगतः 'he went home;' वर्त्म तीर्णः 'having crossed the road;' अहं पदवीम् अवतीर्णोऽस्मि 'I have descended to the road;' अहं नगरीम् अनुप्राप्तः 'I reached the city;' आवाम् आश्रमं प्रविष्टौ स्वः 'we two have entered the hermitage.' But observe, that its active use is generally, though not invariably, restricted to verbs which involve the idea of 'motion,' and to a few neuter verbs. The following are other examples: पक्षिण उत्पतिताः 'the birds flew away;' स मृतः 'he died;' व्याधो निवृत्तः 'the fowler returned;' स भक्षयितुं प्रवृत्तः 'he proceeded to eat;' स प्रसुप्तः 'he fell asleep;' ते स्थिताः 'they stood.'

a. Occasionally this participle is susceptible of a present signification; thus, स्थित 'stood' may sometimes be translated 'standing,' and भीत 'fearing.'

b. The neuter of the passive participle is sometimes used as a substantive; thus, दत्तं 'a gift;' खातं 'an excavation;' अन्नं 'food;' दुग्धं 'milk.'

---

* This instrumental or passive construction, which is so prevalent in Sanskṛit, has been transferred from it to Hindí, Maráthí, Guzerátí, and other dialects of India. The particle *ne* in Hindí and Hindústání corresponds most clearly to the Sanskṛit न *na*, the final letter of the commonest termination for the instrumental case; and this particle can never occasion any difficulty if so regarded.

Active Past Participle.

897. This participle is much used (especially in modern Sanskṛit and the writings of commentators) to supply the place of a perfect tense active. It may govern the case of the verb; as, सर्व्वं श्रुतवान् 'he heard every thing;' पत्नी पतिम् आलिङ्गितवती 'the wife embraced her husband;' राज्ञो हस्ते फलं दत्तवान् 'he gave the fruit into the hand of the king;' तत् कृतवती 'she did that.' This participle may also be used with the auxiliaries *as* and *bhú*, 'to be,' to form a compound perfect tense; thus, तत् कृतवान् अस्ति 'he has done that;' तत् कृतवान् भविष्यति 'he will have done that.'

Indeclinable Past Participles.

898. The sparing use made in Sanskṛit composition of relative pronouns, conjunctions, and connective particles, is mainly to be attributed to these participles, by means of which the sense of a clause may be suspended, and sentence after sentence strung together without the aid of a single copulative. They occur in narration more commonly than any other kind of participle; and some of the chief peculiarities of Sanskṛit syntax are to be traced to the frequency of their occurrence.

899. They are generally used for the past tense, as united with a copulative conjunction, and are usually translatable by the English 'having,' 'when,' 'after,' 'by,' see 555; thus, तद् आकर्ण्य निश्चितम् एव अयं कुक्कुर इति मत्वा छागं त्यक्त्वा स्नात्वा स्वगृहं ययौ 'having heard this, having thought to himself "this is certainly a dog," having abandoned the goat, having bathed, he went to his own house.' In all these cases we should use in English the past tense with a conjunction; thus, 'When he had heard this, he thought to himself that it must certainly be a dog. He then abandoned the goat, and, when he had bathed, went to his own house.'

a. It is evident from the above example that the indeclinable participles often stand in the place of a pluperfect tense, a tense which does not really exist in Sanskṛit.

b. But although they always refer to something past, it should be observed that they are frequently rendered in English by the present participle, as in the fifth sentence of the story at 930.

900. Another, though less frequent, use of them is as gerunds in *do*; thus, नराः शास्त्राण्य् अधीत्य* भवन्ति पण्डिताः 'men become wise *by* reading the S'ástras;'

* As the Latin gerund is connected with the future participle in *dus*, so the Sanskṛit indeclinable participle in *ya* is connected with the future passive participle in *ya*.

भार्य्या अप्य् अकार्य्य-शतं कृत्वा भर्त्तव्या 'a wife is to be supported even *by* doing a hundred wrong things;' किं पौरुषं हत्वा सुप्तं 'What bravery is there *in* killing a sleeping man?'

901. The termination त्वा *twá* of this participle is probably the instrumental case of the same affix of which the infinitive termination (*um*) is the accusative; see 459. *a*. There can be little doubt that the indeclinable participle bears about it much of the character of an instrumental case. It is constantly found in grammatical connexion with the agent in this case; thus, सर्व्वैः पशुभिर् मिलित्वा सिंहो विज्ञप्तः 'by all the beasts having met together the lion was informed;' सर्व्वैर् जालम् आदाय उड्डीयतां 'by all having taken up the net let it be flown away.'

a. Another and perhaps stronger proof of its instrumental character is, that the particle अलं, which always governs the instrumental case, is not unfrequently joined with the indeclinable participle; thus, अलं भोजनेन, 'enough of eating,' is with equal correctness of idiom expressed by अलं भुक्त्वा; see 918. *a*.

Future Passive Participles.

902. The usual sense yielded by this participle is that of 'fitness,' 'obligation,' 'necessity' (see 568); and the usual construction required is, that the agent on whom the duty or necessity rests be in the instrumental case, and the participle agree with the object; as, त्वया प्रवृत्तिर् न विधेया 'by you the attempt is not to be made.'

a. Sometimes, however, the agent is in the genitive case; thus, द्विजातीनां भक्ष्यम् अन्नं 'boiled rice is to be eaten by Bráhmaṇs.' Compare 865, note.

903. Occasionally the future passive participle may yield a sense equivalent to 'worthy of,' 'deserving of;' thus, कश्य 'deserving a whipping;' ताडनीय 'worthy of being beaten;' मुसल्य 'deserving death by pounding;' वध्य 'worthy of death.'

904. If the verb govern two accusatives, one may be retained after the future passive participle; as, नयन-सलिलं त्वया शान्तिं नेयं 'the tear of the eye is to be brought to assuagement by thee.'

905. Occasionally the neuter of this participle is used impersonally; in which case it does not agree with the object, but may govern it in the manner of the verb; thus, मया ग्रामं गन्तव्यं, 'it is to be gone by me to the village,' for मया ग्रामो गन्तव्यः. So also, त्वया सभां प्रवेष्टव्यं 'by you it is to be entered into the assembly.'

a. The neuter भवितव्यं (from भू) is thus used, and, in accordance with 841, requires the instrumental after it, as well as before; thus, केनापि कारणेन भवितव्यं 'by something it must become the cause,' i. e. 'there must be some cause;' स्वामिना सविशेषेण भवितव्यं 'a ruler ought to be possessed of discrimination;' मया तव अनुचरेण भवितव्यं 'I must become your companion.'

906. Similarly, the neuter of शक्य may be adverbially used, and impart at the same time a passive sense to the infinitive; thus, पवनः शक्यम् आलिङ्गितुम् अङ्गैः for पवनः शक्यः &c. 'the breeze is able to be embraced by the limbs' (S'ak. Act III). Again, शक्यम् अञ्जलिभिः पातुं वाताः 'the breezes are able to be drunk

by the hollowed palms;' विभूतयः शक्यम् अवाप्तुं 'great successes are able to be obtained.'

907. It is not uncommon to find this participle standing merely in the place of a future tense, no propriety or obligation being implied, just as the past passive participle stands in the place of a past tense; thus, नूनम् अनेन लुब्धकेन मृगमांसार्थिना गन्तव्यं 'in all probability this hunter will go in quest of the deer's flesh,' where गन्तव्यं is used impersonally; त्वां दृष्ट्वा लोकैः किञ्चिद् वक्तव्यं 'when the people see you, they will utter some exclamation;' यदि पक्षी पतति तदा मया खादितव्यः 'if the bird falls, then it shall be eaten by me.' See also the eleventh sentence of the story at 930.

908. The neuter of this participle is sometimes used infinitively or substantively, as expressive merely of 'the indeterminate action' of the verb, without implying 'necessity' or 'fitness.' In such cases इति may be added; thus, वञ्चयितव्यम् इति 'the being about to deceive;' मर्त्तव्यम् इति 'the being about to die:' but not always; as, जीवितव्यं 'life.'

Participial Nouns of Agency.

909. The first of these nouns of agency (580) is constantly used in poetry as a substitute for the present participle; implying, however, 'habitual action,' and therefore something more than present time. They are sometimes found governing the same case as the present participle, but they are always united with the word which they govern in one compound; thus, पुरञ्जय 'city-conquering;' प्रियंवद 'speaking kind words;' जलेचर 'going in the water;' सरसिज 'lake-born.' The word which they govern is often in the crude base; thus, तेजस्कर, 'light-making' (see 69), from *tejas* and *kṛi*; मनोहर, 'mind-captivating,' from *manas* and *hṛi* (64); बहुद, 'giving much,' from *bahu* and *dá*; आत्मज्ञ, 'self-knowing,' from *átman* and *jñá* (57. *b*).

910. The second (581) is sometimes, but rarely, found as a participle governing the case of the verb; thus, वाक्यं वक्ता 'speaking a speech;' बहुमार्गगां वोढा 'bearing the Ganges.'

911. The first and second species of the third (582. *a*. *b*), like the first, have often the sense of present participles, and are then always united with the crude base of the word which they govern in one compound; thus, मनोहारिन्, 'mind-captivating,' from *manas* and *hṛi*; कार्य्यसाधक, 'effective of the business,' from *kárya* and *sidh*. They may sometimes govern the case of the verb whence they are derived, and may then be compounded, or not, with the word which they govern; thus, ग्रामेवासिन्, 'dwelling in a village,' or ग्रामे वासिन्; मुकुलानि चुम्बक 'kisser of the buds' (Ratnávali, p. 7).

SYNTAX OF CONJUNCTIONS, PREPOSITIONS, ADVERBS, &c.

Conjunctions.

912. च 'and' (727) is always placed after the word which it connects with another, like *que* in Latin, and can never stand first in a sentence, or in the same

place as 'and' in English; thus, परिक्रम्य अवलोक्य च 'walking round and looking.' Unlike *que*, however, which must always follow the word of which it is the copulative, it may be admitted to any other part of the sentence, being only excluded from the first place; thus, तनयम् अचिरात् प्राची इव अर्कं प्रसूय च पावनं 'and having after a short time given birth to a pure son, as the eastern quarter (gives birth to) the sun.'

a. Sometimes two *cha*'s are used, when one may be redundant or equivalent to the English 'both;' or the two *cha*'s may be employed antithetically or disjunctively, or to express the contemporaneousness of two events; thus, अहश्च रात्रिश्च 'Both day and night;' क्व हरिणकानां जीवितं च अतिलोलं क्व च शरास् ते 'Where on the one hand is the frail existence of fawns? Where on the other are thy arrows?' क्रन्दितुं च प्रवृत्ता स्त्रीसंस्थानं च ज्योतिर् उत्क्षिप्य एनां जगाम 'no sooner had she began to weep, than a shining apparition in female shape, having snatched her up, departed' (S'ak. Act V). Observe—When क्व, 'where?' is used as in the above example, it implies 'excessive incompatibility.'

b. Sometimes च is used as an emphatic particle, and not as a copulative; thus, किं च मया परिणीतपूर्वा 'Was she indeed married by me formerly?'

913. तथा 'so,' 'likewise' (727. *a*), frequently supplies the place of च; thus, अनागतविधाता च प्रत्युत्पन्नमतिस् तथा 'both Anágata-vidhátá and Pratyutpanna-matis' (names of the two fish in Hitop. book IV).

914. हि 'for,' तु 'but,' वा 'or' (727. *a*, 728. *a. b*), like च, are excluded from the first place in a sentence; thus, पूर्वावधीरितं श्रेयो दुःखं हि परिवर्त्तते 'for happiness formerly scorned turns to misery;' विपर्य्यये तु 'but on the contrary;' एनां त्यज वा गृहाण वा 'either abandon her or take her.'

915. यदि 'if' and चेत् 'if' (727. *b*) may govern the potential or conditional (see 891), but are also used with the indicative; thus, यदि जीवति भद्राणि पश्यति 'if he live, he will behold prosperity;' यदि मया प्रयोजनम् अस्ति 'if there is need of me;' तृष्णा चेत् परित्यक्ता को दरिद्रः 'If avarice were abandoned, who would be poor?'

Prepositions and Adverbs.

916. Of all the internal evidences of the antiquity of Sanskṛit, there is none more decisive than the sparing use which this language makes of prepositions, in expressing the dependence of one word upon another. Indeed, the employment of these aids to syntactical combination may be regarded as a result of modern refinement, incompatible with the simplicity of the most ancient languages. Thus, even the Greek, which is copiously provided with prepositions, made comparatively little use of them in the days of Homer, and was satisfied to express most of the relations of the words in a sentence by the cases of its nouns. But let it not be imagined that few prepositions exist in Sanskṛit. On the contrary, they exist in great abundance, as we have shown at 729. Of these, however, only three are generally used in government with nouns, viz. आ, प्रति, and अनु; the latter two being usually placed *after* the word which they govern. Examples will be found at 730.

a. Other examples of आ are, आ मणिबन्धनात् 'as far as the wrist;' आमृत्योस् 'till death;' आसमाप्तेस् 'to the completion;' आ व्रतस्य समापनात् 'till the completion of his vow;' आ शरीर विमोक्षणात् 'till his release from the body;' आजन्मनस् 'from birth.'

917. Adverbs are often used as prepositions, or rather *postpositions*, in government with nouns. The following examples illustrate their construction as described at 731.

a. न दण्डाद् ऋते शक्यः कर्तुं पाप विनिग्रहः 'the restraint of crime cannot be made without punishment;' शतं जन्मानि यावत् 'for a hundred births;' सर्प विवरं यावत् 'up to the serpent's hole;' पुत्रेण सह 'along with his son;' हेतुं विना 'without cause;' अपराधेन विना 'without fault;' विवराद् वहिर् निःसृत्य 'creeping out of the hole;' अवलोकन क्षणात् प्रभृति 'from the moment of seeing (him);' जन्मप्रभृति 'from birth;' ततः प्रभृति 'from that time forward;' उपनयनात् प्रभृति 'from the time of investiture;' धनस्य अर्थे, or more usually धनार्थे, 'for the sake of wealth;' तस्याः कृते or तत्कृते 'for her sake;' पुत्र हेतोस् 'for the sake of a son;' तन्निमित्ते 'on that account.' उपरि, with the genitive, occurs rather frequently, and with some latitude of meaning; thus, नाभेर् उपरि 'above the navel;' सिंहस् तस्य उपरि पपात 'the lion fell upon him;' मम उपरि विकारितः 'changed in his feelings towards me;' तव उपरि असदृश व्यवहारी 'not behaving properly towards thee;' पुत्रस्य उपरि क्रुद्धः 'angry with his son;' नाभेर् ऊर्द्ध्वं 'above the navel;' नाभेर् अधस्तात् 'below the navel;' वृक्षस्य अधस्तात् 'beneath the tree;' भोजनानन्तरं 'after eating;' राज्ञः समीपं 'near the king;' पितुः सकाशाद् धनम् आददाति 'he receives money from his father;' मांसं शुनोऽग्रे निक्षिप्तं 'flesh thrown before the dog;' मम समक्षं 'in my presence.' साक्षात् may take an instrumental; as, अन्यैः साक्षात् 'before others;' अस्माकं पश्चात् 'after us;' प्राङ् निवेदनात् 'before telling;' प्राग् उपनयनाद् 'before investiture;' भोजनात् प्राक् 'before eating;' स्नानात् पूर्वं 'before bathing;' विवाहात् पूर्वं 'before marriage.' प्राक् may take an accusative; as, प्राग् द्वादश समाः 'before twelve years are over;' अभिवादनात् परं 'after saluting;' तदवधेर् ऊर्द्ध्वं 'after that period;' संवत्सराद् ऊर्द्ध्वं 'after a year,' i. e. 'above a year having expired;' विवाहाद् अर्वाक् 'after marriage;' अर्वाक् सञ्चयनाद् अस्थ्नां 'after collecting the bones;' फलम् अन्तरेण 'without fruit;' भर्तुर् अनुमतिम् अन्तरेण 'without the consent of her husband;' वाटिकाया दक्षिणेन 'to the right of the garden;' प्राणि हिंसा व्यतिरेकेण 'without injury to living beings.'

918. अलं, 'enough,' is used with the instrumental, with the force of a prohibitive particle; as, अलं शङ्कया 'away with fear,' 'do not fear.'

a. It is also used with the indeclinable participle; as, अलं विचार्य 'enough of consideration;' see also 901. *a.*

b. It is sometimes followed by an infinitive; as, न अलम् अस्मि हृदयं निवर्तयितुं 'I am not able to turn back my heart.'

919. मात्रं 'even,' 'merely,' when compounded with another word is declinable;

as, उत्तरमात्रं न ददाति 'he does not even give an answer;' न शब्दमात्राद् भेतव्यं 'one ought not to be afraid of mere noise;' शब्दमात्रेण 'by mere sound;' वचनमात्रेण 'by mere words.'

920. तथा and यथा, when used as correlatives, are equivalent to the English 'so that,' and the Latin *ita ut*; thus, यथा स्वामी जागर्त्ति तथा मया कर्त्तव्यं 'I must so act that my master awake,' i. e. 'I must do something to make my master awake.' So also, त्वं न जानासि यथा गृहरक्षां करोमि 'Do not you know that I keep watch in the house?'

a. ईदृशं, तादृशं, and यादृशं, may be used in the same way; thus, तादृशम् अनायुष्यं न किञ्चिद् विद्यते यादृशं परदारगमनं 'nothing is so opposed to length of life as attention to the wife of another.'

b. यत्, as well as यथा, is used for 'that;' thus, अयं नूतनो न्यायो यद् अरातिं हत्वा सन्तापः क्रियते 'this is a new doctrine, that having killed an enemy remorse should be felt.'

921. किं, 'why?' may often be regarded as a mark of interrogation which is not to be translated, but affects only the tone of voice in which a sentence is uttered; as, जातिमात्रेण किं कश्चित् पूज्यते 'Is any one honoured for mere birth?'

a. It sometimes has the force of 'whether;' as, ज्ञायतां किम् उपयुक्त एतावद् वर्त्तनं गृह्णाति अनुपयुक्तो वा 'let it be ascertained whether he is worthy to receive so large a salary, or whether he is unworthy;' मन्त्री वेत्ति किं गुणयुक्तो राजा न वा 'the minister knows whether the king is meritorious or not.'

922. वत् as an affix of comparison or similitude (724) may be compounded with a word in the crude base, which if uncompounded would be in the accusative case; thus, आत्मानं मृतवत् सन्दर्श्य 'showing himself as if dead;' आश्चर्यवद् इदं पश्यति 'he regards it as a wonder.'

923. The negative न is sometimes repeated to give intensity to an affirmation; thus, न न वक्ष्यति 'he will not not say' = वक्ष्यति एव 'he will certainly say.'

924. The indeclinable participle of *dis* with *ut* is sometimes used adverbially to express 'on account of,' 'with reference to,' 'towards,' and governs an accusative; thus, किम् उद्दिश्य 'On account of what?' तम् उद्दिश्य 'with reference to him.'

925. The indeclinable participle of रभ् with आ ('to begin') is used adverbially to express 'from,' 'beginning with,' and may either govern an ablative or be placed after the crude base; thus, निमन्त्रणाद् आरभ्य श्राद्धं यावत् 'from the time of invitation to the time of the S'ráddha.' निमन्त्रणारभ्य would be equally correct.

926. The interjections धिक् and हा require the accusative; as, धिक् पापिष्ठं 'Woe to the wretch!' and the vocative interjections the vocative case; as, भोः पान्थ 'O traveller!'

ON THE USE OF THE PARTICLE इति.

927. All the languages of the East are averse to the use of the *obliqua oratio*. In Sanskrit it is rarely admitted; and when any one relates the words or describes the sentiments or thoughts of

another, the relator generally represents him as speaking the actual words in his own person.

a. In such cases the particle इति (properly meaning 'so,' 'thus') is often placed after the words quoted, and may be regarded as serving the purpose of inverted commas; thus, शिष्या ऊचुः कृत-कृत्या वयम् इति 'the pupils said, "We have accomplished our object;"' not, according to the English or Latin idiom, 'the pupils said *that they had* accomplished their object.' So also, कलह-कारी इति ब्रूते भर्त्ता 'your husband calls you "quarrelsome,"' where कलह-कारी is in the nominative case, as being the actual word supposed to be spoken by the husband himself in his own person. So again, युष्मान् विश्वास-भूमय इति सर्वे पक्षिणो मम अग्रे प्रस्तुवन्ति 'all the birds praise you in my presence, saying, "He is an object of confidence,"' where the particle इति is equivalent to 'saying,' and the word विश्वास-भूमयः is not in the accusative, to agree with युष्मान्, as might be expected, but in the nominative, as being the actual word supposed to be uttered by the birds in their own persons. In some cases, however, the accusative is retained before इति, as in the following example from Manu: अज्ञं बालम् इत्य् आहुः 'they call an ignorant man "child."' But in the latter part of the same line it passes into a nominative; as, पितेत्य् एव तु मन्त्रदं 'but (they call) a teacher of scripture "father."' II. 153.

928. In narratives and dialogues इति is often placed redundantly at the end of a speech. Again, it may have reference merely to what is passing in the mind either of another person or of one's self. When so employed, it is usually joined with the indeclinable participle, or of some other part of a verb signifying 'to think,' 'to suppose,' &c., and may be translated by the English conjunction 'that,' to which, in fact, it may be regarded as equivalent; thus, मर्कटो घण्टां वादयति इति परिज्ञाय 'having ascertained *that* it is a monkey who rings the bell;' पुनर् अर्थ-वृद्धिः करणीया इति मतिर् बभूव 'his idea was *that* an increase of wealth ought again to be made;' धन्योऽहं यस्य एतादृशी भार्य्या इति मनसि निधाय 'reflecting in his mind *that* I am happy in possessing such a wife.' The accusative is also retained before इति in this sense; as, मृतम् इति मत्वा 'thinking that he was dead.' In all these examples the use of इति indicates that a quotation is made of the thoughts of the person at the time when the event took place.

929. Not unfrequently the participle 'saying,' 'thinking,' 'supposing,' &c., is omitted altogether, and इति itself involves the sense of such a participle; as, बालोऽपि न अवमन्तव्यो मनुष्य इति भूमिपः 'a king, even though a child, is not to be despised, *saying to one's self*, "He is a mortal;"' सौहार्दाद् वा विधुर इति वा मय्य् अनुक्रोशात् 'either through affection or through compassion towards me, *saying to yourself*, "What a wretched man he is;"' अयं वराहः । अयं शार्दूल इति वन-राजिषु आहिण्ड्यते 'There's a boar! Yonder's a tiger! *so crying out*, it is wandered about (by us) in the paths of the woods.'

CHAPTER X.

EXERCISES IN TRANSLATION AND PARSING.

STORIES FROM THE HITOPADEŚA TRANSLATED AND PARSED[1].

930. THE following two stories are taken from the 4th book of the Hitopadeśa. A literal translation and grammatical analysis are given to both stories. All the rules of combination are observed, but the words are separated from each other in accordance with 26. In the two cases where such separation is impossible, viz. where a final and initial vowel blend together into one sound, and where crude words are joined with others to form compounds, a dot placed underneath marks the division.

STORY OF THE SAGE AND THE MOUSE.

1st sentence. अस्ति गौतमस्य मुनेस् तपोवने महातपा नाम मुनिः। 'There is in the sacred grove of the sage Gautama a sage named Mahátapás (Great-devotion).'

2d. तेनाश्रमसन्निधाने मूषिकशावकः काकमुखाद् भ्रष्टो दृष्टः। 'By him, in the neighbourhood of his hermitage, a young mouse, fallen from the beak of a crow, was seen.'

3d. ततो दयायुक्तेन तेन मुनिना नीवारकणैः संवर्द्धितः। 'Then by that sage, touched with compassion, with grains of wild rice it was reared.'

4th. तदनन्तरं मूषिकं खादितुम् अनुधावन् विडालो मुनिना दृष्टः। 'Soon after this, a cat was observed by the sage running after the mouse to devour it.'

5th. तं मूषिकं भीतम् आलोक्य तपःप्रभावात् तेन मुनिना मूषिको बलिष्ठो विडालः कृतः। 'Perceiving the mouse terrified, by that sage, through the efficacy of his devotion, the mouse was changed into a very strong cat.'

6th. स विडालः कुक्कुराद् बिभेति। ततः कुक्कुरः कृतः। कुक्कुरस्य व्याघ्रान् महद् भयं। तदनन्तरं स व्याघ्रः कृतः। 'The cat fears the dog: upon that it was changed into a dog. Great is the dread of the dog for a tiger: then it was transformed into a tiger.'

7th. अथ व्याघ्रम् अपि मूषिकनिर्विशेषं पश्यति मुनिः । 'Now the sage regards even the tiger as not differing at all from the mouse.'

8th. अतः सर्वे तत्रस्था जनास् तं व्याघ्रं दृष्ट्वा वदन्ति । 'Then all the persons residing in the neighbourhood, seeing the tiger, say.'

9th. अनेन मुनिना मूषिकोऽयं व्याघ्रतां नीतः । 'By this sage this mouse has been brought to the condition of a tiger.'

10th. एतच् छ्रुत्वा स व्याघ्रः सव्यथोऽचिन्तयत् । 'The tiger overhearing this, being uneasy, reflected.'

11th. यावद् अनेन मुनिना जीवितव्यं तावद् इदं मम स्वरूपाख्यानम् अकीर्त्तिकरं न पलायिष्यते । 'As long as it shall be lived by this sage, so long this disgraceful story of my original condition will not die away.'

12th. इति समालोच्य मुनिं हन्तुं समुद्यतः । 'Thus reflecting, he prepared (was about) to kill the sage.'

13th. मुनिस् तस्य चिकीर्षितं ज्ञात्वा पुनर् मूषिको भव इत्य् उक्त्वा मूषिक एव कृतः । 'The sage discovering his intention, saying, "Again become a mouse," he was reduced to (his former state of) a mouse.'

Observe in this story four peculiarities: 1st, the simplicity of the style; 2dly, the prevalence of compound words; 3dly, the scarcity of verbs; 4thly, the prevalence of the past passive participle with the agent in the instrumental case for expressing indefinite past time, in lieu of the past tense active with the nominative: see 895, with note.

First sentence.—*Asti*, 'there is,' 3d sing. pres. of the root *as*, 2d conj. (see 584). *Gautamasya*, 'of Gautama,' noun of the first class, masc. gend., gen. case (103). *Munes*, 'of the sage,' noun of the second class, masc. gend., gen. case (110): final *s* remains by 62. *Tapovane*, 'in the sacred grove,' or 'grove of penance,' genitively dependent compound (743); the first member of the compound formed by the crude noun *tapas*, 'penance,' *as* being changed to *o* by 64; the last member, by the loc. case of *vana*, 'grove,' noun of the first class, neut. (104). *Mahátapá*, 'great devotion,' relative form of descriptive compound (766); the first member formed by the crude adjective *mahá* (substituted for *mahat*, see 778), 'great;' the last member, by the nom. case of *tapas*, 'devotion,' noun of the seventh class, neut. (164): final *s* dropped by 66. *a*. *Náma*, 'by name,' an adverb (713). *Munih*, 'a sage,' noun of the second class, masc., nom. case (110): final *s* passes into Visarga by 63. *a*.

Second sentence.—*Tena*, 'by him,' instr. case of the pronoun *tat* at 220. *Áśrama-sannidháne*, 'in the neighbourhood of his hermitage,' genitively dependent compound (743); the first member formed by the crude noun *áśrama*, 'hermitage;' the last member, by the loc. case of *sannidhána*, 'neighbourhood,' noun of the first class, neut. (104). The final *a* of *tena* blends with the initial *á* of *áśrama* by 31. *Múshika-śávakah*, 'a young mouse,' or 'the young of a mouse,' genitively dependent compound (743); the first member formed by the crude noun *múshika*, 'a mouse;' the last, by the nom. case of *śávaka*, 'the young of any animal,' noun of the first class (103): final *s* becomes Visarga by 63. *Káka-mukhád*, 'from the beak (or mouth) of a crow,' genitively dependent compound (743); the first member formed by the crude noun *káka*, 'a crow;' the last, by the abl. case of *mukha*, 'mouth,' noun of the first class, neut. (104); *t* being changed to *d* by 45. *Bhrashṭo*, 'fallen,' nom. case, sing. masc. of the past pass. part. of the root *bhranś* (544): *as* changed to *o* by 64. *Dṛishṭah*, 'seen,' nom. case, sing. masc. of the past pass. part. of the root *dṛiś*: final *s* becomes Visarga by 63. *a*.

Third sentence.—*Tato*, 'then,' adv. (719): *as* changed to *o* by 64. *Dayá-yuktena*, 'touched with compassion,' instrumentally dependent compound (740); the first member formed by the crude noun *dayá*, 'compassion;' the last, by the instr. case of *yukta*, 'endowed with,' past pass. part. of the root *yuj* (670). *Tena*, see second sentence. *Muniná*, 'by the sage,' noun of the second class, masc. gend., instr. case (110). *Nívára-kaṇaih*, 'with grains of wild rice,' genitively dependent compound (743); the first member formed by the crude noun *nívára*, 'wild rice;' the second, by the instr. plur. of *kaṇa*, noun of the first class, masc.: final *s* becomes Visarga by 63. *Sanvarddhitah*, 'reared,' nom. case, sing. of the past pass. part. of the causal form of the root *vṛidh* (549): final *s* becomes Visarga by 63. *a*.

Fourth sentence.—*Tadanantaram*, 'soon after this,' compound adverb; the first member formed with the pronoun *tat*, 'this,' at 220; the second, by the adverb *anantaram*, 'after,' at 731 and 917. *Múshikam*, noun of the first class, masc. gend., acc. case (103). *Kháditum*, 'to eat,' infinitive mood of the root *khád* (458, 868). *Anudhávan*, 'pursuing after,' 'running after,' nom. case, sing. masc. of the pres. part. Paras. of the root *dháv*, 'to run,' with the preposition *anu*, 'after' (524). *Viḍálo*, 'a cat,' noun of the first class, masc. (103), nom. case: *as* changed to *o* by 64. *Muniná*, see third sentence. *Dṛishṭah*, see second sentence.

Fifth sentence.—*Tam*, acc. case of the pronoun *tat* at 220, used as a definite article, see 795. *Múshikam*, see fourth sentence. *Bhítam*, 'terrified,' acc. case, sing. masc. of the past pass. part. of the root *bhí* (532). *Álokya*, 'perceiving,' indeclinable part. of the root *lok*, with the prep. *á* (559). *Tapah-prabhávát*, 'through the efficacy of his devotion' (814), genitively dependent compound (743); the first member formed by the crude noun *tapas*, 'devotion,' *s* being changed to Visarga by 63; the second, by the abl. case of *prabháva*, noun of the first class, masc. (103). *Tena*, see second sentence. *Muniná*, see third sentence. *Múshiko*, nom. case: *as* changed to *o* by 64. *Balishṭho*, 'very strong,' nom. case, masc. of the superlative form of the adj. *balin*, 'strong' (see 193): *as* changed to *o* by 64. *Viḍálah*, see fourth sentence: final *s* becomes Visarga by 63. *Kṛitah*, 'changed,' 'made,' nom. case, sing. of the past pass. part. of the root *kṛi* at 682: final *s* becomes Visarga by 63. *a*.

Sixth sentence.—*Sa*, nom. case of the pronoun *tat* at 220, used as a definite article (795): final *s* dropped by 67. *Viḍálah*, see fourth sentence. *Kukkurád*, 'the dog,' noun of the first class, masc. (103), abl. case after a verb of 'fearing' (855): *t* changed to *d* by 45. *Bibheti*, 'fears,' 3d sing. pres. tense of the root *bhí*, 3d conj. (666). *Tatah*, 'upon that,' adv. (719): *as* changed to *ah* by 63. *Kukkurah*, 'the dog,' nom. case (103): final *s* becomes Visarga by 63. *Kṛitah*, see fifth sentence. *Kukkurasya*, 'of the dog,' gen. case (103). *Vyághrán*, 'for the tiger,' noun of the first class, masc. (103), abl. case after a noun of 'fear' (814. *d*): *t* changed to *n* by 47. *Mahad*, 'great,' noun adj. of the fifth class (142), nom. case, sing. neut.: *t* changed to *d* by 45. *Bhayam*, 'fear,' noun of the first class, neut. (104), nom. case. *Tadanantaram*, see fourth sentence. *Vyághrah*, nom. case: final *s* becomes Visarga by 63. *Kṛitah*, see fifth sentence.

Seventh sentence.—*Atha*, 'now,' inceptive particle (727. *c*). *Vyághram*, acc. case. *Api*, 'even,' adv. *Múshika-nirviśesham*, 'as not differing at all from the mouse,' relative form of dependent compound (762); the first member formed by the crude noun *múshika*; the second, by the acc. case of the substantive *viśesha*, 'difference,' with *nir* prefixed: or it may be here taken adverbially, see 776. *Paśyati*, 3d sing. pres. tense of the root *dṛiś*, 1st conj. (604). *Munih*, see first sentence.

Eighth sentence.—*Atah*, 'then,' adv. (719). *Sarve*, 'all,' pronominal adj., nom. case, plur. masc. (237). *Tatra-sthá*, 'residing in the neighbourhood,' anomalous compound, in its character resembling a locatively dependent; the first member being formed by the adverb *tatra* (720), 'there,' or 'in that place;' the second, by the nom. plur. masc. of the participial noun of agency of the root *sthá*, 'to remain' (587): final *s* dropped by 66. *a*. *Janás*, 'persons,' noun of the first class, masc. gend. (103), nom. case, plur.: final *s* remains by 62. *Tam*, acc. case of the pronoun *tat* (220), used as a definite article (795). *Vyághram*, 'tiger,' noun of the first class, masc. gend. (103), acc. case. *Dṛishṭwá*, 'having seen,' indeclinable past participle of the root *dṛiś* (556). *Vadanti*, 'they say,' 3d plur. pres. of the root *vad*, 1st conj. (599).

Ninth sentence.—*Anena*, 'by this,' instr. case of the demonstrative pronoun *idam* at 224. *Muniná*, see third sentence. *Múshiko*, nom. case: *as* changed to *o* by 64. *a*. *Ayam*, 'this,' nom. case of the demonstrative pronoun at 224: the initial *a* cut off by 64. *a*. *Vyághratám*, 'the condition of a tiger,' fem. abstract noun of the first class (105), acc. case, formed from the substantive *vyághra*, 'a tiger,' by the affix *tá* (80. XXIII). *Nítah,* 'brought,' nom. case, sing. masc. of the past pass. part. of the root *ní* at 532.

Tenth sentence.—*Etach,* 'this,' acc. case, neut. of the demonstrative pronoun *etat* at 223: *t* being changed to *ch* by 49. *Chhrutwá,* 'overhearing,' indeclinable participle of the root *śru* (676 and 556). श्रुत्वा becomes छ्रुत्वा by 49. *Vyághrah,* nom. case: final *s* becomes Visarga by 63. *Sa-vyatho,* 'uneasy,' relative form of indeclinable compound, formed by prefixing the preposition *saha* to the fem. substantive *vyathá* (769): *as* changed to *o* by 64. *a.* *Achintayat,* 'reflected,' 3d sing. 1st pret. of the root *chint,* 10th conj. (641): the initial *a* cut off by 64. *a.*

Eleventh sentence.—*Yávad,* 'as long as,' adv. (713): *t* changed to *d* by 45. *Anena,* see ninth sentence. *Jívitavyam,* 'to be lived,' nom. case, neut. of the fut. pass. part. of the root *jív* (569, 905. *a,* 907). *Távat,* 'so long,' adv. correlative to *yávat* (713). *Idam,* 'this,' nom. case, neut. of the demonstrative pronoun at 224. *Mama,* 'of me,' gen. case of the pronoun *aham,* 'I,' at 218. *Swarúpákhyánam,* 'story of my original condition,' genitively dependent compound (743); the first member formed by the crude noun *swarúpa,* 'natural form' (see 232); the second, by the nom. case of *ákhyána,* noun of the first class, neuter (104): *m* retained by 60. *Akírti-karam,* 'disgraceful,' accusatively dependent compound (739); the first member formed by the crude noun *akírti,* 'disgrace;' the second, by the nom. case, neut. of the participial noun of agency *kara,* 'causing,' from *kṛi,* 'to do' (580). *Na,* 'not,' adv. (717. *a*). *Paláyishyate,* 'will die away,' 3d sing. 2d fut. Átm. of the compound verb *paláy,* formed by combining the root *i* with the prep. *pará* (783).

Twelfth sentence.—*Iti,* 'thus,' adv. (717. *e;* see also 928). *Samálochya,* 'reflecting,' indeclinable part. of the compound verb *samáloch* (559), formed by combining the root *loch* with the prepositions *sam* and *á* (784). *Munim,* acc. case. *Hantum,* 'to kill,' infinitive mood of the root *han* (458, 868, and 654). *Samudyatah,* 'prepared,' nom. case, sing. masc. of the past pass. part. of the compound verb *sam-ud-yam,* formed by combining the root *yam* with the prepositions *sam* and *ut* (545).

Thirteenth sentence.—*Munis,* nom. case: final *s* remains by 62. *Tasya,* 'of him,' gen. case of the pronoun *tat* (220). *Chikírshitam,* 'intention,' acc. case, neut. of the past pass. part. of the desiderative base of the root *kṛi,* 'to do' (550 and 502), used as a substantive (896. *b*). *Jñátwá,* 'discovering,' indeclinable part. of the root *jñá* (556 and 688). *Punar,* 'again,' adv. (717. *e*): *r* remains by 71. *e.* *Múshiko,* nom. case: *as* changed to *o* by 64. *Bhava,* 'become,' 2d sing. imperat. of the root *bhú* (585). *Ity* answers to inverted commas, see 927. *a:* the final *i* changed to *y* by 34. *Uktwá,* 'saying,' indeclinable part. of the root *vach* (556 and 650). *Múshika,* nom. case: final *s* dropped by 66. *Eva,* 'indeed,' adv. (717).

931. STORY OF THE BRÁHMAṆ AND HIS WEASEL.

अस्त्य् उज्जयिन्यां माधवो नाम ब्राह्मणः। तस्य ब्राह्मणी
प्रसूता। सा बालापत्यस्य रक्षार्थं ब्राह्मणम् अवस्थाप्य स्नातुं
गता। अथ ब्राह्मणस्य कृते राज्ञः पार्वणश्राद्धं दातुम्
आह्वानम् आगतं। तच् छ्रुत्वा ब्राह्मणः सहजदारिद्राद्
अचिन्तयत्। यदि सत्वरं न गच्छामि तदान्यः कश्चिच् छ्राद्धं
ग्रहीष्यति। किन्तु शिशोर् अत्र रक्षकः कोऽपि नास्ति तत्
किं करोमि। यातु। चिरकालपालितम् इमं पुत्रनिर्विशेषं

---

[1] See 584; the final *i* becomes *y* by 34. [2] Loc. case of *Ujjayiní;* see 106. [3] Proper name, noun of 1st class at 103; *as* becomes *o* by 64. [4] 713. [5] Nom. case of *Bráhmaṇa,* noun of 1st class at 103; final *s* becomes Visarga by 63. *a.* [6] 220. [7] 80. XXV. [8] Past pass. part. of the root *sú,* 'to bring forth,' with the preposition *pra,* 532 and 647. [9] 220. [10] *Bála,* 'young,' crude base; *apatyasya,* gen. case of *apatya,* noun of 1st class, neuter, at 104; see 755. [11] *Rakshá,* f. 'protection,' crude base; *artham,* 'for the sake of,' adv.; see 731, with note, and 917. [12] Accus. case of *Bráhmaṇa.* [13] Indecl. part. of the causal of the root *sthá,* 'to stand,' with preposition *ava;* see 566 and 587. [14] Infinitive of the root *sná,* 'to bathe,' 2d conj.; see 458, 868, and 200. [15] 545, 896, and 200. [16] 727. *c.* [17] Gen. case; see 103. [18] 731 and 913. [19] 149. [20] *Párvaṇa,* crude base; *śráddha,* noun of 1st class, neut., at 104; see 743; 'a funeral ceremony in behalf of three ancestors.' [21] Infinitive of the root *dá,* 'to give,' 3d conj.; see 458, 868, and 663. [22] Nom. case, sing. of *áhwána,* 'invitation,' noun of 1st class, neut., at 104. [23] Past pass. part. of the root *gam,* 'to go,' with preposition *a;* see 783, 545, and 896. [24] 220, 49. [25] 49, 556, and 676. [26] *Sahaja,* 'natural,' 'inborn,' crude base; *dáridrád,* abl. case of *dáridra,* 'poverty,' abstract noun of 1st class, neut., formed according to 80. XII, see 755: final *t* changed to *d* by 45. [27] 3d sing. 1st pret. of the root *chint,* 'to think,' 10th conj.; see 641. [28] 790. *a,* 760. [29] 717. *a.* [30] See 602. [31] For *tadá anyah* by 31. [32] 228, 49. [33] 49. [34] See 699, 414. *a.* [35] 728. *b.* [36] Gen. case of *śiśu,* m. 'a child;' see 111. [37] 720. [38] Nom. case of *rakshaka,* 'a protector,' noun of 1st class, masc., at 103. [39] 229. [40] 31, 584. [41] 220. [42] 227. [43] See 682 and 873. [44] See 644 and 882. *a.* [45] *Chira,* 'long,' crude base; *kála,* 'time,' crude base; *pálitam,* 'cherished,' accus. case of *pálita,* past pass. part. of the root *pál,* 'to cherish,' 10th conj.; see 538. This is a complex compound, the whole being an accusatively dependent (see 739, 821), involving a descriptive, 755. [46] 224. [47] See seventh sentence of the last story, p. 331.

[48]नकुलं [49]बालक.रक्षार्थं [50]व्यवस्थाप्य [51]गच्छामि। [52]तथा [53]कृत्वा
गतः। [54]ततस् [55]तच्च [56]नकुलेन [57]बालक.[58]समीपं [59]तूष्णीम् [60]आगच्छन्
[61]कृष्ण.सर्पो [62]व्यापादितः [63]खण्डितश् [64]च। [65]ततोऽसौ [66]नकुलो
[67]ब्राह्मणम् [68]आयान्तम् [69]अवलोक्य [70]रक्त.विलिप्त.मुख.पादः
सत्वरम् [71]उपागम्य ब्राह्मणस्य [72]चरणयोर् [73]लुलोठ। ततोऽसौ
[74]ब्राह्मणस् तं [75]तथाविधं [76]दृष्ट्वा [77]मम [78]पुत्रोऽ[79]नेन [80]भक्षित [81]इत्य्
[82]अविचार्य्य [83]व्यापादितवान्। [84]अनन्तरं [85]यावद् [86]असाव् [87]उपसृत्य

---

[48] Accus. case of *nakula*, 'a weasel,' 'ichneumon,' or 'mungoose,' noun of 1st class, masc., at 103. [49] *Bálaka*, m. 'a child,' crude base; *rakshá*, f. 'protection,' crude base; *artham*, 'for the sake of,' adv.; 731, with note. [50] Indecl. part. of the causal of *sthá*, 'to stand,' with prepositions *vi* and *ava*, 566. [51] See 602. [52] 721. [53] 556. [54] 719; final *s* remains by 62. [55] 720. [56] Instrum. case, 103. [57] See above. [58] 731. [59] 717. *e*. [60] Pres. part. of the root *gam*, 'to go,' 524, with preposition *á*, 'to come,' 783. [61] *Kṛishṇa*, 'black,' crude base; *sarpo*, 'a snake,' nom. case of *sarpa*, noun of 1st class, masc., at 103; *as* becomes *o* by 64: see 755. [62] Past pass. part. of the causal of the root *pad*, with *vi* and *á*, 'to kill,' 549. [63] Past pass. part. of *khaṇḍ*, 'to tear in pieces,' 538; final *s* becomes *ś* by 62. [64] 727, 912. [65] 225; initial *a* cut off by 64. *a*. [66] Nom. case; *as* becomes *o* by 64. [67] Accus. case, 103. [68] Pres. part. of *yá*, 'to go,' 524, with preposition *á*, 'to come,' 783. [69] Indecl. part. of the root *lok*, with preposition *ava*, 'to see,' 'to observe,' 559. [70] *Rakta*, 'blood,' crude base; *vilipta*, 'smeared,' crude base of past pass. part. of the root *lip*, 'to smear,' with preposition *vi*; *mukha*, 'mouth,' crude base; *pádah*, nom. case of *páda*, 'foot,' noun of 1st class at 103. Complex relative compound, the whole being the relative form of descriptive, involving a dependent and an aggregative, 771. [71] Indecl. part. of the root *gam*, 'to go,' with prepositions *upa* and *á*, 'to approach,' 564. *a*. [72] Loc. case, dual, of *charaṇa*, 'a foot,' noun of 1st class, masc. or neut., at 103, 104; see 862. *b*. [73] 3d sing. 2d pret. Parasmai of the root *luṭh*, 'to roll,' 364. [74] Final *s* remains by 62. [75] *Tathá*, 'so,' adv., 721; *vidha*, 'kind,' 'manner,' relative form of adverbial compound, 796. *b*. [76] Indecl. part. of *dṛiś*, 'to see,' 556. [77] 218. [78] Nom. case of *putra*, 'a son,' noun of 1st class at 103; *as* becomes *o* by 64. *a*. [79] 224 and 64. *a*. [80] Past pass. part. of the root *bhaksh*, 'to eat,' 538. [81] 719. *e*, 928, and 929; final *i* becomes *y* by 34. [82] Indecl. part. of the causal of the root *char*, with preposition *vi* and negative prefix *a* (726), 'without deliberating,' 566. [83] Past active part., formed from the past pass. part. *vyápádita*, 'killed,' 553. [84] 731. [85] 713. [86] 225 and 37. [87] Indecl. part. of the root *sṛi*, 'to go,' with preposition *upa*, 'to approach,' 560.

पश्यति[८८] तावद्[८९] बालकः सुस्थः[९०] स्वपिति[९१] सर्पस् तु[९२] व्यापादितस्[९३] तिष्ठति[९४] । तत उपकार.करं[९५] नकुलं निरूप्य[९६] सन्तप्त.चेताः[९७] स[९८] परं[९९] विषादम्[१००] उपगतः[१०१] ॥

---

[88] See 604. [89] 713. [90] Nom. case of *su-stha,* 'in a good state,' 'safe,' from *su,* 'well,' 726. *f,* and *stha,* participial noun from *sthá,* 'to stand,' 580. [91] See 655. [92] 728. *a,* 914. [93] 784. [94] See 587. [95] *Upakára,* 'benefit,' crude base; *karam,* 'causing,' accus. case of *kara,* participial noun from *kṛi,* 'to make,' 580; see 739. *b.* [96] Indecl. part. of the root *rúp,* with preposition *ni,* 'to look at,' 564. [97] *Santapta,* 'scorched,' 'tormented,' 'distressed,' crude base; *chetáh,* 'mind,' nom. case, masc. of *chetas,* noun of the 7th class, neut., at 164. *a;* see 767. [98] 67. [99] Accus. case of *para,* adj. m. f. n. 'excessive,' 187. [100] Accus. case of *vishádа,* 'grief,' 'despondency,' noun of 1st class, masc., at 103. [101] Past pass. part. of *gam,* 'to go,' with preposition *upa,* 543, 896, and see 844.

932. *Translation.*

'There lives in Ujjayiní a Bráhmaṇ named Mádhava. His wife bore him (a son). She, having stationed the Bráhmaṇ (her husband) to take charge of the young child, went to perform ablution. Meanwhile a message came from the king for the Bráhmaṇ to perform the Párvaṇa S'ráddha. On hearing which, the Bráhmaṇ, from his natural neediness, thought to himself, "If I do not go quickly, some other Bráhmaṇ will take the S'ráddha. But there is none here (that I may leave) as a guardian to the child. What then can I do? Come, having stationed this long-cherished weasel, dear to me as a son, in charge of the infant, I will go." Having so done, he went. Presently a black serpent, silently approaching the child, was killed by the weasel and torn in pieces. By and by the weasel, seeing the Bráhmaṇ returning, quickly running to meet him, his mouth and feet smeared with blood, rolled himself at the Bráhmaṇ's feet. Then that Bráhmaṇ, seeing him in such a condition, hastily concluding that he had eaten the child, killed him. Afterwards, no sooner did he come up than he beheld the infant slumbering safely, and the black serpent lying dead. Then looking at his benefactor the weasel, and bitterly repenting (of his precipitation), he experienced exceeding grief.'

EASY SENTENCES TO BE TRANSLATED AND PARSED.

933. Note—The numbers over the words in the following sentences and fables refer to the rules of the foregoing grammar. Those words which cannot be translated by a reference to the rules are explained in regular order at the foot of the page. Observe, that *cr.* stands for *crude base*; *c.* for *class* or for *case*; *s.* for *substantive*; *m.* for *masculine*; *f.* for *feminine*; *n.* for *neuter.*

स आगच्छतु । ताव् आगच्छतां । आवाम् आगच्छाव । ते उपविशन्तु । तौ शृणुतां । ते शृण्वन्तु । अहं तिष्ठानि । युवां तिष्ठतं । वयम् उत्तिष्ठाम । स करोतु । त्वं कुरु । वयं करवामहै । स चिन्तयतु । त्वम् अवधेहि । ते ददतु । यूयं दत्त । भवान् एतु । कुत्र भवान् वसति । यूयं कुत्र वसथ । भवान् शेतां । ते शेरतां । नरः स्वपितु । ते सर्वे सुषुपुः । नरो गृहं याति । युष्माभिः किञ्चिद् भोक्तव्यं । वयं शास्त्रम् अध्ययामहै । अस्माभिः शास्त्राण्यध्येतव्यानि । त्वम् अन्नं भुंक्ष्व । मयान्नं भुज्यतां । त्वया दुग्धं पीयतां । यूयं जलं पिवत । यद् अहं जानामि तद् युष्मान् अध्यापयिष्यामि । मा दिवा स्वाप्सीः । नदीं मा गाः । मा शब्दाद् बिभीत । मा मां निरपराधं बधान ॥

रात्रिशेषे विद्यार्थी शयनाद् उत्तिष्ठेत् ॥

मातापित्रोस् तुष्ट्या सर्वस्य तपसः फलं प्राप्यते ॥

नर s. m. (1st c. 103) 'a man.' गृह s. n. (1st c. 104) 'a house.' शास्त्र s. n. (1st c. 104) 'a book,' 'a sacred treatise.' जल s. n. (1st c. 104) 'water.' रात्रिशेषे genitively dependent (743); *rátri*, cr. 'night;' *śeshe*, loc. c. of *śesha*, s. m. (1st c. 103) 'end.' शयन s. n. 'a bed;' *-nád*, abl. c., *t* becomes *d* by 45. तुष्टि s. f. (2d c. 112) 'gratification;' *-shṭyá*, instr. c. तपस् s. n. (7th c. 164) 'penance;' *-sah*, gen. c. फल s. n. (1st c. 104) 'fruit;' *-lam*, nom. c.

ईरिणे वीजम् उप्त्वा कर्षकः फलं न [783.p]प्राप्नोति ॥

शूकरोऽन्नघ्राणयोग्यदेशान् निरसनीयः ॥

रात्रिर् भूतानां स्वप्नार्थं [586]भवति दिनं च कर्म्मानुष्ठानार्थं ॥

[755.a]वहिःशौचं [759]मृद्वारिभ्याम् [755.a]अन्तःशौचं रागद्वेषादित्यागेन [682]क्रियते ॥

न [717.f]जातु कामः कामानाम् उपभोगेन [610]शाम्यति ॥

व्यसनस्य च मृत्योश्च व्यसनं कष्टम् [471, 680]उच्यते ॥

[916.a]आमृत्योः श्रीसिद्ध्यर्थम् उद्यमं [684]कुर्यात् ॥

[778.b]अद्भिर् गात्राणि शुध्यन्ति [764]मनस् [728.a]तु निषिद्धचिन्तादिना दूषितं सत्याभिधानेन ॥

ईरिण s. n. (1st c. 104) 'a barren soil;' *-ne*, loc. c. वीज s. n. (1st c. 104) 'seed;' *-jam*, acc. c. उप्त्वा indecl. part. (556), 'having sown,' from root *vap*. कर्षक s. m. (1st c. 103) 'a husbandman.' शूकर s. m. (1st c. 103) 'a hog.' अन्नघ्राणयोग्यदेशान् complex compound (770. *a*); *anna*, cr. 'food;' *ghráṇa*, cr. 'smelling;' *yogya*, cr. 'suitable,' 'fit;' *deśán*, abl. c. of *deśa* (1st c. 103), 'spot,' 'place,' *t* becomes *n* by 47. निरसनीय fut. pass. part. (570), 'to be driven away,' 'to be expelled,' from root *as*, with prep. *nir*. भूत s. n. (1st c. 104) 'a living being;' *-tánám*, gen. pl. स्वप्न cr. 'sleep;' *artham*, see 760. *d*. दिन s. n. (1st c. 104) 'day.' कर्म्म cr. 'business;' *anushṭhána*, cr. 'performance;' *artham*, see 760. *d*. रागद्वेषादित्यागेन complex compound (772); *rága*, cr. 'passion;' *dwesha*, cr. 'hatred;' *ádi*, cr. 'et cetera;' *tyágena*, instr. c. of *tyága*, s. m. (1st c. 103), 'abandonment.' काम s. m. (1st c. 103) 'desire,' 'object of desire;' *-mah*, nom. c.; *-mánám*, gen. c. pl. उपभोग s. m. (1st c. 103) 'enjoyment;' *-gena*, instr. c. व्यसन s. n. (1st c. 104) 'vice;' *-nasya*, gen. c. मृत्यु s. m. (3d c. 111) 'death;' *-tyoś*, gen. c., *s* becomes *ś* by 62. कष्ट adj. (1st c. 187) 'painful,' used here as superlative, 'the most painful.' श्री cr. 'prosperity,' 'fortune;' *siddhi*, cr. 'attainment,' 'accomplishment,' see 34; *artham*, see 760. *d*. उद्यम s. m. (1st c. 103) 'effort,' 'exertion.' गात्र s. n. (1st c. 104) 'a limb;' *-tráṇi*, n. pl. शुध्यन्ति 3d pl. pres. Parasmai, 'are purified,' from root *śudh* (4th c. 612). निषिद्धचिन्तादिना complex compound (764); *nishiddha*, cr. 'forbidden;' *chintá*, cr. 'thought;' *ádiná*, see 764. दूषित past pass. part. (549), 'polluted,' 'defiled,' from causal of root *dush* (4th c.). सत्याभिधानेन Tat-purusha or genitively dependent (743); *satya*, cr. 'truth;' *abhidhánena*, instr. c. of *abhidhána*, s. n. (1st c. 104), 'speaking.'

विषाद् अप्यमृतं ग्राह्यं[573, 699] बालाद् अपि सुभाषितं[755. a] ॥

श्रद्दधानः सञ्जात.क्रोधाय कस्मैचित्[238] प्रतिक्रोधं न कुर्यात्[681] ॥

सूर्येऽस्तमिते गृहस्थेना.तिथिर् न प्रत्याख्येयः सायम्भोजने निवृत्तेऽपि तस्मै[220] भोजनं देयं[663, 571. a] ॥

अतिथिषु ज्ञातिषु च कृत[767. a]भोजनेषु ततोऽन्नाद्[834] अवशिष्टं[834] भार्य्यापती[761] पश्चाद्[715] अश्नीयातां[696] ॥

यावत्[713. a] पुरुषो भाषते तावत्[713. a] प्राणितुं न शक्नोति[679] यावच्च प्राणिति तावद्[713. a] भाषितुं न शक्नोति ॥

हस्तौ रक्ता.क्तौ न रक्तेन किन्तु[728. b] विमल.जलेन विशुद्धौ

विष s. n. (1st c. 104) 'poison.' अमृत s. n. (1st c. 104) 'nectar.' बाल s. m. (1st c. 103) 'a child;' *-lád*, abl. c., *t* becomes *d* by 45. श्रद्दधान s. m. (1st c. 103), 'a believer,' from *śrat*, an indecl. prefix implying 'belief,' and *dadhána*, 'having,' pres. part. Átm. of *dhá*, see 664. सञ्जातक्रोधाय Bahu-vríhi or relative form of descriptive (767. *a*); *sañjáta*, cr. 'excited,' 'roused;' *krodháya*, dat. c. of *krodha*, s. m. (1st c. 103), 'anger;' see 853. *a*. प्रतिक्रोध s. m. (1st c. 103) 'anger in return.' सूर्य s. m. (1st c. 103) 'the sun;' *-ye*, loc. c., see 840. अस्तमित past pass. part. (531), 'having gone to its setting,' 'having set,' from *astam*, acc. c. of *asta*, 'the western mountain,' and *ita*, past pass. part. of *i*, 'to go,' see 645. गृहस्थ s. m. (1st c. 103) 'a householder;' *-sthena*, instr. c. अतिथि s. m. (2d c. 110) 'a guest,' *s* becomes *r* by 65. प्रत्याख्येय fut. pass. part. (571. *a*), 'to be refused,' from root *khyá* (2d c.), with prep. *prati* and *á*. सायम्भोजन s. n. (1st c. 104), 'evening meal,' 'supper,' from *sáyam*, indecl. 'evening,' and *bhojana*, s. n. 'meal,' see 755. *a*; *-ne*, loc. c., see 840. निवृत्त past pass. part. (531), 'being ended,' from root *vṛit* (598), with prep. *ni*. ज्ञाति s. m. (2d c. 110) 'a kinsman,' 'relative;' *-tishu*, loc. pl., see 840. पुरुष s. m. (1st c. 103) 'a man.' भाषते 3d sing. pres. Átmane, 'speaks,' from root *bhásh* (1st c.). प्राणितुं infin. (458), 'to breathe,' from root *an* (2d c. 326), with prep. *pra*. प्राणिति 3d sing. pres. Parasmai, 'breathes;' see 326. हस्त s. m. (1st c. 104) 'a hand;' *-stau*, nom. c. du. रक्ताक्तौ Tat-purusha or instrumentally dependent (740); *rakta*, cr. 'blood;' *aktau*, nom. du. of *akta*, past pass. part. (539), 'soiled,' from root *añj* (7th c. 668). विमलजलेन Karma-dháraya or descriptive (755); *vimala*, cr. 'clean,' 'pure;' *jalena*, instr. c. of *jala*, s. n. (1st c. 104), 'water.' विशुद्ध past pass. part. (539), 'cleansed,' 'purified,' from root *śudh*, with prep. *vi*; *-ddhau*, nom. du.

भवतस्[585] । तथैव[717.c] मूर्ख.जनितं दोषं न मूर्ख एवा.पहन्ति किन्तु विद्वान्[168.a] ॥

[727.b]यदि जन एकाकी जीवति[603] न किञ्चित्[228] त्यजति[596] न कस्यापि[229] त्यागेन दुःखम् अनुभवति[783.c] न च केनापि[229] त्यज्यते[596] ॥

धातूनां सुवर्ण.रजता.दीनां मूषायाम् अग्निना[110] ध्मायमानानां मल.द्रव्याणि[757.a] दह्यन्ते[610] ॥

अल्प.धनान्य्.अपि[766.a] कुलानि वेदा.ध्ययन.युक्तानि महतीं[142] ख्यातिम् अर्जयन्ति ॥

देहो विविध.व्याधीनाम् आश्रयः क्षुत्.पिपासा.शीतो.ष्ण.पीडितो विनश्वर.स्वभावोऽस्ति[584] ॥

मूर्खजनितं Tat-purusha or instrumentally dependent (740); *múrkha*, cr. 'a fool;' *janitam*, acc. c. of *janita*, past pass. part. (549), 'occasioned by.' दोष s. m. (1st c. 103) 'mistake,' 'fault.' अपहन्ति 3d sing. pres. Parasmai, 'removes,' 'takes away,' from root *han* (2d c. 654), with prep. *apa*. जन s. m. (1st c. 103) 'a man.' एकाकिन् adj. m. f. n. (6th c. 188) 'alone;' *-kí*, nom. c. masc. दुःख s. n. (1st c. 104) 'grief,' 'pain.' धातु s. m. (3d c. 111) 'a metal;' *-túnám*, gen. pl. सुवर्णरजतादीनां complex relative compound (772); *suvarṇa*, cr. 'gold;' *rajata*, cr. 'silver;' *ádínam*, see 772. मूषा s. f. (1st c. 105) 'a crucible;' *-sháyám*, loc. c. ध्मायमान pres. part. pass. (528), 'being melted,' from root *dhmá*, 'to blow' (1st c. 269). कुल s. n. (1st c. 104) 'a family;' *-láni*, nom. pl. वेदाध्ययनयुक्तानि Tat-purusha or dependent (745); *veda*, cr. 'the Veda,' 'holy scripture;' *adhyayana*, cr. 'study;' *yuktáni*, nom. pl. neut. of *yukta*, past pass. part. 'intent on,' 'attached to.' ख्याति s. f. (2d c. 112) 'celebrity,' 'honour.' अर्जयन्ति 3d pl. pres. Parasmai, 'they obtain,' from causal of root *arj*. देह s. m. (1st c. 103) 'the body;' final *s* becomes *o* by 64. विविधव्याधीनां Karma-dháraya or descriptive (755); *vividha*, cr. 'various;' *vyádhínám*, gen. pl. of *vyádhi*, s. m. (1st c. 103), 'disease,' 'sickness.' आश्रय s. m. (1st c. 103) 'abode,' 'seat.' क्षुत्पिपासाशीतोष्णपीडितो complex compound, the whole being a dependent, containing an aggregative (771); *kshudh*, cr. 'hunger,' *dh* becomes *t* by 42; *pipásá*, cr. 'thirst;' *síta*, cr. 'cold;' *ushṇa*, cr. 'heat;' *píḍito*, nom. c. of *píḍita*, past pass. part. (538), 'afflicted,' 'suffering from.' विनश्वरस्वभावो Bahu-vríhi or relative form of descriptive (766); *vinaśwara*, cr. 'perishable,' 'frail;' *swabhávo*, nom. c. of *swabhávo*, s. m. (1st c. 103), 'nature.'

यं मातापितरौ क्लेशं सहेते सम्भवे नृणां ।
न तस्य निष्कृतिः शक्या कर्तुं वर्षशतैर् अपि ॥

934. FABLES* TO BE TRANSLATED AND PARSED.

॥ कथा १ ॥ STORY I.

एकस्मिन् प्रदेशे कश्चिद् गोमायुर् नाम शृगालः क्षुत्क्षामकण्ठ इतश्चेतश्च परिभ्रमन् वने सैन्यद्वयसङ्ग्रामभूमिम् अपश्यत् । तस्यां च दुन्दुभेः पतितस्य वायुवशाद् उद्धतशाखाग्रैर् हन्यमानस्य शब्दम् अशृणोत् । अथ क्षुभितहृदयश् चिन्तयामास । अहो विनष्टोऽस्मि । तद् यावन्

क्लेश s. m. (1st c. 103) 'trouble,' 'pains.' सम्भव s. m. (1st c. 103) 'rearing,' 'bringing up;' *-ve*, loc. c. निष्कृति s. f. (2d c. 112) 'acquittance,' 'discharge of a debt or obligation.'

गोमायु s. m. (3d c. 111) 'a jackal,' a proper name; *-yur*, nom. c., final *s* becomes *r* by 65. शृगाल s. m. (1st c. 103) 'a jackal;' *-lah*, nom. c. (63). क्षुध् s. f. (8th c. 177) 'hunger;' *kshut*, cr., for *kshudh* by 42. कण्ठ s. m. n. (1st c. 103, 104) 'the throat;' *-ṇṭa*, nom. c., final *s* dropped by 66. परिभ्रमत् pres. part. Parasmai (524), 'wandering,' from *bhram*, 'to wander' (1st c.), with prep. *pari*, 'about' (783); *-man*, nom. c. masc. वन s. n. (1st c. 104) 'a wood;' *-ne*, loc. c. सैन्यद्वयसङ्ग्रामभूमिम् Tat-purusha or dependent (745); *sainya*, cr. 'army;' *dwaya*, cr. 'two' (835. *a*); *san·gráma*, cr. 'battle,' 'war;' *bhúmim*, acc. c. of *bhúmi*, s. f. (2d c. 112), 'ground,' 'field,' 'site.' दुन्दुभि s. m. (2d c. 110) 'a kettle-drum;' *-bheh*, gen. c. (63); *-bhim*, acc. c. वायुवशाद् Tat-purusha or dependent (743); *váyu*, cr. 'wind;' *vaśád*, abl. c. of *vaśa*, s. n. (1st c. 104), 'power,' 'force;' *vaśád* for *vaśát* by 45. उद्धतशाखाग्रैर् complex compound (770. *a*); *uddhata*, cr. of past pass. part. 'raised,' lit. 'struck up,' from root *han*, see under *ut* at 783, and compare 545; *śákhá*, cr. 'branch;' *agrair*, instr. c. pl. of *agra*, s. n. (1st c. 104), 'point,' 'end.' हन्यमान pres. part. pass. (528), 'being struck,' from *han*, 'to strike' (654); *-nasya*, gen. c. शब्द s. m. (1st c. 103) 'noise,' 'sound;' *-bdam*, acc. c. The nom. c. occurs in next page. क्षुभितहृदयश् Bahu-vríhi or relative form of descriptive (761, 766); *kshubhita*, cr. of past pass. part. 'agitated,' 'shaken,' from root *kshubh* (539); *hṛidayaś*, nom. c. masc. of *hṛidaya*, s. n. (1st c. 104, 108), 'heart,' 'mind.' विनष्ट past pass. part. (531), 'lost,' 'undone,' from root *naś* (4th c. 620), with prep. *vi*; see under *vi* at 783: see also 895.

* Selected from the Pancha-tantra.

नास्य प्रोच्चारितस्य दृष्टिगोचरे गच्छामि । तावद् अन्यतो व्रजामीति । अथवा नैतद् युज्यते सहसैव पितृपर्यायागतं वनं त्यक्तुं । उक्तं च

भये वा यदि वा हर्षे सम्प्राप्ते यो विमर्शयेत् ।
कृत्यं न कुरुते वेगान् न स सन्तापम् आप्नुयात् ॥

तत् तावज् जानामि कस्यायं शब्द इति धैर्यम् आलम्ब्य व्यमर्शयत् । यावन् मन्दं मन्दं प्रतिगच्छति तावद् दुन्दुभिम् अपश्यत् । यावच् छाखाग्रैर् वायुवशाद् धन्यते तावच् छब्दं करोति । अन्यथा तूष्णीम् आस्ते । ततश्च सम्यक् परिज्ञाय समीपं गत्वा स्वयम् एव कौतुकाद् अताडयत् ।

प्रोच्चारित past pass. part. (549), 'made to utter a sound,' 'made to give forth a noise,' 'uttering a loud voice,' from causal form of root *char* (1st c.), with prep. *pra* and *ut* (48, 783); *-tasya*, gen. c. दृष्टिगोचर Tat-purusha or dependent (743) 'the range of the sight;' *drishṭi*, cr. 'sight;' *gochara*, 'range,' 'limit,' lit. 'range of a cow's pasturage;' *-re*, loc. c. व्रजामि 1st sing. pres. Parasmai, 'I will go,' from root *vraj* (1st c.); see 873. पितृपर्यायागत Tat-purusha or dependent (745); *pitṛi*, cr. 'father,' 'ancestor;' *paryáya*, cr. 'succession,' 'inheritance;' *ágatam*, acc. c. of *ágata*, 'come,' past pass. part. (545) of root *gam*, 'to go,' with prep. *á*; see under *á* at 783. भय s. n. (1st c. 104) 'fear,' 'fearful thing,' 'danger;' *-ye*, loc. c. हर्ष s. m. (1st c. 103) 'joy,' 'pleasure,' 'happiness;' *-rshe*, loc. c. सम्प्राप्त past pass. part. (531), 'obtained,' 'arrived,' 'happened,' from root *áp* (5th c. 681), with prep. *sam* and *pra*; *-pte*, loc. c. विमर्शयेत् 3d sing. pot. Parasmai, 'he may consider,' 'deliberate,' 'hesitate,' from root *mṛiś* (10th c.), with prep. *vi*. कृत्य s. n. (1st c. 104) 'act,' 'action,' 'that which is to be done;' *-tyam*, acc. c. वेग s. m. (1st c. 103) 'impetuosity;' *-gán*, abl. c., *t* becomes *n* by 47. सन्ताप s. m. (1st c. 103) 'remorse,' 'repentance,' 'pain;' *-pam*, acc. c. धैर्य s. n. (1st c. 104) 'firmness,' 'boldness,' 'courage;' *-ryam*, acc. c. आलम्ब्य indecl. part. (564), 'having taken hold of,' 'having rested on,' 'having recourse to,' from root *lamb*, with prep. *á*. व्यमर्शयत् 3d sing. 1st pret. Parasmai, 'he reflected,' 'he considered,' from root *mṛiś*, with prep. *vi*. मन्दं adv. 'slowly,' from *manda*, 'slow;' see 713. छाखाग्रैर् for शाखाग्रैर् by 49; see उद्धत-शाखाग्रैर् in last page. सम्यक् adv. 'truly,' 'accurately.' परिज्ञाय indecl. part. (561), 'having ascertained,' from root *jñá* (688), with prep. *pari*. कौतुक s. n. (1st c. 104) 'curiosity,' 'sport;' *-kád*, abl. c. (45).

भूयश्च हर्षाद् अचिन्तयत् । अहो चिराद् एतद् अस्माकं महद् भोजनम् आपतितं । तन् नूनम् एतन् मांस.मेदोऽसृग्भिः पूरितं भविष्यति । ततः परुष.चर्मा.वगुण्ठितं कथमपि विदार्य एकदेशे छिद्रं कृत्वा संहृष्ट.मनाः प्रविष्टः । परं चर्म विदारयतो दंष्ट्रा.भङ्गः सञ्जातः । अथ तद् दारु.चर्म.विशेषम् आलोक्य निराशीभूतः ॥

॥ कथा २ ॥ STORY 2.

कस्मिंश्चिद् अधिष्ठाने चत्वारो ब्राह्मण.पुत्राः परं मैत्री-भावम् उपागता निवसन्ति स्म । तेषां त्रयः सर्व.शास्त्र.पा-

---

भोजन s. n. (1st c. 104) 'food;' *-nam*, nom. c. **आपतित** past pass. part. (538), 'happened,' 'befallen,' from root *pat*, with prep. *á*. **मांसमेदोऽसृग्भिः** Dwandwa or aggregative (749); *mánsa*, cr. 'flesh;' *medas*, cr. 'marrow,' *as* becomes *o* by 64. *a; asṛigbhih*, instr. c. pl. of *asṛij*, 'blood' (8th c. 176. *d*). **पूरित** past pass. part. (549), 'filled,' from root *pṛí* (10th c. 640). **परुषचर्मावगुण्ठितं** complex compound (770); *parusha*, cr. 'harsh,' 'hard;' *charma*, cr., for *charman*, 'skin,' 'hide,' 'leather,' see 57; *avaguṇṭhitam*, acc. c. of *avaguṇṭhita*, 'covered,' past pass. part. (538) of root *guṇṭh*, with prep. *ava*. **विदार्य** indecl. part. (566), 'having torn,' from causal of root *dṛí*, with prep. *vi*. **एकदेशे** Karma-dháraya or descriptive (755) 'in one spot;' *eka*, cr. 'one;' *deśe*, loc. c. of *deśa* (1st c. 103), 'spot,' 'place.' **छिद्र** s. n. (1st c. 104) 'a hole;' *-dram*, acc. c. **प्रविष्ट** past pass. part. (531), 'entered,' 'penetrated,' 'pierced,' from root *viś*, with prep. *pra;* see 896. **परं** adv. 'afterwards,' 'then,' 'but,' 'nevertheless.' **चर्मन्** s. n. (6th c. 152) 'skin,' 'hide,' 'leather;' *-rma*, acc. c. **विदारयत्** pres. part. Parasmai (524), 'tearing,' 'rending asunder,' from causal of root *dṛí*, with prep. *vi; -yato*, gen. c., final *as* becomes *o* by 64. **दंष्ट्राभङ्गः** Tat-purusha or dependent (743); *danshṭrá*, cr. 'tooth;' *bhan·gah*, nom. c. of *bhan·ga* (1st c. 103), 'breaking,' 'fracture.' **सञ्जात** past pass. part. (545) 'produced,' 'happened;' *-tah*, nom. c. **दारुचर्मविशेषं** complex relative compound (771); *dáru*, cr. 'wood;' *charma*, cr., for *charman*, 'skin,' see 57; *viśesham*, acc. c. of *viśesha*, s. m. (1st c. 103), 'property,' 'attribute.' **आलोक्य** indecl. part. (564), 'perceiving,' 'seeing,' from root *lok*, with prep. *á*. **निराशीभूत** past pass. part. (532), 'disappointed,' from *nir* 'not,' *áśá* 'hope,' *bhúta* 'become;' see 788.

अधिष्ठान s. n. (1st c. 104) 'a place,' 'a town;' *-ne*, loc. c. **पर** adj. m. f. n. (1st c. 187) 'great,' 'excessive;' *-ram*, acc. c.

रगाः परं बुद्धिरहिताः । एकस् तु शास्त्रपराङ्मुखः केवलं बुद्धिमान् । अथ कदाचित् तैर् मिलित्वा मन्त्रितं । को गुणो विद्याया यदि देशान्तरं गत्वा भूपतीन् परितोष्यार्थोपार्जना न क्रियते । तत् सर्वथा सर्वे देशान्तरं गच्छाम इति । तथानुष्ठिते किञ्चिन् मार्गं गत्वा तेषां ज्येष्ठतरः प्राह । अहो अस्माकम् एकश् चतुर्थो मूढः केवलं बुद्धिमान् । न च विद्यां विना राज्ञां प्रतिग्रहः केवलबुद्ध्या लभ्यते । तद् अस्मै स्वोपार्जनाविभागं न दास्यामः । तद् एष निवृत्य स्वगृहं गच्छतु । अथ द्वितीयेनाभिहितं । अहो सुबुद्धे विद्याहीनस् त्वं । तद् गच्छ गृहं । ततस् तृतीयेनाभिहितं । अहो न युज्यते कर्तुम् एवं । यतो वयं बाल्यात् प्रभृत्येकत्र क्रीडिताः । तद् आगच्छतु । महानुभावोऽस्मद्-

बुद्धिमत् adj. m. f. n. (5th c. 188) 'possessed of intelligence,' 'intelligent,' see 140; *-mán*, nom. c. मन्त्रित past pass. part. (530), 'planned,' 'deliberated,' from root *mantr* (10th c.). गुण s. m. (1st c. 103) 'merit,' 'advantage;' *-ṇo*, nom. c., *as* becomes *o* by 64. विद्या s. f. (1st c. 105) 'learning,' 'knowledge,' 'science;' *-dyáyá*, gen. c., final *s* dropped by 66. *a; -dyám*, acc. c. परितोष्य indecl. part. (566), 'having propitiated,' 'having pleased,' from causal of root *tush*, with prep. *pari*. मार्ग s. m. (1st c. 103) 'a road,' 'a way;' *-rgam*, acc. c. प्राह 3d sing. 2d pret. Parasmai, 'he said,' 'he addressed,' from root *ah*, with prep. *pra;* see 384 and 783. *p*. मूढ past pass. part., used as adj. (1st c. 187), 'ignorant,' 'foolish,' from root *muh;* see 539, 305. *a*. प्रतिग्रह s. m. (1st c. 103) 'donation,' 'countenance,' 'favour;' *-hah*, nom. c. केवलबुद्ध्या Karma-dháraya or descriptive (755); *kevala*, cr. 'mere;' *buddhyá*, instr. c. of *buddhi*, s. f. (2d c. 112), 'intelligence.' स्वोपार्जनाविभागं complex compound (770); *swa*, cr. 'own,' see 232; *upárjaná*, cr. 'earning,' 'acquisition;' *vibhágam*, acc. c. of *vibhága*, s. m. (1st c. 103), 'share.' गृह s. n. (1st c. 104) 'house,' 'home;' *-ham*, acc. c. अभिहित past pass. part. (533), 'said,' 'spoken,' 'accosted,' from root *dhá*, with prep. *abhi*. बाल्य s. n. (1st c. 104) 'childhood;' *-lyát*, abl. c. क्रीडित past pass. part. (538), 'played,' 'sported,' from root *kríḍ*. महानुभाव Bahu-vríhi or relative form of descriptive (761); *mahá* for *mahat*, cr. 'great,' 'noble,' see 778; *anubhávo*, nom. c. (64. *a*) of *anubháva*, s. m. (1st c. 103), 'disposition.' This compound is equivalent to the English, 'a good fellow,' 'a fine fellow.'

पार्जितस्य वित्तस्य संविभागी भवतु । तथानुष्ठिते तैर्
मार्गम् अतिक्रामद्भिर् अटव्यां मृतसिंहास्थीनि दृष्टानि ।
ततश्चैकेनाभिहितं । अहो पूर्वाधीतविद्यायाः प्रत्ययः क्रियते ।
किञ्चिद् एतन् मृतसत्त्वं तिष्ठति । तत् सदभ्यस्तविद्याप्र-
भावेण प्रत्युज्जीवयामः । ततश्चैकेनाभिहितं । अहम् अस्थि-
सञ्चयं कर्तुं जानामि । द्वितीयेनाभिहितं । चर्ममांसरुधिरं
प्रयच्छामि । तृतीयेनाभिहितं । अहं सञ्जीवनं करोमि । तत
एकेनास्थिसञ्चयः कृतः । द्वितीयेन चर्ममांसरुधिरैः संयो-
जितः । तृतीयो यावज्जीवितव्यं योजयितुं लग्नः । तावत्
स बुद्धिमता निषिद्ध उक्तश्च । एष सिंहः । यद्येनं सजीवं
करिष्यसि तत सर्वान् अप्यस्मान् व्यापादयिष्यतीति । ततस्

वित्त s. n. (1st c. 104) 'wealth,' 'riches,' 'property;' *-ttasya*, gen. c. संविभागिन् agt. (582. *a*), 'a participator,' 'a sharer,' from root *bhaj*, with prep. *sam* and *vi; -gí*, nom. c., see 159. अटवी s. f. (1st c. 106) 'a forest,' 'a wood;' *-vyám*, loc. c. पूर्वाधीतविद्यायाः complex compound (770); *púrva*, cr. 'former,' 'formerly;' *adhíta*, cr. 'studied;' *vidyáyáh*, gen. c. of *vidyá*, which see. प्रत्यय s. m. (1st c. 103) 'test,' 'trial,' 'ascertainment.' मृतसत्त्वं Karma-dháraya or descriptive (755); *mrita*, cr. 'dead;' *sattwam*, nom. c. of *sattwa*, s. n. (1st c. 104), 'animal,' 'beast.' सदभ्यस्तविद्याप्रभावेण complex compound (770); *sad* for *sat*, cr. 'well,' 'good,' see 45; *abhyasta*, cr. 'exercised,' 'practised,' 'learnt;' *vidyá*, cr. 'science;' *prabhávena*, instr. c. of *prabháva*, s. m. (1st c. 103), 'power.' प्रत्युज्जीवयामः 1st pl. pres. Parasmai, 'we will cause to live again,' 'let us resuscitate,' from causal of root *jív* (603), with prep. *prati* and *ut;* see 48 and 873. प्रयच्छामि 1st sing. pres. Parasmai, 'I will provide,' 'I will furnish,' from root *yam*, with prep. *pra;* see 270 and 873. सञ्जीवन s. n. (1st c. 104) 'bringing to life;' *-nam*, acc. c. अस्थिसञ्चयः Tat-purusha or dependent (743); *asthi*, cr. 'bone;' *sańchayah*, nom. c. 'collecting,' 'gathering together.' संयोजित past pass. part. (530), 'furnished,' 'endowed,' from root *yuj* (see tables at 583), with prep. *sam; -tah*, nom. c. लग्न past pass. part. (531. *a*), 'intent on,' 'busied about,' from root *lag*, see 896; *-gnah*, nom. c. निषिद्ध past pass. part. (539), 'prohibited,' 'forbidden,' from root *sidh*, with prep. *ni* (see 616 and 783. *l*). सिंह s. m. (1st c. 103) 'a lion;' *-hah*, nom. c. व्यापादयिष्यति 3d sing. 2d fut. Parasmai, 'he will kill,' 'he will destroy,' from causal of root *pad*, 'to go,' with prep. *ri* and *á*, 'to kill;' see 784.

तेनाभिहितं । धिग् मूर्ख नाहं विद्यां विफलतां नेष्यामि । ततश्च तेनाभिहितं । तर्हि क्षणं प्रतीक्षस्व यावद् अहम् एनं समीपतरुम् आरोहामि । तथानुष्ठिते यावत् संजीवः कृतस् तावत् त्रयोऽपि ते तेनोत्थाय व्यापादिताः । स च बुद्धिमान् सिंहे स्थानान्तरे गते वृक्षाद् अवतीर्य गृहं गतः ॥

॥ कथा ३ ॥ STORY 3.

कस्मिंश्चिज् जलाशये शतबुद्धिसहस्रबुद्धिनामानौ द्वौ मत्स्यौ प्रतिवसतः स्म । तयोर् एकबुद्धिर् नाम मण्डूको मित्रताम् आजगाम । एवं ते त्रयोऽपि जलतीरे कियन्तं कालं सुभाषितगोष्ठीसुखम् अनुभूय पुनर् जलं प्रविशन्ति । अथ तेषां कदाचिद् गोष्ठीगतानां जालहस्ता धीवराः प्रभूतैर्

मूर्ख s. m. (1st c. 103) 'a fool;' *-rkha*, voc. c. विफलता s. f. (1st c. 105) 'unprofitableness,' 'uselessness;' *-tám*, acc. c. समीपतरु Karma-dháraya or descriptive (755); *samípa*, cr. 'near,' 'neighbouring;' *tarum*, acc. c. of *taru*, s. m. (3d c. 111), 'a tree.' आरोहामि 1st sing. pres. Parasmai, 'I ascend,' 'I mount,' from root *ruh* (1st c.), with prep. *á*. उत्थाय indecl. part. (561), 'having risen (into life),' from root *sthá* (587), with prep. *ut;* see under *ut* at 783.*j*. वृक्ष s. m. (1st c. 103) 'a tree;' *-kshád*, abl. c., see 45.

शतबुद्धिसहस्रबुद्धिनामानौ complex relative compound (771); *śatabuddhi*, cr. 'Hundred-devices,' name of a fish; *sahasrabuddhi*, 'Thousand-devices,' name of a fish; *námánau*, see 152 and 154. मत्स्य s. m. (1st c. 103) 'a fish;' *-tsyau*, nom. du. एकबुद्धिर् Bahu-vríhi or relative form of descriptive (766) 'One-device,' name of a fish; final *s* becomes *r* by 65. मण्डूक s. m. (1st c. 103) 'a frog;' *-ko*, nom. c., see 64. मित्रता s. f. (1st c. 105) 'friendship;' *-tám*, acc. c. सुभाषितगोष्ठीसुखं complex compound (770); *su*, indecl. 'good;' *bháshita*, cr. 'discourse;' *goshṭhí*, cr. 'conversation;' *sukham*, acc. c. of *sukha*, s. n. (1st c. 104), 'pleasure,' 'happiness.' जल s. n. (1st c. 104) 'water;' *-lam*, acc. c. प्रविशन्ति 3d pl. pres. Parasmai, 'they enter,' from root *viś* (6th c.), with prep. *pra*. धीवर s. m. (1st c. 103) 'a fisherman;' *-ráh*, nom. pl. प्रभूत past pass. part., used as adj. (1st c. 187), 'many,' 'abundant,' from root *bhú*, with prep. *pra;* see 532.

मत्स्यैर् व्यापादितैर् मस्तके धृतैर् अस्तमयनवेलायां समायाताः । तं च जलाशयं दृष्ट्वा ते मिथः प्रोचुः । अहो बहुमत्स्योऽयं ह्रदो दृश्यते स्वल्पसलिलश्च । तत् प्रभातेऽत्रागमिष्यामः । इत्युक्त्वा स्वगृहं गताः । ते च तद् वज्रपातसदृशं वचः श्रुत्वा परस्परं मन्त्रयाञ्चक्रुः । तत्र मण्डूकोऽब्रवीत् । भो भद्रौ शतबुद्धिसहस्रबुद्धी किम् अत्र कर्तुं युज्यते । पलायनम् अवष्टम्भो वा । तच् छ्रुत्वा सहस्रबुद्धिर् विहस्योवाच । भो मित्र मा भैषीर् वचनश्रवणमात्रेणापि । आगमनम् अपि तेषां न सम्भाव्यते भविष्यति वा । तदा स्वबुद्धिप्रभावेण त्वाम् आत्मानं च रक्षिष्यामि । यतोऽहम् अनेकजलगतीर् जानामि । तच् छ्रुत्वा शत-

---

मस्तक s. m. (1st c. 103) 'the head;' *-ke*, loc. c. धृत past pass. part. (532), 'placed,' 'held,' from root *dhri.* अस्तमयनवेलायां Tat-purusha or dependent (743); *astamayana*, cr. 'sunset;' *veláyám*, loc. c. of *velá*, s. f. (1st c. 105), 'time.' समायात past pass. part. (532), 'arrived,' 'came,' from root *yá*, with prep. *sam* and *á*. प्रोचुः 3d pl. 2d pret. Parasmai, 'they said,' from root *vach*, with prep. *pra;* see 375. *c*. ह्रद s. m. (1st c. 103) 'lake,' 'pond;' *-do*, nom. c., see 64. उक्त्वा indecl. part. (556), 'having said,' 'having spoken,' from root *vach*. वचस् s. n. (7th c. 164) 'speech,' 'discourse;' *-chah*, acc. c., see 63. मन्त्रयाञ्चक्रुः 3d pl. 2d pret. Parasmai, 'they consulted,' 'they deliberated,' from root *mantr* (10th c.); see 385. *a*. भद्र adj. m. f. n. (1st c. 187) 'good,' 'excellent;' *-drau*, voc. du. पलायन s. n. (1st c. 104) 'flight,' 'departure;' *-nam*, nom. c. अवष्टम्भ s. m. (1st c. 103) 'stopping,' 'staying;' *-mbho*, nom. c., see 64. विहस्य indecl. part. (564), 'having smiled,' from root *has*, with prep. *vi*. मित्र s. n. (1st c. 104) 'a friend;' *-tra*, voc. c. श्रवण s. n. (1st c. 104) 'hearing,' 'listening to.' आगमन s. n. (1st c. 104) 'arrival,' 'coming;' *-nam*, nom. n. सम्भाव्यते 3d sing. pres. passive, 'will take place,' 'will happen,' from causal of root *bhú* (585), with prep. *sam;* see 496, 873. स्वबुद्धिप्रभावेण Tat-purusha or dependent (743); *swa*, cr. 'own;' *buddhi*, cr. 'intellect;' *prabhávena*, instr. c. of *prabháva*, s. m. (1st c. 103), 'power.' रक्षिष्यामि 1st sing. 2d fut. Parasmai, 'I will preserve,' from root *raksh* (1st c.). अनेकजलगतीर् complex compound (770); *aneka*, cr. 'many;' *jala*, cr. 'water;' *gatír*, acc. c. pl. of *gati*, s. f. (2d c. 112), 'movement;' final *s* becomes *r* by 65.

बुद्धिर् आह । भो युक्तम् उक्तं सहस्रबुद्धिना । वचनश्रव-
णमात्राज् जन्मस्थानं पितृपर्यायागतं त्यक्तुं न शक्यते ।
तन् न क्वचिद् अपि गन्तव्यं । अहं त्वां स्वबुद्धिप्रभावेण
रक्षिष्यामि । मण्डूक आह । भद्रौ मम तावद् एकैव बुद्धिः
पलायनविषया । तद् अहम् अन्यं कञ्चिज् जलाशयं
सभार्योऽद्यैव यास्यामि । एवम् उक्त्वा मण्डूको रात्रिम्
आसाद्यान्यं जलाशयं गतः । अथान्येद्युस् तैर् यमकिङ्क-
राभैर् मत्स्यबन्धिभिः प्रभात आगत्य जालैर् आच्छादितो
ह्रदः । सर्वेऽपि मत्स्यकूर्ममण्डूककर्कटादयो जलचरा जाले
निबद्धा गृहीताः । तौ च शतबुद्धिसहस्रबुद्धी सभार्यौ
पलायमानौ चिरम् आत्मानं गतिविशेषविज्ञानैः

पलायनविषया Bahu-vríhi or relative form of dependent (762); *paláyana*, cr. 'flight;' *vishayá*, nom. fem. of *vishaya*, s. m. (1st c. 103), 'subject,' 'of which flight is the subject,' 'relating to flight;' see 762. *a*. **रात्रि** s. f. (2d c. 112) 'night;' *-trim*, acc. c. **आसाद्य** indecl. part. (566), 'having reached,' 'having arrived at,' from root *sad* (10th c.), with prep. *á*; *rátrim ásádya*, 'having arrived at the night,' i. e. 'when the night had arrived.' **यमकिङ्कराभैर्** anomalous compound (777); *yama*, cr. 'Death,' 'the god of hell;' *kin-kara*, cr. 'a servant,' 'a messenger;' *ábhair*, instr. c. pl. of *ábha*, adj. (1st c. 103), 'like,' 'resembling;' *s* becomes *r* by 65. **मत्स्यबन्धिभिः** Tat-purusha or genitively dependent (743); *matsya*, cr. 'fish;' *bandhibhih*, instr. c. of *bandhin*, noun of agency, 'a catcher,' 'a killer,' see 582. *a*. **आगत्य** indecl. part. (564. *a*), 'having come,' from root *gam*, with prep. *á*. **जाल** s. n. (1st c. 104) 'a net;' *-lair*, instr. pl., see 65. **आच्छादित** past pass. part. (530) 'covered;' *-to*, nom. c., see 64. **मत्स्यकूर्ममण्डू-ककर्कटादयो** complex relative compound, involving an aggregative (772); *matsya*, cr. 'fish;' *kúrma*, cr. 'tortoise;' *mandúka*, cr. 'frog;' *karkata*, cr. 'crab;' *ádayo*, nom. pl. of *ádi*, s. m. (2d c. 110), 'beginning;' see 772. **निबद्ध** past pass. part. (544), 'caught,' 'confined,' from root *bandh*, with prep. *ni*; *-ddhá*, nom. c. pl.; final *s* dropped by 66. *a*. **पलायमान** pres. part. Átmane (526), 'running away,' 'trying to escape,' from root *i*, with prep. *pará*, see under *pará* at 783; *-nau*, nom. du. **गतिविशेषविज्ञानैः** complex compound (770); *gati*, cr. 'movement;' *viśesha*, cr. 'variety,' 'difference;' *vijñánaih*, instr. c. pl. of *vijñána*, s. n. (1st c. 104), 'knowledge.'

कुटिलचारेण रक्षन्ताव् अपि जाले निपतितौ व्यापा-[784, 530]
दितौ च ॥

॥ कथा ४ ॥ Story 4.

अस्ति[584] कस्मिंश्चिद्[228] वनोद्देशे कश्चित्[228] पुलिन्दः । स च पापर्द्धिं कर्तुं[682] वनं प्रति[730. b] प्रस्थितः । अथ तेन[220] प्रसर्पता महान्[142] क्रोडः समासादितः । तं दृष्ट्वा[604] कर्णाकृष्टनिशितसायकेन समाहतः । तेनापि[220] कोपाविष्टचेतसा बालेन्दुद्युतिदंष्ट्राग्रेण पाटितोदरः पुलिन्दो गतासुर् भूतले प्रापतत् ।

कुटिलचारेण Karma-dháraya or descriptive (755); *kuṭila*, cr. 'crooked;' *chárena*, instr. c. of *chára*, s. m. (1st c. 103), 'motion.' रक्षन्तौ nom. du. masc. of *rakshat*, pres. part. Parasmai (524), 'preserving,' from root *raksh*. निपतितौ past pass. part. (538), 'fallen,' 'fell,' see 896, from root *pat*, with prep. *ni*.

वनोद्देशे Tat-purusha or genitively dependent (743); *vana*, cr. 'wood;' *uddeśa*, s. m. (1st c. 103), 'quarter,' 'region;' *-śe*, loc. c. पुलिन्द s. m. (1st c. 103) 'a mountaineer,' 'a countryman;' *-ndah*, nom. c. पापर्द्धि s. f. (2d c. 112) 'hunting,' 'chase;' *-rddhim*, acc. c. प्रस्थित past pass. part. (533), 'set out,' 'set forward,' from root *sthá*, with prep. *pra*; see under *pra* at 783, and see 896. प्रसर्पता instr. c. sing. of *prasarpat*, pres. part. Parasmai (524), 'proceeding onwards,' 'creeping forwards,' from root *sṛip*, with prep. *pra*. क्रोड s. m. (1st c. 103) 'a boar,' 'a hog.' समासादित past pass. part. (530), 'met,' 'encountered,' from causal of root *sad*, with prep. *sam* and *á*. कर्णाकृष्टनिशितसायकेन complex compound (770); *karṇa*, cr. 'ear;' *ákṛishṭa*, cr. 'drawn,' 'pulled;' *niśita*, cr. 'sharp;' *sáyaka*, s. m. (1st c. 103), 'an arrow;' *-kena*, instr. c. समाहत past pass. part. (545), 'killed,' from root *han* (2d c., see 654), with prep. *sam* and *á*. कोपाविष्टचेतसा complex relative compound (771); *kopa*, cr. 'rage;' *ávishṭa*, cr. 'possessed,' 'filled with;' *chetas*, s. n. (7th c. 164), 'mind;' *-sá*, instr. c. बालेन्दुद्युतिदंष्ट्राग्रेण complex compound (770); *bála*, cr. 'young;' *indu*, cr. 'moon;' *dyuti*, cr. 'brightness;' *danshṭrá*, cr. 'tusk' (80. XXIV); *agra*, s. n. (1st c. 104), 'point;' *-greṇa*, instr. c. पाटितोदरः Bahu-vríhi or relative form of descriptive (766); *páṭita*, cr. 'rent,' 'ripped up;' *udara*, s. n. (1st c. 104), 'belly,' 'stomach;' *-rah*, nom. c. गतासु Bahu-vríhi or relative (767); *gata*, cr. 'gone,' 'departed;' *asu*, s. m. (3d c. 111), 'breath,' 'life;' *-sur*, nom. c., see 65. भूतल s. n. (1st c. 104) 'the ground,' 'the earth;' *-le*, loc. c. प्रापतत् 3d sing. 1st pret. Parasmai, 'he fell down,' from root *pat* (1st c.), with prep. *pra*.

अथ लुब्धकं व्यापाद्य शूकरोऽपि शरप्रहारमात्रवेदनया
पञ्चत्वम् उपागतः। एतस्मिन् अन्तरे कश्चिद् आसन्नमृत्युः
शृगाल इतस्ततो निराहारतया पीडितः परिभ्रमंस् तं
प्रदेशम् आजगाम। यावद् वराहपुलिन्दौ पञ्चत्वम् उपा-
गतौ द्वावपि पश्यति तावत् प्रहृष्टो व्यचिन्तयत्। भो
अनुकूलो मे विधिः। तेनैतद् अचिन्तितं भोजनम् उप-
स्थितं। तद् अहं तथा भक्षयामि यथा बहून्यहानि मे
प्राणयात्रा भविष्यतीति। तत् तावद् एनं स्नायुपाशं
धनुःकोटिगतं भक्षयामि। इत्येवं मनसा निश्चित्य स्नायुं

लुब्धक s. m. (1st c. 103) 'a hunter;' *-kam*, acc. c. व्यापाद्य indecl. part. (566), 'having killed,' from causal of root *pad*, with prep. *vi* and *á*. शूकर s. m. (1st c. 103) 'a boar,' 'a hog.' शरप्रहारमात्रवेदनया Tat-purusha or dependent compound (745); *śara*, cr. 'arrow;' *prahára*, cr. 'wound;' *mátra*, cr. 'mere;' *vedaná*, s. f. (1st c. 105), 'sensation,' 'perception;' *-nayá*, instr. c. पञ्चत्व s. n. (1st c. 104) 'death,' 'the state of return to the five elements.' उपागत past pass. part. (545), 'underwent,' 'went to,' from root *gam*, with prep. *upa* and *á;* see 896, 844. अन्तर s. n. (1st c. 104) 'interval;' *-re*, loc. c. शृगाल s. m. (1st c. 103) 'a jackal.' निराहारता abst. s. f. (1st c. 105 and 80. XXIII) 'the state of being without food;' *-tayá*, instr. c.; see 769. *a*. पीडित past pass. part. (538), 'distressed,' from root *píḍ*. परिभ्रमत् pres. part. Parasmai (524), 'wandering about,' from root *bhram* (1st c.), with prep. *pari;* this root is also of the 4th c., see 275; *-man*, nom. c., *s* added by 53. प्रदेश s. m. (1st c. 103) 'spot,' 'place,' 'region;' *-śam*, acc. c. वराहपुलिन्दौ Dwandwa compound (751); *varáha*, cr. 'a boar,' 'a hog;' *pulindau*, nom. du. masc. of *pulinda*. प्रहृष्ट past pass. part., used as adj. (1st c. 187), 'pleased,' 'delighted,' from root *hṛish*, with prep. *pra;* see 539. व्यचिन्तयत् 3d sing. 1st pret. Parasmai, 'he reflected,' 'he thought to himself,' from root *chint* (10th c., see 641), with prep. *vi*, 783. अनुकूल adj. m. f. n. (1st c. 187) 'favourable;' *-lo*, nom. c., see 64. विधि s. m. (2d c. 110) 'destiny,' 'fortune;' *-dhih*, nom. c., see 63. *a*. भोजन s. n. (1st c. 104) 'food;' *-nam*, nom. c. प्राणयात्रा Tat-purusha or genitively dependent (743); *práṇa*. cr. 'life;' *yátrá*, s. f. 'the means of going,' 'the means of supporting,' see 80. XXIV; *-trá*, nom. c. स्नायुपाशं Tat-purusha or genitively dependent (743); *snáyu*, cr. 'sinew;' *páśa*, 'string;' *-śam*, acc. c. धनुःकोटिगतं Tat-purusha or dependent (745); *dhanus*, cr. 'bow,' see 63; *koṭi*, cr. 'the end,' 'the point;' *gata*, see 739. *a*. निश्चित्य indecl. part.; see under *nir*, 783. *m*. and 560.

भक्षयितुं[641. b] प्रवृत्तः[806, 781]। ततश्च त्रुटिते पाशे तालुप्रदेशं निदार्य चापकोटिर् मस्तके शिखावन् निष्क्रान्ता[781, 846]। सोऽपि तद्वेदनया तत्क्षणान्[718] मृतः[806]॥

त्रुटित past pass. part. (538), 'cut,' 'divided,' from root *truṭ* (6th c. 388. *b*); *-ṭite*, loc. c., see 840. तालुप्रदेशं Tat-purusha or genitively dependent (743); *tálu*, cr. 'palate;' *pradeśa*, s. m. (1st c. 103), 'region;' *-śam*, acc. c. निदार्य indecl. part. (566), 'having pierced,' 'having penetrated,' from causal of root *dṛí*, with prep. *ni*. चापकोटिर् Tat-purusha or genitively dependent (743); *chápa*, cr. 'bow;' *koṭi*, s. f. 'point;' *-ṭir*, nom. c., see 65. मस्तक s. m. (1st c. 103) 'the head;' *-ke*, loc. c. शिखावत् indecl.; *śikhá*, 'a tuft,' as of hair, &c.; *vat*, 'like,' affix of similitude, see 724; *t* becomes *n* by 47. वेदना s. f. (1st c. 105) 'pain,' 'agony;' *-nayá*, instr. c.

SCHEME OF THE MORE COMMON SANSKṚIT METRES.

1st class of Metres, consisting of two lines, determined by the number of SYLLABLES *in the half-line.*

Śloka or *Anushṭubh* (8 syllables to the half-line or Páda).

935. THE commonest of all the infinite variety of Sanskṛit metres is the Śloka or Anushṭubh. This is the metre which chiefly prevails in the great epic poems.

It consists of four half-lines of 8 syllables or two lines of 16 syllables each, but the rules which regulate one line apply equally to the other; so that it is only necessary to give the scheme of one line, as follows:—

1	2	3	4	5	6	7	8	‖	9	10	11	12	13	14	15	16
•	•	•	•	⏑	⏓	⏓	•	‖	•	•	•	•	⏑	—	⏑	•

Note—The mark • denotes either long or short.

The 1st, 2d, 3d, 4th, 9th, 10th, 11th, and 12th syllables may be either long or short. The 8th, as ending the half-line, and the 16th, as ending the line, are also common. Since the line is considered as divided into two parts at the 8th syllable, it is an universal rule that this syllable must end a word, *whether simple or compound* *.

---

* There is, however, one example in the Hitopadeśa of a compound word running through a whole line.

The 5th syllable ought always to be short. The 6th may be either long or short; but if long, then the 7th ought to be long also; and if short, then the 7th ought to be short also. But occasional variations from these last rules occur.

The last 4 syllables form two iambics; the 13th being always short, the 14th always long, and the 15th always short.

Every S'loka, or couplet of two lines, ought to form a complete sentence in itself, and contain both subject and predicate. Not unfrequently, however, in the Rámáyaṇa and Mahábhárata, three lines are united to form a triplet.

936. In the remaining metres determined by the number of *syllables* in the half-line, each half-line is exactly alike; so that it is only necessary to give the scheme of one half-line, or quarter of the verse (Páda).

Note, that in printed books each quarter of the verse, if it consist of more than 8 syllables, is often made to occupy a line.

937. *Trishṭubh* (11 syllables to the half-line).

Of this there are 22 varieties. The commonest are—

	1	2	3	4	5	6	7	8	9	10	11	
938. *Indra-vajrá,*	—	—	∪	—	—	∪	∪	—	∪	—	•	‖
939. *Upendra-vajrá,*	∪	—	∪	—	—	∪	∪	—	∪	—	•	‖

There is generally a cæsura at the 5th syllable.

Note—The above 2 varieties are sometimes mixed in the same stanza; in which case the metre is called *Upajáti* or *Ákhyánakí.*

	1	2	3	4	5	6	7	8	9	10	11	
940. *Rathoddhatá,*	—	∪	—	∪	∪	∪	—	∪	—	∪	—	‖

941. *Jagatí* (12 syllables to the half-line).

Of this there are 30 varieties. The commonest are—

	1	2	3	4	5	6	7	8	9	10	11	12	
942. *Vanśa-sthavila,*	∪	—	∪	—	—	∪	∪	—	∪	—	∪	∓*	‖
943. *Druta-vilambita,*	∪	∪	∪	—	∪	∪	—	∪	∪	—	∪	∓	‖

944. *Atijagatí* (13 syllables to the half-line).

Of this there are 16 varieties. The commonest are—

	1	2	3	4	5	6	7	8	9	10	11	12	13	
945. *Mañju-bháshiṇí,*	∪	∪	—	∪	—	∪	∪	∪	—	∪	—	∪	∓	‖
946. *Praharshiṇí,*	—	—	—	∪	∪	∪	∪	—	∪	—	∪	—	∓	‖
947. *Ruchirá* or *Prabhávatí,*	∪	—	∪	—	∪	∪	∪	∪	—	∪	—	∪	∓	‖

* The mark ∓ is meant to show that the last syllable is long at the end of the half-line, but long or short at the end of the line.

948. *Śakwarí* or *Śakkarí* or *Śarkarí* (14 syllables to the half-line).

Of this there are 20 varieties. The commonest is—

	1	2	3	4	5	6	7	8	9	10	11	12	13	14	‖
949. *Vasanta-tilaká,*	—	—	⏑	—	⏑	⏑	⏑	—	⏑	⏑	—	⏑	—	⏓	‖

950. *Atiśakwarí* or *Atiśakkarí* or *Atiśarkarí* (15 syllables to the half-line).

Of this there are 18 varieties. The commonest is—

	1	2	3	4	5	6	7	8	‖	9	10	11	12	13	14	15	‖
951. *Málinì* or *Mánini,*	⏑	⏑	⏑	⏑	⏑	⏑	—	—	‖	—	⏑	—	—	⏑	—	⏓	‖

There is a cæsura at the 8th syllable.

952. *Ashṭi* (16 syllables to the half-line).

Of this there are 12 varieties; none of which are common.

953. *Atyashṭi* (17 syllables to the half-line).

Of this there are 17 varieties. The commonest are—

	1	2	3	4	5	6	‖	7	8	9	10	11	12	13	14	15	16	17	‖
954. *Śikhariṇí,*	⏑	—	—	—	—	—	‖	⏑	⏑	⏑	⏑	⏑	—	—	⏑	⏑	⏑	⏓	‖

Cæsura at the 6th syllable.

	1	2	3	4	‖	5	6	7	8	9	10	‖	11	12	13	14	15	16	17	‖
955. *Mandákrántá,*	—	—	—	—	‖	⏑	⏑	⏑	⏑	⏑	—	‖	—	⏑	—	—	⏑	—	⏓	‖

Cæsura at the 4th and 10th syllables.

	1	2	3	4	5	6	‖	7	8	9	10	‖	11	12	13	14	15	16	17	‖
956. *Hariṇí,*	⏑	⏑	⏑	⏑	⏑	—	‖	—	—	—	—	‖	⏑	—	⏑	⏑	—	⏑	⏓	‖

Cæsura at the 6th and 10th syllables.

957. *Dhṛiti* (18 syllables to the half-line).

Of this there are 17 varieties; one of which is found in the Raghu-vanśa—

	1	2	3	4	5	6	7	8	9	10	11	12	13	14	15	16	17	18	‖
958. *Mahá-máliká,*	⏑	⏑	⏑	⏑	⏑	⏑	—	⏑	—	—	⏑	—	—	⏑	—	—	⏑	⏓	‖

959. *Atidhṛiti* (19 syllables to the half-line).

Of this there are 13 varieties. The commonest is—

	1	2	3	4	5	6	7	8	9	10	11	12	‖	13	14	15	16	17	18	19	‖
960. *Śárdúla-vikríḍita,*	—	—	—	⏑	⏑	—	⏑	—	⏑	⏑	⏑	—	‖	—	—	⏑	—	—	⏑	⏓	‖

Cæsura at the 12th syllable.

961. *Kṛiti* (20 syllables to the half-line).

Of this there are 4 varieties; none of which are common.

962. *Prakṛiti* (21 syllables to the half-line).

	1	2	3	4	5	6	7	‖	8	9	10	11	12	13	14	‖	15	16	17	18	19	20	21	‖
963. *Sragdhará,*	—	—	—	—	⏑	—	—	‖	⏑	⏑	⏑	⏑	⏑	⏑	—	‖	—	⏑	—	—	⏑	—	⏓	‖

Cæsura at the 7th and 14th syllables.

964. Of the remaining metres determined by the number of syllables in the half-line, *Ákṛiti* has 22 syllables, and includes 3 varieties; *Vikṛiti* 23 syllables, 6 varieties; *San̄kṛiti* 24 syllables, 5 varieties; *Atikṛiti* 25 syllables, 2 varieties; *Utkṛiti* 26 syllables, 3 varieties; and *Daṇḍaka* is the name given to all metres which exceed *Utkṛiti* in the number of syllables.

965. There are two metres, however, peculiar to the Vedas, called *Gáyatrí* and *Ushṇih*. The first of these has only 6 syllables to the quarter-verse, and includes 11 varieties; the second has 7 syllables to the half-line, and includes 8 varieties.

a. Observe, that when the half-line is so short, the whole verse is sometimes written in one line.

b. Observe also, that great license is allowed in Vaidik metres: thus in the

966. *Gáyatrí,*

which may be regarded as consisting of a triplet of 3 divisions of 8 syllables each, or of 6 feet of 4 syllables each, generally printed in one line, the quantity of each syllable is very irregular. The following verse exhibits the most usual quantities:

1 *a*	*b*	2 *a*	*b*	3 *a*	*b*
• • • •	⏑ – ⏑ • ‖	• • • •	⏑ – ⏑ • ‖	• • • •	⏑ – ⏑ • ‖

but even in the *b* verse of each division the quantity may vary.

2d class of Metres, consisting of two lines, determined by the number of SYLLABLES* in the WHOLE LINE (each whole line being alike).

967. This class contains 7 genera, but no varieties under each genus. Of these the commonest are—

968. *Vaitálíya* (21 syllables to the *whole* line).

1	2	3	4	5	6	7	8	9	10 ‖	11	12	13	14	15	16	17	18	19	20	21
⏑	⏑	–	⏑	⏑	–	⏑	–	⏑	– ‖	⏑	⏑	–	–	⏑	⏑	–	⏑	–	⏑	•

There is a cæsura at the 10th syllable.

969. *Aupachchhandasika* (23 syllables to the *whole* line).

The scheme of this metre is the same as the last, with a long syllable added after the 10th and last syllable in the line; the cæsura being at the 11th syllable.

970. *Pushpitágrá* (25 syllables to the *whole* line).

1	2	3	4	5	6	7	8	9	10	11	12 ‖	13	14	15	16	17	18	19	20	21	22	23	24	25
⏑	⏑	⏑	⏑	⏑	⏑	–	⏑	–	⏑	–	– ‖	⏑	⏑	⏑	⏑	–	⏑	⏑	–	⏑	–	⏑	–	•

There is a cæsura at the 12th syllable.

* This class of metres is said to be regulated by the number of feet or instants in the line, in the same way as the 3d class. But as each line is generally distributed into fixed long or short syllables, and no option is allowed for each foot between a spondee, anapæst, dactyl, proceleusmaticus, and amphibrach, it will obviate confusion to regard this class as determined by syllables, like the 1st.

3d class of Metres, consisting of two lines, determined by the number of FEET *in the whole verse (each foot containing generally four instants or mátrás).*

971. Note—Each foot is supposed to consist of four instants, and a short syllable is equivalent to one instant, a long syllable to two. Hence only such feet can be used as are equivalent to four instants; and of this kind are the dactyl (— ◡ ◡), the spondee (— —), the anapæst (◡ ◡ —), the amphibrach (◡ — ◡), and the proceleusmaticus (◡ ◡ ◡ ◡); any one of which may be employed.

Of this class of metres the commonest is the

972. *Áryá* or *Gáthá*.

Each line consists of seven and a half feet; and each foot contains four instants, excepting the 6th of the second line, which contains only one, and is therefore a single short syllable. Hence there are 30 instants in the first line, and 27 in the second. The half-foot at the end of each line is generally, but not always, a long syllable; the 6th foot of the first line must be either an amphibrach or proceleusmaticus; and the 1st, 3d, 5th, and 7th feet must not be amphibrachs. The cæsura commonly takes place at the end of the 3d foot in each line, and the measure is then sometimes called *Paṭhyá*. The following are a few examples:

1	2	3	4	5	6	7	
— —	◡ — ◡	◡ ◡ —	— ◡ ◡	— ◡ ◡	◡ — ◡	— —	—
◡ ◡ —	◡ — ◡	◡ ◡ —	— —	◡ ◡ —	◡	— —	◡
— —	◡ ◡ —	— —	— —	— ◡ ◡	◡ — ◡	— ◡ ◡	—
◡ ◡ —	— ◡ ◡	◡ ◡ —	◡ — ◡	— —	◡	— ◡ ◡	—
◡ ◡ —	— ◡ ◡	— —	◡ ◡ —	— ◡ ◡	◡ — ◡	— —	◡
◡ ◡ —	◡ ◡ ◡ ◡	— ◡ ◡	— —	◡ ◡ —	◡	— —	—
— ◡ ◡	◡ — ◡	◡ ◡ —	— ◡ ◡	— ◡ ◡	◡ — ◡	— —	—
— —	◡ — ◡	— —	◡ ◡ ◡ ◡	◡ ◡ —	◡	— —	—
— ◡ ◡	— —	— ◡ ◡	— —	— —	◡ ◡ ◡ ◡	◡ ◡ —	—
◡ ◡ ◡ ◡	◡ ◡ ◡ ◡	— —	— —	◡ ◡ —	◡	— —	◡

973. The *Udgíti* metre only differs from the *Áryá* in inverting the lines, and placing the short line, with 27 instants, first in order.

974. There are three other varieties:—In the *Upagíti*, both lines consist of 27 instants; in the *Gíti*, both consist of 30 instants; and in the *Áryágíti*, of 32.

INDEX I.

OBS.—The numbers refer to the number of the rule.

ABSTRACT nouns, 80. IX. X. XII. XXIII. 81. V. 85. IV.
Accentuation, 24.
Adjectives, 184; syntax of, 824.
Adverbial compounds, 760.
Adverbs, 712; syntax of, 917.
Affixes; forming nouns, substantive and adjective, 80; forming adverbs, 718.
Agency, nouns of, 579.
Aggregative compounds, 746.
A'kṛiti, a kind of metre, 964.
Alphabet, 1—26.
Anomalous compounds, 777.
Anubandhas, 75. *c*.
Anunásika, 7.
Anushṭubh, a kind of metre, 935.
Anuswára, 6.
Aorist, see Third preterite.
Ardha-visarga, 8. *a*.
Ardhákára, 10.
A'ryá, a kind of metre, 972.
A'ryágíti, a kind of metre, 974.
Ashṭi, a kind of metre, 952.
Atidhṛiti, a kind of metre, 959.
Atijagatí, a kind of metre, 944.
Atikṛiti, a kind of metre, 964.
Atiśakwarí, a kind of metre, 950.
A'tmane-pada, 243.
Atyashṭi, a kind of metre, 953.
Augment अ *a*, 260, 260. *a*. *b*.
Avyayí-bháva compounds, 760.
Bahu-vríhi compounds, 761.
Base, of nouns, 74, 77; formation of base of nouns, 79, 80—87; inflection of, 88—183; of verbs, 244; formation of the base of verbs, 256—517.
Benedictive, 242; terminations of, 246; formation of the base of, 442; syntax of, 890.
Cardinals, 198; declension of, 200.
Cases of nouns, 90.
Causal verbs, 479; terminations of, 480; formation of the base of, 481; passive form of, 496; syntax of, 847.
Chandra-vindu, 7.
Classes, of nouns, 79; of verbs, see Conjugation.
Classification of letters, 18.
Collective or Dwigu compounds, 759; nouns, 80. XII. XXIII.
Combination (euphonic) of vowels, 27; of consonants, 39; of the finals of verbal bases with terminations, 296.
Comparative degree, 191, 194; syntax of, 829.
Comparison, degrees of, 191, 192; syntax of, 829.
Complex compounds, 770.
Compound consonants, 5.
Compound verbs, 782, 787.
Compound words, 733—737; Tat-purusha or Dependent, 739; Dwandwa or Aggregative, 746; Karma-dháraya or Descriptive, 755; Dwigu or Collective, 759; Avyayí-bháva or Indeclinable, 760; Bahu-vríhi or Relative, 761; Complex, 770; Anomalous, 777; changes undergone by words at the end of, 778.
Conditional, 242; terminations of, 246, 247; formation of the base of, 456; syntax of, 891.

Conjugational tenses, 241, 248.

Conjugations of verbs, summary of, 249; three groups of, 257; first group of, 259; second and third groups of, 290. 1st conj., 261; examples, 587: 2d conj., 307; examples, 644: 3d conj., 330; examples, 662: 4th conj., 272; examples, 612: 5th conj., 349; examples, 675: 6th conj., 278; examples, 625: 7th conj., 342; examples, 667: 8th conj., 353; examples, 682: 9th conj., 356; examples, 686: 10th conj., 283; examples, 638.

Conjunction (euphonic), see Combination.

Conjunctions, 727; syntax of, 912.

Consonants, 1; method of writing, 4; compound, 5; pronunciation of, 12; combination of, 39.

Crude form or base, 77.

Daṇḍaka, a kind of metre, 964.

Declension; general observations, 88; of *nau*, 'a ship,' 94; of 1st class of nouns in *a*, *á*, *í*, 103—109; of 2d class in *i*, 110, 112, 114; of 3d class in *u*, 111, 113, 115; of 4th class in *ṛi*, 127—130; of 5th class in *t* and *d*, 136—145; of 6th class in *an* and *in*, 146—162; of 7th class in *as*, *is*, and *us*, 163—171; of 8th class in any other consonant, 172—183.

Degrees of comparison, 191, 192; syntax of, 829.

Demonstrative pronouns, 223.

Dependent compounds or Tat-purusha, 739—745.

Derivative verbs, 460.

Descriptive compounds or Karma-dháraya, 755.

Desiderative verbs, 498; terminations of, 499; formation of the base, 500; causal form of, 506; nouns, 80. XXII; adjectives, 82, 111.

Deva-nágarí alphabet, 1.

Dhṛiti, a kind of metre, 957.

Dwandwa or Aggregative compounds, 746.

Dwigu or Collective compounds, 759.

Euphonic combination of vowels, 27; of consonants, 39.

Examples of verbs, see Conjugations.

First preterite, 241, p. 102; terminations of, 246, 247; formation of base of, 260, 261, 272, 278, 283, 307, 330, 342, 349, 353, 356; syntax of, 884.

Frequentative verbs, 507; Átmane-pada frequentatives, 509; Parasmai-pada frequentatives, 514; nouns, 80. XXII.

Future, first and second, 386; terminations of, 246, 247; formation of the base of, 388; syntax of, 886, 887.

Gáyatrí, a kind of metre, 965, 966.

Genders of nouns, 89.

Gíti, a kind of metre, 974.

Guṇa change of vowels, 27, 28, 29.

Hard consonants, 18. *a*. *b*, 20. *b*, 39.

इ *i*, inserted, 388. *a*, 391, 392; list of roots ending in vowels inserting or rejecting *i*, 394; list of roots ending in consonants rejecting *i*, 400.

Imperative, 241, p. 102; terminations of, 246, 247; formation of the base of, 261, 272, 278, 283, 307, 330, 342, 349, 353, 356; syntax of, 882.

Imperfect tense, see First preterite.

Indeclinable compounds, 760.

Indeclinable words, 712; syntax of, 912.

Indefinite pronouns, 228.

Indicative mood, 241, p. 102.

Infinitive, 458; formation of the base of, 459; syntax of, 867.

Intensive verb, see Frequentative.

Interjections, 732; syntax of, 926.

Interrogative pronouns, 227.

Jagatí, a kind of metre, 941.

Karma-dháraya or Descriptive compounds, 755.

Kṛiti, a kind of metre, 961.

Letters, 1; classification of, 18; euphonic combination of, 27.

Metre, scheme of the more common kinds of, p. 350.

Moods, 241, p. 102.
Multitude, nouns of, 80. XII. XXIII.
Nágarí alphabet, 1.
Nominal verbs, 518—523.
Nouns, formation of base of, 74; declension of, see Declension; syntax of, 802.
Numbers, of nouns, 91; of verbs, 243.
Numerals, 198—215; syntax of, 206, 835.
Numerical symbols, 216.
Optative, see Potential or Benedictive.
Ordinals, 208.
Pada or voice, 243.
Parasmai-pada, 243.
Parsing, exercises in, 930.
Participial nouns of agency, 579.
Participles, present, 524, 526; past passive, 530; past active, 553; of the 2d preterite, 554; past indeclinable, 555; adverbial indeclinable, 567; future passive, 568; of the 2d future, 578; syntax of, 892.
Particle, 878.
Passive voice, 243. *a*, 253; passive verbs, 461; terminations of, 462; formation of the base of, 463.
Patronymics, 80. XII. 81. VI.
Perfect, see Second preterite, Third preterite.
Persons of the tenses, 244.
Possessive adjectives, 84. I. II. p. 51, 85. VI. VII; pronouns, 231.
Potential, 241, p. 102; terminations of, 246, 247; formation of the base of, 261, 272, 278, 283, 307, 330, 342, 349, 353, 356; syntax of, 879.
Prakṛiti, a kind of metre, 962.
Prepositions, 729, 783; syntax of, 916.
Present, 241, p. 102; terminations of, 246, 247; formation of the base of, 261, 272, 278, 283, 307, 330, 342, 349, 353, 356; syntax of, 873.
Preterite, see First preterite, Second preterite, Third preterite.
Pronominals, 236, 240.
Pronouns, 217; syntax of, 836.
Pronunciation, of vowels, 11; of consonants, 12.
Prosody, 935.
Reduplication, rules for, 331, 369.
Relative pronouns, 226; compounds (Bahu-vríhi), 761.
Root, 74, 75.
S'akwarí, a kind of metre, 948.
Sandhi, rules of, see Combination.
San-kṛiti, a kind of metre, 964.
Second preterite, 364; syntax of, 885.
Soft letters, 18. *a*, 20. *b*, 39.
Sonant letters, 18. *a*. *b*, 20. *b*, 39.
Superlative degree, 191, 192.
Surd consonants, 18. *a*. *b*, 20. *b*, 39.
Symbols, 6.
Syntax, 794.
Tables of verbs, 583.
Tat-purusha or Dependent compounds, 739—745.
Tenses, 241, p. 102.
Terminations, of nouns, 91; of verbs, 246, 247.
Third preterite, 415; syntax of, 888.
Translation, exercises in, 930.
Trishṭubh, a kind of metre, 937.
Udgíti, a kind of metre, 973.
Upagíti, a kind of metre, 974.
Ushṇih, a kind of metre, 965.
Utkṛiti, a kind of metre, 964.
Vaitálíya, a kind of metre, 968.
Verb, 241; syntax of, 839.
Vikṛiti, a kind of metre, 964.
Viráma, 9.
Visarga, 8, 61.
Voices, 243.
Vowels, 1, 2; method of writing, 4; pronunciation of, 11; combination of, 27.
Vṛiddhi change of vowels, 27, 28, 29. *a*.
Writing, method of, 26.

INDEX II.

OBS.—The numbers refer to the number of the rule.

अ affix, 80. I. II. III. XII.

अक affix, 80. IV.

अक्षि 'an eye,' 122.

अग्नि 'fire,' 110.

अञ्च् 'to stretch,' 385.

अञ्ज् 'to anoint,' 347, 668.

अथु affix, 82. VI.

अद् 'to eat,' 317, 652.

अदत् 'eating,' 141. *c.*

अदस् 'this' or 'that,' 225.

अधी 'to read,' 311, 372. *a.*

अध्वन् 'a road,' 148.

अन् 'to breathe,' 326.

अन affix, 80. V. 85. I.

अनडुह् 'an ox,' 182. *d.*

अन्तर 'another,' 777. *b.*

अन्य 'other,' 236.

अपेक्ष्य 'with reference to,' 'than,' 833. *a.*

अप्सरस् 'a nymph,' 163. *a.*

अम्बा 'a mother,' 108. *c.*

अय् 'to go,' 385. *c.*

अर affix, 80. VIII.

अर्च् 'to worship,' 371.

अर्थ् 'to ask,' 642.

अर्य्यमन् 'the sun,' 157.

अर्वन् 'a horse,' 158.

अर्ह् 'to deserve,' 608.

अल affix, 80. VIII.

अलं 'enough,' 901. *a,* 918.

अल्प 'a few,' 240.

अल्पमति 'narrow-minded,' 119.

अल्पविद्य 'possessed of little learning,' 108.

अवधीर् 'to despise,' 75. *a.*

अवाच् 'southern,' 176. *b.*

अश् 'to eat,' 357. *a,* 696.

अश् 'to obtain,' 'to pervade,' 371. *a,* 681. *a.*

अश्मन् 'a stone,' 153.

अस् 'to be,' 322, 364. *a,* 369, 584.

अस् 'to throw,' 622.

अस affix, 86. I.

असृज् 'blood,' 176. *d.*

अस्थि 'a bone,' 122.

अस्मत् 'I,' 218.

अह् 'to say,' 384.

अहन् 'a day,' 156.

आ affix, 80. XXII.

आक affix, 80. VIII.

आत्मक 'composed of,' 'consisting of,' 769. *f,* 774.

आत्मन् 'soul,' 'self,' 147, 222.

आदि 'beginning with,' 'et cetera,' 764, 772.

आप् 'to obtain,' 351, 369, 681.

आरभ्य 'beginning from,' 925, 793. *b.*

आरु affix, 82. VI.

आलु affix, 82. VI.

आशिस् 'a blessing,' 166.

आस् 'to sit,' 317.

आस् 'to remain,' with pres. part., 877.

इ 'to go,' 310, 372, 645.

इ affix, 81. I. II. III. VI.
इक affix, 80. XIII.
इत् affix, 84. II.
इत affix, 80. XXI. *c*.
इतर 'other,' 236.
इति 'so,' 927.
इत्नु affix, 82. VI.
इदं 'this,' 224.
इन् affix, 85. V. VI.
इन affix, 80. XVI.
इन्ध् 'to kindle,' 347.
इमन् affix, 85. IV.
इर affix, 80. VIII.
इल affix, 80. VIII.
इष् 'to wish,' 282, 370, 637.
इष्ठ affix, 192, 80. XIX.
इष्णु affix, 82. V.
इस् affix, 86. II.
ई affix, 80. XXV. XXVI. XXVII.
ईक्ष् 'to see,' 605.
ईड् 'to praise,' 325.
ईदृश 'so like,' 234.
ईन affix, 80. XVI.
ईय affix, 80. XV.
ईयस् affix, 192.
ईश् 'to rule,' 325, 385.
उ affix, 82. I. II. III.
उक affix, 80. VIII.
उख् 'to move,' 370.
उत्पलचक्षुस् 'having lotus eyes,' 166. *a*.
उदञ्च् 'northern,' 176. *b*.
उद्दिश्य 'with reference to,' 924.
उन्द् 'to moisten,' 347.
उपगो 'near a cow,' 134. *a*.
उपानह् 'a shoe,' 182. *e*.
उर affix, 80. VIII.
उल affix, 80. VIII.
उशनस् 'Venus,' 170.
उष् 'to burn,' 385. *c*.
उष्णिह् a kind of metre, 182. *b*, 965.
उष्मन् 'the hot season,' 148.
उस् affix, 86. II.
ऊक affix, 80. VIII.
ऊर्ज् 'strong,' 176. *h*.
ऊर्णु 'to cover,' 316.
ऋ 'to go,' 334, 378.
ऋण् 'to go,' 684.
ऋध् 'to flourish,' 371, 680.
ऋभुक्षिन् a name of Indra, 162.
ॠ 'to go,' 358.
एक 'one,' 200.
एतत् 'that,' 223.
एध् 'to increase,' 600.
एय affix, 80. XIV.
एर affix, 80. VIII.
क affix, 80. VIII. XVII.
कतिचित् 'a few,' 230.
कथ् 'to say,' 286, 643.
कम् 'to love,' 440. *a*.
कर्मन् 'an action,' 152.
कल्प affix, 80. XXI.
कश्चित् 'any one,' 228.
काम 'desirous,' with infinitive, 871.
कारिन् 'a doer,' 159.
कास् 'to shine,' 385. *c*.
किं 'who?' 'what?' 227.
किं 'why?' 921.
कियत् 'how many,' 234. *b*.
कुन्थ् 'to pain,' 'to be pained,' 362.
कुमार् 'to play,' 75. *a*.
कुमारी 'a girl,' 107.
कुमुद् n. 'a lotus,' 139. *a*.
कुर्वत् 'doing,' 141. *c*.
कू 'to sound,' 432.
कृ 'to do,' 355, 364, 366, 368, 682, 683, 701.

कृत् 'to cut,' 281.
कृतवत् 'who made,' 140. *a.*
कृष् 'to draw,' 606.
कॄ 'to scatter,' 280, 627.
कॄ 'to hurt,' 'to kill,' 358.
कॄत् 'to celebrate,' 287.
क्लृप् 'to make,' 263.
कोऽपि 'any one,' 229.
क्री 'to buy,' 689.
क्रोष्टृ 'a jackal,' 128. *c.*
क्लिश् 'to harass,' 697.
क्षण् 'to kill,' 684, 685.
क्ष्णु 'to sharpen,' 396. *a.*
क्षिण् 'to kill,' 684.
क्षिप् 'to throw,' 274, 279, 635.
क्षिप् 'to throw,' freq., 710.
क्षु 'to sneeze,' 396. *a.*
क्षुभ् 'to agitate,' 694.
खन् 'to dig,' 376.
खलपू 'a sweeper,' 126. *b,* 190.
खिद् 'to vex,' 'to torment,' 281.
ख्या 'to tell,' 437. *a.*
गतभी 'fearless,' 123. *b.*
गम् 'to go,' 270, 602.
गम् 'to go,' freq., 709.
गुप् 'to protect,' 271.
गॄ 'to evacuate,' 432.
गॄ 'to sound,' 358.
गै 'to sing,' 268, 374, 595. *a.*
गो 'a cow,' 133.
गोरक्ष् 'cow-keeper,' 183. *b.*
ग्रन्थ् 'to tie,' 362, 375. *f,* 693.
ग्रस् 'to swallow,' 286.
गुह् 'to conceal,' 271, 609.
ग्रह् 'to take,' 359, 699.
ग्रह् 'to take,' freq., 711.
ग्रामणी 'chief of a village,' 126. *a.*
ग्लै 'to be weary,' 268, 595. *b.*
घस् 'to eat,' 377.
घुष् 'to proclaim,' 643. *a.*
घृण् 'to shine,' 684.
घ्रा 'to smell,' 269, 588.
च 'and,' 912.
चकास् 'to shine,' 75. *a.*
चक्ष् 'to speak,' 321.
चक्षुस् 'the eye,' 165. *a.*
चतुर् 'four,' 203.
चन्द्रमस् 'the moon,' 163.
चमू 'a host,' 125.
चर् 'one who goes,' 180.
चर्मन् 'leather,' 153.
चि 'to gather,' 350, 367, 583.
चित्रलिख् 'a painter,' 175.
चिन्त् 'to think,' 641.
चेत् 'if,' 915.
चुर् 'to steal,' 284, 638, 639.
छद्मन् 'a pretext,' 153.
छिद् 'to cut,' 667.
छुर् 'to cut,' 388. *b.*
जक्ष् 'to eat,' 290. *b,* 326.
जगत् 'moving,' 142. *a.*
जन् 'to be born,' 276, 376, 434, 617. *a.*
जन् 'to produce,' 339, 666. *b.*
जन्मन् 'birth,' 153.
जरस् 'decay,' 171.
जरा 'decay,' 108. *d.*
जलपी 'water-drinker,' 126. *a.*
जागृ 'to be awake,' 75. *a,* 316, 385. *d.*
जाग्रत् 'watching,' 141. *a.*
जि 'to conquer,' 263, 590.
जिगदिस् 'desirous of speaking,' 166.
जीव् 'to live,' 267, 603.
जुह्वत् 'sacrificing,' 141. *c.*
जॄ 'to grow old,' 277, 358, 375. *g,* 437. *a.*
ज्ञा 'to know,' 360, 688.
ज्या 'to grow old,' 361.

डी 'to fly,' 274, 395. *a*.
त् affix, 84. I.
तक्षन् 'a carpenter,' 150.
तत् 'he,' 220.
तन् 'to stretch,' 354, 583, 684.
तन affix, 80. XVI.
तनु 'thin,' 118, 119. *a*.
तन्त्री 'a string,' 'a wire,' 124.
तम affix, 191, 80. XIX.
तर affix, 191, 80. XIX.
तरी 'a boat,' 124.
ता affix, 80. XXIII.
तादृश 'such like,' 234.
तादृश 'so,' 801. *a*, 920. *a*.
तावत् 'so many,' 801, 838, 876.
ति affix, 81. V.
तिर्यञ्च् 'going crookedly,' 176. *b*.
तु affix, 82. VI.
तु 'but,' 914.
तुद् 'to strike,' 279, 634.
तृ affix, 83. I. II.
तृण् 'to eat grass,' 684.
तृप् 'to be satisfied,' 618.
तृह् 'to kill,' 'to strike,' 'to hurt,' 345, 348, 674.
तॄ 'to cross,' 364, 375. *g*.
त्यज् 'to abandon,' 596.
त्यत् 'he' or 'that,' 221.
त्र affix, 80. VII. VIII.
त्रा affix, 80. XXIV.
त्रि 'three,' 202.
त्रुट् 'to break,' 388. *b*.
त्रै 'to preserve,' 268.
त्व affix, 80. IX.
त्वत् 'thou,' 219.
त्वदीय 'thine,' 231.
दंश् 'to bite,' 271.
दघ्न affix, 80. XX.
दण्डादण्डि 'mutual striking,' 793.
ददत् 'giving,' 141. *a*.
दधि 'ghee,' 122.
दय् 'to pity,' 385. *c*.
दरिद्रा 'to be poor,' 75. *a*, 328, 385. *d*.
दह् 'to burn,' 610.
दा 'to give,' 335, 663, 700.
दातृ 'a giver,' 127, 129. *b*.
दामन् 'a string,' 153.
दिव् 'to play,' 275.
दिवन् 'a day,' 156. *a*.
दिश् 'to point out,' 'to exhibit,' 279, 439. *a*, 583.
दिश् 'a quarter of the sky,' 181.
दिह् 'to anoint,' 659.
दीधी 'to shine,' 329.
दुर्मनस् 'evil-minded,' 164. *a*.
दुह् 'to milk,' 327, 660.
दुह् 'one who milks,' 182.
दृश् 'to see,' 270, 604.
दृश् 'to see,' causal, 704.
दृश्वन् 'a looker,' 148.
दॄ 'to tear,' 'to rend,' 358, 367. *c*.
दे 'to pity,' 379.
देवेज् 'a worshipper of the gods,' 176. *e*.
देशीय affix, 80. XXI.
दोस् 'an arm,' 166. *b*.
द्युत् 'to shine,' 597. *b*.
द्रु 'to run,' 368, 592.
द्रुह् 'to injure,' 623.
द्रुह् 'one who injures,' 182.
द्वयस affix, 80. XX.
द्वि 'two,' 201.
द्विमातृ 'having two mothers,' 130.
द्विष् 'to hate,' 309, 657.
द्विष् 'one who hates,' 181.
धनवत् 'rich,' 140.
धनिन् 'rich,' 159, 160, 161.

धर्मविद् 'knowing one's duty,' 138.
धा 'to place,' 336, 664.
धामन् 'a house,' 153.
धी 'understanding,' 123.
धीमत् 'wise,' 140. *a*.
धू 'to agitate,' 280, 358, 367. *b*, 677.
धृ 'to hold,' 285.
धे 'to drink,' 438. *b*, 440. *a*.
धेनु 'a cow,' 113.
ध्मा 'to blow,' 269.
ध्यै 'to meditate,' 268, 595. *b*.
ध्रू 'to be firm,' 432.
न affix, 80. VI.
नदी 'a river,' 106.
नप्तृ 'a grandson,' 128. *a*.
नम् 'to bend,' 433.
नश् 'to perish,' 620.
नह् 'to bind,' 624.
नामन् 'a name,' 152.
निज् 'to purify,' 341.
नी 'to lead,' 590. *a*.
नु 'to praise,' 280, 313, 396. *a*.
नु affix, 82. IV. VI.
नृ 'a man,' 128.
नृत् 'to dance,' 274, 364, 583.
नॄ 'to lead,' 358.
नौ 'a ship,' 94.
पच् 'to cook,' 267.
पचत् 'cooking,' 141.
पञ्चन् 'five,' 204.
पति 'a lord,' 121.
पथिन् 'a road,' 162.
पद् 'to go,' 434.
परिमृज् 'a cleanser,' 176. *e*.
परिव्राज् 'a religious mendicant,' 176. *e*.
पा 'to drink,' 269, 589.
पा 'to protect,' 317.
पाण्डु 'pale,' 187.
पाद् 'a foot,' 145.
पाप्मन् 'sin,' 148.
पितृ 'a father,' 128.
पिपक्ष् 'desirous of cooking,' 166.
पिपासु 'thirsty,' 118.
पिश् 'to organize,' 'to form,' 281.
पीवन् 'fat,' 150.
पुंस् 'a male,' 169.
पुट् 'to contract,' 388. *b*.
पुण्य 'holy,' 191.
पुनर्भू 'twice-born,' 126. *b*.
पुरःसर 'preceded by,' 777. *c*, 792.
पुरुष 'a man,' 107.
पुष् 'to nourish,' 357. *a*, 698.
पुष् 'to be nourished,' 621.
पू 'to purify,' 358, 364.
पूर्व or पूर्वक 'preceded by,' 'with,' 777. *c*, 792.
पूषन् 'the sun,' 157.
पृषत् 'a deer,' 142. *a*.
पॄ 'to fill,' 285, 358, 367. *c*, 640.
प्यै 'to grow fat,' 399. *b*.
प्रच्छ् 'to ask,' 282, 381, 631.
प्रत्यञ्च् 'western,' 176. *b*.
प्रशाम् 'quiet,' 179. *a*.
प्राछ् 'an asker,' 176.
प्राञ्च् 'eastern,' 176. *b*. *c*.
प्रिय 'dear,' 187.
प्री 'to please,' 285, 690.
प्रेमन् 'love,' 153.
बन्ध् 'to bind,' 362, 692.
बलिष्ठ 'strongest,' 193.
बलीयस् 'stronger,' 167, 193.
बहुनौ 'having many ships,' 134. *a*, 190.
बहुरै 'rich,' 134. *a*, 190.
बुध् 'to know,' 262, 364, 583, 614.
बुध् 'one who knows,' 177.
बुद्ध्या 'under the idea,' 809. *b*.

ब्रह्महन् 'the murderer of a Bráhman,' 157.
ब्रू 'to speak,' 314, 649.
भक्ष् 'to eat,' 643. *b*.
भञ्ज् 'to break,' 347, 669.
भवत् 'your honour,' 143, 233.
भस् 'to shine,' 340.
भानु 'the sun,' 111.
भारवाह् 'bearing a burden,' 182. *c*.
भार्या 'a wife,' 107.
भिक्ष् 'to beg,' 267.
भिद् 'to break,' 343, 583.
भी 'fear,' 123, 333, 666.
भीरु 'timid,' 118. *a*, 187.
भुज् 'to eat,' 346, 668. *a*.
भू 'to be,' 263, 367. *b*, 585, 586.
भू 'to be,' causal, 703.
भू 'to be,' desiderative, 705.
भू 'to be,' frequentative, 706, 707.
भू 'the earth,' 125. *a*.
भूपति 'a king,' 121.
भृ 'to bear,' 332, 368, 583.
भृ 'to blame,' 'to nourish,' 358.
भ्रंश् 'to fall,' 276.
भ्रज्ज् 'one who fries,' 176. *g*.
भ्रज्ज् 'to fry,' 'to roast,' 282, 381, 632.
भ्रम् 'to wander,' 275, 375. *f*.
भ्राज् 'to shine,' 375. *f*.
भ्राश् 'to shine,' 375. *f*.
भ्री 'to fear,' 358.
म affix, 80. VIII.
मघवन् a name of Indra, 155.
मज्ज् 'to be immersed,' 633.
मत् affix, 84. V.
मत् 'I,' 218.
मति 'the mind,' 112.
मथिन् 'a churning-stick,' 162.
मद् 'to be mad,' 275.
मदीय 'mine,' 231.
मधु 'honey,' 115.
मन् 'to imagine,' 684.
मन् affix, 85. II.
मनस् 'the mind,' 164.
मन्थ् 'to churn,' 'to agitate,' 362, 693. *a*.
मय affix, 80. XVIII.
मर affix, 80. VIII.
महत् 'great,' 142.
महात्मन् 'magnanimous,' 151.
महामनस् 'magnanimous,' 164. *a*.
महाराज 'a great king,' 151. *a*.
मा 'to measure,' 274, 338, 664. *a*.
मा 'not,' in prohibition, 882, 889.
मांसभुज् 'flesh-eater,' 176.
मात्र affix, 80. XX.
मात्र 'merely,' 'even,' 919.
मि affix, 81. IV.
मिद् 'to be viscid,' 277.
मुच् 'to let go,' 'to loose,' 281, 628.
मुह् 'to be troubled,' 612.
मुह् 'foolish,' 182.
मूर्द्धन् 'the head,' 150.
मृ 'to die,' 280, 626.
मृग 'a deer,' 107.
मृज् 'to cleanse,' 'to wipe,' 324, 651.
मृदु 'tender,' 118. *a*, 187.
मृष् 'one who endures,' 181.
मेधाविन् 'intellectual,' 159.
म्ना 'to repeat over,' 269.
म्लै 'to fade,' 268, 374, 595. *b*.
य affix, 80. X. XI.
यकृत् 'the liver,' 144.
यज् 'to sacrifice,' 375. *e*, 597.
यज्वन् 'a sacrificer,' 148.
यत् 'who,' 226.
यदि 'if,' 880. *a*, 891, 915.
यम् 'to restrain,' 270, 433.

या 'to go,' 317, 644.
याच् 'to ask,' 364, 392.
यावत् 'as many,' 801, 838, 876.
यु 'to join,' 'to mix,' 313, 357, 396. *a*, 583, 686, 687.
यु affix, 82. VI.
युज् 'to join,' 346, 670.
युज् 'to be fitting,' 702.
युवन् 'a youth,' 155.
युष्मत् 'you,' 219.
र affix, 80. VII.
रभ् (with आ) 'to begin,' 601. *a*.
रम् 'to sport,' 433.
राज् 'to shine,' 375. *f*.
राज् 'a ruler,' 176. *e*.
राजन् 'a king,' 149.
राज्ञी 'a queen,' 150. *a*.
रि 'to go,' 280.
री 'to go,' 358.
रु 'to sound,' 313, 396. *a*.
रु affix, 82. VI.
रुद् 'to weep,' 326, 653.
रुध् 'to hinder,' 344, 671.
रुन्धत् 'hindering,' 141. *c*.
रूप 'composed of,' 'consisting of,' 769. *f*, 774.
रै 'wealth,' 132.
रोमन् 'hair,' 153.
ल affix, 80. VIII.
लक्ष्मी 'fortune,' 124.
लघिमन् 'lightness,' 150.
लघिष्ठ 'lightest,' 193.
लघीयस् 'lighter,' 193.
लभ् 'to take,' 601.
लभ् 'one who obtains,' 178.
लिप् 'to anoint,' 281, 437.
लिह् 'to lick,' 327, 661.
लिह् 'one who licks,' 182.
ली 'to adhere,' 358.
लुप् 'to break,' 281.
लू 'to cut,' 358, 691.
व affix, 80. VIII.
वच् 'to speak,' 319, 650.
वत् affix, 84. IV.
वत् 'like,' 922.
वद् 'to speak,' 599.
वधू 'a wife,' 125.
वन् 'to ask,' 684.
वन् affix, 85. III.
वप् 'to sow,' 375. *c*.
वम् 'to vomit,' 375. *d*.
वर affix, 80. VIII.
वर्त्मन् 'a road,' 153.
वर्मन् 'armour,' 153.
वल affix, 80. XVI.
वल्ग् 'one who leaps,' 183.
वश् 'to choose,' 'to desire,' 320, 656.
वस् 'to dwell,' 607.
वह् 'to carry,' 611.
वा 'or,' 914.
वाच् 'speech,' 176.
वारि 'water,' 114.
वाह् 'bearing,' 182. *c*.
विच् 'to distinguish,' 346.
विज् 'to separate,' 341.
विद् 'to know,' 308, 583.
विद् 'to find,' 281.
विद्वस् 'wise,' 168. *a*.
विन् affix, 85. VII.
विभ्राज् 'splendid,' 176. *e*.
विविक्षु 'desirous of entering,' 166.
विश् 'one who enters,' 181.
विश्वसृज् 'the creator of the world,' 176. *e*.
विष् 'to divide,' 341.
वी 'to go,' 312.
वृ 'to surround,' 368.

वृ 'to choose,' 675.
वृत् 'to be,' 598.
वृहत् 'great,' 142. *a.*
वॄ 'to choose,' 358. See वृ.
वे 'to weave,' 379.
वेमन् 'a loom,' 150.
वेवी 'to go,' 'to pervade,' 75. *a.*
वेश्मन् 'a house,' 153.
व्यच् 'to deceive,' 282, 383, 629.
व्यथ् 'to be pained,' 383.
व्यध् 'to pierce,' 277, 615.
व्यय् 'to spend,' 383.
व्ये 'to cover,' 379.
व्योमन् 'sky,' 153.
व्रश्च् 'to cut,' 282, 630.
व्रश्च् 'one who cuts,' 176. *g.*
व्री 'to choose,' 358.
व्ली 'to choose,' 358.
शक् 'to be able,' 679.
शकृत् 'ordure,' 144.
शम् 'to be appeased,' 619.
शालिवाह् 'bearing rice,' 182. *c.*
शास् 'to rule,' 290. *b*, 323, 658.
शासत् 'ruling,' 141. *a.*
शिव 'the god S'iva,' 'prosperous,' 103, 104, 105.
शिष् 'to distinguish,' 672.
शी 'to lie down,' 315, 646.
शुचि 'pure,' 117, 119. *a*, 187.
शुचिरोचिस् 'having brilliant rays,' 166. *a.*
शुभ् 'to shine,' 252.
शुभ 'fortunate,' 187.
शुष्मन् 'fire,' 148.
शॄ 'to dissolve,' 367. *c.*
शॄ 'to hurt,' 358.
शो 'to sharpen,' 374.
श्रन्थ् 'to loose,' 'to string,' 362, 375. *f*, 693. *a.*
श्रि 'to have recourse,' 367. *a*, 395. *a*, 440. *a.*
श्री 'prosperity,' 123.
श्रु 'to hear,' 352, 367. *b*, 368, 676.
श्वन् 'a dog,' 155.
श्वश्रू 'a mother-in-law,' 125.
श्वस् 'to breathe,' 326.
श्वि 'to swell,' 395. *a*, 437. *a.*
श्वेतवाह् 'Indra,' 182. *c.*
स for सह 'with,' 790. *a.*
सक्थि 'a thigh,' 122.
सखि 'a friend,' 120.
सजुस् 'an associate,' 166.
सञ्ज् 'to adhere,' 426, 597. *a.*
सङ्ग्राम् 'to fight,' 75. *a.*
सद् 'to sink,' 270, 599. *a.*
सन् 'to give,' 354, 426. *b*, 684.
सनाथ 'possessed of,' 'furnished with,' 769. *d.*
सम्यञ्च् 'fit,' 176. *b.*
स्म particle, 878.
सरित् 'a river,' 136.
सर्व 'all,' 237.
सर्वशक् 'omnipotent,' 175.
सह् 'to bear,' 611. *a.*
सात् affix, 789.
साधु 'good,' 187.
सामन् 'conciliation,' 153.
सिच् 'to sprinkle,' 281.
सिध् 'to accomplish,' 364.
सिध् 'to succeed,' 273, 616.
सीमन् 'a border,' 150.
सु 'to bring forth,' 647.
सु 'to press out juice,' 677. *a.*
सुन्दर 'beautiful,' 187.
सुपथिन् 'having a good road,' 162.
सुपाद् 'having beautiful feet,' 145.
सुभ्रू 'having beautiful eyebrows,' 125. *b.*

सुमनस् 'well-intentioned,' 164. *a.*

सू 'to bring forth,' 312, 647.

सृ 'to go,' 368, 437. *a.*

सृज् 'to create,' 625.

सृप् 'to creep,' 263.

सेनानी 'a general,' 126.

सेव् 'to serve,' 364.

सो 'to destroy,' 276. *a*, 613.

सोमपा 'a drinker of Soma juice,' 108. *a.*

स्तम्भ् 'to stop,' 695.

स्तु 'to praise,' 313, 368, 648.

स्तृ 'to spread,' 678.

स्तॄ 'to cover,' 'to spread,' 358, 678.

स्त्री 'a woman,' 123. *c.*

स्था 'to stand,' 269, 587.

स्नु 'to drop,' 'to trickle,' 368, 396. *a.*

स्नु affix, 82. VI.

स्फुट् 'to expand,' 388. *b.*

स्फुर् 'to glitter,' 388. *b.*

स्पृश् 'to touch,' 636.

स्पृह् 'to desire,' 288.

स्मि 'to smile,' 591.

स्मृ 'to remember,' 367. *c*, 594.

स्व 'own,' 232.

स्वन् 'to sound,' 375. *f.*

स्वप् 'to sleep,' 326, 665.

स्वयम्भू 'self-existent,' 126. *c.*

स्वसृ 'a sister,' 129. *a.*

हन् 'to kill,' 318, 654.

हन् 'to kill,' freq., 708.

हरित् 'green,' 95, 136, 137.

हविस् 'ghee,' 165.

हा 'to quit,' 'to abandon,' 337, 655.

हाहा 'a Gandharba,' 108. *b.*

हि 'to send,' 378.

हि 'for,' 914.

हिंस् 'to injure,' 673.

हु 'to sacrifice,' 333, 662.

हृ 'to seize,' 593.

ह्री 'to be ashamed,' 333. *a*, 666. *a.*

ह्री 'shame,' 123.

ह्वे 'to call,' 595.

LIST OF COMPOUND CONSONANTS.

CONJUNCTIONS OF TWO CONSONANTS.

क्क *kka*, क्ख *kkha*, क्ण *kṇa*, क्त *kta*, क्थ *ktha*, क्न *kna*, क्म *kma*, क्य *kya*, क्र or क्र *kra*, क्ल *kla*, क्व *kwa*, क्ष *ksha*. ख्य *khya*, ख्व *khwa*. ग्घ *ggha*, ग्ध *gdha*, ग्न *gna*, ग्भ *gbha*, ग्म *gma*, ग्य *gya*, ग्र *gra*, ग्ल *gla*, ग्व *gwa*. घ्न *ghna*, घ्य *ghya*, घ्र *ghra*, घ्व *ghwa*. ङ्क *ṅ-ka*, ङ्ख *ṅ-kha*, ङ्ग *ṅ-ga*, ङ्घ *ṅ-gha*, ङ्भ *ṅ-bha*, ङ्म *ṅ-ma*.

च्च *chcha*, च्छ *chchha*, च्ञ *chña*, च्म *chma*, च्य *chya*. छ्य *chhya*, छ्र *chhra*. ज्ज *jja*, ज्झ *jjha*, ज्ञ *jña*, ज्म *jma*, ज्य *jya*, ज्र *jra*, ज्व *jwa*. ञ्च *ñcha*, ञ्छ *ñchha*, ञ्ज *ñja*.

ट्ट *ṭṭa*, ट्ठ *ṭṭha*. ठ्य *ṭhya*. ड्ग *ḍga*, ड्ड *ḍḍa*, ड्ण *ḍṇa*, ड्ढ *ḍḍha*, ड्भ *ḍbha*, ड्य *ḍya*, ड्र *ḍra*. ढ्य *ḍhya*, ढ्र *ḍhra*. ण्ट *ṇṭa*, ण्ठ *ṇṭha*, ण्ड *ṇḍa*, ण्ढ *ṇḍha*, ण्ण *ṇṇa*, ण्म *ṇma*, ण्य *ṇya*, ण्व *ṇwa*.

त्क *tka*, त्त *tta*, त्थ *ttha*, त्न *tna*, त्म *tma*, त्य *tya*, त्र *tra*, त्व *twa*, त्स *tsa*. थ्न *thna*, थ्य *thya*, थ्व *thwa*. द्ग *dga*, द्घ *dgha*, द्द *dda*, द्ध *ddha*, द्न *dna*, द्ब *dba*, द्भ *dbha*, द्म *dma*, द्य *dya*, द्र *dra*, द्व *dwa*. ध्न *dhna*, ध्म *dhma*, ध्य *dhya*, ध्र *dhra*, ध्व *dhwa*. न्त *nta*, न्थ *ntha*, न्द *nda*, न्ध *ndha*, न्न *nna*, न्म *nma*, न्य *nya*, न्र *nra*, न्व *nwa*, न्स *nsa*.

प्त *pta*, प्थ *ptha*, प्न *pna*, प्प *ppa*, प्फ *ppha*, प्म *pma*, प्य *pya*, प्र *pra*, प्ल *pla*, प्व *pwa*, प्स *psa*. ब्ज *bja*, ब्द *bda*, ब्ध *bdha*, ब्ब *bba*, ब्भ *bbha*, ब्य *bya*, ब्र *bra*. भ्य *bhya*, भ्र *bhra*, भ्व *bhwa*. म्ण *mṇa*, म्न *mna*, म्प *mpa*, म्फ *mpha*, म्ब *mba*, म्भ *mbha*, म्म *mma*, म्य *mya*, म्र *mra*, म्ल *mla*.

य्य *yya*, य्र *yra*, य्व *ywa*.

र्क *rka*, र्ख *rkha*, र्ग *rga*, र्घ *rgha*, र्च *rcha*, र्छ *rchha*, र्ज *rja*, र्ण *rṇa*, र्त *rta*, र्थ *rtha*, र्द *rda*, र्ध *rdha*, र्प *rpa*, र्ब *rba*, र्भ *rbha*, र्म *rma*, र्य *rya*, र्व *rva*, र्श *rśa*, र्ष *rsha*, र्ह *rha*.

ल्क *lka*, ल्ग *lga*, ल्द *lda*, ल्प *lpa*, ल्ब *lba*, ल्भ *lbha*, ल्म *lma*, ल्य *lya*, ल्ल *lla*, ल्व *lwa*, ल्ष *lsha*, ल्ह *lha*.

व्न *vna*, व्य *vya*, व्र *vra*, व्ल *vla*, व्व *vva*.

श्च *ścha*, श्न *śna*, श्य *śya*, श्र *śra*, श्ल *śla*, श्व *śwa*. ष्क *shka*, ष्ट *shṭa*, ष्ठ *shṭha*, ष्ण *shṇa*, ष्प *shpa*, ष्म *shma*, ष्य *shya*, ष्व *shwa*. स्क *ska*, स्ख *skha*, स्त *sta*, स्थ *stha*, स्न *sna*, स्प *spa*, स्फ *spha*, स्म *sma*, स्य *sya*, स्र *sra*, स्व *swa*, स्स *ssa*. ह्ण *hṇa*, ह्न *hna*, ह्म *hma*, ह्य *hya*, ह्र *hra*, ह्ल *hla*, ह्व *hwa*.

CONJUNCTIONS OF THREE CONSONANTS.

क्क्ण or क्क्ण *kkṇa**, क्ष्ण *kshṇa*, क्थ्न *kthna*†, क्ष्म *kshma*, क्क्य *kkya*, क्ख्य *kkhya*, क्त्य *ktya*, क्थ्य *kthya*, क्ष्य *kshya*, क्त्र *ktra*, क्त्व *ktwa*, क्ष्व *kshwa*. ग्घ्य *gghya*, ग्ध्य *gdhya*, ग्न्य *gnya*, ग्भ्य *gbhya*, ग्र्य *grya*, ग्ध्व *gdhwa*. ङ्क्त *n·kta*, ङ्क्य *n·kya*, ङ्ख्य *n·khya*, ङ्ग्य *n·gya*, ङ्घ्य *n·ghya*, ङ्क्ष *n·ksha*.

च्च्य *chchya*, च्छ्य *chchhya*, च्छ्र *chchhra*, च्छ्व *chchhwa*. ज्ज्ञ *jjña*, ज्ज्व *jjwa*. ञ्च्य *ñchya*, ञ्छ्य *ñchhya*, ञ्च्व *ñchwa*, ञ्ज्व *ñjwa*.

ट्ट्य *ṭṭya*. ड्ड्य *ḍḍya*, ड्भ्य *ḍbhya*. ण्ट्य *ṇṭya*, ण्ठ्य *ṇṭhya*, ण्ड्य *ṇḍya*, ण्ड्र *ṇḍra*.

त्क्र *tkra*, त्न्य *tnya*, त्प्र *tpra*, त्स्न *tsna*, त्त्य *ttya*, त्थ्य *tthya*, त्म्य *tmya*, त्र्य *trya*, त्स्य *tsya*, त्त्र *ttra*, त्त्व *ttwa*, त्र्व *trwa*, त्स्व *tswa*. द्द्य *ddya*, द्ध्य *ddhya*, द्भ्य *dbhya*, द्र्य *drya*, द्व्य *dwya*. ध्व्य *dhwya*‡, ध्न्व *dhnwa*. न्द्ध *nddha*, न्त्म *ntma*, न्द्म *ndma*, न्ध्म *ndhma*, न्त्य *ntya*, न्थ्य *nthya*, न्द्य *ndya*, न्न्य *nnya*, न्त्र *ntra*, न्द्र *ndra*, न्ध्र *ndhra*, न्त्व *ntwa*, न्द्व *ndwa*, न्ध्व *ndhwa*, न्य्व *nywa*, न्त्स *ntsa*.

प्स्न *psna*, प्त्य *ptya*, प्स्य *psya*, प्त्र *ptra*, प्ण्व *pṇwa*, प्त्व *ptwa*, प्ल्व *plwa*, प्स्व *pswa*§. ब्ज्य *bjya*, ब्ध्य *bdhya*, ब्भ्य *bbhya*, ब्भ्र *bbhra*,

---

* As in सृक्क्णा from सृक्कन्.

† सक्थ्ना from सक्थि.

‡ साध्व्योः from साध्वी.

§ प्रेप्स्वोः from प्रेप्सु.

ब्ध्व *bdhwa.* भ्र्य *bhrya.* म्प्य *mpya,* म्ब्य *mbya,* म्ब्ल *mbla,* म्भ्य *mbhya,* म्प्र *mpra,* म्भ्र *mbhra.*

र्क्ष *rksha,* र्ष्ट *rshṭa,* र्ण्ण *rṇṇa,* र्त्त *rtta,* र्द्ध *rddha,* र्ग्य *rgya,* र्घ्य *rghya,* र्च्य *rchya,* र्ण्य *rṇya,* र्त्य *rtya,* र्प्य *rpya,* र्ब्ब *rbba,* र्य्य *ryya,* र्ष्ण *rshṇa,* र्ह्म *rhma.*

ल्क्य *lkya,* ल्ग्य *lgya,* ल्प्त *lpta,* ल्प्य *lpya.*

श्च्य *śchya,* श्र्य *śrya.* ष्ट्य *shṭya,* ष्ण्य *shṇya,* ष्ट्र *shṭra,* ष्ट्व *shṭwa.* स्त्य *stya,* स्त्र *stra,* स्त्व *stwa,* स्थ्न *sthna,* स्थ्य *sthya,* स्न्व *snwa.* स्म्य *smya,* स्र्य *srya,* स्र्व *srwa.* ह्न्य *hnya,* ह्म्य *hmya,* ह्व्य *hwya.*

CONJUNCTIONS OF FOUR CONSONANTS.

क्त्र्य *ktrya,* क्ष्म्य *kshmya.* ङ्क्ष्ण *n-kshṇa,* ङ्क्ष्म *n-kshma**, ङ्क्त्य *n-ktya,* ङ्क्ष्य *n-kshya,* ङ्क्त्र *n-ktra,* ङ्क्ष्व *n-kshwa.* ण्ड्र्य *ṇḍrya.* त्त्र्य *ttrya,* त्स्न्य *tsnya,* त्स्म्य *tsmya.* द्ध्र्य *ddhrya.* न्त्र्य *ntrya,* न्त्स्य *ntsya,* न्त्स्व *ntswa,* न्ध्र्य *ndhrya.* प्त्र्य *ptrya.* र्क्ष्य *rkshya,* र्त्त्य *rttya,* र्त्र्य *rtrya,* र्त्स्य *rtsya,* र्द्ध्र *rddhra.* ल्प्त्य *lptya,* ल्प्स्म *lpsma.* ल्प्स्य *lpsya.* ष्ट्र्य *shṭrya.*

CONJUNCTIONS OF FIVE CONSONANTS.

ङ्क्ष्ण्व *n-kshṇwa* †, ङ्क्त्र्य *n-ktrya* ‡. र्ङ्क्ष्म *rn-kshma* §, र्ङ्क्ष्व *rn-kshwa* §, र्त्स्न्य *rtsnya* ‖, र्द्ध्र्य *rddhrya.*

---

* चाकाङ्क्ष्मि Intens. of काङ्क्ष्. † दङ्क्ष्ण्वोः from दङ्क्ष्णु.

‡ मङ्क्त्र्योः from मङ्क्त्री. § As in अताङ्क्ष्म, अताङ्क्ष्व, from root तृंह्.

‖ As in कार्त्स्न्यं.

CORRECTIONS.

Page 160, line 17, *for* form III; see 441. *read* form II.; see 435.

P. 166, l. 2, *for* 681 *read* 682

P. 178, l. 22, *for* 459 *read* 559

P. 197, l. 13, *for* 316 *read* 317

P. 215, l. 19, *for* तर्पेष्य *read* तर्भेष्य

P. 216, l. 15, *for* पाषणीय *read* पोषणीय

Page 77, line 16, *for* कर्मेन् *read* कर्म; line 17. *for* नानन *read* नाम